10–20 February 2023

Dear Peter Faber,
Thank you for your support of,
and inspiration to, operation Benjamin
—and now operations Jacob & Gideon—
With best wishes,

JEWISH ANZACS

MARK DAPIN was born in Leeds, England, in 1963. His family are of Ashkenazi and Sephardi Jewish descent. He grew up in Aldershot, 'home of the British Army', where the only other Jews were in the cemetery. His great-grandfather was in the British Army at the time of the Boer War. His grandfather was an air raid warden in the East End of London during the Blitz in World War Two. His father was a British Army national serviceman in the 1950s. Mark's 2010 novel *Spirit House*, about Jewish POWs on the Burma Railway, was shortlisted for the *Age* Book of the Year and the Royal Society for Literature's Ondaatje Prize, and longlisted for the Miles Franklin Literary Award. His first military history, *The Nashos' War*, about the Australian national service scheme and Vietnam, won an Alex Buzo Shortlist Prize and the People's Choice Prize at the Waverley Library Awards for Literature (The Nib), and was shortlisted for the NSW Premier's Award for Non-Fiction. Mark is a PhD candidate in Military History at UNSW Canberra.

JEWISH ANZACS

JEWS IN THE AUSTRALIAN MILITARY

MARK DAPIN

SYDNEY
JEWISH
MUSEUM
HOLOCAUST
AND AUSTRALIAN
JEWISH HISTORY

NEWSOUTH

A NewSouth book

Published by
NewSouth Publishing
University of New South Wales Press Ltd
University of New South Wales
Sydney NSW 2052
AUSTRALIA
newsouthpublishing.com

National Library of Australia
Cataloguing-in-Publication entry
Creator: Dapin, Mark, author.
Title: Jewish Anzacs: Jews in the Australian military / Mark Dapin.
ISBN: 9781742235356 (hardback)
       9781742242705 (ebook)
       9781742248189 (ePDF)
Notes: Includes index.
Subjects: Australia – Armed Forces – Minorities – History.
       Jewish soldiers – Australia.
       Jewish Australians – Wars.

Design Josephine Pajor-Markus
Cover design Blue Cork
Cover images FRONT Meeting of Australian Jewish soldiers outside the YMCA's Jewish Soldiers' Hut, London, after World War One. Australian War Memorial, H01295; colourised by Luke Causby. BACK Clockwise from centre: Jake Kleinman; Walter Karri Davies; Berrol Mendelsohn; Edna Goulston; Wilfred Beaver; Sol Levitus; Philip Allen. See picture sections and picture credits list for details.
Printed in China

All reasonable efforts were taken to obtain permission to use copyright material reproduced in this book, but in some cases copyright could not be traced. The author welcomes information in this regard.

This book is printed on paper using fibre supplied from plantation or sustainably managed forests.

This project was assisted by funding from the Commonwealth Government's Saluting Their Service Commemorative Grant program.

SYDNEY JEWISH MUSEUM
HOLOCAUST AND AUSTRALIAN JEWISH HISTORY

100 YEARS OF ANZAC
THE SPIRIT LIVES
2014 - 2018

THE CENTENARY OF ANZAC JEWISH PROGRAM
Patrons: Major General Jeffrey V. Rosenfeld AM OBE KStJ; Wesley E. Browne OAM

UNSW
AUSTRALIA

Contents

Foreword

by Major General Jeffrey V Rosenfeld

The 2014–18 Centenary of Anzac Commemorations include anniversaries of the Anzac landings at Gallipoli, the other battles of World War One, as well as significant anniversaries of World War Two and subsequent wars. Many Australians have become aware of those transformative events in Australia's history for the first time and many young Australians have learnt about the sacrifice of fellow Australians of similar age who went to war many years before they themselves were born. Those who visit the war graves at Gallipoli and on the Western Front are often brought to tears.

The Australian Jewish community should be incredibly proud of the Jews who have made such an extraordinary contribution to the defence of Australia and our allies, particularly when one considers the relatively small size of the Jewish community. Following more than 2000 years of persecution, Jews have an abiding respect for human rights and a deep appreciation of the fragile nature of freedom and democracy. I believe this is essentially why so many Jewish Australians have taken up arms. By the end of World War Two, more than 7000 Australian Jews had served in the defence of Australia, with thousands more serving in the Australian Defence Force (ADF) subsequently. At least 340 have made the supreme sacrifice: they are honoured with details of their final resting place or memorial in the Appendixes to this book.

Remembrance (*Zachor* in Hebrew) is a central tenet of Judaism. It is the solemn duty of the Federal Association of Jewish

Ex-Servicemen and Women (FAJEX) and its state affiliate organisations to remember and pay our respects to those Jewish Australians who have served Australia and its allies in times of war and particularly to commemorate those who lost their lives. This duty includes raising awareness in the community, and educating the current and following generations about the courage and sacrifice of Australian Jews who have served in the ADF.

I believe *Jewish Anzacs* will become the definitive account of Australian Jews at war and peacekeeping for many years to come and will thus help to perpetuate the memory of those who have served. Equally, any lingering doubt about the loyalty of Australian Jews to Australia and the Crown is dispelled in these pages. Australian Jews have had the same hopes, dreams, and a desire to fight for freedom and the creation of modern Australia as have non-Jews.

Mark Dapin presents a succinct history of each of the conflicts, wars and operations in which Australia has taken part from the nineteenth century to the present day. However, what makes *Jewish Anzacs* unique is his interweaving of the many remarkable lives and personal accounts of Jewish Australians – both passed and still living – who have served in uniform: from all three services, wearing many different ranks from diggers to generals, and in diverse occupations. Their experiences reflect and supplement those of all our Australian servicemen and women.

The stories of three Jewish soldiers who were recommended for the Victoria Cross, the highest military honour – 'For Valour' – are no less extraordinary than the stories of all other VC recipients. During the Boer War, West Australian Walter Karri Davies humbly declined a VC for his outstanding bravery at the Relief of Ladysmith. Issy Smith sailed back to England from Melbourne at the outbreak of the Great War to rejoin his old Manchester Regiment. He was awarded a VC for rescuing wounded comrades from No Man's Land during the Second Battle of Ypres – on 26 April

1915, the day after the Anzacs had landed at Gallipoli. There, Leonard Keysor's daring actions, throwing back Turkish bombs at the Battle of Lone Pine in August 1915, resulted in his award of a VC.

While several excellent biographies of General Sir John Monash have been published, Mark Dapin accords General Monash the special attention he deserves. He is indisputably one of Australia's greatest sons. It is often stated that his exceptional leadership of the Australian and allied troops to victory on the Western Front and his pride and openness in being Jewish were the reasons anti-Semitism was limited in Australian society at that time and well beyond.

Mark Dapin has uncovered the stories of many more World War Two servicemen and women, bringing back to life dozens of characters: from the amazing exploits of Group Captain Julius Cohen in North Africa and the leadership of Lieutenant Colonel Paul Cullen there and in New Guinea, to the humorous experiences of private soldiers and the terrible privations of prisoners of war in Europe and Asia.

Moreover, Mr Dapin has brought the record of Jews in operations with Australia's military forces up to date, citing experiences of men and women in post-World War Two actions such as Korea, Vietnam, Iraq and Afghanistan – demonstrating the continuing commitment of Jewish men and women to service in the ADF to this day. As a member of the ADF, I served with the United Nations Assistance Mission to Rwanda in 1995–96. Being witness to the aftermath of a genocide of nearly one million innocent people personally affected me, more so as a Jew. I continue to ask myself how the world could have watched this genocide unfold, despite the murder of six million Jews by the Nazis during the Holocaust and the more recent genocide in Cambodia. Australia's peacekeepers, including Australian Jewish servicemen and women, continue to confront such challenges.

Let us ensure, 'Never again'!

I commend Mr Peter Allen and the Committee of the Centenary of Anzac Jewish Program, together with the Sydney Jewish Museum, for securing funding from the federal government's Saluting Their Service Commemorative Grant program that enabled the commissioning of Mr Dapin to write this book, and for guiding the project through to its successful publication and book launch.

Jewish Anzacs should be read by all members of the Jewish community and by all Australians who believe that our way of life is worth defending. I thank Mark Dapin for helping to rediscover and remember those Jewish men and women of our defence forces who sacrificed so much for Australia.

Lest We Forget.

Major General Jeffrey V Rosenfeld AM OBE KStJ
Former Surgeon General (Reserves), Australian Defence Force
Co-Patron, Centenary of Anzac Jewish Program
Patron, Federal Association of Jewish Ex-Servicemen and Women
    (FAJEX)
Patron-in-Chief, Victorian Association of Jewish Ex &
    Servicemen & Women Australia Inc. (VAJEX Australia)

Preface

by Peter M Allen

The genesis of *Jewish Anzacs* can be traced to 2008, when I discovered that my distant cousin, Private Lionel Harold Levy, was one of the 'Lost Diggers of Fromelles' and that my great-uncle, Sergeant Morris Phillips, was awarded a DCM at the Battle of Fromelles, 19–20 July 1916, with the AIF on the Western Front in France.

So, there was no question that on 19 July 2010, my wife Gloria and I would attend the dedication of the first Commonwealth War Graves Cemetery in almost fifty years, commemorating the reinternment in the Fromelles (Pheasant Wood) Military Cemetery of 250 lost soldiers, 96 of whom were identified.[*] A Jewish memorial service was conducted and, at the grave of Lieutenant Berrol Mendelsohn – the only one of some dozen 'Lost Jewish Diggers of Fromelles' to be identified, including Private Joseph de Pass Joseph, believed to be the youngest Jewish digger killed in action in World War One, aged just 16 – I thanked the driving force behind the discovery of the soldiers' mass graves, Lambis Englezos AM. It is largely due to Lambis' inspiration, and his dogged determination to ensure that the lives of our Australian servicemen and women are never forgotten, that I set out on this journey. It is up to all of us to ensure their due recognition by recording the collective memory

---

[*]   In 2016 I joined Lambis Englezos again in France, at commemorations marking the Centenaries of the Battles of Fromelles and Pozières. By then, an amazing 150 of the 250 'Lost Diggers of Fromelles' had their headstones named. Sadly, neither my cousin Lionel Levy nor any more of the Jewish soldiers who made the supreme sacrifice there have been identified – but efforts to find them continue.

of all our Australian soldiers, sailors and airmen/women, no matter what their backgrounds or affiliations may be, and whether Christian, Jew or neither.

I learned that thousands of Australia's Jewish community have served in the Australian armed forces, from the Sudan campaign in 1885 through to the recent actions in Afghanistan and Iraq, exemplifying the rich multi-denominational and multicultural thread woven through Australia's military history, and our shared values of freedom, peace and tolerance. Hundreds of them have given their lives in the service of our country.

Jews came from all corners of Australia and the globe – perhaps less of the former and more of the latter, as compared with the general population – from Albany to Zeehan, from Aberdeen (Scotland) to Vilna (Lithuania), and willingly enlisted for duty in the Australian forces, displaying their gratitude for living in this tolerant, safe haven. Chaplain Rev. David Freedman reported from France in 1916 that 'the Jew is here, too, side by side with his fellow-citizens, striving, fighting and dying for the sacred cause of the British Empire'.

I read that in South Africa, Nurse Rose Shappere served in both Boer and British hospitals. In World War One, Jews enlisted voluntarily in the AIF in no lesser proportion than those in the general population, with General Sir John Monash being the most famous, despite being considered by some as an 'outsider'. The number of historians who believe that Monash turned around the course of the war on the Western Front is still growing. Some even contend that a Jewish soldier, Sergeant Issy Smith, was actually the first Australian to receive a VC in World War One. Born Israel Smilovich, Issy went on to reenact his exploits with a British regiment in the 1926 film *Mademoiselle d'Armentières* before returning to live in Australia. Lieutenant Leonard Keysor VC (Lone Pine) also reenacted his exploits in a film after the war – but at some personal risk. Many actions of Australian Jews in World

War Two are also the stuff of Boys' Own adventure stories – in stark contrast to those who suffered terribly as POWs on the Thai-Burma railway.

Although there have been two landmark publications recording the contribution of Jews to Australia's military forces – the *Australian Jewry Book of Honour, the Great War, 1914–1918* (Hon. Lieutenant Harold Boas, 1923) and *Australian Jewry's Book of Honour, World War II* (Gerald Pynt, 1974) – it is now acknowledged that both of these books are incomplete and contain several inaccuracies with regard to names of those who served. Furthermore, there has been no publication regarding Jewish members of the Australian Defence Force (ADF) from 1788 to World War One, between the wars, or since World War Two.

It became clear to me that a complete history of the contribution of Jews and the Jewish community to Australia's military history has not been compiled, written or published and that the Centenary of Anzac years would be the appropriate, if not last, opportunity for that to happen. However, this book is not intended to be a comprehensive history, nor a textbook. Rather, *Jewish Anzacs* is created as a sweeping narrative of unique and extraordinary true stories, set against the broad backdrop of Australia's defining military participation on the world stage, that will appeal to Jews and non-Jews, whether or not they are interested in military history. It also tracks some families through their generations of service and follows the paths of the Jewish chaplains as they ministered to all the troops in conflicts across the globe.

In 2011, I commenced discussions with Russell Stern, then President of the Australian Jewish Historical Society (AJHS), who was researching the identities of Australian Jews who had enlisted in the armed forces. I prepared a detailed submission to the Executive Council of Australian Jewry (ECAJ) that was wholeheartedly accepted – and the Centenary of Anzac Jewish Program (CoAJP) was launched on Anzac Day, 25 April 2012, under the auspices of the ECAJ, the Federation of Australian Jewish Ex-Service Associations (FAJEX) and the AJHS. The CoAJP's purpose is to initiate, develop and coordinate activities, grants and donations across every state and the ACT, culminating with the proposed opening of an Australian Jewish War Memorial at the ACT Jewish Community Centre on the Centenary of the Armistice, 11 November 2018. The key project of the CoAJP is the preparation and publication of this up-to-date record of Jews in the Australian military.

WHEN I HEARD MARK DAPIN SPEAK AT THE SYDNEY JEWISH Writers Festival in August 2012 and I read his historical fiction *Spirit House*, I knew that we had found our author. He wrote about my parents' generation, and their experiences in World War Two and after the war, as though he had lived that with them: as Australian Jews, living in and fighting for Australia. So I was delighted when, in 2013, Mark agreed to take on the project.

A submission to the Department of Veterans Affairs led to their announcement just before Anzac Day 2014 of a Saluting Their Service Major Commemorative Grant to the Sydney Jewish Museum (SJM) towards funding of the book – and for which we are extremely grateful. Similarly, a year later, the Department approved several Anzac Centenary Local Grants for a range of Jewish Anzac commemorative services, honour rolls, exhibitions and educational projects, across twenty-five electorates in all states and the ACT, coordinated by the CoAJP.

Mark had initially thought there would be only a limited amount of material for the manuscript, but soon came to realise that, rather than having difficulty finding sufficient material to include, the difficulty would be deciding which material to exclude. Indeed, Mark declared that there may be a whole book waiting to be written about Walter Karri Davies alone, as well as other characters he has since researched for this book.

Mark and his partner Claire Waddell scoured more sources than I could have imagined, and he travelled on numerous occasions around Australia and to Europe in search of new and better information. Mark made special efforts to interview servicemen and women, particularly those who had served after World War Two. When I suggested that he might have included them in this book in greater detail than I had anticipated, Mark quite rightly reminded me that none of the post–World War Two stories had ever been told before – and, without this book, would probably never be told at all, so these stories were the most historically important part of the book, and a gift to future generations.

The CoAJP's publicity also had some success in eliciting new information. For example, Tasmanian Beth Sandor alerted us that she had three Crawcour uncles, each of whom had lost a leg as the result of their service in World War One. And in January 2016, when Mark thought he had finished his research, we discovered an incredible resource: the unpublished diary of Robert Patkin, a World War Two POW in Europe, which was held by his family in Melbourne.

The other challenge of this project was to assemble and clarify the provenance of the names and numbers of Jews in the armed forces: a massive task, undertaken by the AJHS' Russell Stern. A brief background to his many years of research and his discovery of almost 2000 more World War Two Jewish enlistments is summarised in Appendix 2. This lists the names of 6798 Australian Jewish men and women who served in the Australian or Allied armed forces in the Boer War, World War One and World War Two, preceded by a Memorial Roll of those 342 Jews who are known to have died on service in the Australian armed forces, merchant navy or Allied armed forces, to date (Appendix 1).

It is acknowledged that despite the title *Jewish Anzacs*, Jewish New Zealanders have not been included in this book unless they served in the Australian forces. Janet Salek of the Wellington Jewish Community is continuing her research.

A detailed list of acknowledgements appears towards the end of the book. I record here especially my sincere thanks to: Warwick Abadee (z"l) (FAJEX/NAJEX), Russell Stern, Peter Wertheim AM (ECAJ), Charles Aronson (SJM), members of the CoAJP Funding and Action Committee, and the NSW Association of Jewish Ex-Servicemen and Women for their efforts, support and encouragement with this project. Most especially, to my dear wife Gloria, who compiled the memorial and cemetery information, helped me edit Russell's enlistment lists and shared her endless patience with my passion to see this book published to the high standard it deserves: I owe you everything.

THE DIVERSE CULTURE YET DEEP-ROOTED LOYALTY OF members of the ADF, Australian Jews and Australians generally – both past and present – was no better exemplified than at the Anzac Centenary Commemorative Service of the NSW Jewish Community, held at the Great Synagogue, Sydney, on 3 May 2015. More than 1100 people of all faiths, ages and status attended. The second of the CoAJP's four Centenary Yahrzeit (Memorial) Candles was lit by Professor Group Captain Lisa Jackson Pulver, RAAF Specialist Reserve (Public Health Epidemiologist), President of Newtown Synagogue and an equally proud member of the Wiradjuri people.

Zachor – 'Remembrance' – is a key part of Jewish tradition and Mark's writing consistently reflects that. In *Jewish Anzacs*, Mark has explored the memories of men and women at and beyond the battlefront: he has given voice to their souls. He has shown how the experience of Jewish servicemen and women is similar to other members of the ADF, and how occasionally their service lives – and deaths – included uniquely Jewish aspects. By using their own words, Mark has captured the best of all these elements, with his characteristic candour, clarity and dry humour.

Ultimately, the publication of this book will provide a fitting, long-term legacy for those thousands of Jewish men and women who have served our country – and in many cases gave their lives – in the continuing struggle for freedom, peace and tolerance, values that all Australians share.

As Jews, we firmly believe that it is incumbent on every generation to pursue the task of recording and commemorating the lives and memories of our parents, grandparents and previous generations. Mark Dapin has more than excelled at that in *Jewish Anzacs*: my eternal thanks to you, Mark.

Peter M Allen
National Coordinator, Centenary of Anzac Jewish Program

In honour of my late parents,
Moya Miriam (nee Levy) (z"l) and Philip Allen (z"l),
who served in World War Two and were staunch members of NAJEX

Dedicated to all members of the Australian Defence Force,
including more than 340 Jewish servicemen
who, in the pursuit of freedom, made the supreme sacrifice.

Wesley Browne OAM
Co-Patron of the Centenary of Anzac Jewish Program
Life member and past President of
the Federation of Australian Jewish Ex-Service Associations
and the NSW Association of Jewish Ex-Servicemen and Women

Prologue

It's a warm, drizzly Melbourne afternoon on 3 December 2014. Felix Sher, the father of the last Jewish Australian soldier killed in action, is driving south-east along the Monash Freeway – a road named in honour of Australia's greatest Jewish general – to visit the Chevra Kadisha Lyndhurst Cemetery and the grave of his son Greg. As the skies clear and the traffic thins, Felix talks softly and deliberately of his own past, and the life of the boy he lost in Afghanistan.

Felix was born in South Africa, where he worked as a financial adviser, dealing in life insurance, pensions and investments. When he left school, he completed a year of compulsory military training, and was then liable for a decade of part-time service. He started out in the armoured corps, went to a light horse regiment, and finished his career as a captain in a logistics unit. He fought twice in Angola. When his ten years were up, he volunteered for two more. Greg was born in South Africa too, the middle brother of three. When Greg was growing up, 'He saw me in uniform on a regular basis,' says Felix. 'Every Tuesday night was parade night.' He pauses. 'It's exactly the same in Australia: for Greg it was a Tuesday night.'

The Sher family migrated to Australia in 1986, when Greg was seven years old. They moved first to Adelaide, then to Melbourne where Greg attended state schools in Doncaster. He wanted to study financial planning and started at university but did not stay. He helped to set up the Victorian Community Security Group (CSG), where he trained the volunteers who protect Jewish events, schools and synagogues, and found his vocation in the Army Reserve. 'He just loved the military,' says Felix. 'That was his life. As kids, him and his brothers used to borrow my uniform and go and play soldiers.' Greg's older brother Steven is a Reserve officer in the RAAF. 'Steven's never served overseas,' says Felix, 'and we've asked him not to. Losing one in that environment is enough.'

When Greg signed up, he marched into the 5th/6th Battalion of the Royal Victoria Regiment, a Melbourne-based Reserve infantry battalion. With 5/6 RVR he worked on security for the 2000 Olympics, and later went to East Timor as part of the United Nations peace-keeping forces. 'My wife was absolutely distraught about what might happen to him and where he was going,' says Felix. But Greg returned unharmed.

Greg was a bodybuilder and a runner, an extremely fit man. He sometimes trained with a younger CSG member, Josh Fink, who was later to become an Australian army officer in Afghanistan. Josh's father Michael was a former amateur boxer and martial arts trainer who had served in Papua New Guinea with the Army Reserve. Josh's grandfather Samuel Fink fought on Morotai in World War Two. In 2004 Greg made it through the ferociously demanding selection process to become a special-forces commando. 'They used to call him "Super-Jew",' says Felix, 'and he took that positively. When they went on exercises, he would trade bacon for more eggs. When he qualified for commandos, they put up a feast of pork and prawns and lobster. And he wouldn't eat, so they went out and bought him Nando's. He was a huge Nando's fan.'

In 2008 a company of Greg's unit, 1st Commando Regiment, was warned for deployment in Afghanistan as part of the Special Operations Task Group (SOTG). Greg remembered the stress it had caused his mother Yvonne when he went to East Timor, says Felix. 'So he decided that, rather than put up with an argument about going to Afghanistan, he was not going to tell me or her. He told us he was going on an exercise in South Australia, but he had told his brothers where he was going.'

Greg grew a beard. Felix remembered from his time in Angola that 'a lot of the fellows grew beards, and just had this look about them'. Then Greg began to sort out his things. 'Bags and bags and bags of his stuff just came out of his room.' On 24 November 2008, Greg left for the airport, where his partner Karen saw him off. 'I just gave him a hug goodbye when he went on his way,' says Felix, 'and that was it. Not long afterwards, a letter arrived. It said Greg was serving in the Middle East! The unit had sent it to me, because I had him down as one of my employees. They were writing to tell the employer what was going on. Then he phoned on Christmas Day. I said to him, "How are you phoning me?" He said, "On a satellite phone." You don't phone on a satellite phone from South Australia. So he had to be over there.' Felix shared his suspicions with Yvonne. She said, 'No, no, no, no. That can't be the case.' He confronted his youngest son Barry. 'I said, "Hey, listen: I know you think I don't know, but I believe Greg's in Afghanistan." And he wouldn't admit it.'

On 2 January 2009 Yvonne and Felix went to Daylesford, Victoria, for a holiday. 'We were having a wonderful time,' says Felix. But, at about 2 am on Monday 5 January, the phone rang in their hotel room. Felix assumed it was a wrong number. Who would call him at the hotel? 'I made a mistake,' he said. 'I'd switched off my mobile. I never switch it off anymore.' The caller was Barry. 'He said, "It's Greg." "What's wrong with Greg? Did he have an accident?" "No. He was killed." "How?" "He was hit by a rocket." "Where?" "Afghanistan. You'd better come home. The military are waiting here for you."

'My wife was behind me,' says Felix, 'listening. How was I going to tell her? There was just no way out. I said to her, "Look, Barry's rung me to say Greg was killed in Afghanistan." And I just remember that shriek, that gasp of horror. We just packed up our things, went downstairs, paid the bill, got into the car. I set my GPS – I didn't think I'd find my way home – and even then, I argued with it. When I came out of the carpark, it said, "Turn left." I turned right. I did about three turns before I settled myself down.'

Waiting for Felix and Yvonne at the family home were two soldiers and a Catholic priest – the army had been unable to contact Australian Defence Force (ADF) Senior Chaplain Rabbi Ralph Genende. 'They told me the story,' says Felix. 'The Taliban had attacked the forward operation base, Patrol Base Qudus. They'd fired two 107-millimetre rockets. One of the rockets fell short, and the other rocket was a dud. It went through a Hesco wall and didn't explode. It went through a container full of water bottles and came out the other side, and it still hadn't exploded, and then Greg was walking past on the other side. It hit him, then it passed through a group of twelve soldiers and didn't touch one, and it hit the wall on the other side of the compound and then exploded. He was hit in the chest.

'I said, "What happens with getting him back? We want him back by Friday, because he's Jewish and we've got to bury real quick. Bring him back now." They said, "Okay, we'll fix it up." Then the Prime Minister phoned us, Kevin Rudd. I said, "Number one: we want him back here as soon as possible. The other thing is, I don't want you to do any post-mortems. We don't desecrate the bodies, and it's not that we don't know what went wrong".'

FELIX HAS ARRIVED AT THE CEMETERY WHERE HIS SON'S body lies. It's a relatively new graveyard, the tombstones clustered sadly near the Chevra Kadisha chapel. 'When Greg was buried here, there were about five graves,' says Felix. 'There was no *shul* there, there was a tent: a *huge* tent that they accommodated everyone in.' Greg's corpse came to the burial society on the Friday after he was killed. 'Down here, there's a wonderful old man," says Felix. 'I said, "Listen: if his face is in good order, I want to see him. If it's not, I'll just leave it as it is." He said, "No, he looks fine." Yvonne didn't know how she would cope, so I went in first. He looked pretty peaceful. Then I helped clean him up a bit, so he wouldn't look too bad for Yvonne. Then she came in, and she never saw him again after that.

'She never,' repeats Felix, 'saw him again.'

Throughout Saturday, the CSG watched over Greg's body. Once the Sabbath was out, 'I took his *tallit*,' says Felix, 'and saw him for the last time.' The funeral was held the next day. It was attended by the prime minister, the leader of the opposition, the minister for defence, the chief of army, the acting chief of the ADF and the acting premier of Victoria. 'There were about six rabbis there,' said Felix, 'about four generals. There were about 5000 people at the funeral.' At the family's request, a rifle company from 5/6 RVR fired a salute. Josh Fink, by then a lieutenant with the Royal Australian Electrical and Mechanical Engineers (RAEME) posted to the 1st Armoured Regiment, was one of the soldiers who escorted the coffin.

Felix parks his car, takes a Disruptive Pattern Camouflage *yarmulke* from the glove box, and covers his head as he walks towards his son's grave. There is a mound of pebbles on the slab – a sign the site has been visited – and a drawing of a figure labelled '*dod*', the Hebrew word for uncle. The picture was made by Felix's granddaughter, Steven's daughter, Greg's niece Ariel Libby Sher. 'The reason is, it's his birthday today,' says Felix. 'You can see on the stone.' The inscription reads:

Gregory Michael Sher
3rd December 1978 – 4th January 2009

'Greg was thirty years, one month and one day,' says Felix. 'It's a beautiful stone they bought. I was here to clean it the other day. I come at least once a month to wash it down.'

The headstone is carved from black marble, and the top slopes from right to left, as if a slice has been cut from a rectangle. In

Jewish tradition, the sloping stone is one of two ways to signify a life cut short. 'The other way was to cut off a corner,' says Felix, 'but we didn't want to do it that way, because the rocket had almost taken off his shoulder. It was a little too graphic.' There is a Star of David at the top right of the stone, and a Commando Regiment cap-badge, with the motto 'Strike swiftly', at the bottom left. 'He asked for that in his funeral plan,' says Felix, 'and he said that he would like us to give his mates a wake. We waited a year because it was too raw to do that kind of thing, and Nando's catered and did not charge a single penny. For four years after Greg's parting, we would go to a Nando's on the 4th of January, and they would bear the cost of the meal, for his mates and us.'

Other small offerings before the tombstone include Ferrero Rocher chocolates – 'He was a huge chocaholic,' says Felix. 'He loved those' – and a bottle of Jack Daniel's premix. 'That was one of his favourite drinks,' says Felix. 'His partner Karen also comes to visit. She brought that for him.'

On what would have been Greg Sher's 36th birthday, his father remembers him with towering dignity and an unmeasurable sense of loss. 'He never really wanted much,' says Felix. 'He wasn't materialistic in any way. He was very altruistic. He'd give of himself. And he certainly gave of himself for this lot.'

1

Birth of a nation

Soldiers, sailors and settlers

There were Jewish soldiers and sailors in Australia even before there was an Australian army and navy. The first Jews arrived in shackles with the First Fleet in 1788. They were a motley collection of convicts, largely of Ashkenazi (East European) descent, but including a clutch of Sephardi (Middle Eastern) felons. But most were British citizens and loyal – if not always honest – servants of the Crown. Among the wretches was milliner Esther Abrahams, a young woman sentenced to seven years' transportation for stealing lace from a London draper. Along with her baby daughter, Rosanna, she was taken on board the *Lady Penrhyn* to the colony of New South Wales. Somewhere on the oceans, Abrahams began a relationship with Lieutenant George Johnston of the Royal Marines. A son, Robert, was born to Abrahams and Johnston in Sydney in 1790, in the first military barracks built by Governor Arthur Phillip. As the Jewish religion is passed down through the mother's line, Robert and his siblings are considered Jews under Jewish law, although Abrahams and Johnston were finally to marry under Anglican rites in 1814. When Robert was seven years old, his father took him to England and enrolled him at a school in Surrey. At thirteen Robert Johnston became the first native of New South Wales to join the Royal Navy. In his long naval career, Johnston ferried British troops to the Battle of Montevideo in 1807, and fought Napoleon at the Battle of Corunna in 1809. He was present at the French storming of the Spanish naval base of Cadiz, and at the subsequent attack on Cape St Mary's where he was 'in

7

command of a rocket boat and narrowly escaped death through the boat being sunk by a round shot, and those who were not killed [were] left struggling in the water until a rescue could be effected'.[1] He was in Chesapeake Bay when the British captured Washington during the War of 1812 against the United States, and also at the British defeat at Baltimore. In 1816 he took leave to return to Sydney to visit his family. While Robert had been away, his father had led the so-called 'Rum Rebellion' of the NSW Corps, which overthrew Governor William Bligh in 1808. Major Johnston had then become Lieutenant-Governor and Esther, the Jewish drapery thief, performed the duties of first lady.

While in New South Wales, Robert discovered and named the Clyde River and found the source of the Warragamba River. He was about to return to the Royal Navy when his father and eldest brother passed away leaving him duty bound to remain and look after family affairs. He was made a Commander of the Royal Navy in 1865 and died in Sydney in 1882 at the age of ninety-two. At his funeral his coffin was carried to the grave by a party of sailors from HMS *Nelson*. Esther's children were not raised Jewish, but her grandson by Rosanna, the *halachically* Jewish parliamentarian George Robert Nicholls, argued hard to win government assistance for Jewish worship – alongside Christian congregations – in the debates that helped cement the separation of church and state in Australia in the 1850s.

The earliest Jewish free settlers followed the convicts in the nineteenth century, and the first military man among them would appear to be John Daniels, who was born in London in about 1818. When Daniels was eighteen years old, he joined his brother in business in South America. A few years later he returned to England and enlisted in the 99th (Lanarkshire) Regiment of Foot, an infantry regiment of the British Army. The 99th sailed out to Australia in 1842. Daniels served as 'sergeant of the regiment in charge of convicts' on Norfolk Island,[2] which was then the most notoriously brutal penal settlement in the British Empire. When the 99th moved to Sydney in 1845, Daniels left the army and made a new home in South Australia. He joined an auctioneering firm run by Emanuel Solomon, an emancipated convict who was later to become the first Jewish member of the South Australian parliament. In 1854 Daniels married Emanuel's niece, Rosetta Solomon. The couple had many children including, in 1860, a son also named John.

Many ruddy and respectable types among Australia's early colonists kept themselves busy – and socially connected – by drilling with part-time volunteer militia units one evening a week. John Daniels Jnr enlisted in South Australia's Volunteer Military Force in 1877. He served four years in D (North Adelaide) Company, and was eventually promoted to lieutenant in the Port Adelaide Company. In 1885 he was posted to the Hindmarsh Company, where he was said to have been appointed to accompany the contingent then being formed for the Sudan.[3]

The NSW Sudan contingent and the extraordinary life of Ernest Simeon de Pass

The Sudan, an arid land in the Nile Valley, was in the throes of a revolt against its Imperial masters, the British-backed Egyptian government. The rebel Sufi 'Dervish' warriors, led by the messianic 'Mahdi' Muhammad Ahmad, hacked their way through various Egyptian forces, and were marching towards Egypt's southern Red Sea ports when the British despatched Major General Charles Gordon, former Governor-General of Sudan, to the Sudanese capital of Khartoum to supervise an evacuation. But Gordon, a hero of the Empire who had quashed a number of earlier uprisings, was not inclined to abandon the territory. Once the majority of British civilians had been returned home, the General, against the express wishes of his government, began to organise the defence of the city. Gordon and his men were besieged for a year until Khartoum finally fell in January 1885. Ten thousand people were massacred as the Dervishes sacked Khartoum, and the General was killed only two days before the arrival of a reluctantly despatched British relief force.

Calls for vengeance rang throughout the mother country and her colonies, but there was also a terrible sadness, felt in the Australian Jewish community as keenly as other reaches of the Empire. News of the General's death did not reach Sydney until Wednesday 11 February. On Friday 13 February, pupils at the Melbourne Hebrew School were lectured about Gordon's life by their head teacher, who spoke at length of the General's heroism, patriotic self-sacrifice and confidence in God. A tablet in Gordon's memory was to be placed in the schoolroom. The next day Rabbi Abrahams of the Bourke Street Synagogue promised that Jews would join in with any 'movement made by their fellow-citizens to perpetuate the memory of the gallant soldier'.[4]

The British resolved to crush the Mahdi, and the colonies were eager to play their part. New South Wales' offer to raise a contingent of men to send to the Sudan was accepted by the government in London, but approaches by Victoria, Queensland and South Australia to join the force were rebuffed, and therefore the services of John Daniels Jnr were never called upon. A contingent of 758 infantry and artillerymen steamed out of Sydney for the Sudan on 3 March 1885 to join a large British force despatched to protect a railway under construction at Sudan's Red Sea port at Suakin, from which it was hoped the Empire would push into Mahdi territory. The ranks of the Australians included the man who was probably the first Jewish Australian soldier to actually go to war, an extraordinary character by the name of Ernest Simeon de Pass.

Ernest was the son of prominent Victorian squatter Michael

de Pass, who in November 1863 came into possession of a large run at Wild Duck Creek, south-east of Bendigo. Michael was the child of Daniel de Pass and Rachel Davis, and the brother of Elliot de Pass. He was born into a distinguished Sephardic family that traced its roots to Portugal but which had spread its branches around the world, from London to the West Indies, South Africa and India. Wherever the de Pass family settled, they seemed to produce military men and adventurers, as well as businessmen and traders. Michael de Pass married Simmy Bensusan. The couple had five daughters and one son, Ernest, who was born in 1861 in Highbury, London, before the family came to Australia. Ernest was twenty-three years old when, in the heady summer of 1885, he enlisted as a private soldier in the Colonial Military Forces bound for the Sudan. He was a single man, who claimed his trade as 'silver refiner' and his religion as 'Hebrew'. He joined B Company of the infantry, in a proud uniform of red tunic, white helmet and blue trousers. He and his comrades boarded the SS *Iberia* to Suakin before huge, cheering crowds, anxious for the men from New South Wales to go overseas and prove that Australians would fight and die for the Empire. Two of the first 'substantial' men of the colony to put down a large sum of money towards financing the contingent were Benn Wolfe Levy and his brother-in-law George Judah Cohen.[5] The Melbourne *Argus* published with approval a patriotic sermon sent from Chief Rabbi Nathan Marcus Adler in London to be read out at synagogues throughout Victoria, and pronounced it 'not a little touching and impressive' that Jews were to beg, with great poetry and passion, for the Lord's blessing on the British soldiers in the Sudan.[6] Melbourne's *Jewish Herald* reprinted a remarkable piece from London's *Jewish World* newspaper which claimed the Jews were 'old enemies of the Soudanese' since 2500 years earlier when 'Asa, King of Judah, chased the dark-skinned hordes pell-mell from the land they had invaded under Zerah, the Kushite'.[7]

THE SUDAN CAMPAIGN SET A HOST OF PRECEDENTS THAT were to be followed in subsequent Australian military engagements: patriotic rabbis, anxious to display the loyalty of their community, declared their support for the war from the *bimah*; strong men volunteered to fight; wealthy men paid for their arms. Sometimes eccentric arguments were mustered by Jews to claim the conflict as one in which they might have a stake, so as to firmly identify their interests with the British Empire. Antisemites denounced the war as being the fault of the Jews – in this case 'the Jews of the Stock Exchange'[8] for having crushed Egyptian patriots and encouraged the scoundrels who replaced them.* The insinuation that the Sudan Campaign was a 'Jewish war' had little resonance with the public, who tended to either embrace the adventure or ridicule the adventurers: a certain Corporal John Monash of the 4th Victorian Rifles wrote of his frustration that the lives of his battalion had been 'made a burden' by the campaign, as their appearance in uniform acted as 'the signal for the display of all the wit of which unwashed Melbourne seems possessed'.[9] However, the idea that wars were fought primarily to further Jewish interests echoed tragically down the next century.

The Sudan Contingent dropped anchor en route to Suakin at the Yemeni sea port of Aden, where the men amused themselves in 'bantering a host of Jews, who offered ostrich feathers for sale'.[10] The Australians arrived in Suakin on 29 March, one week after a bloodbath at the staging post of Tofrek, in which the Empire had lost about 300 men and the Dervishes perhaps 2000. The contingent, however, did little fighting. The infantry were issued with light khaki jackets and trousers in place of their impractically

---

* *The Freeman's Journal* (4 April 1885) reported the British government had bought up shares in the Suez Canal and 'these shares are now held by wealthy money-lenders in England – mostly Jews it is said – and when these and other commercial interests became imperilled, the war was commenced'.

colourful uniforms and had a brief skirmish, in which three men were lightly wounded, on 3 April, but spent most of their time camped around the railway. By 17 May, the survivors of the contingent were safely on board the SS *Arab*, ready for the next day's return journey to Australia. They had lost only nine men – to typhoid and dysentery, rather than enemy action – and acquired a donkey as a mascot.

Throughout all this excitement John Daniels Jnr continued his successful career in the South Australian military unhampered by his remoteness from any war. In 1887 he became captain in charge of A (East Adelaide) Company. He was later quartermaster of the First Regiment and in December 1900 reached the rank of major. Meanwhile, the rather unsatisfactory Sudan episode had done nothing to dampen Ernest de Pass's martial ardour. He left Australia to settle back in England, where in 1890 he married Lizzie Maria Roe of Market Harborough, Leicestershire, and later took over her family's brush-making business. In January 1900 he signed up as a private soldier in a volunteer cavalry regiment, the Imperial Yeomanry, to go to South Africa and fight the Boers. He gave his age as thirty-nine, his trade as 'nil', and said he had never before been in the military, including the militia. He was 5ft 8in tall and 161 lbs, with a 40-inch chest, a tattoo of his initials on his right arm, a 'wound' on his knee and claimed his religion as 'Church of England'. Although de Pass may have converted to marry Roe, it was not unusual for a Jewish soldier to enlist in the Imperial forces as a Christian – particularly, perhaps, a man such as de Pass, who rarely filled out similar forms in the same way. He fought for two years in South Africa, where a Frederick Charles de Pass was also serving with the Canadian Mounted Rifles, and a John de Pass with Warren's Mounted Infantry. Ernest Simeon returned home in March 1902, whereupon he was granted a commission as quartermaster with the temporary rank of lieutenant, and paid a war gratuity of £15. De Pass was next heard of in June

1905, when he was described in a press report, rather startlingly, as a man who had 'fought through five wars and holds the record for volunteer service in the British Empire'. He was living in Naphill, Buckinghamshire, near the town of High Wycombe, when it was reported that his servant Jack Simla, a 'negro', had run away to the workhouse at nearby Saunderton on 'the foolish advice of his neighbour, who thought he saw in the presence of a black servant the beginning of an effort to introduce slavery into Buckingham-shire'. According to the report: 'When Mr de Pass arrived at the workhouse and claimed his "slave" back again, Jack's eyes glis-tened, and his face lit up with smiles.' It had all been a mistake. Simla was not de Pass's slave, but a boy de Pass had met during a trade expedition two years before, in what is now Ghana. 'The statement made at a meeting of the High Wycombe guardians that I brought him from his parents is an absolute fabrication,' said de Pass, who promised to send Simla 'back to West Africa ... with every penny of his accumulated wages'.[11]

Extraordinarily, Ernest Simeon de Pass, who must have been at least fifty-two years old, next enlisted in His Majesty's armed forces on 9 September 1914, when he joined the Oxford and Buck-inghamshire Light Infantry, one month after Britain declared war on Germany. He gave his age as forty-eight, and cited prior mili-tary service with the Australian Sudan Contingent, and the Impe-rial Yeomanry in South Africa. He had now lost both height and weight, standing at 5ft 7in and 154 lbs. His son Geoffrey Pamrial Barbe de Pass joined the same regiment and went to France as a lieutenant on 10 April 1916, but Ernest Simeon was discharged due to sickness on 1 March 1916. He had been appointed the reg-imental quartermaster sergeant but had begun to feel nervous and irritable. The Medical Board noted that 'the most marked nervous symptoms were loss of voice, weakness of vision and sleeplessness'. This was held to be caused by the 'stress and strain of work due to ordinary military service of a most exacting nature, leading to nervous breakdown' and was 'largely the result of active service with local volunteer corps and climate of Africa and Australia both as civilian and volunteer'. It was also recognised that he was 'old for his position and worked very hard'. By the time of his discharge, de Pass was claiming to have also served in the Anglo-Zulu War of 1879 and the First Boer War of 1880–81. He was a loss to the regiment. His commanding officer described him as being of 'very good' military character, 'thoroughly trustworthy and fitted for any responsible work'. He was granted a pension but, astonishingly, he appears to have joined the British Army again before the end of World War One. On 22 October 1918, according to the *London Gazette*, an Ernest Simeon de Pass was granted a commission as a temporary second lieutenant.[12]

2

Australia's armed forces emerge

Jews in the militia and the rise of John Monash

By the time the British Army left Australia in 1870, there were volunteer militias in every town and city. Wide variations existed in the potential military effectiveness of these units, in which commissions could be purchased by the socially ambitious, and whose messes also offered an entry into middle-class society. Although the volunteers were expected to help defend Australia from attack, some militia units appear to have acted as little more than dressing-up-and-drinking clubs. The departure of the British led to the formation of permanent, paid defence forces, which tended to draw their foot-soldiers from the less moneyed classes, but the volunteers remained as an enthusiastic military resource. John Daniels Jnr's comrades in the South Australian colonial forces included relatives on his mother's side, such as Benjamin Solomon, who had a longer connection with the SA military than any other man in the nineteenth century. Solomon had joined the artillery as a gunner in 1860, was gazetted a lieutenant in 1877, became Australia's first Jewish lieutenant colonel in 1897, and was still serving (in South Australia) during the Boer War.

In 1900, when Dr George Hains of Gladstone, South Australia, was granted a commission as lieutenant surgeon in the Gladstone Mounted Rifles, he joined only two other Jewish officers in the SA militia: Benjamin Solomon and the tireless Captain and Quartermaster John Daniels Jnr. Daniels was president of the First Battalion committee, a body of non-commissioned officers and men elected to manage the gymnastic, sporting and social affairs of the regiment, and for a time was also honorary secretary of the Naval and Military Club of South Australia. When he gave up his position at the club, he was presented with 'a handsome liqueur stand' by the club's president, Lieutenant Colonel Solomon.[1] The Solomon family was a mainstay of the SA militia. The Lieutenant Colonel's son, Lance Corporal Reg Solomon, was a member of the Field Artillery, and Reg's cousin, Len Solomon, was in the Pioneer Corps. Another cousin, Walter Samuel Solomon, eventually went to the Boer War with the 6th Contingent from New South Wales.[2]

There were Jews scattered in the militias throughout Australia, but the Tamworth Company of the 4th Regiment NSW Infantry was rare in that it boasted two Jewish officers, Captain Albert Joseph and Lieutenant Eric Hyman, whose brother, Arthur Hyman, held a commission in the NSW Mounted Rifles.[3]

ALONGSIDE THE MILITIA GREW THE RIFLE CLUBS, WHICH were often run by militia officers. These organisations, whose early members included sporting shooters, gradually evolved into militia themselves, albeit in a rather ad hoc manner. When Isidore Isaacson of Stawell, Victoria, was gazetted a lieutenant in 1889, the *Jewish Herald* described his unit as 'the Rifle Ranges [sic], the new branch of the military forces of the colony'. The paper also reported that a Captain Joseph of the Torpedo Corps had been promoted to the rank of major.[4] The Victorian Mounted Rifles (VMR) emerged from the rifle clubs, and its Jewish officers included Myer Evergood Blashki (who was later to make a different name for himself as the painter Miles Evergood). The young Blashki, one of fourteen children of the prominent Melbourne watchmaker and jeweller Phillip Blashki, was an 'all-round sportsman: swimmer, runner, boxer, horseman and tennis player'.[5] In 1890 Myer Blashki was commissioned a lieutenant in the 2nd VMR, where he remained for four years, the first in a long march of his family members to serve in the Australian military. In March 1900 his brother Henry Blashki convened 'a meeting of gentlemen' to form a rifle club in South Yarra.[6]

In 1884 the young Melbourne University student John Monash joined the university's D Company of the 4th Battalion, Victorian Rifles. Monash was born in West Melbourne in 1865, the son of German-speaking Polish Jews Louis Monash and Bertha Manasse. He was the grandson of a rabbi but neither of his parents had any real involvement with the Australian Jewish community, and in 1874 the family moved to the small Riverina town of Jerilderie in New South Wales where Louis ran a general store and John attended a one-teacher bush school. In 1877 Monash was enrolled in Scotch College, Melbourne. When he turned thirteen he was *barmitzvah* at the East Melbourne Synagogue, but by the time he reached university he thought of himself as agnostic.

Monash was a student of arts and engineering, a polymath immersed in mathematics who also played the piano, ran the student newspaper, spoke at student debates, and wrote with clarity and fluidity. He was also popular with women. At one time or another, four of Phillip Blashki's daughters – Minnie, Jeanette, Rose and Eva – all hoped to marry him,[7] but Monash was troubled by their orthodoxy and they by his irreligiosity. As a student, Monash was an enthusiastic and dedicated soldier in a milieu that still attracted more than its share of dilettantes and drunks. He was promoted to colour sergeant, and despaired at the indiscipline of some of his comrades. In turn, they nicknamed him 'Corporal Potash' for his fastidiousness. D Company was disbanded in 1886, its military utility in doubt. In March 1887 Monash was working as a civil engineer when he joined the North Melbourne Battery of the Garrison Artillery, where he was quickly promoted to lieutenant. He struggled to modernise thinking within the artillery and to abolish the traditional but useless practice of musketry. He designed his own gun, the 'Stanley-Monash', to be used in more realistic artillery drills. It was a great success. Monash initially had difficulty with marksmanship, but through practice became the battalion's finest marksman. In 1891 he married Hannah Victoria Moss in a Jewish ceremony. He added a law degree to his accomplishments, became a prolific lecturer in military matters, and continued his battle to push the military towards a better understanding of science. His married life may have been a series of triumphs and reverses – he and Victoria separated for a while during 1894–95 – but his army career was one long advance, and he was promoted to captain in October 1895.

The Jameson Raid and the Jews

When prospectors discovered gold in the Transvaal in the mid-1880s, a scrappy and truculent landlocked backwater in southern Africa suddenly became a wealthy and alluring place to live. The Dutch farmer-settlers commonly known as Boers, who had been the first white people to arrive en masse at the foot of Africa, were joined by vast numbers of immigrants from other, less blessed parts of the world, including about a thousand Australians fleeing hard times at home. Life was tough and success elusive for most of those who descended upon Johannesburg with grand dreams of easy fortunes. Even Walter 'Karri' Davies, a Western Australian Jew who was 'as strong and upright as the timber he had come to sell from his father's vast Western Australian estate',[8] found it difficult to prosper. Karri Davies – who adopted the name of the trees that grew in his family's forest lands at Karridale and fed his father's timber mills – was the son of Maurice Coleman Davies and Sarah

Salom, a Jewish couple who married in Adelaide in 1858. Karri Davies was Australia's most celebrated Jewish soldier in the days before World War One, and was acclaimed as a hero throughout the British Empire, only to become lost in history as European wars eclipsed colonial conflicts and the sun set on the Imperial dream.

Karri Davies arrived in South Africa in 1893 to open new markets for the family timber business. He expected to be treated like any other white man (black Africans were considered a species aside) but the Boers refused to grant political rights to new arrivals, who remained foreigners, or *uitlanders*, in the eyes of the governments of the autonomous colonies of the Transvaal and the Orange Free State. 'We had no political rights,' wrote Karri Davies in 1896, 'and it had been made impossible for us to ever obtain them. We contributed over three-fourths of the revenue of the country, but only a fraction of it was being spent on us. We objected to the corruption of the Government. We had no proper water supply, although the rainfall yearly was ample. The sanitation of the town was disgraceful. The educational laws were such that it was impossible for us to educate our children, except at great expense.'

The Boers feared the economic domination of a small and newly minted 'randlord' class of wealthy miners, and gold and diamond traders, many of whom were Jewish. But the *uitlanders*, rich and poor, demanded the same rights as British citizens in other parts of South Africa and when their 40 000-signature petition was ignored by the government, they began to stockpile weapons. Members of a Reform Committee of prominent Johannesburg citizens – whose ranks included the Jewish randlord (entrepreneur) Lionel Phillips, as well as Cecil Rhodes' brother, Colonel Frank Rhodes, and Karri Davies – asked the administrator of neighbouring Matabeleland, Leander Starr Jameson, if he would cross the border and come to the aid of a planned uprising. Jameson agreed but the rebellion was repeatedly delayed until Jameson lost patience. With a force of 600 men, he 'invaded the country without our knowledge and against our wishes', wrote Karri Davies, 'and upset the whole of our arrangements'. Jameson had hoped to spark the rebellion, and indeed on 31 December 1895 armed *uitlanders* hoisted the Transvaal flag and took over Johannesburg.

The rebels were told the Boers were anxious to avoid a civil war and that if the Reform Committee sent a deputation to the capital, they would win most of what they wanted. 'Whilst we held the rifle in one hand,' wrote Karri Davies, 'we were still prepared to extend the other in friendship if they would meet us half way.' The committee offered themselves as hostages, to ensure that the Boers would allow Jameson to leave the country unmolested. 'After making this arrangement with us,' wrote Karri Davies, 'the Government sent a large force out, who met and captured Jameson and his men.' Although the British government supported the aims of the raid, it would not endorse the raiders. The Reform Committee met Sir Hercules Robinson, the British governor of neighbouring Cape Colony, who told them if they did not lay down their arms, Jameson and his men would be shot. 'It is now a matter of history that this statement was untrue,' wrote Karri Davies. The committee asked the former chief justice of the Transvaal, Nicolaas Jacobus de Wet, 'whether he believed the Transvaal Government was acting in good faith towards us, or whether, having disarmed us, they might not take measures against us,' wrote Karri Davies. De Wet promised, on behalf of the British government, that 'not a hair of a man's head in Johannesburg' would be touched.

'In the face of this,' wrote Karri Davies, 'we were arrested and sentenced as follows: The four leaders to death, and the fifty-nine others to two years' imprisonment, a £2000 fine, or another year's imprisonment and three years' banishment.' Karri Davies was not among the four condemned, but he was a prisoner. He and his comrades felt they had been entrapped and that the British government had reneged on a promise of protection. But they pleaded guilty to the charges that were laid against them, as they were told by their counsel that their guilty plea would help the leaders, and their own crimes would be reduced to technical offences. Neither assurance proved reliable, and Karri Davies and the others were each sent to prison for two years.

The other members of the Reform Committee – even the leaders – were gradually released, with fines and bonds and on promises to play no further part in the politics of the Transvaal. The last two prisoners were Karri Davies and his great friend Captain Aubrey Woolls-Sampson, who swore they would never compromise. 'Our refusing to sign an appeal or petition to this Government is not pig-headedness,' wrote Karri Davies. 'We prefer to serve our sentence to degrading ourselves by asking this Government for anything.'[9]

Karri Davies fully intended to join another uprising against the government. He and Woolls-Sampson chose honour above all, and they never gave in. It was an extraordinarily idealistic, principled and inflexible stand, and characteristic of the way Karri Davies carried himself through life.

Jameson was handed over by the Boer government to the British, sent to London for trial, and sentenced to fifteen months in Holloway Prison. The other British raiders were shipped out with him, and some gave evidence in court. These included a mercurial Jewish adventurer named Henry Laurence Bernstein, a Melbourne man who had left Victoria several years previously to seek his fortune in South Africa. Bernstein was the son of a Jacob Bernstein, formerly of Dunedin, New Zealand, and Rachel Marks. He was born in 1872 and apparently joined the British South Africa Force in August 1893 and fought in the first Matabele War, which began when that force invaded Matabeleland in November. Bernstein was commissioned as subaltern in charge of the machine-gun battery, in a conflict which was noted for the savage efficiency with which the British guns slaughtered the local warriors. Bernstein was wounded in battle, promoted to lieutenant and, by his own testimony, publicly thanked by the commandant for bringing in the baggage wagons. In August 1894, he joined the New Matabeleland Mounted Police, whose ranks provided many of Jameson's raiders. After the Jameson Trial, in 1897, the Colonial Office seems to have appointed Bernstein to accompany the Niger Expeditionary Force as an instructor in machine-gunnery.[10] This was not the last time history was to hear of Henry Bernstein and his machine guns.

The Second Boer War

The Boers had seen the Jameson Raid as a declaration of war. In the following years, in the eyes of both the government and its most dedicated foes, the conflict was cold but never dead. While Karri Davies was imprisoned for his part in the Johannesburg uprising, he had sworn that his 'little Union Jack' would fly over the Boer capital of Pretoria within five years.[11] The Second Boer War broke out on 11 October 1899, to the surprise of nobody. It was fought by the British under the pretext of rights for the *uitlanders*. The Boer governments of Transvaal and the Orange Free State united to attack the Cape Colony with well-armed units made up largely of ordinary citizens (*burghers*) mustered into local 'commando' units, although each Boer state also possessed full-time, professional artillery. The Boers were expert marksmen and horsemen, and the early battles went their way.

While there had long been a small number of Jewish soldiers in the British Army, Britain's Jews were not much stirred by martial passion until the Second Boer War. The conflict in South Africa coincided with a revival of interest in military affairs among the Jews of Europe. In Medieval times, Jews had occasionally soldiered in Muslim armies, but in Europe, as a reviled minority, they saw little to gain from military adventuring, and much to lose should the heat of war turn upon them – as it so often did. But in the nineteenth century, the nature of European armies slowly changed and the idea of a citizen soldier, driven by patriotism, replaced older notions of a bloodthirsty sell-sword or a press-ganged peasant. Jews fought in the French Revolution for the promise of emancipation, and across Europe came to adopt the new nationalistic thinking, and take public pride in bearing arms in common cause with gentiles in France, Italy, Austria and Germany.

In the decades immediately before the Second Boer War, Australia's *Jewish Herald* regularly published news of the growing number of Jews in foreign armies. The question was asked whether the descendants of Judah Maccabee – who had led the revolt that had restored Jewish worship to the Temple in Jerusalem in 164 BCE – could become a warrior people once again. In July 1880 the paper reported there were 20413 Jewish soldiers, exclusive of officers, in the Austrian army.[12] The next year it was noted in a foreign despatch that there were now 30603 Austrian Jewish soldiers. An excitable story supposed that 'in the same proportion, there must be enrolled in the German army about 25000 and in the Russian about 50000 men'. From these figures, the writer argued, 'The Jews of those three countries can place in the field 100000 trained men, and Abraham had only 318 men. Neither King David nor the Maccabees had so large an army. If the three Kaisers would send their Jewish soldiers into the field, and Rothschild furnish the money, they could take Palestine and some of the adjacent countries.'[13] This line of thought so animated the *Jewish Herald* that the item was repeated verbatim one month later.[14]

In addition to the global low-key Jewish military renaissance were factors singular to both Australia and South Africa. The Jewish population of Australia had never faced significant, organised antisemitic violence. Most saw themselves as British above all, and some felt the need to prove themselves worthy of the empire that had granted them equal rights wherever English was spoken – with the rare exception of South Africa. Nor were the Calvinist Boers from afar seen as great friends of the Jewish people: as Reverend David Isaac Freedman told his Perth Hebrew Congregation in October 1899, in the Transvaal it had been proposed that 'even if the so-called Outlanders were granted a conditional franchise, yet the Polish and Russian Jews should be excluded'. A nation such as this, said Freedman, 'had still to be taught an elementary lesson of civilisation'.[15] The Boers deserved a beating, and the Jews stood with the rest of the Empire, cudgels in hand.

Globally, there was also a current of thinking that blamed Jews for the conflict with the Boers, an idea seized upon with grubby enthusiasm by the radical nationalists at the *Bulletin* magazine and the antisemitic populists at Melbourne's extravagantly misnamed newspaper the *Truth*. The British Empire, they believed, was guided by the hidden hand of the Jews to protect the profits of the rapacious Jewish randlords. The *Truth* merrily referred to the Australian contingents eventually raised for South Africa as 'Cohentingents'. Sections of the labour movement were equally hostile.

When it was suggested by Rabbi Hermann Adler, the Chief Rabbi of the British Empire, that there were many pseudonymous British Jews at the front, the satirical newspaper *Punch* claimed the statement was made to correct 'the popular impression that the war in South Africa was being fought for and not by the Jews'.[16] But there were Jews fighting on the Boer side too. An apocryphal story was widely circulated to illustrate the dilemma faced by Jewish soldiers. The anecdote, reprinted in several Australian newspapers, took the form of a letter written by 'one of the Jewish soldiers of the Queen' who was in 'the thick of one of the engagements', charging through a hailstorm of bullets in pursuit of the Boers. 'Just as I was near one of them he dodged me,' the alleged soldier wrote. 'When I was within a few paces of him he turned round and was preparing to fire at me. Then I saw he hesitated, and, to tell the truth, I hesitated too, for I could see he was a young Jew ... But I remembered it was Briton v. Boer, and Jew or no Jew it is all the same in war. I recollected that thousands of Jews were saying Dr Adler's prayer for the success of our arms, so I did my duty. I heard the poor chap say something in Hebrew as I hit him.'[17] Since there were, at best, 250 Jews fighting on the side of the Boers in the entire course of the war,[18] the odds for one of them engaging in individual combat with a Jew on the other side were low, and for the British soldier's actions to be governed by the echoing words of a rabbi shows a remarkable degree of piety. But the moral was clear: in a life-or-death situation, Jews on either side would pause before striking a co-religionist, but the Briton (which, of course, included the Australian) would put his loyalty to the Queen before Hebrew fellow-feeling.*

At the start of the Second Boer War in October 1899, there were hardly 200 Jews in the Territorial Army in Britain, but perhaps 1000 British Jews volunteered to fight in South Africa.[19] Among Australians, at least eighty-eight verifiably Jewish men answered the call, a number roughly proportionate with Jewish numbers in the general population. The first Jews to fight were those who, like Karri Davies, were already settled in South Africa. They included Jewish Australians who had arrived before the Jameson Raid, such as Ballarat rabbi Israel Morris Goldreich's sons Samuel and Leisser.

In June 1899, 15 000 British troops under the command of Sir

---

*   Similar stories were later told during World War One, when there was a much higher – but still negligible – chance of two Jews facing each other on the battlefield. For example, Maurice Smith, the son of VC winner Issy Smith, wrote of his father: 'At Neuve Chapelle in France he had captured a prisoner, and was just on the point of bayonetting him, when something held him back. He did not bayonet the man, but took him prisoner, and placed him where the prisoners were received. There on searching the man, he found that the German was wearing a Jewish token.' (Smith, Maurice, 'Issy Smith VC', *Australian Jewish Historical Society Journal*, November 2006, p. 183)

Redvers Buller were despatched to the British colony of Natal in the hope of cowing the Boers or defending the colony in case the united forces of Transvaal and the Orange Free State should attack. Karri Davies, who had been released from jail by the Boer president, Paul Kruger, on the occasion of Queen Victoria's Diamond Jubilee in 1897, joined a group of friends to raise a regiment, the Imperial Light Horse (ILH). More than 5000 men applied for the 500 places in the ranks of the ILH, spurred on by the huge popularity of Karri Davies and his fellow commander Woolls-Sampson. Many of the recruits selected were Australians.

In October, the uncowed Boers invaded both the Cape Colony and Natal. Samuel Goldreich joined Bethune's Mounted Infantry, a corps raised in Durban, Natal, under the command of Lieutenant Colonel Edward Cecil Bethune. Leisser manned the guns with the Cape Garrison Artillery. The small number of Australian Jewish women in South Africa included Rose Shappere, who had been the first Jewish woman in Victoria to qualify as a nurse. Rose had taken herself to the Transvaal in early 1899, spurred on by rumours of war. Like so many men of her generation, it seems, she hoped to test herself under fire. Rose's brother, 22-year-old Lieutenant Harry Shappere, was a member of the Royal Horse Artillery, a British regiment stationed in Meerut, India. As Harry's regiment was idle, he volunteered to go to South Africa with the Royal Field Artillery, and left India for Durban on 5 October 1899. Harry, an expert horseman, quickly established himself as his troop's "'dare-devil" and rough rider',[20] but it was said that 'for nerve and pluck, there are few that can equal and none that can surpass' his sister.[21]

Rose Shappere was the first nurse to join the Boer commando but, when she found the Boer ambulance would only treat Boers, she travelled south-east to join the British division at Ladysmith, Natal. After she arrived, Ladysmith was isolated when a Boer commando cut railway and telegraph links with another base at Dundee, and a force, including five squadrons of the ILH, was despatched from the division to confront the commando at Elandslaagte on 21 October 1899. One squadron of the ILH, under a Captain John Charles Knapp, became separated from the main force. Knapp failed to receive the order to withdraw when Boer fire had destroyed the Natal Artillery's ammunition wagon, and headed blindly into a trap. Karri Davies rode after them – one man with no cover, under heavy fire – and caught up with Knapp and led his squadron to safety. Karri Davies' commanding officer, General Sir John French, wanted to recommend him for a Victoria Cross, but Davies refused the honour, as he had pledged from the start to serve without reward. He was later gazetted to become a Companion of the Order of the Bath but insisted his name should be removed from the honours list.[22] He was a storybook hero, a man who embodied the values considered the finest by his age and whose deeds were widely celebrated in both Britain and Australia. The fact that he was a Jew went broadly unreported.

Much the same could be said of Rose Shappere, who was in Ladysmith when the Boers laid siege to the division on 2 November. Eventually the Boers allowed the British wounded to be moved outside the garrison and encamped in nearby Intombi. 'There I had charge at one time of eighty-four patients,' said Shappere. 'The tents were badly pitched; in the windstorms they nearly blew down, and actually went down in the rain. The tents filled with water, and the poor patients, who were lying on the ground, were simply wetted through and through … The patients were laid out to dry, they were given a sun bath. But the want of food and comforts was the worst of the siege. Even our starving stomachs revolted at the food and the drink, and as for the patients, all that we could give them at night was water; in the day they were allowed half a pint of milk. It was terrible in every phase, and in the midst of it shells would come flying into the hospital. It was very hard work, too; going from tent to tent with orderlies who did nothing, and delirious and dying men to attend to.'[23] By February

1900 Harry and Rose's mother in St Kilda was suffering 'great anxiety' as she had not heard from either of her children for months.[24]

Karri Davies and the ILH fought to defend Ladysmith at Gun Hill and then at Wagon Hill on 6 January 1900, when a large force of Boers attacked a much smaller number of Light Horsemen in a push to smash through into Ladysmith. Many of the ILH were killed and Karri Davies, among others, was wounded. He wrote home to his brother Herb, 'Hearing the Boers were only 100 yards on our flank and on the hill I went to tell Major Miller-Wallnutt of the Gordons as he did not seem to know they were there … and our own men were on the top of the ridge within nine or ten yards of the Boer on the other side of the valley. I was afraid the Gordons would shoot our men. So when I crawled up to Major Wallnutt I told him I would take a few men forward and look with the glasses to see if I could see the Devils. He said he would come and so we crawled along on our bellies and I saw the Boers going up on the other side of the valley and said, "I can see them, lend me your rifle." We were all ordered to carry rifles so as officers could not be distinguished from men. He said, "I have no cartridges", at which I remarked, "Dam". He said, "Never mind, I'll get some", and crawling over to one of his men he got a package as I half turned and took his rifle. The next thing I felt a smack like a steam hammer on the spine. So I said, "Can you move your legs if your spines hit?" and he remarked you could not. Well, at first I could not, but after a bit I found I could. He said, "You're hit, let me tie you up." I said, "No it is too much [for] our little lot. I am right and will go back for reinforcements," so I started rolling back and they potted at me all the way as I rolled. My khaki britches had washed white so they were a good target. I saw the devil aim at me as you could see the smoke from the black powder. He was about 100 or 120 yards off. I got a bit back and one of the Gordons came and I wrote a note and had it sent to the Colonel for more men. The Gordons then tied me up and then as they were firing at us like H— I rolled walked and tumbled down the hill.' A man gave Karri Davies a drop of rum. 'Good thing rum,' he wrote, 'when you are hit in the bottom. When I got to the bottom of the hill I arrived in a cosy little place kept warm by the Boer shrapnel which were arriving quite in a hurry. I then heard the Colonel had been hit so sent our orderly in full split for reinforcements. The doctor then came along and sent an ambulance as he said I looked green. I got down all right and found we had nine officers hit.'

Many British soldiers were sacrificed in bayonet charges at Wagon Hill, and the ILH lost men fighting to save them. 'The way the army is run is rotten,' wrote Davies, 'and it is a lucky job we were only fighting Boers and not a European power.' But he still had faith in the justice of the British cause, and wrote that he hoped he would live to see that 'the result of our staying fourteen months in gaol has helped to make South Africa a better place for mankind to live in'.[25]

SIR REDVERS BULLER AND HIS NATAL FIELD FORCE LOST battles at Stormberg, Magersfontein and Colenso, in what was later referred to as 'Black Week'. Their early attempts to relieve Ladysmith met with disaster at Spioenkop on the Tugela River. The first Jewish Australian killed in the Boer War was 40-year-old Mark Goldstein, the fourth son of the late Rabbi Louis Goldstein of Melbourne. Impatient with the delay in raising a unit in Australia, Goldstein had taken himself to Cape Town, where he had joined the Natal Carbineers on 10 January 1900. He died in February, shot through the neck while trying to help a comrade in the Battle of Tugela Heights, six miles from Colenso.[26]

Goldstein was among a number of volunteers from prominent Jewish families, including Samuel and Leisser Goldreich; Leopold Wolfe Cohen, the son of George Judah Cohen, president of the Great Synagogue, Sydney; Samuel Harris, the son of Nathan

Harris, past president of the Perth Hebrew Congregation; Percy Hollander, the son of Jacob Hollander, past president of Ballarat Hebrew Congregation and president of the Zionist Movement in Sydney; and Alfred Solomon Saunders, the eldest son of Moses Saunders, who had presided over early religious services in Western Australia. The relatives of Jewish politicians were also well represented. Walter Solomon of the 6th Australian Contingent was related to two of Australia's first Federal parliamentarians, Elias Solomon (a nephew of Emanuel Solomon) and Vaiben Louis Solomon; and Louis Eleazar Phillips, of Cameron's Scouts, was the brother of Pharez Phillips, another member of that same parliament. Mark Frederick Collins' half-brother Charles was the first mayor of Narrabri, succeeded by Collins' full-brother Albert Ernest. (Charles later became the Member of the Legislative Assembly for that constituency, to be succeeded, once again, by Albert Ernest.) But their enthusiasm was not shared by John Monash who was now in his mid-thirties, a capable and enthusiastic soldier, with a cauldron of innovative ideas bubbling in his head. If Monash chose not to join the fight in South Africa, the chances were he would never go to war and would remain all his life untested and unfulfilled. Nonetheless, he decided to remain in Australia to attend to his business interests and family. 'This is certainly not an occasion where patriotism demands the making of any personal sacrifices,' he wrote to a junior officer who had asked Monash whether he should volunteer.[27]

The Boer War populated common English speech with new words borrowed from Afrikaans and indigenous languages. Men wrote home with stories of the flatlands known as *veldt*; the granite hills called *kopjes*; the *neks*, which were passes between hills; the *dongas*, dry creeks or river beds; the black people derided as *kaffirs*; and the *kraals*, a word used to describe both a cluster of *kaffir* huts and a cattle pen. Australian soldiers sent accounts of the pom-poms, automatic weapons despatching one-pound shells loaded with bullets, which exploded like a body of men firing independently, and much of their correspondence was printed in local newspapers.

A letter home from Samuel Goldreich gave one of the first published reports of the early months of the war by a Jewish soldier. Goldreich had been at Spioenkop and Colenso. 'What we have to go through on two biscuits a day (sometimes a little more or less) seems utterly impossible for a human being to do,' he wrote. 'For instance, saddle up at 3.30 am, patrol all day, with a chance of an encounter with the enemy in the hot sun, return to camp about 7 pm, go at once on picket all night, and patrol next day. This goes on for weeks, and notwithstanding the poor scoff food we are all in grand health, which I put down more to excitement than the food.' The soldiers' life agreed with the rabbi's son. 'I can honestly say that I am enjoying myself,' he wrote, 'and have never felt better in my life.'[28] But in besieged Ladysmith in December 1899, Rose Shappere later wrote, 'All the patients were simply dying of starvation. We had run short of medicine, stimulants and all medical comforts … It was an awful Christmas day. One never to be forgotten, blazing hot, and patients dying all round you, and very little comfort could we give them.'[29] Karri Davies, who had organised cricket matches and other sporting events throughout the siege, bought up all the toys in town and gave them away at a Christmas party for Ladysmith's 250 children.[30] Rose's brother, the dashing Henry Shappere, was also in Ladysmith at the time of the siege. The siblings met by accident, and hardly recognised one another as they had been apart for so long.[31]

On 28 February 1900 the siege was broken by squadrons of the Natal Carbineers and the ILH. Karri Davies left Ladysmith for other battles. By this time, Rose Shappere was exhausted and sick. 'Once I broke down for three days and had to take to my bed,' she wrote, 'and again for two days, and then I broke down again eight days before the convoy came. I got rheumatics from having to sleep in a soaking bed while on night duty. With hard work, anxiety and no food, I was a skeleton.'[32] She was invalided to Mooi River, and then recuperated in England, before returning to the war in South Africa. While in London, she gave an angry interview to a newspaper. 'I never really shall know how we nurses ever managed to come out of the siege alive,' she said. 'I never realised before that the human frame could stand so much. In the first place, the military hospital camp at Intombi was grossly mismanaged. Everything was to our disadvantage ... Everything seemed to go wrong ... I couldn't trust my orderly, who would steal my patients' food on the first opportunity. Towards the end the strain grew unbearable. Many and many a time have I gone on duty at six in the morning, to leave off at eleven at night with the same programme next day. Many and many a time have we all been compelled to go into the enteric wards without so much as a cup of tea; while our beds – well, I've gone in soaked through and through, and fagged out, to find my bed soaking as well. Again, the cooking – I wonder we ever did any. No sooner would a fire be lighted than down would come the teeming rain, absolutely deluging everything.'[33] Rose Shappere was Mentioned in Despatches.

Back home in Australia, contingents from every state had been raised in a carnival of jingoistic zeal. There was a handful of Jewish military veterans in the state contingents. Sydney-born Charles Lima Braun had sailed Australian waters with the Royal Navy torpedo gunboat HMS *Karrakatta* and Braun was reportedly still honorary secretary of the ship's football team in 1899.[34] But in January 1900, he steamed out of Sydney on the *Southern Cross* with the 1st NSW Mounted Rifles. Braun was described as an 'honorary instructor of the Life Saving Society, who passed with honours and a bronze medal the examination for First Aid, and made top score out of 400 men in the shooting test' when he was recommended as sergeant for the second contingent to leave New South Wales.[35] His brother Benjamin Henry Braun, a sign-writer who had left

Australia two months earlier with the first NSW contingent, was already in South Africa. On board the *Southern Cross* with Charles Lima Braun was Mark Frederick Collins, a Jewish lance corporal in Braun's C Squadron. The ship arrived in South Africa in February. For a short time, when their lieutenant left for another unit, Braun took charge of the squadron and Collins was third in command. The Rifles marched to Poplar Grove among an army of about 30 000 troops. They rode past the site of the battle of Paardeberg and the British defeat that became known as Bloody Sunday. 'Dead horses were there in hundreds,' wrote Collins, 'and vultures in thousands.' The men 'commandeered' 208 sheep and goats and three head of cattle from local farms, and on 10 March were fired upon by Boers; five of Collins' comrades were wounded and one killed.[36]

Sergeant Major Harry Wollstein had been a lieutenant in the Cameronians, or Scottish Rifles, in the British Army. He had served the Empire in India, New Zealand and the First Boer War, and was living quietly in Queensland when he joined the 2nd Queensland Mounted Infantry as a private. His military value was clear and, before leaving camp, he was promoted to corporal. On the voyage to South Africa in January 1900 he was promoted to sergeant and soon after he arrived, he became company sergeant major. In April he wrote from near the Orange Free State capital of Bloemfontein that the place had hardly changed since he was last there, eight years before. He had fought in the Battle of Driefontein, in which Imperial forces sustained heavy casualties breaking the Boer Line, and the old soldier was clearly back in his element. 'I am feeling "fit as a fiddle",' he wrote, 'and as hard as nails – never have felt sick or sorry for a moment since I got on board at Brisbane, and have not stopped any bullets as yet, although I came very near doing so at Driefontein.'[37]

SAMUEL HARRIS WAS TWENTY-FOUR YEARS OLD WHEN HE went off to war with the second contingent of West Australian Mounted Infantry, No. 4 Division. He had been an officer in the senior cadets in Victoria, and brought his commission with him to the Perth Regiment in 1894. He was a member of the Fremantle Polo Club and well known in the Jewish community. Harris was given a farewell by the intensely patriotic Reverend Freedman, who named him as the only Jewish officer so far in the Australasian contingents. As midnight approached, Lieutenant Harris was hoisted onto the shoulders of his friends, who sang hearty, patriotic songs, while his mother stood silently in the corner, her eyes filled with tears.[38]

On 5 May 1900 the West Australians working as scouts for the British officer General Pole-Carew moved forward to the Vet River to attack a Boer position near the village of Brandfort and drew artillery fire from behind some *kopjes*. British guns replied, but the Boers hit one of the batteries. The British called in naval guns and at about 3 pm a message came from the General for an officer and two men to volunteer to find a crossing over the river. 'This meant a big risk as we had to steal right round, and under the enemy's position,' wrote Lieutenant Harris. 'Eventually volunteers were called for from among the officers, of whom there were fourteen, and I think they all offered to go. However, I was the selected one.' He took his two men, left one of them by the riverbed with their horses and crawled with his corporal for about 800 metres until they came to a crossing that would be navigable with artillery. 'I wrote my report,' he remembered, 'taking care to note that the house close by us was flying a white flag from the roof.' When he got back to the column, Lieutenant Harris was told Lord Roberts, the leader of the British forces in South Africa, had ordered the division to take the *kopje* that commanded the drift over the river. They marched to about 750 metres from the enemy when 'we were greeted with a perfect hail of bullets', wrote Harris. 'Down we went. There was not a particle of shelter, but we all lay close ... I never lay closer to anything than I did to the ground when that firing was going on. We replied with volley after volley, and with good effect, for after about a quarter of an hour, though it seemed a month, their fire ceased somewhat, and we then advanced by rushes from the right, until our right flank was in line with the farmhouse that was flying the white flag. They then opened a hellish fire from this building; and being at a closer range, this took greater effect ... and my helmet was shot clean through from right to left ... We then received the order to put in three volleys of magazine fire, fix bayonets, and charge ... When we got on the kopje their fire ceased, to our cheers and "Give 'em the same, boys." We all got down behind rocks, completely blown, and so ended the warmest bit of fighting for the day, and I trust I may never get into such a tight place again ... Next morning, I am pleased to say, the house from which we were fired at was blown up with all its contents.'[39]

Harris rose to the rank of captain and then commander of the 2nd WA Mounted Rifles but proved to be a controversial officer; he was criticised for cowardice by one of his soldiers and accused of 'more than questionable' conduct at the front by his commandant, but praised and supported by his colonel. He disappeared in South Africa, possibly with some missing money, and was reported to be in gaol in Johannesburg in 1904.[40]

There was never a stain on the honour of Karri Davies: 16 May 1900 saw the liberation of Mafeking, which had been besieged since October 1899, and Davies was the first man to ride into town, at the head of a line of troopers of the Imperial Light Horse. He was also one of the first men in Johannesburg when the city fell on 31 May. The Transvaal capital of Pretoria surrendered on 5 June. 'Once more we are back in the rotten old place,' Karri Davies wrote to Herb, 'but there is not that pleasure in coming here which I always expected to have, this is due to the war not being over and until the war is quite over and this proclaimed a British Colony I will not feel happy.'[41]

The *Sydney Morning Herald* published 'A Woman's Letter from London', in which a correspondent showered praise on Jewish soldiers. 'On the field of battle,' she wrote, 'the Queen's Jewish officers go to the front and fight like Englishmen in the hottest corners of every engagement.'[42] Her letter drew a furious response from 'An Australian Jew' incensed by the suggestion that Jews could only be 'like' Englishmen. 'They fight for England's flag and Queen, and yet they are only like Englishmen,' he fumed. 'Wherefore the distinction?'[43]

THE LARGEST OF THE LAST SET-PIECE BATTLES OF THE WAR was fought on 11–12 June 1900 at Diamond Hill, where Imperial forces drove the Boers out of striking distance of Pretoria. During the chaos, Charles Braun of the NSW Mounted Rifles shot a Boer and took the man's brother prisoner on the field. On the second day of the fighting, wrote Braun, 'The ground was rough and boggy, and a lot had to dismount.' The men from New South Wales charged a line of sniping Boers. 'You should have heard the row,' wrote Braun. 'Some cheered, others yelled, a lot more swore. Only about twelve in our own company had bayonets fixed. Some were lost, others would not fix through being used as picket pegs, but still we went. The butt end of a rifle is good enough. Spotted a chap waiting for a shot; took aim, and fired. As I did so, saw another of his breed taking aim my way. Dropped to the ground, told my mate, [Cuthbert] Fetherstonhaugh, to do likewise, but the bullet went so close to his cheek that it scorched him. Followed up, and came on the fellow I had fired at. His mate turned out to be his brother, who had been trying to carry him away. He waved a white handkerchief and asked for water. I offered him a drink. He said: "Nay, my brudder." Had a look at his brother, poured water down his throat; he was bleeding at the mouth, and died quickly. The bullets came pretty close then, and the shells were bursting everywhere, so got under cover and kept the Boer with me. He had thrown away his rifle, and I took what ammunition he had. Had a yarn with him in broken English. Told me his brother was a field cornet, and had three farms. While we were talking a shell burst very close. Told him to keep down, but he said "The Lord watch me." "Yes," I said, "but that won't stop you from following your brother." Then there was a shout to me to bring on the prisoner. Made a start, but the bullets were thick. A pom-pom struck near us, and the Boer dropped on his stomach and would not move despite the great faith he professed.'[44] Late in 1900 Braun was invalided to England for several months with enteric fever, or typhoid. He returned to South Africa and gained a commission in the Imperial Army.

On 13 June Samuel Goldreich wrote, 'I was sent to the hospital in consequence of the old wound breaking out again, caused by knocking my hand up against a box of ammunition … I am sorry to have to say that the members of my squadron (E) have been nearly all killed or wounded. Out of the original 118, including officers, there are only seven of us left, namely, one officer and six men.'[45] The squadron had been ambushed about nine kilometres northwest of Vryheid. They were surrounded by Boers, who set ablaze the dry grass to create a smokescreen from behind which they poured fire into the encircled troops, killing the commanding officer and preventing the rest of the column from reaching their entrappèd comrades.

But in July, Goldreich wrote to say he had been able to get out of hospital and 'back again to the front': 'We come in contact with the Boers nearly every day. Only yesterday thirty of us had a go with the Boers. They numbered over fifty and had cover at a farmhouse while we had bare veldt.' The *Jewish Herald* printed the letter with pride, as evidence that Goldreich had 'proved himself a thorough British soldier in every way'.[46] When in March 1900 Trooper Louis Eleazar Phillips sailed to South Africa with the twenty-five men chosen for Cameron's Victorian Scouts the paper had similarly been quick to claim that Phillips was 'a typical Australian, a stalwart Hebrew, 6ft 2in in height, and will evidently give a good account of himself in the fight with the Boer'.[47]

Leopold Cohen had left Australia about ten years before to work as a merchant banker in London, where he and a number of colleagues had chosen to go to the war in the Honourable Artillery Company of the City of London Imperial Volunteers. Cohen served for about eight months, alongside five other 'Jewish gentlemen'. Upon his return to Australia, he was interviewed by the *Jewish Herald* and said he had joined Colonel Paget's column in the middle of May. Paget's guns were escorted by the Australian Bushmen to their first battle at Lindley, after which Cohen fought in fifteen further engagements, including Bethlehem and Stabbert's Nek.[48] Leo's father George Cohen and uncle Benn Wolfe Levy contributed £1000 to the despatch of the Australian Bushmen's Contingents, just as they had earlier helped to fund the NSW adventure in the Sudan.

Karri Davies' youngest brother Frank also went to the war. He travelled to South Africa with a WA contingent as a press correspondent but then gained a commission in the Rhodesian Field Force and was shot in the leg while attached to the WA Bushmen. His complicated situation caused some confusion in the newspapers of the time, when a Lieutenant Davies was reported as being wounded at Koster River with the Bushmen, even though there was no record of Davies ever having joined them.[49]

When Henry W Goldring, aged twenty-seven, had applied for the NSW Bushmen's Corps in January 1900, he described himself as a 'good rider and good shot' with 'many years' bush experience'.[50] He left Mafeking with the Bushmen on 1 August 1900 and fought a skirmish with the Boers on 5 August. They had seven men wounded, camped for the night, and woke up to find they were surrounded by the enemy. 'They shelled the camp and fired upon us,' wrote Goldring, 'and we made good use of our time with our rifles. Our lads with the big guns shelled the Boers and scattered them in all directions; we chased them for a few miles and then lost sight of them. We had to fight against big odds: we had only 1000 men and the Boers had 5000, so you can tell we had a rough time. They caught one of our lads, and while two of the Boers were on guard one went to sleep, and he strangled the other and got back safe to us. There were ten men missing; seven of them came back, but the others are still missing.' Goldring was tired of fighting. 'I don't think any of us will be sorry when it is over,' he wrote, 'we are sick of the way we have been fooled about.'[51]

The Boers hoped to bring the war to the British by attacking Natal. In September 1900 Samuel Goldreich and Bethune's Mounted Infantry rode to Wakkerstroom, a Transvaal town on the Natal border, to help keep the enemy out of the colony. 'Work commenced early in the morning,' wrote Goldreich, 'and lasted until late in the afternoon, taking one ridge and then another, and at last entering the town, to the great delight of the English population … Four of our infantry men, whilst out on the flank, went to a farm which was flying the white flag, and as soon as they got about thirty yards from it the Boers, in hiding of course, opened fire on them. They killed one, wounded another, and the other two were taken prisoners … We left a garrison at Wakkerstroom, and marched on to Utrecht, which occupied another three days, just the same as the former march, but we had the pleasure of seeing a couple of those "white flag farms" blown up …We garrisoned at Utrecht and started for Vryheid and had the same rough time for another five days. Crossing the Blood River we spotted a good party of Boers evidently in waiting for us, but a salvo from the battery of artillery made them change their minds, and they cleared for the very identical place (Scheeper's Nek) where we were ambushed last May … Before we could come into action, however, the artillery were at it again, and much to our disappointment they cleared again. The veldt was strewn with dead horses, shot in ambush. We bivouacked that night close to the battlefield. We fenced in our poor dead comrades and officers' graves with barb wire, and set in stones on top of them, "BMI, RIP".'[52]

The conventional war in South Africa was over by October. The Boers had lost both of their capital cities and most of their territory. However, while their armies had been driven from the field, many Boers had not been defeated in their hearts. The commandoes launched a guerrilla war against the British that was set to bring out the worst in the Empire, and bring yet another term into everyday use in Europe: 'concentration camp'. And even as the Boers fought to prevent their states from disappearing, a new nation was born in Australia, at war in both South Africa and China.

The Boxer Rebellion

Even in the heady years of the birth of patriotism and the reawakening of the Jewish military spirit, Jews were most likely to enthusiastically endorse a war when 'there could not possibly be Jews on the other side'.[53] The battle to quash the Boxer Rebellion in China pitted the European imperial powers of Russia, France, Britain, Austria-Hungary, Germany and Italy – all nations with substantial Jewish populations – allied with the US and Japan, against an uprising of Chinese peasants. The allied powers had divided China into spheres of influence and seemed likely to ultimately break up the country. The so-called 'Boxers' sought to drive them out, attacking foreigners, missionaries and Christians in northern China, and laying siege to the legation quarter in Peking.

Ever eager to come to the aid of the Empire, Australians lined up to sail to China, and the colonies of New South Wales, Victoria and South Australia raised volunteer naval brigades. In addition to their militias, the colonial governments had acquired a handful of warships including, in South Australia, the British-built flat-iron gunboat HMAS *Protector*, which comprised the entire South Australian Navy. The *Protector* left Australia for China on 6 August 1900 with at least one Jewish sailor on board, a South Australian named Jacob John Davis who was apparently the son of an old Crimea soldier. The *Protector* was supposed to take part in a battle for the forts of Shan-hai-kwan but, by the time the ship arrived, the Chinese had fled before the assault of the gunboat HMS *Pygmy*. The *Protector* sailed on down the coast to Ch'in-huang-tao but, poised once again to drive the Boxers from the forts, she discovered the Russians had already conquered them. The South Australians were unable to find a role in the fighting, and the *Protector* left north China on 7 November 1900. She was cleaned and replenished in Hong Kong, and then decommissioned from the Royal Navy to steam home as a South Australian vessel once more. Jacob John Davis arrived back in Adelaide on 6 January 1901.

Davis' service in Chinese waters caused excitement in the Jewish press, where it was embraced as another detail in the picture of loyal engagement in Imperial wars. The London *Jewish Chronicle* was especially keen on the China deployment and equated the scourge of Boxerism with the evil of antisemitism.[54] There were perhaps 1000 Jews among the allied forces, and the *Chronicle* included Davis in its 'Typical Portraits of Jewish Soldiers who served in the International Contingents in China'. Davis looks the toughest of them all, dark-eyed and pugnacious, and wearing the tally of the *Protector* around his cap.[55] In Australia, the *Jewish Herald* mused that, with all the recent talk of the Jewish soldier, little was ever heard of the Jewish sailor.[56]

On 1 January 1901, in the final days of the *Protector*'s voyage from Hong Kong, the ship sailed in celebrations for the Federation of Australia's self-governing colonies into the Commonwealth of Australia. Two months later, control of the various militias passed from the states to the Federal government, and the Australian Army was born – technically in a state of war. When the new Commonwealth Parliament was opened in Melbourne, the WA military delegation to the ceremony included Karri Davies' brother Frank.[57]

The guerrilla war against the Boers

Only a small number of Australians fought in both the Boxer Uprising and the Boer War but they included a single Jew: Jacob John Davis left Australia with the 5th South Australian Imperial Bushmen on the troopship *Ormazan* on 9 February 1901, barely a month after he had returned from China. Davis was lightly wounded during rifle practice at Winburg in the Orange Free State on 5 September, but ultimately returned home safely.

The Australians in the Cape were now battling the 'bitter enders', the Boers who refused to give up. The war took a darker turn, as civilians who supported the guerrillas were rounded up and isolated from the commandoes in often brutal concentration camps, and Boer leaders such as General De Wet were chased down. Among De Wet's pursuers was a Jewish officer, Captain Joseph Ernest Joseph of the 4th Queensland Imperial Bushmen. St Kilda–born Joseph, who grew up in Gympie and ran his own business as an assayer in Mackay, had a long history in the Queensland militia. He had first served for three years in F Company at Mackay, then joined the local Mounted Infantry as a private solider. He was promoted to sergeant major and then lieutenant, before gaining a captain's commission and command of M Company in October 1898.[58] He was probably the most senior Jewish soldier to leave Australia for the war, although he was, of course, outranked by Karri Davies in South Africa.

In February 1901 Joseph sent a letter to a friend in Mackay, describing the hunt for De Wet in the north-west of the Cape

Colony. His men were sixty yards from a *kopje* when the enemy suddenly opened fire. 'We dismounted,' wrote Joseph, 'hoping the firing would slacken; but it got hotter and hotter. We had not a particle of cover, so I ordered the men to fall back on our supports … We had only twenty-four all told, and the Boers had 200, as we found out afterwards. I saw all the men gallop away, including one of the two who had gone up the kopje, and then got on my horse and started back myself. The bullets were whizzing, spitting, and cracking above us, in the ground around us, and on either side. I saw five men fall, and thought I would have no company left … The Boers kept the fire on us for 1500 yards, and then our guns came up and got at them. I at once saw how many men got back, and then went round the flank to the front again to look after the remainder. More troops were sent up to turn their flank and they then retired. We all at once galloped out to pick up the dead and wounded.' He found only one man hurt, although four horses had been shot. 'Rain came on as we resumed our march,' he wrote. 'G Company was sent out to reconnoitre a kopje on the left front and to hold it until some other troops came up. This we did, and whilst there, the advanced guard had some more fighting.' Joseph relished the action. 'Thus so far we had not done badly,' he wrote, 'seven fights in three days – and things were humming, everybody being jubilant in the hope of at last penning De Wet up.'[59]

By April 1901 Rabbi Goldreich's elder son, Leisser, had been promoted to bombardier. His second son, Samuel, now a lance corporal, wrote home from Edenburg that they had been travelling from Dewetsdorp to Springfontein when his squadron detached from the main body of Bethune's Mounted Infantry in order to escort a few families to another column. As they rode back to their comrades in the corps, 'We were all trotting along in open order until we came to a very nasty pass running through a large range of kopjes … where we had to close in and walk our horses through the pass. We had got about half-way through when volley after volley in very quick succession came into us from the hills on our right, and in less time than it takes to write we were scattered all over the left-hand side hills, and making our way in ones and twos as best we could over the hills and down to the flat on the other side, where we pulled up and dismounted to have a shot at them, the Boers having by this time come into the edge of the hills. When they volleyed at us in the pass, they killed seven horses and wounded three men, and also took three prisoners, whom they released after they had taken everything they had from them, and it is nothing short of a miracle that the whole lot of us were not killed or wounded on the spot. They were firing explosive bullets, and as they hit the ground and burst they frightened the life out of our horses, and away they galloped like the wind, and I can assure you that my horse never went so fast in all his life. He doesn't mind ordinary Mausers, but he strongly objects to explosives. Our three men that were collared counted forty-two Boers, and they said they had as many more, on the hills around but I don't think they were far short of a hundred. The following day we saw half-a-dozen of them, wounded one, and took the rest prisoners, so that was some little consolation.' In the country around Dewetsdorp, they 'got on the track of a commando, which we followed, and surprised them whilst off-saddled for some scoff (food). We put a volley into their horses, and they all stampeded and cleared. The Boers (ninety-two of them) made for a donga, and put up a fight for three hours, when they surrendered. A Boer on the left put up a white flag, and one of our squad (sergeant major's) stood up, and was shot through the stomach by one on the left, who said afterwards that he did not see the white flag. Two other of our men that were lying next to the sergeant major when he fell jumped up to his assistance, and they were also shot. All three of them died; and we buried them next day.'[60]

In May Rabbi Goldreich travelled to the local school's flag day in Coleraine, a small pastoral town in western Victoria, as the guest of Captain Louis Lesser, a Jewish militia officer who gave generously to the Ballarat Hebrew Congregation. Lesser, an officer in the rifle brigade, led his troops through their manoeuvres. During the speeches that followed, Rabbi Goldreich spoke of his sons who had taken leave in Cape Town, where they had been urged to accept their discharges. 'My patriotic boys firmly replied, No!' said Goldreich. 'Never would they leave until British supremacy was firmly established in South Africa!'[61] Mark Collins returned home unhurt, and was interviewed by the Sydney *Hebrew Standard*. He said he had visited the synagogues in Johannesburg and Pretoria, and in Cape Town Synagogue he had met 'Mr A Vecht of Hunter's Hill, Sydney'.[62] Similar experiences were to be reported in future wars by Jewish Anzacs, many of whom explored local Jewish sites and regularly bumped into stray Jewish Australians in unlikely settings.

Samuel Pollock, a fish-hawker from Colac, Victoria, who enlisted as a boundary rider in the 5th Victorian Mounted Rifles, was wounded on 12 June at Wilmansrust, east of Pretoria, in a battle he described as a 'terrible disaster' and an 'awful affair'. The last deployments of Victorians suffered the heaviest casualties of any Australian contingent, and Wilmansrust was their bloodiest defeat. Eighteen Australians were killed and eleven wounded. 'It was a Mauser bullet that hit me,' wrote Pollock, 'going in at the rear of my ankle on the right side, through the round bone, and coming out at the bottom of the foot on the left side. It made a clean hole, not breaking any bones. The range from which they were firing at was fifteen yards when I was hit, the Boers having got into the camp between the outposts without being seen. They surrounded the camp under cover of darkness, creeping to within fifteen yards of our lines, and opened a most murderous fire upon us from all sides. It came so suddenly that we were all confused for a second how to act. I happened to be on my knees at the time, placing my coat behind my saddle for a pillow, having laid down my blanket to turn in for the night, but almost the first shot that was fired hit me in the foot. The bullets were flying around us like hail. Throwing myself down flat on the ground I rolled behind my saddle for cover, but how I missed getting hit from the cross fire I cannot say, as the bullets were hitting the flaps of the saddle and flying off, four going through the seat, and one passing clean through my night cap, drawing a little blood, but doing no damage to speak of. My wound was nothing to what some of our poor fellows received. Four had their legs shattered (I mean the bones of their legs) and two of them have since had their legs amputated.'

'It has been a very rough time for this contingent,' wrote Pollock. 'During the six months we have been in action we have had thirty-four killed, three died of enteric fever, and sixty-three wounded – a terrible record for such a short time … As far as I can see, when our time is up the war will be no nearer the end than it is today. I will be very glad to return to Victoria.'[63]

Samuel Goldreich wrote home to tell his father he had been made a corporal, and had a 'rather severe experience' in Orange River Colony. While riding back towards their column, Goldreich and two other men were fired upon by a large party of Boers: 'As soon as we got about 500 yards from them we came to a very deep donga, and in went the horses. The Boers kept on firing at us, but could not do any damage. We dismounted in the donga, and were looking about for a way out, when there was a shout of "Hands up." We looked up, and about twenty paces from us on top of the donga on either side we saw a crowd of Boers. There was nothing left but to surrender. While we held our hands up a Dutch boy, about fourteen years of age, fired at us, but luckily he missed, and one of the other Boers went for him. They took everything from us – horse, saddle and bridle, rifle, bandolier, spurs, field-glasses, and put a number of questions to us, but otherwise treated us well. It was Brand's commando, about 200 strong (a nice little lot for three men to get among), and I must say they were a very decent lot, quite above the ordinary Boer.

47

'After keeping us for a few hours the commandant gave us a pass, and pointed out a road, which he told us to take, that would lead us to Bethulie, forty odd miles away. The pass was to get us through Boer patrols and pickets, which we continually passed, and by which we were challenged. We only had our overcoats. The nights were bitterly cold. We could only walk in the daytime, and it took us three days to travel to Bethulie, where, luckily, we picked up the column. The colonel congratulated me on our escape … I don't want to be a prisoner any more, as we only had one onion between us the whole time we were on the road – a three days' journey from *Yom Kippur*.'[64] Writing from Dordrecht in November, Goldreich at last seemed weary of the enemy and the war. 'We only wish they would make a stand,' he wrote, 'and finish the thing.'[65]

Leo Goldspink of Carlton was attached to the Second Imperial Light Horse as the war drew to a close. He wrote home in December 1901: 'An awful thunderstorm occurred one night whilst we were out on the veldt. Two men in our regiment were killed by the lightning, and several others were stunned. The First Imperial Light Horse had one man killed. Their camp was also rushed by Boers. We had pickets out, and towards 1 am were aroused by the cry, "Stand to arms," besides the firing of volleys. What with the roar of thunder, the flashing of lightning, the din of warfare and the stampeding of horses and cattle about the camp, it was a night to be remembered for a life time. The ground was like a quagmire, with the water in some places up to our knees.' Goldspink predicted the war would be 'practically ended in a few months'. He wrote, 'There are whole regiments of Boers in the field, commanded by British and colonial officers. It is only the prejudiced and ignorant old Boers who are now fighting against us.'[66] A peace treaty was finally signed in May 1902. At a special thanksgiving service to mark 'the glorious conclusion of the unhappy war', Rabbi Goldreich, patriot nonpareil, deplored only two stains on Britain's victory: that anti-war parliamentarians had done 'more mischief in prolonging the war than the Boers themselves'; and that Queen Victoria had not lived to see the day.[67]

Australia literally came of age during the Boer War. The last Australians to sail to South Africa to fight went as members of the Commonwealth Horse, the first truly Australian unit to go to war. The victories of Australian volunteers – and their supposed superiority over their allies – were proclaimed as proof that the Australian soldier had arrived. All over the world, elements in Jewish society were struggling to reclaim a long-lost fighting heritage. But in Australia alone, the idea of a Jewish military revival and the creation of a new and martially confident state were born simultaneously and grew up together.

A CURIOUS AFTERWORD TO JEWISH AUSTRALIA'S BOER WAR was the mystery of Charles Lima Braun, who had returned to South Africa after coming home to Australia. His father, Benjamin Braun, crossed the Indian Ocean to bring him back to New South Wales in 1905. Father and son sailed on the steamer *Euryalus*, but enteric fever had robbed Charles Lima Braun of his memory. When the *Euryalus* berthed at Port Melbourne, Charles walked up the pier and disappeared. His suit, underwear and hat were found on the beach, but there was no sign of Charles. He was eventually discovered looking into the window of a chemist shop by an old friend, whom he did not recognise, and whom he told his name was not Charlie. He vanished again and, when rediscovered, could not identify his mother in a photograph and appeared to have been living from the proceeds of pawning his coat and watch.[68]

A more abiding mystery was that of the former Jameson raider Henry Bernstein. While Karri Davies led the relief of Mafeking, Bernstein pursued an extraordinary and mysterious military career that would see him sniping from the margins of world history for the next three decades and beyond. In July 1898, Bernstein arrived in Tasmania from Lagos, where he had apparently been a captain of 'a Lagos battalion'. While in the African bush, Bernstein had been wounded and a companion of his shot by 'the chief of a tribe'. Bernstein, in turn, shot the chief dead and, as a memento of the adventure, brought the chief's head home in a box.[69] He then supposedly published a book about his experiences, entitled *Life with the Niger Expeditionary Forces* – although, if he really did write it, no copy appears to have survived. He had later found a job as inspector of machine guns with the Maxim Nordenfelt Company, and had been invited to reorganise the native artillery in Brazil, 'which position he filled for about twelve months, when he had to relinquish his position owing to the revolution'. By his own account, Bernstein next commanded an expedition into the South American interior, when five of his men were killed by 'native Red Indians' and two died of fever. In November 1901 he was reported to be chief of artillery in the army of the Republic of Bolivia. When Bernstein had reached Bolivia, he had been given the rank of major and attended a military review during which he 'took the liberty of telling the President of the Republic, General Pando, that his artillery was practicing tactics that were obsolete twenty years ago'. Bernstein had given the president a practical exhibition of modern artillery which supposedly so impressed Pando, his minister of war and other officers, that the next day they made Bernstein chief of artillery, 'with full power to reorganise the same'. Some or all of these events may actually have occurred. A newspaper report suggested Bernstein would soon be back in Europe to procure modern machine guns for Bolivia, and that he would be remembered by numerous friends in Melbourne.[70] It was to be several years until Bernstein was heard from again, with his confusing interventions into World War One.

The Defence Act and the militia

Rabbi Francis Lyon Cohen was born in Aldershot, the home of the British Army, and in England had been a Jewish military chaplain and a founder of the military-style Jewish Lads' Brigade. Cohen came to Australia in 1905 as Rabbi of the Great Synagogue, Sydney. He took up his role at a time of concerned debate about the defence of the nation. In 1907 the Protectionist Party Prime Minister Alfred Deakin announced that his government planned to introduce a bill committing all male Australians to a period of compulsory military training. That same year, Rabbi Cohen set out to enhance his Chanukah Confirmation (*batmitzvah*) Service by adding a military element. This service was perhaps the largest gathering seen at the Great Synagogue to that date, as a regimental order was issued for a voluntary 'church' parade, and about seventy non-Jewish servicemen turned up to fill the benches. All but one of the known Sydney Jewish members of the Commonwealth, permanent, naval, military, volunteer and cadet forces attended. Although their number was 'only about a dozen and a half', they at least outnumbered the eleven confirmees. The Jewish officers were Lieutenant Colonel George Michaelis (formerly Commandant of the Australian Rifles, and the first Jew to reach the rank of colonel in Australian forces), Lieutenant Darrell A Bensusan of the 1st Infantry Regiment, Lieutenant Lawrence W Phillips of the NSW Lancers, and Boer War veteran Lieutenant Percy E Hollander of the Australian Field Artillery.

Australia's Jewish community was largely un-pious and uninvolved with religious affairs outside – and sometimes even inside – of high holy days. But no matter what genuine sway the clergy held over the community, Rabbi Cohen was confident of his own influence. 'I, at least, can entertain hopes of a greatly increased representation of Jews in the Citizen Forces in the near future,' he said, 'when I call to mind the striking growth in the number of Jewish soldiers and sailors that rewarded my annual Chanukah exhortations in England.' He looked forward to conscription. 'We shall anticipate compulsion,' he declared, 'and of our own accord hasten to submit ourselves to organised defensive training, and zealously strive to increase our personal value to our country, regarding our participation in the task of safeguarding the peace of the realm as a high privilege as well as a sacred duty.'[71]

Lieutenant General Robert Baden-Powell's Scouting movement came to Australia in 1908, offering boys a premilitary experience inspired in part by Baden-Powell's deployment of cadets during the siege of Mafeking. Scoutmaster Harold Cohen, a militia officer, oversaw the formation of two patrols of Judean Boy Scouts at the Great Synagogue, and Roy Hector Blashki, a senior army cadet, was appointed the first patrol leader. Many future Jewish soldiers were to first put on khakis as Judean Scouts. But it does not seem that the rush to join the armed forces anticipated and encouraged by Rabbi Cohen actually occurred and his views were possibly not congruent with those of his congregation. The Deakin government fell, but the Australian Labor Party backed conscription, and a Defence Act, which brought universal military service to Australia, was passed in the Federal Parliament in 1909. Under the new scheme, cadet training – which had been around since the mid-nineteenth century – would become compulsory for all boys between the age of twelve and eighteen, and every man was compelled to enrol in the Citizen Military Forces (CMF) until he was twenty-five. The 1910 military Chanukah service was a disappointment. The *Jewish Herald* was acerbic about the 'large, though by no means crowded, attendance' and judged it 'almost hopeless to expect that our community will concern themselves, much less become enthusiastic, about anything'. But new faces among the officers included Lieutenant Arthur W Hyman of the NSW Mounted Rifles, Lieutenant GF Benjamin of the 9th Australian Infantry, and Roy Hector Blashki's elder brother, Lieutenant Eric

Phillip Blashki of the 3rd Battalion Senior Cadets. Rabbi Cohen used the ceremony to welcome the new universal training scheme – which would not come into effect until the following year – and the obligation for Jewish youths to register and enjoy the 'honour of being the pioneers in this new development of British citizenship'.[72] While the impact of any rabbi's words on Australian Jewry can easily be overstated, and might at times be misunderstood as reflecting – rather than directing – communal feeling, there was Jewish involvement in the militia far out of earshot of the Great Synagogue's *bimah*. In the furthest reaches of Australia, a solitary Jew manned the defences of the nation. After thousands of years of Ashkenazi migration, Louis Goldstein, formerly of Elizabeth Bay, found himself second lieutenant of the Australian Garrison Artillery on Thursday Island.[73]

More recent currents of migration were subtly changing the make-up of the Jewish community in Australia. Jews from Russia and Poland began to arrive in their hundreds in the later nineteenth century, driven from their homes by pogroms and progressively more crippling antisemitic legislation. Very small numbers of Palestinian Jews – generally of Eastern European birth – also fled displacement for Australia. Russian-born Eliazar Margolin, who had spent some time in Palestine in his youth, came to Australia in 1902. At first, he spoke little English – and it seems his enunciation was never entirely clear – and worked for a time as a greengrocer's assistant, but Margolin had an aptitude for soldiering that had been honed in his teens in defence of the *moshava* of Rehovot, south of Tel Aviv. In 1911 he formed and commanded the Collie Company of 1st Battalion, WA Infantry Regiment. A story in his local newspaper later recalled that Second Lieutenant Margolin had taken 'an intense interest in the cadet movement' but that 'for some time he was handicapped by his imperfect knowledge of the English language'. According to the story, 'The boys at Collie still remember the time when he marched them practically up against a wall, and could not recollect the term "halt" and stopped them by holding up both his hands and yelling "stop".'[74] Other Jewish officers appointed as lieutenants of cadets included Bertie Crook, Eric G Goldring, Percy H Goldstein and Henry WR Meyer. Isadore Basser of Lithgow, a Jewish member of an Australian contingent of cadets who travelled to the UK for the coronation of George V, won second prize for cadets at the annual rifle shooting carnival at Bisley, Surrey.[75]

The Royal Military College of Australia was opened at Duntroon in 1911. It offered a four-year officer training course, modelled on the curriculum at the Royal Military Academy Sandhurst in England. Duntroon would turn gentlemen into full-time career officers, with courses evenly split between military and academic subjects, and training provided also in dining and deportment. The first riding instructor at Duntroon was the Boer War veteran Lieutenant Harry Shappere.

A report of Rabbi Cohen's 1911 Chanukah service in Sydney made the rather extravagant assertion that 'the Hebrew nation claims to possess the greatest record of military achievement in the world's history'.[76] A similar service was also held, for the first time, in Melbourne, attended by fifty officers and cadets, and commanded by Major Harold Cohen of the Field Artillery Brigade.* The congregation included Major Isidore Isaacson and Lieutenants Henry and Dalbert Hallenstein. The Hallenstein brothers were the golden children of the union of two families of cousins, the wealthy Michaelis and Hallensteins, mainstays of the Victorian Jewish community, who owned a successful tannery business. Dalbert, in particular, was almost a prince of Melbourne Jewry. The Melbourne service was addressed by the chief minister of the St Kilda Hebrew Congregation, Reverend Jacob Danglow, who

---

*   Cohen, who had joined the artillery in May 1901, was to go to both world wars and receive a DSO and two Mentions in Despatches in World War One.

had attended to Jewish soldiers at CMF training camps since 1908. At Kilmore, Victoria, with the 5th Australian Infantry Regiment, Reverend Danglow first met John Monash,[77] who was then a lieutenant colonel, in command of the Victorian section of the new Australian Intelligence Corps. In a militia awash with poor quality officers, Monash stood out for his uncompromising intellect and his commitment to soldiering as a science. He was fascinated, even enthralled, by the logistics of battle, although he had still come no closer to war than war games at Seymour and Avenel. In 1913, twenty-six years into his military career, Monash was finally made a full colonel, and Commander of the 13th Infantry Brigade.

3

World War One: 1914 to 1918

The road to Gallipoli

World War One broke out on 28 July 1914, when Austria-Hungary invaded Serbia. It began in the Balkans but spread rapidly across Europe, a plague carried in the bacteria of military alliances. It pitted the Triple Entente of the British Empire, the Russian Empire, France and their allies (including, eventually, the United States) against the Central Powers of Germany and Austria-Hungary along with the Ottoman Empire.

On 3 August, Germany declared war on France and invaded Belgium. The next day, Britain declared war on Germany. The Australian government had already offered a contingent of troops to fight for the Empire, a proposal accepted by the British on 6 August. Even before a larger army could be raised for service in Europe, an Australian Naval and Military Expeditionary Force was enlisted to capture German New Guinea, and the Australians bested the German garrison at Rabaul. Melbourne-born Lieutenant Wilfred Norman Beaver, a Jewish public servant and former militiaman with the Australian Field Artillery, who had been a commissioned officer in the Armed Constabulary of Papua since December 1905, seems to have been 'the first British soldier to enter German territory' anywhere in the world.[1] At the outbreak of the war Beaver was despatched by the government of Papua to take command of the armed constabulary on the Anglo-German frontier of Papua and New Guinea, and led the force for six months until the German surrender. He later enlisted in the 60th Battalion of the 1st Australian Imperial Force (AIF), and was killed in Flanders in 1917.

Notwithstanding the rather scrappy and unsatisfying experience of the Boer War, Australia considered itself a country that was yet to fully prove its worth in battle, and Australia's Anglo-Jewish community felt the deficiency twofold, as both British Australians and emancipated Jews. The 1911 census had counted 17 287 Jews in Australia, comprising 0.35 per cent of a population of 4 940 000.* Like their contemporaries in the wider community, young Jews rushed to enlist, encouraged by exhortations from the clergy and the press.

The *Jewish Herald* published a sorrowful and prophetic editorial, blaming the outbreak of the terrible war on the selfish, duplicitous machinations of the ruling class throughout Europe – although it would countenance no criticism of Britain. 'Whatever the motives or objects of the other belligerents may be, her cause is indubitably a just and honourable one; and every citizen of our Empire will applaud the action of the Imperial Government, and cheerfully make whatever sacrifices are needed in its support,' swore the *Herald*. 'In every one of the armies there are large numbers of Jewish soldiers; and we may be confident that, as they have always done, they will acquit themselves worthily as men, even in cases where they know full well that their efforts will be repaid by the contempt, insult, and persecution of the rulers for whom they offer up their lives.'[2]

The Great War has come to be remembered as hell on earth, a prelude to the Apocalypse, but the greatest worry for many young Australians in 1914 was that it might end before they got there.

---

*   Although demographers agree that up to 20 per cent of Jews today do not identify themselves as 'Jewish' on official documents, there is no accepted figure for the under-reporting of Jewishness in Australia in the years before World War One.

The first Australian doctor to reach the fighting was Sydney-born radiography pioneer Herschel Harris, who enlisted in England. Harris initially served at the Australian Voluntary Hospital in France. He wrote home to a friend in Sydney that the hospital, which was then at Saint-Nazaire on the Breton coast, was daily flooded with hundreds of wounded men, including many frightened, demoralised Germans who were ready to commit suicide rather than fall into the hands of the French. However, the wounded British officers with whom he spoke all agreed that 'the tide has turned now, and that we have the Germans well in hand … The officers say that the Germans are great cowards. Their heavy artillery is very good and the firing very accurate … When the British cavalry charge the Germans give in at once, and throw down their arms and hold up the white flag. At the present time both sides are entrenched, and if a man is shot he remains there, for none dare to go to his assistance … We breakfast at 7.30 each morning, and work as long as there is anything to do. There is not any grumbling – each man does his best. Our staff is now 100 men, with twenty nurses and thirty motors. I am provided with a special motor ambulance for my X-ray apparatus. I have had some 200 cases, and most of them of remarkable interest. One man was shot in the right shoulder and the bullet went through his lung and liver, passed through his intestines and came out through the skin. He is now quite well again. Another man was shot twice in the leg; one bullet was found in his trousers, and the casing of the bullet was left in the wound. He is also recovering.' To a doctor, wrote Harris, 'The experience which one gets here is well worth going for. Not one of us would miss it.'[3]

Back home, some young Jews feared they might not be chosen for the front. David Conroy, born Abraham Levene in Glasgow in 1892, was a labourer on the railways in Sydney when he enlisted in the AIF on 27 August 1914, at the age of twenty-two. Although he had taken care to Anglicise his name, he declared his religion as 'Jewish'. When Conroy quit his job and signed up, he was not sure he would be able to remain a member of the AIF. He wrote to his mother in England that the officers 'were always picking out all the fellows who did not seem to be up to much and either discharging them or else putting them in the 2nd Contingent. As I had no previous training I stood as good a chance as anyone of being rejected.' But the initial medical testing had not been oner-ous: 'When I got in front of the doctors I had to strip naked and then was examined. First of all, I had my eyes examined and when I had passed that I was examined by another doctor who sounded my lungs, punched me in the chest, had a look at my teeth, told me to hop and jump about a bit and then passed me.'[4]

The AIF at first comprised only one division of infantry, the 1st Division, and the 1st Light Horse Brigade. It had expanded rap-idly as, in response to enormous enthusiasm for military service, within weeks three infantry brigades were filled and a fourth was being raised: the 4th Infantry Brigade, under the command of John Monash. Reverend Danglow of the St Kilda Hebrew Congregation wrote to congratulate Monash on his appointment. Monash, who was not often given to making declamations about his Judaism, replied, 'With the help of many fine men who are going to serve under me I hope to be able to sustain the honour of Australia, of British Armies and, not least, of the Jewish Community.' Monash attended the Military Chanukah service on 14 December and, at the reception that followed, publicly declared, 'I am, and always shall be, fully conscious of my responsibilities as an Australian soldier, citizen and Jew.'[5]

The first contingent steamed out of Albany, Western Australia, on 1 November 1914. The troop transports were escorted by bat-tleships, including HMAS *Sydney* and the Japanese vessel HIJMS *Ibuki*. They headed first for Colombo, Ceylon. On 17 November, wrote Conroy, 'when we were about half way between Albany and Colombo we saw the Japanese boat turn to her left and steam away for all she was worth. About an hour later we heard that the *Sydney* was in action with the *Emden* and had been so for some hours.'[6] The *Emden* was a German cruiser engaged by the *Sydney* off the Cocos Islands, and hit perhaps a hundred times by the Australian guns. The captain had to run his ship aground to save it from sinking. He lost 133 men from his crew of 376. Three men on board the *Sydney* were also killed, and a fourth later died of his wounds. There were apparently two Jewish sailors on board the *Sydney*, including Able Seaman Jack Levy, a Sydney man born in 1895 who had joined the navy as a sick-berth attendant in August 1913.* At least one German-Jewish sailor was killed on the *Emden*, a man born in 1893 in Lauenau in Lower Saxony with the name of Gustav Levy. The Battle of Cocos was likely the first time Australian Jews faced other Jews in combat, in a fratricidal clash of Levy versus Levy.** 'We heard that the *Emden* had been sunk,' wrote David Conroy. 'Soon after we had received this news we saw the Japanese boat returning to her former position on our right. The band then played "God Save the King" and we all got half a day's holiday.'

Instead of going straight to the Western Front as they had hoped, Conroy and his mates had learned they were to stay in Egypt. 'I would never have turned in my billet and spent about 18 or 20/- in train fares etc had I known that we would not be sent to the Front,' he wrote. 'However, I reckon "it is of no use crying over

---

*   Levy was to remain in the navy through two world wars and his entire working life. He transferred to the Reserves in 1954, and retired as a lieutenant commander with an MBE.

**   Jewish casualties in the RAN included Stoker Roy David Justice of Thoona, Victoria, who had joined the service in December 1913. Justice saw action in the German New Guinea campaign and the pursuit across the Pacific Ocean to the South Atlantic of the German naval officer Maximilian von Spee, whose East Asia Squadron had included the *Emden*. Stoker Justice died in an accident on board the steam pinnace of the HMAS *Australia* in March 1916, while the vessel was alongside Rosyth, Scotland.

spilt milk" and the only thing one can do is to take it all in good part and hope that we shall either be relieved by another Force and sent to the Front or else be given the opportunity of having a smack at the Turks.' Conroy assured his mother he had as much chance of getting 'hurt or shot' in Egypt as he did of 'becoming a multimillionaire within the next few minutes'.[7] He was killed at Gallipoli in Turkey on 23 July 1915.

The 1st Division pitched their tents at Camp Mena, near Cairo, where they were charged with protecting the Suez Canal from the Ottoman Turks. A second contingent of Australians followed, including Colonel Monash's 4th Brigade, which landed in Egypt in January 1915, a part of the New Zealand and Australia Division of the recently formed Australian and New Zealand Army Corps (ANZAC).* All the troops went through a period of dubiously effective training with the idea that they would be sent to the Western Front.

Samuel Weingott was a tailor's cutter born in Sydney, New South Wales. He was twenty-one years old when he enlisted on 24 August 1914, the 127th man to sign up for the 1st Battalion. For the majority of Anzacs, their voyage to Egypt was the first time they had left their home country. The war offered them all the chance to see something of the world, but the particular geography of the tragedy gave the Jewish Anzacs the opportunity to engage with the Jewish world. In Egypt, and subsequently Palestine, they found windows into the age of the Bible. When Samuel Weingott reached Cairo, he wrote home to his father, Harris ('Harry'): 'I met a Hebrew Egyptian, who took a great interest in me. There are twenty synagogues in Cairo, and last Saturday he took me to the principal one. The building is wonderfully elaborate, and

---

*   While this book uses the term 'Anzacs' to describe the troops of the 1st AIF, it does not record the experience of Jewish New Zealanders unless they fought in Australian units.

altogether different to ours in Sydney. Instead of candles there are electric lights, and many electric fans are also in evidence. As soon as I arrived the "servant of the church", as he is called, gave me a *tallit* ... Instead of the Rabbi taking the *Sefer Torah* from the ark, as they do in Sydney, an auction sale is held, and the highest bidder is the chosen one ... I have very much pleasure in saying that this honour was bestowed upon me; I swelled with pride when I carried the *Sefer* round. Everyone leaned over the side as I passed by, and kissed it.' He was then called up to the *bimah* to read from the *Torah*. 'I feel that this honour is the greatest that can be paid to a Jew,' he wrote, 'and I shall never forget it!'[8]

A week later Weingott wrote, 'I go to *shul* every *Shabbos*, and experience no difficulty in getting the necessary leave. Afterwards I take a quiet stroll through the Jewish quarter, and am made welcome by the many friends I have made. Next Friday I am invited to partake of gefilte fish at the house of one of them.' He visited the synagogue in Old Cairo on the site where Moses was supposed to have prayed for the last time before leaving Egypt, and was awed by what he was told was the world's oldest *Sefer Torah*.[9] In April, with the festival of Passover approaching, Weingott knew his stay in Egypt was coming to an end. 'There are many Jewish refugees here from Palestine,' he wrote, 'and I am doing my little for them by giving some of my clothing to the society formed for their help ... We are allowed leave for the first two and last two days of Passover, but it is impossible to get the whole eight days, owing to our expecting to leave at any time.'[10]

In January 1915 Dalbert Hallenstein, the favourite cousin of Reverend Danglow's wife, followed Archie and Grant Michaelis and became the third member of the family firm Michaelis Hallenstein to volunteer for active service. Dalbert was a much-loved young man and was given a send-off by employees and staff at Federal Hall. His father Reuben spoke briefly to say that the evening would always remain in his memory and that he 'hoped his boy would come back and they would all meet happily again later'.[11] Dalbert was called to the *Torah* at St Kilda Synagogue, where he had been *barmitzvah*. Reverend Danglow told the congregation that the Jewish community 'were fully and painfully conscious of the fact that the British Empire, of which they were so proud to form a part, was in serious danger' and 'they were gratified when they saw their young men responding readily, as was but right, to the call of their King and country'.[12] Although he perhaps had a larger audience – and even the judgment of history – in mind when he spoke, Danglow's heart was with Hallenstein, whose father was a past president of the St Kilda congregation and his grandfather one of its founders. Captain Keith Levi, the son of another past president, Joseph Levi and his wife Kate (the sister of Karri Davies) was also leaving for the front, and Danglow said he would be the first Jewish doctor to go overseas with the AIF. Signaller Morris Israel, whose parents had sung in the synagogue choir, was sailing to the Middle East too. Danglow prayed that God would watch over them all, and that before long they would be back in the synagogue to thank God for their safe and happy return. Instead, he was forced to watch as the young men of his congregation disappeared, one by one – at first to the trenches and then, as the war dragged on, to the grave.

'On the first Sunday we suffered hell'

In April 1915 the Anzacs left Egypt, sailing not for the Western Front but for Turkey. Along with larger numbers of British, French and Indian troops, they were despatched to open up another front against the enemy and secure the Russian navy's access to the Black Sea via the straits of the Dardanelles and Bosphorus. The Gallipoli Peninsula was also to be a staging point for the eventual invasion of Constantinople, which lay about 270 kilometres to the north-east. Like so much of Turkey, the area had a Jewish history. The peninsula's port town of Gelibolu (Gallipoli) itself had been home to a sizeable Jewish population since at least the thirteenth century although the old Jewish Quarter, with its two nineteenth-century synagogues, had been destroyed by an earthquake in 1912. But the Anzacs never reached Gallipoli town. The assault force waded ashore at a nameless bay between Ari Burnu and Hell Spit, later known as Anzac Cove. Captain Eliazar Margolin, the Russian-born Jewish officer from Collie, Western Australia, arrived at Anzac on that first day, as did Samuel Weingott, Sidney Diamond, a 21-year-old piano tuner who received the Distinguished Conduct Medal for his actions in the Gallipoli landings, and Harley Cohen, a 21-year-old Sydney clerk who had joined the 4th Battalion AIF on 17 August 1914.

Harley Cohen had been driven to enlist by a great sense of urgency. Men were allotted service numbers according to the order in which they arrived at the recruiting office: Cohen was number 27. He charged onto the beach in the first landing at nine o'clock in the morning of 25 April, and 'rushed through the scrub into the firing-line,' he said later. 'Men were dropping like skittles, and as an officer was yelling for someone with a knowledge of first aid and no one answered, I chipped in, and did a bit of it. When I'd bandaged up a few of the worst cases I resumed the job I went out there for, and that was to give the Turkish first-aiders some work to do. The Turks seemed to have screened themselves so thoroughly that we could not see them, and volunteers were called to go out and locate them.'[13] Cohen and half a dozen of his comrades crawled out in search of the enemy.

'It was night,' he wrote home to his father, 'and we did not have much chance of returning, so we shook hands with our nearest pals and set out.'[14] Cohen said, 'Curiously enough, though the ground was continually swept by machine guns, not one of us was hit.'[15] He wrote, 'We reached the hill, from which we drove off a few Turks, using the bayonet freely on them, but we had then to lie down, as we had drawn the fire of the Indians, who, with the Turks, imagined we were the enemy, but we came through.'[16] He said, 'When we gained a bit of a ridge, where we could observe things, we found we had no water. I was sent back for it, and to report, and then returned to the observation point. On the way I noticed one of our wounded, who must have been left as the first crowd of our boys swept forward, in that wonderful charge, directly on landing. I could not pick him up then, as my mates needed the water badly, but coming back my mates picked him up, and got him safely into our lines, in spite of the fact that by rising and carrying him they faced almost certain death.'[17]

The first Jewish Anzac killed at Gallipoli* would seem to be 24-year-old Private Godfrey Sherman, 9th Battalion, a banker from Woollahra, New South Wales, who went missing on 25 April and whose body was never found. His parents were later informed by Sherman's returned comrades that their son was killed by shell-fire. Sherman, whose parents had married in the Great Syna-gogue Sydney, had enlisted as a Roman Catholic, which was not uncommon for a Jewish soldier. In addition, however, a crucifix and rosary beads were listed among his belongings, which were perhaps keepsakes from his girlfriend, a Miss K Cleveland-Coxe of Bondi, whom he had listed as his next of kin and whose exist-ence he had hidden from his family. Sherman's father had to sign a number of statutory declarations attesting that he was actually related to his late son, a process which clearly caused him pain. But the suffering was not over for the Sherman family. Godfrey's younger brother Leslie (who enlisted as a Jew) was to die at Ypres

---

* Corporal Lionel Marks, a 23-year-old clerk from Carlton, Victoria, who was Jewish but enlisted in the 1st Battalion as 'C of E', also died on that day or shortly afterwards. The army's inquiry heard he had his head blown off by a Turkish shell. Lionel's brother, Alfred Marks, a private in the British Army, was also killed in action in the Dardanelles.

in 1917. None of the possessions of either man were ever returned to their father.

Other Jewish soldiers were wounded on the first day in Gallipoli. Herbert Bloustein, a clerk from Ballarat who had been appointed company quartermaster sergeant with the 5th Battalion, wrote home: 'When we landed on Sunday we got terribly mixed up ... As we were just advancing into the firing line to the support of another company of our battalion, a shrapnel pellet hit me just at the base of the neck, glanced off the bone, and lodged in the muscle of my chest. I was quite stunned for a few minutes, and was bleeding pretty freely. I had the impression that I could not move my right arm. I gradually moved it a little, and then found it was quite free. I had not fired a shot up till that time, having seen no one to fire at ... I was in a trench on Monday with about forty others, and they were from all brigades and battalions. On Wednesday we were relieved, and retired to muster under cover of the hills overlooking the sea. The ground we have to work over is awful. It is thick scrub everywhere. The enemy's snipers were picking off a lot of our men, being able to creep up close to the trenches under cover of the bushes.'[18]

On 26 April Colonel John Monash arrived on the beaches. Samuel Weingott had become separated from his battalion and attached himself to the 5th Battery, which engaged the enemy for the whole day. 'Their guns do awful damage,' he told his diary. 'The biggest majority of our chaps seem to be wiped out.' He heard that his older brother Alexander ('Alec') had been wounded, then Samuel was 'nearly killed through a falling cliff'. On 30 April he wrote from rest camp, 'Snipers still keep going and bag a lot of chaps on the beach. An Indian caught one and cut his head off.'[19]

On 27 April Captain Eliazar Margolin was in the thick of the fighting. His signaller, the artist Ellis Silas, wrote in his diary, 'There is a pale moon – any minute we are expecting the enemy to rush the trenches – we have no reserves. I ask Captain Margolin to let me make his dugout more secure, as every time he has to give a message he has to expose himself – after some persuasion he permits me to do so, though at the same time asking me if I had completed my own dugout. However, after having made his position apparently secure and arranged the bushes the better to make it less conspicuous, I had no sooner vacated the position and he had got into my place, than he was struck in the mouth by a bullet. "Good God!" I exclaimed, "have they got you Sir?" "My God!" he yelled, "they have caught me at last." But, after the first shock, he said to me, "I thought they had got me then, Silas; what shall I do? I mustn't let the boys see I have been hit." However, I said he had better have it attended to. Just at that moment a shot struck the parapet close to my face; I thought my turn had come; although it was nearly dark the snipers seemed well on to this par- ticular dugout. A body was lifted out of the trench; I thought it was a wounded man; I asked if he was dead – then I saw the top of his head – oh God! The Turks seemed to be going to rush us – Margy grabbed hold of a rifle; I asked him if he was going to use it – "My word, yes," he said, "I want something I can fight with."'[20]

Harley Cohen wrote home from Gallipoli after seven days' fierce fighting: 'Most of my chums are dead but my dearest pal is still with me, alive and unwounded, like myself.'[21] Every day in the trenches brought a fresh horror for the living. On 6 May the corpses around Samuel Weingott's trench began to smell. Then Weingott was 'very nearly blown to pieces by the enemy's heavy gun fire'. In the days that followed, a sergeant major had his head blown off while shaving; two shells landed in Weingott's trench and one buried itself in the parapet alongside Weingott but did not explode. 'The other blew one man to pieces, wounded one.' Then the 'Armoury Sergeant has his brains blown out by shrapnel whilst inspecting trenches … Mate of mine shot through the heart whilst asleep … Shell explodes in our trench, killing or seriously wound- ing Captain Hill … Terrible sights. Men alongside of me blown to pieces … Many lose their nerves. Trenches blown to pieces. Work all night fixing them up … Enemy come right on top of trenches but repulsed. Hundreds lying dead outside our trench.'[22]

The letters of Monash give a lyrical account of trench life in May. He sat 'within a hundred yards of the firing line' where 'the rattle of musketry, and the boom of cannon' never ceased,[23] crouched in his ramshackle headquarters between points the Anzacs called Pope's Hill and Courtney's Post, in front of the depression that became known as Monash Valley. 'The noises of the battlefield are numerous and varied,' he wrote, 'and after a little while it is quite easy to distinguish the different sounds. The bullet which passes close by (say within ten or twenty feet) has a gentle purring hum, like a low caressing whistle, long drawn out. The bullet which passes well overhead, especially if fired from a long range, has a sharp sudden crack like a whip, and really feels as if it is very close. Our own rifle-fire listened to, of course, from behind the firing-line or in it, sounds like a low rumble or growl. Our machine guns are exactly like the rattle of a kettledrum. The enemy's rifle and machine-gun fire, on the other hand, sounds as if it were directly overhead, in a medley of sharp cracks like the explosions of packets of crackers just overhead, even though the fire is actually coming from the front, a half mile away. The enemy's shrapnel sounds like a gust of wind in a wintry gale, swishing through the air and ending in a loud bang and a cloud of smoke, when the shell bursts. Unless one gets in the way of the actual fragments of the shell itself, the Turkish shrapnel does very little harm. Our own artillery is the noisiest of all, both the discharge of the guns and the bursting of the shells being ear-splitting, with a reverberating echo that lasts twenty or thirty seconds.'[24]

Arthur Abraham (aka Adrien) Jacobs, the eldest of four Jewish brothers from South Australia who fought in World War One, had also relaxed into the deadly routine. 'Compared with the first week,' he wrote home from Gallipoli on 12 May, 'what we are now experiencing is a pleasant holiday. On the first Sunday we suffered hell, and the following Monday and Tuesday were about as bad; but the enemy are now apparently tired, and only now and again do they give us anything to do. They send us plenty of shrapnel, however, but we are fairly accustomed to the whistling of the shells, and know how to dodge. No one seems to care a hang for rifle bullets. At the moment of writing – the platoon to which I belong is in the firing line – shrapnel is bursting over us; but nobody is taking any particular notice of it. It is also raining slightly.'[25]

Jacobs, a former journalist with the *Register* in South Australia, had enlisted in the 10th Battalion at the first opportunity. His service number was 66. The Jacobs boys were so desperate to go to war that both Arthur and the next oldest brother Solomon (aka Sullivan) William Jacobs enlisted in the 10th Battalion twice. David Jacobs went to Egypt, France and Belgium with the 27th Battalion and 5th Field Ambulance and was wounded in action. The youngest brother, Emmanuel (aka Martin Edward) Jacobs served with the 32nd and 50th battalions but was under-age when he signed up at sixteen, and had to be sent home from France.*

Every man at Gallipoli saw his share of death, but it was the troops of the Field Ambulance who bore witness to each mangled corpse and mutilated survivor. Harold Emanuel Collins, who was born in 1892 in Malvern, Victoria, but grew up in Paddington, New South Wales, had joined the AIF on 15 August 1914, and served as a stretcher-bearer at Gallipoli. On 5 May Collins wrote in his diary, 'We went up to the firing line at 6.30 pm to see if there was any wounded to bring down. Just as we got up to the top of the hill we saw a doctor cutting the remaining shreds holding his left arm just below the shoulder. The poor beggar, only a lad, was

---

* A fifth brother (or possibly half-brother), Charles Isaac (or possibly Isaac Charles) Jacob, is thought to have fought in the Boer War with British forces and served in German East and West Africa in World War One.

screaming with agony while we tied a putty around the tops to stop the artery. My mate Joe Barnes took the arm away and buried it, the chap was conscious all the time.' On 19 May, 'The Australians repelled an early morning attack on their right flank,' wrote Collins, 'when the AMC went up to collect the casualties, they found about six wounded men in stretchers and about six men who could walk. There were three dead so it was not necessary to bring them down. While our squad was bringing a patient down, we had to go across an open space. The Turks evidently could see us and they sent six shells after us [and] we had to run for our lives … The poor beggar we had must have suffered as we ran with him. He was shot through the eye, and it came out of his left jaw.' During an armistice for the Turks to bury their dead, 'Our stretcher-bearers took stretchers outside our firing line and went half way to the Turks' trenches where there was white flags and they could not pass beyond them,' wrote Collins. 'Our men took the dead Turks (who were in a very decomposed condition) down to the half way mark where the Turks had a big hole dug. We got some of our own men who had been lying there since the first Sunday. I went out and had a look around, it is a sight that I never want to see again. There was a sort of a natural trench coming to a point just in front of our trench, well there was a dead Turk on his hands and knees while at the bottom there was about twenty. I suppose as they crawled up this slight incline they were shot. You could not walk two paces without encountering a dead Turk.'[26]

On 25 May a German submarine sank HMS *Triumph* in sight of the Australian troops, seventy-eight men drowned and Samuel Weingott read a burial service from his prayer book. Harold Collins saw it too. He wrote, 'She sunk in ten minutes, settling down by one o'clock. She had a horrible list then she gradually [sank], gaining momentum as she went, until she was over altogether … I have seen dead men lying about by the hundred, have seen men's arms and legs torn off but nothing has made me feel like crying

70

as I did when I saw that stately and majestic old battle-ship go down.'[27] On 29 May Weingott wrote, 'One shell burst in my face and although unwounded I was knocked out for a few minutes. My rifle was twisted beyond recognition.' But only two days afterward Weingott was 'still going day and night' and wrote, 'I have quite recovered from my awful experience and feel pretty fit once more.'[28]

Where others saw chaos, death and cruelty, Monash found order, life and kindness. 'We have got our battle procedure now thoroughly well organised,' he wrote. 'To a stranger it would probably look like a disturbed ant-heap with everybody running a different way, but the thing is really a triumph of organisation. There are orderlies carrying messages, staff officers with orders, lines of ammunition-carriers, water-carriers, bomb-carriers, stretcher-bearers, burial-parties, first-aid men, reserves, supports, signallers, telephonists, engineers, digging-parties, sandbag-parties, periscope-hands, pioneers, quartermaster's parties, and reinforcing troops running about all over the place, apparently in confusion, but yet everything works as smoothly as on a peace parade, although the air is thick with clamour and bullets and bursting shells and bombs and flares. The remarkable intelligence and initiative of the men is most helpful. Most of my officers are now men who have been promoted from the ranks for gallantry in action, and they are really fine.

'Also they are humane and gentlemanly fighters. I saw a sight today which is to the eternal credit of Australian soldiers. After we had retaken the temporarily lost trenches, we found about sixteen or seventeen Turks in a sap both ends of which we held. The men might have easily killed the lot. But they waited while an interpreter was sent for, and the Turks were persuaded to surrender – all while the men's blood was up, and they had seen their mates blown to bits by these very men. But this is not all. Scarcely had these Turks been disarmed and lined up to be searched, when our boys crowded round them with water-bottles and biscuits which they devoured ravenously, and then gave them cigarettes, and all the while lines of stretcher-bearers were carrying past our dead and wounded.'[29]

But the men received questionable orders based on optimistic intelligence, and vastly underestimated the enemy. On 30 May Collins wrote, 'Sir Ian Hamilton told us that he had authentic reports stating that the Turks were getting very short of ammunition, so our lads were told to shout and kick up as much row as they could every three hours and make the Turks fire and waste as much ammunition as they could. It worked twice, they must have frightened hell out of them.'

On 1 June Samuel Weingott was proud to be appointed lance corporal in charge of his section. The next day he heard his lieutenant say that he 'would make a good NCO' because he 'wasn't at all afraid'.[30] On 5 June Weingott lay dead, with a bullet in his belly. He had been wounded at Steel's Post and died on board the hospital ship *Sicilia*. He was buried at sea, and as the army noted, he 'especially asked not to receive a Christian burial'. His father wrote a letter asking for his son's death certificate. His ordinarily clear signature was smudged, as if his hand had become suddenly unsteady, or he had shed a tear onto his notepaper.[31]

Harry Weingott was already broken-hearted. Unknown to Samuel, Alec was also dead. Alec, another tailor's cutter, was shorter, darker and broader than his brother Samuel, and had joined up a month after him. He too had been shot in the stomach at Gallipoli, on 26 April after he had been ashore for only about two hours. He was evacuated to Alexandria, where he died in hospital. His father was spared few details. A Sergeant Kenward, who was attending Alec in hospital in Alexandria, wrote to tell him that, 'We dressed his wounds (abdominal), but an operation was necessary to extract the bullets. Owing to weakness, the surgeons decided to wait a while. On May 2nd, he seemed to rally, and it was decided to operate, but, I am sorry to say, his vitality could not stand the strain, and I decided to stay with him until the end, which occurred that night. He was buried with all the full rites of his religion the next day at Chatby Military Cemetery, Alexandria.'[32] Harold Collins wrote to Rabbi Cohen, 'I was very sorry for Mr Weingott losing his two sons: I knew them both personally and we were often together over here.' On the battlefield Collins had found an *arba kanfot*. 'It may have belonged to one of Mr Weingott's sons, if so, I will only be too pleased to give it to him.'[33]

For Collins, the horror only intensified as the days passed, as if Gallipoli were trying to outdo itself with awfulness. 'There was a very bad accident last night,' he wrote on 4 June. 'We had to relieve a squad … We had just put our blankets down when an awful explosion took place immediately in front of us, I thought that they must have had a gun there but then I heard moans and a chap calling for help. I knew it was something serious, so I ran up to one of the chaps, who was hit, to see what I could do. He had his left leg just below the knee hanging by the skin and it was twisted around a telephone wire. As the artery was not bleeding I did not apply pressure, but supported his head for he was conscious and talking rationally all the time. He offered York his wire cutters, to cut the wire so as he could liberate his leg, but Tom got his smashed up leg away and we lifted him on to level ground. As the doctor was away Sid cut the hanging part away with his jack knife. So as to ease him, I gave him an opium tablet while Tom and Sid did his other leg (which was broken at the knee). By that time the doctor came along and he saw that we had done our work alright, so he just injected morphia to ease the lad. The lad was a corporal belonging to headquarters signallers, asked me to let him have a look at it as he knew his leg was off. He was cracking jokes all the time and he said, what a funny looking cove I will be with a wooden leg. Then there was two killed and fourteen wounded. They said it was one of our own guns that did the damage.'[34]

On 6 August 1915 the Anzacs attempted to break the deadlock at Gallipoli by capturing the hills of Chunuk Bair and Hill 971, in what became known as the Battle of Lone Pine. The Anzacs took the main Turkish trench, which was their target, and defended it with countless gallons of their blood, but the offensive was ultimately a failure. Monash's 4th Brigade was tasked with assaulting Hill 971 from the left, but they got hopelessly lost. Monash was always willing to give credit where credit was due, even when he felt it was owed to himself. Now a brigadier general, he wrote home that, from his point of view, operations had 'been brilliantly successful, notwithstanding that the main object, the conquest of the whole mountain range, has not yet been achieved.' At 9.30 pm on 7 August, Monash's brigade took the lead and, he wrote, 'My column swept out of Reserve Gully into black darkness for its two-mile march northward along the beach into enemy territory. It was like walking out on a stormy winter's night from a warm, cosy home into a hail, thunder, and lightning storm. We had not gone half a mile when the black tangle of hills between the beach road and the main mountain-range became alive with flashes of musketry, and the bursting of shrapnel and star shell, and the yells of the enemy and the cheers of our men as they swept in, to drive in the enemy from molesting the flanks of our march.

'By eleven-thirty we had reached the farthermost point of the beach road, and came abreast of the northern end of the mountain range. My column had the role of a vast turning movement, to get completely around the enemy's right as it faced the sea. From this point we turned sharp into the foothills of the main range, with a tangle of gullies and low ridges covered with prickly gorse ... The 13th Battalion was advanced guard and had scarcely entered the defile of the valley of the Aghyl Dere when the head of the column was met with volleys of fire from the ridges. My orders to the troops were to march with empty magazines, and fight with the bayonet only. Our boys rushed the ridges and drove out the enemy from them. The great difficulty was to keep the right direction in the dark ... I had to go forward personally to the head of the column to push things along, and put vigour into the advance. By dint of yelling and swearing I got the head of the column going on, and soon, as company after company deployed and dashed forward, I had the whole brigade going in fine style, and they swept forward in a magnificent dash of two miles, on a front of fully a mile, carrying everything before them, and just as day broke we established ourselves on a line of ridges overlooking the valley of Asma Dere. As the light became brighter the sight of the battlefields was one to remember. Our own losses were about 300, of which the 15th Battalion bore the brunt, but I counted fully 500 Turkish dead and wounded ...

'We dug hard all day Saturday, and Sunday was another sleepless night, during which I was ordered (much against my advice) to make another sortie to ascertain the enemy's strength on the opposite ridge. In this operation I lost nearly 1000, mostly very lightly wounded, but the operation proved very useful in further dislocating the enemy and delaying his counter-attack. When he did counter-attack late on Sunday afternoon we were already well established and we beat them off easily, killing hundreds of them ... I am more than satisfied with the work of the brigade, although the men are beginning to lose condition physically, and the reinforcements are not up to the same high standard as to physique and training as the original brigade. I think that now I have scarcely 600 left of the [4500] men who marched through the city of Melbourne on 18 December last, and a ragged, dirty, bearded crew they are ... I personally captured two Turks, who had crawled into a hole. I heard a slight movement near me and soon spotted them. They crawled out quite tamely when challenged, and holding up their hands gave themselves up. We captured a Turkish bivouac, and I now have a Turkish officer's folding bedstead and copper bathtub as my share of the loot.'[35]

Harley Cohen was hit at Lone Pine. 'I've a piece or two of shrapnel in my right eye,' he said, 'and I've got a mate who has lost his left eye, but we linked arms and used our two good eyes.' Both were invalided home. After the battle Captain Harold Jacobs of the 1st Battalion wrote that his trench was 'so full of our dead that the only respect that we could show them was not to tread on their faces, the floor of the trench was just one carpet of them, this in addition to the ones we piled into Turkish dugouts'.[36]

The Jewish VCs

The AIF's first Jewish VC was Leonard Maurice Keysor, born in London in 1885. Keysor's father was a furniture broker who imported clocks and also ran a coffee house. The boy was educated at refined Jewish boarding schools in England, where he excelled at sport, especially cricket, football and rowing. He left England at the age of seventeen for Quebec, Canada, where he spent a decade adventuring and farming, and learned to shoot and ride. 'I never knew such a boy, even when he was a child, for pluck,' said his mother. 'He would do anything, and was hard to discipline.'[37]

In 1913 Keysor departed Canada to join his brother Stanley and sister Madge, who had moved to Australia. When war broke out, Keysor was working as a clerk in Sydney. He was among the first 1000 men to enlist in the 1st Battalion AIF. When he entered the army, he took the precaution of knocking a year off his age (he enlisted as twenty-seven when he was actually twenty-eight) and the social shackles off his religion. He proclaimed his faith as 'Church of England', although he was openly Jewish thereafter.

Keysor sailed from Sydney on HMAT *Afric* as a private soldier with H Company, 1st Battalion, 1st Division AIF and landed at Gallipoli on 25 April. In August 1915, already an expert bomb-thrower with a bowler's arm, Keysor was battling through the maelstrom of Lone Pine. The Turks showered the Australians with cast-iron hand grenades which – as has often been pointed out – were a similar size to cricket balls. Keysor stood among the bombs as they rained down, and replied to the barrage with improvised Australian 'jam-tin' grenades. 'He generally carried on his job from a raised platform in the side of the trench,' wrote a comrade. 'His "jam-tin" bombs always drew a response from the Turks, but Keysor seemed to bear a charmed life, and he did not know the meaning of fear.'[38]

On 7 August, according to Keysor's citation for the Victoria Cross, he was in a trench under heavy bombardment by the Turks when he 'picked up two live bombs and threw them back at the enemy at great risk to his own life, and continued throwing bombs, although himself wounded, thereby saving a portion of the trench which it was most important to hold.' The next day the wounded Keysor 'successfully bombed the enemy out of a position from which a temporary mastery of his own trench had been obtained, and was again wounded. Although marked for hospital he declined to leave, and volunteered to throw bombs for another company which had lost its bomb-throwers. He continued to bomb the enemy till the situation was relieved.'[39]

He wrote home to his sister Madge, 'My word, it was a grand affair, but, unfortunately, there was a terrible lot of casualties. I had a slight cut on the mouth.'[40] His Jewishness was immediately acknowledged. His mother told the press, 'As a co-religionist I should have been proud of him – but my own son – well, it's simply glorious.'[41]

With only a brief passage of time, Keysor's deeds became exaggerated, and the Imperial idol – whose dark Semitic features watched schoolboys and housewives from cigarette cards and biscuit tins – grew from hero to superhero. According to the book *Deeds that Thrill the Empire*, he 'not only hurled our bombs at the enemy, but managed to cover with overcoats and sandbags the bombs which the enemy threw at us. Others he caught in their flight without letting them explode.'[42] The men at the time were unconvinced. One Frank Lesnie, a London-born Jew in the trenches with the AIF, wrote home, 'You might have read that a favourite trick here is to catch the Turkish bombs, throw them back again and so hoist them with their own petards. A spectator would think and witness otherwise. The moment a bomb is seen to drop over the parapet, there is a muddy rush for the four corners of the globe; so much so, that one trench is called by the name of "The Racecourse".'[43]

But Keysor's feat of grenade-catching – which appears never to have been claimed by Keysor himself – was already orthodoxy when a Russian journalist sought out the AIF to visit the hut where lived 'the greatest wonder of the whole Australian camp – the famous, wonderful Keysor, about whom I had read so much, whose portrait I had seen in shop windows and on sweet boxes. Keysor, who had been so much praised in the papers. But, good heavens, is this he? A small, weak, plain man, not at all like a hero. Is this the man who for fifty hours on end protected his comrades from the Turkish hand grenades, catching them and throwing them back, like children's tennis balls? ... I looked at his face, which was not young, at the long, winding line of his mouth, and in a moment it struck me: "Listen, you are a Jew, aren't you?" He smiled an ancient Jewish smile. His features were sharp and frowning. A typical youth of Odessa. He treats himself sometimes ironically, sometimes with the greatest respect, triumphantly. "Yes, we are Jews from Persia."' The journalist asked Keysor to talk about his deeds, but he modestly refused. 'He shook his head lazily. "It isn't worthwhile. I have so often told the story. And, besides, what did I do in particular? Others were doing more, only no one saw them, whereas they happened to notice me."' On prompting, Keysor showed the Russian his VC, 'the rarest distinction in the world'. The journalist marvelled, 'The King himself receives him at his palace, the papers publish his biography, his figure in wax is set up in Madame Tussaud's Museum, and the crowd that meets him in the street greets him.'[44]

Keysor was the AIF's first Jewish VC, but two other Jewish VCs of World War One also had Australian connections and one of them, the Egyptian-born Issy Smith, is widely claimed as Australian (as well as British but never, it could be noted, as Egyptian). The first Jewish VC of the war was Sudan veteran Ernest Simeon de Pass's younger cousin, Frank Alexander de Pass, who died near Festubert, France, on 15 November 1914. Frank, born in England, had graduated from the Royal Military College Woolwich and transferred to the Indian army. It was as a lieutenant in the 34th Prince Albert Victor's Own Poona Horse that Frank displayed 'conspicuous bravery' in 'entering a German sap and destroying a traverse in the face of the enemy's bombs, and for subsequently rescuing, under heavy fire, a wounded man who was lying exposed in the open'. Dryly, the citation continues, 'Lieutenant de Pass lost his life on this day in a second attempt to capture the aforementioned sap, which had been re-occupied by the enemy.'[45] De Pass was awarded his medal the following year, and his story became celebrated in Australia. The sacrifice was linked explicitly with the cause of the Jewish people, by the Jewish and secular press alike. The Perth *Sunday Times* predicted, 'This young soldier's heroism will not soon be forgotten, and neither will the honourable part which the Jewish community is playing in the war. There are only a quarter of a million Jews in the United Kingdom, and many of them are men of alien birth, who are not eligible to wear the King's uniform, yet no fewer than 10000 Jews are serving in the British Army and Navy. In proportion to the number of able bodied males capable of bearing arms, none of the composite communities which make up the British Empire have a better record than the Jews.' A letter from Frank's father Elliot, written to a friend in New Zealand, was published in the *Hebrew Standard*. Even in grief, Elliot de Pass related the sacrifice of his son to the fight against antisemitism. 'Whilst we weep in the privacy of our home, we neither repine nor show any lack of courage to the world,' he wrote. His consolation was the thought that his son's VC might 'help to lessen the prejudice against his race, that [it] is obsessed by the love of gain, that care little for the more immortal virtues, and value their lives more than their country's weal'.[46]

ISSY SMITH WAS BORN IN EGYPT IN 1890 TO RUSSIAN PARENTS who were French citizens living in Alexandria. His birth name was Israel Smilovich and he was to lead a celebrated and vigorous life, a big man who was a giant among his people. He stowed away on a ship to England at the age of eleven and went to school in the East End. To earn money, he sold fish. He left school at fourteen and enlisted in the British Army two weeks before his sixteenth birthday. He changed his name on the recommendation of the recruiting sergeant, from one of the most Jewish names imaginable to a title that almost seemed a joke, or a question: Issy Smith?

But Smith also took a third name, 'Jack Daniels', and it was as Daniels he fought as a professional boxer in England and, occasionally, France. Daniels/Smith faced Bermondsey journeyman Young Lilley a surprising twelve times between 1907 and 1913. As Issy Smith, he became the middleweight boxing champion of the First Battalion, Manchester Regiment. He served in South Africa and India but left the army in 1912. He subsequently migrated to Australia, where he worked for a while in Melbourne. In 1914, as Jack Daniels, he fought three times against Alf Morey, who had won the Australian lightweight title the year before. Still on the army reserve list, Smith was called up at the start of the war. He was said to have taken part in the Australian capture of German New Guinea, but no army records document his part in this action.

Smith took a passage out of Australia with the AIF convoy

via Egypt in December 1914, and rejoined his regiment, the Manchesters, to fight in France. He was wounded several times on the Western Front. On 26 April 1915, the day after the Anzacs had landed in Gallipoli, Smith's battalion suffered heavy casualties from enemy shellfire at a position near Ypres in Belgium. At about eleven o'clock in the morning, Smith later told an interviewer, 'We halted in a field for rest, but we had not time to take our equipment off before shells were rained on us from a German aeroplane, and many were killed. We then got the order to run for cover and leave everything behind us. I left my pack behind me, and when we went to look for cover I suddenly remembered I had left my cigarettes behind. I went back to get the cigarettes out of my pack, and it was lucky I did, for when I had gone a short distance a Jack Johnson dropped among my platoon and killed or wounded about fourteen of them. Then we got orders to fall in, and word was passed along the line that the artillery would commence a bombardment at 1:20. This lasted for forty minutes, and was followed by five minutes of rapid fire. Our platoon was leading, with Lieutenant Robinson in charge. After our long march we were almost breathless with fatigue, but just then we got orders to fix bayonets and charge.

'The Germans yelled like madmen when they saw cold steel coming on them. Our commander was hit, and I got my field dressing out and bandaged him. There was heavy machine-gun fire at this time. I carried the commander about two or three hundred yards, before I got to a first-aid post, and on my way I saw Lieutenant [WM] Shipster running up and down with ammunition for the machine gun.

'Lieutenant Shipster was a man who knew no fear. He saw me bending under the weight of another wounded man, Sergeant Rooke, of the Manchester Regiment, and said "Don't falter, old chap; I shan't be long, and will give you a lift." The place was swept by heavy fire at this time, and Lieutenant Shipster had not gone twenty yards, when he was shot in the neck.

'I said to Sergeant Rooke: "Lie here a minute while I bandage Lieutenant Shipster." I rolled down the hill with my hands by my side, and reached the officer. I carried him to where Sergeant Rooke lay. I removed Sergeant Rooke a few yards, and then Lieutenant Shipster a few yards, and so on, alternately, until I reached our trenches, where I found the [4th] Suffolks in support. A Lieutenant Priestly came out of the trench and took Lieutenant Shipster in. I brought Sergeant Rooke to safety, and, then exhausted, I fell down, not able to move. An officer gave me his flask, and said, "There is brandy in this, take a drop, and it will revive you." I said that I would not, as I was a teetotaller, and intended to remain one, no matter what happened, but I was dreadfully weak.

'I rested for half-an-hour, and then went back to my company to learn that Lieutenant Robinson was missing. A few hours afterwards I went out to look for him, but could not find him. I saw a lot of our wounded lying about, and with the help of our stretcher-bearers managed to take them all out of danger. We were relieved by the Highland [Light] Infantry about three o'clock on the morning of 27th April, and we went back and received a good meal – the first for two days. I was slightly gassed, and was carried to the first-aid post, and lay there very sick for about twenty-four hours, but would not leave the battalion, as I wanted to see the fight through.'[47]

In this engagement, which became known as the Second Battle of Ypres, the Germans had used poison gas on their enemies for the first time. Smith was sent to Britain to recuperate from his gassing, and there he was awarded the Victoria Cross by George V at Buckingham Palace on 16 October 1915. At the announcement of his VC, Smith was a patient at Dublin University Voluntary Aid Detachment hospital, which was 'besieged' by the local Jewish community when they heard the news. They took Smith to a city hotel where, according to the *Evening Mail*, 'They feted him to their hearts' content.' The reporter noted this was 'a somewhat more emotional event than most people would associate with the Jewish character. However, there was one man amongst them who seemed proof against all this fine sentiment, and that was Issy Smith, the hero of many a battle. Issy had lived in blood these ten months, and now he was hardened at the killing business, and talks of the most terrible carnage as if it were one of the small things in life. There is one thing which he cannot understand, and that is why we make a fuss of our heroes.'[48]

The fact that Smith was Jewish was known to all, and widely reported in Australia. He was lauded in the *Jewish Herald* in the context of the 'Three Jewish VCs', in a story highlighting the decorations of Keysor, Smith and de Pass.[49] On 10 November 1915 the Adelaide Hebrew Congregation gathered to say farewell to the Jewish South Australians who were leaving that week for the war. Reverend Abraham Tobias Boas said he envied the boys 'the opportunity of going to the battlefield in the cause of the country which they love', and said, 'were it not for old age I would also have offered my services'. He referred to 'our Issy Smith' and voiced the usual hope that 'all working for the cause would remove the false accusations that we were lacking in patriotism and loyalty'. On behalf of the soldiers, Sergeant Morris said they 'hoped they would all distinguish themselves as their comrade Issy Smith had done'.[50]

Back in England, Smith tasted the gratitude felt for his courage by some sections of the British public. He was directed to take part in a recruiting drive, which took him to Leeds, Yorkshire, a northern English city with a large Jewish community. Smith walked into the Grand Restaurant in Boar Lane with an Australian friend and, according to press reports, 'refreshments, of the teetotal kind, were called for'. However, 'The waiter declined to serve the soldier, and the proprietor, being interviewed, repeated the refusal to serve the man in uniform, on the ground that he was a Jew.' The incident was reported in the Australian press. The *Sunday Times* of Sydney wrote it was 'not to be wondered at that he proposes to make his home in Australia'.[51] When the recruiting tour was over, Smith returned to the Middle East to fight. In Baghdad he was wounded once more. He received the Russian Cross of St George and Palm for rescuing a wounded Russian soldier (Smith also held the French Croix de Guerre with Palm) and was witness to the fall of Jerusalem in 1917. After the war, 'Jack Daniels' fought his last boxing match in Broken Hill on 2 December 1922. Issy Smith returned to live in Melbourne, where at least he could get a cup of coffee.

Last days at Gallipoli

While the war raged on in Europe, the Anzacs remained pinned down at Gallipoli. They were joined by fresh troops from home, who could do little but die beside them. Among the reinforcements headed for the Dardanelles was Private Frank Bernard Hershorn Lesnie, the London-born labourer who had shown his scepticism about the possibility of fielding bowled bombs. Lesnie had declared himself as Jewish on his attestation paper, but chose to serve as Frank Bernard. He had come to Australia at the age of seventeen, apparently to make a home for his mother. When war broke out, he mocked her suggestion that he might return to England. 'I was greatly amused at being asked to save up some of the filthy lucre, take a trip to England and enlist there instead of Australia,' he wrote. 'Australia, the home of workers, will suit me in the capacity of a worker or a soldier. I have a love of freedom which would have been denied me, had I joined a home regiment.' He left Sydney on the SS *Kanowna* with about 1000 other men of the 17th Battalion AIF, most of them raw recruits, on 19 June 1915. 'We stopped at Adelaide,' he wrote, 'but were not allowed to leave the ship. We determined, however, to get ashore at the next port, which we managed after a great deal of trouble. Arriving at Fremantle, the Major in charge positively asserted that we would get no leave whatever. He then took a walk round the ship and saw here and there that the soldiers were climbing over the side into some small boats. His next move was to post a double guard throughout the ship, which stopped the escapade for the time being. In the meantime, coaling was going on at both sides of the ship. The men refused to allow the coalers to go on with their work until leave was granted. The Major realised that the men were in earnest and consented to their demands. This will just serve to show you the independence of the Australian. If the same thing had been done in the British Army a Court Martial would have followed. Having obtained our leave, the next thing to do was to make the most of it. I took a train to Perth and enjoyed a very nice holiday. On coming back to the *Kanowna* a rumour went round that four men of the 19th were sober. The natural results of a holiday in Perth were perceived the same night and the following day. I witnessed twenty-four fights in three hours, which was followed by a general scrum. We retired to bed that night some with black eyes, others with a few bruises and aching limbs. The next day some of the men took to pelting a few officers with orange peel and apple cores. One man who had drunk well but not too wisely, thought he was taking part in a swimming race and dived into the water with all his clothes on. He was picked up before reaching the wharf.'[52]

On 23 August Karri Davies' nephew Keith Levi was shot through the head at Cape Helles.[53] Although he had gone to Egypt with the Light Horse reinforcements in February, Levi had been attached to a British regiment, the Hampshires, at the time he was killed. He had previously worked at the hospital at Heliopolis, on transports of wounded men between the Dardanelles and Alexandria, and at the rest camp of Imbros. He had been a regimental medical officer with the Hampshires' 29th Division for less than a month.

But other men were frustrated not to have reached the front.

Bombardier Stanley Octavius Benjamin of Melbourne who, before the war, had presented a long paper proposing 'A System of Raising Military Forces in the Commonwealth' to the Jewish Literary and Debating Society,[54] wrote from Alexandria: 'Much to my disappointment, I am still in Egypt and not yet at the front. This is not because we are in want of training, but because there is no use at present over at Gallipoli for a Field Artillery Ammunition Column, to which I was attached on arriving in Egypt. However, my chance is sure to come sooner or later. May it be sooner.'[55]

In 1915 the festivals of *Rosh Hashanah* and *Yom Kippur* fell respectively on 27 August and 5 September, while Benjamin was still in Egypt. He wrote, 'I had already started to make enquiries about the dates of the Days from one of the many Jewish refugee boys from Syria, etc., who come round the camps in Alexandria selling cigarettes, tobacco, soap, matches, etc., or to take away washing.' Like many other Jewish Australian troops, he had eaten with the always hospitable Slutzkin family, prominent Melbourne Jews who had settled in Palestine in 1905 but evacuated to Egypt.* Benjamin had also enjoyed a service at the handsome Synagogue on Rue Nebi Danial, along with other Anzac troops and English and French soldiers. However, the rabbi was from Italy and 'his sermon was delivered in Italian', wrote Benjamin, 'so, I could not understand it'.[56]

Jewish people in World War One had an apparently inexhaustible capacity for meeting one another in unlikely situations. Julius Leonard Neustadt, a Sydney-born 'merchant and agent', had served for eighteen months in the Australian Rifle Regiment, where he held the rank of corporal, but was initially refused a place in the AIF due to 'deficient chest measurement'. When the chest expansion thought necessary in a soldier was lessened, as

---

*   Rose Slutzkin, the wife of patriarch Lasar Slutzkin, was a sister of Aaron Blashki, and aunt to Dr Eric Blashki and Lieutenant Roy Hector Blashki.

thousands of big-chested men were slaughtered in the trenches, Neustadt was admitted to the 23rd Battalion AIF, and sailed for Gallipoli on 30 August 1915. On 2 September HMAS *Southland*, a troop carrier steaming about four hours ahead of Neustadt's ship, was torpedoed by a submarine. When they reached the wreckage, 'We launched boats to rescue those who were hanging onto rafts etc,' wrote Neustadt. 'Much to my surprise among the rescued was Theo Levy and I'm glad to say he seemed none the worse for his ducking though they say they were on the raft for four hours and were thrown into the water twice – once in launching the boat and once the raft capsized … I fixed Theo up with some clothes etc, and we slept alongside one another under the wagon and talked of old times.'*

Neustadt landed at Anzac Cove on 4 September. The next day was *Yom Kippur*, the Day of Atonement, when Jews are expected to fast and pray. 'I will be justified in fasting on the food we get here,' wrote Neustadt. 'Still, I will try and make a little difference in that day.' Neustadt's cousin Jack Marks Levy, an 'agricultural expert and journalist' from Melbourne, was posted to Headquarters as a warrant officer in Ordnance and by 17 September he had found Neustadt a job too. 'All my work is to keep the accounts of clothes and equipment for the Brigade,' wrote Neustadt. 'This job is more in my line. I have a decent little dugout near HQ and Jack and I mess together.' On 19 September Theo Levy visited and played solo for a while. Jim Joseph brought Neustadt cigarettes on 28 September, and the next morning he enjoyed the further luxury of egg for breakfast and a sponge bath in a tin. He described it as a 'gala day'.

---

* Theodore Harold Levy, a clerk from Coleraine, Victoria, went on to serve close to five years in the army, during which he fought at Gallipoli, transferred to the Anzac Provost Police in France, was promoted to lieutenant, made a temporary captain and eventually awarded an MBE by King George V.

A number of Jewish Australians, including members of the Michaelis family, had been in England when the war broke out, and so had joined the British Army. On 23 September Lieutenant Grant Michaelis was killed in the Dardanelles. Michaelis, a cousin of Dalbert Hallenstein, had grown up mostly in St Kilda and Geelong but moved to England in about 1911. He had been an officer in the part-time Territorial Forces and had volunteered for the Expeditionary Army. The death toll mounted but Arthur Jacobs, the South Australian former journalist, remained confident of victory. 'Like an insidious poison,' he wrote, 'slow, but sure, we are eating into the vitals of the Turkish Army on Gallipoli, losing a few men here and there, but making the Turks pay a terrific toll for those who have gone … At present everything seems peaceful, and the dull boom of the guns seems just like the surf breaking heavily on a rocky shore. And further away there is the sound of heavy rifle fire, but it seems as if someone were operating a Brobdingnagian typewriter.'[57] On 4 October Jacobs was hit by an enemy grenade and evacuated from the peninsula. 'My introduction to a Turkish "firetail" bomb was disastrous,' he wrote home from hospital in London. 'When I reached England I gave up all hope of keeping my leg, as septic poisoning had set in, and the wound would not heal. The surgeons at this hospital are wonderfully skilful, and after a series of operations cleared the muscles of the calf of the poisonous germs, and today is the third on which I have been up on crutches.'[58]

On 9 October another cousin of Julius Neustadt, Julius Bloom, a clerk from Sydney, dropped by Neustadt's trench. 'He looks well,' wrote Neustadt, 'though working pretty hard and is suffering a bit from prickly heat and diarrhoea. He had tea with me and said it was a nice change for him. Fixed him up with a razor and a tin of jam.' Despite the dangers, it was possible to escape from Gallipoli for weeks at a time. Monash and others took leave in October in Alexandria, Egypt, where Roy Hector Blashki was training with the Field Artillery. The city seemed flooded with Jewish officers. On 26 October, Blashki wrote in his diary, 'Heard General Monash was in Alexandria staying at Savoy Palace Hotel so called on him, found him and introduced myself. Had an interesting yarn to him for a couple of hours, also met his nephew, Lieutenant Eric Simonson (just arrived in Egypt with reinforcements).'* Two days later, Blashki wrote, 'Met Major Margolin (WA, 16th Battalion) and he gave me the address of his relations in Cairo', and on Friday 29 October Blashki had 'tea' with Monash, Margolin, Dalbert Hallenstein and others.[59] Back in the trenches, on 1 November Julius Neustadt received a letter from Saddler Sergeant Sylvester Browne, who was in Egypt with the 1st Australian Light Horse Regiment (ALH). Brisbane-born Browne, one of at least fifty-seven Jewish soldiers in the ALH, had been a member of the 9th Light Horse militia regiment before the war and was the first of a family of soldiers to enlist in the AIF. His brother Roy George later resigned from the 7th Light Horse (NSW Lancers) to join the AIF and saw active service in England. A third brother, Gunner Louis Browne, fought in France with the 4th Field Artillery. Their youngest sibling, Sapper Maurice H Browne, joined the army at eighteen years old, and served in Australia with the Mining Corps.

At his trench in Gallipoli, Neustadt continued to receive mail and visits from other Jewish troops. Julius Bloom was a regular caller until 5 November, which Neustadt called 'one of the saddest days', when a friend of the Blooms, Harold Herman, broke

---

*   Lieutenant Eric Simonson became the second of Monash's nephews to arrive at the front, following Aubrey Moss, who worked for some time as his uncle's aide in Gallipoli. Eric's brother Paul Simonson later served as Monash's aide de camp in France. Astonishingly, Monash's alcoholic cousin, the 45-year-old pharmacist Karl Roth (NAA B2455 Roth, Karl Charkel service record), also turned up in Gallipoli in November, as a private soldier with the 22nd Battalion. Monash did his best for Roth, a chaotic widower struggling with his addiction, and saw that he was transferred to the 4th Field Ambulance.

the news of Julius' recent death. According to a Red Cross report he died while 'sitting in the firing line at No. 6 Post, near Quinn's Post ... in a support trench near at hand, reading a letter he had just received from his mother, when a Turkish mine exploded under the trench'.[60] 'He was over with us yesterday and spent a pleasant day,' wrote Neustadt, 'We buried him this morning at Anzac.'[61] Harold Collins was evacuated from Gallipoli with a hernia on 8 September, and later transferred to the Australian Flying Corps (AFC).*

Harold Herman was hit by a bullet at Quinn's Post on 19 November and died the next day on the hospital ship *Somali*. His body was given to the ocean, which had become both a battlefield and a burial ground. On 23 October 1915 the New Zealand transport ship SS *Marquette* had been sunk while heading for Salonika. About four hours' steam from its destination, it was torpedoed by an enemy submarine and disappeared under the waves in twenty minutes. Thirty-two New Zealanders were among those who died, including ten nurses. On board the *Marquette* was Roland Benjamin from Auckland, whose home unit had been decimated in the sinking, and who was by 1916 attached to the Australian Medical Corps. He wrote to his mother from Salonika: 'My four mates have gone. All except one died from exposure, as the water was bitterly cold, and most of us were in it for eight hours. A young fellow named Clark and I hung on to a piece of timber from

---

*   There were a number of Jews in the RAAF's modestly sized predecessor, the AFC, in World War One. Harold Collins joined in November 1916, and was promoted to technical quartermaster sergeant in France, and eventually re-mustered as a master mechanic. At the end of the war, Collins was awarded the Meritorious Service Medal (MSM). Flight Lieutenant Bernard Freiman of Footscray, Victoria, won his wings in 1917. Flight Lieutenant David Altson of Melbourne saw brief active service in France. Monash's nephew Eric Simonson transferred to the AFC in September 1917 and later enlisted in the RAAF in World War Two. Air Mechanic Edgar Emanuel Hansman died at sea in December 1917 (his brother, Private Hyam Joseph Hansman, had been killed in Flanders three weeks earlier). Flight Lieutenant Robert Sydney Lasker was lost over France in 1918.

the hatchway cover, and were the last to be picked up by a French torpedo boat. We were in a very exhausted condition, being nearly frozen ... I lost everything I possessed, and landed here with only a pair of short pants, shirt, drawers and singlet, and three shillings in cash, everything else having gone down with the ship ... I was about fifty yards away when the *Marquette* took the final plunge. It was a magnificent and dreadful sight. She went down bow first, and at the finish the stern was straight out of the water, just like the pictures we have seen of sinking ships, with men struggling all round her. On arrival at Salonika we were taken on board two hospital ships, and received all the attention possible ... My wristlet watch went for one hour after being in the water, but is now full of rust. My old carved pipe and all my little knick-knacks are now with Davy Jones.' He wrote again, once he had had a chance to look around Salonika, bemoaning more than anything the loss of his pipe ('I had it in my mouth when I went into the water, but after a while I took it out and put it in my pocket, and it must have been washed out'). However, he was able to find some comfort in his surroundings. 'The Salonique Jewess is supposed to be the finest-looking woman in the world,' he wrote, 'and from the samples I have seen I can quite believe it.'[62]

In October 1915 Reverend Freedman of Perth had been appointed the first Jewish chaplain on active service with the AIF. He disembarked at Gallipoli on 9 December 1915, and later wrote, 'Though there was no set attack on either side, the crack of rifle and the boom of shell never ceased. I have not been out of the firing line all the time. In fact, when I was in the front firing trench I felt safer than in a gully or a dug out. Walking up and down gullies one was continually turning to see shells fall and burst. Being delayed one afternoon for half a minute I had the good fortune to avoid walking right into a bursting shell.'[63] Gallipoli proved an extraordinary experience for Freedman, who recorded his hardships with good humour, and adopted the fighting man's obsession with rations. He wrote to the president of his congregation in Western Australia: 'Some of the nights especially were the most beautifully awful I have spent in my life. Most of the time in the night I spent in doing voluntary sentry duty, as I preferred walking to sleeping. However, by breakfast time I forgot all about the "comforts" of the night, and immensely enjoyed my tin of sardines and biscuits. At one breakfast I ate a large tin of sardines, all to myself – a thing I never did before – so I must be thoroughly enjoying life.' Freedman met with Brigadier Monash and also Major Margolin, who had become known for his courage under fire. In addition, Freedman held prayer services, one of which was attended by members of the Zion Mule Corps, a British formation largely made up of Jewish refugees from Palestine and, apparently, the first regular Jewish fighting unit to go to war since Biblical times. The mule corps had come ashore at Gallipoli among the first wave of troops on 25 April. 'The Zion Mule Corps men did not understand a word of English,' wrote Freedman, 'and our men did not know Yiddish, and only very little of Hebrew, so that I had to make the service a regular mix-up thing. The Zion men mostly speak only Hebrew and Arabic.'[64]

In the week that Freedman arrived, Monash received new orders. 'Like a thunderbolt from a clear blue sky,' he wrote, 'has come the stupendous and paralysing news that, after all, the Allied War Council has decided that the best and wisest course to take is to evacuate the Peninsula, and secret orders to carry out that operation have just reached here. The secret is known so far to only a small handful of men … The first thing to do is to secure as great a measure of secrecy as possible. This operation of withdrawal is going to be every bit as critical and dangerous an enterprise as the first landing, and if the Turks were to get the slightest inkling of what was intended, it would mean the sacrifice of at least half our men. As it is, it will mean the sacrifice of some men, and of vast quantities of munitions and stores. At a conference of the commanders it was decided to put up the bluff that, owing to the severe winter conditions, it is intended to form a winter rest-camp at Imbros, and take the brigades and battalions there by turn. In this way we should be able in two or three stages to remove about two-thirds of the total army, leaving the remaining third to man the defences very lightly, and then finally to make a bolt for the beach, in the dead of night and into boats which will be in waiting. It is of course an absolutely critical scheme, which may come off quite successfully or may end in a frightful disaster. But orders are orders. I need not say I feel very unhappy. Being bound to secrecy, I can take none of my staff or COs into my confidence. I am almost frightened to contemplate the howl of rage and disappointment there will be when the men find out what is afoot, and I am wondering what Australia will think at the desertion of her 6000 dead and her 20000 other casualties.'[65]

Lesnie was at the evacuations. 'Two weeks previous,' he wrote, 'orders to our troops were to cease firing. The Turks wondered what we were up to and sent about fifty of their men over the parapets from their second line of trenches to their first. Had we opened fire not one of them would have seen daylight again. They got off scot free and silence reigned supreme. Next morning, at break of daylight, four Turks took a walk over to our trenches to see what the game was. Three made a hurried retreat to their own trenches, the fourth fell right into the trench, pushed one bayonet aside and was butchered a second later. There was absolutely no justification for the killing, the man would have been more useful alive than dead. At the end of three days the silence stunt was over. In the meantime, the Turks had got up a stunt of their own, in the shape of a gun and started shelling our trenches about 100 yards to the right of us. I saw a few arms and legs go up in the air and did not look that way again. That was the preliminary to the evacuation. Our idea evidently was to see whether the Turks would come over in the event of there being silence. The ruse worked successfully as

events proved. A day before the advance party left we were introduced to [the] intended scheme. We had an idea as to what was
going to happen, but could not possibly believe that they would
carry out such a thing. Mind you, we all wanted to get away from
the peninsular [sic], but did not agree with the manner of leaving.
The night before a large fire was lit on the beach; the blaze could
be seen for miles around and the Turks shelled heavily. December 18th at 4 pm the advance party, with muffled feet, was waiting
patiently at the top of Quinns Post. Darkness approached, and we
started sneaking off the peninsular [sic] with our tails between our
legs. One wharf was lit up by a fire while we marched at the back
of the fire, then on to another wharf some fifty yards away.'⁶⁶

'The last hours passed most wearily,' wrote Monash. 'Every
crack of a rifle, every burst of rifle-fire, every bomb explosion,
might have been the beginning of a general attack all along the
line. By ten o'clock our numbers had been reduced to 170 in the
brigade, 700 in the whole New Zealand and Australian Division,
and about 1500 in the whole Army Corps, spread along a front over
eight miles. This meant that if at any point along this great line the
Turks had discovered the withdrawal, and if only a few of our men
had given way and allowed our lines to be penetrated, the whole
of this last 1500 would have had a very hard fight of it, and many
would have left their bones on Gallipoli.

'Down dozens of little gullies leading back from the front lines
came little groups of six to a dozen men, the last closing the gully
with a previously prepared frame of barbed wire, or lighting a fuse,
which an hour later would fire a mine for the wrecking of a sap or
a tunnel by which the enemy could follow ... All these little col-
umns of men kept joining up ... there was no check, no halting, no
haste or running, just a steady, silent tramp of single file, without
any lights or smoking, and every yard brought us nearer to safety.'⁶⁷
But the withdrawal was not entirely disciplined. Chaplain Freedman left Gallipoli on a lighter crowded with Australian troops. He

94

wrote, 'We were still tied up to a little pier, and though everything was being done to keep the enemy from getting a hint of what was a-foot, our lads were singing choruses at the top of their voice.'[68]

The men were conveyed by small tugs onto battleships. 'The following night the second party marched to the beach without any casualties,' wrote Lesnie. 'One per cent of the troops were left behind and evacuated Gallipoli on the third night ... When the last batch was out at sea, Walkers Ridge, Lone Pine, Courtneys, Quinns Post, etc., were all blown up.'[69] Monash was satisfied with the operation. 'We had succeeded in withdrawing 45 000 men,' he wrote, 'also mules, guns, stores, provisions and transport without a single casualty, and without allowing the enemy to entertain the slightest suspicion. It was a most brilliant conception, brilliantly organized and brilliantly executed, and will, I am sure, rank as the greatest joke – and the greatest feat of arms in the whole range of military history.'[70]

One of the last men to leave the peninsula was Major Eliazar Margolin, who had taken temporary command of the 16th Battalion, and wrote home that only one officer and ten men had been left behind when he departed Gallipoli, and they had followed him ten minutes later.[71] When Collie man Sergeant Watkins later returned to Western Australia on a recruitment tour, he named Margolin as 'the bravest man who ever set foot on the Peninsula'.[72] The AIF withdrew to Egypt having lost 8141 men, including at least thirty-six Jewish Anzacs, many of whom were temporarily buried under makeshift crosses or sunk to the bottom of the sea.

Anzacs in Egypt

Julius Neustadt had been evacuated sick from Gallipoli in November. He recuperated in Alexandria, where he was regularly visited by his friend Sylvester Browne of the 1st Australian Light Horse.

Meanwhile, elements of the ALH were preparing for action in the Middle East. Private Maurice Sussman, a clerk born in Gloucester, New South Wales, had left Australia for Egypt on 30 September 1915 with the 6th Light Horse Regiment. Sussman and his comrades rode out of Mex Camp near Alexandria on 8 December to do battle with the Senussi Arabs, a Sufi sect aligned with the Ottoman Empire. Sussman fought as part of the Western Frontier Force (WFF), a colourful gathering of soldiers from exotic corners of the British Empire. The WFF grouped at the Mediterranean seaport of Mersa Matruh and the Light Horse rode out to face the Senussi before dawn on Christmas Day 'accompanied by artillery, machine guns and armoured cars, half a battalion of Sikhs and a battalion of NZ Rifles (Infantry)', wrote Sussman. 'The Infantry marched along the coast, and we made a wide detour. At six o'clock the niggers were firing at us at a range of about 400 yards and the bullets flew thick and uncomfortably close. My troop was first into action and having a good little officer we fired with deliberation and made every shot tell. The niggers fell here and there, then wavered and retreated a little to the right whither we had been instructed to try and drive them. Their shots became erratic so we became more confident and stood up to take aim as one would pot rabbits. A couple of our horseholders and several horses were shot but not seriously. We then joined our squadron and galloping several miles again dismounted and engaged the enemy. With the assistance of the artillery we succeeded in driving them into a big waadi or ravine. Here the New Zealanders put in some fine work and ending with a bayonet charge accounted for 200 dead and took many prisoners. The Sikhs fought like tigers often going into the caves in the sides of ravines (where the snipers were busy) and rooting the Arabs out would bash them over the head by way of a feeler and tickle them up with the bayonet. They are savage warriors and every time one shot an Arab he would jump with a wild shout of fiercesome [sic] joy…

'We had a gun-boat handy pumping in lead and as a result the enemy's big guns were put out of action early in the day. At sundown we knew that victory was complete and a tired and weary infidel was gathering up the remnants of his whiskers and with the blessings of Allah in his trousers, was fast fleeing into regions whither we were not inclined to follow. We captured 380 camels, 13 000 sheep, many goats, asses and mules, one month's food supply, the whole of their convoy, 16 000 rounds of ammunition, sixteen shells and a lead pencil. When we counted up their dead we found that something like 600 of their number had said his last prayer in his whiskers and assigned his estate to Allah. Among the effects of the dead were German officers' trousers, German literature and military books and BLOOD. Our total casualties (killed and wounded) were sixty-nine on Xmas Day ... Thank God the troop to which I belonged No 2 of B Squadron returned unscathed for since our first scrap we seemed to regard each other as brothers.'

A few days later Sussman was a member of a party that went to make peace with a Bedouin chieftain. 'I learned that the Chief's terms of Peace were that he would give us two towns including Salome if we would let him have Egypt,' wrote Sussman. 'I suggested that they might throw in Belfield's Pub and the Salon de Luxe so long as we had peace. Anyhow there was no scrap but we burned all the villages along the road home. After that we could never get near the niggers they would spot us a long way off in the desert and then run like Hell and moreover the country was too rough to give our horses any chance of following them.'[73]

Bloodied and blooded at Gallipoli, the main body of the Anzacs expanded and reorganised in Egypt. In Cairo, Chaplain Freedman harangued a Major Maxted of Ordnance to ensure that a correct emblem marked Jewish graves. 'I requisitioned and submitted a design for fifty memorials,' he wrote, 'and after a good deal of trouble Major Maxted agreed to have them made after this pattern, which is that of the Shield of David, the sides of the triangles being wide enough to take the name, number and battalion of the deceased soldier.' On 10 February 1916 Freedman was appointed chaplain to all Jews in the Allied armies of the Mediterranean Expeditionary Force. He made his headquarters at Ismailia, in the north-east of Egypt, 'it being near the railway and in the centre of the work'. His greatest difficulty was finding transport to reach the various units. 'I used all sorts and conditions of conveyance,' he wrote, 'GS wagons, motor lorries, horse, ammunition wagons, mule carts, and camels. I frequently had to walk many miles over the desert. Often I had to go without meals, as my work took me away from my own camp, at times from seven in the morning till eleven and twelve at night, and some messes forgot I was stationed far away. On the other hand, I experienced great kindness from many messes, both British and Australian.'[74]

The thoroughness with which Chaplain Freedman approached his responsibilities shows in a diary entry from early in his posting: 'To Port Said twice. Reported at Headquarters of 15th Corps and arranged for number of men to celebrate the Passover as guests of the President of the Congregation. Visited the Turkish Consulate Hospital and 15th Stationary Hospital. Called on Jewish men in Notts and Derby Regiment, 1st Lowlands AMC, Signal Camp and Details Camp of 13th Division. Rowed out to Monitor M.23 to see a Jewish sailor.'[75]

Morris Michelson had been in the US when war broke out, working as a publicity agent for *Sunset* magazine. He immediately returned to Melbourne and joined the AIF at the age of thirty-seven. He was in Egypt for Purim in March 1916. At Purim, Jews remember their biblical deliverance from Haman the Agatite, who had planned to exterminate all the Jewish people in the Persian Empire, but was foiled by the King of Persia's secretly Jewish wife Queen Esther. Purim, like Chanukah, is a celebration of victory in war. The story ends with a royally sanctioned uprising of the Jews against their would-be murderers, which leaves tens of thousands of enemy dead. Jewish people traditionally celebrate their survival with feasting, gift-giving and drinking wine. 'Every Saturday afternoon, we Jewish boys were entertained by the President of the Portuguese Congregation,' wrote Michelson, 'and I assure you it was entertaining. We went into the Jewish quarter in old Cairo for Purim, and there was some festivity. In the streets, most of it. Free food of the best for us all, and free liquor to our heart's content. We did have a good time. We attended a Jewish wedding … I was attracted one day by a procession in the street.' It turned out to be the prelude to a ritual circumcision. 'A brass band led the way from the house to the *shul*. After this, came a girl, dressed as a bride, carrying the tiny baby on a silver platter. After her came a band of children, dressed in white with wings on shoulders, representing angels, and after them marched the friends and relatives. The ceremony took place in the *shul*, and was followed by a great feast. We joined up and carried on.'[76]

Many Jewish soldiers in Egypt at Passover were taken in to private houses for *Seder* dinners. In Port Said the president of the Jewish community put them up in the Jewish Hotel. Chaplain Freedman took services and preached in both Alexandria and Cairo, and was impressed by the hospitality of the local communities. 'I could not help feeling how good it was to be a Jew,' he wrote. In Alexandria the soldiers were not allotted hosts for a *Seder* until after the evening synagogue service, and Freedman was concerned some men would end up without a home to visit. However, he wrote, 'I was most agreeably surprised at the expeditious way in which our soldier guests were introduced to their hosts, and at the smoothness with which everything was carried out … in a few minutes not a soldier was left. There were some disappointed ones, but they were the representatives of the families for whom there was no soldier left to take home.' The chaplain himself spent the first night of *Pesach* with the Aghion family, at a dinner including Captain Evelyn and Lieutenant Anthony de Rothschild. On the second night, he ate with the Slutzkins. 'Their home is always wide open to the Jewish soldier,' he wrote, 'and I believe every Sabbath eve there are at least half-a-dozen soldiers at their table.'[77]

Dalbert Hallenstein, Captain Eric Hyman of Tamworth, and Lieutenant Alroy Cohen spent the first night of Passover with Cattaui Pasha, a leader of Egyptian Jewry. The next morning Hallenstein, through Major Reuben Laman Rosenfield, was invited to the private synagogue of the Massari Pasha family. 'When the service was over,' wrote Hallenstein, 'they insisted on the two of us and Hyman stopping to breakfast, and that again was most interesting, as the dinner of the previous night we had *matzo*, quite different to the English cucumber, cheese, and tea.'[78]

Harry Barrkman was a proofreader and journalist at the Melbourne *Argus*, who enlisted in the 14th Battalion AIF in June 1915 at the age of twenty-two, but his reports from overseas were printed in the *Jewish Herald*, and often focussed on specifically Jewish subjects. Barrkman attended a *Seder* led by Chaplain Freedman in a mess hut, along with forty or fifty other soldiers, including Brigadier John Monash, whose attitudes to religion had softened. This was Freedman's last service in the desert 'not far from where the Children of Israel* crossed the Red Sea'. He read from a small *Sefer Torah* given to him by Cattaui Pasha. Freedman described the scroll as 'enclosed in a wooden case, which is flat bottomed so that the surface stands direct with it'.** At the reading of the Law, Monash stood by the *Torah* and those men called to the Law included Major

---

*   The Jews in their Biblical exile were referred to as 'the children of Israel' and, in the many centuries before the establishment of the modern State of Israel, Jews (or 'Hebrews') were often known as the 'people', 'children' or 'nation' of Israel — or, in their totality, simply 'Israel'.

**   This scroll, which was much later dubbed 'The Anzac Torah' by Melbourne lawyer Joe Lederman, was brought to Australia by Rabbi Freedman when he returned from the front. It spent decades in storage in the Western Australian Museum before it was handed back to the Perth Hebrew Congregation in September 2003.

Eliazar Margolin and Captain Eric Hyman, both of whom were to play their parts in the drama in Palestine to come. At the end of the service, wrote Barrkman, 'cigarettes, though very incongruous at the moment and day, but, nevertheless, excusable in the conditions, were distributed. These cigarettes were kindly provided by the JYPA [Jewish Young People's Association] and were very much appreciated for three reasons – firstly, for the kindness generosity and spirit which prompted their sending; secondly, because they were of good quality; and thirdly, because they were "Baksheesh", which, no doubt, being Jews, appealed to them greatly.'[79]

Freedman worked for a week in the desert, and found the climate difficult to cope with, even for a West Australian. 'The sun burnt us, the dust-laden wind choked us, and the sand baked us,' he wrote.[80] Freedman often found himself in situations not generally associated with the rabbinate. He visited the Western Australian Light Horse to borrow a horse to ride out to the trenches in the company of Captain Collick, Archdeacon of Kalgoorlie and chaplain to the regiment. 'He was good enough to offer to accompany me, and act as my guide,' wrote Freedman. 'I am not sure if he is not sorry, and if he is, it is entirely his horse's fault. I rode the Adjutant's horse, a fine animal and most respectful to the padre, even though he bears the threatening name of "Submarine." The name of the horse the Archdeacon rode I do not know, nor do I wish to know; and if Captain Collick knows, I think he would like to forget it. When we started out I could not make out why my "Submarine" turned up his nose with disgusted contempt at the Archdeacon's mount and why he would not keep to his side. But I found [out] when we approached the first camel on our way. "Submarine" merely sniffed and passed on quietly, but his companion reared and kicked and plunged, and did everything which no self-respecting horse, with an Archdeacon riding him, would ever think of doing.' When the two mounted chaplains approached the first army camp, like characters in a bar-room joke, Collick's mount bolted, 'and at the second camp he finished a second bolt by throwing the Archdeacon head over heels'.

'Fortunately,' wrote Freedman, 'the throw was made in soft sand, and no hurt was sustained. The Archdeacon enjoyed all this immensely. I did not. It was at a time that large bodies of Turks were reported to be in our neighbourhood, and we were expecting an attack daily. I told the Archdeacon it would be bad enough if we were captured by the Turks, but it would be much worse if we had to carry him back with wounds inflicted by one of his own regiment. I was glad when we got back safely to the stables.'[81]

As the bodies had piled up halfway across the world, young Jewish Australians had continued to volunteer to fight. Several Jewish families had a number of boys in the services. For example, Corporal Albert Solomon, of the South Australian Solomon family, who was wounded in action and invalided home from Gallipoli, had three brothers in uniform. Four of the sons of John and Julia Hains of Port Adelaide joined the AIF: Philip, Ivan, Harold and Morris. Private Morris Hains was killed at Gallipoli in August 1915, less than three months after he enlisted. And pain poured from every word of a letter sent by the twice-bereaved Harry Weingott to the Recruiting Officer at the Board of Health Sydney in January 1916. He wrote that he understood another of his sons, Barry, had been classed as fit for military service, subject to inoculation: 'I wish, however, to inform you that he is under the age of twenty-one and that he should have first obtained his Father's consent. You will possibly know that I have already lost two sons at the landing at Gallipoli, and it breaks my heart to give my consent for another boy to leave for the front. As however he appears to be determined to go I will not withhold my consent and will have to sign any papers that are necessary.'[82] 'Barry' or Barron Weingott fought in France and survived. The youngest of the Weingott boys, Issacher (or Issy), was a half-brother to Samuel, Alec and Barron, born on 23 April 1911. A disquieting photograph (see image 11) exists of the small boy dressed in full army uniform, his hands clasped behind his back like a solemn soldier doll. It was a portent of Issy's life to come.

The Western Front

There had been Jews in the AIF in Europe almost since the war began, men such as Corporal Phillip Laurence Harris, a Denili-quin-born Sydney journalist who was later to become editor of the 'trench newspaper' *Aussie*. While in France with the Australian Ammunition Park, Harris was unable to observe the 1915 Jewish New Year 5676 but later contemplated the Day of Atonement, *Yom Kippur*, on its eve, *Kol Nidre*. 'Although from the day we arrived in the field cannonading was incessant,' he wrote, 'on *Kol Nidre* night not a gun was fired. It was a brisk moonlit night, and the peaceful aspect of things was not disturbed. I sat with a friend "listening to the silence" till near midnight. Certainly no *Kol Nidre* service was ever half so impressive as this service of silence.'[83] Dr Eric Blashki, one of twelve members of the extended Blashki family to serve in World War One, was also 'somewhere in France', comparatively well equipped. 'In most places the aid post consists of a bit of a "dug out" or cellar,' he wrote, 'which has to serve as living, sleeping and working room, while here we have surgery, waiting room, living room, kitchen, and stretcher-bearers' quarters, good upholstered furniture, oven in kitchen, stove in parlour, and, above all, enough room in a shell-proof cellar to duplicate the lot.' While comforta-ble, Blashki was not necessarily safe. 'Sandbags out here are very necessary, and until recently we could not get enough. We dare not move out without gas helmets, and we always carry two each with us.'[84]

Harris, with a journalist's raised eyebrow for exotic detail, wrote home of a service held for Jewish soldiers in France by Rabbi

Michael Adler, the son of the late Chief Rabbi Hermann Adler, and now Senior Jewish Chaplain to His Majesty's Forces. The event took place in a hilltop monastery in France, where the Kaiser's nephew Prince Maximillian had died early in the war, after being shot by a British patrol. Harris attended with other Jews from the Australian Ammunition Park, Private Jack Cohen and Private Frederick Julius Detmold. 'No doubt, this quaint old monastery has seen some strange sights,' he wrote, 'but surely none more unusual than these trench-worn, muddy Jewish soldiers making its old walls echo to the strains of Hebrew hymns.'[85]

In March 1916 the first Anzac infantry units were transferred to Europe to serve in France and Belgium. Early casualties included St Kilda-born Private Eric Blaubaum, who grew up in Melbourne, where his father Reverend Elias Blaubaum was Rabbi Danglow's predecessor as minister of St Kilda Hebrew Congregation. Eric had moved to New Zealand to work for Michaelis Hallenstein in Dunedin. He enrolled in the Otago Infantry in October 1915, and travelled with them to Egypt, then France, where he met his death on 3 June 1916. Eric had a brother, Captain Ivan Blaubaum, who was serving in the Army Medical Corps in France and another brother in camp with the Field Artillery in Maribyrnong, Victoria. Dalbert Hallenstein wrote home, 'I had the misfortune to have to break the news to Ivan of Eric having been killed. I found it quite by accident myself in the *Daily Chronicle* list of 28th June, and about three days ago, when being on parade for the General's inspection, Ivan rode up and did not know anything, when I, of course, had to sympathise with him and tell him. He is only ten minutes' ride from here, and so I have gone over to him every day. He is taking it like a man, and does not appear to fully grasp it, which is a good thing. I am very sorry for the others at home, as they are sure to feel it, and then to worry about Ivan, but for the present no need to, as he and I as well are about thirty miles behind the firing line, being Army Corps Headquarters Mtd. Troops, and running no danger whatever. When it is clear weather we can sometimes just hear the distant rumble of the guns, and being on a high hill can see through my glasses the smoke of the explosions of enemy shells a long way away in the afternoons when the sun is behind.'[86] Hallenstein had been transferred from a support company to the 14th Machine Gun Company in July, and was happy with his posting. 'The tactics are altering since the Lewis gun has come,' he wrote, 'and the Vickers is front line artillery, as I get on to targets 2800 yards in front of me, and in rear of Fritz's line. One thing, in this sector my guns have got him bluffed, and I keep him fairly quiet of a night – always into him as soon as he opens up, and always get the last shot. There is no doubt about it, the MG's are one of the great things in this war ... One never gets out of hearing of the guns, as they are going some-where, if not with you, for at least twenty miles each side of you that you can hear, and when a big show is on probably forty miles, and they never cease day or night with their "sssh crrruuf", or in the distance their passage through the air like rolls of thunder, and then you hear the night owl, that is me, chattering away at the rate of 600 a minute, and even so, always getting the last word in. It is all very fine to see on the cinema, but you miss the row and the real sights, and calls for stretcher-bearers.'[87]

The 5th Division fought the Australians' first big engagement on the Western Front on 19 July 1916 at Fromelles, a village in northern France. The Allied assault on German positions was supposed to draw German attention from the Somme eighty kilo-metres south, where one of the bloodiest battles in world history had been raging since 1 July, but it was a catastrophic failure of inadequate planning, inexperienced artillery and a suicidal attack over easily defendable terrain. Waldo Hyman Zander of the 30th Battalion, a Brisbane-born warehouseman who had shipped out as a sergeant and been promoted to second lieutenant, wrote some years later, 'Zero hour approached (6 pm) and then as our bar-rage increased, over went the 31st and the 32nd Battalions. We began to move up Cellar Farm Avenue to carry out our role of the night – "carrying parties". The way was blocked here and there by direct hit [sic] by enemy shells on the communication trenches, but the men soon jumped out and passed these obstructions. The front line was reached at last and we made our way along it to our appointed places. Dead seem everywhere – one man had got a hit from a shell and half his face was blown away. He lay across the duckboard track, blocking it. A sergeant stepped forward and shifted him to one side, while another person covered the dead man's face with a bloodstained tunic lying near. It seemed all so terrible to us – those dead lying all around – but we were not used to the sight of dead then. Further along the line a dump of ammunition was alight, and as the flames got a further grip, the cartridges started to explode. Their sharp staccato explosions could be heard clearly against the dull crashes of the heavy shells burning nearby. We passed this dump and reached our position.

'The Bosche wire at last! We saw how our trench mortars and artillery had made great gaps in it, and through these gaps we hurried … We had been told that on no account were we to help either of the Battalions ahead of us, as our work was entirely "carrying" supplies up to them, also food, water etc. But once up there it was the greatest trouble to get our chaps to go back to their carrying. They wanted to step up there and "box on" with their chums in the 31st and 32nd, and to bag a few Fritzs if possible. My particular job was to stay in the Hun old front line, and to contact supplies as they came up, directing them to whatever point of the line required them most …

'As the night wore on our artillery seemed to slacken in volume, but the Bosche's, if anything, increased. It was pitch dark, and one could only get glimpses of things by the flashes of exploding shells. The Hun sent some incendiary shells over, and these set alight to anything they came in contact with when they burst, their flickering flames throwing a ghostly light over the dead and debris lying about. One poor wretch who had his arm blown off by a shell was crawling painfully across No Man's Land, endeavouring to reach shelter and aid when one of these diabolical incendiary shells burst nearby, splattering him with its burning contents. By the light made by a bursting shell he was seen to be frantically trying to smother the flames that were eating into his flesh, tearing up handfuls of mud and earth in his endeavour and agony. His screams could be heard for a second or two – then silence! … His body we passed the next morning, one side cruelly charred and burnt.

'At last we got to our own line and manned it. We cast our eyes around – what a changed scene! How different it was to the one we saw when we made our way along it the night before. The Hun barrage had played havoc with the trenches – huge gaps yawned here and there, parapets in places were blown entirely in, fire bays completely wiped out, and the whole place littered with dead and debris. In the afternoon parties were called for to go and collect wounded and dead in No Man's Land. Although the men were dead tired and weary there was no trouble in getting the numbers required, the men being only too willing to go and see if they could find their mates lying perhaps dead or wounded in the open between the two lines of trenches.'[88] Zander was later promoted to captain and Mentioned in Despatches.

Fromelles was a tragedy for the Australians, who lost 5533 men and gained no ground. Those killed included at least twelve Jewish diggers, among them Joseph Hart, whose mother, upon receiving a picture of his grave, wrote to the army requesting the cross be removed and replaced by a small square tablet, as her son was 'a Jewish boy'.[89] Gallipoli survivors such as Sydney-born Lieutenant Berrol Mendelsohn and Melbourne-born Bezelle Rabinovitch also perished at Fromelles. (Bezelle's twin, stretcher-bearer Eliezer Rabinovitch, died in France in 1918, and a third brother, Boaz, joined the RAN in 1920.) The desperate sadness of Fromelles was compounded by the fact that many hundreds of men – including ten Jewish Anzacs – were buried together in mass graves, their remains intermingled with their comrades'. Many, such as former cab driver Lionel Harold Levy of Sydney, were for a long time listed simply as 'missing in action', which robbed their families even of the certainty they needed to grieve.*

In battle, the misery continued at Pozières, a village in the heart of the Somme battlefield, where three attacks on German positions, from 23 July to 7 August, left thousands of Australians dead, including at least sixteen Jews. However, the final assault, which culminated in hand-to-hand fighting between Anzacs and Germans, was a success, and the enemy was permanently dislodged. Melbourne-born diamond setter Lance Corporal John Cohen had been rejected once by the army, on account of chest problems, but managed to enlist on his second attempt in September 1915. Before the war Cohen had been a colour sergeant with the 60th Infantry Regiment (North Carlton) CMF. He fought in the Brigade Trench Mortar Battery at Pozières in July 1916. 'One of our corporals received shell shock and went silly,' he wrote, 'another man got killed, dead and wounded were lying about everywhere. I felt very sick, all day stretcher-bearers were being killed and they could not get the dead and wounded out. One thing I saw myself was two stretcher-bearers carrying a badly wounded man out and a shell landed in the stretcher and blew all to pieces. Things went fairly well till about 4 pm and then I was buried twice in quarter of an hour and then again at 5 pm. Three in every ten men were either wounded or killed or buried. It was terrible, the enemy had the range to an inch. At 9.30 pm we were out to dig a trench as we were attacking at 10.30 pm. We dug our trench and went over in

---

*   In 2010, 250 of the 'Lost Diggers of Fromelles' were disinterred from mass graves
     at Pheasant Wood and individually reburied at the new Fromelles (Pheasant
     Wood) Military Cemetery. The dead who could be identified included Lieutenant
     Berrol Mendelsohn.

waves of men. We had a certain part to take and we had to take it at all costs. There were six waves attacked before the wave I was in, then we attacked and the enemy were best part killed or taken prisoners or wounded and I had not a scratch on me. I accounted for five or six Germans with bombs and we had orders to bayonet all wounded Germans and they received it hot and strong. You bet the sights were terrible, brains hanging out, heads bashed in, arms and legs apart from bodies, then at 11.15 the enemy big guns opened fire and it was perfect hell. I did not lose my nerve for a minute, men went silly but it was this time that I was hit and the Germans were going to try a counter attack, well my OC said, "Corp, you try and get out of this and get away to a dressing station." I did get out with luck, three miles walk with three pieces of shrapnel in my leg and a hole right through.'[90] The wound in his leg was 'terrible', he wrote from hospital in France. He told his father he did not know how long he would be laid up, but hoped the war would be over by the time he recovered.[91] He wrote to his parents, 'Everything I possessed I lost in the charge. My gas helmet, my shrapnel helmet, my big pack and my small one, my belt and my coat was fairly ribboned off my back. But I got out with my life. If ever I get into a spot like that I will be able to get out alive, don't worry.'[92] He was killed in action near Baupame on 4 March 1917.

Frank Lesnie also fought at the Somme. 'We relieved the first lot of Anzacs,' he wrote. 'On our way to the firing line, we passed through the former "Hun" trenches, with their elaborately prepared dugouts … It would be impossible to describe the sickening state of the trenches; suffice it to say that we were walking over the bodies of our own boys and also the "Huns". The horrible sight of the maimed dead and the stenches arising to one's nostrils served to show us how terrible and gruesome this war could be. Some of us went into the firing line and others were ordered into the supports. The German artillery kept a good barrage fire on our supports and communication trenches. Thanks to the efficiency of our aeroplane observers, a few of their guns were put out of action. We were in the trenches nine days, and every day seemed a week and every night was a month ... The Huns bombard the reserves and supports very heavily at night, always fearing an attack; this prevents our reinforcements from coming up, or causes heavy casualties when they do attempt to get through. We crouched in reserve for four solid nights, waiting for our turn to come, that is waiting for a shell to lob in the trench and take us on a very long journey. Five and six inch shells were falling on both sides of the parapet, sometimes near enough to bury a man in a small dugout. The force and explosion of a shell like this would make a large hole, the displacement of earth in its turn would push the side of the trench inwards and so completely bury anyone sitting in the trench near the explosion. We got to know the particular battery which played on our trench so regularly. The moment the shell left the gun five miles behind the Huns' firing line, we would listen and the whine and whurr of it would gradually get closer, while we would crouch and cuddle up; then whizz bang – an ear splitting noise, lumps of dirt falling all over us, the smell and smoke of the shell filling our heads till we'd hold our breath; then an anxious inquiry all round if everything is OK or anybody hurt. Once every two minutes this would occur, the comments after each were always the same – "By — that was a close 'un", or "To hell with the gunners, strafe 'em, — 'em." ... Sometimes a man might be hit with a lump of shrapnel, the back-wash from our own guns. Travelling back from the explosion a distance 400 yards or more, a piece of shrapnel falling flat would make a small bruise, but a jagged edge on it might penetrate the flesh and cause a wound. High explosives were used to a great extent and are the cause of most deaths and terrible gaping wounds. The last night of our picnic the guns played havoc with the German trenches, a continuous bombardment being kept up; the 18th and 20th battalions were sent over the parapet, gained their objective whilst we dug a trench some forty yards behind them, going for our very lives. In a couple of hours that trench was dug, and the day broke with a glimpse of the pock marked ground around us. Hardly a square foot of ground had been left untouched by our shells. There were shouts of "Kamerad, mercy, kamerad", and two or three dozen Huns came running towards our lines with their hands up and their faces showing that their morale and calibre had been torn to pieces by the previous night's bombardment. Here and there the Huns would be hiding in shell holes and when things were getting too hot for them, out they'd crawl and give themselves up. Our artillery bombardment must have been terrific, for the Huns were completely demoralised. I am well out of range of the guns for the present, but it will soon be our turn to go in again, and can only hope that my luck will stand good.'[93] Lesnie was killed in action at Warlencourt on the Somme in March 1917.

Reverend Danglow was to lose another valued member of his St Kilda Hebrew Congregation when Second Lieutenant Maurice Edward Kozminsky of the 7th Battalion was killed in another terrible battle at Mouquet Farm, north of Pozières, on 19 August 1916. Although he had been a company director at Austral Hat Mills when war broke out, Kozminsky had joined the AIF as a private. He was killed while in charge of a party digging a trench as the battalion attacked German lines. His parents received a heartfelt letter from a Captain Charles Goddard, AIF: 'Kos was an old pal of mine, and it was with no surprise that we met on the field, as it's only his sort that are doing their bit. Only a few days before he was killed we had dinner together. We chatted over old times, and discussed the recent fighting on the Somme. It was Kos's first scrap, and he did good work. I afterwards met his Colonel, who spoke very highly of him, stating Kos was one of the bravest; in fact, too brave.'[94] Elsewhere on the front on 19 August was Roy Hector Blashki, now a forward artillery observer who had been appointed liaison officer for a night-time raid. Blashki arranged lines of communication then joined the officer commanding the attack in a dugout on the front line. 'Firing started at 10.30,' Blashki recorded in his diary, 'and we gave the Hun a pretty warm time. But it did not take him long to wake up and he retaliated in about thirty seconds from our first sound bursting. We kept in telephone communication with … HQ till 10.47 at which time the wires were all cut. Just then the first men of the raiding party reported back and a minute or so later I was ordered to send the signal to shorten. Wire being cut, I fired the rockets but a shell burst and either by the concussion of that or their own backfiring, the rockets fell. Only two out of four (two was the signal) were seen to go up and they were too low to be seen so the fire continued till midnight. The OC said send back a "runner" with a report and I sent the order to cease firing by the same orderly but the order was not received as I learnt later the orderly had been killed on the way in Penny Avenue. As fire was still continuing at midnight I went back to have it stopped. I met some linesman at old D3 on Rue Petillon and got them to send the message through.' Blashki reported, 'Total casualties in the raiding party were two officers and about ten others killed and ten wounded and a number of other casualties from enemy shell-fire in the lines.'[95]

In September 1916 Dalbert Hallenstein wrote, 'I went over and spent the evening with some of our cavalry, and Ivan Blaubaum is their medical officer. He looks well and seems all right. The poor beggar found Eric's grave and put up a wooden memorial, as they are not yet allowed to place anything of a permanent nature on graves up close.'[96]

On 23 October, Lieutenant Herbert Abraham Ansell of the 8th Brigade Machine Gun Company was killed in action near Baupame. Born in Hobart, Ansell was one of about a dozen members of Tasmania's small Jewish community to fight in World War One.* Gunner Walter Napthali of Adelaide wrote to Rabbi Abrahams to reassure the minister that he was 'still amongst the lucky ones', and even though the *Chronicle* had reported 'somebody of the same name as wounded, it has no reference whatever to my substantial self'. Napthali was an artilleryman, but he was filled with despair at the devastation made by guns and bombs. From an unnamed position on the front he wrote, 'It would make your heart bleed to see what must have been once a lovely city now a mass of ruins. The finest stately buildings with gaping holes in the walls – that is, if walls are still standing – and what were once imposing terraces now piles or masses of bricks and dust. In no street will you see any two houses with roofs on them, and the whole of the insides have been torn out or blown out. To crown it all, not a solitary inhabitant; if the streets are not deserted, there are only soldiers. Whether all the civilians got away alive is not known to this day – and this is the twentieth century.'[97]

On 27 and 28 November Chaplain Freedman held *Rosh Hashanah* services on the Western Front. The second service was 'in a loft within sound of the guns', wrote Dalbert Hallenstein, 'and attended by all of us who could in the vicinity'.[98] Hallenstein continued to mark time by its distance from the death of his cousin. 'This time last year I was, as also poor Grant, whom I have often thought of lately, in Gallipoli,' he wrote.[99]

For *Yom Kippur* Harry Barrkman was still with the 7th Battalion in France. His commanding officer refused him leave, but his company commander exempted him from front duty. Barrkman spent *Kol Nidre* isolated among his comrades, 'depressed and dejected' and composing bad sentences: 'Where were the choice and appealing eatables dear to the Jewish heart, and which made

---

* Other Tasmanians included Private Hyman Glasser, who was gassed in France in June 1917, and brothers Henry and Felix Bloch, who were born in Deloraine and both served with the 6th Brigade's Field Artillery. Felix was killed in action on 17 August 1918, near Harbonnières in France. He was buried by Lieutenant Colonel Harold Edward Cohen at a service attended by his Tasmanian cousin, Simeon Sternberg.

the table groan under their weight?' he asked. 'Where was that great candle – a monument of grease … ?' He looked around and saw instead – unsurprisingly – soldiers eating army rations. 'Bread there was, but not the plaited variety with the poppy seeds; fish there was also, but, alas! it was not such as our mothers and wives cook to such a delightful golden brown colour; meat, yes, meat also, but instead of a sweet fowl there was Maconochie's tinned meat; but why go further – there was not even a drop of wine to make *"Kiddush"*.' But Barrkman took consolation from his prayer book, and by sunset, he fancied he heard the sound of the *Shofar*, the ram's horn blown at both *Rosh Hashanah* and *Yom Kippur* – although it turned out to be just an army bugle.[100]

AS A GENERATION OF AUSTRALIANS WAS DECIMATED AMID the carnage in France, and it became apparent that the war was not going to be over by any Christmas soon, the rate of volunteers for the AIF slowed. The men who had signed up in 1914 had known they were young and fit and Australian and would live forever. But, by the final months of 1916, every town and city in the country had lost its fittest and best, and the great adventure did not look quite so attractive to youths whose elder brothers and cousins lay buried overseas. In October 1916 the government of Billy Hughes staged a referendum in an attempt to win majority support for conscription. Keysor's sister Madge wrote to a newspaper, appealing to the women of Australia to follow her lead and vote their men to war: 'I have listened well to every possible argument and reason put forth by those who want us women to vote "No" … Their arguments are lies and their reasons are those of cowards.' Madge Keysor's letter was perhaps the result of a collision between Jewish Imperial loyalty and the rise of 'white-feather' feminism. Australian women had won the right to vote in Commonwealth elections in 1902, whereas the women of England remained disenfranchised.

In Madge Keysor's eyes, as 'almost the only women in the world who have an actual voice in the making of laws', Australians had to 'show that the trust in us is not misplaced when a great crisis is reached which needs courage and justice to carry it through'.[101] Now that women had the vote, they should vote 'like men'; just as now that Jews enjoyed the freedoms offered by the British Empire, they should defend them like Christian soldiers.

Roy Hector Blashki was an authorised witness for his battery in the referendum. He wrote home, 'From the way all the men talk a great majority seem to be opposed to conscription. There is some idea that if the rest of the available men came away the labour market will get swamped by immigrants.'[102] The measure was narrowly defeated at the referendum, which returned 1 087 557 votes in favour and 1 160 033 against.

Jewish Anzacs in Palestine

In February 1916 Saddler Sergeant Sylvester Browne of the ALH wrote home from Benhasa, Egypt, 'The habits of the natives and the way they dress, and the manner in which they conduct the funeral service (of which we have seen many since our stay here) are similar to the customs of our forefathers which we read about in Scripture. (I really think they must be the "lost tribe".)'[103] By the middle of the year the Anzac infantry divisions had mostly shipped out from Egypt to Europe, but Light Horse regiments stayed behind in the Middle East, where they fought both Turkish troops and Turkish-aligned Arabs as part of the Egyptian Expeditionary Force (EEF). Not all the mounted infantrymen rode horses, as Australians also made up more than half of the 1st Imperial Camel Corps. The EEF fought the battle of Romani, where they evicted the Germans and Turks from the Suez Canal, won a stirring, if almost accidental, victory at Maghaba, and slowly pushed towards Palestine, capturing the large Turkish garrison at Rafa in January 1917. By March they were in Gaza. Two Allied assaults on Gaza had failed when in June all the mounted infantry of the EEF were placed under the command of the Australian General Henry Chauvel, and designated the Desert Mounted Corps. On 31 October 1917, in what has become a celebrated moment in Australian military history, the 4th Australian Light Horse and New Zealand Mounted Rifles charged across an open, treeless six-kilometre plain to the town of Beersheba and overran the Turks, smashing open the door to Southern Palestine. The fortuitously named Morris Israel, a Gallipoli veteran who had been farewelled by the St Kilda Hebrew Congregation at the same service as Keith Levi and Dalbert Hallenstein, was awarded the Military Medal for his bravery at Gaza and Beersheba, and was promoted to sergeant of the 2nd Signal Squadron Australian Mounted Division.[104] Major Eric Hyman of Tamworth received the Distinguished Service Order (DSO) in November 1917 for his actions at Beersheba on 31 October when he 'led his squadron full gallop at a Turkish redoubt against heavy odds', according to his recommendation for the decoration. 'The redoubt was strong, manned by enemy machine guns and rifles. The Enemy opened up a very heavy fire but the charge was so vigorous and skilled that the enemy was overrun and his fire silenced in a few minutes thus enabling the Regiment to carry on the assault and complete the capture of Beersheba. This Turkish redoubt was the main enemy defence obstructing the Regiment in the above attack. Sixty dead Turks were afterwards found in their trench.'[105] Major Hyman was originally recommended for a VC, which he did not receive, but the award of the DSO caused excitement among both Jews and residents of Tamworth, where Hyman, a farmer, was well-known both for his militia days and his exploits on the cricket pitch, where he was 'one of Tamworth's foremost bats and wicket keeps'. According to the *Jewish Herald*, it was said that 'upon the entry of the British Forces into Jerusalem Major

Eric Hyman was to be made Military Governor of the city'.[106] The *Tamworth Daily Observer* had more modest ambitions for the local man: it wrote, 'Private information has been received that Major Hyman has received his lieutenant-colonelcy.'[107] Neither piece of intelligence turned out to be correct.

The assault on Beersheba marked the beginning of the end of Turkish rule in Palestine. On 2 November British Foreign Secretary Arthur Balfour wrote the letter that became known as the Balfour Declaration, in which he stated, 'His Majesty's government view with favour the establishment in Palestine of a national home for the Jewish people, and will use their best endeavours to facilitate the achievement of this object, it being clearly understood that nothing shall be done which may prejudice the civil and religious rights of existing non-Jewish communities in Palestine, or the rights and political status enjoyed by Jews in any other country.' At least rhetorically, the foundations for the state of Israel had been laid.

On 9 December Jerusalem fell to the Allies. With the Anzacs was Louis Salek, a Jewish New Zealander, who had been working as a wholesale druggist in Melbourne when the war broke out. He enlisted in the AIF and went to Gallipoli with the Medical Corps, but after five months he was invalided to Malta, wounded and shell-shocked. He wrote home, 'I am glad I am a Jew because the way I have been treated is beyond words. The Jews in Malta have treated us like kings: everybody's house is open to us Friday night and Saturday.' After convalescence, he told a Wellington weekly newspaper that 'in Jerusalem he saw the ancient flag of Judah flown for the first time for about 2500 years'. The Zionist banner was unknown to most, the description offered by the paper almost comical: 'The colours are blue and white with a device like a double triangle in the centre.'[108] Many years later, Salek revealed it had been his own flag. 'At a small private *shule* ... owned by a Pasha in the heart of Cairo,' he wrote, 'auction was always held for honours of being called up. As I was about to be sent to Palestine the buyer of the honours passed this honour to me and afterwards it was suggested that a flag be made and taken by me to Palestine. This suggestion was accepted by the owner of one of the largest stores in Cairo, Mr Cicurel, who made the flag and on the instructions of Mr Leyzer Slutzkin (late of Melbourne, Victoria, Australia) … the flag was taken by me to Palestine and after I left Jaffa I stayed at the half way place called then "Enab" and then at the fall of Jerusalem, the day General Allenby took over the city I went to the top of David Tower and tied the Jewish flag … From the top of the tower the Jewish people in a small village Buckharlia (below the wall over a small stream) cried out at the sight of the Star of David … The flag was later taken down by Headquarters instructions and was taken to the oldest *shule* in the world [where] the women looked during the service through a grill half way up the wall from the outside … later the flag was taken by me and brought home to New Zealand.'[109]

For some of the Jewish diggers, the journey to Palestine was a homecoming. Sergeant Major Max Steigrad was born in Jaffa in about 1892, the son of Samuel Steigrad and Pearl Grunstein. The Steigrads migrated to Australia in 1905, leaving behind Pearl's sister Genende and her family, including Max's cousin Avram Sternblitz. Max Steigrad, a tailor, joined the AIF in August 1915. He was five foot four-and-three-quarter inches, only just tall enough to be a soldier. He joined as a private and went to Egypt with the service corps. In March 1916 he transferred to the Camel Transport Corps, where he quickly became Company Quartermaster Sergeant, then Company Sergeant Major. He was Mentioned in Despatches on 7 June 1917. He wrote to his brother from Palestine on 27 November 1917, 'The situation here is too awful for words. Much has been said about the Belgium atrocities, but in dealing with the Jews the Turks have out-Hunned the Huns in frightfulness. The Turks have all along suspected the Jews of sympathising with the Allies. They accused them of spying, and blamed them for all their reverses, and they therefore drove them out from all the southern towns and chased them into the hills. Those who survived the wholesale massacres are now hiding in the hills without food or shelter, and they are at the mercy of the Bedouins ... The other day I was with the scouts in a village south of Gaza. I rode past a native hospital where they were treating some refugees. I dismounted and saw many sad cases, the work of the brutal Turks. There were old men and women and babies lying all over the place, and their cries were pitiful. I approached an old couple; the man was badly wounded, one leg in splints and the other was tied to the tent pole; the woman was thin and worn out, she looked about sixty-five. I asked her whether they were Jews, and she said: "Yes, we are from Kastinia; this is my husband; a Turkish officer shot him, they took all our money, they parted us from our children; they shot him in the hip and then broke his leg." Her voice seemed somehow familiar, so I asked for her name. Well, I got it, and my blood almost froze. I had to lean against the pole for support. Why, it was our own Aunt G[enende], mother's sister, and the hopelessly wounded man was no other than Uncle E—. When I recovered from the shock I told her who I was, and the poor woman threw herself on me ... When she had told me what they had gone through I no longer wondered that she looked fully sixty-five years old when she is just forty-two! When the Turks raided their town they shot as many men as they could, and took away their sons and daughters, God knows where. The wounded and the dead were left in a wadi for two days and two nights exposed to the rain and cold. Many died, and the rest were brought in by our ambulances. Thus have the Jews paid for our victory in Palestine ... I did all I could to relieve their suffering; I gave them my blankets, and, finding that they were only allowed native rations – that is, hard black bread – I bought all I could afford at the canteen – and distributed it amongst some of the sufferers. There they are, and thousands like them, rich and poor, men and women and infants all herded together, with hardly any bedding or blankets, dying from misery and starvation.'[110] Steigrad later met his cousin Avram Sternblitz, who was a member of the Jewish self-defence organisation Ha Magen ('The Shield') and who passed on intelligence to the Allied forces. According to one source, 'The Turks put a price on Avram's head and came close to killing him twice. They got as far as putting a noose around his neck and the burn marks from the rope were visible for the rest of his life. Avram was rescued by his father Hirsch and other members of Ha Magen in a shoot-out with his Turkish captors in which Hirsch was severely wounded in the leg. On another occasion Avram escaped his Turkish pursuers by riding into the desert. He survived by drinking his horse's urine.'[111] Steigrad took up an Imperial commission in the Egyptian Camel Transport Corps in May 1918.

In later life Sylvester Browne would claim to be the first Jewish soldier of Imperial forces to enter the ancient land of Israel. In March 1918 he attended Passover celebrations in Palestine. He wrote home, 'I consider myself very fortunate at having the luck to be here, as this thing is now history, never to be wiped off the slate but carry on for ever and ever. The two Jewish Chaplains were there, and many influential Jewish people from Cairo and Alexandria, and all the leading Zionists. There were about 200 English Jewish soldiers, two French, four from South Africa, and two Australians. Properly speaking, I was the only Australian soldier, as the other man had only been in Australia six days before joining up. For the first night *Seder* I went round to my friend's place, Mr Samuel Raffolli, and later in the evening we went round to where all the soldiers were, to finish up.

'At 3.30 the reception took place, all the "Makkaba" women and men, girls and boys, wearing their colours (not having their uniforms yet). They were headed by the leading Makkabi, carrying their beautiful standard (the Flag of Zion). They marched through the streets to the reception hall, and there lined themselves up into a guard of honour for us in the garden of the hall. We were all formed up and marched through them, and were placed in a most prominent position, with all the Makkabi (Maccabean Society) round us, and were then officially received. There were very many speeches in their own tongue (Hebrew), afterwards explained in English by the Jewish Chaplains. This went on for two hours. Then we sang "God Save the King" and the Hebrew National Anthem. (The whole of the Jewish population were outside, and it was a gala day.)' Browne noted that the colours of the flag were the same as the colours of his regiment – pale blue and white.[112]

LION HARLAP OF WESTERN AUSTRALIA, WHO HAD SERVED first as a provost in the AIF then as a trooper in the 10th Australian Light Horse, wrote to the officer commanding at Australian Head-quarters in Cairo on 5 November 1918 to ask to be discharged in Egypt when the time arrived, rather than return to Australia. 'I am a Hebrew,' he explained, 'and I was born at Odessa, Russia on July 21st 1898 and at the age of eighteen-months I arrived in Palestine where I resided until the year 1909 when I left for Australia. On March 1915 I enlisted in Perth, Western Australia, in the Austral-ian Imperial Forces, of which I am still a member. My family are still in Palestine and reside at Rehovot (Dieran) where we have property. Whilst there with the Forces I was gratified to find my parents and sisters still alive although my father who has suffered so much at the hands of our enemies has aged considerably, is suf-fering from a weak heart and is now unable to continue to work our land. At the joyful meeting with my family we have decided that it is absolutely necessary for me to live in Palestine.'[113] His request was granted.

But the Jewish Anzac who had the greatest impact on the his-tory of Israel was Eliazar Margolin from Collie, Western Australia, who had been awarded the DSO for his work at Gallipoli. Margolin had volunteered early for the AIF and was wounded in both the Dardanelles and France. He was widely recognised as an excellent officer and in June 1917 appointed lieutenant colonel in command of the 14th Battalion in the field. He was Mentioned in Despatches in 1917 but invalided to London and adjudged by the AIF to be no longer fit for active service. He petitioned furiously to remain overseas and when his request was turned down, he resigned from the AIF to take a commission with the 38th Battalion, Royal Fusiliers. The 38th was one of five battalions comprising the so-called 'Jewish Legion' raised by the British Army from British subjects and volunteers from around the world. The Zion Mule Corps had disbanded in Egypt in May 1916 and many former muleteers joined the 38th Battalion. Lieutenant Colonel Margolin took command of the battalion in March 1918, telling his men 'our aim is to participate in the fighting on the front of Eretz Israel and the liberation of our homeland',[114] which was a controversial reading of the Balfour Declaration. At his former home in Rehovot, he helped raise a 40th Battalion from among Palestinian Jews. In September the 39th and 40th battalions joined with the Anzac Light Horse and other units to chase the Ottoman forces back to Turkey in the last great battle of the Palestine campaign at Megiddo. Margolin was then made the first Jewish military governor of a district of Palestine, to the pride of the *South Western Times*, which wrote 'probably the war holds no greater record of advancements together with deserved merit than that of this young man who rose from the humble position of a greengrocer's assistant to that of a Military Governor within a few short years, by sheer force of pluck, merit and study'.[115]

The chaplain to the Jewish Legion was a Latvian-born British rabbi named Leib Aisack Falk who, like Margolin, was destined to play a part in the history of both Palestine and Australia.

Monash on the Western Front

John Monash had moved to the Western Front around Armentières in northern France in June 1916. In July he was promoted to major general and given command of the 3rd Division, which he trained in England on Salisbury Plain and at Lark Hill. The 3rd came to France in November. In January 1917 Monash described life on the front line with his customary command of detail: 'I suppose the popular idea of the public as to the doings of the army in France is that there is one or at most two rows of deep trenches all along the front, in which we stand glaring at the enemy standing in a similar trench on the other side of a strip of territory called No Man's Land – all our people (and his) standing side by side, if not shoulder to shoulder, and throwing things at him, and trying to dodge the things he throws at us. Holding the line does not mean anything like this at all, for the great bulk of our activities, measured both by numbers employed and by their importance, has very little to do with the front-line trenches.

'The whole of my sector, which is nearly five out of the ninety-two miles of the British front, is actually held defensively by only one platoon of each of four companies, of each of four battalions, while all the other nine battalions, all the artillery and engineers, and all the administrative services, have all sorts of work to do which not only has nothing to do with the trenches, but often takes them many miles in the rear. The front line is not really a line at all, but a very complex and elaborate system of field works, extending back several thousand yards, and bristling with fire trenches, support and communication trenches, redoubts, strong points, machine-gun emplacements, and an elaborate system of dugouts, cabins, posts and observation cells. Life in the front system is very arduous and uncomfortable, and a front-line battalion stays in only six days, during which each platoon is changed round, so that at the worst a single man seldom does more than forty-eight hours'

continuous front trench duty in every twelve days, and every forty-eight days the whole brigade gets relieved by the reserve brigade
and goes out for a complete rest, or for work in the back area, for a
clear twenty-four days. At least, all this is in my particular system –
designed to spread the stress on the personnel as widely as possible.

'The four battalions in the front line have a great deal of work
to do – besides actual fighting. The mere problem of feeding and
warming absorbs fully one-third of the total energies of a front-
line unit. The carrying, cooking and distributing of food, and fuel,
and dry clothing, the service of intercommunication and carrying
of munitions absorbs fully half the strength at any one time. The
remainder are engaged either in repairing damages to the defences
by weather or by enemy shelling, or on actual sentry duty or in
raiding and patrolling. The officers of a front-line battalion get
very little rest, they are almost constantly on duty for their whole six
days' tour, particularly the adjutant, the commanding officer, and
the signalling officer. Out of a battalion of 1000, not more than say
600 are actual fighting men, the rest being scattered far and wide,
as drivers and grooms, batmen and messengers, runners, guards,
police, stretcher-bearers, and orderlies of all kinds; of the 600 not
more than half are available for fighting, except in an emergency.

'The Pioneer Battalion of 1000 is split up into all sorts of trade
activities – running carpenters, blacksmiths, wheel-wrights, sad-
dlers, plumber's and bricklayer's shops, and works of all kinds all
over my area. The Engineers are similarly scattered, in small parties, chiefly as gangers to infantry working parties, but also in the
more technical trade works such as bridging, demolition, mining,
main-drainage, concrete work, roads and special constructions.
They are all high-class tradesmen in civil life. The Artillery are
the only ones who have scarcely anything else to do but to fight
and shoot, but even they have constant work, not only in their
own maintenance, and that of their wagon-lines and horses (in
some cases miles in rear), but also in the upkeep and repair of their

gunpits and guns and ammunition. The divisional area extends back from the front upwards of twenty miles, and my responsibilities include the administration of the whole area and all the civil and military population which it contains ... The infantry offensive action consists of patrols, who creep right up to the enemy lines and bomb them, and in continual raids, one every two or three days, from fifty to 300 men strong.'[116]

Monash's fascination for the order among the chaos was in no part a love of killing. In March he wrote, 'I hate the business of war, the horror of it, the waste, the destruction, and the inefficiency. Many a time I could have wished that wounds or sickness, or a breakdown of health would have enabled me to retire honourably from the field of action – like so many other senior officers. My only consolation has been the sense of faithfully doing my duty to my country, which has placed a grave responsibility upon me, and to my division which trusts and follows me, and I owe something to the 20 000 men whose lives and honour are placed in my hands to do with as I will.'[117]

Arthur Jacobs had been through seven surgeries in the UK to fix the foot that had been wounded at Gallipoli. He was sent home to Australia on 21 February 1916 but re-embarked for active service in January 1917. His brother Solomon, who had enlisted in 1915 but was sent home with asthma in January 1916, re-enlisted as 'Sullivan' and was back in France by March 1917. The two brothers met with their younger brother David while Arthur was on leave in London. Both David and Solomon had been lightly wounded in action. After the family reunion, Arthur returned to his old regiment. He was desperately disappointed by the outcome of the first conscription referendum. 'We are terribly short of men,' he wrote. 'Unless further reinforcements arrive from Australia – and they are already three months overdue – this draft will be the last one that can be sent. Other regiments are in like predicament. If we cannot get the men to replace the wastage, our battalions will have to be reinforced by Englishmen. This will mean that the Australians will lose their individuality; and, once that is gone, our fighting power will depreciate. The fighting is very heavy, and the real battles have only just begun. Had the result of the Australian referendum been the other way, it would have weakened the morale of the Hun to a very great degree.'[118]

Australian troops took part in assaults on the Hindenburg Line of German defences, which stretched from the north coast of France to the Belgian border near Verdun. The first of the bloody battles at Bullecourt in northern France was fought on 11 April. Harry Barrkman wrote, 'We were lined up in a sunken road, and in the part I was in we were 800 yards from the German trench. The ground over which we had to advance was literally as flat and clear as a billiard table but with a covering of a cloth of snow to replace the customary green. In some places our boys had to advance as much as 1700 yards to come in contact with the opposing forces. Four-thirty am and the tanks (twelve in number) went ahead with a quarter of an hour's start. Five minutes to go; four minutes; three minutes; two minutes; one minute. Mental prayers were hastily said, and then: "First wave, advance!" Half a minute's interval and the second wave "Forward", and so on until all the waves were launched on the field of sacrifice. We were led to believe that the position would be easily won and held, but great heavens, what a mistake! The position was certainly easily taken, but then the Germans took a hand in the matter, also. No sooner had we set ourselves in motion than the enemy opened up a deadly machine-gun fire upon us. I saw numbers of men go down but no effect was produced on our ranks. Through the storm of death-producing hail of lead we advanced in open order, quite unconcerned. With rifles slung, and most people carrying either a shovel or pick-axe – their hands encased in sheepskin gloves – our men moved forward through it all with such a showing of quiet contempt that proved them to belong to a class of the bravest order.'[119]

Facing the Hindenburg line at the town of Reincourt with the 16th Battalion was Lieutenant Daniel Aarons, who had grown up in Broken Hill and enlisted in the AIF as a private in February 1915. Aarons went over with the first wave of the infantry charge and led his men across unbroken enemy wire and into the trenches. When his company commander was killed, Aarons assumed command, reorganised the company, and led bombing attacks on the enemy.[120] But the main attacks were poorly planned and led to massive casualties. 'Slowly but surely the enemy drove back our forces from line to line,' wrote Barrkman. 'Every scrap of ammunition had been fired off resulting from a search of the equipment of dead men, outnumbered and outgeneralled, but certainly not outfought, the fight came gradually to an end after a fierce battle of about seven hours' duration.' Neither armour nor artillery were used to their best effect. The tanks intended to support the attack either broke down or were quickly put out of action by enemy fire. In any case, wrote Barrkman, 'With only a short start ahead of us they had no opportunity of reaching their objectives and machines as they were then, we passed them long before they even got close to the wire entanglements.'[121] Artillery held its fire for fear of hitting Australian troops, whose position in the field was unclear. A fellow officer of the 4th Brigade remembered Aarons' attempt to have fire called in, after Aarons had 'been through Hell, and had lost 60 per cent of his men'. Lieutenant Colonel HW Murray wrote, 'We could see the Germans massing behind their lines; could see them swarming about the houses of Reincourt, free from danger, without so much as one shell to hinder them. It soon became evident that we could not hold out without bombs and artillery support. We sent back two volunteer runners with joint messages, but no response came. All this time we were being shot at freely, and heavy bomb attacks were made while our own supplies of bombs gradually ran out. Aarons bravely volunteered to attempt the journey back to headquarters with a message in the hope that by bringing the weight of an officer's personal report on the position artillery assistance would be afforded, while bombs would be brought up under cover of the artillery fire. It was extremely dangerous to move at all in the rear of the lines we had occupied for even on a solitary man a regular barrage of machine gun and rifle fire was directed. The chance of anyone getting through was at least ten to one against. None knew that better than [Lieutenant] Aarons, but undeterred, and as a last desperate measure to save the remnant of the brigade and retain what had cost so much to win, he volunteered to go. To get through it required a very level head and coolness – both these I could see he possessed, and I felt that if any had a chance of getting our message back he was the one. He got back; but still we got no help, for it was now too late! The Germans had pressed their attack home before assistance could be given us.'[122] Aarons was awarded the Military Cross. Harry Barrkman was wounded and captured by the Germans – one of 1170 Australians who became POWs that day. 'As soon as we were taken prisoner,' he wrote, 'and were being taken to the rear of the German positions, our guns opened up a deadly fire on the enemy trenches. Their aim was wonderfully accurate, but oh! how many of our own men were laid low by our own shells. Had they opened fire before we attacked there is no knowing what the result might have been … As we passed through the German lines we could see the German reserve trenches positively full of fresh vigorous troops that had been brought up after our clearly given warning.'[123] Barrkman, ordinarily so voluble in his correspondence, was only permitted to send a couple of lines on a postcard on isolated occasions during his imprisonment. The last his parents heard from him was that he was interned at Hameln and was 'quite well', although he had been 'batting on a bad wicket lately'.[124] He survived the war to write a rather cheerful unpublished memoir of his imprisonment, the burden of which was lightened by the fact he could speak German.

The fighting continued along the Hindenburg Line. Captain Charles Leedman, a Sydney-born surgeon from a prominent Western Australian Jewish family, had been posted as RMO to the 54th Battalion in January. He wrote home from France, 'Fritz has frequently objected to my walking the earth and tried to blow me up skywards – but he has not succeeded yet – and merely accumulates extra remarks about his ancestry and the usual retort about his parentage ... My word, it's bitterly cold! ... My word, I could do a fancy feed and wash.'[125] Leedman refused to allow the fighting to dampen his exuberance. 'If I put my nose far out of this joint,' he predicted later, 'Fritz will probably take my head off with it. If you can spread your imagination on an artillery bombardment on each side for twenty-four hours a day and seven days a week, and then place your abode in a ditch in between it and hope to blazes Fritz misses your little spot, then you've got it. Am in first rate nick: seeing France and "Buds" flying mud, bits of villages, bits of Fritz and every damd [sic] thing on earth.'[126] Leedman was finally hit when the Germans shelled his Regimental Aid Post at Sunken Road on the Hindenburg Line on 14 May. He was only lightly wounded, but one of his men was killed and another seriously hurt. Leedman remained at his post the whole day, tending to patients under fire, and was subsequently awarded the Military Cross.

Monash's 3rd Division played their part in the costly victory at Messines in June, then the British and Australians pushed north towards Ypres, to relieve the French. On 11 July, Daniel Aarons was promoted to Captain. On that same day, his elder brother, Private John Fullarton Aarons of the 16th Battalion, was killed in action at Ploegsteert Wood in Flanders. Roy Hector Blashki, who had been Mentioned in Despatches on 1 July, wrote home to his parents on 30 July, 'Before this letter leaves France there will probably be the biggest battle the world has ever known ... If anything should happen to me I hope you will look on it with more pride than grief. It is not going to be an easy job as far as I can see, but I will feel better able to go through with it if I can feel that you realise my place as a pawn in the game, whose sacrifice may at any time be demanded to further our cause – the greatest and most honourable of all. However, I hope for a whole skin.'[127] He died on 3 August 1917, only days after he had been promoted to captain. An enemy shell set fire to an ammunition dump and Blashki rushed out from under partial cover to extinguish the flames when another shell exploded at his feet. A lieutenant at the scene wrote to Blashki's parents to say, 'His man, Wilson – great rough fellow though he be – cried like a child and the sorrow of his men is eloquent proof of their affection for him … Though I am twice Roy's age he has by his character and example, helped me many a time, and his memory will do so in the future. Roy was religious. I am not of your faith, but the religion that has produced a man like Roy is a good one, and to his religious beliefs he was true.'[128] Blashki's commanding officer wrote that the action which resulted in Blashki's death had been not only voluntary but officially forbidden: 'Ammunition may be replaced but not a splendid man as he had proved himself time after time. He was one of the most sterling and conscientious men I ever had anything to do with.'[129]

The Battle of Polygon Wood, which cost 5770 Australian casualties from 26 September to 3 October 1917, was a successful but blood-soaked confrontation on the path to assaults at Menin Road and Broodseinde Ridge. Dalbert Hallenstein wrote home after the battle, 'I was in charge of the "hop over" part of my Company, and am the only officer out of three of us to come out "OK". The skipper, a grand fellow, was also killed when looking over the line the next day. Before he went out to it, he told me he would get me a decoration for the show … You never saw anything like it, and you can't imagine how these boys of ours went forward and took the place … and then when Fritz counter-attacked just before dusk, with one gun and with a grand team we had a whole battalion cheering as at each burst of fire we just wiped everything out that came through the barrage, and again next morning one of my Sergeants did the same thing. That's the time when you feel you would not be anything else but a machine gunner.' Hallenstein claimed a 'charmed life' as 'nothing could get through my clothes, though I was hit innumerable times'.[130]

The Allies eventually took Ypres from the Germans at the Battle of Passchendaele, where the Anzacs were among the forces that recaptured Passchendaele Ridge to the east of the town. At Broodseinde Ridge they fought their most successful attack, after which Monash cabled Melbourne, 'All well. Division again brilliantly victorious in "greatest battle of war".' He wrote home, 'A fine bag of prisoners is pouring in. All are most elated, particularly at the fine feat of pulling off so big a job with only three days for all our local preparation. In using the words "greatest battle of war", I quote from a letter the Commander-in-Chief sent me yesterday.'[131] For all Monash's evident satisfactions, there were terrible, heartbreaking frustrations, too. 'Our men are being put into the hottest fighting and are being sacrificed in hair-brained ventures, like Bullecourt and Passchendaele,' he wrote.'[132]

Arthur Jacobs, now a sergeant, had a letter printed in the *Register* describing the special training he had undertaken for 'tea parties', or raids into enemy-held territory. 'To get to the enemy's line is a long job,' he wrote, 'for those composing the "tea party" must crawl on their stomachs and avoid detection. Getting back is another business – a case of each man for himself, and the Hun take the hindmost. No man's land becomes a veritable hell, for the Bosche artillery sets us a barrage to protest the raiders reaching their own line. Then the "guests" are encumbered with prisoners, and their task is far from easy. Yet ninety out of 100 men would sooner take part in a raid than do line work. To use one man's expression, "You get your money's worth, even if you do hand your cheque in." One hour's excitement in this game is worth more than a month in the firing line.'[133] By the time the letter was published, Sergeant Jacobs had been killed at Broodseinde. His brother Solomon later told the Red Cross that, on the evening of 1 October, the 10th Battalion was dug in near Zonnebeke, and Arthur had been in a trench 50 metres behind Solomon's. 'We were subjected to a very heavy bombardment, at 8.30,' said Solomon. 'Some of the men of my brother's platoon came into my trench and informed me that my brother's trench had been blown in and that my brother had been killed.' They found his body in pieces. 'We buried him where he was killed as it was impossible to carry him out as we were repelling a counter attack.' Arthur, he noted, had eighteen surgical incisions in his left leg from all the operations he had suffered after his bomb wound at Gallipoli.[134]

Jewish women at war

One female Jewish Australian doctor and at least seven nurses went to the war. Eveline Rosetta Cohen was described by the *Hebrew Standard* as 'one of the first Jewesses to take a medical degree and to practice in this country'.[135] Born Eveline Rosetta Benjamin in Hobart Town in 1879, she began her medical work at Melbourne University but left Australia for Scotland in 1905 to study medicine at Edinburgh University. She graduated in 1909 and joined the Royal College of Surgeons in Ireland in 1910. The next year, she married Henry Cohen, who served on the Western Front, and became Dr Eveline Cohen. In late 1916 she became attached to the British Royal Army Medical Corps (RAMC) as a civilian surgeon, and spent the following year with the Women's Medical Unit RAMC in Malta, largely treating casualties from fighting in Salonika. She came back to Australia to visit her family in June 1918 and stayed at the Sydney household of Phillip Blashki's youngest son David, who was married to her elder sister Lydia Benjamin.

She told the local press she hoped to return to Europe to serve in France, but she saw out the last days of the war at the Cambridge Military Hospital in Aldershot.

Among the nurses was Nellie Isaacs of St Kilda, who was a member of the AIF but served first with the British in India, then transferred to Salonika via Alexandria. From South Australia came Sophia Daniels, daughter of John Daniels, who was perhaps the first Jewish soldier in Australia, and sister of the indefatigable militiaman Major John Daniels. Sophia Daniels joined the AAMC at the age of forty-five and served at the British general hospital at Abassia, Egypt. She was invalided home with a uterine fibroid and recuperated at the Caulfield Military Hospital. Adelaide-born sisters Miriam Adelaide and Rosey Bennett served in England and France. Ballarat-born Adelina Marks served at Australian hospitals in Egypt. Emillienne Dubrulle was a French-born nurse living in Western Australia who served with the British in India.

Leah Rosenthal of St Kilda was the sister of Lieutenant Samuel Rosenthal of the 58th Battalion who was killed in France in September 1917. Leah had joined the British Queen Alexandra Imperial Military Nursing Service in 1915, and was posted to the 33rd Casualty Clearing Station in France. She wrote home of a *Yom Kippur* service in 1917: 'The hall was packed with Jewish boys, and about six officers. I was the only woman present.' There were only five nurses remaining at the casualty clearing station – the rest of the staff and the patients had been moved to a safer place – but she felt the 'honour in being maintained in that most dangerous spot'. She sent home souvenirs to her family, including a heavy fragment of shell labelled 'piece of shell that hit this hospital, and wrecked the church'. She also posted the cap of a bomb that almost hit, and described how she had to wear a gas mask on her shoulders while crossing the hospital compound.[136] Rosenthal was still in France a year later and, once again, she was the sole female at the British military *Yom Kippur* service. She reported that this time, the rabbi had to improvise, using biscuit tins with a curtain in front of the Ark to hold the *Torah*.

Monash's 'perfect battle'

Recruitment continued as wounded men came home and the dead were buried where they fell. After his discharge, Harley Cohen toured Australia with a company of entertainers who called themselves 'The Gallipoli Strollers', comprising eight veterans of the Dardanelles who were no longer fit for active service but eager to encourage other men to go to war. A reviewer of a Strollers concert noted, 'Though several members still show outward signs of their injuries, their entertaining capabilities are in no way marred'.[137] During his long tours up and down the country, Cohen, who performed with an eye-patch over his missing eye, played a number of his own compositions, including the music-hall hit 'They Were There, There, There', a song about Gallipoli which brought him national celebrity. By the end of the war, he was the face of a patent medicine – Dr Sheldon's New Discovery cold remedy – which, testified Cohen, was even better than his luck at Gallipoli.

Despite the efforts of the Strollers, the Anzacs remained in desperate need of more manpower. In December 1917 the Hughes government announced a new conscription referendum with a modified proposal that would see a smaller number of unmarried young men, chosen by ballot, pressed into service to man a 6th Australian Division. This time Leonard Keysor himself was quoted in favour of compulsory service. The papers published an extract from a letter to his brother Stanley, in which Keysor, now a lieutenant with the 42nd Battalion in France, said, 'I am disgusted at the want of reinforcements on this side. There are heaps of men who have been fighting now for over three years and are badly in need of rest, and they still go on for want of men to take their places.

It is a fearful shame that there is no conscription in Australia.'[138] The second time around, the conscriptionists were defeated by a marginally increased majority, and it became clear that Australia was going to have to rely exclusively on voluntary recruitment for the rest of the war.

Monash had won enormous respect for his abilities from the British High Command, and he was an obvious candidate for the new position of commander of a single Australian Army Corps. But casually antisemitic forces within the Australian establishment hissed against him. Even before the formation of the independent corps had been approved, the influential war correspondents Keith Murdoch and CEW Bean had cabled Prime Minister Hughes to warn against appointing Monash as Australian commander-in-chief. 'We do not want Australia represented by men mainly because of their ability, natural and in-born in Jews, to push themselves,' wrote Bean.[139] Although Bean was later to resile from his views, he continued his whispering campaign against Monash and his 'Jewish capacity for worming silently into favour without seeming to take any steps towards it'.[140] Bean's sentiments were hardly isolated among his milieu. Will Dyson, Australia's first official war artist, predicted Monash would get the job as 'he must always get there on time, on account of the qualities of his race; the Jew will always get there'.[141]

Monash did win command of the new corps from 1 June. His Jewishness had, of course, worked against him rather than in his favour, but this was impossible to grasp for high-born men such as Bean, who accepted success as a birthright. Monash wrote home to declaim his triumph: 'For all practical purposes I am now the supreme Australian commander, and thus at long last the Australian nation has achieved its ambition of having its own Commander-in-Chief, a native-born Australian – for the first time in its history. My command is more than two-and-a-half times the size of the British Army under the Duke of Wellington, or of the French

Army under Napoleon Bonaparte, at the battle of Waterloo. Moreover, I have in the Army Corps an artillery which is more than six times as numerous and more than a hundred times as powerful as that commanded by the Duke of Wellington.'[142]

Reverend Jacob Danglow, who had lost so many young men of his congregation to the slaughter, replaced Freedman as the Anzac military chaplain at the front. While he had been away, Freedman had been elevated from reverend to rabbi. He had been Mentioned in Despatches and proved himself as a spiritual soldier. Back in Perth, he was feted with a civic reception. The *Jewish Herald* wrote, 'Shells and bombs have burst only a few yards away from Major Freedman and his billet has been shattered in his absence, yet he went on with his work of encouraging the fighters, sympathising with the sick and wounded, and burying the dead, serenely and uncomplainingly oblivious, to all appearances, of the messengers of death that dogged his footsteps. Yet, with the help of a stout heart and a robust constitution, he did not, "report sick" once, and he is even willing and eager to go back. But his own congregation want him, and they have been calling him by cable and letter for twelve months.'[143]

Chaplain Danglow served for a much shorter period than Freedman. When he arrived in England en route to France in 1918, several newspapers carried a report of the 'rather unique' happenstance that Danglow was 'fortunate enough to have exactly "*minyan*" at the Sabbath and Sunday services he conducted during the passage from Australia'. On board were 'the chaplain, six soldier lads, a Jewish Red Cross passenger, a steward and a sailor of the ancient faith', comprising 'probably the only Hebrew congregation afloat during those days'.* Although Danglow's was

---

* It was not entirely true to say this was the first floating Anzac military minyan. In August 1917 Morris Michelson had written, 'On our hospital ship from France I discovered that we had a minyan of Jewish chaps on board. We held service every

not the first synagogue at sea, it had certain singular characteristics: 'On *Shavuot* the absence of flowers was compensated for by cakes and other available delicacies. But perhaps the strangest and most solemn services of the voyage were those conducted in the danger zone, when the chaplain, and his tiny congregation assembled, clad in their life-jackets, in the cabin constituting the *"shul"* and invoked the Almighty to prosper their hazardous voyage.'[144] Danglow had a farewell dinner in London before his departure for France, at which he dined with Dalbert Hallenstein, among others. He wrote home to his wife that Hallenstein, who was on leave, 'looked tall, broad, tired and well'.[145]

The Australian Army Corps under Monash charged on to victory. The General was an original, independent military thinker, who rarely felt bound to repeat the mistakes of the past. On the recapture of Villers-Bretonneux in April 1918, he wrote of his conviction that 'the true role of infantry was not to expend itself upon heroic physical effort, not to wither away under merciless machine-gun fire, not to impale itself on hostile bayonets, nor to tear itself to pieces in hostile entanglements' – he cited Pozières and Stormy Trench and Bullecourt – 'but on the contrary, to advance under the maximum possible protection of the maximum possible array of mechanical resources, in the form of guns, machine guns, tanks, mortars and aeroplanes; to advance with as little impediment as possible; to be relieved as far as possible of the obligation to fight their way forward; to march, resolutely, regardless of the din and tumult of battle, to the appointed goal; and there to hold and defend the territory gained; and to gather in the form of prisoners, guns and stores, the fruits of victory.'[146]

The routing of the Germans at Hamel on 4 July was, for

Shabbos and yours truly acted as Chazan. You know I ought to be able to daven a bit, seeing the stock I came from.' (*Hebrew Standard of Australasia*, 25 January 1918)

Monash, the perfect battle. 'No battle within my previous experience … passed off so smoothly,' he wrote, 'so exactly to timetable, or was so free from any kind of hitch. It was all over in ninety-three minutes. It was the perfection of team work. It attained all its objectives; and it yielded great results … The attack was a complete surprise, and swept without check across the whole of the doomed territory. Vaire and Hamel Woods fell to the 4th Brigade, while the 11th Brigade, with its allotted Tanks, speedily mastered Hamel Village itself. The selected objective line was reached in the times prescribed for its various parts, and was speedily consolidated. It gave us possession of the whole of the Hamel Valley, and landed us on the forward or eastern slope of the last ridge, from which the enemy had been able to overlook any of the country held by us … The Tanks fulfilled every expectation, and the suitability of the tactics employed was fully demonstrated. Of the sixty tanks utilised, only three were disabled, and even these three were taken back to their rallying points under their own power the very next night. Their moral effect was also proved, and, with the exception of a few enemy machine-gun teams, who bravely stood their ground to the very last, most of the enemy encountered by the tanks readily surrendered.'[147] At Hamel, Monash's triumph was the successful integration of infantry, armour, artillery and airpower, but one Jewish Australian officer was awarded the Military Cross for a conventional foot-soldiers' action. Captain Morris Lewis of the 44th Battalion, a tailor from Perth, had led the approach march of an attack on enemy trenches east of Hamel on the day of the battle. During the German counter-attack that bled from night into the next day, Lewis led a party forward and drove 'the enemy from the trenches, inflicting severe casualties on them and capturing several prisoners and four machine guns'. It was judged that 'the success of the latter operation was entirely due to the coolness and bravery with which Captain Lewis handled the situation'.[148] On 11 August 1918 Monash was knighted in the field by King George V. He was the first man for 200 years to be honoured this way. In the months that followed, he established his headquarters at Menin Gate in the east of Ypres. The town, he wrote, 'once a marvel of medieval architectural beauty, lies all around us a stark, pitiable ruin'.[149]

At Mont St Quentin in August–September, Monash fought a fluid, imaginative battle, reacting spontaneously to enemy movements and decisively turning the war to the Allies' favour. Reverend Danglow held a *Rosh Hashanah* service at Bussy on 5 September. It was attended by more than seventy Jewish soldiers, but not Dalbert Hallenstein. The minister learned from Captain Alroy Cohen of Monash's personal staff that Hallenstein had been killed in action three days before. He had been going forward to attack the Germans at Mont St Quentin when he was hit by a fragment of high-explosive shell. His body was buried next to a trench. In his diary Danglow wrote, 'I was dumbfounded. My heart became cold. I lost interest in the Service and wanted to get away.' He told his wife May, 'I am making a desperate effort to pull myself together so as to do my duty as best as I should. I am some miles behind the front line and it has been pointed out to me that my best work can be done among the soldiers as they come out on rest. They have no time for me when they are actually fighting.'[150] Danglow struggled to recover from the loss of Hallenstein. He wrote, 'He was such a noble boy, so brave and modest, and he had cheerfully endured so much during his long period of active service. I grieve to think of what Australian Jewry has lost through his death.'[151] Three weeks later Danglow presided over a funeral near Péronne, and took the opportunity to visit Hallenstein's grave. Danglow's biographer wrote, 'He found it easily and added a Star of David to the foot of the white cross and wrote underneath the Hebrew word "Shalom". With the aid of his batman, he gathered up some wild flowers, separated them into bunches for various members of the family and in pencil wrote whom they were from.'[152]

THE WAR WAS CLEARLY COMING TO A CLOSE WHEN, AT THE end of 1918, Leonard Keysor returned to Australia on six months' leave to take part in an army recruiting campaign with ten other VC winners. At a meeting on 2 November 1918 of Sydney Zionists to commemorate the first anniversary of the Balfour Declaration, Keysor was presented with war bonds and a gold cigarette case. One speaker deliberately painted Keysor's experience among those of the fighting Jews of Europe. 'The Jews were always loyal,' he said, 'and France had shown her appreciation of her Jews by conferring on them 139 decorations of the Legion of Honour, 127 military medals and 700 Croix de Guerre.' Percy Marks pointed out that France was also 'the first country to put the Jews on equal footing with their compatriots'. And the republic's reward had been 1000 Jewish heroes. Keysor received his gifts, followed by three wildly enthusiastic cheers, and said he 'found it very difficult to make a speech, because he had never yet had such a reception from the Jewish people, and he felt it more deeply than they could imagine … He was very proud to be there, he was very proud to be one of the Australian Army, and he was prouder still of being a Jew.'[153] Turkey surrendered that same night.

Leah Rosenthal, the nurse who came to symbolise Australian Jewish women's contribution to the war, had been awarded the British Associate Royal Red Cross medal, and was now attached to a medical unit following the Allied advance through the ruins of France. Six days before the Armistice was signed, Rosenthal wrote home from a small town near Valenciennes: 'The town had the French flag flying from nearly every window. The scene was very gay, but it was terrible to see the white, thin faces of the people, especially the little children. These people had been four years in the power of the Germans, and had never tasted meat all that time, just bread and grease, and vegetables sometimes. The field ambulance men who arrived before us saw most pathetic sights. The whole population was ravenous. Those who were given food

simply bolted it down their throats without any attempt at masti-
cation. One man ate steadily for two hours, and even then was not
satisfied, our soldiers had to give him another meal. When they
first arrived our men saw women cutting up dead horses and fighting in the streets for the flesh. We are quartered in a large school.
It has been a magnificent building, but when we took possession it
was in a dreadful state of filth and neglect. The Huns had cut off
the water supply, destroyed the drainage pipes, and battered part of
the building with bombs. The engineers came along before some
of the bombs exploded, and so saved the place from being entirely
demolished. In a few days we had it converted into a clean and
comfortable hospital.'[154]

The war ended with Germany's surrender on 11 November
1918. On Armistice Day, Reverend Danglow wrote from Amiens,
'The price of victory has been a ghastly one … Were it not for
the loss of so many of our brave boys, including our Dalbert, how
happy we would all feel but it was even little Dalbert who made
this great day possible.'[155] Few servicemen turned up for the 1919
Military Chanukah service at the Great Synagogue. Nonetheless,
the rabbi told the congregation they would not leave the synagogue
without loving recollection of the seventy-three NSW dead among
648 names on the synagogue's roll of honour. And so their names
were remembered on their *yahrzeit*, called out in alphabetical
order, from Samuel Asher, Stanley Benjamin and Roy Blashki to
Alex Weingott, Samuel Weingott and Jacob Wertheim. All dead.[156]
However, while the lost were evoked as heroes, the wounded were
barely recalled. Isaac, Maurice and Samuel Crawcour – the three
sons of Leon and Rosa Crawcour of Melbourne – were all severely
wounded in France. Maurice enlisted twice, having been invalided
out after breaking his leg in 1916. Each brother lost a right leg as a
result of the war. But not every war-related death occurred during
the fighting. Isaac Crawcour was found shot in his bed in Sydney
in August 1938. Maurice told the coroner that a Melbourne doctor

had treated his brother, and had told him that nearly everyone who suffered in war as his brother had suffered committed suicide.[157] But the Crawcour family fought on. The boys' cousin Sydney Crawcour, a doctor, enlisted in both the 1st and 2nd AIF.

How many Jews served in World War One?

Chaplain Freedman knew at the height of the war, just as the *Jewish Herald* had foreseen in 1914, that the Jewish fighters – the VC winner, the four DSOs, the three Military OBEs, the fifteen MCs and the scores of other Jews who were decorated or Mentioned in Despatches; the dead, the wounded, the maimed and the living – would be forgotten, and the old stereotypes of shirker, coward and profiteer would resurface. 'The Jew is here, too,' he wrote, 'side by side with his fellow-citizens, striving, fighting, and dying for the sacred cause of the British Empire. We think that the general public know well already; it does not. For ever statements have to be made, and articles written, pleading that the Jews are doing their duty. Even at this moment many are ignorant of the part Jews are playing in the war. When the war is over, the knowledge with many will be very vague.'[158] Lieutenant Harold Boas, the son of Reverend Boas and the YMCA's Jewish representative with the AIF, had spent the war years in Britain and occasionally France assisting the Jewish chaplains, identifying Jewish troops and attending to their needs. When he came home he compiled registers of the living and the dead. He counted rolls and enrolments and painstakingly added to his master list those names he identified as Jewish, and in 1919 estimated that there had been 2000 Jews in the AIF, out of a population of 17 287 Jews in Australia.[159] His research made the backbone of his memorial work, *Australian Jewry Book of Honour, the Great War, 1914–1918*, which listed the names of 1542 Australians who served overseas, including 218 who died, and also 147

New Zealanders, including fifteen who died.[160] When Boas published his book in 1923, its specific object was 'to place on permanent record Australian Jewry's practical part in the Great War, and to establish beyond question that Jewish citizens of the Empire, no less than members of any other faith, are prepared to share the full burden of its citizen responsibilities as well as its privileges'. Similar projects had been completed in other parts of the world – most heartrendingly in Germany where, by the war minister's own anti-semitically motivated count, more than 100 000 Jews had served in the army, 80 per cent of them in the front line; 35 000 were decorated and 12 000 gave their lives for the Kaiser. Many Jewish veterans of the German military lived on to be told by the Nazis that their race had betrayed the German nation and thousands later died in Hitler's concentration camps.

Boas' numbers were long accepted – or perhaps simply repeated – by Australian academics, but in Australia, there was no official military religion count, and obstacles existed to arriving at an accurate figure. Boas interviewed a number of Australian Jews who had enlisted under another denomination, 'mostly Church of England', and asked them 'pointedly' to explain their reasons. 'They may be summarized under the misconceived notion that to be designated a Jew was to start in the army under a disadvantage,' he wrote. 'Men lacked the moral support of numbers when they first went into camp, and being but an isolated unit, without even a direct representative padre, their character was not sufficiently strong to resist the temptation to take the line of least resistance. Others, I am sorry to say, with an education and a knowledge sufficient to have guided them otherwise, adopted a similar course out of mere snobbery.' It is possible, of course, that many considered the religion of their birth to be irrelevant to their service, since they were fighting primarily for the Empire rather than the faith of their fathers. However, several nominal apostates had apparently approached Boas themselves, to ask to have their papers altered to reflect their true religion. 'I must confess,' wrote Boas, 'that some of these wrong denominations were discovered immediately prior to the granting of special leave during the High Festivals. Whether there is any significance in this relationship is not for me to say here. Certainly the possibility of fourteen days' leave for the New Year Day of Atonement Festivals, and eight days for Passover Festival, may be accepted as an excuse for suggesting that not all were guileless in this respect.

'On these occasions,' Boas added dryly, 'I not only had to deal with the Jew who was nominally a Christian, but had to deal with many Christians who were pseudo-Jews – temporarily anyhow.'[161] Reverend Danglow was confronted with and confounded by a more eccentric case. 'I travelled a great distance to see a soldier whose name was on my list,' he wrote. 'When I introduced myself to him he grinned and told me he was not a Jew. He had stated that he was one just for a joke. Needless to say I failed to see any humour in the situation and told him so.'[162]

By 1940, Boas claimed that 2304 Jews served in the AIF, including more than 300 who died, but no updated lists were published to corroborate these larger figures.[163] The latest research indicates Boas may have overestimated the number of Jews in the AIF – if, that is, the definition of a Jew is taken as any person who has a Jewish mother, or a person with non-maternal Jewish ancestry who considers themselves to be Jewish. Russell Stern (see Appendix 2) suggests that at least 1288 verifiably Jewish men embarked with the AIF; another 115 Australians joined Empire forces in the UK, New Zealand or South Africa; thirty Jews signed up with the RAN; and more than 120 volunteered for the AIF but were not posted overseas. Stern identifies a further 138 servicepeople who may have been Jewish, but there is insufficient evidence to establish their background with certainty. Thousands of service records have not yet been examined and the exact extent of Australian or overseas recruitment remains unknown. However, it seems at least 1553 verifiably Jewish Australians served in uniform in World War One.

Old soldiers

At least ten of Australia's Jewish Boer War veterans also served in World War One. Walter Karri Davies was given a colonel's rank and appointed Provost Marshall at San Francisco. Maurice Barnett, who had served in South Africa with the Scottish Horse, was gassed on the Western Front in August 1918 but survived. James Edison Ikin, who fought in South Africa for several years, enlisted twice in World War One, first in the Artillery as 'Church of England' and then in the Service Corps as Jewish. Fennel Phillips went to the Boer War with the 5th Victoria Mounted Rifles, and World War One with the Service Corps. Alfred Solomon Saunders was in both South Africa and Gallipoli. Jacob John Visbord fought in South Africa and was wounded in France. The story of Ernest Simeon de Pass has already been told. Walter Solomon, of the prominent South Australian family, was perhaps the only Australian to serve in the Boer War and World Wars One and Two, although he converted to Christianity sometime after his return from South Africa, and actually went to the world wars with the Salvation Army. Leslie Maurice Menser of Sydney, whose father Morris Menser had been an early member of the volunteer militia in New South Wales, died of wounds in France on 10 April 1917. Leslie had been a volunteer infantryman before the Boer War, had served in South Africa with the Australian Bushmen, and had been wounded in the leg. He was still in the Cape when World War One broke out, and he fought to drive the Germans out of South West Africa; he then returned to Australia to enlist in the AIF as a private. He died a sergeant, aged about forty. His mother had two grandsons in France, and another son in training with the AIF. Poor Charles Lima Braun lost his life in June 1917 in the army in India, aged fifty-three. It is difficult to know what to make of the contribution to World War One of the enigmatic Henry Bernstein. According to a historian of espionage, Bernstein applied to work for the Secret Intelligence Service (SIS) at the Admiralty in London under the name of Enrique Lorenzo Bernstein. His record apparently showed he had helped out British espionage in the past, but that did not convince the director of naval intelligence who, upon receiving Bernstein's application, called the police – his suspicions aroused by the fact that, for the last eighteen months, Bernstein had been touring British music halls as a conjurer by the name of Lu Chang. Bernstein's flat was searched, and plans for a missile were found, as well as codes and ciphers. He was charged under the Official Secrets Act, imprisoned in Brixton, and was about to be deported when he was recognised by SIS director Sir Mansfield Cumming as 'a very noted international spy' and taken on the books of the naval intelligence division. He now called himself Henry Lawrence.[164] The world would hear from him again.

4

Between the wars

Peace, and the rise of fascism

World War One started slowly but ended suddenly, and the demobilisation of the AIF was a complex and laborious process. The task of organising the return of the troops fell to Lieutenant General John Monash with his great love of the tiny details within vast plans. As Director General of Repatriation and Demobilisation of the Australian Troops in Britain and Europe, he oversaw a system which ensured those who had served overseas for the longest period would come home first. The Jewish Anzacs left in London with no enemy to fight were given the gift of the YMCA's Jewish Soldiers' Hut in the Strand, which was opened on 25 January 1919 by Monash himself. The idea for the hut had been promoted by Rabbi Freedman, who saw it as not only – or even primarily – a recreational facility, but as a reminder that a large number of Jews were actually serving in the war. 'Every religious denomination has a hut,' he wrote. 'A building marked with the legend "The Jewish Soldiers' Hut" would show the hundreds of thousands of troops moving in and out of the big base, that the Jew is here, too, side by side with his fellow-citizens, striving, fighting and dying for the sacred cause of the British Empire.'[1]

The weeks after the Armistice ground into months for the troops in Europe. In April 1919 Reverend Danglow attended a debate at the Jewish Soldiers' Hut and later in the month left for Paris to spend the first days of Passover with men who had obtained special Paris Passover Leave. He estimated there were as many as 700 American and Australian Jewish soldiers present at the Passover service at the Synagogue Rue de la Victoire. 'The utmost cordiality prevailed between our American comrades and our own boys,' he wrote, 'and the stirring "cooees" given by the latter ... came right from our hearts and were obviously appreciated by our kind hosts and fellow Jews from the land of the "Stars and Stripes".'[2] The *Seder* for troops in the UK was arranged by Harold Boas at the Jewish Hut and included many members of the British Army's Jewish Legion.

The troops of the AIF awaiting repatriation in Europe were encouraged to take up opportunities of work or occupational training. West Australian bootmaker Henry Isaac Rothbaum of the 4th Machine Gun Battalion, who had been wounded in action in France, was granted leave without pay to work for the boot and shoe manufacturer Harris Goodman in Hackney, London. He also used his time in the city to meet and marry the tailor Minnie Rauchwerk.

Even after the war was over, young soldiers continued to die thousands of miles from their families. On 23 April 1919 Reverend Danglow buried the Russian-born Australian Private George Breitman of the 3rd Battalion, who had been awarded the Military Medal in April 1917 and who died from pneumonia at the Tidworth Military Hospital in Wiltshire. Breitman was interred at Willesden Jewish Cemetery, the fourth Australian soldier to be put to rest there.

Reverend Danglow sailed home in June. Monash returned in December. On his way back to the eastern states, Monash stopped in Western Australia and laid the foundation stone of the Memorial to Fallen Jewish Soldiers in Kings Park, Perth. The memorial, a column bearing the Star of David at its peak and a Lion of Judah at each corner of its base, was held to be the only Jewish war memorial in the world erected in a national reserve. On 12 December 1920 Monash, now a civilian, unveiled the Record Tablet of the soldiers of the St Kilda Hebrew Congregation who had volunteered for the front. Among the 112 names were nineteen dead. Monash told the congregation, which overflowed outside the synagogue, that 'the Jews of Australia had shown that they were Australians first'.[3] Monash was also present on 11 November 1923 at the opening of the NSW Jewish War Memorial, the Maccabean Hall in Darlinghurst, and was on hand to unveil the Jewish War Memorial at Melbourne General Cemetery on 14 December 1924. The comradeship of the trenches was renewed for some in communal organisations: a Jewish Returned Soldiers' Club was established in New South Wales in 1920, and a Jewish Returned Soldiers' Circle formed in Victoria in 1929.

For years the nation talked about how the veterans should be rewarded for their sacrifice, giving the *Truth* the opportunity to reprise its favourite antisemitic canard. The returned men were being made 'promises galore', noted the newspaper, just like the pledges that had earlier been 'handed out to the misguided patriots who fought to make South Africa safe for the German Jews'.[4] The meaning was unmistakable: even after General John Monash and the hundreds of men who had died on the battlefield, and all the boys who had lost their arms, legs or eyes fighting for the British Empire, the Jews were an alien people with their own agenda, and a part of the recent enemy. At the *Bulletin*, where decades of encrusted antisemitism could not be washed off by the blood of the dead, the homecoming of Colonel Harold Cohen was met with both a cheer and a sneer. 'He has had charge of the 6th (Artillery) Brigade,' wrote the newspaper, 'and though the authorities persistently omitted to make him a General, he did good work with it, and repeatedly harassed the unspeakable Hun to the verge of frenzy. He has a CMG and a DSO, and with luck he should be entitled to write even more of the alphabet after his name.' However, the

Bulletin could not help but note that, 'Like most persons named Cohen, he is outrageously affluent'.[5] Yet, of the Jewish Cohens who lost their lives in the war, Private Alexander Cohen, killed in France, was a sign-writer; Private George Cohen, killed in Belgium, was a jockey; Private Joseph Cohen, who died at Polygon Wood, was a cigar-maker; and Private Solomon Cohen, who enlisted as Charles Cohn and died of wounds in France, was a ship's steward.

A bizarre episode of inchoate antisemitism assailed the post-war reputation of Eliazar Margolin, who had remained in Palestine at the end of the war in command of his own First Jewish Battalion of Judea. The battalion, a Hebrew-speaking unit of the British Army, used a menorah as its cap badge and often seemed to follow an agenda set by Margolin rather than the British. In 1920 Margolin and his men independently suppressed Arab anti-Jewish riots, and the despairing British disbanded the unit in 1921. In May 1921 Margolin's war record came under attack in the Australian Senate during a speech by Senator 'Pompey' Elliott, who had been a popular and heavily decorated senior officer in the AIF. Elliott complained that the great Captain Jacka VC, while fighting in France, had once been superseded in the command of the 14th Battalion by 'an illiterate Polish Jew, who could not correctly spell the name of the officer he had superseded, and who had stayed behind in a safe position whilst officers and men of the 14th Battalion went into action at Messines Ridge'. Elliott said, 'The General Staff had shown no knowledge of the temperament of the Australian rank and file when they appointed such an officer to the command, and his coming to the 14th Battalion had almost caused a mutiny.'

Brigadier General Senator Edmund Drake-Brockman, whom Margolin had served as second-in-command in France, rose to Margolin's defence. Margolin, he said, certainly was 'a Jew born in Russia', but he had come to Australia twenty years previously and his conspicuous bravery and ability had earned him the DSO at Gallipoli. He happened to have sprained his knee at Messines, which is why he could not, on that occasion, go forward with his men, and 'the man who Senator Elliott had styled as an illiterate Jew certainly spoke broken English, but he spoke fluently French, German, Russian, Arabic and Yiddish'. Elliott, in reply, admitted that he had never personally met Margolin.[6] Monash himself then weighed in for Margolin with a letter to the press stating that the 'implied calumny' against Margolin was ridiculous, and that Margolin was 'a gallant, cultured gentleman, of fine physique and engaging personality, ardently loyal to Australian soldiers and ideals'.[7] Elliott came back with the insistence there was a cloud over Margolin at Messines, and feigned talking about his knee when, as Monash knew, the slander was not meant for his joints but for his race. Margolin returned to Western Australia soon afterwards, and went into business. In 1922 Rabbi Leib Aisack Falk, former Chaplain to the Jewish Legion and associate of Margolin, came to Sydney as assistant minister of the Great Synagogue, and became a relentless and influential advocate for Margolin's favoured brand of patriotic Zionism.

At the end of the war, the Australian military shrank back to the size of a peacetime force. Some professional Jewish soldiers remained in the army. Dashing Harry Shappere did not retire from the Australian Instructional Corps until 1922, and was always remembered as a popular character at the Royal Military College. A memoirist of Duntroon wrote that there were 'officers who became long-term residents and none more famous than the renowned Shappere, the riding instructor from 1912 to 1923, a specialist whom Duntroon suited and who suited Duntroon'. Shappere arrived as a lieutenant and left as quartermaster and honorary major.[8] In 1921 the public servant CS Daley attended a charity race meeting in Acton. He wrote, 'Major Shappere, in red jacket and black velvet cap, mounted upon a grey horse, appeared to be in charge of the course, and I asked him for advice about the horses. He said "lend me your card" which I did, and he ticked off a horse in the list for each of the six races. I backed these on the "tote" and they all won. "Shap", as he was called, certainly knew the horses of the district.'[9]

The AIF ceased to exist in 1921. Compulsory military training was suspended, at first for men in rural areas and then, in 1929, for everyone else. The military became an all-volunteer force. Captain Norman Packer, a doctor from Sydney, who had been attached to the British Army and served at Aden, Mesopotamia and India, died in December 1922 in Cologne, Germany, where he was stationed with the army of occupation in the Rhineland. He was thrown from a horse while hurrying to attend to a man injured in an accident. An ignominious mischance befell Leonard Keysor in 1927, when he was injured in Hounslow, Middlesex, while playing himself in the silent film *For Valour*. During a re-enactment of the key scene in which Keysor picked up and threw back enemy bombs at Gallipoli, one of the props exploded prematurely, burning his face, breaking his jaw and lacerating his arm and knee. He went to hospital for treatment – as he had refused to do at the Dardanelles – and found he was hurt worse than he had been at Lone Pine.

The pretensions of World War One to be the 'Great War' were shattered by the far greater war that was to follow, the seeds of which had been sown in the Treaty of Versailles, whose terms humiliated Germany more than the nation could bear. The 1930s saw the Great Depression and the rise of fascism, especially in Germany, Italy and Spain, but also, in far smaller ways, throughout the rest of Europe and the independent dominions of the British Empire. Australia's own homegrown fascist movement, the New Guard, was particularly anaemic and not notably antisemitic. When the forces of reaction gathered to whisper about the need for a strong leader, a firm hand, a man to crush the communists, rein in the excesses of democracy and make the trains to Flinders Street Station run on time, the name they came up with was General John Monash. In a celebrated response to one of the many overtures he received throughout the 1920s and early 1930s, implying that he should somehow seize the government for himself, Monash wrote: 'What do you and your friends want me to do? To lead a movement to upset the Constitution, oust the jurisdiction of Parliament, and usurp the Governmental power? If so, I have no ambition to embark on High Treason, which any such action would amount to. What would you say if a similar proposal were made by the Communists and Socialists ... ? Depend upon it, the only hope for Australia is the ballot box, and an educated electorate. You and your people should get busy and form an organisation as efficient, as widespread, and as powerful as that of the Labour Party.'[10] Monash enjoyed immense prestige in the post-war years. He was head of the State Electricity Commission of Victoria, Vice Chancellor of Melbourne University, and president of the Zionist Federation of Australia and New Zealand. He left his mark on Australian military thinking by demonstrating that battles could be more easily and intelligently won with the carefully planned integration of every available military element, from armour and artillery to cavalry and cooks. Monash died from a heart attack in 1931. His state funeral was the largest yet seen in Australia, with more than 300 000 mourners gathered along the route of the procession from State Parliament House past the Shrine of Remembrance – whose construction Monash had championed – to Brighton Cemetery.

Some Jews continued to follow Monash's path of progress through the militia. Paul Alfred Cohen, who had been posted to the Garrison Artillery in the days of compulsory military service in 1927, was commissioned as a lieutenant in 1931 and as a captain in 1935, and was to become – as Paul Alfred Cullen – the most senior Jewish soldier in World War Two. But the great mass of young men, both within the Jewish community and outside, unconsciously followed the advice given by Monash to the father whose son wanted to go to military school: 'If a boy has any aptitudes with which he can enliven and enrich his mind, do not let him live the life of a

153

soldier in times of peace. There is nothing more narrow or more deadening than the walls of administrative routine, textbook, and regulation by which he will be surrounded. Let him find his great life interest in whatever he is fitted to practise. If the day of fighting should come, he will be then the more useful because he will be at his very best in whatever he is best suited to accomplish.'[11]

Adolf Hitler became Chancellor of Germany in 1933. Under new laws, all Jews and other non-Aryans were excluded from the civil service, the medical and legal professions and agriculture. At first, Jewish war veterans and their families were allowed to keep government jobs, but this exemption was later revoked. Jews were barred from schools and universities, from journalism and from the ownership of newspapers. In May 1935 military service was restricted to Aryans, and in November the Nuremberg Laws prohibited sexual relations between Aryans and Jews, and stripped Jews of their citizenship and civil rights. Many Jews fled while it was still possible to leave. A few began to find their way to Australia, sometimes to a tepid welcome.

In October 1935 the Italian fascist dictator Benito Mussolini invaded Abyssinia. Many of the soldiers of the Army of the Ethiopian Empire, under Emperor Haile Selassie, were armed with only spears and bows and arrows, although others had rifles of various ages and conditions, and the largely untrained Ethiopian infantry was supported by antiquated artillery and a risible air force. The Emperor's men were defeated in May 1936 by much larger and better equipped Italian forces, who poisoned more than 100 000 Ethiopians with illegal mustard gas. The Italians argued that they were provoked by the Ethiopians' use of illegal dum-dum bullets, which exploded inside the body. Although Haile Selassie's plight was met with indifference throughout Europe, claims were made that the dum-dum bullets had been supplied by a British manufacturer. It seemed a Colonel Pedro Lopez had approached Bates and Co of Birmingham to obtain samples of their soft-nosed bullets and a letter, which he had dictated himself, stating their origin. This letter then appeared in the Italian press. Subsequently, a Colonel Gustav Mezler had approached an Abyssinian official in London with the offer to supply the Ethiopians with large quantities of arms and ammunition, and induced him to sign a document authorising Mezler to purchase weapons for the Abyssinian government. This, too, had fallen into the hands of the Italians.[12]

But who were Lopez and Mezler? Their trail led to Melbourne-born Henry Bernstein – veteran of the British South Africa Force, the Matabele Wars, the Jameson Raid, the Niger Expeditionary Force, the Bolivian artillery and the British Secret Service – who was now living in London as Henry Lawrence. In the early hours of a May morning, Bernstein/Lawrence was confronted on his doorstep by a journalist from the *News Chronicle*, who wrote: '"I am three personalities, but only one man," said Lawrence, flinging wide his arms to accentuate the words ... He stood in a half-open doorway clad only in a white nightshirt, and glanced frequently up and down the deserted street as though afraid of what lurked there. His forehead was covered with perspiration, despite the cold night. A woman's voice from the darkness screamed, "Tell them the authorities have sworn you to secrecy." However, a hectic cross-examination broke down Lawrence's reserve, and the confession poured out tumultuously, as though he were relieving himself of a burden.' Astonishingly, Henry Lawrence, formerly Henry Bernstein, revealed that he had also been both Colonel Gustave Mezler and Colonel Pedro Lopez, but swore that his actions had been motivated solely by patriotism. Indeed, he predicted, 'Time will reveal that I am the most patriotic man in the country.' Next, 'Lawrence's wife, a blonde, grey-eyed woman, full of charm, but utterly weary, took up the story. She said that the strain had been frightful. She had not slept for nights. "We have been married twenty years, and have never had any money ... My husband learned a great deal about weapons while employed by a large firm of British armament manufacturers. All through the episode of the dum-dum bullets he worked in closest conjunction with the Italian Embassy, which employed him. Before taking the job he wrote to the British Government saying that if he found that the Italians were working against Britain he would let them know."' Anyway, she said, the Italians 'had let him down in every way, and never paid him a penny, except expenses. "The trouble is that he is over-trusting," she added.'[13]

It turned out that Bernstein had first visited Bates and Co towards the end of the Gran Chaco War between Paraguay and Uruguay, looking to buy rifles. The London *Daily Mail* alleged Bernstein had become a Secret Service agent in 1919 in Constantinople, when it was thought he had been in contact with the Communist International. The White Russian Secret Service had sworn to kill him, but he had escaped in a fishing boat from Odessa. Like much else said about Henry Bernstein, there is a chance this may have been true. The dum-dum bullets episode marked the end of the public career of a man who was probably the first Australian-born Jewish soldier to go to war. He was a character who had lived a life on the edge of history and perhaps, once or twice, did something to change its course a little – but to what end remains unclear.

In the same year as the Ethiopians fought Mussolini's fascists in Africa, a microcosm of the democratic and communist world stood against General Francisco Franco's Falangists in Spain. The Spanish Civil War began in 1936 as a rebellion by a group of right-wing military officers against the elected left-wing government of Spain. Hitler's Germany and Mussolini's Italy supplied arms and men to Franco's rebels, while Stalin's Soviet Union and the Mexican Republic gave aid to government loyalists. Some 40 000 foreigners fought for the loyalist cause in the International Brigades: Jewish people from all around the world converged on Spain to fill their ranks (some 5000–7500 international volunteers were Jewish[14]) but there were very few Jews among the small number of Australians who fought. Australian Communist Sam Aarons arrived at the war in June 1937 and was attached to the Transport Section at Brigade HQ as a chauffeur. He sent regular despatches to the Australian *Weekly Worker*, in which he attacked fascism and Trotskyism with equal venom, and pronounced victory as inevitable even when all hope was lost. But it would be impossible to overlook the earnest idealism in his heart. 'In the auto park here,' he wrote, 'there are all nationalities, English, Scotch, Americans, Romanians, Poles, Chinese, etc., with myself the sole Australian. They are unfortunately separated a good deal, due to the language difficulty, but a spirit of real comradeship exists which is immensely stimulating and thrilling, because each and every one is animated by the same desire, is here because of his hatred of fascism and war, and love for democracy and progress. And the park is a minute cross-section of Spain today, where the people of whatever nationality or creed or colour are in the overwhelming majority determined that not only shall fascism not be victorious in Spain, but that right here on Spanish soil, shall the grave of international fascism be dug. And it will be, of that there is no doubt.'[15] Aarons returned home in September 1938 and began propaganda work for the Spanish Relief Committee. Franco's bombing raids were aimed at civilians, he said. 'Whole blocks of tenements and houses were often destroyed by one bomb. In Granollers, north of Barcelona, I saw about 500 people, mostly women and children in the market square, killed … The people go mad with fear … I have seen people running backwards and forwards between the doubtful shelter of two brick walls. The people do not sleep. Barcelona was bombed for five hours one night, and when at last the inhabitants were able to leave their shelters most of them were in a pitiable state, white-faced and crying.'[16] Nevertheless, he said that life in many places went on as usual, literacy levels had improved, and the Loyalists were certain that if all foreigners were withdrawn, they could win the war in months. Spain fell on 1 April 1939. But for all his self-deception, Sam Aarons knew he was fighting the first battle of the next war. In 1938 he wrote, 'Sometimes, as I listen to a fascist plane humming overhead, invisible in the night, I wonder whether he is after us or some unprotected villages in the rear, and then I like to think of Sydney, for to me it represents peace. But if you represent peace to me, what do I represent to you? We ought also to represent peace to you. Australia at war would mean that the things I have seen in Madrid would happen to the people and cities I know and love.'[17]

On 19 November 1938 the Nazis in Germany and Austria initiated the super-pogrom that became known as Kristallnacht, in which more than 1000 synagogues were burned, almost 100 Jewish people killed, and 30 000 were arrested and sent to concentration camps. On Kristallnacht the promise of the Holocaust was carved with shards of broken glass. In its aftermath a small number of German and Austrian Jews made their way to Australia.

1 previous page 'Lieutenant-Colonel Solomon's connection with the South Australian Military Force dates back further than that of any other officer or private', wrote the *Hebrew Standard* in 1900. Benjamin Solomon joined the South Australian Artillery as a gunner in 1860, aged sixteen. He was commissioned lieutenant in 1877, was Commanding Officer of the SA Garrison Artillery by 1899, transferred to Artillery Brigade Headquarters as Brigade Quartermaster 1900, and represented the Brigade at the Commonwealth celebrations in Sydney, January 1901.

2 right Officers of the 4th Contingent (Queensland Imperial Bushmen) bound for the Boer War, pictured with Lord and Lady Lamington, at Government House, Brisbane, in May 1900. Captain Joseph Ernest Joseph (back row, sixth from left) was an assayer in Mackay who became one of the most senior Jewish Australian soldiers in South Africa. He was promoted to Major in 1904.

3 above These profiles of St Kilda nurse Rose Shappere and her brother Harry appeared in the *Sydney Mail*'s 'Soldiers of the Empire! Departure of Australians for South Africa' supplement in 1899.

4 right Colonel Walter Karri Davies took his middle name from the timber grown by his family in Karridale, Western Australia. Karri Davies was a hero of the Boer War who raised the Imperial Light Horse regiment, survived the siege of Mafeking, and refused to accept the Victoria Cross.

5 *above* Captain Daniel Sidney Aarons, 16th Battalion, stretchered to a first aid post in Belgium, 1917.

6 *right* John Fullarton 'Jack' Aarons followed his younger brother Daniel (above) to enlist in Perth in July 1916, initially in the 51st Battalion. He was transferred to his brother's battalion in 1917 and was killed two months later. Daniel took this photo of Jack's original grave marker at Trois Arbres Cemetery, Steenwerck, France.

7 *opposite page* Sidney Diamond of the 6th Battalion on furlough at Giza, Egypt, after the horror of the Gallipoli landings when he was awarded a DCM for displaying 'greatest courage and decision of character'. Diamond, an English-born piano tuner, served in the AIF for more than four years. He received a commission and fought on the Western Front.

8 King George V knights Lieutenant General Sir John Monash at Chateau Bertangles on 12 August 1918, in recognition of Monash's pivotal role in the Battle of Hamel, which is often considered the turning point for Allied victory in World War One. It was the first knighthood bestowed on a commander in the field in nearly two centuries.

9 Lieutenant General Sir John Monash (seated) with his two nephews and aides-de-camp Captain Aubrey Moss (left) and Captain Paul Simsonson (right), and Major Walter Berry (centre) of the Australian Corps Headquarters at Chateau Bertangles in the Somme, 20 July 1918.

Private L. KEYZOR, V.C.

10 In the early 20th century tobacco manufacturers began inserting picture cards into packets of cigarettes. They became popular collectibles and in 1917 Melbourne company Sniders & Abrahams Tobacco printed a series of cigarette cards depicting Australian VCs, including this one honouring Leonard Keysor, the AIF's first Jewish VC recipient.

11 Issacher Weingott served as a signaller in World War Two and wrote a diary of his experience at the fall of Rabaul in 1941. This picture was printed in the *Sydney Mail* in 1915 as six-year-old Issacher had recently collected '£33 for the Australian Wounded Fund' after two of his half-brothers had fallen at the Dardanelles.

12 Private Mark Albert Buttel, a butcher of Redfern, NSW, enlisted in the AIF in 1914. He served at Gallipoli and then on the Western Front. In 1916 he sent this signed portrait home to his mother. The following year he was captured at Riencourt and spent the remainder of the war in POW camps. He survived and returned to Australia in 1919.

Mother With Best Love from Mark

13a left Lieutenant Berrol Lazar Mendelsohn was killed in action on 20 July 1916 at the Battle of Fromelles, aged twenty-five. In 1921, his mother Abigail wrote to Army Records: 'I am still waiting and hoping that the grave of my darling son has been found, but so far have not had that consolation.'

13b above Mendelsohn was one of the identified soldiers among the 250 'Lost Diggers of Fromelles', a resolute effort led by Lambis Englezos AM. Mendelsohn's headstone was consecrated on 19 July 2010 at the dedication of the new Fromelles (Pheasant Wood) Military Cemetery by Jewish chaplain Rabbi Saunders.

14 and 15 Harold Collins (pictured on opposite page, and at far right in image above) was a stretcherbearer in the 1st Field Ambulance at Gallipoli, then transferred to the Australian Flying Corps in late 1916 and became a master mechanic. He was an avid photographer and founding member of NAJEX.

16 *above* Chaplain Reverend David Freedman raises a *Torah* given to him by a congregation in Alexandria, Egypt, in April 1916, at a service in the field (probably Salisbury, England in 1917 or 1918). This scroll has become known as the 'Anzac Torah'.

17 *right* Dr Eric Blashki of the Royal Army Medical Corps was one of twelve members of the extended Blashki family to serve in World War One.

18 *above* Meeting of Australian Jewish soldiers
outside the YMCA's Jewish Soldiers' Hut, the
Strand, London after World War One. (Back
row, left to right) Unidentified, Isard Zeltner,
unidentified, Michael Levy, Henry Myers; (front
row, left to right) William Dennerstein, Harris
Mendelsohn, Chaplain Jacob Danglow, Harold
Boas, Emanuel Eilenberg, Wolfe Zeeng.

19 *below* Australian, British and American soldiers
and sailors raise their cups at a Passover Seder
service at the YMCA's Jewish Hut, April 1919.

20 above Sergeant Maurice Sussman, of the Australian 6th Light Horse Regiment, wrote letters home telling of his brigade's battle with the Senussi Arabs and his attempts to make peace with a Bedouin chief in 1915.

21 right Lieutenant Wilfred Beaver, 60th Battalion AIF, may have been the first World War One British soldier to enter German territory anywhere in the world when he led the Papuan Armed Constabulary into German-administered New Guinea in 1914. He was killed at Polygon Wood in 1917.

22 Roy Browne (centre) and his three brothers fought in World War One. Roy and his sons Adrien (left) and Wesley (right) served in World War Two.

5

World War Two: 1939 to 1945

The world on the brink of disaster

The world was on the brink of unthinkable disaster, and the Jewish people were about to enter the darkest period of their history on 30 August 1939, when Rabbi Falk, now acting Chief Minister of the Great Synagogue, gave a radio address evoking the memory of the Maccabees for a new generation. 'If the principles of justice and righteousness are to be trampled underfoot,' said the rabbi, 'if the right of small nations to live is to be challenged, if the unity and greatness of the Empire is to be threatened, then we Jews will consider it a religious act to take up arms for the defence of those sacred principles. The spirit of the Maccabeans of old still flows in the life-blood of modern Israel. Should the hour strike when the Empire calls its sons to defend its flag, Israel will respond with a mighty "Here am I".' The Jewish population of Australia was still very small: the 1933 census had counted only 23 000 Jews, although by 1939 numbers had been bolstered by 7000–8000 European refugees from Nazism. As a hostage to the future, Rabbi Falk assured his 2UE listeners that the refugees in Australia would stand by the Empire too.[1]

Two days later, on 1 September 1939, Germany invaded Poland from the west. On 3 September France, Britain, Australia and New Zealand declared war on Germany, with Canada and South Africa quickly following suit. Russia invaded Poland from the east. The

NSW Jewish ex-servicemen's annual meeting was attended by a record number of members. The president, Simon Joseph Guss, said, 'I feel somewhat that we are not meeting as ex-servicemen but as men who are on the threshold of a new era of service. The Hun is again plunging the world into an orgy of blood to satisfy an insatiable lust of conquest. We who, in our own small way, helped to ... smash Germany in 1914–1918 feel that this time that country must be shown that savagery and brutality cannot be tolerated and brutes must be taught in the only way they can understand.'[2]

Under cover of the Nazi-Soviet Pact, the Soviet Union over-ran the Baltic states and parts of Romania, and Europe plunged deeper into hell. Many Jewish refugees in Australia were now citizens of enemy powers. Historically, it had been a favourite ploy of antisemites to find Jews forced into a restricted situation and then abuse them for the consequences as if they were choices. So it was that in different times and places, Jews were restricted from trades and occupations, then told they were economic parasites; herded into ghettoes, then denounced for being clannish; and barred from military service, then labelled cowards and shirkers. 'Enemy aliens' in Australia were not allowed to join the services, and were about to be caught inside the familiar pincers. Under the National Security (Aliens Control) Act, they had to register at their nearest police station, provide four photographs of themselves, and give a written undertaking not to engage in actions prejudicial to the safety of the British Empire. They were not permitted to change the name by which they were known in August 1939, and if they did not report for registration, they could be locked up in internment camps.

In practice, only resident foreigners thought to pose a real risk to national security were likely to find themselves in the camps, although they were later joined by luckless captives from the British troopship *Dunera*, and other more recent refugees, but some of the most vehement and highly motivated anti-Nazis in Australia were prevented from joining the struggle against Germany until aliens were finally taken into military 'employment companies' in 1942.

Early enlistments

The 2nd AIF was raised at the end of 1939, and Australia's British citizens, among them many Jews, rushed to enlist in that period of intense patriotic enthusiasm and thirst for action that tended to accompany the outbreak of any war. The AIF was to be made up entirely of volunteers, while other men – outside of protected occupations – were conscripted into the Citizen Military Forces (CMF) for home defence and could not be compelled to serve outside Australian territories. The Jewish Chaplain to the CMF was Rabbi Falk.

On 20 November 1939 Robert Patkin, a 21-year-old salesman from Caulfield, Victoria, enlisted in the Australian Army. Patkin had been a cadet at Melbourne Grammar School and later joined the volunteer Royal Melbourne Regiment. 'So, when war was declared it was an opportunity to combine my military knowledge with adventure,' he wrote. 'The army gave me a little piece of paper and sent me home with details of what to bring the following day when I would go into camp. The most important item was, that I was to bring a cut lunch. The following day I returned with a cut lunch, [was] put into a bus and transported to the Melbourne Showgrounds, given a straw palliasse to sleep on and locked into a large pavilion which was used, I think, for animal exhibits. There would have been some hundreds of men to each of these pavilions and everyone was dressed in varieties of clothing. Some people wore militia uniforms, others wore day clothes as if they were going to the office, labourers were wearing their work clothes … The following day the army issued us with khaki drill trousers and a jacket and a soft khaki hat. We used to call these uniforms "giggle suits", because when we put them on we looked like people who should have been incarcerated somewhere else. They also gave us a pair of boots. After the clothing was issued, men were lined up and asked what arm of the forces they would like to go into. Approximately ninety percent had absolutely no idea, so they were just led into various units that the army decided to put them into.'[3] Patkin joined the infantry, the 2/6th Battalion of the 17th Brigade of the 6th Division.

While Patkin trained at Puckapunyal near Seymour, Victoria, Europe went up in flames. Germany took Denmark and Norway. The Soviets attacked Finland. Winston Churchill replaced Neville Chamberlain as British Prime Minister on 10 May 1940, and left the appeasement policy to the savage judgment of history. Germany invaded France and, as was by now customary, violated the neutrality of Belgium, as well as Holland and Luxembourg. British and French troops were beaten back to Dunkirk and evacuated to Britain. Italy, too, declared war on France and Britain. The Germans took Paris, the Italians invaded France through the Alps, and an armistice was signed, carving France into German and Italian zones, but leaving unoccupied the collaborationist Vichy France regime in the south, under Marshal Philippe Pétain. French possessions from North Africa to Indochina also fell under Vichy French control.

One of the first Australian heroes of the war was Flight Lieutenant Julius Allan Cohen, who was born in Moree, New South Wales, and grew up in Sydney. In 1935 Cohen joined the Royal Australian Air Force (RAAF) and became an officer cadet at Point Cook, Victoria. The next year he graduated with his wings – and the lowest marks ever recorded for 'officer qualities'.[4] He was sent to London in 1939 with others from 10 Squadron to pick up Sunderland flying boats to fly them home for the RAAF. When war broke out, the Australians and their Sunderlands were needed in Europe and were therefore attached to the British Coastal Command. At first they were used to search for U-boats. 'It sounds exciting,' said Cohen at the time, 'but it is really most prosaic, flying by instruments over a featureless ocean. The only breaks in the monotony are the meals of bacon and eggs, hot joints and other delicacies. We live a hotel life in the air. It is an armchair sort of warfare.'[5]

But the Australian squadron of Sunderlands soon became furiously active. They were used largely for convoy escorts, but they also carried British diplomats and politicians on sensitive and often dangerous missions. On 25 June 1940 Cohen piloted a flying boat carrying the British Minister for Information Duff Cooper and the then Commander in Chief of the British Field Forces Lord Gort to Rabat in Morocco, in an attempt to persuade former leaders of the French Government in Morocco to side with the Allies, rather than throw in their lot with Vichy France and the Axis powers. The party was unsure what kind of a welcome it might expect in North Africa. Cohen landed in the sea, found a mooring position, dropped off Cooper and Gort, then received an urgent coded message from London warning that their mission was probably in vain as Vichy France was already in the ascendancy in Morocco. Cohen resolved to deliver the message to the diplomats but, he later wrote, when he called to the shore for a boat, he found 'nobody would take any notice and come out to us'.

'I had one of the aircraft's dinghies inflated,' wrote Cohen, 'and a couple of us started to paddle for the shore. That's when a police boat headed us off and forced our return to the aircraft. We tried setting out from the other side of the aircraft, but the same thing happened and we were turned back. By then it was getting dark, so I ordered all the Sunderland's lights turned on. This quickly got attention because there was a blackout in force and the local authorities were fairly nervous. A boat came round near us, its occupants calling out "Le blackout, le blackout" and pointing to our lights, but we took no notice. Eventually the boat came alongside, and my first officer (an RAF pilot officer named Derek

163

Stewart) and I hopped aboard. I put my service revolver into the back of the fellow in charge of the little pinnace and politely asked him to take us ashore, which he did.'

When they reached the shore, a British consular official was ready to meet them, but he was surrounded by French police who would not allow him to get close. Cohen and Stewart were ordered back to the Sunderland and told an armed guard would be placed on board, but Cohen managed to convince the French police that Stewart was the man in charge which meant that Stewart had to go back to the aircraft while Cohen could stay ashore with the consul. 'For some reason that ruse worked,' wrote Cohen, although they were tailed by police cars, which waited for them outside the consulate gate.

At the consulate, Cohen was told Gort was addressing French officers at the Balima Hotel, while Cooper attended another meeting. 'There seemed little prospect of me being able to reach either of them,' wrote Cohen, 'with police cars cruising up and down outside the Consulate, but then it was decided that a female member of the staff would try to smuggle me to the Balima in a consular car. That was the plan, and accordingly I climbed into the back seat of this sedan and got down on the floor. My lady driver carefully draped a blanket over me to conceal my presence, and then we drove out the gate. We were immediately pulled up by the police, who used torches to inspect the inside of our vehicle. They also opened the boot, but after they found no-one there they said to her, "Off you go." Of course, we were still followed, so my driver took me as close as she dared and then pointed out to me along the blacked-out street where I needed to go.

'I got out of the car and headed off, but I hadn't gone very far before there was a call from behind telling me to stop. I kept moving, and whoever was following fired a couple of shots in what I presumed was my direction. "Well bugger you," I thought and since I still had my fully-loaded revolver, I pulled it out and fired off a couple of rounds in return. It would have been a miracle if I hit anybody, but that wasn't really my aim.'

He found Gort at the hotel speaking to an unreceptive crowd of French officers and was about to whisk him away when both men were apprehended by French police, driven to the station, and left alone in a locked room. 'When I looked at the lock I could see that it was only an ordinary kind of lock,' wrote Cohen, 'nothing reinforced, so it should be susceptible to a bit of brute force. We hadn't been searched at all, so I still had my revolver around my waist, I pulled this out and fired a shot that blew the lock apart, and we stepped out into the corridor.

'The noise brought people racing along the narrow passageway. I turned in their direction and fired a couple of shots, and I have a recollection of two men falling down. I don't know for sure how much damage I did to either of them, but it was very close range and I would be surprised if I didn't kill the poor fellows. Nonetheless, that ensured that the others didn't reach us before we made it to the front door and got back outside. Strange to say, the car that had just brought us there was still sitting where we left it, with the same policeman still behind the wheel. He must have heard the shots, I would have thought, but didn't have enough time to react.

'We hopped into the car pronto – Gort in the back, me in the front – and I stuck the revolver in the driver's ribs and told him to take us to the quay. He was gabbling away in excitement, but I couldn't follow what he said and just kept jabbing him in the ribs with the barrel of the weapon. On reaching the jetty we jumped out and I called to our aircraft. It was moored well out, in a different position to where it was when I'd left it. The French had made Derek move – they were a very big nuisance. Luckily, my yells were heard by our blokes in the Sunderland and they sent the dinghy in to collect us.' Cooper eventually joined them on the Sunderland and, wrote Cohen, 'It wasn't long afterwards that a couple of police boats with armed crews came out and started circling around us.' Five minutes before dawn, Cohen blindfolded himself, and Stewart let him know to remove the blindfold once there was enough light for take-off, to ensure his vision would be clearer in the sunrise. 'Then we slipped our moorings,' wrote Cohen, 'and I just gave it full bore. We taxied at speed down the river and out through the harbour, past all the fishing boats at their moorings. I damaged the float on the port wing dodging one boat – it wasn't so much smashed as left flopping, as a couple of pins had got knocked out … The police boats were pursuing us, but we didn't have to worry about them unless we tipped over – they certainly couldn't catch a flying boat that was almost on the point of airborne.'[6] Cohen was awarded the Distinguished Flying Cross (DFC) for his heroics at Rabat, but the full story of the gunfights and jail escape was not told until more than thirty years later, apparently to save the feelings of Lord Gort who was, after all, Commander in Chief of British Forces when he allowed himself to be gently taken prisoner by the dubious gendarmes of Morocco.

Cohen was feted in the press throughout the war. It was somehow easier to make a hero from a flier than a digger, and Cohen had the glamour and dash to play the part as if it were scripted. When he later flew Catalinas against the Japanese in New Guinea, Cohen, who was known in the RAAF as 'Dick' – a small step in his gradual transition to the post-war Sir Richard Kingsland – was described by an unimaginative journalist as 'tall dark and handsome' but also 'one of the most popular all-round blokes in the Australian Air Force'. According to the *ABC Weekly*, the Catalina crews 'idolised Dick Cohen, and it was quite common to see junior members of the Air Force pointing out this curly-haired laughing airman to the new arrivals'. In the late afternoon, Cohen could apparently be seen 'striding down towards his aircraft with his crew. Once aboard he ceased to be a wing commander but became one of the mob. Off came his shirt and cap, and with a towel slung around his neck he would jockey his aircraft out into the harbour for a take-off which the Japs always had good reason to regret.'[7] The reader can almost hear Cohen whistling 'Colonel Bogey'.

EARLY IN 1940 ROBERT PATKIN COMPLETED HIS INFANTRY training, took his final leave, and was told to prepare to depart from Australia. 'Everything was supposed to be secret,' he wrote. 'We were not allowed to talk about any of our movements.'[8] The first Australian soldier stepped onto a troopship to start out for battle on 9 January 1940: 30-year-old Captain Paul Alfred Cohen, who had enlisted in the militia twelve years previously, marched his men on board SS *Otranto* cheered on by vast crowds of Sydneysiders. Paul was the son of Sir Samuel Cohen, a prominent Jewish business-man who had been president of the Great Synagogue Sydney and founding president of the Jewish Welfare Society – Paul himself was a founding member of Temple Emanuel, Sydney's first lib-eral/reform synagogue. Cohen was given command of B Company, 2/2nd Infantry Battalion, 16th Brigade, 6th Division. In September 1941, he was to change his name to Paul Alfred Cullen – appar-ently to protect himself if he was captured by the Nazis – and as Cullen he went on to become the most distinguished Jewish Aus-tralian solider in World War Two, rising to the rank of lieutenant colonel and receiving a DSO and Bar for his actions in Papua New Guinea.

Robert Patkin was promoted to sergeant, and left Australia with his comrades on the troopship HMT *Neuralia*. They sailed to Egypt, and took a troop train to Palestine, where they disembarked at Beit Jirja, south of Tel Aviv. 'From Beit Jirja we did our training in the desert,' wrote Patkin. 'At this stage we were given proper equipment, armaments and weaponry. We were very fit and spent some three to four months in the desert with the odd leave into Tel Aviv and Jerusalem. Whilst we were on our way from Australia to

El Kantara before arriving in Palestine, the Italians declared war on the Allies so we now had the Italians as enemies in Libya. We knew when we had finished training in Palestine we would move into Egypt, and from Egypt we would go to Libya to fight the Italian Army.'[9]

Like their predecessors in the 1st AIF, some young Jewish Australians took advantage of their leave time in the Middle East to explore religious sites in Palestine. Sergeant Albert Hertzberg of Bellevue Hill, New South Wales, spent four days in Jerusalem. 'I decided that on Saturday I would go to *shule*,' he wrote home. 'I made friends with many fine Jewish men of about twenty-five years of age who wear beards, let their hair grow long and curl it and wear big black hats. They are the very *frum* Jews and there are not many of them ... I thought it would be a *mitzvah* if I prayed at the Wailing Wall ... There were many hundreds of Jews – rich and poor praying at the Wall. I, in uniform, took out my Singer's Prayer Book and also davened. Well, you can imagine, Jews all around me. Could it be possible that this Australian is a Jew? However, I prayed and when I was about to go I was rushed by many Jews to talk to me. When they saw my *Arba Kanfot* they nearly fainted – an Australian wearing an *Arba Kanfot*! Although I was invited home for Sabbath dinner by many Jews, rich and poor, I declined because in the afternoon I decided to go for a trip to the Dead Sea and Jericho.'[10]

Lieutenant David James Benjamin of the 16th Battalion, writing home at Chanukah, was less impressed with the Holy Land. Benjamin was a legal clerk from Sydney who went on to become a lieutenant colonel and Chief Legal Officer of the Australian Army Legal Corps. The *Hebrew Standard* chose to précis his letter, stifling Benjamin's naturally lively prose into its own turgid, incurious argot: 'It was Chanukah, and candles were everywhere. The huge electric Menorah over one of the principal buildings was, however, not illuminated: because of war precautions ... A feature that strikes the visitor is the fine parade beach – of course it is not so spectacular as Bondi.'[11] But Benjamin enjoyed a dip in the Mediterranean and appreciated the view from his hotel window. He spent part of his leave happily in the company of Rabbi Lazarus Morris Goldman, formerly the assistant minister at Toorak Road Synagogue, Melbourne, the first Jewish chaplain posted overseas with the 2nd AIF.

HMAS *Sydney* and the war at sea

There were Australian Jewish sailors patrolling the Mediterranean while the troops in the desert made ready to fight. Berny Nathan Shilkin, a sick-bay attendant, had joined HMAS *Sydney* at Fremantle on 30 August 1939, and he later gave an account of his war experiences to a journalist. According to the reporter, Shilkin told his story 'slowly, briefly and modestly, as one who had been merely an onlooker at a very uninteresting game of cricket'. The *Sydney* had joined the British Mediterranean Fleet in May 1940 and was in port in Alexandria when the Italians declared war. On 21 June, the ship bombarded the Italian military base in Baria, Libya, turning the port into 'a hazy smoky mess', said Shilkin. On 28 June, the *Sydney* intercepted three Italian destroyers heading towards Libya. The Australians fired on the *Espero*, the flagship of the convoy, 'and hit her engine room,' said Shilkin, 'bringing her to a standstill. We started to chase after the other two but were signalled to go back and sink our victim. Never was there a ship more game. As we shortened range and blasted the *Espero* with our guns, she kept firing at us. She was all ablaze but she kept firing with everything she had, and at the very end loosed her torpedoes. Her flag fluttered until the end. It was like cold-blooded murder. We lowered two lifeboats and took forty-seven survivors, of whom three subsequently died.' The *Sydney*'s generosity towards the routed enemy was impeccable. For any men who might have survived the wreck but been unable to board the Australian ship, 'We left a cutter loaded with provisions, clothing, lamps and signal books,' said Shilkin. 'The prisoners we took were well cared for. Donations from among our sailors kept them well-clothed and for four days while attending to these men no one slept.' The Battle of the *Espero* Convoy was the first surface engagement of Allied and Italian ships in World War Two. The *Sydney* left her prisoners in Alexandria, and on 7 July set out with the fleet to attack the Italian fleet at Calabria. On 9 July, said Shilkin, 'We sighted the enemy formation and action started about ten o'clock in the morning. The enemy turned to run, laying a smoke screen and firing as they went. The 7th cruiser squadron (HMAS *Sydney*, HMS *Orion*, HMS *Neptune*, HMS *Gloucester* and HMS *Liverpool*) penetrated the screen and the enemy turned to attack. The squadron then led them back on the battleships and as soon as they saw that action with bigger ships was imminent, they turned to run again. The destroyer *Zefiro*, knowing full well that what she had to do meant disaster and destruction, turned across the British fleet, running right across its path, and laid a smoke screen so as the other ships could get away. She was blown to pieces. We chased the Italians up to the heel of Italy and then the danger of shore batteries forced us to turn away.' This indecisive engagement with the Italian fleet became known as the Battle of Calabria.

On 18 July the *Sydney* left Alexandria with a screen of five destroyers for anti-submarine work. 'About 7.30 am on the following morning,' said Shilkin, 'the two destroyers astern broke wireless telegraphy silence and informed the *Sydney* that they had seen two enemy ships. At breakfast the action alarm went and at 8.30 we opened up fire. The ships were the Italian cruisers *Giovanni Delle Bande Nere* and the *Bartolomeo Colleoni* – much faster and carrying heavier anti-aircraft defences. They were oncoming to engage in line astern (one behind the other) with the *Giovanni* in front. At 19 000 yards we scored a direct hit on the aft gun turret of the

Giovanni, which turned away and allowed the *Colleoni* to engage us. We closed to about 12 000 yards and hit her midships. She stopped. We signalled to HMS *Havoc*, one of the destroyers, to come up and torpedo the *Colleoni*. Then we gave chase to the *Giovanni*, which got away. During the engagement we sustained a direct hit on the funnel. Our reward for [the Battle of Cape Spada] was a double ration of butter. Consequently, there was enthusiasm about sinking a battleship so that we could each have a tin of jam.'

In August the *Sydney* bombarded Stampali, a seaplane base in the Dodecanese. Next the Australians, together with HMS *Hex* and HMS *Orion*, attacked the newly built aerodrome at Scarpanto. 'Here we had lucky escapes,' said Shilkin, 'and but for the *Hex* might have been sunk. Two torpedo boats were heading straight for us when the *Hex* cut right across their bows and with heavy gunfire sunk the two.'[12]

The *Sydney* returned to Sydney on 9 February 1941 to a jubilant public welcome. Berny Shilkin left the ship in Sydney on 29 August 1941. On 19 November, the *Sydney* was off the coast of Western Australia when sailors spotted a vessel that identified itself as a Dutch merchant ship. The 'Dutch' ship sent a distress signal, and as the *Sydney* moved in closer, the foreign vessel – actually the German auxiliary cruiser *Kormoran* – opened fire. In the subsequent battle, the *Sydney* was sunk, taking every man down with her in the worst naval disaster in Australian history. The *Kormoran* was also scuttled after the fighting, although most of the German crew were rescued. The 645 drowned Australian sailors included canteen manager Maurice Opas and assistant steward Lionel Rothbaum, the only son of Harry Isaac Rothbaum, the AIF machine-gunner who had married the tailor Minnie Rauchwerk in London in 1919. Minnie died in 1935, and the widower Harry had re-enlisted in the army in June 1940, at the age of fifty. Lionel had signed up with the RAN in September 1940, when he was not quite eighteen, and joined the *Sydney* on 9 July 1941. He was nineteen when he died.

Another Jewish Australian sailor barely survived the sinking of his ship one month later, on 19 December 1941. Able Seaman (later Sub Lieutenant) Stanley Lands of Bellevue Hill, New South Wales, had joined the RAN at twenty years old in August 1940. He was posted to England for anti-submarine training at the land establishment HMS *Osprey*, and was attached to the destroyer HMS *Stanley* when it was sunk by a U-boat in waters west of Portugal. 'It really was a ghastly affair,' Lands wrote home. 'Like a horrible nightmare. When we were hit I was in the cabinet from where we operate on the bridge. There were two of us there at the time and we were blown to the top of the cabinet … We immediately bashed open the door and by that time the ship had broken. When we stepped out of the cabinet it was into the water, or perhaps I should say the oil, which was thick on the surface, and began swimming. That will show you how quick it all was. As far as I can guess, I should think it took no longer than about a minute and a half before she practically vanished.

'The lad with me could not swim, but he had a lifebelt on, so I went to try and help him. Then I suddenly realised that I myself had no lifebelt on, so might endanger both our lives. Seeing a log of wood nearby I swam to that and pushed it to this lad, then just had to swim away as best I could with all my clothes on, and find something to keep me afloat.

'I eventually found another piece of debris and hung on until I heard a voice saying there was room on a big cork float I could hang on to about thirty yards away. So I let go of my log and swam over, guided by their voices. Though it was pitch black in the early hours of the morning and there was a thick coating of stifling thick oil everywhere, I managed to remain fairly calm.

'After about an hour we gradually drifted with the swell and waves out of the oil which had kept us comparatively warm and the sea fairly calm. Then, of course, it became very cold and rough and soon we were hardly able to talk without our teeth chattering. It was not until about another one-and-a-half hours that we were picked up. They said they did not expect to find any survivors at all, what with the explosion and the sheets of flame they saw in the distance.

'As it was, only about one-seventh of our complement were picked up, twenty-five out of 140. At the beginning on our float there were about ten of us, and we could not recognise one another for oil, and could only recognise chattering voices. By the time we were picked up there were only four of us left. A couple went off their rocker and were raving, and the others slipped off saying, "They won't see us in the darkness." "I'm too cold." Gosh, it was horrible.

'One of the four of us had a couple of broken ribs. At first he complained of a pain in the shoulder and then, after a while, said he could not hold on much longer. Fortunately I saw not far away four legs of a table sticking up, so I swam over and brought this table back. We laid his body across the table and put his two arms over the cork float, and I am glad to say he came through OK … Also, one of the lads that sank without a murmur was a particular pal of mine on board. I held him up for about an hour, slapping his face, trying to make him hang on, but eventually I got a cramp in the arm holding him and had to let him go. We were absolutely frozen and exhausted when we were picked up and hauled on board. We could do nothing ourselves and had to be washed by the lads on the ship that picked us up. They washed us in kerosene and shale petrol, and then with soapy water.

'Then they wrapped us up in blankets and we slept through until about midday. One thing, I am fortunate in being an Aussie, and being used to the surf and waves going over my head. Once we were out of the oil patch the waves were coming over our heads and that was when a lot of them became panicky. The same applies, too, when I first slid into the oil, for, instead of gasping, I began to regulate my breathing so as not to swallow any oil.' He was incredibly lucky. 'All I received was a "busted" nose,' he wrote, 'and a few stitches and, naturally, cuts and bruises all over the body.'[13]

The Middle East 1940–1941

Bardia to Tobruk

Paul Cullen was promoted to Major while his battalion was encamped in Egypt, and he led his men into battle against the Italians in January 1941. Mussolini had half a million troops in Egypt, Libya and Abyssinia, and the Australians joined the British attempt to push them back. The fresh troops of the Australian 6th Division replaced the 4th Indian Division, which had driven the enemy out of Sidi Barrani, an Egyptian port on the Mediterranean. The first Australian campaign of the war was a great success. The diggers passed through Sidi Barrani to the village of Sollum, on the Libyan border, where they came under shell fire. The assault came from a battery of Italian medium guns south of Bardia, on the Libyan side, and Major Cullen is claimed to be the first Australian soldier to be hit by an enemy weapon. Cullen was touched by fire from the guns – and nicknamed 'Bardia Bill' by the Australians – but was not seriously wounded. Two days later, he joined the British as they crossed the border, and became the first Australian soldier of the war to step on Libyan sand, before returning to his men for the push west. Dr Clive 'Tom' Selby, Regimental Medical Officer (RMO) to the 2/1st Infantry Battalion, 6th Division, sent a long and detailed letter home describing the subsequent fighting. On 4 January 1941 Selby was outside Bardia. He wrote, 'At 4 am we moved off to the start line following a tape and at 4.30 am our barrage started … It wasn't nearly as noisy as I expected but the shells just seemed to miss one's head; I heard later, they just did! – and as they went past sparks flew out of them and they made a sharp crack.

'Suddenly a tremendous and unbearable thundering in my ear threatened my whole reputation. In a flash, as a drowning man is supposed to see his past, I could see my future – evacuated in disgrace with a minor medical condition. The troops would say I had "chickened out". The thunder was a beetle's footsteps on my eardrum. I pulled my waterproof ground-sheet over my head and, breaking all rules – all lights were strictly forbidden – I shone a torch into my ear. God and the beetle were on my side. The intruder crawled out and I continued my life in forward areas and had many other opportunities for thanksgiving.

'We didn't have a death in the battalion since its formation till fifty yards from the wire, which I put down partly to the way I shooed flies and poked my stick down thousands of drains. In the tank ditch were some funny lights going past which we discovered afterwards were explosive anti-tank bullets and machine guns firing exactly down the ditch. By this time it was almost light … The British Matilda tanks came up and the first one faltered and had to back and fill and then crashed over. That was the most dramatic moment and, Oh boy, what a relief! I got my stretcher bearers to help the engineers to fill the ditch to let the tanks get in. The whole of the attack on the Western Desert pivoted on that little incident's success. Incredible!! When the second one went over, my stretcher bearers followed me out of the ditch and through the wire without faltering. I left some behind, in the ditch to establish a Regimental Aid Post [RAP]. I found some wounded just through the wire and fixed them up and the stretcher bearers, except two, took them back. The battalion had gone on and I went to see if they wanted an aid post further forward. At this time we were in the centre of the enemy's defensive barrage and I can only say it is incredible the way one can walk through the stuff and not get hurt. I actually sheltered behind a thing I found out later was their aiming mark, a wooden tower observation post. I went on and took cover in their second line of defences ... While we were there I got word of some wounded down a gully and we were definitely machine-gunned getting there. I wore a Red Cross brassard. I had the breeze up but the two coves who had come for me used to say "You bastards!" every time a bullet whizzed past and we actually laughed. The little spurts from the bullets in the dust on either side looked like a locust's egg repository on a gum tree branch.

'When I got to the little dugout "X", I found a shell had landed on some of our chaps. They were dropping everywhere around. Even if the Italian infantry had no stomach for fighting, their artillery was first class and one could judge their good morale and our good counter-battery fire from the unhappy sight of dead gun crews still round their guns. An Italian doctor had stopped the bleeding and couldn't do enough for them. Outside the dugout was a low stone wall and behind this were several wounded. I collected the bits of one boy and covered him with a groundsheet to save the feelings of his comrades.

'Poor Sergeant Meredith, the Intelligence Sergeant, had a hand almost off and I stopped and treated him for some time ... I went back and got caught in another barrage on the way to the RAP and found my stretcher bearers and Corporal Kelly had done marvellous work in the tank ditch and by this time ambulances had come up and taken some wounded away. We worked there for a while and then Strutt, my driver, drove Jenny almost down the ravine to "X" and we got some wounded out of the hole with some difficulty. I think they respected my Red Cross armband this time as I was not fired on but when they found the dugout was full of men a sniper with a Breda gun kept popping bursts over the entrance ... We worked then in the ditch and got two Italian doctors and stretcher bearers to fix the hundreds of Italian wounded.

'We got shelled badly but the field ambulance stretcher bearers got Italian trucks and evacuated all except about 100 who had to stay in the ditch all night. We got rid of all the Aussies, though. Field ambulance stretcher bearers were not supposed to work forward of the RAP but their commander ... did not reprimand me for this. It was hard work putting on dressings in dugouts and trucks, sometimes in the dark. I had a bit of bully beef and "turned in" leaving the Italian doctors to look after their own ... Next morning we moved a thousand yards to a concrete strongpoint and were fairly busy. In the afternoon, I got a message that a shell had landed fair in the middle of a pit in which was one of our mortars. Three chaps were blown up ... One chap had his greatcoat covered with mincemeat which had been his best friend. I gave him my coat and a cigarette ... We fixed them up and the bearers took them back and I went down a gully with Sergeant [Allen Vivian] Craske – "Crackers", a most lovable and bright cove, from the anti-tank company ... Things were fairly quiet until we stopped a direct hit on the RAP. It was concrete and we all happened to be in the deep part but it was a funny feeling ... After tea that night, they got me out to see "Crackers", whom some bastard of a sniper had got coming up the gorge where they had accounted for some tanks. He had just died in the ambulance and I confess I was so tired I had a bit of a weep in the dark part of the dugout. My driver and I then had to go and cheer up Dick Digby, the mortar officer, who was blown up with his men, but not hurt, only terribly shocked. That was the most difficult part of the whole show.

'I then brought in the two "Iti" doctors and gave them a meal. That night I couldn't sleep. I had to get up and treat more Italians and after that some men from another battalion arrived and we had to make cocoa and give them treatment until morning ... The most touching part was today. I had to work hard and didn't get breakfast till midday treating a lot of chaps who had wounds and sores but didn't "let on" during the action. I remember one whose feet were absolutely raw but he thought I was too busy to worry.

The coves kept bringing me presents – two fowls, a barometer, an automatic pistol, surgical instruments, etc.'[14]

Selby's letter is noteworthy for its extraordinary clarity and power. Its candour might stem from the fact it was addressed to a soldier brother, Benjamin, who was a lieutenant in the Sydney University Regiment and later a captain in New Guinea, but there seems to be little else like it in Jewish-Australian war-time correspondence. The Australian Jewish press, which had regularly published personal stories of the fighting in World War One, largely restricted itself to printing letters about religious services in exotic locales in World War Two. Among the rare exceptions were two letters from Libya by Lassalle Harris Spielvogel of the 2/5th Infantry Battalion. Lassalle was the son of Nathan Frederick Spielvogel, a well-known Jewish writer and chairman of the Dads' Association formed to look after the interests of serving men. Lassalle's first letter began, 'I am writing on the note paper of the Chief of the Italian Artillery Batteries, as a result of our advance on Bardia ... We began our advance on Bardia at 5 am on 3rd January, after about 140 guns of our artillery had put over a four-hour barrage. The carriers (three) had the job of scouting about 1000 yards in front of the troops to make sure there were no enemy gun posts. Our engineers had done a marvellous job of cutting the wire and making bridges across their Italian tank traps. We were under heavy fire for all the time. The carriers had the proud honour of leading the 5th through the wire. Everything went beautifully until we reached a small valley which the boys have since named "Hell's Valley".

'We had just arrived in this position when a section of Italian mortars and field guns Wiz bang!!!!! Our mortar section went into action and in twenty minutes the engagement was over. Then the prisoners began to roll in – by six o'clock in the evening 16 000 prisoners had been taken. Only one battery of guns was still firing on us and our guns could not find them until a Lysander gave them their range and most of them went to whichever portion of Hell is reserved for Italians … The next morning we did our job. Two carriers … were sent out to clean out a machine-gun post that was holding up our infantry advance. We charged over a hill and straight at a wall that was lined with machine guns about twenty yards apart. After Corporal Frankie Walker (my carrier commander) had fired thirty shots into the first gun they started to run out like rats from burrows. Altogether the two carriers are credited with bringing in 700 prisoners. This then allowed our advance to go on. We had a couple of bullet marks on the carrier but the armour-plate is so good that it hardly marked it. The Italians are supposed to have had about sixteen Brigades.' Spielvogel described himself as 'well and happy and looking forward to our next little bout with the enemy with keen anticipation'.[15]

During the battle for Bardia, Lance Corporal Cyril Solomon Pearlman, a Ballarat-born Jewish former schoolteacher with the 2/6th Infantry Battalion, ran an observation post for two days under heavy shellfire. He received a Military Medal for his work which 'helped to make possible control of the operations and materially influenced the conduct of the battle'.[16] Pearlman, who was later promoted to captain, had a sister, Lieutenant Celia Pearlman, serving with the Australian Army Nursing Service in the Middle East, as well as a brother in the 2/14th Battalion and another in the 15th Field Ambulance.

The 6th Division took Tobruk on 22 January and Benghazi on 7 February 1941. In March Lassalle Spielvogel wrote, 'At Bardia the Italians left hundreds of wonderful diesel trucks and thousands of gallons of desiline (Diesel fuel), however they did what the Russians did to Napoleon at Moscow – burnt everything trucks, cars, fuel, petrol, oil and all that might prove of any use as a means of transport … Our RAA Forces did a wonderful job. Since we have been in the front we have not seen one Italian plane. A few days ago our armoured tanks captured sixty-five enemy planes. I received a letter from [brother Phil Spielvogel] a few days ago. He reports the only trouble he has was the price of beer at Papua – anyway he is better off than we are – we get none!! ... We were very short of water but the Italians were very decent – they left us gallons of it. I had my first decent wash for nearly a month. Tobruk Harbour is excellent and when a number of sunken vessels are removed it will be very valuable. We are now camped right alongside the sea – but it has been bitterly cold – so no swimming. It is said here that we will be doing a victory march in July – and that all Colonial troops will be home by September.'[17] But the only men home by September were the wounded and the sick.

Oddly, there was a semblance of Jewish communal life at Tobruk, where the docks were worked by Palestinian stevedores, and the Polish Brigade, which included a number of Jews, assisted in the defence of the city. The British Rabbi Louis Isaac Rabinowitz conducted a service at the Tobruk synagogue that was attended by fifty Jews from various armies.[18] Rabbi Israel Brodie, once a minister in Melbourne but now a chaplain with the RAF, was also at Tobruk until June. The city was put to siege on 10 April 1941, when it was attacked by German and Italian troops under the command of Lieutenant General Erwin Rommel. On the first day of the siege, Dr Zelman Schwartz, one of Melbourne's leading eye specialists and a captain in the AAMC, was killed. The men dug in and Tobruk held out. Sergeant Rupert Michaelis wrote home to his mates at Cronulla Surf Club to describe his dugout. The *Sydney Morning Herald* obtained his letter and reported: 'Michaelis is proud of his modern war-time dwelling-place. Built beneath solid rock, over which there is about three to four feet of earth, his dugout, like others, is about 9ft by 5ft and electric light has been installed. Ventilation and natural light is not forgotten, Michaelis's method of obtaining this being through the construction of a window and the installation of a concrete pipe, 4-inch in diameter, with a kerosene tin on top. Sergeant Michaelis still has his sleeping bag and mosquito net, the only one in his "district." The net is invaluable, he says, against the attacks of flies.'[19]

On 15 June, Bombardier Robert Alick Shmith, a Jewish artilleryman from Melbourne who had been Mentioned in Despatches, was killed in the siege. 'Just how bad was life in Tobruk?' asked Brigadier Philip Masel of the 2/28th Battalion. 'Tobruk had developed into a war of nerves and in such circumstances every man reacts differently. Furthermore, the reaction depended upon the individual's job. The fighting troops were not often a target for the 3317 German planes which appeared over Tobruk from April to September, but they were subjected to the strain of patrols and shelling. The B echelon troops did not have to patrol, but they did have to go regularly into the much bombed town to obtain stores and supplies. Curiously enough, few men seemed to envy the job of others. Storemen preferred to be dive-bombed; riflemen preferred to go on patrol.

'Everybody had to put up with the dust, the flies and fleas, and the uncertainty of the future. Everybody had to suffer the extreme shortage of water and the unpalatability of the canned rations. With the possible exception of the bully beef, the food – the sausages, the herrings in tomato sauce, and the baked beans – were all singularly unappetising. Canned fruit, when it appeared, was on the scale of one tin to eighteen men.

'There was little in the way of serious disease; but there was plenty of dysentery and sandfly fever, and every scratch was likely to fester and was always slow to heal. Letters from and to home were the only recreation, and the occasional loss of mail between Alexandria and Tobruk was treated as a major disaster.

'For the riflemen this was a war by night. By day they had to dig in the heat and the dust – dig down through rocky stratum which threatened to break their backs and their shovels. All they had to look at was the brown, sun-baked desert which scarcely seemed to be worth an ounce of sweat let alone a drop of blood ...

But something had sprouted in the sand desert: a sense of reliance on the next chap ... the basis of esprit de corps. Oddly enough, another great salvation came from the enemy, from the notorious Lord Haw-Haw whose nightly broadcasts were heard with the greatest pleasure by those whom he was addressing as "rats".'[20]

Lord Haw-Haw was the nickname given to William Joyce, a former member of the British Union of Fascists who broadcast propaganda for the Nazis throughout the war and was hanged as a traitor in 1946, still blaming the Jews. Joyce dubbed the Allied defenders of Tobruk 'poor desert rats' and the diggers adopted the name with pride. The 'Rats of Tobruk' even struck their own unofficial medal, made from pieces of a downed German bomber and featuring the image of a rat sitting upright and looking curiously like a kangaroo.

By July 1941, a sign on the wall of the synagogue at Tobruk read 'Out of bounds, Jewish soldiers'. When it was visited by David Benjamin, now a major, the building had been abandoned. Everything portable had been removed, from the seating to the light fixtures. All that remained was the *bimah* and an empty ark without a curtain, and pages from prayer books and torn covers scattered about the floor. The study hall, or *beth midrash*, had been hit by a bomb. Major Benjamin made a souvenir of a vermillion envelope and a blank receipt form inscribed 'Comunita Israelitica, Tobruk', and wrote with wonder that 'even in an outpost of Italian Empire there was a synagogue – somewhere where a wandering soldier could go and be a Jew in the house of God'.[21] Benjamin knew a number of other Jewish soldiers at Tobruk, including Michaelis; Colin Pura, a journalist who later became editor of the troops' newspaper *Guinea Gold*; Dr Stan Goulston, who was awarded the Military Cross for his actions as medical officer to the 2/1st Pioneer Battalion; and Captain Hedley Freedman, son of the late military chaplain Rabbi David Freedman, and a great friend of Masel, whom he was to succeed as adjutant of the 2/28th Battalion.

So in September 1941, in the absence of a chaplain, Major Benjamin chose to hold a *Rosh Hashanah* service at Tobruk. 'I turned up at the concrete cave in fear and trembling,' he wrote home. 'How was "my baby," our New Year Service going to turn out. It turned out very well indeed. Thirty-one men were there, British and Australian. The majority of them I did not know ... We started off at 11 am and finished at 11.45. We had to stand all the time as the British Unit, which lent us a cave, could not lend us chairs. The Hebrew part was read by Sergeant [Maurice] Sherwood, a Palestinian, serving with the AIF and one of the Divisional interpreters. He read it very nicely, but of course with Sephardic pronunciation. That did not matter to me as I can now follow it pretty well, but it was a little troublesome to some others who could not. Lieutenant Freedman (son of the Rabbi) couldn't be there for operational reasons so Sherwood substituted. The latter will read for us on *Yom Kippur*. The English part was shared among four of us, Captain Rose (a Melbourne MO), Rupert [Michaelis] and Colin [Pura] and myself. I read the Prayer for the Royal Family and announced the pages in the Prayer Book. Unhappily, we were short of books.'[22] There were other Jewish Australians at Tobruk who may not have attended the service, among them Sydney-born Albert Rosen, who had held a commission in the militia before the war but enlisted in the AIF as a private. Rosen was seven months in Tobruk, and quickly made his way back up the ranks to lieutenant.

But even rats cannot hold out forever. Most of the Australians evacuated Tobruk between August and October, and were replaced by British troops. Masel wrote, 'For the first time a man noticed that his mate had lost a stone or more in weight; that his body was marked with desert sores that refused to heal; that his clothing was reduced to a last faded, tattered pair of shorts and a shirt. For the first time one became conscious of a craving for eggs and chocolate – a craving so strong that it took months to be satisfied. Above all, one lost one's veneer of fatalism, patience and philosophy. To hell with the thought of chasing Rommel back to Derna! All that mattered now was to get aboard that warship before Higher Command changed its mind … My unhappiest moment in Tobruk was when I was told that Dick Legrove and myself, together with ten ORs, were to remain behind for a few days to assist the [British] to settle in.'[23]

The attrition of the siege took its toll on every man. At Rabbi Goldman's Purim service in Palestine the following year, 'The congregation included a squad of diggers just back from Tobruk,' he said. 'As it eventually became obvious, most of them neither had attended Purim Services before, nor did they know the ritual. For, when during the reading of the *Magillah*, the mention of the name of Haman evoked the traditional stamping by the congregation and also in this instance, a loud rattling by the children, the Diggers promptly dived under seats. Ruefully they confessed noise was a warning of an air raid.'[24]

Fighting in Greece

In October 1940 the Italians had invaded Greece, only to be forced out by the Greeks. The Germans eventually went to help their hapless ally and the British, joined by Australians and others, came to the aid of the Greeks. At the same time as Rommel and his men bombarded Tobruk, the Germans drove Allied troops from the Aliakmon River, forcing them to retreat to the Thermopylae Line. The defenders of Greece included the Australian 2/2nd Battalion, where Major Paul Cullen was now second-in-command.

Cullen's men fought a rear-guard action against the Nazis at Tempe Gorge in Northern Thessaly on 18 April 1941. Cullen wrote: 'My mate, Sergeant Tanner, hit the third enemy tank with his anti-tank rifle, but the bullets were just bouncing back. It was that close … We were forced back [and] I was facing the front, like all good soldiers should, leaning forward, in a sunken road with my men, and we only had rifles, for God's sake, when a German tank came round the corner and turned its turret in our direction … fired a burst of machine-fire, killed the two men alongside me, and it went through the breast pocket of my tunic, and clipped the lucky sovereign that Mummy had given me, to her darling little Paul, to protect me. The last two German tanks in that area approached the highway [to Larisa]. They were only about a couple of hundred yards away, and down that highway the Anzac corps was departing.

'All that was left between these last two German tanks and the highway behind was an area of ploughed field about the size of a couple of football fields. I can see it now with a line of poplar trees at the back, and behind the poplar trees was the highway, and the Anzac Corps was rumbling along it … the transport officer, lined up his B echelon. "B echelon" is the transport drivers, the cooks, the clerks, batmen, few signallers, etc. He lined them up and as the two tanks approached he fired a volley, of pistols for God's sake, against these wonderful German Mark 4 tanks. I shouldn't think the tanks even knew they had been fired at … Corporal Bill Cameron, a signal corporal, had a twenty-litre can of petrol and his cigarette lighter and he scrambled aboard the leading tank and tried to light the petrol but couldn't. There is nothing tanks like less than having petrol poured over them, so the two tanks wheeled round within fifty yards of the highway. As they wheeled round to go back they threw Corporal Cameron off into the ploughed field and one of the tanks ran over him … They ran over his thigh but the pressure per square inch of a tank is not that great and in a ploughed field he wasn't killed. [The tanks] scuttled but by then the Anzac corps had gone.'[25]

Robert Patkin was at Brallos Pass on 22 April, when the routed Allied troops were ordered to evacuate to Crete. Patkin was among the men charged with delaying the German advance to cover for the withdrawal. 'At this stage, we had no air force left,' he wrote, 'so therefore we had no air cover whatsoever, which gave the Germans an absolute free hand to machine-gun and bomb us with Stukas and Messerschmitts and our losses began to grow … overnight we withdrew down the peninsula. Early in the morning, in convoy, my company was about to cross the Corinth Canal when we were detached from the main force by an English brigadier and told that we were to defend the Corinth bridge. We set up positions on the northern side of the bridge (which is the Athens side) and the Allied army rolled across the canal and were evacuated or captured, as the case may be, some days later. But in the meantime, we took up defensive measures and on 26 April 1941, early in the morning, were very heavily strafed by Messerschmitts and following the strafing, German transport planes came over and dumped the German paratroopers on top of us. We were a company of approximately 120 men. The Germans had 2000 paratroopers. It was a very fierce battle on the ground, but before the paratroopers had actually hit the ground we were able to use, with great effect, the Thompson submachine gun (which the American gangsters used in Prohibition days). These were marvellous weapons to shoot the paratroopers as they came down. Finally they landed, and of course we were completely outnumbered and many of our men were wounded and killed …

'Because of the number of Germans that landed on top of us an organised defence was not possible. So the order was given, "Every man for himself". Myself, and three men from my platoon decided to try and make it to the hills, which would have been three or four miles away. But to get to the hills we had to go through a vineyard which would have been perhaps thirty or forty acres in the immediate area of the paratroop drop. We had to climb up an embankment, cross a railway line, go down the embankment to get into this vineyard, where we felt we would get cover and crawl through and see what was on the other side, and eventually make the hills in the distance. However, as we crossed over the railway line, immediately below us were two German paratroopers with their automatic weapons pointed at us. They were on my extreme left at the bottom of the mound we were clambering over. They fired at us and threw grenades. A friend, Keith Carter, was on my immediate left, and unfortunately for him, he took the full brunt of the fire and was killed instantly. Pieces of him splattered across myself and my other two men and we went to ground and lay down, pretending that we had been shot. The Germans were still on their knees with their weapons pointed at us, but they stopped firing, thinking no doubt, that they had killed the lot of us. After some minutes they moved away, and we were left to ourselves. We then decided to lay still until evening and escape during the night-time, but this was not to be, because a German patrol came along and kicked us back into life and we were captured.'[26]

The Allies were pushed out of mainland Greece and then Crete. Cullen returned to Australia via Ceylon. The next time he was to fight would be as Lieutenant Colonel Cullen in New Guinea.

Back in the Middle East

Many Australian troops had remained in the Middle East. Trooper Hyman ('Hymie') Pearlman was a Jewish wool-classer from Bog-gabri, New South Wales, who had served in the Australian Light Horse before the war. He joined the AIF in 1939, at the age of twenty-seven, as a trooper in the 2/7th Australian Cavalry Regiment, and reached Palestine in January 1941. Pearlman, who kept a detailed diary throughout his eventful years in the army, took leave in Tel Aviv and met with the Bravermans, relatives of family friends. 'As the local people robbed the Australian soldiers in a shameful fashion I did a lot of shopping with Ben [Braverman] who was very fluent in Hebrew, French, Yiddish and Arabic,' wrote Pearlman. 'I could buy at half the price with Ben's assistance.' He toured Jerusalem, Jericho and the Red Sea, then the mosques and pyramids of Egypt. While the infantry was fighting in Libya, the Light Horse (now, of course, motorised) waited in their camps for equipment to arrive. Pearlman took eight days' leave at Passover and stayed at the Victoria Hotel in Cairo with a Jewish airman, Flying Officer Keith Nettheim. They joined a local family for the *Seder* nights and met 'a Jewish chap named Mathew' who introduced them to a couple of Egyptian girls 'with whom we did some big courting', wrote Pearlman.[27] At the fall of Greece, Pearlman and the Light Horse shipped out to Cyprus.

Still in the Middle East, Lassalle Spielvogel managed to visit a kibbutz. 'It is almost incredible seeing what those people have done,' he wrote. 'Nine years ago, twelve families of seventy-two Jews arrived from Poland and bought 200 acres of land. Now there are 520 souls, and they have 500 acres. No one in the settlement is given money unless it is for the annual fourteen days leave. They make their own clothes, shoes, build their own homes from wood that is grown on their own land and cut at the saw mills. This group had seventy cows and a stud farm of horses. They also had a concrete factory. There were hundreds of poultry and incubators for turkeys and ducks. The flower nursery was very complete – the flowers are sent to Tel Aviv and Jerusalem for sale. The communal nursery for the children is conducted by trained nurses who look after the kiddies whilst the parents are at work. The whole settlement has its meals in one big dining room. It would be useful if some of our Australian farmers could be shown how 520 people on 500 acres of land pay £2000 a year interest on the loan and still show profit. It is a really wonderful place. The lucerne is waist-high.'[28]

Gunner Norman Joseph of Bondi continued a tradition as old as the Boer War when he disembarked in Palestine in 1941 and met his sister, Sister Zeryl Joseph, a nurse attached to the Queen

Alexandra Imperial Military Nursing Service. With a number of other Jewish soldiers, Joseph went to Rehovot for *Yom Kippur*. 'Col Milingen was called to hold the *Torah* aloft,' he wrote, 'and make a complete circle and I was given the dressing of the *Torah*. Myer Morris, of Newcastle, took us to another *shule*, where they were two-and-a-half hours ahead with the *davenning* – so all went home for a rest ... I went home with a Pole and his wife; they had resided in Palestine for seventeen years.'[29] Cecil David Super, a fur-cutter from North Carlton, wrote home: 'I have arrived in Cairo for *Rosh Hashanah* and I am now waiting in the crowded Jewish Club, there being about 350 to 400 Jewish soldiers gathered there from all corners of the British Empire. I sat there talking, to an Australian Lieutenant whom I knew, when I noticed an air force officer enter. He looked very smart. I recognised him immediately, despite the fact that he had shaven his beard off. It was Rabbi [Israel] Brodie, formerly of Melbourne. I stood up and went over to him. He recognised me immediately and stretched out his hand and said "Cecil, Cecil", as if he could hardly believe his eyes; at the same time he put his left arm around my shoulders ... For a moment or two we were too full of emotion to speak. Then we had a good old chat about different things, including good old Aussie. We then adjourned to the Synagogue which the Club contained. There was a large congregation of soldiers of all ranks from a Lieutenant Colonel downwards. The service began, and I can say without exaggeration that it gave me an indescribable thrill to hear Rabbi Brodie's voice again. He gave us a rousing sermon, one of his usual dramatic and eloquent speeches, full of fire and magnificent language. It was worth the whole journey through the desert to hear that one service. I have always been an admirer of his, but never in my wildest dreams did I expect to hear him preach in Cairo on *Rosh Hashanah*.'[30]

Hymie Pearlman saw no action – but most of the tourist sites – in Cyprus, and the Light Horse was shipped back to Haifa in August 1941 to then spend months waiting around in Syria. Pearlman took leave in Tel Aviv and met a girl who spoke English, French, German, Arabic and Hebrew. 'She is very keen to get married,' wrote Pearlman, 'and is quite open about it, and even stressed what a wonderful wife she would make me. Poor girl, I felt sorry for her ... She quoted the three theories on essentials a good wife requires, as written by Freud (a companion, a good cook and a passionate mistress). Well, well.'[31]

Pearlman was always hungry for the company of women. In January 1942 he was in Tel Aviv for the last time, waiting to finally be shipped to battle, when he found out that Lieutenant Celia Pearlman, a stranger to him, was serving at 7 Australian General Hospital in Rehovot, and applied for leave to visit her on the grounds that she was his cousin (which she was not). 'She turned out to be quite a nice little girl and was pleased to see me,' he wrote. 'She was expecting her brother when my name was announced and got a shock to see a stranger at the door ... Sister Pearlman's brother Cyril won a MM.'[32]

Some Jewish soldiers found war brides in the Middle East. Sergeant Phillip Solomons AIF of Adelaide married Betty Tamches, the joint secretary of the Jewish Welfare Club in Cairo. His wife spoke four languages – French, English, Hebrew and Arabic – and her arrival in Adelaide provoked some local curiosity. After gentle questioning from a women's-page journalist, Betty pronounced Australian food as 'good'. The meat was lovely, she said, although prepared a little differently from Egypt, and she thought perhaps Australian women chose more muted colours for their clothes.[33]

In March Sergeant Raymond Shaw, a pilot with 450 Squadron RAAF, had just returned to the fighting from forty-eight hours' leave in Alexandria and Cairo when he wrote home: 'I travelled over 1300 miles by air just for that forty-eight hours, a break from the dust sand and storms of the desert, the pleasure to put on clean clothes (my blue uniform), to wash, to sleep between sheets and to order what food I desire – prawns and chicken – to go dancing with a charming Jewish girl I met in Alexandria. She is very pretty and attractive French ... All this I crammed into forty-eight hours and then back to Libya and fighting with a real charming dust storm to welcome me back.'[34]

Shaw, whose father ran the Hotel Allawah in Allawah, New South Wales, was a Jewish former display designer who enlisted in the RAAF as 'C of E'. He had joined up at eighteen years old in May 1940 and trained in the UK as a fighter pilot. He had arrived in the Middle East in September 1941, and was still bursting with bravado and the invulnerability of youth. In March 1942 he wrote, 'The other day while on patrol the Germans and Italians tried to dive bomb Tobruk which is visited pretty often and we got into a glorious dogfight, although unfortunately out to sea. After being attacked by some German fighters I managed to beat them off and damaged one and then diving down I saw a Macchi 202 (the latest Italian fighter and very good) attacking one of our planes from behind. I turned and dived on him and shot him down spinning with black smoke into the sea and also saved our plane. I was very pleased and at the present I am the top scorer in the squadron having shot the most planes down since the squadron has been up the desert. This is my second plane, the other being a German bomber since I have joined this squadron about six weeks ago.' Shaw advised his father, to 'do what war work you can now as the Japs are at New Guinea for an attack on Australia. Take my rifles out of the old kit bag – oil them and get plenty of ammunition, also [dig] slit trenches ... I trust since I have shot these planes down that you will be proud of me and I have destroyed about combined £50 000 of German products besides their crew and that if you remember when I first asked you to sign the recruiting paper was what I set out to do – much more damage than if I was in the army as what you wanted me to do.'

Shaw displayed the typical concerns of a young pilot – 'My

moustache is growing strongly,' he wrote, 'although fairly fair' – and an anxious Australian, fighting halfway across the world: 'I am constantly hoping to come back home and have a go at the yellow B—,' he wrote, 'however I am glad to read about American reinforcements constantly arriving and now General MacArthur – the Japs will never take Aussie.' He believed he had a future. 'I have been recommended thru the CO for a commission, have taken a medical and everything is definitely on the way at last – I am the senior sergeant here – have the most flying experience, have shot the most planes down and am leading formations of fighters, a job which is always done by a senior officer and so very soon I should be an officer. I like this Australian Squadron very much – there is a camaraderie, good feeling of fellowship which is lacking in English squadrons.'[35]

Later in the month, he wrote, 'So far since I joined the squadron I have shot down a Jun 88 (German high-speed bomber), a Macchi 202 (an Ity high-speed fighter) and damaged a Messerschmitt 109F (a German latest high-speed fighter). The latter occurred in a "show" when I was attacked by six of them and a running fight took place for about eighty miles. It was very hectic with the Germans doing their utmost to get rid of an accursed Australian for they know Australians are fighting against them and they don't like it. However everything came off alright. I never got hit but I put a good burst into one of them and he fell away black smoke pouring out and so with that they broke off and home I came a very relieved young boy.'[36] Shaw was shot down over Libya on 29 May. 'A fellow member of his Unit came to visit my mother after the war,' wrote his sister, 'and told us the shocking story, of how his plane was discovered two days after he was shot down, and he was still in it, and alive, but he died on the operating table. When I think of him sick, injured in the heat of the desert with no water, my heart breaks. I wish we had not been party to that awful information.'[37]

War in the Pacific

The fall of Singapore

The most catastrophic moment of the war for Australia was the fall of Singapore in February 1942. Australia's post–World War One defence policy had pivoted around Britain's dubious idea of a 'Fortress Singapore', a base in South-East Asia from which British and Commonwealth troops might hold off any enemy advance towards Australia and deny the Japanese navy command of the sea. By 1941 it was clear that a successful defence of Singapore would have to take in the whole of the Malay peninsula, and British, Australian and Indian troops were despatched to South-East Asia. Melbourne-born Captain Dr Victor Brand was posted as MO to the 2/29th Infantry battalion, which sailed for Singapore as part of the 8th Division in July 1941. Brand and his men were encamped at Segamat, Malaya, halfway between Kuala Lumpur and Singapore, when Japan entered the war in December, all but simultaneously attacking the US fleet in Pearl Harbor and landing in the Philippines, Thailand, Malaya and Hong Kong. The Japanese thrust proved ferocious and unstoppable, but the 8th Division struggled to help hold them off. Brand kept a corrosively honest and angry diary of his part in the brief, bloody and terrible Malaya Campaign, beginning on 17 January 1942, when the 2/29th went to oppose the Japanese who had landed at Muar. On his way to the battle, Brand met the chaotic flight of Indian troops under enemy mortar fire, pursued by Japanese tanks. Australian anti-tank guns knocked out some of the Japanese armour, briefly delaying the encroaching slaughter, but on the evening of 18 January, wrote Brand, 'We felt pretty sure that the Japanese would not let the night pass without an attack, for they had already been held up for twenty-four hours … Suddenly from the C Coy front a solitary voice screamed out horribly – "They got me – Oh they got me!" Another few minutes of intense silence and then a terrible outcry – Japanese yells and screams, bursting grenades – then the yells of our men – "Come on you yellow bastards!" This lasted for some time. The Japanese made two or three determined attacks but each was driven off without yielding an inch of ground. The night was pitch black, and the wounded brought to the RAP had to be dressed by touch – a horrible job.'

The battle drove men insane. 'Scotty McGovern was brought over with four or five bayonet wounds,' wrote Brand, 'and he gave me a hair-raising few minutes as I felt for his wounds. "Doctor – you must believe me for the sake of the other boys," he whispered intensely in an eerie Irish accent. "That Major and his black men; they're signalling to them. They buried me alive!" – he repeated. He appeared to believe that he had been buried alive and was dead, and my hair stood on end and my spine tingled. He had some crazy idea that Major Whitman and his Indian sappers were Fifth Columnists, and in spite of my commands to keep quiet, he persistently reiterated his terrible charges. The other wounded had to be dressed and I was infuriated to find that one body I was pawing proved to be a dead Japanese.'

The next day, Brand worked without shelter under a rain of mortars, saved scores of men's lives and refused to leave behind the wounded when the battalion withdrew. He was awarded an MC for his heroism, but he almost cracked. 'Shells began to fall on and around our position,' he wrote. 'The barrage was severe and it was a terrible thing for men who had never before experienced shell fire. We could hear the faint reports of the guns in the distance and then the crescendo scream of the shells and the ear-splitting crash of the burst. The actual blast of the explosions was quite severe. Everyone took cover in their trenches. The Indians who had no trenches dug, were panic stricken. Some piled in on top of our wounded, others ran around hysterically and refused to lie down ... When the barrage ceased, the RAP was flooded with wounded, and a few trucks were sent off with casualties to try and get through to Bakri … While we were loading these trucks, Indians, wounded and unwounded, stormed us, crying, pleading to be taken, and they had to be kept off by force … Fighting was heavy; automatic fire seemed to come from all directions. Mortaring was constant and an artillery barrage began to open up. The area became a frightful shambles. Wounded and killed were lying everywhere. Wounded were being twice and thrice wounded in the trucks … There were fearful sights. I can never forget one of our men who was wounded in the neck. I found him pacing aimlessly along the road, his swollen tongue protruding from his mouth. I could do nothing but give him some morphia and beg him to sit down and rest. During this time messages were coming through by wireless encouraging us with news that relief was coming. But as time went on we lost hope.

'Passing by the ambulance Pte Browning pointed to his foot with a wry smile and said "They got me again, Doc!" I had to hurry away to restrain my emotion, but when I saw Lieut. Hackney I broke down. I remember crying bitterly and repeating "They're machine-gunning the wounded in the trucks" while Hackney stroked my hand and muttered "Don't worry, there's help coming soon". I left him and rushed away to find Lt. Col. Anderson. Still crying I tried to say something to Major Kidd lying on the roadsides. He must have thought I was mad.'

Later, wrote Brand, 'Lynch and I had given up all hope of getting out alive and I think most of the others felt the same. We had kept jokes going, but now when our eyes met we would shake our heads grimly. I wondered how my wife would take it and felt sad and desperate. A stretcher bearer told us that wounded were collecting at a house about thirty yards down the road, and as Lynch and I walked towards it the scream of a shell sent us to the ground. It burst near us and Lynch said "It got me". We found that he had a long deep slash on his right ankle, but luckily no bones were broken. I put him in a nice deep drain, waist deep in water and as I went off, his face parted the bushes and peering out he called after me "If anything happens don't forget to give me the drum". As I was working under this house we heard some trucks on the road suddenly begin to start up, and I saw the ambulance move up the road. Word came through that Lt.-Col. Anderson had ordered a withdrawal to the north. All wounded who could not walk were to be left in the trucks. I later heard that the ambulance had made a desperate dash on to the bridge where it was met with such a heavy burst of fire that it went over into the river.

'I went up and got Lynch out of his drain and we began to walk through the rubber together with some walking wounded. One man with an arm wounded supported Lynch on one side whilst I held him on the other. After some distance we came to a stream – a branch of the Simpang Kin. As we approached I asked Lynch if he could swim. He said "No", so I told him to grasp our backs and kick his legs and we plunged into the water without losing a step or waiting to discard any weight. I immediately went under and when I rose saw my tin hat floating down stream. Out of the corner of my eye I could see men struggling in the water, and a plane swooping down with its guns rattling. Many men were drowned here, but somehow we got across.'[38]

Within weeks, the Australians had been pushed to the tip of the peninsula. On 8 February, the Japanese invasion force crossed the straits into Singapore, driving the Australians to the south coast. The next day Neville Milston, a Jewish signaller from Leichhardt, New South Wales, wrote, 'Crowded roads with trucks troops on side of road. Indians panicked at opening of shell bombing, ran across road, some were knocked down or crushed between trucks. One pleaded with me, and I let him get on back of our vehicle. Glow in sky very pronounced, from fires, shelling … Heavy bombing all day.' On 11 February Milston woke to find his unit gone and 'MG and rifle bullets whizzing just overhead, Japs in extreme proximity'. He searched for his unit all morning, but paused for a drink at Raffles at 10.20 am. On 13 February, he was sent up as infantry attached to anti-tank guns. On Orchard Road in the after-noon, there was 'fire just going out from Armd Car being shelled. Police Station opposite just bombed, eight buried by our gun crew. Search for snipers in A/car that evening'. The next day he found 'AIF shot dead in gutter, two Malay police dead in Police Station'.[39] On 15 February, British troops down the road raised the white flag.

When Singapore fell after only seventy days of fighting in the Malay peninsula, Winston Churchill called it the worst disaster in British military history. The British commander, Lieutenant General Arthur Percival, unconditionally surrendered on behalf of all Allied troops, and nearly 15 000 Australians – many of whom had never fired a shot – were captured. But Maurice Ashkanasy, Assistant Adjutant General for the AIF in Malaya, swore he would never be taken prisoner. 'I walked down to the waterfront through Japanese lines,' he said, 'picking up a party of English soldiers along the way. We secured a still usable lifeboat from a ship that had been bombed and sunk and was resting against a jetty. There were forty-two of us in the boat. To avoid the Japanese, we decided not to go to the nearest point but to go to Intraplura River further to the north. We rowed for eighty miles, all taking turns, half-hour on, one hour resting. We rowed through a minefield, bailing all the while because the boat was leaking. At Karimon Island in mid Sumatra we were able to get two baskets of limes and two of green peanuts. We lived on them for five days. After five days we met an Assistant Dutch Commissioner who was waiting at the entrance of a river to surrender to the Japanese. I made an agreement on behalf of King George with Queen Wilhelmina by selling our lifeboat to the Dutch navy for towage up the river. For five days they towed us towards an RAF station at Pakenbaroe.

'As our boat came around the bend in the river in the late afternoon we sighted a bus, with the engine running, full of RAF personnel, and two officers racing for a car. They thought we were the Japanese. They said some extremely rude things to us. Two minutes later and we would have missed them. They were the last evacuating party. We went over the Sumatra mountains to Fort de Kock where we were given food and transport to Padang on the West Coast of Sumatra. I was endeavouring to get a Chinese junk to sail the Indian Ocean. An old British cruiser *Danair* pulled in and took us off. We landed in Java where the Battle of Java was taking place. We managed to get on to a Dutch cargo vessel escaping to Australia. We were bombed on the way but the ship made it to Fremantle. We reached Australia three weeks after the fall of Singapore.'[40]

Japan's entry into the war challenged many young Australian men who had not yet volunteered to serve overseas. For the first time, there was a chance that Australia itself might be threatened. Dr Geoffrey Kaye, a Jewish medical practitioner from Melbourne, wrote to his sister Vera Silberberg from 2 Australian General Hospital in the Middle East to advise her on a military future for her sons, John and Frank. He said it was time for them to sign up, if the family agreed. 'I had hoped, most devoutly, that the need might not after all arise,' wrote Kaye who had joined the RAAMC in November 1939. 'When I enlisted, I hoped for a short, even if a sharp, war.' However, 'There is in our family a certain tradition of giving service when it is required. We have never been military-minded people, nor should I imagine that (with exceptions, of course) we have made very good soldiers. But we have taken our part and done our best ... I can well imagine that John and Frank are anxious to do as much as their seniors have done.* There is the

---

*   Geoffrey Kaye's elder brother, Gerald Kaye, was born in Melbourne but moved to London, where he served in the Westminster Dragoons from 1911–13. He fought with distinction in the British Army in World War One and reached the rank of major. During World War Two, he trained troops in Australia. Kaye's grandfather was in the Prussian Guards.

further consideration that they are young, and of an age to see the element of adventure in soldiering. God wot, it is not very apparent to those of us who are older.' Kaye had an eye to the future. 'It will not be easy to live in the post-war world,' he went on, 'knowing that one has had no part in its birth-pangs ... If we lose, our world lapses into a cosmic asylum for criminal lunacy. We cannot escape this dilemma ... Is it not obvious how your lads, now that they are old enough to make their own decisions, will also decide?'[41]

Frank Silberberg joined the navy, John Silberberg went to the RAAF.

Changi and the Burma Railway

By February 1942 Australian troops were in desperate need of rein-forcements, in part because about 15 000 men of the 8th Division of the 2nd AIF had disappeared behind barbed wire in Changi, where they were held among the 87 000 POWs captured by the Japanese during the invasions of Malaya, Singapore and the Dutch East Indies. There was a jail at Changi, built by the British colonial authorities in 1936, but most POWs were kept in camps nearby, with Australians largely confined to the former British barracks at Selarang. There were Jews in every camp. By the end of the war, there was even a synagogue, Ohel Jacob, built in Changi to serve a congregation which worshipped under the Dutch Rabbi Chaim Nussbaum.

The Japanese had never planned to take such a large number of prisoners, and at first had no idea what to do with them. In May 1942 when a chance came to leave behind the boredom of Changi for an unknown destination, many prisoners were excited and eager to go. In his diary Milston wrote, 'Much preparation today, packing gear etc, for move tomorrow of about 2000 AIF. Were addressed by Brigadier Callaghan acting CO AIF. Informed us that we were not going on a pleasure cruise, and neither were we going straight home to Australia. However his speech seemed to indicate that we were going on a journey whose ultimate destination was good old Aussie ... Took with us as much plain rice as we wished, a meat, rice and veg pie in a tin, four biscuits and some peanuts, for the rest of the day. Marched up to the main square of the camp and waited for the trucks. Boarded vehicles with the packs of the force, 750 of us going, first with the gear, the remainder of the 3000 following at 11.30 and 2.30 that day. We arrived at the wharves about 8.40 or so. The docks have had a terrible knocking about some of the concrete sheds with steel and iron girders being completely razed to the ground. The whole day we sat around in the sun, trying to get what little shade we could. We were on a very dirty oily tarry piece of ground opposite the wharf, where the ship we later boarded was berthed. Indian and Malay labourers were loading coal on to trucks and pushing them to some other place. The rest of the force arrived during the day, having being transported in large trucks. About 6.30 we commenced to form up to move on board. The ship was a cargo vessel, named the *Toyohashi Maru* ... Some of us had to give a hand to load flour, and clothes, on board by means of a sling. Just after midnight we were given a meal of rice and meat and veg (cold) from tins. We moved up the gangplank very slowly and moved across the crowded decks to one of the hatchway entrances. Down below was as hot as Hades, the hold having been divided up into small compartments wherein to sleep and put our gear. Straw mats were spread on the floor, the roof in some partitions being about 3'6" high, in others 4'6" high, with an iron ceiling making the heat almost unbearable. It was electrically lit even in the day, as in this hold, being a small one, light came through the one solitary entrance only. We slept as if dead that night, and next morning awoke covered with sweat and feeling as though we were in a Turkish bath. It was very crowded some having no or little opportunity to stretch out their legs when lying down ... Most of our company was moved from this hold at 12 am. Friday to the biggest hold on the ship. The new quarters were exceptionally cramped, with a very low wooden ceiling, but as this hold has two entrances and boards raised on deck and air vents it is cooler than the other we were first in. The foodstuffs and clothes are kept on the floor below us and when goods have to be hauled out which occurs every day for the kitchens, some chaps have to move their gear so as to allow the boards under them to be removed ... We eat in messes of about eighteen men. Lunch Friday consisted of dried rice about two-thirds to three-quarters of our dixies full per man, and about half a teacup or one-quarter of onion stew or soup. This has been our meal now three times a day ... There are two ships in our entourage, ours is the front one ... The poop portion is entirely occupied by Japanese soldiers and seamen, the top being occupied by a railed deck wherein a machine gun trains forward and [is] able to cover a large portion of the ship. A range finder or the theodolite for the AA guns is near it and an armed soldier constantly on guard. From the front of the poop forward to the Cabin portion is thrown open to us. Tarpaulins have been erected, and are very welcome but the decks are always so crowded and a spot to sit down on is often hard to find. The latrines are on the bow side and are the roughest I have ever seen.' Later in the journey he wrote, 'Much bargaining going on all day between Seamen and Soldiers, and AIF. Cigarettes are of course the items our lads require and bargain such valuables as watches, fountain pens, pencils, etc, also torches and Malay dollars. At first our lads were to be found as they are still at the doors to the Jap's quarters bargaining, but lately the Japs have been coming amongst us with bottles of mysterious tablets and also cigarettes, wanting watches, pens, cig. cases, cut-throat razors (not safety) etc. Whilst on deck this morning looking at photos in [my] wallet, a ... seaman came up, and displayed great interest in photos and wallet. He pointed to mother's photo with mine and said what was meant to be "wife". To save argument I agreed. He displayed almost childish interest and joy in recognising my photo amongst the snaps. Then he said "cigarettes"? apparently wishing to buy it for smokes. On my refusing he just smiled and went away. Several others also looked at it and said "wife" when they see mother's and my photo together. The last chap said "thank you" after examining the wallet and contents, and all were very polite and friendly.'[42]

They dropped anchor in Burma on 23 May, unloaded the ship and were marched to Tavoy, a rainy river port in the south-east of the country, where they were ordered to begin to build on the site of an aerodrome recently abandoned by the British. Before the war, the idea of a Thai-Burma railway had been canvassed by British, German and Japanese engineers, who had all discounted it because – even with modern tools – the jungle, the monsoons, tropical disease and the almost impassable terrain would make the job impossible without vast expense and huge loss of life. But tens of thousands of diseased, abused and starved POWs, along with hundreds of thousands of 'coolies', began the project in June 1942 and finished it in sixteen months, largely with implements that wouldn't have looked modern in the Iron Age. And they died of cholera, of beriberi, of malaria, of malnutrition and of dysentery.

Milston's diary is one of the few journals written by an Australian soldier on the Burmese side of the border, and probably the only diary of life on the line by an Australian Jew. And Milston felt his religion keenly – as well as his diary, he carried his *siddur* with him throughout the war. 'Roll call 8 am and 8 pm each day,' wrote Milston. 'Jap guards make sure all are present. Orders to shoot anyone leaving small area outside hangar. One Jap on guard at this end of hangar all the time. Remainder at other end, and at desk near the entrance. Dysentery and diarrhoea cases taken away this morning in truck, that is, some of them. Rained again several times today enabling us to bathe, etc. Working party out all day digging holes, carrying bricks and on aerodrome. Saturday 3rd May ... Work on oil drums this morning, carting empty drums, several hundreds, across drome. I pushed mine with a stick, also kicked some, and hand-rolled others! ... Sunday morning 31st May. Doctor will only see diarrhoea and dysentery cases ... Told to eat no rice, only light stew. Flies are very bad. Water position not good. Has to be carted for kitchen from wells, some distance away. Water for washing etc, rainwater only. Most out working today, rolling full oil-drums etc. Announced by Maj Jacobs that we are now under new Jap commander, a Lieut, who is a better man apparently than the previous one. Will be paid in POW currency when in working parties @ 10c per day for men, 15c NCOs (Sgts only), 25c officers. Officers are now quartered in hut 150 yards away from this stony-floored hangar. June 1st. Monday ... Japs wrote our names down this morning, a very slow process, and later called them out to us. We had difficulty in recognising our names but answered to them. They also asked some their ages and seemed pleased!! This of course only applied to us on the working party. More AIF arrived. Our gear we left at wharf is reported OK at Tavoy. My blanket and biv sheet is there, along with many others, also kit bags, etc, so here's hoping. June 2 ... Eight men made a break for it early this morning. Supposed to have Pris. compass and map. Good luck to them!! Brig made speech about it last night. Said he thought it was not advisable at present, as difficulties are immense, and repercussions may be severe on remaining men and officers ... Japs in mild turmoil over eleven shovels not returned to shed. June 5 ... Our L/Cpl has been unanimously named "George" by us five on his party. He cycles to work, carries bayonet but no rifle. Rumour persisting Germans have capitulated. Also have used gas. "Oh to see the old Granny Herald for accurate news again!!" Announced on evening parade by Brig, that Jap officer has informed him that eight men have been captured and are in Tavoy jail. Brig indicated that this was to

be taken more or less with a grain of salt, until we know for certain
… Brig in car with Japs passed us on road. Returned shortly after
with truck with eight men who had escaped and were now captured. About six guards on truck!!! Graves had been dug during
afternoon, and the men were tied to posts in a kneeling position,
blindfolded and shot by sixteen Japanese guards in two volleys at
a distance of eight or nine feet! Their gear was put in the graves by
Jap orders. The Brigadier very strongly objected to the shooting,
pointing out that it was absolutely contrary to the Geneva conven-
tion articles for Prisoners of War. Cold-blooded murder! Nobody,
not even the Padres, were allowed to speak to them. The Padre
said a service over each grave. June 7. Sunday. Free day unless
called on by Nipponese for special party. At Church Parade Padre
called for special prayer for "men who died yesterday doing their
duty to King and country". George, our guard on the road had
sent Burmese to Tavoy on June 5 to get cigars, he produced them
yesterday and we five received one cigar each.'[43]

The conflict in New Guinea

New Guinea was a quiet posting for Australian troops before
Japan entered the war. Melbourne-born Philip Henry Napoleon
Opas was sent to 11 Squadron RAAF at Port Moresby at the end
of 1940. 'My war was not all bad,' he wrote. 'In fact, until the
Japanese messed it up for me, it was quite pleasant.'[44] He had a
commission pending, he was married, and his wife joined him
in New Guinea for a few months in 1941. Her arrival coincided
with the delivery of the first Catalina seaplanes to Moresby. Opas
had enlisted on the same day as his brother Athol Louis Opas.*

---

*   Their sister Bobbie went into uniform too and manned anti-aircraft guns in the
     Atherton Tableland.

'The day we joined up was the last time I saw him,' he wrote.

Lassalle Spielvogel's brother Phil was also stationed in Moresby. By September Dick Cohen was in town too, in charge of 11 Squadron, his first command. Phil Spielvogel wrote home, 'Our services on Sunday evening and Monday, the First Day of *Rosh Hashanah*, were definitely the first ones ever held in Papua. Many of the chaps come from country towns and although very eager to attend, most of them had not been inside a *shule* for many years. Phil Opas and I read the service between us but as our Hebrew was not very strong we had to read portions in English. But even if the procedure was not strictly according to the ritual we, nevertheless, showed our appreciation of the fact that we were Jews and proud to try to carry on the traditions of our forebears. We hope to get a *minyan* on *Yom Kippur* consisting of Squadron Leader Cohen, Corporals Opas and Finkelstein, LAC Solomon, Goldsmith, Private Rothman, Messrs Roth, Stafford and Davis and myself. Though we have no *Sefer Torah* nor a *Shofar* we shall fast and say our prayers, and remember we are an exiled remnant of the Children of Israel.'[45] In the end Cohen could not make it to the service, but the other men fashioned a *Shofar* from a ram's horn and sounded the ritual *tekiah*, *shevarim* and *teruah*.

The idle days in Port Moresby did not last. 'The first day of the Pacific War, I saw a dead body for the first time,' wrote Opas. 'In fact, I saw eight dead bodies, close friends. On a night operational flight, December 8, Catalina A24-15 crashed on take-off into a hill at Fairfax Harbour. I had eaten with some of the crew that day. The plane was laden with nearly 5000 litres of fuel and armed with eight 114kg bombs. I was Orderly Sergeant. I took a party across the harbor in a launch but we had to watch helplessly as the Cat burned. We could not get near it for eight hours. Bombs exploded and ammunition and fuel made a terrible spectacle of pyrotechnics. When we got there, I saw a blackened arm sticking out of a blister, a Perspex turret located on each side of the fuselage from which side guns operated and on the starboard side. I pulled. The arm came away in my hand. I was sick and very little use afterwards.'[46]

In January 1942, Sergeant Pilot Lionel Van Praag of the RAAF was reported missing during air operations in Java. Sydney-born Van Praag was a national celebrity, the country's most prominent speedway racer, who had won the inaugural world championship for Australia in 1936. The son of a tram conductor, he was movie-star handsome, a cigarette-card hero who had joined the RAAF in August 1941. Van Praag had been flying an unarmed RAAF Douglas transport plane returning to its base in Darwin when the aircraft came under attack. With him were Flying Officer Noel Webster, Sergeant Eric Picker and Corporal Fred Mason. One of the crew said later, 'Suddenly, machine-gun bullets cut through the fuselage. We looked back and there was a Japanese "Zero" on our port tail. Van Praag went to the rear of the machine to get the Mae Wests (self-inflating life preservers). No sooner had he left than bullets blew the instrument panel to bits. We looked round again and there was another Jap "Zero" shooting up our wing tips on the starboard. Pilot Officer Webster put the Douglas into vertical dive. The "Zeros" followed us down, firing all the way. As we flattened out over the water, the Japanese got in a final burst and sheered off, probably thinking we were goners. When we landed, the Douglas blew to bits, throwing us into the water. There was a rough sea. On top of a wave we saw land – the island of Sumba, twenty-five miles away.'[47] The men had three Mae Wests, three revolvers and an empty petrol tin. Picker had never swum more than twenty-five yards, and Mason, who was badly wounded, lost consciousness after an hour. Van Praag was in the water, grazed by three Japanese bullets. He later told a journalist that he and Webster had no choice but to tow their two comrades to safety. 'We donned Mae Wests,' he said, 'but one of them had a faulty valve. Noel, and then I, broke teeth in trying to tighten the valve, which we finally bound with a strip of my shirt. During the thirty hours we were in the water, we talked about everything but our plight. It rained several times, and we'd open our mouths to catch the drops, but often as not, we'd get a mouthful of salt water. We had a gallon tin of water with us, but we didn't know how long it would last. We restricted ourselves to two mouthfuls at a time, and nobody took a drop more. Cramps worried Noel and me for about half an hour. Fortunately we had it at different times, and we were able to ease one another's burdens. When land seemed reasonably close, our stocks rose, but then I saw a shark fin cutting through the water towards us. I yelled "shark," and we all started shouting and firing our revolvers. The noise was terrific and the shark disappeared. A little later, we saw a shark making towards Noel. My gun was underwater, but I fired and yelled. To my amazement, the gun operated, and the shark grazed Noel's leg as it sheered off. But my shot punctured Noel's Mae West, and he used the now nearly empty water tin to keep him afloat. When anyone wanted a drink after that, Noel had to swim. Next afternoon we made the breakers, and, discarding my Mae West, I caught a shoot and made the beach. The others quickly followed. None of us could walk so we crawled up the beach to the shade of a rock, and fell asleep at once. We awoke to find Islanders staring at us. They took us to a tiny village, and from there we rode fourteen miles on horses to a town where we reported to the military authorities.'[48] The news that Van Praag was safe quickly reached home, and Van Praag and Webster were awarded the George Medal.

But the hero of the skies over New Guinea remained Julius 'Dick' Cohen. 'His Catalinas, night after night, through all sorts of weather, kept up their hammering of the Japanese – at Rabaul, at Lae, at Salamaua – in fact, anywhere Dick Cohen hunted them out,' reported *ABC* magazine. Cohen was the pilot 'who turned the clumsy Catalina into a dive bomber over Rabaul, whose sheer brilliance got him out of several scraps with Zeros, and who time after time left the Jap ack-ack gunners floundering as he escaped low over a hill or down a narrow valley.'[49] Another Catalina pilot told a newspaper reporter, 'Cohen, whose squadron usually was on reconnaissance work in New Guinea, planned his attacks with amazing thoroughness. One night we followed Cohen out to a Jap base, where we knew several transports and supply ships were congregated. We took our comparatively slow-moving planes to a great height. Then every light in Cohen's machine was switched on, and he dived like a ground-going rocket. It was the signal for us to follow. We dived after him in our blacked-out plane. Others in the squadron dived, too. Soon, great fires were raging below us. We could see one ship afire from stern to stern. Cohen got the credit for that shot. The Japs, taken completely by surprise, opened up with a few "ack-ack" bursts. But Cohen led his squadron in again and more bombs were dropped. Soon everything below us looked like a kids' giant bonfire on Guy Fawkes' night.'[50]

The Japanese bombed the port of Rabaul, on the north-eastern tip of New Britain, in January 1942. Rabaul's only defenders were a small RAAF contingent and the 1400 AIF and militia troops who made up Lark Force, under the command of Colonel John Scanlan. Dr Tom Selby's brother David commanded the anti-aircraft battery in town.* Lieutenant David Selby wrote on 4 January, 'We had been warned of the approach of enemy planes and far out to sea, flying high over Watom Island, we saw them coming, in perfect arrowhead formation, eighteen heavy long-range bombers flashing silver in the bright sunlight. It seemed impossible to believe that they were bent on destruction, so serene and beautiful did they look. The excitement of the men was intense and they laughed and chattered like a lot of schoolgirls ... Only six men of the battery had seen a shot fired previously and many faces were white and tense as the bombers flew straight towards the gun posi-

---

*   The oldest Selby brother, Esmond, was to become second-in-command of the 9th
        Infantry Battalion.

tion … For these were the first shots to be fired at an enemy by a Militia unit, and the first shots to be fired from Australian territory at an invading enemy.' The Japanese bombardment continued for days. Selby wrote, 'As the enemy came over, time after time, usually at a height of about 16 000 feet, there was nothing the infantry could do but cower in their slit trenches and watch the cottonwool puffs unfold amongst the formation. But they felt that someone was hitting back, the enemy was not getting it all his own way and at least did not dare to come down to a height where he could be a real menace … The morale of the men was magnificent. On quiet mornings they would go to the cliffs facing the northern sea and call "Jap, Jap, Jap, come and play with us." There were excited cheers when the telephone bell sounded at the command post and raiders were announced on their way, groans when the message was merely a complaint our ration return was late or an explanation that we would have to be satisfied with pineapple instead of papaw as our fruit ration for the day.'[51]

But January 1942 was a time of defeat and retreat for the Allies. When the Japanese overran Rabaul only the RAAF had an evacuation plan. On 23 January the soldiers of Lark Force were told it was every man for himself, and Selby took to the hills and led some of his men on a trek to the Catholic mission at Lemingi in the interior and on to the east coast of New Britain. At the same time as Selby's party started out, Signaller Issacher Weingott, the half-brother of the World War One diarist Samuel Weingott, set off with a group of mates along the same trail. Incredibly, Issacher kept a diary too. 'As we were walking down the road the Jap planes machine-gunned and bombed the road,' he wrote, 'so we thought it time to take to the jungle. We cut our way through jungle and finished up in a deep gully.'[52] On 26 January they passed Selby's party, which had joined Y Company – 'composed of the odds and ends', wrote Selby, 'postal unit, mess waiters, clerks, everyone who was out of a job'[53] – under the command of Captain Frank Shier.

Each party made it to Lemingi, where Selby was delighted to find many more of his men. All the groups eventually moved off. On January 29, wrote Weingott, 'We had to cross three rivers and at one of these Captain Shier's party were stumped they couldn't cross. One of our chaps … took a bush rope across and fastened it. With the aid of this we managed to cross, but one of Captain Shier's party was washed away and two chaps rushed in and helped him out. The chap was unconscious as he had hit his head on a rock.'[54] On 1 February, Weingott's party made it to the coast. Food was scarce. The men had to buy taro from the locals and plead for help from missionaries. Weingott's party shot a pig and dynamited a river for fish. Throughout their journey, other small parties of ragged, exhausted Australians passed by. Selby met one more of his own men, the badly wounded gunner Max Hazelgrove, in a 'native' village. Hazelgrove had been in a party that had surrendered to the Japanese at Tol. 'They were well treated,' wrote Selby, 'given a good meal of rice and Australian bully beef. Next morning they were taken out into the jungle in small groups of about ten and either shot or bayonetted in the back.'[55] Weingott's party found another escaped prisoner whose 'hands were tied behind his back for two days before he found someone to undo them [and] his wrists were all festered'.[56] He, too, told the story of the Tol Plantation massacre. The men skirted Tol.

On 12 February, Weingott's men watched parties of Japanese land from a destroyer. The Australians headed further south, and made a raft to try to cross a river. Weingott's party included a man who could not swim. 'We put him and our gear on top of the raft and swam,' wrote Weingott, 'pushing and pulling the raft across the river. All the time we were crossing it we were thinking of crocodiles as the river was supposed to be alive with them. Kept walking until we came to another river. As it was dark we lit a fire. Just as we were trying to dry our clothes two koons [sic] came across the river in a canoe and took us across. We went as far as a native village. These koons seemed very sulky and didn't seem to like us staying. Next morning as we were leaving we tried to shoot a pig. Just as we did the koons opened fire on us. Seeing the Japs were close we thought the Japs were on us. We made a dive into the bush and it took us about four hours to get back to the track.'[57]

The walking grew tougher as the men grew weaker. Selby's party had to trek through the night. 'Even at midday we were enveloped in a sort of eternal moist twilight,' wrote Selby. 'The vigour of the jungle growth had a ferocity which was frightening. Everything from the slenderest vine to the mightiest tree strove fiercely and relentlessly to reach the light. High above everything towered the gigantic erima trees, and parasitically entwined around their trunks and branches, vines of every imaginable description strove to climb above the jungle darkness. Grasses, shrubs, bushes and the lesser trees were all engaged in the same bitter struggle, the weaker ones strangled and choked by their more vigorous neighbours. Here and there some prolific vine had completely strangled the tree by which it had climbed to the day-light, and the dead tree, rotting away, had left the matted vine standing erect with no visible means of support … At night time the brightest stars and even a full moon were completely blotted out, and no matter how near one walked to the man ahead, it was impossible to see even the dim outline of his figure. Here and there a fallen log or dead tree trunk would glow in the hard white light of a mass of fungi, or a friendly firefly would flitter ahead of us down the track, but these were the only signs of light in that impenetrable gloom. That night, as the leaders stumbled over obstructions in the path, the word would be passed down the column in a tired, dead voice, "Roots", "Vine", "Log", "Slippery patch". Our bones and muscles ached till we felt that we could scarcely stand; when we stopped for a rest, we grew so stiff we felt that we could never move on, our bodies, clammy with sweat, growing cold in the night air. Our boots felt like masses of lead and our packs seemed to weigh tons. My steel helmet bowed my head down. Still we kept on, stumbling, slipping and falling.'[58]

Selby's men found a local uprising had taken place at Drina, where villagers had murdered the plantation manager, raped his wife, destroyed or stolen everything, and were apparently planning to ambush the Australians. Selby executed the ringleader of the revolt and Selby's party made camp at the plantation on 27 February. For Weingott's men, 5 March was the hardest day of the trek. 'We followed the beach and it was coral,' he wrote, 'and as we were nearly all bare footed the coral cut our feet. In places we had to climb cliffs and cling on to jungle vines. The sea was breaking over rocks under us. After this we came to a river. Met a koon and he had a small canoe. I was crossing with him when the canoe sunk … if it hadn't been for the koon I would have been drowned. I left [the] party to try and push on to a village taking two packs. I came to a river which did not look deep. I started to wade across but went out of my depth and was washed on to a sand bank. Went on to a village called Pomi. I sent two koons back to help the rest of our party.'[59] They were starving but there was no food at Pomi. One of the men seemed to be cracking up. Everyone was feeling the strain. While the largest number of men – including Selby and the medical officer – remained encamped at Drina, Weingott's party had to stay with others in Wunung plantation because there was not enough food at Drina. By now, many men had died and most of the survivors were too sick to work. But on 9 April, both Selby's and Weingott's parties were rescued by the *Laurabada*, a diesel yacht belonging to the administrator of Papua. They had been in the jungle more than three months.

The Japanese attacks on Australia

On 19 February 1942, the Japanese launched a massive air raid on Darwin, sinking US and Australian ships in the harbour, damaging the RAAF base, wrecking the infrastructure of the town and killing at least 243 people. Lieutenant Zelman Cowen was a Melbourne-born Naval Intelligence officer posted to naval headquarters in Darwin. 'There were two raids during the morning,' Cowen remembered. 'The first raid came from the Japanese aircraft carriers. It was the same group as had bombed Pearl Harbor. It was a very big air-raid. The sky was literally full of aeroplanes. Some stupid wit said, "Thank God we've got an air force." In fact, none of them was ours, they were all Japanese. We saw the dive bombers diving on the ships in the harbour, and diving on the harbour facilities. I remember seeing an American destroyer – the *Peary* – sinking, blazing, and it was really a pretty shaking experience because we had very little with which to resist; negligible planes, very little of anything except anti-aircraft fire. The anti-aircraft people did a very impressive and very brave job, but overall it was a catastrophe. Dive bombers diving [make] a very unpleasant sound, and also Japanese fighters were machine-gunning, strafing. They went off, and there was an unearthly quiet after all of that tremendous noise, followed very suddenly [by] the mother and father of all explosions. The *Neptuna* had been tied up at the wharf and the *Neptuna* had a cargo of explosives, but the fire got to the explosives. The ship blew high into the air. I don't think I've ever heard a noise like that in my life. It was appalling. And then the next wave of Japanese planes came over, principally land-based bombers that came from the Dutch East Indies, and they made their way to the airfield and they dropped their bombs on the airfield ... Then they went away and we were really just totally ineffective.'[60]

JACK ROSEN, A LIFELONG MERCHANT SEAMAN, DIED ON THE *Neptuna* that morning. Rosen's was another Jewish family which had every eligible member assisting the war effort.*

In the months that followed the devastation of Darwin, Japanese planes repeatedly hit the north and west of Australia, bombing Townsville in Queensland, Katherine in the Northern Territory and Wyndham, Derby, Broome and Port Hedland in Western Australia. Darwin itself was raided sixty-four times. Many people believed the Japanese planned to invade – although, in truth, they had neither the capacity nor the intention to do so. In February 1942 small Japanese reconnaissance planes were spotted over Melbourne, Sydney and Hobart. Slit trenches were dug in front of St Kilda synagogue to protect it from attack, and investigations were made into the safety of the *Torah* scrolls in the event of an air raid. On the night of 31 May/1 June, three Japanese midget submarines stole into Sydney Harbour and, while aiming for the much larger USS *Chicago*, torpedoed and sank HMAS *Kuttabul*, a former ferry which served as a dormitory ship for Australian sailors who had not yet received their posting. Asleep on board the *Kuttabul* was twenty-year-old Stoker John Samuel Asher, a Jew from Meningie, South Australia, who drowned with twenty of his comrades. On 8 June, Japanese submarines targeting Sydney Harbour Bridge surfaced and fired ten shells, nine of which hit Rose Bay and Bondi. Reginald Marks, a Jewish instructor at the headquarters of the St John Ambulance, was on medical duty and came to the aid of the

---

*   Jack Rosen had five brothers: Henry was chief saloon waiter on the merchant ship *Macdhui* and was at Port Moresby when the Japanese attacked in June 1942. He was manning one of the ship's anti-aircraft guns, under a maritime-union deal which had merchant seaman paid a bonus for defending their vessels, when he died at his post. Alf, who had been awarded the DSO in World War One, had gone missing fighting the Germans in Europe with the British Army in 1941. Albert was seven months at Tobruk, Emmanuel was a sergeant in the RAAF and Woolf was an AIF commando.

first civilian injured by enemy fire that night – who turned out to be Edward Hirsch, a Jewish refugee from the Nazis.

Alarmed by the intimate reach of the enemy, Prime Minister John Curtin introduced amendments to the Defence Act which permitted conscripted CMF men – who were already fighting in the Australian territory of New Guinea – to be sent to war in most of the South-West Pacific area.

The battles for El Alamein

The battles for El Alamein in Egypt in 1942 halted Rommel's advance towards Alexandria in June 1942, and saw the Germans forced back to Tunisia in December. Among the Jewish Australians who died in the months of heavy fighting was Captain John Harris Samuels, RMO of 2/15th Battalion and a former Rat of Tobruk, killed in action near El Wishka on 25 October 1942. Also killed was Arthur Moses, who had been a jackaroo in Queensland before he enlisted in the AIF. Moses shipped out to England along with his brother Hubert. They were both sent to the Middle East, but Hubert stayed in Egypt and Palestine while Arthur went to Syria. Arthur was injured in an accident, then transferred to the 2/28th Battalion. In El Alamein, Arthur Moses was hit by an anti-tank shell and buried near the battlefield on 2 November 1942.* Rabbi Goldman officiated at a *Yom Kippur* service at El Alamein, close to the battlefield. The fifty men at the service, in the tent generally used for holding courts martial, included AIF troops and an Australian serving with the South Africans, as well as Palestinian and English soldiers. Philip Opas was temporarily back in Australia when he heard his commission had come through. 'It was here

---

* The Moses boys' older brother Braham also served, as a gunner in the north of Australia.

that I learned that Athol was missing,' he wrote. 'My parents clung to hope when there was none. The first telegram reported him missing; six months later, the message was missing believed killed; another six months and he was missing presumed dead. This was followed by the return of his effects.' Athol had left Australia to take part in the Empire Air Training Scheme (see 'The other war in the air', p. 248); he had fought in the Battle for Britain, flown twenty missions over Europe and had then travelled to the Middle East with his 108 Squadron RAF. Philip inherited his brother's logbook, read it and wrote, 'In August 1942, he was engaged every second night in bombing Tobruk, then held by Rommel. On the fifth of these operations, the night of August 12–13, he failed to return. He was never found. He was aged twenty-one.' Athol Opas' name is carved on a memorial tablet at El Alamein Cemetery. 'Immediately under his name is that of his bosom friend Maurice [Mo] Shapir. They were at school together, enlisted the same day, and had regimental numbers three digits apart. They trained together in Canada, fought in the same squadron, and died in the same way, three days apart,' wrote Philip. 'After Athol's death, I became hell-bent on revenge and wanted to fight the war single-handed, killing as many of the enemy as possible.'[61]

The Australian 9th Division, which had been involved in some of the worst fighting in El Alamein, left North Africa for Australia in January 1943. The temples of Jerusalem, the pyramids of Gaza, the souks, mosques and deserts became postcard memories for a new generation of Australian servicemen, who had returned to lands where their fathers had fought more than twenty years before. For Jewish Australian soldiers, sailors, airmen and nurses, the roots ran deeper and the memories stretched further.

On the home front

As news leaked out of Nazi atrocities in Europe, few Jews needed convincing that this was 'their' war although, as usual, Nazi and other antisemitic propaganda was dedicated to spreading the canard that the Jews would not fight. Eric Butler, a prominent pre-war antisemite, had warned in 1940 that 'a stream of Australian youth is leaving to be smashed to bloody pulp in the second war to "save democracy", which like the first war, was fomented by Jewish International Finance, will be financed and controlled by the same group and will mean their undisputed world domination'.[62] But in some corners, attitudes were shifting. Even Monash's one-time nemesis CEW Bean had changed his views about the Jews, first refuting the idea that they had avoided front-line service in the German Army during World War One, and later campaigning in favour of the quixotic dream of a Jewish homeland in the Kimberley. 'If there is any sincerity in our professions of what we are fighting for (God help us if there isn't),' wrote Bean, 'I don't see how we can decently refuse these courageous people the chance to "have a go".'[63]

However, the decorated World War One veteran Harold Cohen, who served in World War Two as honorary Red Cross commissioner in the Middle East, and later as brigadier at Land Headquarters, somehow remained a focus for prejudice. In March 1942 a Western Australian newspaper published a short item entitled 'A True Story', under the byline 'Contributed': 'A society dame (Melbourne) thought she would like to billet two American soldiers, so she rang the head office, which replied: "Yes, madam, we can send you two." She made one stipulation: "They must not be Jews." The day they were to arrive she invited all her bridge-party pals to come and welcome them. They arrived – Two Dinkum American Soldiers (niggers). Colonel Cohen had answered the phone (a Jew).'[64] The tale is surely apocryphal, mess-hall humour, but the joke would be meaningless if it did not reflect something about the ideas of the day.

A pamphlet entitled 'Jews and the War' was published in Melbourne in 1943 by the Jewish Council to Combat Fascism and Anti-Semitism. It opened with a barrage of statistics from World War One – including the assertion that 170 825 Jews were killed in action while fighting for the various powers – but the bulk of its pages were devoted to the current conflict. 'In the first world war Jews fought according to their nationality,' it read. 'In the present war – for the first time in the history of modern wars – they are spared this choice: all Jewish sympathies are for one side.'[65] The pamphlet talked of the adventures of Harry Levy, Ralph Coyne and Eric Lipman, the three Jews among the forgotten commandoes of Timor, who did not surrender after the Japanese invaded and instead continued to fight a guerrilla campaign until they were withdrawn and sailed home with the RAN; of Paul Cullen and his brother George, who was also a decorated soldier; and of Flight Lieutenant Peter Isaacson and Wing Commander Dick Cohen.

Flying Cohens throughout the world had attracted the attention of the press when it became known that the RAF's Wing Commander Lionel Cohen, DSO MC, a veteran of the Boer War and World War One, was probably the oldest active serviceman in the world. Extraordinary headlines were written such as 'Jew flyer, 68, raids Nazis'.[66] Cohen had been awarded his decorations as a younger man in the army, but joined the RAF aged sixty-four and became a wing commander in 1940. As an air gunner and observer (navigator) he flew in Norway, the North Sea, the Atlantic and North Africa, was twice Mentioned in Despatches and eventually received the DFC. By one account, the sky – and the land and sea – had become crowded with armed Cohens of all ages, shapes and sizes, jostling for space in the order of battle. A Perth newspaper printed an extraordinary story from the UK that listed air-force

Cohens of Britain and Australia. 'Who now will forget the "King of Lampedusa"?'[67] it asked, of the now largely forgotten RAF Sergeant Pilot Sydney Cohen, a tailor from Clapton, London, who got lost on his way back to base in Malta in June 1941, and had to land his Swordfish plane on the tiny Sicilian island of Lampedusa, where he would have been forced to surrender to the large Italian garrison, if the garrison had not got in first. To his surprise and bafflement, Cohen was met by an Italian officer and a group of soldiers waving white sheets. They were tired of Allied raids and wanted to give up. 'When my plane had been refuelled I took the surrender chit to an American camp in Tunisia,' said Cohen.[68] The story in the *Western Mail* went on to list British Pilot Officer Edward Laurence Cohen, DFC; Flight Lieutenant G Cohen, Mentioned in Despatches; Squadron Leader Mark Cohen and Flight Lieutenant Gerald Cohen, Glasgow brothers, both Mentioned in Despatches; Squadron Leader Ronald Joseph Cohen (NZ), Air Force Cross; and Sergeant Schiller Cohen, of New York, DFC, Air Medal and ten Oak Leaf Clusters to the Air Medal, before shifting its focus back to Australia and onto the ground with nods to Lieutenant Colonel Paul Cohen (now Cullen) and Captain George Cohen. 'The priest has turned warrior,' it announced, 'from the Arctic to the Antipodes.'[69]

The Employment Companies

Those Jewish refugees from Germany and Central Europe who had been classed as 'enemy aliens' at the start of the war were not permitted to join the armed forces. For some prominent conservatives, the wretched families who had fled the Nazis were objects of suspicion rather than sympathy. Archie Cameron, the former leader of the Country Party, now a member of Robert Menzies' United Australia Party, declared that certain refugees had been deliberately planted in Australia by the Germans while others were so perfidious that 'one of the best jobs that Adolph [sic] Hitler ever did for Germany was to push some of [them] out of his country'.[70] He offered them no succour and denied them any possibility of redemption. 'I have heard talk of "friendly aliens",' he said. 'I do not know what a friendly alien is. I know that when my country is engaged in a life and death struggle with Germany and Italy any man of German or Italian birth is an enemy alien. If he is friendly to this country, then he must be a traitor to his own, and I do not think it is our part to encourage treason.'[71] Recent migrants such as Alfred Ulmer, an Austrian, remained subject to severe reporting procedures. 'We, as refugees, were all anxious to do something for the war effort,' said Ulmer. 'There was a hut where the fountain is in Martin Place, where you could put your name down and they called you up. All of us who went there and wanted to join, so to speak, were knocked back because of our original nationality.'[72]

Famously, more than 2000 anti-fascist 'enemy aliens' – the majority of them Jewish refugees – were transported from England to Australia on board HMT *Dunera*, whose decks and holds they were forced to share with Axis POWs and Nazi sympathisers. The 'Dunera Boys' were subject to the constant bastardry of guards who beat and robbed them, and when they arrived in Australia in September 1940, they were interned in camps around Tatura, Victoria, and near the NSW Western Riverina town of Hay. Rabbi Danglow came to see the Jewish detainees at Hay and Tatura, in visits his biographer describes as 'disastrous'.[73] Danglow seemed to share the government's feeling that it was impossible to tell friend from foe. When three hundred internees organised themselves into an Orthodox group, Danglow refused to arrange a supply of *kosher* food for them. In the end, it was Rabbi Falk who arranged *kosher* food and services and took responsibility for the people of Hay Camp, while Danglow continued to visit Tatura.

In 1942 Jewish refugees were officially reclassified as 'friendly aliens'. Hundreds left the camps to join the British and Australian armies, although in Australia they were still largely confined to home service. New CMF Employment Companies were raised specifically to recruit 'aliens' for labouring work, typically loading and unloading supply ships and trains. Jewish troops were concentrated in 5, 6 and 8 companies. 'It was a bit of a disappointment,' said Alfred Ulmer, who joined 3 Employment Company, 'because we thought somehow that we'd be doing something better than just shifting boxes and bags etc ... We got rifle training, we got gas-mask training, and we all had a rifle but no ammunition.'[74]

Kurt Lewinski, who had arrived in Australia on the *Dunera*, kept a diary in German which he translated and synopsised rather unhelpfully after the war. He was interned at Tatura, where most of the Jews desperately wanted to fight the Germans. One of Lewinski's comrades was rejected because his eyesight was not up standard. 'Blast it!' wrote Lewinski. 'The order of the day is now, take a pencil and paper, copy the eye-testing chart (both sides) they've got in the examination room – through a window. Learn to recite them by heart! Sorry to have to cheat you, Australia – but in war every kind of tactics is permissible! That's the way to do it, if you want to be in this show!' Lewinski joined 8 Employment Company along with hundreds of other Dunera Boys. He greeted with despair the news of Nazi atrocities in Europe and realised his family in Germany had probably been slaughtered. 'God damn those Nazi bastards for all they have done to mankind,' he wrote, 'and may He grant us to be victorious over them soon. To achieve this I will do my share here, work, work, work, work! Loading, unloading, shifting, stacking, re-stacking, stencilling, and what not. Boxes, bags, iron bars, straw, vegetable, ammunition.'[75] Danglow held a Chanukah service for 6 Employment Company in December 1942. By this time, his attitude to the former detainees appears to have changed entirely, and he did whatever he could to help any person who was released from the camps. The men of

6 Employment Company are immortalised in the painting *Tocumwal – Loading the Train*, a dark, gloomy portrait of four huddled, withdrawn 'civilian soldiers' exhausted after a day's work carting haulage from goods trains at the change of gauge between Victoria and New South Wales. The painter, Yosl Bergner, was an Austrian Jew who grew up in Poland and came to Australia in 1937, on a ship where he met and befriended another young Jew leaving Europe, Yosl Birstein.

Bergner joined 6 Employment Company and his tent mates at Tocumwal included his friend Birstein and Viennese refugee Frank Klepner. 'Our tent was a small ghetto,' said Bergner, later.[76] Klepner remembered Tocumwal as 'hot and dusty' and said 'the crows seemed to be the worst thing. They pecked us as we walked along'. The rotten meals in the camp were improved after a week-long hunger-strike and the men generally got on well, and often discussed Russian literature and listened to classical music.[77] Birstein wrote Yiddish poetry and Bergner painted not only what he saw around him but what he knew to be happening in Europe: the destruction of the ghettoes, the Jewish people set aflame. 'In the camp we read in the tent by the light of a kerosene lamp,' wrote Bergner, 'there was no electricity. I painted at night and hundreds of mosquitoes and crickets got stuck on the wet paintings.

'The officers were Australians and they felt very superior to us,' wrote Bergner. 'Once, they brought along some prisoners of war dressed in red convicts' uniforms. They looked Jewish. I came up to them and shouted in Yiddish, "Yidn, Yidn, why were you arrested?" They turned out to be Italians. The German Jews in the Labour Corps wanted to assimilate. They sang, Valtzing Matilda, and wanted to be instant Australians, and when we spoke Yiddish between us they'd say to us, "*Nur nicht Juedlen.*" They had all changed their names to super-English-sounding names. When they were on guard duty no one left the camp. When I was on guard, everyone went out.'[78]

23 previous page Australian soldiers and nurses on leave in Palestine visit the Western Wall, Jerusalem in 1940.

24 above Flight-Lieutenant Peter Isaacson celebrates with champagne after flying the first Lancaster bomber to Australia, c. 1943. Isaacson won the Distinguished Flying Cross after an air raid on Berlin. His mother Caroline and sister Barbara both served in the Australian Women's Army Service.

25 right Dashing Flight Sergeant Sol Levitus was a bomber pilot with 450 Squadron RAAF, shot down over Germany in June 1942. His remains have never been found.

26 *top left* Rabbi Falk and his three sons all served during World War Two (left to right): Gerald Falk, Chaplain Falk, telegraphist Balfour Falk of the RAN, and David Falk.

28 *above* Staff Sergeant David Falk in Finchhaven, New Guinea, manning a 40-millimetre Bofors anti-aircraft gun.

27 *left* Captain Paul Cullen (right) in Tobruk, 1941. Cullen, born in Newcastle, NSW, changed his surname from Cohen so as not to be victimised if captured by the Germans, but he was never taken prisoner. He won the DSO and Bar for his actions at Kokoda, and rose to the rank of Major General in the post-war Australian Army.

29 Captain John Einfeld at the bima in the synagogue at headquarters, New Guinea Force, Lae, in August 1944, assisting Chaplain Goldman (right) with a Jewish New Year service.

30 Blowing the *shofar* in New Guinea (date unknown).

A Jewish service for Allied troops in New Guinea (date unknown).

2 Trooper Hymie Pearlman of the 2/7th Cavalry Regiment kept an astonishing diary of his part in bloody fighting in New Guinea, 1942. Pearlman (left) is pictured riding a mate, rather than a horse.

33 Signaller Philip Allen of HQ Company 47 Battalion, on Buin Road, Bougainville, 1945. Allen said, 'If it hadn't rained continuously for three weeks from July 1945, the Australian troops would have moved closer to the Japanese base and they would have fought a major battle, probably killing many soldiers. During those three weeks the first atomic bomb was dropped.'

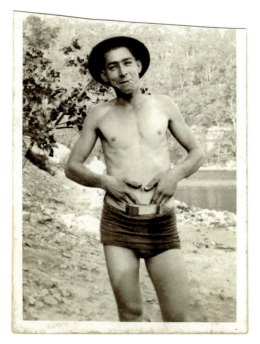

34 Dental surgeon Sydney Levine left a fascinating and thoughtful record of his military experiences in Australia and Morotai, New Guinea, during World War Two.

35 Brisbane-born Cyril Borsht piloted Lancasters for Bomber Command. Borsht was shot down over Holland in 1944 and spent the remainder of the war as a prisoner of the Germans. He retained his sense of humour in captivity, and produced a sketchbook of often whimsical but always accomplished cartoons.

36 Cyril Borsht's POW identification papers.

37 above A naval salute was formed at the Great Synagogue for the 1944 wedding of WRANS Third-Officer Elvira Sloman to Lieutenant Neville Adelstein, who served in New Guinea. Others in the bridal party were (left to right) David Joel and Helen Sloman, unidentified and Jean Solomon. Elvira's father Louis Sloman was wounded at Gallipoli.

38 right Edna Goulston, the sister of Tobruk doctor Stanley Goulston, graduated from the first WRANS officer training class in 1943 and was appointed to the Radar Division at the Navy Office.

THE MAN WHO DIVEBOMBED WITH A FLYING-BOAT

Wing-Cdr J. A. COHEN
did the unusual in an unorthodox manner.

1

"WE SEEM TO BE GETTING STRONGER IN THE AIR NOW, UP HERE IN THE NORTH."

"YAIRS, BUT THAT BLOKE DICK COH WAS HERE EARLY IN THE ... PIE WILL DO ME. HE CER- ... TA SHOWED 'EM HOW TO FLY ... SH"

"IT LOOKS AS THOUGH WE'LL HAVE TO GET OUT, -- QUICK!"

"I AM DESOLATED MESSIEURS, THAT WE MUST TAKE THE ORDERS FROM OUR GOVERNMENT IN FRANCE, BUT IT IS REQUESTED THAT MILORD AND M. COOP AIRE REMAIN FOR THE PRESENT...."

2

But Wing-Cdr Cohen's flying adventures did not begin in New Guinea. The scene is Rabat, Morocco, on June 25, 1940. France has fallen, and Lord Gort and Mr Alfred Duff Cooper have gone to North Africa on behalf of the British Government to see if the Frenchmen there will carry on the fight.

3

"WE SHALL HAVE TO HURRY, COMMANDER THE FRENCH ARE TRYING TO DETAIN US."

"THAT'S ALL RIGHT, SIR, THEY H BEEN AT ME TOO; BUT I AM GO TO TAXI OUTSIDE THE HARBOU AND WE'LL TAKE OFF FROM THER"

But in Rabat Harbour a Short Sunderland flying boat was waiting under the command of Cohen, then a Flt-Lt.

4

With superb airmanship, Flt-Lt Cohen took off from the rough sea and got his craft and important passengers safely back to England. For this he got the DFC.

5

"CATALINAS, THEY CALL THEM, THEY'RE AMERICAN JOBS."

"HANDY LOOKING CRA I WONDER HOW MUC WE CAN DO WITH TH"

Some time later he was transferred back to Austr with other Australian Short Sunderland officers crews.

6

8 Cohen, now a Sqd-Ldr, was soon to
[see] what could be done with Catalinas.
[...], in her swift southward push, reached
[...] and seized Rabaul, former capital
[...] ew Guinea. Immediately she set
[...] reinforcing it, and using it as
[...] e for air attacks farther south.

"THERE'S RABAUL, BOYS, WE'RE GOING IN OVER THE TARGETS. KEEP FORMATION, BUT I'M GOING TO ACT INDEPENDENTLY."

A raid on Rabaul . . . .

At 7,000ft the squadron encountered heavy fire, but the [l]eader did an amazing thing . . . .

Though he nearly tore the wings from his heavy ship, Dick Cohen succeeded in his unheard-of manoeuvre. The machine shuddered out of its dive, went skimming across the water, and gradually rose to clear the crater of the volcano and get safely home.

Power divebombing in a Catalina!

10

"SHE'S A NEW TYPE, BOYS, I'M GOING TO SEE WHAT I CAN GET OUT OF HER!"

And so Dick Cohen set the tradition of gallant deeds in New Guinea, but he did not rest content with that.

12   Next Week.—Lieut Wallach, R.A.N.R., D.S.C.

39 Wing Commander Julius Cohen of Moree, NSW, was a dashing comic strip-style hero who actually appeared in his own comic strip in the *Argus* in 1942.

1 left Jewish ex-servicemen and women march in Melbourne in 1956, led by John Einfeld, president of FAJEX, the national umbrella organisation of the five state Jewish ex-service associations. First row, right to left: Mark Goldstein (NAJEX president), Lewis Lipert (SAJEX president), Harry Grose (VAJEX), Absalom Halprin (NAJEX). Second row, right to left: David Southwick (VAJEX), Meryl Slutzkin née Cohen (VAJEX), Harry Goldstein (NAJEX), unidentified and (no glasses) Michael Arnold (SAJEX).

40 opposite top left Captain Henry Gayst (left) of the Royal Australian Army Medical Corps at the regimental aid post at The Hook, Korea, in July 1953.

42 above Hilda Zinner of Double Bay, NSW, worked for the Australian Red Cross in Vietnam in 1966 and saw to the casualties from the battle of Long Tan.

43 Major Scott Leonard was born in Wollongong, NSW, joined the army in 1988, and has served in East Timor and Iraq. He is pictured above in front of the menorah at B'nai Baghdad, the International Jewish Congregation in Baghdad.

44 Major General Professor Jeffrey Rosenfeld, a veteran of Rwanda, Bougainville,
East Timor and Iraq, was already a qualified neurosurgeon when he joined the
Reserves in Victoria in 1984. He is one of Australia's senior military surgeons and
has a particular expertise in the treatment of bomb blast injury.

45 In 2008, Arthur Shisman, from
Melbourne, won the 1st Armoured Regiment's
Soldier of the Year award and went to
Afghanistan as a tank driver. He was at Patrol
Base Qudus when Greg Sher was killed.

46 Captain Jake Kleinman graduated from Duntroon in 2007 and was posted to 7RAR. He has been on two tours to Afghanistan, and in 2009 he was awarded a DSM for his leadership in the Battle of Kakarak in Uruzgan province. He was base commander of Patrol Base Qudus when Greg Sher was killed.

47 Special Forces Commando
Greg Sher, pictured above in East
Timor in 2003, was a founder of
the Community Security Group in
Melbourne and was tragically killed
in Afghanistan in a rocket attack
on Patrol Base Qudus in Uruzgan
Province, Afghanistan, on 4 January
2009.

48 An armourer on Patrol Base
Qudus made a Star of David from
aluminium piping for Sher's on-
base memorial service and ramp
ceremony.

In November 1943 the men at Tocumwal were joined by German Jewish refugee Helmut Newton, who had been living in Singapore at the outbreak of the war, and who was deported from the colony as an enemy alien in 1940 and interned in Australia for eighteen months. Newton, who was to become a world-famous fashion photographer, wrote an unpleasant memoir of his employment-company service, characterised largely by outlandish sexual boasts. He was one of several German-Jewish photographers in the employment companies. At Tocumwal, Newton became friends with Henry Talbot, a Dunera Boy with whom he was to set up a studio in Melbourne after the war. Another photographer, German-born Max Adolf Devries, worked in 4 and 6 Employment Companies, and his son Graham was to serve in the Vietnam War. A comrade of Devries', Cary Roth, created a strange and likeable record of a typical day in camp in the form of a detailed narrative poem, illustrated by another refugee, Tim Walton. Roth describes a morning parade:

> The corporals yell and the sergeants shout
> Until every single man is about
> When from some dirty office scroll
> They read the names and call the roll
> They can neither pronounce some names nor spell
> But they make no mistakes if you are AWL[79]

The initial enthusiasm of the volunteers quickly turned into something close to the cynicism of professional soldiers. By the end of the war, wrote Kurt Lewinski, 'I would be lying if I said I still like it! You just can't toss heavy weights across the Australian map for three years and still claim to enjoy it, unless you're nuts … I won't do one iota more than called to do – but not one iota less either.' But he felt the army had made him a man. 'There is no trace left of the former feeble, timid youth who was like a leaf tossed around by an icy, hard wind from one place to another,' he wrote. 'Wearing a uniform makes a terrific change.'[80]

Throughout the war, genuine enemy POWs were interned in camps in Australia, most notoriously at Cowra in the Central West of New South Wales, where they lived under the guard of Australian troops and were offered the care of Australian medical personnel, including Captain Sydney Levine (later Major). Levine had joined the CMF as a dentist in June 1940 and enlisted in the AIF in August 1942, hoping to go overseas. He understood what was at stake in the war – his diary included scrapbooked cuttings of newspaper stories about Nazi atrocities in Europe – and became increasingly desperate to do more. Meanwhile, he regularly provided dental treatment at Cowra, where about 6000 enemy personnel were detained, including a large number of Japanese soldiers. 'They are true to the pictures painted of them,' he wrote. 'They bow and hiss as depicted and appear most humble these sons of heaven. Most of them play baseball all day and they have very dirty mouths … I use a Jap Sgt as interpreter – he was shot down over Darwin in the first raid. I discussed with him their feelings on being taken prisoner. He spoke of the shame he felt and that he could never go back – disgraced his family etc. Very concertedly he said "Jap are just not captured".'[81]

Levine often felt bored and frustrated with home service. 'I am very war weary,' he wrote, 'although I have never been in action or danger as yet – so much of my life is speeding past me never to be recovered and so I often wonder whether I have played much of a part in the enormous war machine.' Conversely, he harboured doubts about the small role he did play in a murderous conflict. 'Healthy mouths means healthy bodies,' he wrote, 'and healthy bodies means more gun fodder and in one way we help to bring about the destruction of young men.'[82]

Women serving in the war

World War Two brought large numbers of women into the Australian armed forces for the first time. About 27 000 served in the Women's Auxiliary Australian Air Force (WAAAF) founded in March 1941; about 24 000 in the Australian Women's Army Service (AWAS) created in August 1941; and more than 3000 in the Women's Royal Australian Naval Service (WRANS) established in 1942. These servicewomen were recruited mainly to free servicemen from non-operational duties on the home front and only the AWAS sent non-medical personnel overseas, in postings to New Guinea towards the end of the fighting. In addition, more than 12 000 women joined medical components of the services – mainly the Australian Army Medical Women's Service (AAMWS) and the Australian Army Nursing Service (AANS) – and worked with the AAMC in hospitals locally and in every Australian theatre of war.

Rabbi Goldman in his travels found three Australian Jewish nurses in the Middle East and one woman, Private Madge Grouse, at 2/1st Australian General Hospital in Bougainville. It is difficult to gauge the number of Jewish women in uniform, and they seem to have left behind few letters or memoirs, but among the Jewish women who joined every service were the daughters of families that had men fighting overseas. Thus Captain Dr Edna Selby, the sister of Tom, David and Esmond Selby, served as a captain in the AAMC. Lynka Caroline and Barbara Joan Isaacson, the mother and sister of flying ace Peter Isaacson, were both in the AWAS. Roberta Opas, the sister of Philip and Athol, was in the WAAAF. Edna Goulston, the sister of Tobruk doctor Stanley Goulston, graduated from the first WRANS officer training class and was appointed to the Radar Division at the Navy Office. At the time, the navy did not even have an attestation form for women. Her paperwork was headed 'Royal Australian Naval Reserve', which was crossed out and stamped 'Women's Royal Aust Naval Service';

and the pronoun 'he' was scored through and replaced with 'she'. Marion Rosebery, who joined the WRANS in January 1945, was the daughter of the popular Major Sidney Rosebery, a doctor who served overseas in both world wars and was Mentioned in Despatches twice in the first, and the sibling of WAAAF Flight Sergeant Beryl Rosebery, former WAAAF Ruth Roubin and Arthur Rosebery, who served in the Middle East with the AIF. The navy was still using the same forms when Marion became a WRAN: the pronoun 'she' was inserted by hand.

Caroline Isaacson was a well-known journalist who spoke and wrote a little about her time in the AWAS. She told a CWA meeting that she had joined up to help the war effort but also to show her children that 'Mum could'. Isaacson managed PR for the women's services. In summer 1944 she took a group of reporters – all of them women – around military bases in New South Wales and Queensland. Caroline's daughter Barbara Joan acted as the trip photographer, and the party visited a Queensland unit where AWAS troops were being trained as anti-aircraft gunners. The journalists found the troops were still 'fresh and energetic and intensely interested in their work', despite the heat and discomfort of their posting.[83] A Shepparton journalist bumped into Caroline's husband, Arnold Isaacson, a Jewish Gallipoli veteran and, according to the reporter, the first man to be promoted from a private soldier to commissioned rank in World War One.* Arnold, now a lowly private in the Home Guard–style Volunteer Defence Corps, said he was quite proud of the fact that he was the lowest ranker in his family. He was also keen to dispel the idea that military service might make men out of women, explaining that 'welfare officers look after them well and the feminine touch is evident in their quarters'.[84]

---

*   Arnold Isaacson became a second lieutenant on 11 January 1915, and was later attached to the staffs of General Birdwood and Lord Rawlinson.

The most extensive interview with a Jewish servicewoman would appear to be that conducted with Adelaide-born physiotherapist Betty Rothstadt, who served in the AAMC under her maiden name of Cohn. She applied to join up while she was a single woman living in Melbourne in 1941. 'I can remember dropping the letter in the box and thinking, "Oh, I've done it now",' she said. 'My mother was a widow and I had to write and tell my mother and she was upset. It wasn't a very happy time. I felt sorry for my mother. She had no idea when she would see me again or had no idea where you were going. You just had "AIF Abroad" marked on your luggage.'

A group of female physiotherapists, along with a number of nurses, boarded the troopship *Mauretania* at Port Melbourne, bound for the 2/4th Australian General Hospital in Egypt. 'Different soldiers were supposed to be guarding the sisters but you never spoke to them,' Betty Cohn said. 'You didn't fraternise with the troops.' The physiotherapists were at first given the rank of sergeant, but were quickly promoted to lieutenants along with the nurses. At Colombo, the women changed ships for the *Nevasa*, which took them to El Kantara. Cohn lived in a tent, with a stretcher bed and a box as her only furniture. 'The sandstorms there are very hot,' she said, 'but you had a summer uniform which you wore and which could be very cold at night in the winter.' She stayed in El Kantara for about eight months. Men from the 2/4th went out to set up a hospital in the Barce region of Libya. 'But by the time they got there to establish it the Germans were coming back again,' said Cohn, 'therefore they came further down and established the hospital in Tobruk.' Cohn went with them to Tobruk. 'We worked in the hospital only for, I think, it was just over a fortnight,' she said, 'and then the British insisted that the 2/4th got rid of all their sisters because the Germans were coming down. And we felt pretty awful.' She met some Italian POWs. 'I worked in the dental unit there,' said Cohn, 'and they had a lot of prisoners of war working around the dental unit. I think they were very happy to be prisoners of war. Happy little men that sang away.'

Cohn was later attached to a British hospital in Egypt, where she worked in a plastic surgery unit. 'They trained a physio from each hospital in plastic surgery because they didn't know which hospital would have a plastic surgery unit,' she said. 'Skin grafts is only part of it. They did much deeper things. They did tendon replacements and awful burns and things like that. I liked it very much because it was very personal work, sort of retraining, re-educating nerves and things.'

Cohn returned to Australia a captain, and married Lieutenant Colonel Leon Eric Rothstadt, a doctor who had also been at El Kantara. Throughout her service, Cohn wore a dogtag that marked her as Jewish. 'And before I left more than one elderly, much older man – could have been my father – said to me, "Please don't wear your religion round your neck", because they thought if I fell into the hands of the Germans what would happen to me. I said, "Yes, I'm always going to." And I did … I never hid the fact that I was Jewish ever.

'Some people think that they are paying you a compliment,' said Cohn. 'They say, "But I never think of you as Jewish." And I said, "Well, it's time you did."'[85]

Civilian women also played a part in the war effort. Jewish women ran first-aid and air-raid classes, made clothes for the forces, and were energetic fundraisers throughout the war, contributing heavily to every national appeal. In addition, mobile canteens in the Middle East, London and Sydney, and the Sir John Monash Recreation Hut for servicemen in Hyde Park, Sydney, were all financed by money raised by Jewish women.

From Kokoda to victory over Japan

The Japanese landed in Papua in July 1942, near Gona on the north coast, intending to take the Kokoda Track over the Owen Stanley Range to Port Moresby. As the Australian troops withdrew along the track under the weight of the Japanese assault, Dr Lynn Joseph, a Jewish medical practitioner from Bondi, New South Wales, was posted to 2/6th Australian Field Ambulance to establish a casualty clearing station near the southern trail head at Owers' Corner. When Colonel Paul Cullen and his 2/1st Battalion arrived at Moresby in September 1942, the enemy were less than 50 kilometres away. Cullen's men were among the troops who drove them back through the island, defeating them at Eora Creek then pushing them back through Alola to Gorari in November. Dr Joseph manned advance stations along the track, tending to men battered by malaria, dysentery, scrub typhus, exhaustion, wounds and insect bites. On 5 November he was posted as RMO to the 2/3rd Battalion. Two days later, 16-year-old Jewish factory hand Joe Rovkin (who had enlisted as 19-year-old Greek Orthodox Joseph Rorkin) was shot in the head on Kokoda. He was the youngest Jewish soldier killed in action in World War Two.

Meanwhile Cullen's troops went into action. 'After a day's rest just short of Kokoda,' remembered Cullen, 'we were ordered to take the foot track east, then take a side path to the north and capture a bridge over the river on the main track, which was a motor road … By late afternoon our leading scout reported that he had reached the motor road. We retired about 300 yards and felled a tree across the raging torrent. A platoon under Warrant Officer Gosnell crossed, made their way through the jungle to the road and overcame the Japanese bridge guard from their rear. I then took the battalion up to the motor road and established a defensive position astride the road at the bridge. We were no sooner in position when the Japs started to attack, with a view to breaking through our line and retreating to the coast. The 2/2nd and 2/3rd battalions were pressing them from the Kokoda side. The Japs had nowhere to go. They attacked all night – unsuccessfully. So they left the road, went through the jungle and retreated by trying to ford the roaring torrent above the bridge. We scored our highest ranking kill. Lieutenant General [Tomitaro] Horii, their force commander, was drowned trying to cross the river. Next day we moved east towards the coast and with one of Eather's battalions killed 300 Japs and captured their food depot.'[86] Cullen fought on through the Soputa area, constantly aggressive and tactically imaginative, pressing back the enemy and inflicting considerable casualties. He was awarded the DSO.

The Japanese were forced back down the track to their coastal strongholds at Buna and Gona. The ferocity of the Australian assault on these positions is captured vividly in the diaries of Trooper Hymie Pearlman, who had arrived in New Guinea with the 2/7th Cavalry Regiment. On 19 December 1942 he wrote, 'At daybreak today we started on our big adventure, from which many of us will never return. Somehow I don't feel frightened, just excited and happy to be having a go. If I do go over the divide, I will have no regrets, as after all, I did volunteer for my country.

'We go through a big area of kunai grass. From the start the Japs were ready for us, MGs were chattering everywhere and snipers are everywhere, shooting at us from trees, they are uncanny as we cannot see where the shots are coming from, and we have to just crawl on into the very face of it. The heat is intense and men are collapsing all over the place. Other groups are cut off by the Japs and are fighting their way out. Dozens are dead already and dozens wounded. How anyone can get through I don't know. Any movement is replied by a burst of Jap MG, the rustle of a blade of grass brings a rattle of shots. Bullets seem to be flying all around me.

'Our section is led by Frank Doolin. I am sub-section leader. We had to retrace our steps and cross over a road and attack that way. Old Frank is leading and a burst of MG fire hit him up the leg and lower abdomen. Scotty replied with his Owen gun and shot the sniper out of a tree, then hell broke loose, a MG pinned me down in a shallow trench, when the firing cooled down Scotty and I pulled Frank into a disused trench and tried to fix him up. Sadly he had died instantly. I felt very sad losing my friend.

'We returned to the Yanks perimeter called "Huggins". I am acting section leader now. I have one good man, Scotty and the other three are very poor ... I saw Mel Grover. He is wounded in both legs. Jack Boyle had an arm shot off, and lots of chaps badly wounded, but able to crawl in under their own "steam". There is no doubt that we have run into a trap. The Japs had everything prepared and why myself and hundreds of us are alive, goodness knows. The Section leader and Sergeant and Troop Leader had a conference and our troop has a sticky job to do. Tomorrow we go and tackle the MG nest on the right of the road. I told my section all details, poor devils, it is like sentencing men to death. Scotty took it well, but Hopping and the rest of my section are terribly frightened. I felt confident myself. The chaps are easily upset. The Yanks here are starving and only have one meal every few days. "By gosh, I'm hungry," they say.'

On 23 December, Pearlman wrote, 'We couldn't get to our MG post. The snipers got onto us and we backed out. Jimmy Cohen was wounded in the hip. I am point man in my section and mostly our section is point. It is a dangerous job, exciting, as one can run into anything at any time. All one's resources and energy is required. The strain of looking into every tree, every tree hole and bit of jungle are a nerve strain. Apart from myself there is no-one who can do point work ... Eric Baldwin asked me not to go point, as he is afraid of losing another section leader, but I can't do any-thing else and I know that I am good at it and with luck and the little bit of intuition I seem to have, may yet keep my troop from getting shot up. We just crawl, or keep very low and wind in and out looking for Jap positions, snipers. The going is mostly through dense knee to ankle depth swamps full of rotted dead men, mostly Japs, some Yanks and, I believe, an Aussie artillery officer.'

On 24 December, he wrote, 'We sleep and eat amongst the dead here and the stink of rotting flesh is everywhere. There must be hundreds dead in an area of forty acres, the drinking water is tainted. We and our clothes and hands stink of dead. I haven't taken my boots off for days and they have been continually wet. We keep on doing patrols and so far have been successful. A big stunt is coming off as half of our regiment got through and are cut off about half a mile up the road and we have to try and rejoin them. As the whole area is doubly watched by the Japs now, we think we are in for a slaughtering, but we have to try. One chap when he heard of it immediately shot his big toes ... We started off badly. Allan Mallard got off the track before we left the Yanks perimeter. Myself and section followed him and a burst of Bren gun from Aussies 39th Batt. killed him. Bad luck and I was lucky as I was next to him and they picked on Allan instead of me. "By the grace of God etc." I rejoined my troop and we moved off in the semi dawn into the unknown. Sam Hordern is in charge of us about 120 strong. We took three bearings and struck nothing, but ran into a big Jap Camp and saw about fifty Japs. We backed out, and then I and my section were given the suicide job of leading on the last stage. I was the leader and with compass and guided by Jap shots and rifle signals from "James' mob" lead the long silent file, moving like a ghost army, half crouching and crawling, doing just as I ordered. I knew, and so did they, that their lives and mine were wholly dependent upon my skill and navigation, sixth sense or whatever scientists call it. Although we didn't know the location of James' perimeter, we had an arrangement by wireless of them firing a few shots at certain intervals. By a miracle I came out in the dead centre of James' perimeter and poked my bearded head through the undergrowth and one of the men nearly shot me by surprise. Then the whole lot filed in. One of the first to see me was Len Edmonds and we were both pleased to see each other. We each thought the other dead. James' men were mad to see us and had given us up for lost. We unloaded our rations and they had a square meal. They were actually starving and I had a block of chocolate. I gave it to Len Edmonds and he ate it like a horse ... Eric Baldwin has persistently put my section in front. He seems to be placing more reliance in me than Corporal Fletcher and when any job starts to get ticklish he calls my section up to take the lead. My boys are bucking a bit, and I don't really blame them! On the last and worst leg of the patrol to James I again [take] over and lead. At one stage I cut my way through wait-a-while vine and crawled on our hands and knees. Poor Jack Hopping had thought his last moments had come. My big test came when I came upon a Jap perimeter with dozens of pits. I didn't know whether they were empty or not. So, leaving the others, I advanced slowly to the nearest one and then rushed it. To my relief it was empty and I then found all had been deserted by the Japs. Lucky for me. So, I signalled the others on and we eventually made James.'

Days later, on 7 January 1943, Pearlman wrote, 'James told Capp he had to send a patrol out to find out what is in front. It is silly here and suicidal and unnecessary. "Cappy" and I have never hit it off too well and he told me to take out a patrol, so I decided two would be enough. I asked for a volunteer and Blair Adams came. He is a good man and I like him. This is the first patrol that has gone out without a corporal as I am not even a lance corporal. We had only gone a few yards and we found a dead Aussie lying across his Owen gun, we took it with us going back. We crawled to within a few yards of the Jap lines and waited. Something made me uneasy and I looked around and about ten yards away was a Jap cautiously surveying the scene, including me. I got in first and gave him two bursts of Owen gun. The Jap's mate ran back and after a while we returned to Cappy who was wondering who did the shooting, and as he expected us to strike big trouble was surprised to see us. The boys said afterwards that we were given up for lost.'[87]

At the end of January the Japanese withdrew defeated from Papua to Lae. They had already lost the Battle of Milne Bay, and were subsequently beaten at Wau. In April, the Allies launched the Salamaua-Lae campaign to try to dislodge them from the island. On 12 May 1943, the hospital ship *Centaur* set sail from Sydney to Cairns, bound ultimately for New Guinea, carrying medical supplies and personnel, including twelve female nurses from the AANS, fifty-three members of the AAMC, and 192 soldiers from 2/12th Field Ambulance.

Dr Isidor Henry Sender of Bondi, New South Wales had boarded the ship in Sydney. Sender, a graduate of Sydney University medical school and former representative footballer, had joined the SUR in 1923 and was promoted to sergeant while completing his degree. He was commissioned into 1st Field Ambulance in 1933, served as RMO with the garrison artillery, and reached the rank of captain before transferring to the AIF in May 1940. He married, then went overseas with the AAMC to the Middle East and Greece. After two-and-a-half years' active service, he was classified as temporarily unfit and evacuated to Australia, where he was discharged as Major Isidor Sender. Back home, he saw for the first time his only child, a son aged one year and ten months. Sender quickly rejoined the AIF and, at thirty-seven years old, embarked on the *Centaur*. The hospital ship, which was fully lit and clearly marked with red crosses, was off North Stradbroke Island when it was struck by a torpedo from a Japanese submarine just before dawn. Altogether 268 Australians, including eleven of the nurses and Major Sender, were drowned, crushed, burned or taken by sharks. Survivors of the attack had to spend thirty-six hours in the water before they were picked up by USS *Mugford*. Many died while awaiting rescue. At least one other Jewish soldier, Warrant Officer Norman Lesnie, the son of Great Synagogue treasurer Harry Lesnie, went down with the *Centaur*. Lesnie at first had enlisted in the Light Horse then transferred to an ambulance unit, and had survived two years overseas. Dr Sender's young brother, Captain Leslie Sender, had enlisted in the AAMC in New Guinea, and was on active service in the territory when his brother was killed. The sinking of the *Centaur*, the worst shipping tragedy that had ever occurred on the Australian coast, was a war crime and another intimation of the apparent ruthlessness of the enemy. It was met with outrage at home and the Australians had a new battle cry – 'avenge the nurses'. Ironically, the *Centaur* had previously rescued nine of the German sailors who survived the sinking of the *Kormoran* after their ship's battle with HMAS *Sydney*.

Amid the ravages of the Salamaua-Lae campaign, Jewish Australian servicemen in New Guinea were able to lead a surprisingly rich religious life. A regular Australian congregation gathered without a rabbi. 'Inspired by the early leadership of Staff Sergeant Dick Diamond,' wrote a Christian chaplain, 'young Jewish men from the Army, Navy and Air Force, together with a few Americans are meeting regularly in our United place of worship for their Friday *shule*. They come from miles around and that, in itself, is evidence of their zeal and earnestness … There are no inducements to attract them, apart from their worship and also their fellowship with other Jews … I must confess that they have inspired me greatly.' The chaplain wrote of 'the earnest, reverent and able leadership' that was being rendered as *chazan* by Rabbi Falk's son, Gunner David Falk:* 'His service is most inspiring, and the servicemen, from [the] Lieutenant Colonel who habitually attends, to the humblest soldier present, co-operate with David in a way that would make your heart glad to see. Staff Sergeant Diamond, as President, is ever ready to give kindly support and advice; my little

---

* The three sons of Rabbi Falk were all in uniform. The youngest, Balfour, was in the navy at Tobruk and elsewhere. His brothers David and Gerald were both in the AIF.

part is to preach the sermon and to lead in some of the devotions.'[88]

Reverend Louis Rubin-Zacks, then chief minister of the Perth Hebrew Congregation, had been scheduled to sail to the Middle East as chaplain to the 2nd AIF at the start of the war, but was forced to postpone his departure due to sickness, leaving Rabbi Goldman to go in his place. Goldman returned home in April 1943 and Rubin-Zacks made his way to New Guinea. He was based in Port Moresby where his work 'included a fair share of excitement,' he wrote, 'due to enemy bombing raids'. In June Rabbi Danglow, now Senior Hebrew Chaplain to the armed forces, also embarked on a three-and-half-month tour of military bases from Central Australia to New Guinea, an effort which, according to his biographer, 'almost killed him'.[89] Rubin-Zacks conducted services for Australian and American servicemen, attended by 500 soldiers at *Rosh Hashanah* and 550 on *Kol Nidre* night, including twenty to thirty Australians on each occasion. 'I have never yet experienced in civil life such a fine body of earnest and devout worshippers, following the services with such keen enthusiasm and attention,' he wrote. 'During the mornings, the continuous drone of planes overhead often drowned our voices, and the last few minutes of *Kol Nidre* were concluded in darkness, due to an air-raid warning. It was most impressive and profoundly stirring, under these conditions, in our Chapel in a clearing in the Jungle, to hear the men join heartily in singing *Yigdal* and *Olam*, and finally to disperse to the age-old tune of *Hatikvah*.'[90]*

On 4 September 1943, at a point east of Lae, the 9th Division staged the first Australian amphibious landing since Gallipoli. The day after the ground troops took the port, men of the

---

*   Rubin-Zacks returned to Australia a sick man in 1944. Chaplain Goldman finished Rubin-Zacks' work in the South-West Pacific, ministering to Jewish Australian troops from New Guinea to the Solomon Islands, Indonesia and Borneo until the end of the war.

7th Division joined US paratroopers in seizing the nearby Nazdab airfield. Nazdab was quickly built up into a huge forward base for the USAF and the RAAF, from which a storm of attacks was launched against Japanese positions in the area. Among the Australian airmen at Nazdab was Wesley Browne, whose father, Roy, and three uncles had served in World War One. Eighteen-year-old Wesley had worn his cadets' uniform when he enlisted in the RAAF in Woolloomooloo, New South Wales, in October 1942. The other recruits 'sniggered', he later wrote, 'but it was not long before we were all dressed similarly'.[91] Wesley was a Judean Scout, and the RAAF assessed him as 'earnest and keen' and 'most emphatic in his desire to do wartime work'.[92] He trained as a wireless operator and arrived in Nazdab on 29 January 1944. One night he hitchhiked to Lae for a Friday-night service in the town. 'I went into a large hut and saw a very large crowd of Americans,' he said, 'and right at the front a few Aussie hats and found two of them were from 2nd Bondi Judean … We celebrated that night by driving around Lae in a jeep singing Scout songs.'[93]

For the rest of the war, the Australian 6th Division, with air and naval support, fought a costly and militarily dubious push against the Japanese in strategically unimportant northern New Guinea. When Colonel Cullen's 2/1st Australian Infantry Battalion returned to New Guinea in December 1944, they threw themselves into the Aitape–Wewak campaign. They succeeded in clearing the Japanese from the coast but Australian casualties were high. Cullen was awarded a second DSO for his actions at the capture of Nambut Hill and beyond. His citation recorded that the 'exceptional success of this battle was entirely due to his own personal supervision of the action which he controlled at all times from positions with his forward company. In the same manner he conducted the battalion's advance to the Anumb River, securing in rapid succession objective after objective. Once again, in the But sector when clearing the high ground to the south, he showed up as a leader and a tactician beyond the ordinary. His skilful manoeu-vring of companies into position in the rear of the enemy for the purpose of establishing patrol bases achieved successful results, completely disorganising and destroying the enemy in this sector. The initial policy and subsequent action carried out so success-fully by Lieutenant Colonel Cullen proved him to be a command-ing officer with courage and outstanding qualities. He, in a large measure, contributed to the success of the Brigade's advance.'

The Allies had also attacked Morotai, the most northern of the Halmahera islands in Indonesia. Bombing of the Japanese began in August, the invasion in September. 'I arrived there after the Japanese had been pushed back from the only useful areas on the island,' wrote Philip Opas, 'that is, where the port and two airfields were located. After that, we did not worry about the Japa-nese. They were harmless. They were cut off from supplies. They had no sea or air support and were left to fend for themselves in the jungle and from occasional foraging in the services' garbage dump … We occupied such a small part of the island that we were prac-tically confined to sitting on the beach looking across the water to the main Halmahera Island where there existed still a large uncon-quered Japanese force.'

Also in the area was Lasar Slutzkin's nephew Frank Slutzkin, who had joined the RAN in December 1942. Slutzkin had been selected for the Officers' Training School at Flinders Naval Depot, then the anti-submarine school at HMAS *Rushcutter* in Sydney. When he had completed the course, he joined the newly refitted corvette HMAS *Geelong*, which sailed up to Milne Bay in New Guinea in April 1944, and spent six months on convoy duties in the South West Pacific. The *Geelong* escorted army resupply ships threatened by Japanese submarines, and was sunk in a collision with the US tanker SS *York* on 18 October 1944. 'I was on one of the dog watches,' said Slutzkin, 'and I could see on the horizon a ship approaching … We had radar and I handed over to the officer taking over from me – I said, "Keep your eye on that ship" ... I then went down to have my evening meal by myself in the wardroom ... Some half-hour later there was a tremendous collision. I got catapulted over the table in the wardroom. Water was rushing down the gangway from the upper deck like a waterfall and I went up this waterfall, I think two steps to the surface. I don't think you could ever do it unless the adrenalin was really flooding ... Everyone was given an action station in case of an accident, and I had something like ten sailors under my direction to man this Carley Raft if we were in a collision. It had been painted to the deck. The first lieutenant was very keen on paint and when we came to release it, it was stuck, so we had to belt it and bash it, and eventually it floated clear, and about twenty or twenty-five hung onto this little Carley Raft, which was built to carry about ten.

'We were up to our waists in water and we floated clear of the corvette, which was visibly keeling to starboard down to the right side. We knew it was going to sink and we just had to float clear. The tanker, immediately after collision, let go lifeboats, and came looking for survivors. We were in the water for about two hours, pitch black. There was one little light attached to our Carley Raft, so wherever they could see a light they came and picked up ... It was an earth-shattering experience that you don't really get trained for, but we laughed and joked through it.'[94]

Lieutenant Asher Joel was a Jewish officer from Sydney who had served in the army in Australia, then organised the Lord Mayor's Patriotic and War Fund and the Australian Comforts Fund, before he was released to the RAN. Joel worked closely with the US in the latter years of the war, and was highly thought of by the American staff. He was the first member of the RAN to be awarded the American Bronze Star, which he received in recognition of his 'meritorious service in connection with combat operations in the SW Pacific area'. Joel worked in public relations for Naval Intelligence and landed with the Americans at Leyte in the Philippines in October 1944. He had previously sailed with HMAS *Australia* in Morotai where, he wrote, 'To keep the ship's company on their toes dawn action stations were held every morning at four am. Alarm bells would ring and a great scurrying of feet and drama would begin. Anti-flash gear was donned, boots pulled on and steel helmets worn on top of the anti-flash gear. You then had to race to your position on the ship. On one particular morning the acorns given to me by my children had fallen out of my pocket and I took it as a bad omen. In the strange half-light that precedes dawn I was scrambling around the deck trying to find my acorns. Heavy boots trod on my hands several times and then I saw one of the nuts. Just as I was about to pick it up a great boot squashed it. I found the other one and thought this was an omen too. I am not going to get killed, I told myself, because I have only lost one acorn, but I might lose an arm or a leg. After landing at Tacloban in Leyte … I planted that acorn.

'When we reached our destination open gunfire raked the shores and we saw great slivers of land sliding into the water. I was standing at my battle station on the bridge wearing my steel helmet. I had not put the strap underneath my chin and when a four-inch anti-aircraft gun opened fire directly beneath me the concussion blew the steel helmet off. I had not anticipated the guns opening up and the shock was quite sudden. Then I saw what I thought was my head falling in front of my eyes. The thought flashed through my mind, "I'm dead, my bloody head's been shot off and I'm watching it." The experience was quite unnerving. While the ships continued to fire a volcano began to erupt on the starboard side of the ship causing every free man to rush to that side to watch the phenomenon. Next thing I heard was [Rear Admiral John] Collins screaming from the bridge. Signals were coming in that the shells we were firing were falling short among the American invasion force. Because of the great number of men who had rushed to the other side of the ship, the angle the guns were firing at had been elevated.'[95]

THE DENTIST MAJOR SYDNEY LEVINE WAS FINALLY SENT overseas in January 1945, to command a dental unit in Jacquinot Bay, New Britain, south of the Japanese base at Rabaul. Levine was angered by the way journalism could make war seem both dynamic and ridiculous. 'Those who came here first say the landing was the funniest thing in the world,' wrote Levine on 12 January 1945, 'unloading parties actually got ashore before the infantry – anyway they were pretty sure that there would be no Japs here.' He pasted into his diary a clipping from the troops' own paper, *Guinea Gold*: 'Fighting troops pushed inland, dripping wet. Rear troops began erecting small tents and "doovers" which they covered with banana-tree leaves.'

Levine wrote, 'This is what happened. The barges which came to take the infantry ashore had all the barges gear so they took a party from the ships to unload this gear ashore and then came back to pick up the infantry. Troops then went ashore, cleared the jungle and made camps while others went to other spots farther along and did the same. This is what the paper account calls "fighting troops pushed inland dripping wet".'

According to *Guinea Gold*, 'The formal taking over by the Australians on a 2500-feet ridge (at Torokina Bougainville) was commemorated by an Australian Lieutenant Colonel in a novel manner. In the presence of a group of us officers he threw first an Australian grenade and then an American grenade at a Jap pillbox thirty yards away. The sector was then formally declared open.'

Levine despaired. 'What is this little war, a football match?' he asked. 'This is one of the stupidest things I have ever heard of. One gets the impression at times that the whole blasted war is a joke – a very tragic one but still a joke with myself as one of the chief clowns.'[96]

The war in the Pacific was settled far from New Guinea. On 6 August 1945 the Americans dropped an atomic bomb on the Japanese city of Hiroshima. On 9 August the city of Nagasaki was similarly destroyed. On the same day Russia declared war on Japan. Sydney-born Captain Max Sernack was in Morotai with a transport unit. 'During the night of August 10th there was pandemonium,' he said, 'and there were shots going up on Morotai where there was no warfare, but all of a sudden, everything went crazy. There were tracer bullets going up in the sky, and then the word came through that the war had ended. That was on the 10th, but it wasn't official until the 15th, so I told my men, "No one is going to die until after the war is finished, keep low, don't take any risks, don't get involved in anything, just wait to see what happens." In between the 10th and the 15th, when it was official, I had to take two amphibious vehicles over to pick up 300 Samurai swords … A special ship came up with a crew for the signing of the surrender. I had to take an amphibious vehicle, which they called ducks, to pick up the interpreters. One comes over the side – in such a mess of a uniform you've never seen, and when he turned around, it was Mr Joseph my Hebrew teacher. I said, "Mr Joseph," … He said, "I'm the interpreter." I said, "What, Yiddish?" He said, "No, Japanese."'[97]

On 15 August the Japanese capitulated. 'It was the most frightening day of the war,' wrote Opas. 'The American troops treated us to a spectacular pyrotechnic display. They were so overjoyed at the prospect of going home that they fired off everything they could find … There was a steady rain of spent cartridges, bullets and shells falling around us. I stayed in my tent, not that it was any protection, but at least I could not see what was happening. Miraculously nobody was hurt.'

'A Japanese major came out of the jungle at a time when I was alone and picking wild passionfruit from a large spreading bush. I was more than a mile from the nearest camp and, to my surprise, he surrendered to me. He had thirty others with him. They were ragged and in poor condition. He saluted and solemnly handed his samurai sword to me in token of surrender … I can still see the major, standing stiffly to attention, proffering the sword … He

had small rimless spectacles and he sported a Chaplinesque moustache. His tears left me unmoved.'[98] Information about the Japanese surrender had to be communicated to every corner of New
Guinea and the Pacific Islands. Private Phil Allen, a Jewish signaller with 47th Battalion, was on patrol in Bougainville when word
of the enemy capitulation reached his base. He was told to remain
where he was until the Japanese officers had broken the news to
their men.

Frank Slutzkin was posted to HMAS *Hawkesbury*, a new riv-
er-class frigate. 'The war ended when we were in Morotai,' he said.
'We took the surrender of the Japanese 5th Army in those areas and
did a march past the various towns around the port ... These were
wonderful experiences for a young twenty-and-a-half-year-old ...
it was like an adventure rather than serious war ... I enjoyed every
minute of it.'

But for the men who had been forced to build the Thai-Burma
railway, the war had been an unrelieved nightmare. Frank Slutzkin's *Hawkesbury* was the only Australian vessel in Singapore Harbour when Admiral Lord Louis Mountbatten took the Japanese
surrender on 12 September 1945. 'We flew a huge Australian flag
from the main mast,' said Slutzkin, 'knowing that there were a lot
of Aussies ashore, and the message got to Changi and they started
streaming – finding their way on board just to hear about things at
home ... until you saw the survivors, you couldn't believe that men
could still be alive when they were just skin and bone. They had
tragic stories to tell. We fed them with bread, butter and jam and
tea, and told them to go easy, because they were starving. We ran
out of food, so we had to send across to the *Nelson* – the flagship
– for more food to keep these soldier survivors alive.'[99] Opas was
responsible for repatriating Allied POWs and the disbandment of
RAAF units and their return to Australia. 'I saw men and women
pathetically watching the arrival of each plane to see if their spouses
had survived,' he wrote. 'The reunion of husbands, wives and

children was indescribable. The grief at the news that there could be no reunion was beyond description.'

Some former POWs were moved to Morotai on their way back home. Shortly before Christmas, Opas was in charge of a Catalina sent from Labuan to Kuching in Sarawak to pick up troops. At Kuching, they learned that Colonel Suga, commandant of Kuching prison, where POWs had been held, had been captured and was to be taken to Labuan for a war-crimes trial. Suga had crucified two Chinese women in the town square for smuggling rice to POWs. 'Before he arrived at Labuan to face trial almost every member of the Australian contingent had volunteered for the firing squad,' he wrote. 'I also put my name down when we returned. However, he foiled us. He asked for a razor to shave before his trial. He was too quick for his guards and slashed his wrists ... I witnessed three hangings of convicted Japanese war criminals ... I could have pulled the lever myself.'[100]

When the Japanese in the Philippines surrendered on 2 September, Hobart-born Sergeant Neil Glasser of the RAAF, the son of Hyman Glasser of the 1st AIF, watched as General Tomoyuki Yamashita, who had led the Imperial Japanese Army down the Malay peninsula in 1942, was marched through Baguio in northern Luzon. 'We were all waiting there,' Glasser remembered. 'We called out, "You bloody bastard!" We just screamed at him, he had killed so many Australian boys.'[101] Later, Glasser came upon a familiar figure berating a group of Japanese POWs. It was Mr Joseph* again. Glasser, too, remembered him from Hebrew lessons.

There was at least one more Jewish Australian serviceman in Manila in 1945. Leading Aircraftsman Sam Morris, the son of Rabbi Isack Morris of Newcastle, New South Wales, attended *Yom Kippur* services in town. The *Kol Nidre* sermon was delivered by the Canadian Rabbi Perry Nussbaum, who had briefly been the

---

*   Presumably Lieutenant Norman Joseph.

Rabbi of Temple Beth Israel in Melbourne. 'On *Yom Kippur* day,' Morris wrote to his father, 'I was quite thrilled to be called to the Reading of the Law. The only other Aussies at Divine Service were Lieutenant Joseph, AIF, [and] a lad named Glasser.'[102] They broke their fast together with salmon rolls and biscuits supplied by the American Red Cross, then attended a dance at a Far Eastern Air Force camp where they met Jewish members of the US Women's Army Corps.

Prisoners of war

A total of 61 806 men were sent to help build a Thai-Burma Railway to supply Japanese troops fighting in British-held Burma and 12 399 died in horrific squalor. It seems that about 100 Australian Jews were prisoners of the Japanese. Although they rarely faced antisemitism from their captors, some did not survive starvation, disease and ill-treatment in the prison camps of Asia and on the Burma Railway. Warrant Officer 2 Victor Blashki, of that illustrious military family, was captured in Malaya and died in Thailand in 1943. Private Leonard Joseph, the brother of Norman and Beryl, was captured in Singapore and spent three years in Thai camps. The diarist Neville Milston went from Khonkhan 'hospital camp' near Thambuzyat to Tamarkan, Thailand, keeping the Burma Railway running and cutting wood to burn on the trains. Milston carried his *siddur* wherever he travelled, and was able to lend it to Sydney-born signaller Gil 'Mark' Hayman for a proxy *barmitzvah* service held for Hayman's 13-year-old son Leon in Tamarkan on 27 September 1944. The extraordinary event was formally witnessed by a Japanese military interpreter and a number of Australian, American, British, Canadian and Dutch POWs; Milston could not make it to the service as he was incapacitated with malaria, although he survived the war to marry Madge Grouse, the Jewish nurse who had served in New Guinea. Captain Dr Victor Brand of Melbourne, who had been awarded the MC for his heroism in Malaya in 1942, operated a simple hospital at Tamuronpat on the Burma Railway in Thailand before he was sent to Changi where he was interned until the war's end.

Robert Patkin was among the small number of Australian Jews captured by the Germans. After he was taken prisoner in Greece in 1941, Patkin was transported to a camp at Marburg (now known as Maribor, Slovenia) on the border of Austria and Yugoslavia. 'My family received news from the Army that their son was "Missing Believed Killed",' he wrote. 'When in a German hospital I was interviewed by a famous German called Max Schmeling (a champion boxer – paratrooper). He spoke excellent English with an American accent and interviewed me with six of my wounded friends – and assured us it would not be propaganda but if we gave a message to our parents, he would make sure it would be heard on the wireless. My cousin, Michael Patkin, in Egypt, heard this message and cabled to my family that he had heard my voice and that I was alive.

'From Marburg,' wrote Patkin, 'I escaped and was caught a fortnight later which wasn't a serious crime in those days. However, I was put on bread and water for fourteen days and locked in a cell, and from there moved to a camp that was meant for escapees. It was called Villach which was near the Italian border. From Villach I escaped and was away for some few days, caught again, and then moved into Bavaria, where I went to a camp in a little village called Hohenfels. I was there for a period of some two years. From this camp, in the very early days, I escaped with a friend and we were out for some few days and were caught and brought back. Eventually the Germans treated escapees as criminals, and escaping became a very serious offence. If you were caught, the likelihood of being shot was enough to put one off the thought of escaping. However, we spent some couple of years in this camp.

My friend, Ian Ramsay, had been in a punishment camp in Poland. (He hit a German officer.) We met up when he had served his time and resumed our friendship. Towards the end of the war the two of us escaped again, and we finally got through to Paris. After spending time in Paris, where the Americans were very kind to us, we returned to England and became part of the Army again, and eventually shipped back to Australia.'[103]

Caroline Isaacson wrote a newspaper story about the problems of former POWs. 'Ever since our men were taken captive,' she wrote, 'many of us have shared their exile in our thoughts and in our hearts, but none of us at home could possibly have realised to the full all that they have had to endure. I know several returned POW, and all are reluctant to speak of their experiences. It is not difficult, however, to piece together, from the little they will say, that cruelties and indignities of many years have left scars as deep in their minds as in their bodies.'[104]

Just as some Jewish Australians were prisoners, others were guards. In the Mansfield family, there was one of each. George Mansfield was a POW in Changi and the Burma Railway, and his grandson was to go to the first Gulf War. George's brother Alan was a sergeant in the commandoes who looked after a number of POWs after the Japanese surrender. Many years later, Warrant Officer Takeo Yamashita of the Japanese Navy wrote to Mansfield to thank him for the kindness with which the commando treated his charges. Yamashita recalled a thick mist hanging over Lake Tondano on 27 September 1945, when he first shook Mansfield's hand. 'Everyone had lost their conscience after a long period of fighting,' he wrote. '… At the time as you were armed with pistol, so was I in my heart. It was my resolution at the worst time, I would kill myself after killing you. After two days, you took off your Colt and approached us and opened your hands for soothing of our feeling. "You are our friends," said you. Whenever you came to the air-base, you taught us simple English conversation.' One afternoon, after a heavy shower, 'we saw a beautiful rainbow across the lake,' wrote Yamashita. 'You took my hand and teaching me the colours of the rainbow one by one and strolled on the pier of the air base. Your pronunciation was rather peculiar to my ears. It seemed to my [sic] as if you said "Tank you" instead of "thank you." … the rainbow is a bridge of dream, a bridge binging [sic] to us happiness and friendship.'

Soldiers tore off Yamashita's rank emblem, cap and band, and the Japanese prisoners had part of their wireless confiscated. When Yamashita protested to Mansfield about the radio, 'You repeated "I am sorry",' he remembered, 'and went back to your HQ. Four days after, you bought [sic] us the parts taken away from us. It was indeed a big surprise … I was moved so deeply.'

The night before Yamashita was transferred to a POW compound, he sent Mansfield a bottle of sake and a cup. Mansfield gave Yamashita his address in Australia and a promise to visit him in the compound. 'I expressed my gratitude saying "TANK YOU",' wrote Yamashita. 'You were pleased to hear my pronunciation and told me my English advanced much. If I had had the slip you gave me, I might have been able to write you earlier. But the slip was taken away by Dutch MP when I got on board the repatriation vessel.

'You requested us the discipline to be very strict, but for other things such as fellowship with each other, you were generous. I have so many things to tell you. Recollecting those, I still shouting "Thank you Mr Mansfield". Perhaps you cannot hear me.'[105]

The other war in the air

All this time, another war had been fought by Australians in the air over Europe. At the outbreak of the fighting, Australia had joined the Empire Air Training Scheme, under which flight crews went through basic training in Australia and then sailed to Canada for advanced instruction. Most served at first in Britain, North Africa and the Mediterranean, leaving little air power to defend Australia once the Japanese joined the war. Several Australian Jewish pilots were posted to Bomber Command in London. Sergeant Sol Levitus, from Rose Bay, New South Wales, was the pilot of a Wellington bomber in a huge raid on Rostock in eastern Germany on 26 April 1942; his rear gunner was Sergeant George Viner. Their aircraft was attacked by a Messerschmitt: 'We didn't see anything before bullets came up from below us,' said Levitus. 'We were silhouetted against the moon and an easy mark for the enemy, who of course was in darkness. Then Viner saw him 100 yards away. Viner fired immediately and the Messerschmitt broke off but attacked again from dead astern and from below. There was another exchange of fire and the Messerschmitt climbed to our port side to try again, but Viner gave it a long burst and saw the bullets cutting into the Messerschmitt's cockpit and starboard engine. He went straight down afire, with smoke pouring in volume from the engine.'[106] Levitus was killed in action on 3 June, shot out of the sky near Düsseldorf. His brother AIF Sergeant Maurice Morris was killed in an accident in 1945.

Peter Isaacson of Melbourne had joined the RAAF in December 1940 and graduated from the Empire Training Scheme. He was initially posted to the Australian 460 Squadron – the same unit as Sol Levitus – where his first operational flight was a 1000-bomber raid in May 1942. He wrote home: 'We went to Essen in the heart of the Ruhr, or, as we call it, "Happy Valley". Everything went well until we had dropped our bombs, and in the evasive action the D/R compass "went for a Burton". I didn't notice this for a while, so we were going round in circles over the target. After I'd checked with the magnetic compass, Bob [Neilsen] took a couple of astro shots which put us about thirty miles east of Essen instead of west, so back we had to go, and to be above Happy Valley alone is no fun, I can assure you. Flak was bursting everywhere and we were lucky to be hit only once or twice. Luckily, no bad damage was done though. Another fifteen minutes had passed, when Ed [Wertzler] in the bomb aimer's department yelled through the intercom, "Fighter below, a little to starboard."

'I immediately dived and turned starboard but not before the b— had fired. The bullets entered the bomb bays and fuselage causing a fair bit of damage … Luckily, Ed, on seeing the Jerry, had hopped into his turret, otherwise he wouldn't be alive today, for some of the bullets pierced the bomb aimer's compartment. As it was, he got three pieces of shrapnel in the leg. This was the only burst the fighter managed to get in, 'cos all three gunners fired and I took evasive action. We had lost about 13 000 feet in about five secs. A fire had started in the bomb bay which Ed, with the help of others managed to put out. Although Ed had been wounded, he said nothing about it 'til the fire was subdued and we were on our way again … After the fight, all the compasses went haywire and I got one of the boys to let me know what the bomb sights were reading. All the way I steered back by this. The rudder trim was damaged, which made the kite pretty difficult to control. I had an SOS sent out when we hit England and put down at the first aerodrome I came to. Ed went to hospital. Everyone seemed to ring up – Group Intelligence, Group Captain, AOC, WingCo, and they all congratulated us … When we saw the kite in the morning, we were amazed at the extent of the damage. We'd been raked from nose to stern with cannon and .303 fire, some of the holes being more than a foot square. The largest was two-feet six-inches wide by one-foot long.'[107]

Isaacson was awarded the Distinguished Flying Medal, then left the squadron to join 156 Squadron RAF of Pathfinder Force, where he picked up the Distinguished Flying Cross after an air raid on Berlin. Altogether, he flew forty-five missions with Bomber Command. Half of all Bomber Command aircrew were killed before they had completed ten missions. Going on averages Isaacson should have died four times.

Other Jewish pilots included Joe Barrington, whose family had anglicised their surname from Benjamin but whose father was a performer in an act called 'Stanley and Bernard, Two Yiddisher Boys and a Piano'. Barrington grew up in Coogee and was working as a wool classer. 'I couldn't see any future,' he says, 'but anyway the war interfered with that.' He got on the Air Force Reserve at nineteen years old in 1939, and was finally able to join the RAAF proper in November 1941.

In 1942 Barrington was sent to the UK on HMS *Esperance Bay*. 'We got into a convoy of fifty ships,' he says. 'But the convoy was attacked by a U-pack, and ships were sunk. I was put on gun duty on a little ramp on a bridge over the water ... In the morning, there were explosions, and the captain came up to me and said, "Take the cover off your gun, man, it's action stations." But I couldn't see anything to aim at. I was sitting in it, swivelling around. I went to bed in the end. Someone else took over. When I woke up in the morning, we were on our own. The convoy had split. Our captain took us due north, right around past Iceland. We got into floating ice packs. It was the time of the breaking up of snow. At night, I'd be lying in my bunk, and I could hear the ice hitting the side of the ship.'

In the UK, they went down to the Australian depot in Bourne-mouth. On the day Barrington arrived, he was sitting down by the water with two friends when an air raid began. 'But before it had started, we went to go out for lunch,' he says. 'The other two said, "Why don't we go out for a beer?" I said, "No, I'll see you later." I never saw them again. They got a direct hit on the pub they were in. They were both killed. Then [the Germans] came over and strafed where we were.'

Barrington joined 451 Squadron RAAF, which had just been hit with a raid and lost two pilots. He stayed there for eighteen months and flew fifty-two missions. 'We were escorting American Liberators that were bombing over Italy,' he says. 'And when they'd done that, when they were on their way back, we could break off and scare to ground whatever was moving.' They moved to an aerodrome in France. 'The Germans had just left,' he says, 'and they very pertinently left some mines that we had to tippy-toe around and know where they were, just to get a meal.' After a number of operations, they were brought back to England, and told they had been chosen, along with No 453 and some British squadrons, to carry bombs on their Spitfires. They practiced dive-bombing at a specially built aerodrome near Goodwin Sands, off the Deal Coast in Kent. 'When we were ready, the squadrons went up to near the Wash,' he says. 'It was probably the nearest point to the target in Holland.' On a raid to blow up a railway line that serviced a hidden German V2 factory, the squadron met with V2 fire. 'Suddenly a rocket went up right in front of us,' says Barrington, 'and it was an astounding thing to watch it slowly go up, far enough away to not worry us, except that when the slipstream from the rocket came, it threw us around like toys.'

They flew daylight raids until the British army moved up into Belgium. The 451 squadron escorted Lancaster bombers on the last massive bombing raid on Germany, when 1000 planes attacked the naval base at Heligoland, an island off Hamburg in the North Sea. 'We were circling around many squadrons of fighters,' says Barrington, 'they were coming as far as the eye could see, from England right to the target area. It was an amazing sight ... Flying above us were two Messerschmitt jets. They came down and they took one running shot – it wasn't exactly at me, but it was at somebody – and disappeared back to base. Because it was the end of the war and they couldn't see the point of being shot down.'

'You wore "dog tags" around your neck to identify you if you needed identifying,' said Barrington. 'It had your name, your number, and your religion. I never had mine on when I was flying because I just decided that if I went down anywhere in Europe I would be at an absolute disadvantage for them to know that I was

Jewish.' He struggled to cope with the deaths of those around him. 'You're so close to people. Closer than you'd ever get in civilian life,' he said. 'You're living and eating and even dying, and that's the worst part when you lose the friends. You've just got to learn to live with it, and get over it … If somebody was shot down they would know who his closest friend was … You had to pack up what was his and you had to sort out what you would send home, and you had to write a letter. That is not easy to do … I couldn't imagine anything worse than that.'[108]

Cyril Borsht of Brisbane did not even tell his mother he was playing first-grade rugby, so it was difficult to break it to her that he was going to become a pilot. However, he had his sisters on his side. 'They could see the facts of it,' he says. 'If I didn't enrol voluntarily, I'd be conscripted, and it would be the army, not the air force. A good Jewish mother can tear her hair out and put on the greatest show on earth. She did that all night.' But Borsht had already signed up. 'It wasn't something she could stop,' he says. Borsht, too, finished up with Bomber Command. The dangers were invisible to him then. 'We weren't a practical generation in that sense,' he says. 'All we could see was that to fly was the ultimate. I used to build model aircraft. Every kid that has stars in his eyes about flying built balsa aircraft. My bedroom was full of all the latest aircraft kits. All my spare time was in building and painting them, hanging them.'

At first, flying was worrying, says Borsht, 'but not frightening – you got a thrill out of it. It became matter-of-fact after a while … There was always a reason why you were in the clouds, and you were always going somewhere or returning from somewhere that had been horrible. But there were a number of occasions when you were sort of free. I can remember when we had a two-engine fail going out on a trip. We were joining 100 aircraft on a daylight bombing raid, and we were all going to meet over the town of Reading in the south of Britain, and on our way down to the meeting, we lost one engine. It just blew up. And, incredibly, before we got to Reading, the other engine blew up. We were carrying something like 10 000 pounds of bombs, and the aircraft just couldn't sustain that. Fortunately, we weren't far from the Channel, so I had to head for the Channel, losing height all the time, and drop my bombs, all on safety, in the Channel. So there was nothing else for us to do but go back to squadron. I've only got two engines out of four, but the Lancaster was a brilliant machine, it flew on two as well as four, and we flew up the middle of the UK, flying more or less on the deck, at about fifty feet, chasing trains and avoiding factories. When we got there, all the fire trucks were out, the ambulances were out, and I put the aircraft down and reported to the CO and that was that – but that was a brilliant trip. We enjoyed that.'

On the bombing raids, they swarmed in massive fleets, a cloud of death ready to burst on the country below. 'You can't see anything,' he says, 'but you can hear the noise of the ack-ack bursting around you. You're on intercom with all the crew, so they're all shouting various comments about what's going on around them, fighters coming in and bombs dropping. It's a panic situation on every aircraft. If you can imagine 500 aircraft converging on one spot, they're all supposed to be at different heights, but that still doesn't make it any easier because if they all get there at the same time, the bloke up top who's dropping bombs is going to hit somebody underneath him, and that happened regularly.'

On 23 October 1944, he was shot down over Holland. When he parachuted out, 'I had this poor old bugger, the engineer, mortally wounded,' he says, 'and I had to get him out. He was the last bloke left in the plane. And I was alright. I could've gone and left him there, I suppose. It wouldn't have made any difference. He could've died in the aircraft as easily as he died in the water. But there was something that said you just can't do it. So I pushed him out the hatch and followed him immediately. I knew from the moment I left that seat that I had very little time, because the aircraft was at 1000 feet when I left my seat. It would've been at 900 feet or less by the time I left the aircraft. So I wasn't counting to ten. Then when I pulled my chute, never having experienced it, the jerk from the chute is quite severe when it opens. I thought I might've caught the tail part of the aircraft. But no, I'm as free as a bird. The next thing, I'm looking down at these spikes sticking out of the water. I didn't know where the rest of the crew were. I dived into a culvert, because I knew the rest of the fleet were about to bomb, and I hid there until it was all over, then the Germans came and got me.'

He later wrote, 'I was marched along a road to a farm, and pushed inside a large barn guarded by a soldier where I was delighted to find other members of my crew … My watch, silver cigarette case, and penknife were taken. (Some time after the end of the war I received a package from the American Army Services enclosing my watch, cigarette case and penknife!!) The guard coveted my prized flying boots and made me take them off – giving me his boots as a swap … We were then moved to Middelburg and were kept captive in the basement of a deserted school. When Glynn Cooper bailed out, he landed on the roof of a farmhouse and slid into a rain barrel, injuring his leg. As he was unable to walk, and as Tom Lonergan and I were the only two uninjured, we had to carry him on our backs. He was much taller and heavier than us, so kept catching his leg on the ground – with much complaint.'

The prisoners were taken to an interrogation camp at Oberursel, 'where we entered solitary confinement for four days in windowless cells about eight feet by four feet,' wrote Borsht. 'My interrogator was Oberfeldtwebel Behrens, a blond, handsome Aryan with an excellent command of English, who knew our bomb-aimer, Tom Laing, the Geordie, both having worked at Newcastle-on-Tyne shipyards.

'Our regulations required us to give the Germans our name,

rank and number – nothing more, and, of course, he claimed he needed much more detail of operations. He lost his charm and his cool over the next couple of days and became increasingly threatening with regards to my religion, threatening to call the SS. In the meantime he was wining and dining Tom Laing, and gathering all the information he wanted, which was not very secret or special.'[109] His interrogator was 'very charming one minute, and then threatening the next', says Borsht. 'He was full of guile and he was prepared to go to any lengths to get information from me that he already had – that was the silly part about it; it wasn't special information, he wanted confirmation.'

'As the turnover of POWs was fairly high,' he wrote, 'we were discharged from Oberursel and trucked to Wetzlar and finally to Sagan Stalag Luft III (the camp from which *The Great Escape* was made) and then to its satellite camp Belaria Stalag Luft IIIA. My POW number was KGFN [Kriegsgefangener] 8702 … On arrival, I was greeted by the Smith brothers, near neighbours of ours in Brisbane, the sons of ex-Police Commissioner Smith. Errol, a bomber pilot, and Cy, a fighter pilot, had been in POW camp for some time. They took me under their wing and warned me of the danger of "going around the bend", and to that end suggested I use my newly issued Red Cross logbook to record events and drawings in camp.'[110] [One of Borsht's drawings has been reproduced in this book – see image 35.] Borsht says, 'There was a Jew in the camp with me, an Englishman from Wigan named [Flight Officer Harry] Lanzetter, and we became very good friends – he and a pilot from Australia who was a good mate of mine, shot down on the same trip, from my squadron. So the three of us formed a little group and we played cards together, we combined our rations, and we used the same cooking appliances, did all our cooking and eating together.'

The war ended for Borsht when the Russians arrived at the camp in 1945. 'They charged through the main gates with great big tanks with women infantry sitting on the sides of them,' says Borsht. 'They roared down the main street, and we thought, this is liberation. We were cheering and getting all excited, and they kept charging through the other end. They kept going. All of a sudden, there we are, the doors are open, everyone's gone – the Germans are gone, the Russians are gone – and our British officer in charge of the camp was telling everybody to be careful, don't take any risks, take it easy, wait.

'The next minute, the Russians were back. They didn't release us, they just hung on to us. They closed the camp off and put their own people in charge. Some blokes had actually got out and started walking and they were quickly rounded up by the Russkies under threat of being shot if they didn't get back to the camp. About a week into their control, the Americans sent a convoy of trucks to pick up all the Allied soldiers – the Americans, the Aussies and the Brits. The Russians stood them up at rifle-point, turned them around and sent them away empty.' The stand-off lasted about a month, then the Russians turned up with a great convoy of trucks 'and they loaded us on, and it was the most frightening, hectic drive I'd ever had over the autobahns ... I thought, I've been through the bloody war and I'm going to be killed by these stupid bastards'. They were traded one-for-one with Russian POWs from the Western side. 'The bridges had all been shot out of the Oder river, so they built a pedestrian, sort of military bridge across. In the middle of the bridge was an American colonel and a Russian colonel, and one by one they marched us across one way, and the Russians the other way. They crossed the bridge 'into heaven', says Borsht. 'The Yanks turned it on. They had the lot: food, bars, women, beds, pictures. We didn't know what to do first, fill our bellies or drink our heads off, so we did both.'[111]

Joe Barrington was in Marseilles at the Liberation. 'We went into a brewery on Toulon,' he says, 'and my job was the messing officer of the pilots' mess. We took a truck and we piled it up with

French beer ... And, instead of going straight back, we said we might see if we could have a look at Marseilles. That day was their day of Liberation, and when we parked the truck everyone wanted to buy us a glass of champagne. We spent the afternoon there. The [French] were rounding up the few Germans that were left in Marseilles, they shaved the hair off all the girls who were friendly to the Germans and marched them down the main street.' When he came back to base, Barrington had a fight with a drunken pilot who called him a 'fucking Jew'.

When the war was over, the squadron was posted to Germany as part of the occupation force. 'We were given a talk on how to behave as the conquerors,' says Barrington. 'For six months, there was no fraternisation. But for me, being Jewish, I found it quite easy. I wouldn't want to fraternise with Germans. The theatres in London were showing Belsen camp that the British had opened up. They brought the whole of the population of Bergen Belsen to come and have a look at the camp and help bury the dead that were lying around.' Barrington's CO in Germany wanted to see the remains of the camp, and asked Barrington if, as a Jew, he wanted to come along. 'When we got there, there was only one hut left,' says Barrington. 'They'd burned all the other huts. We went inside, there was a guard on duty, and the ovens were there, that they used to get rid of the bodies. There was a huge pile of shoes on the ground in one part of the camp. It was like a pyramid. I don't know why, but they buried the bodies but kept the shoes.'

The invisible war

The history of Australian Jewish military participation in World War Two was first recorded by Gerald Pynt and Jack Epstein in *Australian Jewry's Book of Honour World War II*, published by the Australian Federation of Jewish Ex-Servicemen and Women

(FAJEX) in the early 1970s. The book tells the stories of many of the most prominent among the Jews who served. While Pynt and Epstein estimated there were about 2400 Jews in the AIF, the most recent figure proposed by Russell Stern (see Appendix 2) is closer to 4200. In addition, there were at least 940 Jews in the RAAF and 120 in the RAN. At least 130 Australian Jews died on active service.

Since the *Book of Honour*, there has been little scholarship about Australian Jewish military history, which has been eclipsed by other concerns that seem more important either to scholars, the Jewish community or both.* There are many more holocaust memoirs written by Jews who emigrated from Europe to Australia than there are personal histories of Australian-born or -raised Jewish soldiers. Everywhere in the world, the Jewish story is focussed on persecution – the plight of refugees; the unspeakable horrors of death camps – followed by redemption in the form of the foundation of the State of Israel in 1948. In Australia, as in many other nations, there is another history: that of a diaspora community that fought the Axis powers with courage, strength and a large measure of military skill. After World War Two, Jewish ex-servicepeople sought to care for their wounded comrades, remember the dead, and keep alive the memory of their military days in the state-based organisations NAJEX, VAJEX, SAJEX, QAJEX and WAJEX, operating under the umbrella of FAJEX. But the greatest lasting impact of World War Two on the community was the post-war migration of about 17 200 Jews, mainly from Europe, that brought the Jewish population of Australia to nearly 60 000 by 1961.

---

*   An exception is the work of Rodney Gouttman, who has published both a
        biography of Eliazar Margolin, *An Anzac Zionist Hero*, and the book *In Their
        Merit: Australian Jewry and WW1*.

6

Cold War conflicts

The Korean War

It seems only a handful of Jews fought in the Australian military during the Korean War, one of the few wars Jews were neither blamed for starting nor accused of shirking. Korea had been occupied by Japan during World War Two, then divided in two by the Allied powers after the Soviet Union declared war with Japan in August 1945, only days before the Japanese surrender. In June 1950 Communist North Korea ('the Democratic Republic of Korea') under Kim Il-Sung, supported by China and the Soviet Union, attacked the supposedly democratic South Korea ('the Republic of Korea'), led by president Syngman Rhee. The South was the only UN-recognised government of Korea, and the UN responded to the North's invasion with the formation of a sixteen-country coalition force under General MacArthur. This United Nations Command (UNC) was dominated by South Korean and US troops, but included substantial numbers from the UK and smaller contingents from Australia and New Zealand (although, at the height of the fighting, there were more Filipinos, Thais, Canadians and Turks than Australians). The first Australians were drawn from the 3rd Battalion, Royal Australian Regiment (3RAR) and the specially recruited K-Force, which included many World War Two veterans who were spoiling for another fight. It might be fair to say that most Jewish men in that category had got it out of their system in the Israeli War of Independence.

The North Koreans initially drove the armies of the South all the way down to the southern tip of the peninsula at Pusan. Then UN forces landed at Incheon near Seoul, and pushed the army of the North back to the very limits of its territory, the border with China at the Yalu River. In October 1950, China entered the war in support of the North and forced the UN into a long retreat. Ferocious fighting eventually ended in a stalemate on the ground around the 38th parallel, and an armistice was signed in July 1953.

The conflict attracted neither coverage nor much comment in the Jewish press, despite the fact that Private John George Brear, the grandson of *Hebrew Standard of Australasia* founder Henry Harris, was fighting with the second Australian infantry regiment to reach Korea, 2RAR. Brear, a World War Two veteran born in 1921, had arrived in Korea on 23 March 1953 and was invalided home 124 days later on 24 July. A message from Australian Army Headquarters to the Harris family – 'Regret to inform you that your son Pte John George Brear was wounded in action in Korea and evacuated to 60 Indian Field Ambulance on 28th May suffering from shrapnel wounds in the left ear. Further information received will be conveyed to you immediately'[1] – comprised almost all the *Hebrew Standard*'s reporting of the war. Although Brear was born of a Jewish mother, Hannah Harris, she had 'married out', and when Brear passed away, aged ninety-three, he was buried in a churchyard and he left his Manly home to the Salvation Army.[2]

Also with 2RAR was Captain Henry Gayst of the RAAMC. Gayst, born in 1922 in Lodz, Poland, had come to Australia with his family in 1926 and joined the army in 1944. Gayst arrived in Korea in March in 1953 and left in August. His widow remembers him saying that he had visited Rabbi Danglow before he went to Korea to ask for dispensation not to keep *kashrut* in Korea, and that when 'he arrived in Korea and said he was Jewish, they said,

"What's a Jew?" They'd never met any.'[3] Gayst too won a small mention in the *Hebrew Standard* when the paper felt a 'breath of fresh air coming from the muggy atmosphere of far-off Korea' at the news of a letter home, in which Captain Gayst had asked his father to contribute for him £10 and 10 shillings to the United Israel Appeal. 'Well done, digger,' said the *Standard*, which was perhaps a measure of how the paper judged the relative importance of Korea and Israel.

Ian Alfred Lyons, a 24-year-old journalist from Bendigo, Victoria, joined the RAAF on 27 June 1940 and gave his religion as 'Presbyterian', although both his parents were Jewish. The RAAF trained him to fly and by 1947 he had completed 1603 flying hours. He had been posted to the Middle East with 3 Squadron in 1941, then to Noemfoor in Dutch New Guinea and to Morotai in 1944. Lyons was a popular man, 'a likeable type of officer who knows the score, but is inclined to dabble about,' in the judgment of his senior officers. As a pilot he was 'keen, game and quite sound leading sections'.[4] In August 1950, Lyons went overseas to join the RAAF's 77 Squadron, the first non-American UN unit to fight in Korea. The squadron sustained casualties supporting UN troops retreating from the North Koreans. Lyons went home, to return for a second brief tour in August 1951. He was awarded an OBE for his work with 77 Squadron where, as operations officer at the three Korean bases, he had apparently displayed 'outstanding enthusiasm and energy'. It was, according to his citation, 'largely due to his foresight and sound planning' that 77 Squadron was able to 'operate continuously in spite of three changes of location'. The commendation continued, 'The success of the Squadron's operations is due in no small measure to his untiring efforts. He has proved a splendid liaison officer, and has won the confidence and high praise of the USAF formation with which No 77 Squadron operates'.[5] Upon his return from Korea, Lyons seemed to lose his drive, although he did not retire until 1967, after years of reports that echoed the appraisal made of him by Group Captain Desmond Douglas in June 1961 as 'a most likeable loyal and intelligent officer who has no ambition whatsoever'.

Harry Epstein of Western Australia was a stoker mechanic on the aircraft carrier HMAS *Sydney* when she sailed to Korea in August 1951. The *Sydney* was attached to the US Seventh Fleet and within five months of fighting, her aircraft were credited with causing more than 3100 North Korean casualties while she lost three pilots and thirteen planes. Epstein came back to Australia with the *Sydney* in February 1952, but returned to Korea with the destroyer HMAS *Arunta* in January 1954, patrolling the waters to help enforce the armistice.

Australia's only Jewish military death during this period was Frederic Bedrich Adler, although exactly what Adler was doing at the time remains slightly unclear. It seems Adler, born in England, had served first in the RAF and later in the Israeli war of independence. He settled in Israel with his mother, but the Israeli air force apparently arranged for him to go back to England for further training as an aeronautical engineer, which in turn led him to Australia. He worked as an engineer at the Aeronautical Research Laboratories, Melbourne, but also served as a pilot officer in the RAAF Reserve. On 16 June 1954, he was an observer (navigator) on a Canberra bomber on a training exercise flying out of RAAF Base Amberley near Ipswich, Queensland, when, it was reported, 'The plane, while taking off, failed to maintain altitude. It tilted; a wing touched the airstrip and the plane cart-wheeled along the ground for a great distance. It disintegrated and its entire load of kerosene jet-fuel ignited.' All three crew members were killed, and 'Air Force personnel gathered the remains of the personnel. Their bodies had been mutilated and badly burnt in the accident.'[6]

Rabbi Dr Alfred Fabian, Jewish chaplain to the Northern Command, remembered, 'There was a Military Funeral with a joint Service for the three men, and later a Jewish Burial Service at

Lutwyche Cemetery at which I officiated (as also at the subsequent tombstone consecration a year or so later) ... PO Adler's mother lived in Israel and I started to correspond with her (later on we met her in Jerusalem ...). She asked that we in Brisbane should take extra good care of her only son's grave and have a memorial service every year at the graveside on his *yahrzeit*. The local QAJEX group assisted me in carrying out this *mitzvah,* and at every anniversary we had a good *minyan* at the grave in Lutwyche of which I sent reports and photos to Mrs Adler.'[7]

At the time of writing, the QAJEX ceremony was still performed at Adler's grave.

National Service and the CMF

The CMF was re-formed in 1948 with the assistance of Colonel Paul Cullen, who was given command of 45 Infantry Battalion. The post-war CMF was organised as a supplement to the regular army, and eventually became the Australian Army Reserve. In 1955 Brigadier Cullen was given command of 15 Infantry Brigade, the next step en route to his final rank of major general. Other Jewish senior officers in the CMF included Alexander Roby, a RAEME officer in the 2nd AIF who became brigadier after the war.

The 1950s saw the introduction of the first post-war national service scheme, a massive project of questionable military value. Although, in its early years at least, it must have involved virtually every young Jewish male in the country, the scheme seems to have left no trace on the Australian Jewish psyche, and is rarely, if ever, referenced in communal histories. When national service commenced in 1951, every eighteen-year-old was required to register for a five- to six-month period of training with either the CMF, Citizen Naval Forces or the Citizen Air Force. CMF service entailed a three-month block, followed by a series of camps and drills alongside CMF volunteers. Those men who joined the navy or air force served their entire term continuously. John Levi, the nephew of Dr Keith Levi who was killed at Gallipoli, joined the Melbourne University Regiment (MUR) in 1953 with 'at least twenty' other Jews, including John Gandel, John Grodack and John Newton. They were to train full-time at Puckapunyal for three months, return to university for a year and drill regularly at the MUR building – 'marching and remembering to turn right and left' – then complete their time at Puckapunyal. The army was 'very nice', says Levi. 'They were treating us with kid gloves because it was the intake of university students, and they formed an entertainments unit so they could put on a musical comedy, which was based on *The Pirates of Penzance*. I ended up the assistant to Private Barry Humphries, painting some of the scenery.' The army 'provided *kosher* food for those who wished to observe', says Levi. 'Poor old Chaplain Danglow came up to Pucka and, of course, he had a lot of braid on. I knew him because Joseph Levi was past president of the St Kilda Hebrew Congregation.' Midway through his time in the CMF, Levi left to attend rabbinical school in the US. En route to the Hebrew Union College in Cincinnati, Ohio, he stopped off in Israel and 'I was the only person who knew how to handle a rifle when we went on excursions', he says.

The scheme was a vast drain on the Australian army, which was forced to divert huge resources to the CMF – whose members had insufficient training to qualify as professional soldiers, and could not be compelled to go overseas – during the time of the Korean War and, later, the Malayan Emergency. For some young men, however, national service training offered a window (and a door) into their vocation. These youths included Harold Karpin, who was born in 1937. Karpin's father, who went by the name of Colin, was a machinist who worked for a number of Jewish firms, one of which had sponsored him to come to Australia from Poland.

'He served in the Australian army as a tailor,' says Karpin, 'and the furthest he got away from St Kilda was the St Kilda football ground. He served out the war a couple of hundred yards from where we lived. He was in transport group, and the soldiers took over the St Kilda football ground; they used to sleep on the grandstands, and underneath one of the grandstands was his tailors' shop. He came out of the war one of the most decorated soldiers in Australia – and possibly America as well – because he was a *ganif*. They used to send things in to get altered and he would take the medals. We had a lot of American medals. And his shop was also the two-up school. He used to sit me up on the bench while they were playing. Now and then, they used to have a gala day. Being transport, they had all the trucks. Actually, when my father was recruited to the transport group, they gave him a truck, which he couldn't bloody drive. He couldn't drive at all. He didn't have a licence. He crashed it and they said, "Okay, go back to being a tailor"'.

Karpin was an apprentice electrician when he went into the CMF with about eight other Jewish boys. 'I absolutely loved it,' he says. 'Something just clicked. I was in the artillery. But nobody knew what to do with us.' He was so taken by the military life that once he had completed his apprenticeship, he joined the RAAF as a barracks electrician. He retired decades later as a squadron leader.

The 'universal' nature of the national service scheme was slowly eroded: at first country boys were excluded – for the same logistical reasons that had exempted them from cadet-conscription in the years before World War One – then the navy and air force left the scheme. By 1959, when national service training was abolished, the program involved only a comparatively small section of the nation's youth, who were chosen at random by birthdate ballot. Many Jewish families effectively ended their engagement with the armed forces after this scheme, which represented the last universal military mobilisation in Australian history to date.

The Cold War and the Malayan Emergency

Australia's full-time military forces struggled to deal with the crush of national servicemen while a real war broke out in Malaya. Like so many post–War World Two conflicts, Malaya was a war that dared not speak its name. It had to be officially referred to as no more than an 'emergency' so as not to nullify the insurance policies of the European rubber planters and tin miners whose business the war was, in part, prosecuted to protect. Australia's enemy in Malaya was once Australia's ally, the Malayan Communist Party (MCP), which had formed the backbone of Malayan resistance against the Japanese in World War Two. Most of Malaya, once a crown colony, was made a British protectorate in 1948 and the MCP rose against Imperial rule and fought a guerrilla campaign that lasted beyond Malaysian independence in 1957, only dwindling to defeat in 1960. In 1962, a further war broke out between independent Malaysia and Indonesia, and Australian military forces lined up with the British and Malaysians to protect the integrity of the infant nation. The Indonesian 'Confrontation', so-named by Indonesia's foreign minister, lasted until August 1966, more than a year after Australia first committed an infantry battalion to Vietnam. Australians were involved on land and in the air during the Emergency and Confrontation, and at least two Jewish Australians fought at sea.

Maurice Kriss was born in London in 1937 and grew up in Birmingham. He describes his childhood as 'murderous'. He says he went to a Hebrew school, which pupils from the nearby Catholic school tried to burn down. 'We couldn't walk to school on our own,' he said. 'We had to walk together with teachers because we'd be beaten up. These are very young children, aged four or five and we used to have to go as a team. Antisemitism was very, very rife at the time. Throughout the whole of World War Two while we were in England, it was like that.'[8] His father, cabinet maker Harry Kriss, was in the British Army during the war, then the family came out to Western Australia in 1947. Maurice says he left school at twelve, joined the Merchant Navy at thirteen and the RAN at seventeen. He trained as an armourer, and was posted first to HMAS *Vengeance* then to the destroyer HMAS *Voyager*. In July 1958 the *Voyager* was in the Straits of Taiwan when a shelling war almost erupted between China and Taiwan. 'The MIGs were coming down breaking their jets on top of the ship,' says Kriss. 'And I was sitting in the turrets with all guns loaded in case they shot at us. And we did that for two days, locked away in there. We had to be relieved in the gun turrets to go to the toilets, because we always had to be armed. The other problem was, we couldn't move the turrets unless we were fired upon, because actually moving the turret is an act of war.' Kriss says he was on an aircraft carrier when a parade was held for 'divisions', from which sailors were divided into their religious denominations for Sunday services. 'We had a Pakistani midshipman on board,' he says, 'and we naturally had Catholics and Protestants. The Catholics could not have a service with the Protestants, so they'd go to different areas of the ship. By the time we went through the Protestants and the Catholics and the Pakistani midshipman, I was the only person out of 3000 people left on the upper deck of the flight deck of an aircraft carrier, and there was all this brass leaning over asking, "What the hell are you?" I said, "I'm Jewish, sir." "Dismissed."' Kriss had made the cardinal error of drawing attention to himself. 'They got me up in New Zealand,' he says, 'before the Auckland Bridge was completed. We were a long way from anywhere, all public transport stopped at ten o'clock. So at midnight one night, I'm in my bunk, I'm asleep, and I got a shake, "Come down to the gangway in your number-ones, your best dress for ceremonial purposes." I thought, What the heck for, at midnight? So I had to find in the dark all my clothes – they were down in the locker – and I got to the gangway and the officer of the days said, "Kriss, you're Jewish, aren't you? I've been reading this book that says you have to walk to the synagogue on a Saturday. I've worked out it's about a nine-hour walk from here to Auckland synagogue. I think you'd better start now." And that was the punishment I got.

'It was an extremely lonely existence,' he says, 'because when we went ashore, I had nothing in common with anybody. I didn't go to the pubs; I didn't go out with the girls. The other problem was, you were at sea for such a long time, and there's nowhere to go. I bought a piano-accordion and taught myself to play.' He met one other Jewish sailor in the RAN, Bobby Moss. Kriss knew Moss's sister Barbara from Blue and White dances at the Great Synagogue. Moss and Kriss bumped into each other at the Manila Hotel in the Philippines when Moss was posted to the aircraft carrier HMAS *Melbourne*. 'I remember him well because he drank too much and threw up into my case with all my clothes in,' says Kriss.[9] Moss also recalls vomiting into Kriss's bag. Moss had also joined the RAN at seventeen, having abandoned a plumbers' apprenticeship, but he had a different experience of navy life. 'There was no racism,' he says. 'I'm only five foot seven, and not once in my naval career did I ever get bullied, or slung shit at. Only in jest. I wouldn't take it anyhow … I was never afraid to tell anyone. Especially when they said, "Are you going to come to church on Sunday?" "No, sorry." Then they'd have me clean the toilets.' Moss grew up in North Bondi and trained as a boxer at Woolloomooloo PCYC, and ended up staying in the RAN until 1980. In 1959 the *Melbourne* was used for the filming of the movie *On the Beach*. 'They did say, "Do you want to stay back and be extras in the movie?" but, being young sailors, we said, "No," and we went to Melbourne and had a drink,' says Moss. In about 1961, he says, on the shore establishment of HMAS *Kuttabul* in Potts Point he became the chaplain's yeoman. 'It was very interesting for a Jewish boy,' he says. 'I had to go in and set up the church for him in Garden Island. The priest would always say, "Bob, would you like to stay?" "No, thanks, pal, I'm alright."' Moss was an able seaman on the *Melbourne* during the

Indonesian Confrontation, but the ship played no real part in the fighting. 'We were just there,' he says. 'We did a couple of exercises with SEATO.'[10]

Former national serviceman Rabbi John Levi was petitioned to join the military chaplaincy by a number of prominent returned men who identified as Liberal rather than Orthodox Jews. 'The ex-servicemen's association was very strong in those days,' says Levi, 'and they wanted to relate to a rabbi who was officially part of the army structure.' In 1960, Rabbi Levi became the alternate chaplain to the military. As national service was over, he ministered to the small number of regular soldiers at Puckapunyal. 'I would meet with [Orthodox chaplain] Chaim Gutnick, and we'd talk about getting Passover supplies to the people at Puckapunyal and so on,' he says. 'Things moved slowly. In fact, they moved so slowly, they never got around to issuing me with a greatcoat. So on Anzac Day, if it was raining, I was wet. In those days, Orthodox and Liberal were daggers drawn, so to have an Orthodox and a Liberal rabbi at the same service, and conduct the service, took some negotiating. Gutnick and I used to take turns in the various prayers at the Anzac Day Memorial Service at Melbourne General Cemetery.'

7

The Vietnam years: 1962 to 1972

When life was a lottery – for some

There were few Jewish soldiers left in the regular army in 1962 when Australia began its creeping commitment to the war in Vietnam. Robert Menzies' Australia was booming, with full employment across all the states, and the military did not seem to offer much of a career to an ambitious young man.

At first only a small team of Australian 'military advisers' (eventually known as the Australian Army Training Team Vietnam or AATTV) was posted to South Vietnam. The men helped train the beleaguered forces of the Army of the Republic of Vietnam (ARVN) to fight an insurgency raised under the flag of the National Liberation Front, whose military arm became known as the Viet Cong (VC). South Vietnam had nine governments between November 1963 and June 1965. They were all under constant military pressure from the VC and their backers in communist North Vietnam, and were generally crippled by a lack of popular legitimacy.

As the CMF member of the Military Board, General Paul Cullen pressed for a CMF battalion to be raised for Vietnam, but the Menzies government favoured a return to the electorally popular policy of conscription. In 1964 national service was reintroduced, in the shape of a scheme which selected by birth-date ballot about one in seven 20-year-old males for two years' service in the army. The government's primary aim was to rapidly build up the strength of the army so it would be large enough to respond to the possibility of simultaneous threats from Indonesia to Malaysia and New Guinea, and – almost as an afterthought – to allow an expanded commitment to the defence of South Vietnam.

As it turned out, the perceived threat from Indonesia disappeared with the massacre of perhaps half a million real and imagined supporters of the Indonesian Communist Party in 1965–66 and the downfall of President Sukarno. Consequently the great majority of national servicemen remained in Australia, but about 15 300 eventually went to Vietnam, while others were posted to Malaysia, Singapore or New Guinea.

Participation by some Jews in the anti-war movement has been recorded faithfully and well.[1] Many leaders of the new left, such as the fiery Maoist Albert Langer, came from Jewish families. Conversely, Jewish involvement in the army has been all but forgotten, although there were Jewish soldiers serving in infantry, armour and engineering corps, as well as the various medical and service units, and even one man in the AATTV. One Jewish soldier was Mentioned in Despatches, another fought as a forward scout. Although the majority of Australians in Vietnam were regular soldiers, it seems most Jewish military personnel were national servicemen.

Ordinary conscripts suffered ten weeks' basic military training at Recruit Training Battalions (RTBs) in Puckapunyal and Kapooka and later Singleton. According to Rabbi Dr Alfred Fabian, by then Senior Jewish Chaplain to the Forces, national service 'brought quite a few orthodox young men into the Army', and some tried to keep *kashrut*. 'A new system was evolved and finally embodied in Army regulations which provided, for the first time, special *kosher* rations for those who would request such food,' wrote Fabian. 'These rations were based on the type of pre-packed meal provided for air travellers by *kosher* caterers.' The rabbi felt these arrangements 'worked quite well, both on an individual and particularly on a collective basis for national service trainees in camp' and, during his occasional visits to the RTBs, he found that when the proper request for *kosher* food had been made, 'the Army had always done the right thing, in spite of high expense and considerable technical difficulties'.[2]

The brightest and fittest men of each national service intake were given the chance to take a six-month officer training course at the newly raised Scheyville Officer Training Unit (OTU) near Windsor, New South Wales. Scheyville was charged with churning out men capable of leading a platoon of infantrymen in half the time it took to produce a junior officer at Portsea. The course was ferociously taxing, mentally and physically, and about one-third of each batch of about 120 cadets failed to graduate. David Roubin – the grandson of Dr Sidney Rosebery, who served in the army in both world wars, and the son of former WAAAF Ruth Roubin – was part of the first OTU intake which marched into Scheyville in April 1965. 'You were on a knife edge all the time,' said Roubin. 'You'd wake up one morning and the guy in the next room wasn't there. You'd go out on a short exercise for two or three days, you'd come back and go to bed and the next morning there'd be five or six gone.' Roubin recalled: 'There were lots of visits from senior military people, lots of visits from politicians. I was the only Jewish boy there. I can remember being visited by so many different chaplains – they'd come and knock on my door and most of them had never seen a Jew before, particularly not in the army. They'd want to know how I was, was I having any difficulties, did I need any special food, all that type of thing. They all came to have a look at me. They were amazed I didn't have horns growing out of my head or a long beard.'[3]

David Buckwalter, born in February 1945, had his number come up in the first national service ballot but was not called into the army until the second intake in September 1965. Buckwalter was born in Glebe to parents who came from Breslau in Germany. His maternal grandfather Martin Maschler was awarded an Iron Cross fighting for the Germans in World War One, but was nonetheless incarcerated in a concentration camp by the Nazis in the 1930s. His grandmother Hilda secured his release, and the family came to Australia. When he received his call-up papers, Buckwalter was working in Melbourne and studying photography part-time at RMIT. He completed his recruit training at Kapooka, then joined 3RAR at Woodside, South Australia, for infantry corps training.

In mid-1965, while the early national servicemen were struggling through their training at the RTBs or the OTU, the first battalion of Australian infantry, 1RAR, had been despatched to South Vietnam. The battalion, which was made up entirely of regular soldiers, came home one year later, to be replaced by 5RAR and 6RAR, each of which contained large numbers of national servicemen. These men formed the core of the 1st Australian Task Force (1ATF) at Nui Dat, a base built at the heart of Phuoc Tuy province, south-east of Saigon.

'After I finished my corps training,' says Buckwalter, 'they were looking for volunteers to do specialist courses. I put my hand up, with fifty-four other blokes, and I did Sigs. Fifty-three of them came home, and the other bloke I carried off the battlefield.' In September 1966 he was attached to A Company 6RAR. He came down with malaria over Christmas and spent three weeks in hospital. When he recovered, the battalion wanted to transfer him to base duties at headquarters. 'I said, "I've got all my mates here,"' says Buckwalter. '"I'll stay in the bloody company." So I put in for a transfer and moved into 3 Platoon.' He gave up his speciality as a signaller to go back into the jungle as a rifleman. 'Many of us decided there and then that the war had definitely got to David,' his CO later wrote.[4]

On 17 February 1967, A Company was dropped by US helicopters into open ground near an abandoned hamlet in Phuoc Tuy province to block an anticipated VC retreat from the area as part of Operation Bribie. However, the VC did not withdraw. They hid in the scrub and attacked the Australians as they came in. Buckwalter remembers, 'The machine-gunner on the helicopter said, "Anybody who gets hit, get back in the helicopter." The machine-gunner in my section and I – later on when we discussed it – said, "How were we going to get back into the helicopter if we'd been hit?"'

'We were dropped in a rice paddy, and we advanced to the scrub line, and that's when the nogs [Vietnamese] opened up. Battle is a very confused state of affairs. The only thing that you know is what you see in front of you. The adrenalin is pumping at 500 miles an hour. I wasn't scared. That doesn't mean I was a hero, it was just the way it was. The next day, we did a sweep through the battle area, and there were eight blokes dead. I was detailed to get them out of there to the paddy field, to chopper them out. Peter Arnold, one of my good mates who'd been with us with 3RAR, was one of them.'

After Bribie, says Buckwalter, 'I'd been looking at trying to get my pay grouping up, so I did the first-aid course.' He was offered a trip to Saigon for a *Seder* with the Americans but, 'Apart from the fact that I didn't particularly have any religious belief, it's a very close team of blokes in an infantry section. You'd do anything for them. I wasn't going to bludge on my mates and get a free trip to Saigon. So I just said, "No thanks, sir".'

A Company was sent to Fire Support Base Horseshoe, on a caldera about eight kilometres south-east of Nui Dat. Fire support bases in Vietnam were built to bring artillery support within range of men who were on patrol outside the reach of the guns of Nui Dat. They were generally temporary, but FSB Horseshoe was a permanent camp that stood guard over the construction of a barrier minefield, a poorly conceived attempt to cut off the VC from their civilian support in nearby villages by laying about 20 000 jumping jack mines between two barbed-wire fences stretching from the

Horseshoe to the coast. Many of the mines were dug up by the VC and reused to kill and maim Australian and ARVN troops.

A Company was supposed to ensure the engineers laid the mines in safety. Late in the morning of 2 May 1967 most of the company was out on patrol while Buckwalter was assisting a cook to prepare food. A US artillery battery came in to replace the Australian unit and the newcomers were not all properly briefed about the minefield. They began to work on securing their positions but, says Buckwalter, one US gunner noticed a defensive site inside the minefield itself. 'When the gunners set up shop, they'd built themselves up sandbags and so forth around the gun. And this gunner decided he would shortcut filling up sandbags and go and get some of this stuff that was already made up.' Although the minefield was enclosed by two high barbed-wire fences, there was a break in the fencing for a road, which was cordoned only by star pickets with two strands of barbed wire strung between them. 'It was easy enough to lift it up and just crawl through,' says Buckwalter, 'and that's what this bloke did. There were international minefield signs on the fence. Either he didn't see them or didn't know what they were.' The mines were laid in patterns of four. 'He trod on a central mine in the first cluster,' says Buckwalter. 'Boom!

'I was on the south-east of the Horseshoe, sitting around doing nothing. I grabbed the medical kit and raced off down the hill. I was dressed in shorts and thongs, which was my basic kit when I was cooking. A long way before I got to the fence, I was in bare feet. I got to the location where the gunner had gone into the minefield, and there was a load of bits and pieces of timber lying around. We didn't know anything about mines. They didn't even show us what they looked like. But I obviously knew if you trod on one it wasn't healthy, so I walked in the minefield using timber to get to that bloke, and then started treating him with shell dressings, morphine. He'd virtually lost one leg – and did lose one leg, but I tried to save it. I strapped both legs together. One leg acts as a brace for the other leg. It immobilises the damaged one. One of the engineers came into the minefield and pointed out where the other mines were in the cluster. There was one a few inches away from his shoulder, and another one near his hip. The guy was in a lot of pain and waving his arms around, so – unbeknownst to me, but the engineer knew what was going on – hitting the mines. But not hitting them hard enough to trigger. So the engineer grabbed his hands and stuffed them down his waist, and restrained him until I'd finished. The Company Sergeant Major had called in a dustoff, blokes turned up with a stretcher and passed the stretcher into us over the fence, we loaded him on, passed him back over the fence, and he was put on the chopper.' The Australians did not realise but an American sergeant was standing outside the minefield and 'copped a bit of shrapnel in the heart and was killed'.

Alpha Company CO Charles Mollison felt that both Buckwalter and the engineer should be decorated, and wrote citations for both of them, but ultimately Buckwalter was only Mentioned in Despatches. Buckwalter's final citation did not reflect his CO's recommendation. 'Why that happened I don't know,' wrote Mollison.[5]

The majority of Australian infantrymen arrived in Vietnam by ship, although replacements and members of support units were more likely to fly in. The vessel that brought the battalions to war was HMAS *Sydney*, a converted aircraft carrier nicknamed 'the Vung Tau ferry', to which Dr Samuel Sakker had been posted as medical officer in 1965. Sakker was born in Harbin, Manchuria, in 1937, to a family that had moved to China before the Russian Revolution. He lived in China through war, revolution and the early years of Communist rule, until the family migrated to Australia in September 1952, two weeks before his fifteenth birthday. Sakker completed his national service in the RAN in 1956, and won a naval scholarship to help him finish a degree in medicine at the University of Sydney. The scholarship carried with it a four-year short-service commission. In 1964 Sakker became a surgeon lieutenant in the RAN. He was on board HMAS *Sydney* on her second trip to Vietnam.

'Apart from the obvious clinical aspect,' he wrote, 'my duties involved planning, instructing, training personnel for the management of casualties throughout a tightly compartmentalized ship at "Action Stations"; to supervising and overseeing the daily health issues; standards of hygiene in the four galleys, numerous toilets; the work and safety in the huge machinery spaces and the movement of heavy equipment. It was a floating city of heavy industry under wartime conditions and with a population of 800–1400 men. Added to this the escort ships did not always carry doctors and I would be winched on board by helo or transferred by jackstay to do a clinic at least once a week and when necessary.

'Australia was also in confrontation with Indonesia, and there were rumours of submarines in the area so that HMAS *Sydney* sailed under strict wartime conditions of darken ship, radio-silence, partial shutdown of compartments and a zigzag course all the way to Vung Tau. There, in the Mekong River delta we anchored and discharged troops and cargo into lighters ... In the near vicinity we could see bombardment by American naval vessels and aircraft. Our anchorage was in danger from enemy swimmers and chained mines floated down the fast-flowing river. Armed sentries in our cutter patrolled around the ship and buoys were placed upriver to intercept the mines.'[6] In April and May 1966 the *Sydney* took 5RAR to Vietnam and brought 1RAR back to Australia. Sakker sailed with both voyages, as did Bobby Moss, who had rejoined the ship. Moss was now a leading patrolman with responsibilities for policing the vessel. The army were 'no trouble', he recalls. 'They didn't do anything. The sailors were working, these guys were just relaxing.' Moss boxed in an inter-services tournament on board ship, and broke the nose of his army opponent. Once the *Sydney* docked at Vung Tau, he says, 'You had the divers going down, but before you had the divers go down, they were dropping one-pound scare charges over the side, just in case there were any Viet Cong divers underneath the water. You'd hear "Boom-boom-boom", and that was done about every hour.' Moss recalls (perhaps apocryphally) saying to Dr Sakker, '"Listen, I've got this rash on my shin." He said, "Oh yeah? Do you play a lot of sport?" I said, "Yeah." He said, "Yeah, I've got the same." And that didn't help me at all.'[7]

In November 1966, the *Sydney* was on exercise off the Fitzroy River in Queensland when she was called to assist an American submarine, USS *Tiru*, which had run aground on Frederick Reef. 'It was beached and had huge waves breaking over it,' recalled Sakker. There was an injured sailor on the *Tiru* and Sakker, as the only medical officer in the area, had to transfer to another ship and then attempt to board the submarine. 'The sailor had been working on the upper deck when a huge wave picked him up,' wrote Sakker, 'tore his lifeline and threw him against a puff dome, injuring his abdomen severely. My transfer to the *Tiru* was postponed to the next day as the seas were too high and the light was fading. In the morning of the 6th of November 1966, with the seas abating slightly, dressed in a wet suit and flippers, I made a hazardous trip in a life raft, hauling it along a gun line fired to and secured on the submarine. The cutter with the other end was positioned just outside the line of breakers maintaining the tension on the line. Timing was crucial and I managed to get on board between two huge waves. The patient was treated with intravenous fluids and attended to in four-hourly shifts until we got to Brisbane ... where he underwent surgery removing eighteen inches of damaged small bowel.'[8]

On 1 January 1968 Sakker was appointed a Military MBE for 'boarding the stranded United States Submarine in rough seas, and for outstanding devotion to duty in treating a seriously injured man in difficult conditions'.[9]

IN EVERY WAR, THERE HAVE BEEN LARGE NUMBERS OF serving Australians of Jewish descent who were not *halachically* Jewish. Stretton Joel, once counted among the few Jewish national servicemen to go to Vietnam,[10] was a cousin of Rabbi John Levi: Joel's father and Levi's mother were siblings. The Joel family were doctors and farmers in Bunbury, Western Australia, but Joel's father, Bernard, 'married out'. When Stretton was twelve years old, he remembers Rabbi Levi asking: "'Stretty, are you interested in Judaism? If you are, I'm happy to fly across and give you some direction and maybe help you along the way." But I'm not a religious person,' says Joel, and he did not go through with it. Joel was called up for national service in 1966 and flown to Puckapunyal, where Rabbi Levi was now the alternate Jewish chaplain. Joel joined the Armoured Corps and went to Vietnam in April 1967.

A SMALL NUMBER OF AUSTRALIAN WOMEN SERVED IN VIETNAM as army nurses or Red Cross workers. The first to arrive in 1966 was the redoubtable Hilda Zinner of Double Bay, a Red Cross veteran of the Malaya Emergency and two postings to Singapore. Zinner's work as head of the Australian Red Cross mission in Vietnam mainly involved caring for patients at the US 36th Evacuation Hospital. Zinner's jeep came under fire on occasion and she saw the terrible casualties of the Battle of Long Tan before she came home in February 1967. On 12 May 1967 more than 250 000 people packed the streets of Sydney to welcome home from Vietnam 1000 Australian troops who had just disembarked HMAS *Sydney*. Zinner joined about 4000 relatives and friends who greeted the ship when it docked at Garden Island, and met some of the men she had looked after in hospital. They insisted she march with them, took her home, where she changed into her fatigues, and transported her back to the march in her jungle boots and greens.

Scheyville graduate David Roubin arrived at the 1st Australian Logistics Support Group (1ALSG) in the port city of Vung Tau in October 1967 as an officer in the Royal Australian Army Ordnance Corps (RAAOC). He had to extend his national service to obtain a posting to Vietnam. He enjoyed his time in Vung Tau, signed up for the regular army, and eventually spent 505 days in Vietnam. Roubin could have been the longest-serving national serviceman in Vietnam. 'I was certainly the longest-serving Jewish nasho there,' he said.[11]

WEST AUSTRALIAN BOB EDELMAN, ALSO A NATIONAL SERVICE-man, was born in Rostov, Russia, in September 1945. His father, who had been a soldier in the Polish army, had fled Poland for Russia and ended up in a work camp, where he met Edelman's mother. Edelman was sent to 1RAR, where he trained as a signaller; he arrived in Vietnam a few weeks before Passover towards the end of the first wave of the Tet Offensive, a nationwide VC uprising backed by units of the North Vietnamese Army. He came by ship to Vung Tau, and was transported by road to Nui Dat. It was one of the most dangerous times for Australian troops in South Vietnam, and 1RAR was to suffer more fatal casualties than any other Australian battalion in the course of the war. 'I had to go out on patrol,' says Edelman. 'We'd been out for two days and I'm on the radio, of course, and I get an instruction to get all my gear together; they've cleared a helipad. A helicopter came in to take me out and take me to a US Army base called Bearcat for a Passover service. It wasn't a Passover really. All they held was a little service amongst the boys in the American army. It was Passover eve. And that was it. Then I got flown back into Nui Dat.'

In May Edelman was taken by helicopter to Fire Support Base Coral, which had been attacked the previous night by a large force of VC surging towards Saigon for a renewed offensive that became known as 'mini-Tet'. 'I was greeted by the sight of nine or ten body bags,' says Edelman. 'And then we had to set up our command post in admin, mainly operating things like supplies and the resupply of ammunition. That was just a tent, and the ammo dump was about ten metres from my pit. I set up my hootchie with Tim Fischer. I'd known Tim from back in Holsworthy. He was a nice enough guy, but he was an officer, so he had to act his part too.' Tim Fischer, who would later become Deputy Prime Minister of Australia, was a Scheyville graduate commanding a transport platoon of 1RAR.

'The second night, we weren't actually on duty,' says Edelman. 'It was about 2 am and we started to get shells, rocket propelled grenades, mortars coming in, and Tim and I had only managed to dig shallow scrapes – a couple of feet deep. So we both grabbed our weapons and helmets and flak jackets, and dived into these pits, and we had our heads down and arses up, hoping and praying that we weren't going to cop one, and luckily we sort of didn't. But our hootchies were attached to a tree, and the tree got hit by a grenade or a rocket and it sprayed shrapnel – what we call a "treeburst" – and Tim got hit with shrapnel across the eyes and the shoulder. I said to him, when I looked up, "I think you've been hit", because I saw blood pouring down his face, and he had blood on his shirt and his shoulder. And I said, "If you don't pull your f—king head in, you're going to get killed! What were you doing with your head up anyway?" He said, "I had to see what's going on."

'The shelling stopped for a bit, and we got a radio call through from C Company. They were out of ammunition for the machine guns. We had quite a few wounded and one guy hit in the pit, so I was nominated to go with the driver of the C Company Land Rover and take some ammunition across. It was pitch black. You couldn't see your hand in front of you. We got clearance to go through the lines but they said, "You're not allowed to use any headlights." But you could use your parker lights. They were to show people where you were, but you couldn't see. We were hanging out the side, following the track, and we picked up barbed wire in the axles of the Land Rover. Eventually the axles locked up on us, but we did manage to get the ammunition across – not all the way through, but most of the way through, and not before tripping off some flares, with the barbed wire being dragged, and having grenades thrown at us by our own blokes; when you trip a flare and they see silhouettes, they don't know what's going on. We managed to call out and stop that, and get out of the Land Rover and into one of the machine-gun pits, and we told them that their ammunition's in the Land Rover *and if you want to go and get it, go and get it.* I wasn't going back out there. If it wouldn't have been for the Yanks, we probably would've been wiped out. I can remember the Dakotas flying around and just spraying the area with machine-gun fire. We were watching the tracers coming out like raindrops.'

Perth national serviceman Warren Austin completed an apprenticeship as a printer with West Australian Newspapers before he marched into Puckapunyal in April 1967. 'I wasn't really looking forward to it,' says Austin. 'I went in on 19 April and within a week it was Passover. In the first day or two, everyone had to go and see a padre, and there was a rabbi there – he was the only army officer I ever saw with a beard – and he sent me to Melbourne for *Seder*. There were two other Jewish fellas there. The three of us were driven to Melbourne and I was billeted by a family and then we were given train tickets and we came back on the train to Seymour.'

Austin was among the few young Jews who tried to keep *kashrut* in training. 'To actually eat completely *kosher* in the army was fairly hard,' he says. 'If I had breakfast, I wouldn't eat the bacon, and at lunchtime there'd be beef and whatever. They would give you one *kosher* meal a day in Australia, that came sealed, in the evening. I got that when I was in Puckapunyal. It always seemed to be such a bother. I said, "Forget it. It's too much of an effort for everybody."'

Austin was posted to the Royal Australian Army Medical Corps and in June 1968 found himself at 8th Field Ambulance in

Nui Dat, rather than the main Australian medical facility at 1st Field Hospital in Vung Tau. Austin worked at first as a clerk, but when casualties arrived, he rushed to attend them as a medic. 'The Americans carried the wounded,' he says. 'If someone came in by road, they'd come to our 8th Field Ambulance, but if the dustoff air ambulance brought people in, they either weren't going to make it to fly the extra distance to Vung Tau, or they were dead. Looking back on it, we were probably fairly basic but a lot of lives were saved by the efforts of ordinary people who only months before had been working in a bank.

'I never suffered from any discrimination,' says Austin. 'In fact, some of the things that people did for me were quite nice. I walked over to the mess one day. We used to have two cooks. I said what's for dinner? "Egg and bacon pie." I said to him, "Oh, that's not much good for me", and I walked off. I thought I'd just go and get some bread and have a tomato sandwich, or whatever. When I went in to get bread, he called out, "Warren!" and he'd made me two vegetarian pasties.'

Geoffrey Cass, another national serviceman from Perth, knew Austin from *cheder*. Cass started his working life as an apprentice to a Jewish cabinet maker. 'I was probably one of the last to go into trades,' he says. Cass was happy to enter the army and eager to get to Vietnam. 'I was twenty years of age and I was looking for a little bit more excitement,' he says. 'I joined 9 Battalion and then sailed across. I wanted to see what it was like in a war zone. I wanted to be part of the action.' He came to Vietnam in November 1968 and stayed until December 1969, rising to the rank of corporal with C Company 9RAR. Being Jewish 'wasn't an issue', he says. 'It's not like I needed to go to *shule* or go to temple or whatever.'

Patrols in Vietnam were led by a forward scout, whose position potentially made him both the first to spot the enemy and the first to step on a mine. 'I was forward scout for a while,' says Cass. 'There was a little bit of trepidation, but after you'd been out for a week or so on a six- or eight-week operation, you became a little bit blasé. I tended to relax a bit out there. You were relieved: you had two scouts rotating, so there was a little bit of time to switch off. We had a couple of ambushes we walked into, one in particular. Luckily, I wasn't on the front that day. I lost a very good friend, but I don't tend to think about it a lot. It was just a job to me. I was getting paid, and I was doing my job.'

Among the few Jewish professional soldiers in Vietnam was Zev Ben-Avi. Born in 1940 he was too old to be drafted, but joined the regular army in April 1968 and went to Vietnam as a corporal with B Squadron 3 Cavalry in August 1969. Ben-Avi served alongside Australia's most famous national serviceman, pop singer Normie Rowe, and was wounded in action, but he saw out his tour and returned to Australia in August 1970. Paul Dion Cohen of Hurstville, New South Wales, had joined the army in August 1952. He enlisted as an ordinary soldier, went through the Royal Australian Engineers' (RAE) School of Military Engineering (SME), climbed up through the ranks, and was posted to New Guinea as a temporary WO2 with 21 Construction Squadron in May 1962. When Cohen returned home, he was promoted to lieutenant. He was a popular and capable officer. His commanding officer at the RAE wrote: 'He performs all tasks with a sense of urgency. He is jovial in his attitude to work and people around him.' More importantly for the army, Cohen proved to be 'an active keen member of the unit Rugby football team' and 'as vice-captain during several matches was a driving force'. In March 1966 Cohen, now a captain, moved with his wife and family to Scheyville, where he became an administration officer at the OTU. He left Scheyville for an instructor's position at the SME in August 1967. His CO recommended he 'should be given an opportunity for [South Vietnam] service in due course'.[12]

Andrew Varga was the Hungarian-born son of a World War Two Jewish partisan. He grew up in Melbourne and was studying part-time at RMIT when he volunteered for national service – an option open to men whose birthdate was not drawn in the ballot. Varga had been an army cadet at South Melbourne Technical School and represented Victoria in judo at Jewish sporting events. His mate Frank Benko, a non-Jewish Hungarian from the same Melbourne suburb, described Varga as 'powerful in the arms, chest and wrist', a man who had 'often beaten all comers in a friendly game of Indian wrestling, or an unfriendly version of the real thing'.[13] Varga said, 'When I was at Puckapunyal doing rookie training, I cannot remember one Jew.'[14] He was, therefore, surprised to arrive in Vietnam in May 1968 to find the commanding officer of his unit, 17 Construction Squadron, was Captain Paul Cohen.

Harold Karpin, the RAAF officer who had joined as an electrician and had performed his national service in the CMF in the 1950s, was posted to Malaysia between 1967 and 1970. Australian casualties from Vietnam had to pass through RAAF Butterworth on their way home. 'My electrician's shop was down near the runway,' he says, 'and 4RAAF hospital was there, and you could see boys coming out on the stretchers to the hospital. It was a pitiful sight.'

National serviceman Noel Turnbull, an artillery officer in Vietnam, grew up in Melbourne with a father who had fought in New Guinea and was Jewish 'when it suited him', says Turnbull. At Puckapunyal, Turnbull remembers: 'We all had to go and see a chaplain, and I said I wasn't religious, which was a terrible mistake in the army. I said, "Well, my grandmother was Jewish", so they sent me to the rabbi. The rabbi said, "My son, you'll get yourself into a lot of trouble in the army if you don't have religion. It's a bit hard for you to become a Jew at this stage. What I suggest is you become an Anglican." And I was very thankful for him: missing church parades was not fun, because they always found some shit job for you to do.'[15] Turnbull was a student at Melbourne University when he was conscripted and he was coached on how to pass the Scheyville entrance tests by Graham Devries, a CMF sergeant in the Psychology Corps and the son of Max Adolf Devries, one of the German Jewish refugees who served in 4 and 6 Employment Companies during World War Two. Devries says he had joined the CMF to get out of national service, but he ended up a national serviceman anyway. Max hadn't wanted his son to be in the army, even the CMF. The war had given him 'a chip on the shoulder about uniforms', says Devries. But Devries was born on 5 May 1945, and his birthdate was drawn in the first ballot. Devries had spoken to officers in the Psychology Corps, and they hoped to bring him into the army as a lieutenant at Eastern Command in Sydney. But first he had to get through Scheyville. He was admitted to the OTU, which 'wasn't surprising', he says. 'As part of the group that administered those tests, I knew the tests. And I think I probably had the intellectual capacity, even without that sort of assistance.' However, he was removed from the course a few weeks before the end. 'The OC Scheyville decided that I didn't fit the profile of an infantry lieutenant,' he says, 'which was quite right. I wasn't the sporting type; I wasn't the fit type. I don't think that the army, as an entity, discriminated against Jewish people; they just didn't cater for them because they didn't understand them, didn't have the facility for it; the army had trouble coping with people who were different.'

He returned to the ranks, and marched into corps training for the Royal Australian Army Service Corps (RAASC) back at Puckapunyal. He was offered a choice of postings, and could have stayed in Australia as a trainer or a librarian, but chose instead to go to 5 Company RAASC at 1ALSG in Vung Tau. 'I had a curiosity,' he says, 'and I was a bit ambivalent about whether we should be there. The newsreels we were shown were of Australian troops going through a village and being waved at by the locals. I'd venture that wasn't open hands they were waving, it was fists.' In Vung Tau, he was an orderly-room clerk, 'a very large square peg with a couple of chips on his shoulder, who thought he was better than everyone else', he says. 'I didn't fit in with my colleagues and, of course, had more in common with some of the officers. I spent most of my evenings writing letters.'

In Vung Tau, Devries met another Jewish national serviceman, Israeli-born Amic Schneider. Just after the Suez Crisis of 1956, Amic's father had convinced his mother to leave Israel so as to keep their children safe from war. They moved from Tel Aviv to Perth, and their son Schneider was conscripted and sent to Vietnam in April 1970. In training, he says, 'I never advertised my religion, but I was very proud to be known as an Israeli. As soon as I said I was Israeli, everybody assumed straight away that I'm Jewish.' Their reaction, he says, was 'very good. It was just after one of the wars, and all the guys in the platoons hated the Arabs'.

Schneider had qualified as a registered general nurse before he went into the army, and so was posted first to the medical corps. But once in Vung Tau, 'I was chosen to join the AATTV,' he says. 'I said, "Whatever for?" "We've looked at your occupation, we've looked at your history, you speak another language." I had to learn Vietnamese. I said, "Okay, I'll join", although I didn't know what I was joining. We went to an American military training base and learned via records and tapes and movies and things, the culture, the language, the behaviour and the thought patterns of the local Vietnamese.'

Schneider lived with other members of the AATTV in the hamlet of Ang Nai, where he would eat lizards and frogs with the villagers. 'Kashrut went out of the window,' he says. 'But unfortunately for me, I met this Jewish colonel from New Jersey. He found out I was an Israeli, and it was coming up to Passover, and he sent me all these packages and boxes of matzo, which I detest, and gefilte fish, which I absolutely loathe. I like middle-eastern food, not European sweet bloody fish dishes. I used to give it to my friends. He really punished me for a week. He decided he was going to take care of me and make sure I ate the right food. Thank God he didn't send me the Bible.'[16]

John Selan was a national serviceman born in Germany and raised in Melbourne. His mother was an Auschwitz survivor, his father a former officer with the NKVD, the forerunner of the KGB. Both of Selan's parents died when he was young, and Selan was raised by Jewish foster families. He started a dental technician's apprenticeship, with part-time study at RMIT, which he was allowed to complete before he entered the army. He says he was given a difficult time during recruit training by an NCO at Puckapunyal in 1970: 'On the first day that they lined us up in the barracks, they called the roll and he called out, "Selan! Where's that from?" Defensively, I said "Poland." And he said, "What is it? Where're you from?" I said, "I was born in Germany." He said, "Oh, you're German." I said, "Not exactly." This questioning went on and, of course, he had on the registry, written next to me, "Jew". I said, "What do you want to know? I'm Jewish, is that what you want?" He said, "Yeah, I just wanted you to say it." So already there was a hundred guys standing to attention he wanted to know I was a Jew. He said, "You're Jewish, are you? I've got a job for you." The huts are about a foot or two off the ground, and you can see underneath them. They're on stumps. They used to drink, and throw the beer bottles underneath the hut. He said, "I want you to crawl under the hut and get all the empty beer bottles and take them to the canteen." In those days, you used to get money back for the empty beer bottles. "You can go and do that, and you can keep the money." I said, "I don't want to do that." He said, "Oh, you're one of those rich Jews, are you?" Through basic training, he rode me the whole time about the fact I was Jewish. When we went to weapons training, he'd pull me up and, if you were running behind someone with your weapon: "You would've killed him. Ah, you wouldn't have cared because you're a Jew, aren't you?" I was lucky because at Puckapunyal there was a dental unit, and they found out I was a qualified dental technician, and they pulled me out of basic training and said, "You'd better come to the laboratory. We've got a lot of work to do. Can you help out?" He wasn't too happy about that, because he perceived that as a Jew I had some sort of contact to get me out of some of basic training.'[17]

David Wittner from Melbourne – whose father Lance Corporal Hymie Wittner had served in the 2nd AIF and in Palestine, Syria and Lebanon – was a qualified radiographer, who trained at Puckapunyal at around the same time as Selan. Wittner remembered, 'For the ten weeks I was at Puckapunyal, one of the NCOs called me "Pork Chop", but I just regarded him as an ignorant sort of dickhead. That didn't worry me. He was a lance corporal and when I was in Vietnam, he came in as a patient, and he noticed I had the two stripes. He acknowledged that and said, "Well done." He was harmless enough.'[18]

Random draws such as the national service ballot can throw up apparently improbable results. David Roubin had two brothers and both of them were called up too. His middle brother Gary was a doctor and still in training when national service was finally abolished. His younger brother Loris tried to avoid the draft by hiding out in Darwin, but eventually found himself not only in the medical corps but in Vietnam. In the army, he said, 'I had a strange name – Loris Roubin – I was singled out for being Jewish.' He arrived at the hospital at 1ALSG on 11 March 1971. *Pesach* fell in April and Roubin remembered a chaplain visiting him in Vung Tau: 'He said, "I believe your Passover is coming up in two days, and I was wondering if you'd like some special food." I hadn't asked for *kosher*. I was eating whatever they served. I said, "No, look, it's all right." He asked, "Is there anything else I could do for you?" The next thing I knew, he had told me to go to the airport at Vung Tau and find my way to Nui Dat. From Nui Dat I could hitch a lift to Saigon, and in Saigon there was a Passover service happening with some Americans in the Free World Building. I hadn't been to Saigon, I hadn't been to Nui Dat. I thought the Free World Building would be a hut somewhere, an American PX. But it was one of the biggest buildings I'd ever seen in my twenty-one years of life – I hadn't been very worldly anyway.

'I found the door and it was just on dark. I'd been running late, and I was wearing my Australian uniform with my slouch hat. I opened the door, and all I could see were lots of people sitting at tables. I felt really shy and intimidated, and I wasn't quite sure if I was even in the right place, and I could hear some Hebrew being sung. They were just about to do the *Kiddush*. And as I walked in, a couple of Americans closest to the door stood up and patted me on my back. And then some more stood up, and a couple started clapping, a slow clap, and then I realised I was the only Australian there. An Australian Jew at a Passover service in Vietnam! This was, like, mind-boggling. They were pushing me along and I was looking for a spare table to sit down on a seat and hide, and there wasn't one. They were pushing me further and further forward, and eventually everyone in this building was standing up and clapping me. The tears started rolling down my face, because Passover is a festival of freedom … All of a sudden, I was feeling Jewish for the first time in my life. I was feeling a unity with other people which I'd never felt. I grew up in the country, in Brisbane, and my Jewishness was really non-existent. There was this table of rabbis and all my life, I'd only ever seen one rabbi, and that was when I was being *barmitzvahed*. People had come from the Philippines, Korea, all of Vietnam and Thailand. It was like I wasn't alone. It was the most amazing thing. I sat at the table with all the rabbis.'[19]

There had been one other Australian national serviceman at the same service – although he only just arrived in time: Captain Dr Ian Isaacs. 'I was a lot more organised for the second night *Seder*,' Isaacs wrote home, 'which had fewer people – about 75–100 … The meal was well presented with chicken soup, gefilte fish and horseradish, and a "TV dinner" of chicken ending with tinned peaches. [I]t was strange however to see copious amounts of Coke served, made "*kosher*" no doubt for the occasion … It was with some reluctance that I left on Sunday morning to come back to Nui Dat.'[20]

At the Passover service in Saigon, Roubin made friends who would later visit him in Vung Tau and take him on trips all around South Vietnam. He said, 'Life was sort of different, but then the bastardisation increased, because I had alienated myself in the group dynamics of the unit by being Jewish and going to the Passover service and having a couple of days off when the others didn't.'[21]

John Selan did not think he would be sent Vietnam. 'I actually said I didn't want to go,' he says, 'but there was a great shortage of dental technicians in the army.' He arrived on 30 August 1971, a month before *Yom Kippur*. He worked at both Vung Tau and Nui Dat and helped dismantle and close down the Nui Dat base, which was handed over to the South Vietnamese on 7 November 1971. Most of the remaining Australian troops in Vietnam were drawn down to Vung Tau and Selan went home on 18 November. Loris Roubin was returned to Australia for compassionate reasons on 25 November. The base at Vung Tau closed in March 1972, leaving only a few dozen 'military advisers' of the AATTV in Vietnam – a mirror image of the situation when the Australian commitment had begun ten years earlier.

Papua New Guinea

The Australian Army was never entirely comfortable with the hundreds of university graduates it had to absorb in the later years of the national service scheme. The army often had little use for their specialities – it had, for example, a low requirement for classicists – and no real idea what to do with highly qualified, self-assured, older men who did not aspire to become officers. So it was that, at the height of the Vietnam War, Australia sent scores of graduate national servicemen – most of them teachers, or 'chalkies' – to Papua and New Guinea, in postings to the Pacific Islands Regiment (PIR).

Since the military threat from Indonesia had abated with the downfall of Sukarno and the end of the Confrontation, the PIR had seemed an unlikely refuge for conscripts: many Australians in the lower ranks of the regiment had been eased out or moved on to make way for local troops. The majority who remained held ranks of sergeant and above – and most national servicemen were privates. And if the regiment was small, its education corps was tiny. In 1964 it had only three members. One of the first national servicemen to swell their ranks was Graham Lindsay, whose Jewish mother's family had come to Australia from London as 'Ten Pound Poms'. His birthday was 6 May 1945, and he was studying to be a teacher when he was called up in the first ballot. 'It hit me right between the eyes,' he says. He was allowed to defer until he had finished his first year of teaching, then he marched into Kapooka in May 1966. Lindsay had been in the CMF for two years, but left before he started teaching. He was not uncomfortable in the army. 'The actual environment didn't bother me at all,' he says, 'but I did tell them when I went in that I wouldn't kill anyone.' After Kapooka he was posted to the medical corps. In August 1966 he was working at 8 Field Ambulance in Puckapunyal, waiting to be sent to South Vietnam, when he was ordered to Watsonia barracks for an interview, and told there were teachers needed in PNG. 'It seemed like a great adventure,' he says, 'and I got out of killing people.' He ended up with the first batch of chalkies at PNG Command, Murray Barracks, Port Moresby, directed to teach NCOs and bring them up to the level of Intermediate Certificate. Lindsay also spent time on a civil-action patrol, travelling around the country cooking food for army crews who went out building roads, repairing electronic equipment for the islanders, and offering medical care. They walked halfway across the Kokoda Track, just for the experience, but had to turn back when one man fell sick. 'Compared to what was going on in Vietnam,' he says, 'compared to what some of our colleagues were going though, we just felt really lucky to be in New Guinea.'

A later Jewish chalkie was Norm Isenberg, whose father Morry had served in World War Two as a forward radar observer with the RAAF in the Northern Territory, and whose uncle Ben Isenberg had fought at the siege of Tobruk. Norm's birthdate was drawn in the seventh national service ballot in 1968, but he was given an automatic deferment to complete his teaching degree at Sydney University. He eventually joined a recruit-training platoon made up largely of regular soldiers at Kapooka in 1970. Isenberg cannot recall seeing a rabbi at Kapooka. 'I chatted to a few of the chaplains,' he says, 'told them I was Jewish. One of them gave me a New Testament in case I wanted to read it. I just said, "Thanks, Sir", and put it in my bag.' Nor does he remember any 'active antisemitism'. He says, 'The only discrimination against me was generally that I was a nasho.' By mid-1970 the education corps in PNG had grown to a strength of about sixty men, most of them conscripts. Isenberg was posted to Port Moresby, mainly running six-week courses for local soldiers, until he left PNG in October 1971.

Nissim 'Nick' Israel had arrived earlier in 1971. As a boy, Congo-born Israel had boarded at Embley Park School in Hampshire, UK. 'It was incredibly bad,' he says. 'There was a lot of anti-Jewish activities with some of the boys. They left me alone because I am able to defend myself. Also, I was one of their top rugby players. So I had some sort of edge on the rest of the Jewish boys in the boarding school. There was also a lot of homosexual activities: I was attacked but managed to punch the shit out of the guys that attacked me. I had my younger brother there in the school as well, and I got the word out that if anybody touches my brother, I'll kill you.' Israel rejoined his family in Sydney at seventeen. When he was called up for national service, he was working as a trainee manager at the Sebel Townhouse Hotel. He graduated from Scheyville and requested first a posting to infantry or armour – 'I wanted to be a warrior,' he says. 'I got the Catering Corps.' Israel was posted to 6th Task Force HQ in Enoggera, Queensland. 'It was on a war footing,' he says. 'They were doing a lot of preparations to send battalions to Vietnam.' He hoped to go to Vietnam too, but a posting came up for a catering officer in New Guinea. 'I said to myself, "Jesus, going to New Guinea will be like going back to Africa",' he says, 'and, in fact, it was. New Guinea was a luxury posting, colonial. Just about everybody had a batman. I had my shirts ironed and my boots and brass polished. I did a lot of scuba diving, a lot of water skiing.'

Israel was in New Guinea until early 1972, when he was returned to Australia with a twisted appendix. He contracted an infection and ended up in the Repatriation General Hospital, Concord, with some badly wounded men from Vietnam. 'I used to go down and have a chat to these guys,' he says. 'A guy had half his head missing. He was blind. A bullet hit one side of his brain and collapsed his cranium.' Nonetheless, Israel still hoped to get to Nui Dat. 'The ramifications of war are not so evident if you're a catering officer,' he says. 'You wouldn't be fighting unless the Vietnamese overran your perimeter and came knocking on your kitchen door.' He says he had been promised the next suitable posting, and he would have stayed in the army to take the job, but by the time he got out of hospital, Australia's Vietnam commitment had all but ended.

In October 1973, when the Yom Kippur War broke out in the Middle East, Israel was a civilian again. He volunteered to go to Israel and fight. 'But they only took people who were doctors, builders, carpenters to rebuild the damage,' he says. 'I think there were enough on-the-ground people in Israel to manage the war.'

8

After Vietnam

From CMF to Reserves

National service was abolished in Australia by Gough Whitlam's new ALP government in December 1972, and both the regular army and the CMF shrank suddenly and dramatically. The doctrine of forward defence, which had brought Australians into Vietnam, was abandoned and in the absence of any immediate threat it was no longer clear what urgent role the defence forces were supposed to play. The CMF was redesignated as the Army Reserve. During the Vietnam years, it had offered a home for those young men least interested in fighting that particular war, and who had joined up only to ensure they would not be drafted. With the end of conscription, the CMF/Army Reserve became, once again, a part-time job attracting men who had a degree of martial enthusiasm, including George Karsai, who was born in Australia in 1954, to Hungarian holocaust survivors. Karsai left school at sixteen and left home at seventeen. He had sales jobs, worked in a pub and drove taxis and in 1973 he signed up as part-time infantryman with the 4th Royal New South Wales Regiment. 'Just because I'm there, and just to see what happens, I put in for *kosher* rations, as a private,' he says. 'And we're in the bush, in Ingleburn. I couldn't believe it: we went out on the Friday night, on the Saturday – *wokka-wokka-wokka-wokka* – a helicopter lands, out passes a white box, "This is for Private Karsai" – *wokka-wokka-wokka-wokka* – it takes off. So I've had this

296

white box, and I was reliably informed it was this *kosher* meal box from Qantas, because they were the only people that made these *kosher* packs. Anyway, next day, we had twenty-eight *kosher* meal requests from my platoon. Needless to say, we didn't pursue that.'

In 1974 Karsai went through jungle training. 'One of the guys, who was not in my platoon, flicked me on the shoulder and said, "Buy me a drink". 'I said, "No, bugger off." He said, "What are you? A dirty Jew or something?" I said, "I happen to be Jewish. Two words to you, 'sex and travel'." He started being stroppy. My section guys took him outside and I believe there was a little bit of what they call "contact counselling".' After about eight years Karsai was promoted to Sergeant. On 7 September 1980, he was married in a military wedding at the Great Synagogue by Australian Army Chaplain Rabbi Raymond Apple. 'Rabbi Apple's wife wanted him to wear his uniform,' says Karsai, 'but he refused.' The next year Karsai went to the Officer Cadet Training Unit (OCTU) in Ingleburn and was commissioned as a second lieutenant. Meanwhile, Norm Isenberg had given up teaching, returned to university to study law, qualified, and gone into partnership with another solicitor. In late 1978 he too joined the Reserves and requested officer training. He was a couple of classes ahead of Karsai at OCTU. Isenberg was commissioned into the artillery in August 1980 but after a year or so with 7 Field Regiment he accepted a new commission to the Australian Army Legal Corps.

THERE WERE ALSO JEWISH WOMEN IN THE RESERVE, SUCH AS Julie Leder, who was born in McKinnon, Victoria. Leder attended a specialty music school where she studied the clarinet. In 1977 she joined the Reserve, with the aim of playing in the band. 'As a musician, you just want to perform with people,' she says. 'The Army Reserve was just another band to me. And I'm not scared of a bit of discipline. Musicians are very disciplined. You have to practice at night instead of going out and getting drunk or something.' However, she says, 'There were no women allowed in the Band Corps – the first woman joined full-time in 1982 – but I had an enlightened bandmaster who needed an extra clarinettist, so he said the way I could get in was to join another corps "on paper" but be "temporarily" posted to the band.' She was paid and badged as Ordnance Corps. 'This lasted for seven years,' she says. 'I was a WRAAC [Women's Royal Australian Army Corps] as well, so I could hide just wearing a WRAAC badge.' It took two years for the army to find a place for Leder on a two-week recruit-training course for women at Georges Heights, New South Wales. 'They were just slack,' she says, 'and couldn't organise themselves. As a woman, I was not permitted to go on the Band's annual camp in Balcombe because there were no women's facilities, so I did my two weeks of annual camp with the Regular Army Band in Melbourne. I'm sure I was a test case to see if I could cope with them and they could cope with me, and if I was okay sharing the men's toilets. Obviously there were no women's band uniforms so I took a bandsman's uniform off the rack and squished myself into it.' She was asked to attend a course for promotion to corporal. 'Military skills were done at Puckapunyal for two weeks,' she says, 'and the music course was at the brand new School of Music at Watsonia where they had women's facilities – but still no women. At Puckapunyal, I had to learn to teach weapons, marching and map-reading. By then I was a high school teacher so to strip and assemble a rifle was just like stripping and assembling a clarinet, saxophone or flute. A year later women were finally permitted in the Band Corps and I could have the band's uniform made-to-measure to fit all of my curves.'

Major General Professor Jeffrey Rosenfeld who, at time of writing, was the highest ranking Reservist in the Australian Army, was already a qualified neurosurgeon when he joined the Reserves in Victoria in 1984, as a direct-entry reserve officer with the rank of captain. 'I felt I owed a debt to Australia,' he says, 'first of all for taking in my father, who was an immigrant from Poland, who came here when he was a little boy. My father got out before the Holocaust. My mother was born in Melbourne, but the family goes back to Poland.' John Monash was second cousin to Rosenfeld's grandfather.

'I wasn't a cadet at school,' says Rosenfeld. 'I was a musician. It came as a shock to all who knew me that I would join the military. Why would this genteel Jewish boy, who'd been involved in music, in culture and the arts and science, and was a studious type, want to join a killing machine, as it were? I joined to serve my country, because of that link to Monash, and … realising that putting on the uniform of the country was really the highest endeavour of any citizen, to defend the country: Not that I went into battle for the country, but I indirectly went into battle.'

By 1989 George Karsai had been posted as a company commander of Sydney University Regiment. He had studied law at UNSW and was now a lawyer in private practice. 'I've never hidden the fact that I was Jewish in the military,' he says, 'I was proud of my cultural identity. Everybody knows. My nickname in the battalion was "General Jerusalem".' At the SUR, however, he believes he faced establishment antisemitism for the first time in his military career. The regiment needed an adjutant, Karsai was qualified, but the training major told him he'd received a delegation from some of his fellow officers who said they did not want a Jew as adjutant of the SUR. Karsai was struggling as a barrister when he accepted a transfer to the regular army as an officer in the Australian Army Legal Corps.

The First Gulf War

On 2 August 1990 President Saddam Hussein of Iraq ordered the invasion of Iraq's oil-rich neighbour, the Emirate of Kuwait. Australia was one of the earliest members of the Coalition that ousted Iraqi troops from Kuwait in the war of January–February 1991, but the ADF played virtually no part in the fighting. One of the few Jewish servicemen in the First Gulf War was Alan Mansfield, the grandson of Changi prisoner George Mansfield. He still had the letters written to his grandfather in the camp, a pile of unanswered mail. He kept the clay pipes George had made as a POW, a cutthroat razor perhaps fashioned from a bayonet, and a tobacco box and matchbox cover made from Japanese Zero aircraft. Alan collected them all in a bag with George's POW armband, which marked him as 'lieutenant in charge of electrical work'. Mansfield was born in 1962, grew up around Brighton and Elwood, and went to school at Melbourne High. In 1981 he signed up for five years in the RAN and ended up serving twenty-and-a-half. 'I think I was the only Jewish person in my intake,' he says, 'because they were a bit concerned about what I would eat and things like that. I said, "I won't eat pork. I don't like the flavour of pork anyway. I keep high holidays, if I can. I'm not going to lose sleep over it if time doesn't permit." And they were quite happy with that.' When the Gulf War broke out, Mansfield was posted to the destroyer HMAS *Brisbane* as a leading seaman, naval stores. The crew knew they would be sent to the Gulf. 'When we first got told, you wouldn't believe the number of people that were ringing up and seeing if you wanted to post off and they could take your place,' says Mansfield. Along with HMAS *Sydney*, the *Brisbane* was attached to the task group shadowing the aircraft carrier USS *Midway*. 'All the way over, we were doing exercises,' says Mansfield. 'Before we left, we got to a stage of going from a defensive posture to action stations – everywhere manned – within three minutes, from half the ship being asleep. Well, sort of asleep. We didn't get much sleep because no-one really had any experience as far as routines and things. You were supposedly six hours on, six hours off. A lot of the time, you were kept below decks. You would only go on the uppers to get rid of some rubbish, or if I was carrying tests for the barrel compressors and things like that, for filling the air tanks on the fire-fighting apparatus.' HMAS *Brisbane* arrived in the Gulf on 6 December 1990, was attached to the US navy battle group from 17 January–28 February 1991, and sailed home without having fired a shot in anger.

Somalia

In January 1993 Australian troops joined the US-led, UN-sanctioned Operation Restore Hope in Somalia. The famine-wracked East African nation had been tortured by a decade of civil war. Rival warlords battled for power and stole and disrupted international aid. The Australian contribution to the military effort was the deployment of 1RAR to secure humanitarian relief in the large sector around the town of Baidoa. There was probably only a handful of Jews in the Australian infantry in the early 1990s, among them Martyn Pincus, the grandson of Cecil Pincus, who had enlisted with his brother Fabian 'Frank' Pincus in World War One. Fabian, who was born in 1900, signed up as an eighteen-year-old in December 1914, went overseas, returned to Australia with pleurisy and was discharged from the AIF in 1915, only to rejoin in January 1916. Cecil and Fabian's youngest brother Hans Ivo Pincus served as a major in the Transport Division, stationed in Adelaide in World War Two. Martyn didn't learn about his family's military history until he was about eleven years old, when he saw a photograph of Cecil and two of his brothers in uniform. 'And I was sort of going, "Why are they in uniform?"' he says. '"What is

World War One and what is World War Two?" But I knew all about the Israeli wars.'

Martyn began studying Electronics at Monash University, where he joined the Reserves. But the degree bored him, and he quit the course but stayed with the Monash University Regiment. He'd been in the regiment about a year when he decided to become a regular soldier. 'It'd given me the opportunity to try before you buy, I suppose,' he says, 'and I thought, "Well, it's not as bad as everyone makes out." But, oh Jesus, when I joined the regular army, I was in for a shock. *It was nothing like the regular army.* The moment you got there, you were just being run around. There was no deciding, "I've had enough, I'll go and sit down for a while." I went from Kapooka, which was fairly tough, to infantry, which was even tougher. It was just really, really punishing and gruelling.' He joined 1RAR. When the officers learned he was Jewish, he says, 'They said, "Oh really? Oh. Okay. What are you doing here? Why aren't you in the Israeli army?" "Well, they're in Israel and I'm Australian."

'When we were doing military history, they were really big on the tactics that had been used in the Israeli wars,' says Pincus. 'We were sitting there in a classroom and they were teaching me about the Israeli military tactics and wars, and I'm going, "Yeah, I've got a fair idea of what you're talking about." They did uphold the Israeli army as a very professional and well-trained fighting force.' Religion was rarely an issue although 'one bloke in particular was quite troublesome', says Pincus. 'The moment he found out I was Jewish, I copped a bit of ribbing. I have memories of him goose-stepping up and down in front of my room one day. So I stuck my head out and I said, "Mate, what the f—k are you doing?" He said, "It's Adolf Hitler's birthday." I just shut my door and went back to bed. He got a medical discharge. It should've been for his head, but he had a botched operation. He got an infection in the hospital and it paralysed him for months.'

Pincus was sent to Somalia as a lance corporal in 1993. 'Malaysia was wet and hot,' he says. 'Somalia was hot and hot. And dusty and horrible, and there was people shooting at you randomly. It was total chaos. We were totally ill-equipped. It didn't feel like everything was well planned. Nothing in the Australian army ever seemed to be very well planned.' Problems included 'simple things like wearing soft hats, because our helmets were so old, they were useless'.

'We were camped out of town, in a flat area,' he says. 'We'd go out from there and into town. I was in charge of a gun group. It was just bizarre: you'd be walking down the road, you'd be crouched down, and all of a sudden the wall behind you would get hit and shower down on you. It was mainly just taking lots of random fire. It could be anything, mainly small arms. The rules of engagement were only to shoot when you had confirmation that people were shooting at you, and you could directly see that they were shooting at you. It was local warlords, local militia, kids with guns really. There were more organised elements, but they weren't what you'd call an army as such. If you got into their patch at the wrong time they'd just shoot at you, with any weapons they had at hand. But if you're in the army and you're worrying about getting killed every second, you're not concentrating on your job.'

The Australians remained in Somalia for seventeen weeks, returning home in May 1993. Pincus left the army three years later. Before he resigned, he spoke to Rabbi Apple, who was by then Senior Jewish Chaplain to the Australian Defence Force (ADF). Since he had spent his career being challenged as to why he wasn't in the Israeli army, Pincus asked the rabbi, '"Is there a path? What's the situation for service-people coming out of other services into the Israeli army?" He said he had no contacts with the Israeli army but he would investigate, but he seemed very reluctant to get involved. So that just petered out.'[1]

Bougainville

In 1988 a civil war broke out on the copper-rich island of Bougainville between the Bougainville Revolutionary Army and the government of PNG. After almost a decade of fighting, the parties began to move towards reconciliation and a multinational Peace Monitoring Group (PMG) under Australian leadership came to the island at the end of 1997. George Karsai deployed as part of the advance party of the PMG, and soon began working on the ceasefire agreement. The warring parties were brought on board HMAS *Tobruk* in April 1998 as the ship waited in Loloho harbour, and the discussions took place in the wardroom. 'There were about twenty-odd clauses to this ceasefire agreement,' says Karsai. 'It was a very basic document. But it got them stopping shooting at each other ... We'd convene as a group for an hour or two, a lot of people made speeches, then there'd be a break, and they'd discuss a particular clause. They'd come to me and say, "What does this mean? We want to give effect to this particular thing." So I would draft the clause. And then they would go to the various cabins, and I would go to the various cabins and explain what the clause meant, or try to write a clause, or they would say, "We don't want that, we want this." So I'd massage the clause. And then once everyone was settled, we'd go back, have another discussion about that clause, put that to bed and go on to the next one. And this went on for thirty-six hours solid.'[2]

Julie Leder went twice to Bougainville with Queensland army bands. 'It didn't bother me,' she says. 'Most musicians want to go on tour.' The bands were taken from camp to village, playing for both troops and local people. 'I had to learn a couple of songs in pidgin English,' says Leder, 'a song called Bullamakow, "I've Got to Get a Cow". Lots of songs with actions, where the kids can follow what I say: "Hi-di, hi-di, hi-di, hi! Ho-di, ho-di, ho-di, ho!" You make the people feel happy, and then do ball-tearers for the soldiers.'[3]

East Timor

Indonesia, which in 1974 had invaded and occupied the former Portuguese territory of Timor L'Este, agreed to a ballot to determine the political future of the province in 1999. A large majority of East Timorese rejected an Indonesian offer of 'special autonomy' in a vote which seemed to signal a move to independence. Indonesia refused to accept the result and provoked, stoked and enabled an explosion of violence against civilians that left 1400 people dead. Australian troops came to East Timor as peacekeepers on 20 September, two weeks after the announcement of the result of the ballot. Several Jewish personnel were deployed to Timor between 1999 and 2004, including Greg Sher, who was later killed in Afghanistan. Jewish officers included Scott Leonard, who grew up in Wollongong, New South Wales, among a small Jewish community that met for services perhaps once a month. In Leonard's second year of high school, his family moved to Sydney. He studied for a year at university and worked through a cluster of odd jobs – including a stint at Lewis' *kosher* delicatessen in Bondi – before he joined the army in November 1988, at the age of twenty-two. 'It was something that I'd wanted to do for a long, long time,' he says, 'and I guess it was a natural progression from ten years in scouting and four years of army cadets, and a general bent towards that outdoorsy, structured kind of work.' He enlisted as an ordinary soldier, as he was initially unable to qualify for officer training because he was colour-blind. He joined the 2nd Signals Regiment at Watsonia but was permitted to transfer to RMC after two years, once the staff 'realised it was doable'. He enjoyed Duntroon, 'played a fair bit of rugby', and, upon graduation, chose to join the RAAMC as a general services officer. After a couple of Medical Corps postings, he was given broader logistical jobs and was posted to Timor as a senior captain in December 1999. 'The disruption from Indonesia had been pushed pretty quickly down towards the border,' he says, 'and that was still bubbling along. We spent a bit of time up in the hills near Dili, helping out a couple of local groups. There was a fair bit of damage. The Indonesians burned a lot, trashed a lot, on their way out.' Leonard arrived a few days before the Tour of Duty – Concert for the Troops, in which an eclectic line-up of Australian rock and pop artists, including Johnny Farnham, Doc Neeson, Kylie Minogue and the Living End played to an audience of about 4000 peacekeepers at Dili Stadium. 'It was a good show,' says Leonard, 'and it became a regular thing. They really revived the whole musos-visiting-deployed-troops-thing à la World War Two or Vietnam.' In the years since Vietnam, says Leonard, the army had lost a lot of its culture and had forgotten how to do things overseas. 'Timor was a real shock in terms of the number of people and the amount of equipment we sent over there,' he says. 'It was a real challenge. We learned a lot.' Almost every officer in the Australian army wanted to deploy to Timor, not only to apply their training, but to acquire military credibility within a fighting organisation. Soldiers who were not posted to Timor were still walking around without any medals on Anzac Day, says Leonard. '"Go to Dili for a dash for cash and medals" was the expression,' says George Karsai. 'We had every legal officer go. From Sydney to Townsville, there was not a legal officer. I was left behind with a couple of others, and we were just frantic; it was so busy, like a one-armed paper hanger in a gale.' Karsai's opportunity to deploy came in 2001. 'Every contact between the Australian troops and militia or Indonesian armed forces was investigated to make sure we obeyed our rules of engagement,' he says. 'I would draft the terms of reference, I would then form part of the investigation team, and we would deploy.' It was not a comfortable posting, even for officers. 'When I arrived there, my jaw hit the deck,' says Karsai. 'We were in a burned-out building with plastic on the windows with gaffer tape. It was still charred. We were sleeping on the floor in what they called a "mozzie dome", a small pup tent with a flyscreen.

Three months into the op, the airfield reconfigured and that threw up a number of demountable buildings. The food was just disastrous. We ate at the UN mess, because the UN lines backed onto ours, and it was atrocious, sometimes inedible.' Karsai and his colleagues bought a rice cooker and started up a curry club. Once a week, they went shopping at the local markets for fresh produce, then returned to their quarters to cook their own meal. 'No pork, I must say,' said Karsai. 'They were very kind to me.'[4]

Julie Leder roughed it in Timor, too, on a six-week tour with the Townsville Army Band. 'We slept on stretchers under our individual mosquito netting and I shared a tent with thirty men,' she says. 'Needless to say I am now an expert at getting into and out of my uniform on my stretcher under a sheet.'[5]

9

The War on Terror

The attack on the Twin Towers

On 11 September 2001 nineteen terrorists hijacked four US civilian aircraft, collided two of them into the Twin Towers of the World Trade Center in New York and a third into the Pentagon in Washington, DC. The fourth plane, which the killers had hoped would crash into Washington DC, was brought down in Pennsylvania when passengers tried to fight off the hijackers. Nearly 3000 people, including the terrorists, died in the attacks. Fifteen of the murderers were citizens of Saudi Arabia. The architect of the attacks was Osama bin Laden, a Saudi prince and *mujahid* – or jihadist – who had been blooded fighting the Soviets in Afghanistan in the 1980s. Bin Laden's organisation, al-Qaeda, had been formed from the jetsam of international volunteers who had infiltrated into Afghanistan to drive out the Russians in the name of Islam – a war on communism partly financed by both the US and Saudi Arabia, with military aid from China and Pakistan.

War in Afghanistan

The Soviets abandoned Afghanistan in February 1989, leaving behind a civil war which, in various forms, wracked the country until the Afghan government was taken over by the Pakistan-backed

Islamists of the Taliban in September 1996. By this time, Bin Laden was living in exile in Sudan, having denounced the Saudi government for allowing US troops to be stationed near Muslim holy sites during the First Gulf War. Bin Laden believed many things in life were controlled by Jews, including the entire US and UK, and that the Israelis hoped to bring the Middle East and the Arabian Peninsula into a Greater Israel. But he declared war on the US in response to what he saw as its continued military occupation of Saudi Arabia. Bin Laden was expelled from Sudan and went to live in the new Islamic Emirate of Afghanistan. Under the Taliban, women were not allowed to go to work, school or university, thieves were separated from their hands or feet, and communists were executed. From the sanctuary of the emirate, Bin Laden planned the September 11 hijackings.

In October 2001 the US demanded the Taliban hand over Bin Laden. Although under pressure from US bombing, the Taliban refused to act unless they were shown binding evidence of Bin Laden's involvement in the assault on New York. On 7 October the US, in alliance with the UK, launched Operation Enduring Freedom, with the stated goal of invading Afghanistan to uproot al-Qaeda from its Afghan bases. The Taliban government quickly crumbled. Its armies fled to the mountains and over the border to Pakistan to escape the Western allies, who had joined forces with anti-Taliban former *mujahideen* of the Northern Alliance.

In December 2001 the International Security Assistance Force (ISAF) was established to help train the new Afghan National Army (ANA) and rebuild a nation devastated by decades of war. The ADF's main contribution to the ISAF effort was Operation Slipper, which first saw Australian Special Forces deployed to Afghanistan along with RAAF planes flying out of neighbouring Kyrgyzstan. In 2003 the re-organised Taliban launched a fresh insurgency. In September 2006 an Australian Reconstruction Task Force (RTF), including infantry, armour and engineers, was deployed to Uruzgan in southern Afghanistan to work with the Dutch task force in the province. They were joined in April 2007 by an Australian Special Operations Task Group (SOTG), including 2 Commando Company, 1st Commando Regiment. The SOTG aimed to disrupt Taliban military systems, and capture or kill key local leaders, who were given codenames and formally targeted as 'objectives'.

A number of Jewish men – and at least one Jewish woman, Major Tanya Haber – served in the Australian army in Afghanistan. One soldier, Greg Sher, was killed by the enemy, and another, Captain Jake Kleinman, was awarded a Distinguished Service Medal. Whereas the Jewish component in other recent wars and operations included business professionals, medical specialists and entertainers – doctors, lawyers and musicians – those who served in Afghanistan were often in combat roles. Arthur Shisman of Melbourne joined the Australian Army in 2005. Shisman was born in the Ukraine in 1982. The family migrated to Australia in 1988, and Shisman's father eventually set up a building business in Melbourne. Shisman attended Sholem Aleichem College, Brighton Secondary College and then Bialik College. His father and grandfather had both completed their compulsory service in the Soviet Union. His great-grandfather, an officer in the Red Army, had been killed fighting the Nazis in 1941. As a teenager, Shisman wanted to join the army; instead he started a university degree – although he preferred to spend his time labouring for his father. 'As soon as I picked up that sledgehammer and the jackhammer,' he says, 'I felt that I was more at home on the building site than at the university, listening to lecturers.' He dropped out of two degree courses and visited Israel, where he saw 'eighteen- or nineteen-year-old girls in uniform everywhere', he says. 'It made me feel a bit guilty, and embarrassed as well – you had young girls doing it and here I am, a bloke. My mum had a close friend in Israel and her daughter was in the Israeli Army, in artillery corps, a combat unit.' Shisman's father, bastardised in the Soviet Army, did not want his son to have anything to do with the military. 'I told my parents I was going into the army two weeks before I was supposed to go,' says Shisman. 'So that came as a big shock to them. They weren't too happy, but they got used to it and they were proud.' He found recruit training difficult. 'I was from a sheltered, isolated environment,' he says. 'I worked hard, I laboured hard, but I was still within the confines of a Jewish suburb, Caulfield, still sheltered by parents. It took a long time to adjust, to understand what needed to be done. I got through recruit training. I have no idea how. I went into IET [Initial Employment Training] for my tank drivers' course, because I'd nominated to go to Armoured Corps. But there were a lot of crusty old sergeants and warrant officers, a lot of screaming. I wasn't used to it. I didn't understand why it was necessary.' He remained in IET for longer than most trainees. 'I just wasn't able to comprehend what these old bastards wanted,' he says. 'Eventually, I got to 1st Armoured Regiment, tentatively. It was basically conditional: "Watch this guy, we're not sure if he can drive a tank or not, so keep an eye on him".' 1st Armoured Regiment was based in Darwin, and Shisman was posted to C Squadron. 'When I got to the unit, they put me into Benjamin "Chuck" Howson's tank straight away,' says Shisman. 'Howson was magnificent. When I got to Darwin, we went on an exercise with the American Marines. I got half an hour's sleep each night, if that. But I didn't care because he was an awesome commander, it was a good crew. It couldn't have fallen into place better for me. I integrated well into C Squadron – head-down, arse-up, that's all I did. I just wanted to prove myself, that I was worthy of being in the squadron, in the regiment. And everything was fine.'

Shisman always hoped to go overseas with the army but never expected it. 'I was told initially, "As a tankie you won't get deployed anywhere",' he says. '"Tankies are like koalas, not to be exported or shot at."' In 2007 the 1st Armoured Regiment became the only unit in the army with Abrams battle tanks. 'I watched the Iraq War from the living room,' says Shisman. 'I saw how these Abrams tanks worked.' Although Shisman imagined he would see out his service in Australia, 'I thought, to work on an Abrams tank, for me, will be good enough,' he says. 'At least I'll be able to say, "I've done my time in the army, I've been on an Abrams: I drove it, I serviced it, I operated from it."

'I loved the Abrams,' he says. 'I was the Regimental Soldier of the Year in 2008, and the reason for it was that love, that passion.' His army nickname was 'Shiz', but 'a few guys called me "the War Bore" as well', he says, '"the War Bore of the Abrams tank".' By this time C Squadron had been disbanded due to lack of numbers, and Shisman had become the operator for the OC of B Squadron. 'In 2008 people started recognising things that I was doing,' he says. He was offered a place on a Combat Fitness Leader's course to qualify him to run the unit's early morning PT sessions, then, 'We had a meeting in March,' he says. 'A rumour started spreading, the squadron met up, and one of the guys said, "Sir, cut the bullshit, what's going on?" And the Squadron Sergeant Major said, "We're going to be deployed, and basically we need to decide who's going to go." And the SSM came up to me and said, "Shizzy, what do you want to do? The Combat Fitness Leader's course, or go to Afghanistan?" My reply was, "Sir, I'll do exactly what I'm told." And he said, "Good. You're going on the CFL course and then you're going to Afghanistan straight afterwards." I was walking away and I had this big smile on my face: I'd got both of them! Not only that, we were told who we were going with – which was the SOTG, the Special Operations Task Group. I couldn't believe it. I thought going to Afghanistan was great, but going with the elite … that was the icing on the cake.'

On Shisman's last exercise in Australia, Talisman Sabre in Rockhampton, he met Allen Volkov, a Jewish family friend in the 2/14th Light Horse, a cavalry regiment based in Queensland. 'Our parents knew each other,' says Shisman. 'His grandmother was very concerned her grandson was going into the army, and she said to my dad, "Get your son to talk to me, maybe we can convince Allen otherwise." I said, "Look, if he wants to go, he wants to go. No matter what you do, you won't convince him."' When Shisman saw Volkov in Rockhampton, 'He'd been in for almost two years,' he says. 'Afghanistan wasn't far away. He knew that it was a matter of time before he got deployed.'

Shisman did not go out of his way to let people in the army know he was Jewish. 'I tried to hide it,' he says. 'I didn't really say that I was Jewish. I did sign up as Jewish, but when I got to the regiment, you filled out a form, and for religion I put "N.A.", even though my dog tags had the "J" that I was Jewish. I thought, "Whoever needs to know knows anyway – and everyone else, what's the point?" But everybody knew anyway. And, basically, if people asked, I said I was Russian. Australians have a culture of taking the piss out of things and I felt that if I was going to let it be known, people would take the piss out of it, and I wouldn't take it lightly. Eventually I would lose my cool and probably do something stupid, and it wasn't part of my plan in the army. What's the point in making headlines for the wrong reasons? Guys made jokes here and there, but it wasn't anything malicious.'

Shisman went to Afghanistan on a five-month deployment in 2008. 1st Armoured Regiment had to leave the Abrams tanks behind in Australia, and travel to Afghanistan with Bushmaster PMV [Protected Mobility Vehicle] armoured cars. 'Our job was basically to take the boys to the battlefield,' says Shisman, 'form a hide and, when they came back, [load them] back in the cars and off we go. Or, when we attacked the compounds, we surrounded the compounds and the boys kicked the doors in. We sat on the gun to act as a perimeter, so nobody could escape. The Bushmasters blocked every bit of exit, along with the snipers, and the shooters were there to get who they needed to get. We were there in the winter, cars were breaking down, we had to tow them, we were always in the mud. It was hard work mentally, because every time you left the wire, apprehension set in on you.' The cavalry never knew when they might hit an Improvised Explosive Device [IED], one of the homemade mines planted by the Taliban to disable vehicles and men. But 'we usually had hunches when something was going to happen', says Shisman. 'In my case, it was no exception when Mick Fussell died; it was no exception when Greg [Sher] died.'

Lieutenant Mick Fussell was a Joint Terminal Attack Controller, whose role was to call in aircraft or gunfire in support of the ground troops. 'He was a short guy,' says Shisman, 'and he was always in front of my Bushmaster in an SRV [Surveillance and Reconnaissance Vehicle]. He always had his slouch hat on.' Early in the morning of 27 November 2008, Fussell was part of a patrol moving along a path towards a compound in the Mirabad Valley where the Australians hoped to find a local Taliban leader, Abdul Hai, 'Objective Rapier'. A warrant officer suggested they should not take the path because it was laced with IEDs, but the OC maintained this was the best chance they would get to reach their objective, and Mick Fussell stepped on a mine. 'I was on piquet,' says Shisman. 'I was the guy looking at them through Ninox [night vision goggles]. I heard a big bang, and I looked to my one o'clock, and I saw it as the smoke went up. The news was broken to us just after I finished piquet. My troop leader came up to me. He said, "Shiz, we need you in your BM." He got us all into the Bushmaster. He told us, "There were two WIAs and one KIA. Lieutenant Fussell passed away earlier tonight." The breath went out of us.' On the return drive to Camp Russell, 'It was a terrible feeling,' says Shisman. 'Nobody was talking in the car: I was used to seeing him, a short fella with a slouch hat, and that was it, I didn't see him anymore, he wasn't there. On the way back, I was just staring at that trunk the whole way through.

'Greg came to Afghanistan on the same day that Mick Fussell

died,' says Shisman, but Shisman and Sher's paths did not cross until January 2009. 'We were looking for Objective Flambard,' says Shisman, 'a Taliban leader in the Baluchi Valley. We thought if we could occupy his house where he lived, he would unmask himself – we were always told that: they would "unmask" themselves, and then *bang!* – and we'd take him out. We wanted to provoke him. It was a four- or five-hour drive from Camp Russell, and we pulled up towards the evening into a patrol base called Qudus. It was an overcast night, and the men could not go into Flambard's compound without overhead surveillance from the Dutch UAVs [Unmanned Aerial Vehicles] to warn them of any waiting ambush. The Dutch didn't want to send up the UAVs – 'They didn't really like to do anything that involved hard work,' says Shisman – so the Bushmaster crews spent the night camped in Forward Operating Base Qudus.

FOB Qudus was commanded by Captain Jacob Kleinman, who was born in Irymple, Victoria, just outside Mildura. His mother and father came to Australia from South Africa in 1979, and his father's first job in the new country was as an orthopaedic surgeon in the Royal Flying Doctor Service, so the family settled in country Victoria. In 1988 they moved to Newcastle, New South Wales. 'There's still a Jewish community in Newcastle,' says Kleinman. 'Dad used to take me to *shule* on Fridays as a kid. Getting a *minyan* was once in a blue moon. I did my *barmitzvah* in Newcastle. I used to come down to Sydney on the weekends and do my *barmitzvah* lessons at the Great Synagogue. At the end of high school, my life basically revolved around playing rugby, going to the gym, drinking beers, chasing girls, going to the beach, all that stuff everyone did in Newcastle.' In 2005 Kleinman went to play rugby for Australia at the Maccabiah Games. 'When I was in Israel,' he says, 'I'd met a lot of kids who did military time and they knew what they wanted to do. I was kind of just floating around. I needed focus. It was something I'd considered throughout high school, and I was twenty-two years old and I'm, like, if I don't do it now, I'm never going to do it.

'I applied originally to be an infantry soldier,' he says, 'and passed the aptitude tests. They said, "Do you want to sit for Officer Selection Board?" I thought, "I just want to join the army as soon as possible."' Kleinman qualified for officer training, enlisted in January 2006, and spent eighteen 'very intense' months at Duntroon. 'You have six days' work a week,' he says. 'Every five-and-a-half months, you have two weeks off. There's so much crammed into it. They equate it to drinking from a fire hydrant. I sucked it up. I was the only Jewish kid in my class. My mates called me "Jewboy" and it didn't bother me. It was like an endearing term. It's like you call a redhead "Blue".' Kleinman graduated in June 2007, went to Singleton for his infantry training, and was then posted to 7RAR in Darwin. He was sent to Afghanistan for the first time in 2008, as part of an Operational Mentoring and Liaison Team (OMLT) embedded with an Afghan unit, living out in patrol bases. 'We were going out on patrols, and we'd try and do some training in between patrols with them,' says Kleinman, 'to try and bring their capability up a bit. It went through stages when there were four Australians with 120 Afghans in the middle of nowhere. I never told them I was Jewish, because that causes problems. I hung out with the guys, learned a bit of Pashto, a bit of Farsi.'

Life was 'biblical' in Afghanistan, says Kleinman. 'Come wheat harvesting, there's still people separating the husks from the wheat with a big bowl, like they did a thousand years ago. It really is remote, except they've got AK-47s and mobile phones. It's a very harsh environment and they're very hard people. Training the Afghans was a hard process because they thought they knew it all, and a lot of them had been fighting for a while. So it was, like, "What're you going to teach me?" I guess you could say they're brave, but they're not very good – and not all of them are brave.' In January 2009 Kleinman was the base commander at Qudus, in charge of about ten Australians and 120 Afghans, when Greg Sher arrived with his commando company.

Both Kleinman and Shisman were watching as the enemy rockets came into the base on Sunday 4 January at 12.55 pm. Qudus, like the other patrol bases, was surrounded by a Hesco wall of earth-filled defensive barriers, inside which sat a collection of Conex shipping containers and tents. When the enemy rocket came in, 'It went through the hessian fence – there was a hole, or a crack, in it,' says Shisman. Its next obstacle was a Conex storing fresh water bottles. 'It went through the water container,' says Shisman, 'we saw the holes – three centimetres or so lower and it would've hit the water. It hit Greg directly, hit the hessian fence that was a few metres from him – boom! – exploded, and killed him.'

'There's a good chance the rocket had been buried underground for a while,' says Kleinman, 'not been stored correctly. The rocket's designed to blow up the moment it hits something, but the fuse had malfunctioned. There were multiple times it should have blown up but it didn't.' Shisman says, 'His body flew into the air. It spun around, he landed on his back, and then they started shooting at us. The left side of his body, from underneath his armpit to his waist, was all covered in blood. A lot of the Bushmaster guys were in tears. A couple of guys, the rocket went straight past their backs. There could've been a lot more casualties. Greg took that rocket for all of us. The ANA started taking pictures of his body. We wanted to confiscate their phones, but they said that they would march off base. Personally, I would've said, "No worries, see you out there." Because we knew – not 100 per cent, but I'm pretty certain – that they were the ones who acted as the spotters for that mortar, and they were the ones responsible for his death: them in collaboration with another spotter.'

Shisman had bumped into Sher on the base, but had not realised he was Jewish. Kleinman did not know Shisman and had never spoken to Sher. None of the men were aware there were at least three Jewish soldiers on that remote base in the Baluchi Valley. An armourer on the base had fashioned Sher a Magen David from aluminium piping, for the memorial service and the ramp ceremony, and 'so he wouldn't lie in chapel under a cross', says Felix Sher. On 7 January, when Shisman came back from Patrol Base Qudus to Tarin Kowt, he phoned his father, who told him Sher was Jewish. 'And when I heard it,' say Shisman, 'I went out and looked at that Star of David, and I stared at it for about ten minutes. I couldn't believe it.'

'The funeral procession was there,' says Shisman, 'everybody paid their respects. The C-130 flew out. On the one hand, I thought, "Shit, he's dead." On the other hand, I thought, "At least he's leaving this place. We still have to be here."'

The US invades Iraq

An unanticipated consequence of the 9/11 attacks, with hitherto unending repercussions, was President George W Bush's decision to invade Iraq and overthrow the regime of Saddam Hussein. Australian soldiers, sailors and air crew were among the forces of the 'Coalition of the Willing' that poured into the Persian Gulf in March 2003. Although Saddam's government was an opportunist sponsor of terrorism, and paid 'pensions' to the families of Palestinian suicide bombers, the dictator was unconnected with al-Qaeda, and there seemed to be scant direct connection between the attacks on the US and the assault on Iraq.

In the run-up to the invasion, the US demanded Iraq give up its weapons of mass destruction. Once Baghdad was taken, after a short war, it became apparent those weapons no longer existed. On 1 May George W Bush appeared in a flight suit on the deck of the aircraft carrier USS *Abraham Lincoln* and announced the end of major combat operations, beneath a banner that read 'Mission Accomplished'. Australian combat troops were quickly withdrawn, as the US occupation of Iraq began. The fugitive Saddam Hussein was captured in December but the Sunni guerrilla forces once loyal to his regime had never surrendered; they had simply gone to ground. They resurfaced gradually – at the same time as rival Shi'a militias were beginning to launch attacks on foreign forces – and first came into mass open combat with the US army in Fallujah, west of Baghdad, in spring 2004.

The US Marines' battle to clear the insurgents from Fallujah was bloody, protracted and initially inconclusive. A second Battle of Fallujah was fought in November, in which US and Iraqi troops battled to clear the city of insurgents. Colonel Jeffrey Rosenfeld, now a veteran of Rwanda, Bougainville and East Timor, was working among a small number of Australians embedded with the 332nd Expeditionary Medical Group, a US Air Force hospital. The US had appealed for specialist medical support, including neurosurgeons. 'I said, "I will go,"' says Rosenfeld. 'My wife, obviously, wasn't that enthralled with the idea. She was concerned that I would come home in a coffin, or that I would be captured by the Iraqi enemy and tortured.' They lived in tents at the hospital. 'We were doing our surgery in fixed Conex boxes,' says Rosenfeld. 'But the surgery was going on around the clock. It was like a very advanced version of *MASH*, working at many times the pace and complexity.' During the Battle of Fallujah, 'There was very tough door-to-door combat. It was hellishly difficult for them to get those enemy fighters out of there. They did, but look at all the casualties. And we were looking after those American Marines, but we were also looking after the injured insurgents, and the families that they were bombing.' The team was confronted with 'the chaos of getting fifty casualties coming on your doorstep at once'. They had to ask, 'How do you sort them out? How do you work out who goes to the theatre first? Who goes to the CAT scanner? Who doesn't get any treatment because they're going to die? Who's left because they're so mildly injured that they don't need any treatment at the moment?' All the while, more patients were coming in. 'The triage has to be done very rapidly,' says Rosenfeld, 'and very expertly, and then the people that need theatre go straight into theatre. There were bombs going off outside our tents at times. We just kept going. You're on an adrenalin rush all the time. You're sort of working twenty-four hours a day – you get some sleep here and there, but it was non-stop.' The most common surgery performed by Rosenfeld was a craniotomy for bomb-blast victims. 'The whole of their body is injured by these bomb blasts,' says Rosenfeld. 'But the head particularly receives that blast wave. It also gets burned from the hot-air blast. The face, the scalp – if they're not wearing their helmet – and the eyes can get injured. And the metal fragments from the bomb pierce various parts of the body, particularly the face, and they go up into the brain. These were horrendous injuries. I became an expert on bomb blasts.'

Australian combat troops returned to Iraq in April 2005. George Karsai, now a lieutenant colonel and a veteran of Bougainville and East Timor, was posted to Camp Victory in Baghdad as the senior Australian legal officer in 2006. Karsai was responsible for the entire Middle East area of operations. 'I got involved in the writing of detention policy,' he says. 'When we captured the insurgents, what did we do with them, how did we treat them. It was a very strict protocol and it was adhered to. I drafted and then administered the rules of operation for our embedded personnel. I got involved in a lot of rules of engagement, order-for-opening-fire interpretation. I found I [gave] more personnel counselling in Iraq than anywhere else. By then, I was older. I was in my fifties. I wasn't the padre, but I thought I was reasonably approachable.' There were 'a lot of domestic issues, with spouses and partners', he says. 'It was not unusual for a spouse of a deployed person to do a couple of things: the deployed person would put all of their money into a joint bank account, and the person staying back in Australia would clear out that bank account. Compounding that problem, they would then say, "I'm leaving", so the army would organise a removal for them. And let's say the married quarter was in Townsville, but this wife wanted to leave her husband who was overseas, clean out the bank account, get a removal, and go to Victoria with the kids and all their possessions – we've got a person deployed who can't go anywhere, can't do anything, and everything at home has fallen apart.'

Another East Timor veteran, Scott Leonard, arrived in Baghdad in November 2007. He was now a major, in his nineteenth year in the army, and posted to the Multi-National Security Transition Command – Iraq (MNSTC-I) as a logistics officer attached to US forces. 'I was in the Green Zone,' he says, 'and by that stage most of the rockets and mortars that were coming in, were coming in at maximum range. So instead of coming in from the side and hitting the big concrete reinforcing walls around the place, they tended to drop straight into the building. And the buildings we were using weren't strong enough to take the weight of any reinforcement on the top, so you took your chances. Before the invasion, it was an Iraqi military barracks, and they supplemented that with your ATCO-style hut, all pretty lightweight stuff, just to add extra office space and storage space as we needed it.' The focus of the command was the training and the re-equipment of the Iraqi Defence Force. 'And that was a classic history-repeating-itself,' says Leonard. 'I was doing pretty much the same job that a number of British logistics officers were there doing in the 1920s, after the fallout from the First World War and the great European divvy-up of the Middle East. The Brits had the mandate in Iraq, and they dismantled the Iraqi defence force and then re-equipped them and retrained them, just like we were doing. And here we were again, doing it all again. And now I see the same equipment getting blown up or used by the bad guys and – what do you know?

– we're starting to build up our presence there. Round and round and round we go. And, unfortunately, people die in the process every time, and you wonder what for.

'We had training teams scattered around the country,' he says, 'a couple of big supply depots. A lot of my work was focused on trying to secure and account for all the equipment coming in from donor countries all over the world, and bringing it in through Kuwait and getting it to the right place in Iraq.' Whole containers of weapons and vehicles and clothing would go missing at every stage in the supply chain. 'Because there were so many countries involved along the way,' says Leonard, 'and merchant ships. It's not like you [call] TNT and their courier will pick it up in Melbourne and their trucks will move it to Sydney and their operator will give it to you. We had so many different people involved along the way that it was very hard to monitor what they were doing. And because the stores were coming from so many different sources, we couldn't even have consistency in terms of GPS tracking devices in the consignments. In some places, like the port in Kuwait, we had some representatives from the US forces but they couldn't be everywhere, and if they started unloading the ship at two o'clock in the morning and our person wasn't there, we'd lost visibility of the shipment again – so it was pretty tough.'

There were always Jewish troops among the Americans stationed in Baghdad. They jokingly called their congregation 'B'nai Baghdad'. 'Every Friday night, we'd get together for a service,' says Leonard. 'Sometimes we'd have twenty or more, depending on who was in town, because a lot of people transited the Green Zone on their way to or from other parts of the country. The core of us were based in the various units inside the Green Zone. I got there just before Chanukah, and stayed through until after *Pesach*, and had a great *Seder* that night. The rabbi flew in, all his supplies complete – all the food, the wine, the cookers, the whole lot. In the grounds of the then US Embassy, they had a demountable building that was the multi-denominational chapel, so we used that. We had a little cupboard for our few supplies: Bill and Noni from Margaret River did the righty by us with some Five Stones *kosher* wine, and managed to ship two dozen bottles over for us.'

Iraq was once the centre of world Judaism. After the fall of Jerusalem, ancient Jewish life came to coalesce around Babylon. Even Fallujah was once a seat of Jewish learning. But, in the face of massive government discrimination and a campaign of synagogue bombings, the great majority of the once 150 000-strong community was airlifted to Israel between 1948 and 1951. Life for the remaining thousands became barely tolerable after the Six Day War, and in 1969 fourteen men – including nine Jews – were publicly hanged on trumped-up charges of spying for Israel. Half a million Iraqis marched and danced past the gallows in celebration, and many more Jews subsequently left the country. By the Second Gulf War, there were perhaps half a dozen left in Baghdad. 'There's been a few efforts over the years since to try and help them to get out, but they want to stay there,' says Leonard. 'We had one lady, in particular, who managed to get into the Green Zone every couple of weeks or so to join us for services.' A Jewish US Army Reserve officer, Stuart Adam Wolfer, worked as a liaison officer with the Iraqi Jews. Wolfer had been thirty-three years old and working for a law firm when he was first posted as a logistics officer in Kuwait in August 2005. At thirty-six, he was called to the Gulf again, to join the staff at MNSTC-I. Leonard knew Wolfer well. He was 'a very nice guy', he says. On 6 April 2008 there was a rocket attack on the headquarters. 'It came in through the roof of the gym at about three o'clock on a Sunday afternoon,' says Leonard. 'The problem was, because the headquarters had been there since day one and a number of locals had worked there over the years, they all knew our routine – and three o'clock in the afternoon was the prime time when many people took a break, and so the gym was full.' Wolfer and another man were killed, but B'nai Baghdad is 'still alive in one form or another,' says Leonard. 'It shifted to Afghanistan a couple of years ago, and some of the people I was with in Iraq have deployed several times since.'[1]

Aaron Chapman arrived in Iraq with 5RAR in January 2009. He was born in Kwajalein in the Marshall Islands, where his father, a former US naval officer, worked as a civilian contractor for the military. 'They had a very small Jewish community there,' says Chapman. 'They used to have a minibus that would come around and collect us all for all the larger Jewish festivals. Everyone on the island was really just temporary. People would come and go all the time, and at times they'd struggle to make a *minyan*.' When Chapman was ten years old, his father took a job in Australia, and the family moved first to Adelaide then to Melbourne. Chapman went to school at Leibler Yavneh College, and left in Year 10. 'I was keen on going back to America and joining the military there,' says Chapman, 'and my dad kind of talked me out of it. He wanted me to be an officer, and join the navy like he did, and my brother did.'* 'Me, being stubborn the way I was, I wanted to join the army. I just had to be different.' He enrolled at the Royal Military College. 'There was a rabbi that came and saw me and he gave me a *siddur* and a *kippah*,' he says. 'He'd just been next door, to ADFA, and I believe there were a couple of Jewish people over at ADFA.' Chapman had been at Duntroon for a year when he decided he did not yet want to become an officer. 'I was only a young person,' he says. 'And so I said, "I'd like to transfer into being a regular soldier, and then I may come back." They weren't too happy. I'd just done twelve months of training and spent a great deal of their money. But, at the same time, they respected the fact that I wanted to gain my experience as a soldier first.' He was sent to 5RAR and, he says, 'It was just the luck of the draw that when I got there they said,

---

* Chapman's brother, David, is a serving officer with the RAN.

"We're gearing up to go overseas." Then I was stoked. The battalion itself was predominantly training for Timor, and one small segment, two platoons, were going to train and go over with Cav to Iraq. I got into the second group, so we did a lot of security-operations training, patrolling urban environments, convoy training, and basically just replicating what we were going to do overseas, as best we could.' Chapman was on the reserve, and when the two platoons went to Iraq, he was left behind in Australia. But on 31 December 2008, when he was preparing to celebrate New Year's Eve with his family in Melbourne, he was ordered to get on a plane back to the battalion and prepare to go overseas. His father and brother were excited for him, he says. 'We were just, like, wow!'

In Iraq the men from 5RAR were charged with providing security for the Australian Embassy and riding with the cavalry when they did their supply runs or transported government officials around the area. 'The Americans had all the facilities,' he says. 'They had taken over the palaces and decked them out. They had a swimming pool. They had all your restaurants like McDonald's and KFC and Pizza Huts. It was crazy. You'd be doing a resupply run up to Baghdad airport, and you'd be going through the Red Zone, which was called Route Irish, one of the most dangerous roads in the world, then you'd get out at the other end and go and have a Slurpee.'

In the army, says Chapman, 'People called me "Chappie" or "Jew", but normally it was just "Chappie". You'd say, "Ah, you slant-eye", to your Asian best mate, then he'd call you a "Jewboy". It's just taking the piss. There are instances, though. When I was in Iraq, there was this Iranian person working with us and he was a real scumbag. He was Australian Army as well – it's a very multicultural environment – and he didn't like me because I'd managed to get on the trip and I was just a new person. And we were on the front of an entry checkpoint, and I was standing out there with him on guard, and some Iraqi Army came up, and they were all armed, and this scumbag said, "This guy's Jewish", just to stir trouble. I was ready to punch his head in, but what do you do? I didn't work with him again after that. I quietly had a word to him afterwards, once I left.'

Australian operations in Iraq ended in July 2009.

Afghanistan 2009–2014

Jake Kleinman's first tour of Afghanistan continued for several months after the death of Greg Sher. At the beginning of March 2009, his OMLT was in FOB Buman, when it was visited by Australian journalists – an event many Australian soldiers fear more than battle. The *Sunday Age*'s Tom Hyland described Buman as a place where the Australians 'listen to their iPods at night and watch the latest movies on their laptops. The Afghans hear the call to prayer during the day and play strident local pop music at night. Some nights their quarters are heavy with the scent of hashish.' Hyland sat in on a meeting with 25-year-old Kleinman and the commander of the ANA troops at Buman, Captain Abdul Qadir Habibullah, a 54-year-old Afghan who had been fighting 'in one army or another' for Kleinman's entire life. Kleinman was trying to discuss the details of the next day's patrol but, wrote Hyland, the ANA commander was not concerned: 'He's got something else on his mind – food. "What about MREs," he asks, referring to the American military rations – meals ready to eat. Will the Australians bring MREs for his men? Sergeant Dean Johnstone, second in command of the Australians at Buman, explains the men will be back in time for lunch. But if they're late, and miss lunch, Johnstone promises to provide rations. But Habibullah insists: "It's very important to provide the MREs first." By now the meeting has gone for fifteen minutes … Habibullah eventually concedes: "It's a short patrol tomorrow, but in future, on long patrols, there must be

MREs." Johnstone has a concession of his own – he'll bring snacks for the Afghan soldiers.'

Kleinman was careful not to publicly despair of his allies, but showed signs of quiet frustration. He said sometimes the ANA would refuse to go into an area because there were enemy around. He'd tell them, 'That's why we have to go there, for security.' In combat, said Kleinman, 'some will engage, some will freeze, some will leave the battlefield ... I've had moments when there's rounds cracking nearby and they've made excuses not to engage, like ... having lunch'.[2]

On 16 March Kleinman's small team was on patrol with a larger number of ANA soldiers near the insurgent stronghold of Kakarak. The Australians under Kleinman's command included Corporal Mathew 'Hoppy' Hopkins, aged twenty-one. Only weeks before, Hopkins had gone home on leave to Newcastle to get married, and be with his bride as she gave birth to their baby on 5 February. 'Matt was kind of on loan to me from another platoon,' says Kleinman. 'He was in my platoon before we became the OMLT.' The patrol was ambushed by insurgent forces with machine-guns and RPGs. During a firefight that lasted two hours, Hopkins was shot dead. Kleinman had lost a mate but, he says, 'At that very point when he got hit, for me as a platoon commander, it just became another issue for me to deal with. It registers that one of the boys was down, because your job is to keep it all working out. So you just do your job and keep the boys focussed on the task.' Kleinman called in an Aeromedical Evacuation but Hopkins was dead on arrival at Tarin Kowt.

From the heavily censored report of the inquiry into Hopkins' death, it seems Habibullah's men did not fight. Prior to the contact, as the patrol drew close to Kakarak, Kleinman had what is described as a 'discussion' with Habibullah about 'the TTP [Tactics, Techniques and Practices] he was employing and the subsequent conduct of the patrol'. There is no further mention of the

ANA until after Hopkins' body was loaded onto the helicopter, when 'the OMLT personnel then re-organised the ANA elements into patrol formation'. The report notes, dryly, 'Throughout the main part of the contact there appears to have been limited involvement by the ANA patrol personnel.'[3]

As for the killing of Hopkins, 'We dealt with it later,' says Kleinman. 'We had another big fire fight about forty-eight hours afterwards, got some artillery in and banged a lot of those guys out.' Kleinman was awarded a Distinguished Service Medal (DSM) for his actions on 16 March.

JASON HYMANS HAD JOINED THE ARMY IN JUNE 2007. HE grew up in Bentleigh, Victoria, and went to school at Brighton Secondary College; was *barmitzvah* at South Caulfield Synagogue, and enlisted in the ADF two weeks after his nineteenth birthday. Hymans was short and stocky, not quite as fit as some of the other recruits. 'I could tac march [tactical road march] alright – my little legs would allow me to do that – I just couldn't run,' he says. 'I couldn't keep up with the big guys.' But he loved the comradeship. 'I met some of the best guys I could ever meet,' he says. 'I was the only Jewish person. Because eighty per cent of the guys in the army had never met a Jew before, I used to get a lot of questions – about little things that they see in mainstream movies, like people stomping on the glass at weddings. Why are you doing that? What's the go with the *payots*, the curls? A lot of them were very interested. They gave me the nickname "the Jew", and I didn't take offence. It was more a term of endearment. Everyone knew who I was. And they got a kick out of it, because every year at *Pesach* the Chief Rabbi would send us *matzo*.'

Hymans served as a private soldier with 6RAR, and was posted to Afghanistan in January 2010. The battalion was flown first to Al Minhad Air Base, Dubai, to acclimatise and complete final training, then taken by Hercules to Tarin Kowt. 'You're kind of lost, just being thrown into there,' he says. 'It wasn't what I'd been expecting. I'd heard from all these Americans they had Pizza Hut and Macca's on their bases – but there's none of that in the Australian ones.' Hymans was only at Tarin Kowt for a couple of weeks before he was moved to Qudus 'with fifteen other Australians, four Dutch, and about fifty ANA soldiers who don't speak a word of English', he says. 'I did a six-week Dari course, so I could speak very basic to the soldiers – but the locals spoke Pashto, so I couldn't talk to them.

'I got on well with the Afghan soldiers,' he says. 'They are quite a friendly bunch. We'd have dinner together. We played volleyball with them. We did our best to bond with them, because these were the guys we were going on patrol with: we needed to trust them with our lives, and they needed to trust us with their lives. Every second day or so, five or six Australians would get divvied up amongst twenty or so Afghan soldiers, and we'd have a destination to go to on the map. We'd make sure they were in the right formation. We weren't training them. We were just trying to guide them, to make sure they were still doing everything they were supposed to be doing. So we'd just pretty much go for a walk, talk to locals on the way, see if they need anything, if there was anything we could do to help them. We were always providing them with resources to build new schools and mosques. We might do a vehicle checkpoint, to search all the cars that were coming through, so the ANA could get the idea of how to do vehicle checkpoints. On patrols they're very relaxed and that's partly because it's their country. We're all, like, "No, you need to face up and watch down the road." They might be turning in and having a cigarette or a coffee or just chatting with their buddies. We have to make sure they stop talking, focus. They were amazing at spotting things out of the ordinary. They'll just point over there and go, "There's a bomb in the ground." They know their land so well, they know what's out of place.

'I was only involved in one contact,' says Hymans, 'in March, the start of the fighting season. It went about an hour. They fired at us, we returned fire. They used to do it a lot, after a quiet period, just to go, "In case you forgot about us, we are still out here." The interpreters we have carry walkie-talkies, and the Taliban use walkie-talkies to talk to one another, so we'd listen in to their conversations. A lot of times, they'd say, "We're going to attack here, we're going to attack there", just to keep us on our toes. They never did, so it's hard not to get a little bit complacent. This time they did attack. It was lucky, because there was an aqueduct next to us. We were able to jump in there and use that as a trench. We had pretty good cover.' There were no casualties. 'I told our interpreter I was Jewish,' says Hymans, 'just because I wanted to see what they'd say. There's no technology there, they don't have TV in the rural areas, so they don't get taught the hatred that the other Muslim countries do. I was telling them, "I'm Jewish ... I'm, like, an infidel ... Israel." They don't know what it is. We were in one of the poorest areas of the country: they don't know what happens outside their village.'

On Friday 20 August Tomas Dale and Grant Kirby, two private soldiers with 6RAR, were killed by an IED. 'I went through basic training with Tomas Dale,' says Hymans. 'They were probably 500 metres away from where I was, and it was that loud that we thought we were hit. When those guys were killed, because I was mates with Dale, my CSM asked me if I wanted to go back to the main base to say farewell, which was really good of him. So I went. I had a bunch of Afghani POWs in the back – these guys that we'd deemed responsible for the bombing. We were taking them to the main base so they could be questioned. I was probably five cars back. Unfortunately, on our way back, we got hit by another IED, which blew up the front car of the convoy, which carried the engineers. The driver broke both his legs and the gunner flew out of the pod and broke his arms and teeth.'

ALLEN VOLKOV, WHOSE GRANDMOTHER HAD PETITIONED Shisman to talk him out of joining the army, was born in Melbourne, where his Lithuanian father and Ukrainian mother run a Russian restaurant. Like Hymans, Volkov went to Brighton Secondary College but he completed his education at Mount Scopus Memorial College. He left school in 2004 and joined the army in 2007. 'Initially, I was quite fat,' he says. 'It took me two or three times to get into the army, because my BMI was too high, so I dropped out of TAFE, concentrated on getting fit, got fit and joined. In Kapooka, I really enjoyed it – in hindsight. I actually got charged for not ironing my polys [polyester parade pants]. So that part of it – the hospital corners, the starchness of uniforms and stuff – didn't sit the best with me, but I liked the rest of it.

'I had a rabbi come out to me,' says Volkov. 'He got me a camouflage *yarmulke*. Putting it on was the going thing with all the boys – "Oh that's cool!" And I got an army *siddur*. My nickname, a lot of the time, was "Jewboy", which I had no issues with because it wasn't out of malice. There was a time when someone did say something out of malice about me being a Jew and, rather than me stepping up, I had a whole footy field of lads just get up to stand up for me. I thought, "Guys, I could've said something."

'I was in the gym and I got a phone call saying I could either go into tanks or cavalry. I had no idea what cavalry did, and I remember asking, "What's going out of Kapooka first?" He said, "Cavalry." I went, "Yeah, sure. Put me on that." I loved it. The esprit de corps was very strong. Even the squadron patriotism – I guess you'd call it – was very strong. The job itself was great. You're extreme four-wheel driving in a vehicle with no limits.

'Towards the end of 2009, we were told there was a manning coming up for Afghanistan. I was excited, pumped. I had a couple of good mates who had already gone.' Another Jewish soldier, Sam Green, had been junior to Volkov in the regiment but was posted to Afghanistan before him. 'I was just, "Get me over there! Get me over there!"' says Volkov. He arrived in mid-2011, and the squadron was based at Tarin Kowt. 'There was a lot of IDF, indirect fire, into the base,' he says. The enemy would 'literally hop onto a rock, have an old mortar round, and light a fuse and fire. They'd try and angle it up into the base. There was a time when we'd get hit once or twice every day, the IDF warning going off and everyone had to go into our chalets – and they'd always hit way out of anyone's chalets.' Within the overall task of mentoring the ANA, the official role of Volkov's unit was manoeuvre support. 'We'd go out to all the different bases all over the Area of Operations, and provide security for resupply runs. However, whatever big mission they wanted to do, whatever backup or reinforcement the other combat teams needed, they would call on us and we'd go in and open up routes, do route recces, put in blocks. We were aware of bad guys going around all the time. Our convoy got blown up a couple of times.' As time passed, they became more aware of smaller indicators of trouble, more experienced and not as anxious. 'We were rolling through, a big convoy, and they were hitting our assets,' says Volkov. 'They were trying to hit the big Mack truck with the fuel, and they hit it and the truck just took the blast, and the guys in the car said, "Yeah, whatever." I remember cruising through and you had a bunch of Afghanis. They'd sit there how they usually did – they'd squat for hours and hours – and you could see he was picking which car to tell old matey down the road to hit. It was surreal. You can't do anything. Your ROEs [Rules of Engagement] don't encompass if he's pointing at your car.'

When his tour was over, Volkov came back to Brisbane. 'My family's in Melbourne,' he says. 'They were all working. They couldn't meet me at the airport. That was fine. I understood that. My girlfriend at the time, she couldn't come either. I was living out of a mate's basement, so I've come back, hired a car, gone to the bottle-o, got myself six beers and passed out in bed. When I got back to Melbourne, I had a big dinner put on for me at the restaurant and a smaller one for my immediate family. Then I understood, for the first time, the effect of me going over there on my parents. I've never seen my dad like that – the relief. That tore me up a little bit.'

JAKE KLEINMAN WENT TO WESTERN AUSTRALIA FOR SAS selection in 2010. 'I finished the twenty-one days,' he says, 'but I didn't get selected. I was sent back to the battalion and deployed to Afghanistan again.' Initially, he worked in an operations/mentor role, but he took leave early in his tour to return to Australia and serve as a groomsman at the wedding of a mate from Duntroon. On his return, he was told he had been posted as the aide to the Commander of Combined Team Uruzgan, US Colonel Jim Creighton. Kleinman spent the rest of his tour accompanying Creighton around the country, and took over some of the responsibility for the Colonel's personal security. 'I'd always go into meetings with him,' he says, 'and sit in the back of the room with my pistol cocked. I've no idea what I'd do with it, because I'm not that great a shot with a pistol, but I was just there to help him out. Between me and the RSM who was always following him around, we had a drill: he would take the colonel, I would engage the target, he would cover me, then I'd fall back to him.' But there were no attempts on Creighton's life – 'Thank God,' says Kleinman. 'It was pretty interesting stuff, but it wasn't what I went over to do. I wanted to be back out there with the boys, be out amongst it again, back out in the patrol bases and being a good infantryman.'

When 5RAR came back from Iraq, says Aaron Chapman, 'A lot of people were going, "Maybe we'll leave. Maybe we'll do something else." I had in my transfer papers to go into Military Police dog handlers, and it came through. Just as I was about to go, they said, "Oi, Chappie, you have a position on the Afghanistan trip but, if you take it, you have to withdraw your MP dog-handler application." So I chose Afghan. It was supposed to be nine months, but we ended up doing just two days shy of ten months – because if it was ten months, they'd have to give you another leave block.' Most of the battalion went to Afghanistan in a battle group in September 2010. Chapman was based in Tarin Kowt, originally as part of the Force Protection Group. They were responsible for security while other troops built Patrol Base Samad. 'We went out to a feature there and just dug in,' he says. 'We had pits, we had our Bushmaster and a swag, and we'd conduct regular patrols in the area with the engineers, and they'd uncover all kinds of weapons cached inside of what they'd call aqueducts. They'd get RPGs out of there, 107 rockets and all kinds of stuff. The Afghan engineers used to patrol with us, and that was a scary thing, because they'd find something and then they'd start banging at it. We were out there for about four weeks, just out in the open, and we had a lot of support – because we had the American Apaches that would go overhead regularly – and that kept a lot of the Taliban at bay: they don't like the choppers. We'd conduct night patrols and sometimes the biggest risk was actually the Americans. One night patrol, we had these little IR things on our helmets, that show up in NVG [night vision goggle] light. And we were patrolling along with the NVGs and, all of a sudden, I see one of my mates was getting lased – which means someone's lining him up with a firearm; and they obviously had night-vision equipment – and I said, "What's that?" And then they see it on me as well, and I'm, like, "Oh shit." Our whole section was being lined up, because they had an American Striker group out on another feature, and they thought we were Afghanis planting things, caching things. So we were trying to turn off these IRs and get on the radio and let the Americans know we're here. It was a very scary situation, because they don't hesitate.'

In April Chapman was told the chaplain wanted to speak to him. 'I thought, Uh-oh, what's happened?' he says. 'It's never a good thing having a padre come and speak to you randomly. He said it'd been organised to transport us to Kandahar for a Passover. It turned out Dad had spoken to one of the rabbis at the *shule*, and he'd spoken to the army rabbi. There was a little bit of animosity about it – not from my own guys, more from higher ranks. Even the way the padre spoke to us, I believe he wasn't too happy about it. I guess they don't like having things that're out of their control.' He was flown about 140 kilometres across the country with David Mafouda, another Jewish private soldier with 5RAR. 'I'd met him before in the battalion,' says Chapman, 'but we were in different companies so we didn't see each other much. We went on a Chinook helicopter at night. It was interesting, flying low in the mountains – all the different patterns they do to try and avoid being shot at. Then we get there, and Kandahar was just a gigantic base. When we went to the *Seder* itself, there was, I think, an American Air Force rabbi, and they had Canadians, American army, air force and navy. There were around twelve of us. After the *Seder*, we spent another day or two there, which was fantastic, almost like rec leave. I did all the shopping for the boys.'

Toward the end of Chapman's tour, 'Things started ramping up,' he says. 'We started getting a lot more Australians injured. A couple of mates of mine got shot. Then they had the green-on-blue incident.' On 30 May 2011 Lance Corporal Andrew 'Chef' Jones was killed by a rogue ANA soldier, who shot him from a tower as Jones used the latrine at Patrol Base Mashal. 'We'd been through there,' says Chapman. 'Of all the people to kill – a cook. It was getting frustrating, losing people right at the end. Everyone was just, like, "Let's just go home before anything happens." You counted down the days. And when they told us we were staying on for an extra month, it was very frustrating.'

Chapman left the army soon after he returned from Afghanistan. 'I actually looked at going back to RMC to finish up,' he says, 'but they said, "No, you'll have to do the full eighteen months again."'

ONE HUNDRED AND THIRTY YEARS AFTER ERNEST SIMEON DE Pass sailed out from Circular Quay on SS *Iberia* to fight the Mahdi Army in the Sudan, there is still some puzzlement at the idea that a Jew might be a foot soldier in the Australian Army. 'I speak to Jews in Sydney,' says Jake Kleinman, 'and they couldn't believe a Jewish guy would join an army that's not the Israeli army. Or you're in the army and they expect you to be a doctor or a lawyer or something. They can't comprehend a Jewish infantry guy.'

One of the last Jewish Australian soldiers in Afghanistan was Captain Josh Fink, the son of a reservist, grandson of a World War Two veteran, and coffin escort at the funeral of Greg Sher. Josh's father Michael says Josh trained heavily in boxing and martial arts, working the bags and hitting the pads in their home boxing gym. In 2007 Josh joined the army. 'He went through Duntroon quite effortlessly,' says Michael. 'It's tough on everybody, but he didn't complain. I think he actually relished it. He enjoyed the activities, the camaraderie.' He was one class behind Aaron Chapman at RMC. Once Josh had graduated, 'everybody was worried he would be deployed', says Michael. The early deployments came and went and 'he got knocked back on two of them, because his senior officers didn't want him to go. They wanted him where he was, because he was very useful to them. On the last one, he finally got accepted to go, and that was the last tour of duty of Afghanistan. We both formulated a plan that we would lie to my mother, because she is the consummate worrier.' Michael says he was not worried about Josh as a Jewish soldier in Afghanistan. 'I was just worried about him as my little boy in Afghanistan.'

But Josh came home safely.

Epilogue

It is the Friday morning before Anzac Day 2015 at the sprawling Gandel Campus of Mount Scopus Memorial College, a large Jewish day school in Victoria. Josh Fink, in his uniform and slouch hat, walks onto the stage at the concert hall to address the school assembly. He looks simultaneously assured in his role and awed by his responsibility. 'I was asked to come here and talk as a man who has graduated from a Jewish school and served in the Australian Army,' he says, 'The values we are instilled, in attending Jewish high schools and primary schools, are part of the reason why I joined the army. The feeling of community, teamwork and mateship is there, but to a different degree.

'I graduated from Leibler Yavneh College, I attended the Royal Military College Duntroon in Canberra in 2007–2008. Upon graduation from there I was posted to 1 Armoured Regiment in Darwin, which is a tank battalion. I served as a lieutenant in charge of logistics for the tank regiment … In 2010 I was posted to 1 Recruit Training Battalion as a platoon commander and recruit instructor. In 2011 I was posted to the School of Armour in Puckapunyal, just north of Melbourne, where I was a troop leader, an instructor and a squadron second-in-command. From there I was posted to 2/4th Support Battalion here in Melbourne and, more specifically, to 3 Recovery Company, in charge of Reserves. Whilst there, I was deployed to Afghanistan in May 2013. My role in Afghanistan was that of a mentor to the Afghan National Army, police, and National Directorate of Intelligence. This was a tri-service organisation in which a Jewish boy from Melbourne was in the heart of a Muslim nation, teaching them how to do their job better in order to defend their homeland and their interests. The contrast is one that should ring home to you now more than ever, now we're sending our people back to Iraq … We are providing mentors. We are instilling this teamwork and mateship into other nations which, frankly, don't even know we exist half the time.'

For a moment, he seems to be fighting back tears.

'And so tomorrow,' he says, 'we are commemorating 100 years of Anzac, the Australia/New Zealand Army Corps landing at Gallipoli. We are not glorifying the war, or sacrifice or bloodshed. We are commemorating the values that we as a nation stand for, and the army has maintained. What we do, why we do it, is for you – to stop these horrible atrocities from appearing at home.

'We go abroad to face this,' says Josh Fink, to a hall packed with students, 'so that you can attend a Jewish school, you can live your life and be free from fear.'

Notes

Note: Quotes from newspaper articles and private papers have been edited to style. Quotes from interviews by the author are not referenced but are distinguished from other sources in that they are reported in the present tense, i.e. 'he says', 'she says'.

1   Birth of a nation
1   *Sydney Mail*, 16 September 1882
2   Obituary, *South Australian Register*, 31 October 1887
3   Obituary, *Register*, 30 November 1926
4   *Jewish Herald*, 20 February 1885
5   *Jewish Herald*, 30 March 1900; *George Judah Cohen: A Memoir*, Sydney, 1937, p. 15
6   *Argus*, 9 April 1885
7   *Jewish Herald*, 17 April 1885
8   Letter to the Editor from 'A Northern Farmer', *Leader* (Melbourne), 21 March 1885
9   Perry, Roland, *Monash: The Outsider Who Won a War*, Random House, Sydney, 2004, p. 28
10   *South Australian Advertiser*, 27 April 1885
11   *New Zealand Herald*, 24 June 1905
12   *London Gazette*, 29 October 1918

2   Australia's armed forces emerge
1   *Jewish Herald*, 23 November 1900
2   *Jewish Herald*, 26 April 1901
3   *Jewish Herald*, 9 December 1910
4   *Jewish Herald*, 26 April 1889
5   Taylor, Kendall, *Phillip Evergood: Never Separate from the Heart*, Associated University Presses, London, c1987, p. 34
6   *Jewish Herald*, 16 March 1900
7   Perry 2004, p. 29
8   Penslar, Derek, *Jews and the Military: A History*, Princeton University Press, New Jersey, 2013, p. 94
9   *West Australian*, 25 August 1896
10   *Australasian*, 28 January 1899
11   Battye Library, MN 371, Papers relating to the Allnutt and Davies families, ACC 1924A-1927A, Walter Karri Davies letter to Herb, dated 13 July 1900
12   *Jewish Herald*, 2 July 1880
13   *Jewish Herald*, 20 May 1881
14   *Jewish Herald*, 17 June 1881
15   *Hebrew Standard of Australasia*, 10 November 1899
16   *Melbourne Punch*, 25 January 1900

17 *West Australian Sunday Times*, 20 May 1900, for example
18 Saks, David, 'Jews on Commando', SAfrica SIG and Jewishgen, 2005. See
    <www.jewishgen.org/SAfrica/commando.htm> (accessed 7 March 2016)
19 Penslar 2013, p. 77
20 *Sydney Mail*, 11 November 1899
21 *Jewish Herald*, 22 December 1899
22 *London Gazette*, 2 August 1901
23 *Jewish Herald*, 20 July 1900
24 *Table Talk*, 8 February 1900
25 Battye Library, MN 371, Papers relating to the Allnutt and Davies families, ACC
    1924A-1927A, Walter Karri Davies letter to Herb, dated 13 April 1900
26 *Hebrew Standard*, 20 April 1900, 7 August 1903
27 Perry 2004, p. 94
28 *Jewish Herald*, 13 April 1900
29 *Age*, 16 May 1900
30 Rethman, Hugh, 'Bravery beyond the call of duty: Walter Karri Davies in the
    South African War 1899–1902' in *Sabretache*, Volume LIII, No. 2, June 2012, p. 21
31 Stern, Russell, 'The Anglo-Boer War 1899–1902: An Australian Jewish Perspective,
    Part II: Rose Lena Shappere', in *Australian Jewish Historical Society Journal*,
    Volume XVII, Part 2, 2004, p. 200
32 *Age*, 16 May 1900
33 *Lismore Chronicle*, 17 July 1900
34 *Mercury* (Hobart), 3 February 1899
35 *Jewish Herald*, 19 January 1900
36 *Evening News* (Sydney), 3 May 1900
37 *Brisbane Courier*, 25 May 1900
38 *Hebrew Standard of Australasia*, 16 February 1900
39 *West Australian*, 4 July 1900
40 Wilcox, Craig, *Australia's Boer War: The War in South Africa 1899–1902*, Oxford
    University Press in association with the Australian War Memorial, Melbourne,
    2002, pp. 379–80
41 Battye Library, MN 371, Papers relating to the Allnutt and Davies families, ACC
    1924A-1927A, Walter Karri Davies letter to Herb, dated 13 July 1900
42 *Sydney Morning Herald,* 28 May 1900
43 *Sydney Morning Herald*, 15 June 1900
44 *Sunday Times* (Sydney), 5 August 1900
45 *Jewish Herald*, 17 August 1900
46 *Jewish Herald*, 31 August 1900
47 *Jewish Herald*, 16 March 1900
48 *Jewish Herald*, 23 November 1900
49 *Inquirer and Commercial News*, 24 August 1900; *Bunbury Herald*, 21 March 1901
50 *South Australian Register*, 1 February 1900
51 *Barrier Miner*, 19 September 1900
52 *Jewish Herald*, 23 November 1900
53 Penslar 2013, p. 136
54 Penslar 2013, p. 136
55 Jewish Museum London, 'Men and Women of Mark in Modern Judea' album of
    newspaper cuttings (c1892–1911), compiled by E de Haas
56 *Jewish Herald*, 17 August 1900

57   *West Australian*, 26 March 1901
58   *Telegraph* (Brisbane), 27 April 1900
59   *Morning Bulletin*, 8 May 1901
60   *Jewish Herald*, 21 June 1901
61   *Jewish Herald*, 23 May 1901
62   *Hebrew Standard of Australasia*, 10 May 1901
63   *Colac Herald*, 3 September 1901
64   *Jewish Herald*, 30 August 1901
65   *Jewish Herald*, 20 December 1901
66   *Age*, 9 January 1902
67   *Jewish Herald*, 20 June 1902
68   *Age*, 18 March 1905
69   *Tasmanian News*, 2 August 1898
70   *Hebrew Standard of Australasia*, 28 January 1899; *Table Talk*, 21 November 1901
71   *Jewish Herald*, 13 December 1907
72   *Jewish Herald*, 6 January 1911
73   *Jewish Herald*, 29 October 1909
74   *South Western Times*, 20 September 1918
75   *Jewish Herald*, 4 August 1911
76   *Sydney Morning Herald*, 16 December 1911
77   Levi, John S, *Rabbi Jacob Danglow*, Melbourne University Press, Melbourne, 1995, p. 61

3   World War One: 1914 to 1918

1   *Jewish Herald*, 19 October 1917
2   *Jewish Herald*, 14 August 1914
3   *Sydney Morning Herald*, 19 November 1914
4   Mitchell Library, State Library of New South Wales, MLMSS 7314, Conroy, David, letter to his mother, 3–6 December 1914
5   Levi 1995, pp. 81–82
6   Mitchell Library, State Library of New South Wales, MLMSS 7314, Conroy, David, letter to his mother, 3–6 December 1914
7   Mitchell Library, State Library of New South Wales, MLMSS 7314, Conroy, David, letter to his mother, 3–6 December 1914
8   *Jewish Herald*, 12 February 1915
9   *Hebrew Standard of Australasia,* 19 February 1915
10   *Hebrew Standard of Australasia,* 30 April 1915
11   *Independent* (Footscray), 23 January 1915
12   *Jewish Herald*, 29 January 1915
13   *Sydney Morning Herald*, 20 0ctober 1915
14   *Hebrew Standard of Australasia*, 18 June 1915
15   *Sydney Morning Herald*, 20 0ctober 1915
16   *Hebrew Standard of Australasia*, 18 June 1915
17   *Sydney Morning Herald*, 20 0ctober 1915
18   *Jewish Herald*, 18 June 1915
19   Weingott, Samuel, transcript of diary from 8 April to 3 June 1915, Australian Jewish Historical Society
20   Mitchell Library, State Library of New South Wales and courtesy copyright holder, MLMSS 1840, Silas diary, 1914–1916
21   *Hebrew Standard of Australasia,* 18 June 1915

22   Weingott, Samuel, transcript of diary from 8 April to 3 June 1915, Australian
     Jewish Historical Society
23   AWM 3DRL/2316 War letters of General Monash: Volume 1, 1934, 14 May 1915,
     p. 61
24   AWM 3DRL/2316 War letters of General Monash: Volume 1, 1934, 16 May 1915,
     pp. 63–64
25   *Register*, 25 June 1915
26   Collins, Harold Emanuel, diary
27   Collins, Harold Emanuel, diary
28   Weingott, Samuel, transcript of diary from 8 April to 3 June 1915, Australian
     Jewish Historical Society
29   AWM 3DRL/2316 War letters of General Monash: Volume 1, 1934, 30 May 1915,
     pp. 72–73
30   Weingott, Samuel, transcript of diary from 8 April to 3 June 1915, Australian
     Jewish Historical Society
31   NAA B2455, First Australian Imperial Force Personnel Dossiers, 1914–1920,
     Weingott Samuel
32   *Hebrew Standard of Australasia*, 18 June 1915
33   *Hebrew Standard of Australasia*, 3 December 1915
34   Collins, Harold Emanuel, diary
35   AWM 3DRL/2316 War letters of General Monash: Volume 1, 1934, 16 August 1915,
     pp. 102–105
36   Quoted in Crawley, Rhys, 'Lone Pine: Worth the Cost?', in *Wartime: Official
     Magazine of the Australian War Memorial*, issue 38, April 2007, p. 16
37   *Western Mail*, 24 December 1915
38   *Courier-Mail*, 8 March 1939
39   *London Gazette*, 15 October 1915
40   *Hebrew Standard of Australasia*, 22 October 1915
41   *Western Mail*, 24 December 1915
42   Quoted in Lockyer, Keira Quinn, *Keysor VC: Gallipoli's Quiet Hero*, self-published,
     Ballarat, 2014, p. 92
43   AWM 1DRL/0415 Private Record, Lesnie, Frank Bernard Hershorn, letter dated
     17 November 1915
44   *Sydney Morning Herald*, 17 July 1916
45   *London Gazette*, 18 February 1915
46   *Hebrew Standard of Australasia*, 11 June 1915
47   *Jewish Herald*, 8 October 1915
48   Quoted in Smith, Maurice, 'Issy Smith VC', in *Australian Jewish Historical Society
     Journal*, Volume XVIII, Part 2, 2006, pp. 186–87
49   *Jewish Herald*, 14 January 1916
50   *Jewish Herald*, 19 November 1915
51   *Sunday Times* (Sydney), 2 January 1916
52   AWM 1DRL/0415 Private Record, Lesnie, Frank Bernard Hershorn, letter dated
     17 July 1915
53   NAA B2455, First Australian Imperial Force Personnel Dossiers, 1914–1920, Levi
     Keith Maurice, p. 42
54   *Hebrew Standard of Australasia*, 3 August 1906
55   NAA B2455, First Australian Imperial Force Personnel Dossiers, 1914–1920,
     Benjamin Stanley Octavius, p. 4

56   *Hebrew Standard of Australasia*, 5 November 1915

57   *Register*, undated letter published 14 October 1915

58   *Register*, 8 February 1916

59   AWM 3DRL/5039 Private Record, Blashki, Roy Hector, diary, 26–29 October 1915

60   NAA B2455, First Australian Imperial Force Personnel Dossiers, 1914–1920, Bloom Julius Sydney, p. 31

61   The Gallipoli diary of Julius Leonard Neustadt, 3 September – 11 December 1915

62   *Jewish Herald*, 10 March 1916

63   *Hebrew Standard of Australasia*, 10 March 1916

64   *Jewish Herald*, 24 March 1916

65   Monash, letter, Anzac, 12 December 1915

66   AWM 1DRL/0415 Private Record, Lesnie, Frank Bernard Hershorn, letter dated 12 January 1916

67   Monash, letter, entering Mudros Harbour, 20 December 1915

68   *Hebrew Standard of Australasia*, 10 March 1916

69   AWM 1DRL/0415 Private Record, Lesnie, Frank Bernard Hershorn, letter dated 12 January 1916

70   Monash, letter, entering Mudros Harbour, 20 December 1915

71   *Collie Mail*, 5 February 1915

72   *Southern Times*, 21 March 1916

73   Sussman, Maurice, unpublished letter to fiancée Rachael Marks, 24 January 1916

74   Freedman, in Boas, Harold, *The Australian Y.M.C.A with the Jewish Soldier of the Australian Imperial Force*, London, 1919, p. 112–13

75   Freedman in Boas 1919, p. 113

76   *Hebrew Standard of Australasia*, 25 January 1918

77   *Hebrew Standard of Australasia*, 11 August 1916

78   Hallenstein, Dalbert, *On Active Service with the AIF: Gallipoli and France, Letters of Dalbert Hallenstein*, self-published, Melbourne, c1920, p. 82

79   *Jewish Herald*, 19 May 1916

80   *Jewish Herald*, 11 August 1916

81   *Jewish Herald*, 11 August 1916

82   NAA B2455, First Australian Imperial Force Personnel Dossiers, 1914–1920, Weingott Barron, p. 19

83   *Hebrew Standard of Australasia*, 19 November 1915

84   *Hebrew Standard of Australasia*, 19 November 1915

85   *Hebrew Standard of Australasia*, 7 January 1916

86   Hallenstein c1920, p. 96

87   Hallenstein c1920, pp. 114–15

88   AWM 2DRL/0171 Narrative of experiences by Captain Waldo Hyman Zander, 30th Battalion AIF, 19 July 1916

89   NAA B2455, First Australian Imperial Force Personnel Dossiers, 1914–1920, Hart Joseph (service #190)

90   AWM 1DRL/0204 Private Record, Cohen, Jack, letter to Mother and Pater, 31 July 1916

91   AWM 1DRL/0204 Private Record, Cohen, Jack, letter to Pater, 29 July 1916

92   AWM 1DRL/0204 Private Record, Cohen, Jack, letter to Mother and Pater, 31 July 1916

93   AWM 1DRL/0415 Private Record, Lesnie, Frank Bernard Hershorn, letter to 'John' dated 13 August 1916

94 *Jewish Herald*, 3 November 1916

95 AWM 3DRL/5039 Blashki, Roy Hector, private diary

96 Hallenstein c1920, p. 122

97 *Jewish Herald*, 17 November 1916

98 Hallenstein c1920, p. 124

99 Hallenstein c1920, p. 126

100 *Jewish Herald*, 15 December 1916

101 *Sunday Times* (Sydney), 15 October 1916

102 AWM PR84/383 Blashki, Roy Hector, letter dated 25 October 1916

103 *Hebrew Standard of Australasia*, 26 May 1916

104 *Jewish Herald*, 22 August 1919

105 AWM28 Hyman, Eric, Recommendation for DSO, 2 November 1917

106 *Jewish Herald*, 15 February 1918

107 *Tamworth Daily Observer*, 22 January 1918

108 'All sorts of people', *Free Lance*, Volume XVIII, Issue 962, 19 December 1918, p. 4

109 Salek, Louis, 'Egypt', original manuscript, 1916

110 *Jewish Herald*, 9 April 1918

111 Piggott, Leanne, *Australia and Israel: A Pictorial History*, Department of Foreign Affairs and Trade, Canberra, 2007, p. 3

112 *Hebrew Standard of Australasia*, 7 June 1918

113 NAA B2455, First Australian Imperial Force Personnel Dossiers, 1914–1920, Harlap Lion, p. 42

114 <adb.anu.edu.au/biography/margolin-eliezer-lazar-7484> (accessed 16 December 2015)

115 *South Western Times*, 20 September 1918

116 Monash, letter, France, 11 January 1917

117 Monash, letter, Menton, 16 March 1917

118 *Register*, 3 July 1917

119 Barrkman, Harry, unpublished memoir, undated

120 MC citation

121 Barrkman, Harry, unpublished memoir, undated

122 'Vacuum Oil Company Promotions – Two Distinguished Soldiers', *Reveille*, Volume 8, No. 7, 1 March 1935

123 Barrkman, Harry, unpublished memoir, undated

124 Barrkman, Henry, POW Red Cross file, p. 7

125 *Westonian*, 21 April 1917

126 *Westonian*, 14 July 1917

127 *Jewish Herald*, 19 October 1917

128 AWM PR84/383 Blashki, Roy Hector, letter from Lieutenant Benson Lewis, 6 August 1917

129 *Hebrew Standard of Australasia*, 12 October 1917; *Jewish Herald*, 19 October 1917

130 Hallenstein c1920, p. 174

131 Monash, letter, France, 4 October 1917

132 Monash, letter, France, 18 October 1917

133 *Register*, 13 October 1917

134 State Library South Australia, <sarcib.ww1.collections.slsa.sa.gov.au/soldier/arthur-abraham-jacobs> (accessed 7 March 2016)

135 *Hebrew Standard*, 24 May 1922

136 *Jewish Herald*, 30 November 1917

137 *Maryborough Chronicle, Wide Bay and Burnett Advertiser,* 25 July 1917
138 For example *Argus,* 5 December 1917
139 Coulthart, Ross, *Charles Bean,* HarperCollins, Sydney, 2014, p. 283
140 Coulthart 2014, p. 287
141 Coulthart 2014, p. 311
142 Monash, letter, Aus. Corps HQ, France, 31 May 1918
143 *Jewish Herald,* 26 July 1918
144 *Jewish Herald,* 15 November 1918
145 Levi 1995, p. 98
146 Monash, John, *The Australian Victories in France in 1918,* Hutchinson, London, 1920, p. 96
147 Monash 1920, p. 56–57
148 AWM28 Lewis, Morris, Recommendation for Military Cross, 8 July 1918
149 Monash, letter, France, 1 October 1917
150 Quoted in Levi 1995, pp. 100–101
151 *Jewish Herald,* 29 November 1918
152 Levi 1995, p. 101
153 *Jewish Herald,* 15 November 1918
154 *Mercury* (Hobart), 1 February 1919
155 Quoted in Levi 1995, p. 103
156 *Hebrew Standard of Australasia,* 26 December 1919
157 *Newcastle Morning Herald and Miners' Advocate,* 10 September 1938
158 In Boas 1919, pp. 122 and 120
159 Boas 1919, p. 50
160 Boas, Harold, *Australian Jewry Book of Honour: The Great War 1914–1918,* Lamson Paragon, Perth, 1923
161 Boas 1919, p. 45
162 Quoted in Levi 1995, p. 102
163 Boas, Harold, 'The Australian Jew in the Great War, 1914–1918', in *Australian Jewish Historical Society Journal,* Volume I, Part IV, 1940, p. 101
164 Smith, Michael, *Six: The Real James Bonds, 1909–1939,* Biteback Publishing, New York, 2011, p. 78

4   Between the wars

1   Boas 1919, p. 120
2   War Diaries of Senior Chaplain O.P.D. for April 1919
3   *Jewish Herald,* 24 December 1920
4   *Truth,* 20 February 1921
5   Quoted in *Jewish Herald,* 24 January 1919
6   *Geelong Advertiser,* 6 May 1921
7   Letter to *Australian* (Perth), 20 May 1921
8   Solomon, Geoffrey David, *A Poor Sort of Memory,* Roebuk Society, Canberra, 1978, p. 124
9   *Canberra Times,* 24 October 1964
10   As quoted in Perry 2004, p. 509
11   *Argus,* 9 October 1931
12   See, for example, *Singleton Argus,* 20 May 1936
13   *Argus,* 25 May 1936
14   Penslar 2013, p. 201

15 *Workers' Weekly*, 13 July 1937
16 *West Australian,* 14 September 1938
17 Quoted in *Workers' Weekly*, 26 July 1938

5 World War Two: 1939 to 1945

1 *Hebrew Standard of Australasia*, 31 August 1939
2 *Hebrew Standard of Australasia,* 21 September 1939
3 Patkin, Robert, 'A view of the 1939–45 World War', unpublished essay, undated
4 Kingsland, Richard, *Into the Midst of Things*, Air Power Development Centre, Canberra, 2010, p. 26
5 *News* (Adelaide), 15 January 1940
6 Kingsland 2010, pp. 70–74
7 Lennard, Haldon, 'Crack pilots of New Guinea War' in the *ABC Weekly*, reprinted in *Hebrew Standard of Australasia,* 10 December 1942
8 Patkin, undated
9 Patkin, undated
10 *Hebrew Standard of Australasia*, 16 May 1940
11 *Hebrew Standard of Australasia*, 9 January 1941
12 *Western Mail*, 5 February 1942
13 Lands, Stanley, 'Three sailors write home', in *Australian Women's Weekly*, 2 May 1942, p. 15
14 Selby, Tom, private letter, in Selby, Clive Herbert, *Dr NX 22*, Selby Family, Melbourne, 2010, pp. 176–81
15 *Hebrew Standard of Australasia*, 20 February 1941
16 NAA B883 VX6746, Second Australian Imperial Force Personnel Dossiers, 1939–1947, Pearlman, Cyril Solomon
17 *Hebrew Standard of Australasia*, 3 April 1941
18 *Hebrew Standard of Australasia*, 4 June 1942
19 *Sydney Morning Herald*, 13 September 1941
20 Masel, Philip, *The Second 28th*, 2/28th Battalion and 24th Anti-Tank Company Association, Perth, 1961, pp. 35–36
21 *Hebrew Standard of Australasia*, 12 September 1942
22 *Hebrew Standard of Australasia*, 16 October 1941
23 Masel 1961, p. 60
24 *Hebrew Standard of Australasia*, 10 June 1943
25 Baker, Kevin, *Paul Cullen: Citizen and Soldier*, Rosenberg, Sydney, 2005, pp. 69–70
26 Patkin, undated
27 Pearlman, Hyman, diary entries dated 23 February, 11 April and 1 May 1941, as published online in Stuart Coppock's *The 2/7th Australian Cavalry Regiment – A Pictorial History*, at www.2nd7thcavalry.com/ (accessed 21 March 2016)
28 *Hebrew Standard of Australasia*, 3 July 1941
29 *Hebrew Standard of Australasia*, 30 October 1941
30 *Hebrew Standard of Australasia*, 6 November 1941
31 Pearlman, Hyman, diary entries dated 2 November 1941, Coppock, <www.2nd7thcavalry.com>
32 Pearlman, Hyman, diary entries dated 2 November 1941, 20 and 24 January 1942, Coppock, <www.2nd7thcavalry.com>
33 *News* (Adelaide), 8 November 1943
34 Shaw, Raymond, letter to family, dated 17 March 1942

35 Shaw, Raymond, letter to family, dated 17 March 1942
36 Shaw, Raymond, letter to family, dated 28 March 1942
37 Letter from Lorraine Havin to Stuart Shaw, 19 July 2002
38 Brand, Victor, 'The diary (Malaya and Singapore) of Captain Victor Brand, MC, RMO 2/29th Battalion', in RW Christie and Robert Christie (eds), *A History of the 2/29 Battalion – 8th Australian Division AIF*, 2/29 Battalion AIF Association, Sale, Victoria, 1983, pp. 68–81
39 Milston, Neville, diary, unpublished
40 Epstein, Jack, Pynt, Gerald and Australian Federation of Jewish Ex-Servicemen & Women, *Australian Jewry's Book of Honour, World War II*, Griffin Press, Adelaide, 1974, pp. 92–93
41 Kaye, Geoffrey, private letter, 22 December 1941
42 Milston, Neville, diary, unpublished
43 Milston, Neville, diary, unpublished
44 Opas, Philip, *Throw Away My Wig*, self-published, 1997, pp. 63 and 67
45 *Hebrew Standard of Australasia*, 7 October 1941
46 Opas 1997, p. 78
47 *Gippsland Times*, 9 March 1942
48 *Hebrew Standard of Australasia,* 9 April 1942
49 *Hebrew Standard of Australasia,* 10 December 1942
50 *Evening Advocate*, 19 May 1942
51 Selby, David, *Hell and High Fever*, Ligare, Sydney, 2008, pp. 15, 18–19
52 Weingott, Issacher, unpublished diary
53 Selby 2008, p. 38
54 Weingott, Issacher, unpublished diary
55 Selby 2008, p. 72
56 Weingott, Issacher, unpublished diary
57 Weingott, Issacher, unpublished diary
58 Selby 2008, p. 104–105
59 Weingott, Issacher, unpublished diary
60 Cowen, Zelman, interview with Jewish Museum of Australia, transcribed and edited by the author
61 Opas 1997, pp. 63–64
62 *Australian*, 25 August 2012
63 Bean, CEW, *War Aims of a Plain Australian*, Angus & Robertson, Sydney, 1943, p. 140
64 *Toodyay Herald*, 27 March 1942
65 Jewish Council to Combat Fascism and Anti-Semitism, 'The Jews and the War', Melbourne, 1943?, p. 6
66 *Courier-Mail*, 3 February 1944
67 *Western Mail*, 28 September 1944
68 *Army News*, 20 June 1943
69 *Western Mail*, 28 September 1944
70 Commonwealth of Australia, Parliamentary Debates: House of Representatives: official Hansard, No. 27, 3 July 1941, p. 878
71 Commonwealth of Australia, Parliamentary Debates: House of Representatives: official Hansard, No. 14, 2 April 1941, p. 544
72 Ulmer, Alfred, interview with Shannon Maguire for the Sydney Jewish Museum Oral History Project Military Exhibition, 30 December 2009

73   Levi, John S, *Rabbi Jacob Danglow,* Melbourne University Press, Melbourne, 1995, p. 227

74   Ulmer 2009

75   Lewinski, Kurt, *19 Wasted Months: Diary and Notes of My Internment*, translated from the German original and copied by the Sydney University Judaica Library, 1940–45

76   Klepner, Frank, *Yosl Bergner: Art as a Meeting of Cultures*, Macmillan, Melbourne, 2004, p. 93

77   Schwartz, Larry, 'Companies dismissed: the "aliens" history forgot', in *The Age*, 23 June 2002

78   Meadows, Julie, *A Shtetl in Ek Velt = A Shtetl at the End of the World: 54 Stories of Growing Up in Jewish Carlton, 1925–1945*, Australian Centre for Jewish Civilisation and Monash University, Clayton, Vic, 2011, p. 165

79   Devries, Max, *A Day in Camp*, unpublished manuscript

80   Lewinski 1940–45

81   Levine, Sydney, private diary, 4 July 1944, p. 15

82   Levine, Sydney, private diary, 1 November 1944, pp. 101–102

83   *Shepparton Advertiser*, 8 September 1944

84   *Camperdown Chronicle*, 30 July 1943

85   AWM S00966, transcript of oral history recording with Betty Rothstadt née Cohn, interviewed by Harry Martin for the Keith Murdoch Sound Archive of Australia, 16 September 1990

86   Baker 2005, pp. 143–44

87   Pearlman, Hyman, private diaries, 7 January 1944

88   *Hebrew Standard of Australasia*, 25 November 1943

89   Levi 1995, p. 236

90   *Hebrew Standard of Australasia*, 25 November 1943

91   Browne, Wesley, private memoir, unpublished, undated

92   NAA A9301 71703, RAAF Personnel files of Non-Commissioned Officers (NCOs) and other ranks, 1921–1948, Browne, Wesley Edward

93   Browne, Wesley, speech to 3rd Rose Bay (Judean) Scout Group, unpublished, undated

94   Slutzkin, Frank, interview with Shannon Maguire for the Sydney Jewish Museum Oral History Project Military Exhibition, undated

95   Joel, Asher, unpublished memoir

96   Levine, private diary, 12 July 1945, pp. 23–25

97   Sernack, Max, interview with Susie Grunstein for the Sydney Jewish Museum Oral History Project Military Exhibition, 13 November 2009

98   Opas 1997, pp. 119–20

99   Slutzkin, Frank, interview with Shannon Maguire for the Sydney Jewish Museum Oral History Project Military Exhibition, undated

100   Opas 1997, pp. 121 and 131

101   Sleigh, Joanna, *Never Wear a Watch*, self-published, 2013, p. 103

102   *Hebrew Standard of Australasia*, 11 October 1945

103   Patkin, undated

104   Isaacson, Caroline, 'Problem of the prisoner-of-war: when he is home', *Argus*, 28 August 1945

105   AWM 3DRL/2663, Yamashita, Takeo, Letter to Mr Mansfield, 1959

106   *West Australian*, 25 April 1942

107   Warner, Denis, *Pathfinder: The Peter Isaacson Story, In the Air – On the Ground*, Crown Content, Melbourne, 2002, pp. 79–81

108   Barrington, Joseph, interview with Noellen Rosen for the Sydney Jewish Museum Oral History Project Military Exhibition, 10 March 2010

109   Borsht, Cyril, *A Life Well Lived*, private memoir, pp. 18–19

110   Borsht, Cyril, *A Life Well Lived*, private memoir, p. 19

111   Borsht, Cyril, interview with the author

6   Cold War conflicts

1   *Hebrew Standard of Australasia*, 12 June 1953

2   *Australian*, 1 December 2014

3   Gayst, N, interview with the author

4   NAA A12372 R/33072/P, RAAF Personnel files – All Ranks, Lyons, Ian Alfred

5   NAA Lyons, Ian Alfred, citation

6   Unit History Sheet, quoted in Ochert, Morris, 'The contribution of three Australian Jewish pilots: 1936–1954', *Australian Jewish Historical Society Journal*, June 2004, p. 288

7   Fabian, Rabbi Dr Alfred, *A Tale of Three Cities: Autobiographical Record of an Australian Ministry, Second Part Brisbane 1947–1962*, unpublished memoir, 1979, pp. 62–63

8   Kriss, Maurice, interview with Shannon Maguire for the Sydney Jewish Museum Oral History Project Military Exhibition, 5 February 2010

9   Kriss, Maurice, interview with the author

10   Moss, Bobby, interview with the author

7   The Vietnam years: 1962 to 1972

1   Mendes, Philip, *The New Left, the Jews and the Vietnam War, 1965–1972*, Lazarus Press, Melbourne, 1993

2   Fabian, Rabbi Dr Alfred, *A Tale of Three Cities: Autobiographical Record of an Australian Ministry, Third Part Sydney 1962 to 1975*, unpublished memoir, 1979, p. 41

3   Roubin, the late David, interview with the author

4   Mollison, Charles S, *Long Tan and Beyond: Alpha Company 6 RAR in Vietnam 1966–67* (3rd ed), Cobb's Crossing, Woombye, Qld, 2006, p. 231

5   Mollison 2006, p. 337

6   Sakker, Samuel, 'Service in the Royal Australian Navy', unpublished memoir

7   Moss, Bobby, interview with the author

8   Sakker, Samuel, 'Service in the Royal Australian Navy', unpublished memoir

9   Wilcox 2002, p. 13

10   Mendes 1993, p. 191

11   Dapin, Mark, *The Nashos' War: Australian National Servicemen and Vietnam*, Penguin, Melbourne, 2014, p. 201

12   NAA B2458 26742, Cohen, Paul Dion, service record, Annual Confidential Report – Officers

13   Benko, Frank, *730 and a Wakey*, Sid Harta, Melbourne, 2010, p. 268

14   Mendes, Philip, transcript of interview with Varga supplied to the author courtesy of Mendes

15   Turnbull, Noel, interview with the author

16   Schneider, Amic, interview with the author

17   Selan, John, interview with the author
18   Dapin 2014, p. 395
19   Dapin 2014, pp. 399–400
20   Isaacs, Ian, Letter to Mum, Dad and Morris, 12 April 1971
21   Dapin 2014, p. 400

8   After Vietnam
1   Pincus, Martyn, interview with the author
2   Karsai, George, interview with the author
3   Leder, Julie, interview with the author
4   Karsai, George, interview with the author
5   Leder, Julie, interview with the author

9   The War on Terror
1   Leonard, Scott, interview with the author
2   Hyland, Tom, 'In the shadow of the valley', *Sydney Morning Herald*, 8 March 2009
3   Australian Defence Force, 'Inquiry Officer's Report into the death of Corporal MRA Hopkins in Afghanistan on 16th March 2009', May 2009

Glossary

arba kanfot – prayer shawl; small tallit

barmitzvah/batmitzvah – ceremony celebrating a boy/girl's coming of age on their thirteenth birthday

bimah – raised platform in a synagogue from which the Torah is read

Chanukah – Festival of Lights, associated with the victory of the Maccabean brothers

chazan – cantor

cheder – traditional primary school, teaching the basics of Judaism and Hebrew

daven – to pray

dod – uncle

frum – pious

ganif – thief

halachically Jewish – recognised under Jewish law

'Hatikvah' – national anthem of Israel

Kaddish – prayer of mourning

kashrut – set of Jewish religious dietary laws

Kiddush – blessing recited over wine for Shabbat or Jewish holy days

kippah – (Hebrew) skullcap worn during prayer

Kol Nidre – declaration recited in the synagogue before the beginning of the evening service on Yom Kippur

kosher – food which is prepared so as to be ritually pure

Magen David – the Star of David

Magillah – scroll read during the festival of Purim

matzo – unleavened bread, eaten at Passover

minyan – quorum of ten men required to recite certain prayers

mitzvah – a religious duty; a good deed

moshava – early Zionist agricultural settlement

'Olam' – full title is 'Adon Olam'; Jewish hymn often sung at the opening of morning service and close of evening service

Passover – Feast of Freedom celebrating the deliverance of Jews from slavery in Egypt

payots – sidelocks

Pesach – Hebrew word for Passover

Purim – festival to celebrate the deliverance from destruction of the Jews of Persia

Rosh Hashanah – Festival of the Jewish New Year, around the month of September, and the start of the high holy days

Seder – a dinner and ceremony to celebrate the exodus on the eve of Passover

Sefer Torah – a handwritten scroll of the holiest book in Judaism

Shabbos/Shabbat – the Jewish Sabbath, or day of rest, from sunset on Friday to Saturday evening

Shavuot – Feast of Weeks; festival of Pentecost

shevarim – one of four characteristic blasts of the shofar

Shofar – a ram's horn, blown like a trumpet

shule – synagogue

siddur – prayer book

tallit – fringed prayer shawl

tekiah – one of four characteristic blasts of the shofar

teruah – one of four characteristic blasts of the shofar

Torah – the first five books of the Bible, the 'Five Books of Moses"

yarmulke – (Yiddish) skullcap worn during prayer

yahrzeit – anniversary of death

Yigdal – Jewish hymn often sung at the opening of morning service and close of evening service

Yom Kippur – the holiest day of the year, known as the Day of Atonement, falling ten days after Rosh Hashanah

Picture credits

Numbers on the left refer to the caption numbers in the picture sections.

1	Searcy Collection, State Library of SA, PRG-280-1-5-340	22	Sydney Jewish Museum collection
2	John Oxley Library, State Library of Qld, 511321	23	Frank Hurley, Australian War Memorial, 004039
3	Trove/*Sydney Mail*, 11 November 1899	24	Argus Newspaper Collection of Photographs, State Library of Victoria, H99.202/4547A
4	Searcy Collection, State Library of SA, PRG 280/1/40/148	25	Sydney Jewish Museum collection
5	Daniel Aarons, Australian War Memorial, P11027.013.002	26	From J. Epstein, G. Pynt & Australian Federation of Jewish Ex-Servicemen & Women, *Australian Jewry's Book of Honour, World War II*, Griffin Press, Adelaide, 1974
6	Daniel Aarons, Australian War Memorial, P11028.001.001		
7	Australian War Memorial, P04013.001	27, 28	Sydney Jewish Museum collection
8	Australian War Memorial, E02964	29	Australian War Memorial, 076010
9	Australian War Memorial, E03186	30, 31, 32	Sydney Jewish Museum collection
10	Sniders & Abrahams, Australian War Memorial, RC09119	33	Courtesy Allen family
		34	Courtesy Levine family
11	Trove/*Sydney Mail*, 25 August 1915	35, 36	Courtesy Borsht family
12	Australian War Memorial, PO4107.002	37	Sydney Jewish Museum collection
		38	Courtesy Goulston family
13a	Courtesy Graeme Mendelsohn	39	Trove/*The Argus*, 31 October 1942
13b	Courtesy Peter Allen	40	Australian War Memorial, P05004.004
14, 15	Sydney Jewish Museum collection, Harold Collins exhibition	41	Adelaide Hebrew Congregation Archive
16	State Library of Western Australia, slwa_b1938213_2	42	Sydney Jewish Museum collection
		43	Courtesy Scott Leonard
17	Source unknown	44	Sydney Jewish Museum collection
18	Australian War Memorial, H01295	45	Courtesy Arthur Shisman
19	Australian War Memorial, H16388	46	Commonwealth of Australia
20	Sydney Jewish Museum collection	47, 48	Courtesy Sher family
21	Darge Photographic Company, Australian War Memorial, DAOF088		

Acknowledgments

Enormous gratitude is due to the numerous people and organisations that have given significant assistance with the contents and publication of *Jewish Anzacs*, including:

Peter Allen, National Coordinator of the Centenary of Anzac Jewish Program (CoAJP), and Gloria Allen; Russell Stern, Immediate Past President, Australian Jewish Historical Society; Major General Jeffrey V Rosenfeld AM OBE KStJ and Wesley Browne OAM, Patrons of CoAJP; Peter Wertheim AM, Executive Director ECAJ and Chair CoAJP Planning Committee; Brian Nebenzahl OAM RFD, CoAJP Planning Committee and Immediate Past President, FAJEX; Charles Aronson, Board Member Sydney Jewish Museum and Immediate Past President NAJEX; other members of the CoAJP Funding and Action Sub-Committee: Trevor Collins, Ralph Hirst, Ruth Lilian OAM, Roger Selby and Gary Ulman; Margaret Beadman, volunteer at the Australian War Memorial; Tony James, Numismatist (incl. research of honours); Jacqui Wasilewsky, Project Manager Community Stories SJM; the Australian Jewish Historical Society; the New South Wales Association of Jewish Ex-Servicemen and Women; the Sydney Jewish Museum.

Sincere thanks to the following organisations and individuals whose generous funding made the publication of this book possible:

The Department of Veterans' Affairs for a Saluting Their Service Major Commemorative Grant; the donors to the Centenary of Anzac Jewish Program, including Kahn Friedlander Foundation, Lowy Foundation, Moriah War Memorial College, NAJEX,

NSW Jewish War Memorial, Pelerman Foundation, JCA, JNF, Sir Moses Montefiore Jewish Home, the S'Team Foundation; Charles and Deidre Aronson, the late Dr Solomon Bard OBE, John Belfer, Errol and Pamela Brown, Garry Browne AM, Wesley Browne OAM and Sari Browne OAM, Gordon Cohen, Neil Cohen and Roy Cohen, David Dinte, Maadi Einfeld, Rodney Ellison, Dr George and Margaret Foster, Jody Glasser and Debbie Sleigh, Professor Kerry Goulston AO, Rhoda Green, Dr Greg Horowitz, Prof Iven Klineberg AM, Ben Lenzer, Dr Max Lenzer, Beverley McLean, Brian Mines, Peter Philippsohn OAM, Joseph Robb, Jeremy Samuel, Robert Schneider, Roger Selby and Zara Selby, Raymond Shaw, John Skala, Ezekiel Solomon AM, Dr Bruce and Allene Symonds, Peng (Patricia) Tan, Claire Trieger, Michelle Urban and Sonia Wilkan.

Mark Dapin would like to acknowledge the following people and organisations:
Firstly, I'd like to thank Peter Allen for his guidance and tireless commitment to this project; and Charles Aronson, Norman Seligman, Jacqui Wasilewsky and, especially, Shannon Maguire at the Sydney Jewish Museum. I'd like to thank Russell Stern for his painstaking research work. Everyone at NAJEX, VAJEX and FAJEX was extremely helpful, particularly Roger Selby at NAJEX, Judy Landau at VAJEX Australia and Warrren Austin at WAJEX. Thanks also to Dr Keith Shilkin at WAJEX. I am hugely grateful to all those who gave up their time for interviews, including Warren Austin, Wesley Browne, Joe Barrington, David Buckwalter, Cyril Borsht, Geoffrey Cass, Aaron Chapman, Graham Devries, Bob Edelman, Josh Fink, Michael Fink, Mrs Gayst, Jason Hymans, Norm Isenberg, Nick Israel, Stretton Joel, Ian Hayat, Harold Karpin, George Karsai, Captain Jake Kleinman, Maurice Kriss, Julie Leder, Scott Leonard, Rabbi John Levi, Graham Lindsay, Alan Mansfield, Bobby Moss, Martyn Pincus, Major General

Jeffrey Rosenfeld, the late David Roubin, Loris Roubin, Amic Schneider, John Selan, Arthur Shisman, Noel Turnbull, David Wittner, Allen Volkov. And special thanks to Felix Sher.

For their information and assistance, thanks to Margaret Beadman, Helen Bersten, Stephen Chapman, Stuart Coppock, Michael Falk, Howard Freeman, Danny Gocs, Gael Hammer, Ben Hirsh, Jean Lamensdorf, Berwyn Lewis, Keira Quinn Lockyer, Philip Mendes, Gareth Narunsky, Vivian Parry, Nerrida Blashki Pohl, David Rosalky, Sue Silberberg, Debbie Sleigh, Michael Solomon, Roslyn Sugarman and Craig Wilcox.

All attempts were made to contact the correct copyright holders. Our thanks for the following book extracts (with permission and courtesy of): Kevin Baker's *Paul Cullen: Citizen and Soldier* (Rosenberg Publishing); Sir Richard Kingsland's *Into the Midst of Things* (Directorate of History – Air Force); Philip Masel's *The Second 28th* (David Warren, 2/28th Battalion and 24th Anti-Tank Company Association); Philip Opas' *Throw Away My Wig* (Rosemary Starr); David Selby's *Hell and High Fever* (Alison Rosenberg); Dr Clive Selby's *Dr NX 22* (Roger Selby).

Our thanks for the following private diaries, letters or manuscripts (with permission and courtesy of): Harry Barrkman (Sandra Barrkman); Cyril Borsht (Cyril Borsht); Harold Collins (Julie Eadie-Edwards); Walter Karri Davies (Jan Watkins); Rabbi Fabian (Miriam Frommer); Sir Asher Joel (Lady Sybil Joel); Geoffrey Kaye (Sue Silberberg); Sydney Levine (Helen Bersten and Joan Rodd) and Neville Milston (Michael, Leah and Richard Milston); Robert Patkin (Tim Patkin); Louis Salek (Rebecca Alford); Sam Sakker (Dr Sam Sakker); Raymond Shaw (Stuart Shaw and Lynne Reading); Ellis Silas (State Library of NSW); Maurice Sussman (Maadi Einfeld); Issacher Weingott (Leveah Hames).

Thanks to the Sydney Jewish Museum's Oral History Project for adding additional interview material; and the Australian

Defence Force for giving permission for me to interview Captain Jake Kleinman.

A special thanks to the wonderful researchers, curators and librarians at the Australian War Memorial, National Archives of Australia, the State Library of NSW and the State Library of Western Australia, in particular Jane Robertson at the Australian War Memorial, Pena Atanasoff at the State Library of Western Australia, Kevin Aston Hoey at the National Archives of Australia, and Deborah Rechter and Peta Cook of the Jewish Museum of Australia. The helpful staff at Mount Scopus Memorial College also deserve a mention.

My editors Marie-Louise Bethune and Tricia Dearborn, and NewSouth Publishing's Emma Driver and Elspeth Menzies, were all wonderful. And my agent Deborah Callaghan came through, as always.

But my biggest thanks must be reserved for my partner, Claire Waddell, who did half the work for none of the praise.

APPENDIXES

Honour rolls of Jewish servicemen and servicewomen

Appendix 1:
Memorial Roll

Those who made the supreme sacrifice

Sergeant Emanuel Eilenberg of Melbourne was in France during World War One with the 4th Division. He wrote to his father to tell of a 'sad old job' he'd had to perform at the funeral of a Jewish soldier: 'The Padre is away on leave, and a little Canadian and myself had promised him to look after that sort of thing during his absence. I met the Canadian at the Mortuary. The coffin is placed on a stretcher mounted on high wheels, four men take the handles, we take up our positions in the front, and the Sergeant in charge of the Mortuary, gives the order – Slow March. Out on to the main road we file; all traffic stops, every officer and man about stands to attention, and salutes as the coffin goes past them. We turn into the burial ground, and halt at the grave: the coffin, covered with the Union Jack, is placed over it. My pal reads the service – mostly in English – [and] the Kaddish, to which I respond in Hebrew. The coffin is lowered, the bugles sound "Last Post", and the grave is filled in. By-and-by, per-haps, tomorrow, will be erected a wooden Magen David. We leave the Cemetery, mount our bikes, and off we go, humming or whistling the latest rag – for that's a way we have in the Army.' (*Jewish Herald*, 10 August 1917)

לזכר עולם

L'Zachor Olam

Remember them forever

On the following pages are the names and cemetery/memorial details
of 342 Australian Jews who died on service
in the Australian armed forces, merchant navy or Allied armed forces.

Lest we forget

Abbreviations

Age   Age at death

DoD   Date of death

Manner   Manner of death:

—   **DOA**: Died of accident

—   **DOI**: Died of illness

—   **DOW**: Died of wounds

—   **DPOW**: Died while prisoner of war

—   **KIA**: Killed in action

—   **POW-P**: Prisoner of war then died as partisan

Memorial   Cemetery or memorial name, location, section.row.grave:

—   **C**: Column

—   **Coll**: Collective grave

—   **J**: Jewish section

—   **P**: Panel

—   **SM**: Special Memorial

PoB   Place of birth

State   State of enlistment

Note: Eligibility for the Memorial Roll is similar to the Australian War Memorial's criteria for its Roll of Honour and Commemorative Roll.

Boer War (South Africa)

NAME	STATE	MANNER	DOD	MEMORIAL OR ACTION
Allen, A.J.	Vic	KIA	9.7.1900	Standerton Cem, Mpumalanga
Goldstein, M.	Vic	KIA	16.2.1900	Tugela River
Levi, J.J.	NSW	DOA	16.12.1901	Jacobsdel Cem/Honeynest Kloof
Marks, A.H.	WA	KIA	30.10.1901	Brakenlaagt
Solomon, H.	WA	KIA	14.4.1901	Jankanistke Farm

World War I

ROYAL AUSTRALIAN NAVY

NAME	POB	MANNER	DOD	AGE	MEMORIAL
Justice, R.D.	Thoona, Vic	DOA	5.3.16	21	Queensferry Cem, West Lothian, UK, 1410

AUSTRALIAN ARMY

NAME	POB	MANNER	DOD	AGE	MEMORIAL
Aarons, J.F.	Hillston, NSW	DOW	11.7.17	35	Trois Arbres, Military Cem, Steenwerck, France, I.T.4
Aarons, M.L.	Carlton, Vic	KIA	8.8.15	28	Lone Pine Mem, Turkey, P51
Abelson, C.	Glamorganshire, UK	KIA	31.1.17	29	Cite Bonjean Military Cem, Armentieres, France, IV.D.9
Ades, S.A.	Cairo, Egypt	KIA	22.8.18	28	Cote 80, French National Cem, Etinehem, France, C.3
Ansell, H.A.	Hobart, Tas	KIA	23.10.16	38	AIF Burial Ground, Flers, France, II.M.30
Asher, J.H.	Hurstville, NSW	KIA	2.9.17	27	Bailleul Communal Cem Ext, Lille, France, III.E.208
Asher, S.	Surry Hills, NSW	KIA	11.7.17	23	Menin Gate Mem, Ypres, Belgium, P23
Barnard, S.H.	Adelaide, SA	KIA	3.5.18	38	Villers-Bretonneux Mem, France, 48 Bn
Barnes, D.	London, UK	DOW	6.6.17	26	Bailleul Communal Cem Ext, Lille, France, III.B.277
Beaver, W.N.	St Kilda, Vic	DOW	26.9.17	35	Lijssenthoek Military Cem, West-Vlaanderen, Belgium, XXIII.C.12
Benjamin, S.O.	Melbourne, Vic	DOW	23.11.16	36	Danzig Alley British Cem, Mametz, Somme, France, IX.P.B
Bishop, S.	London, UK	DOW	28.8.18	26	Daours Communal Cem Ext, France, VII.A.19
Blashki, R.H.	Sydney, NSW	KIA	3.8.17	23	Vlamertinghe New Military Cem, West-Vlaanderen, Belgium, VIII.C.15
Bloch, F.L.	Deloraine, Tas	KIA	17.8.18	20	Heath Cem, Harbonnieres, Picardie, France, IV.J.10
Bloom, J.S.	Paddington, NSW	KIA	5.11.15	24	Shrapnel Valley Cem, Turkey, I.D.21
Breitman, G.	Chechelnik, Russia	DOI	19.4.19	22	Willesden Jewish Cem, Brent, UK, KK.2
Brodziak, C.E.M.	Sydney, NSW	KIA	31.8.18	27	Peronne Communal Cem Ext, France, V.P.1
Cohen, A.	Sydney, NSW	DOW	26.9.17	19	Lijssenthoek Military Cem, West-Vlaanderen, Belgium, XXV.D.12
Cohen, G.	Melbourne, Vic	DOW	22.9.17	35	Lijssenthoek Military Cem, West-Vlaanderen, Belgium, XXIV.F.1A
Cohen, H.	Bristol, UK	KIA	3.10.18	21	Villers-Bretonneux Mem, France, 19 Bn
Cohen, John	Melbourne, Vic	KIA	4.3.17	22	Warlencourt British Cem, Pas de Calais, France, VI.J.24
Cohen, Joseph	Carlton, Vic	KIA	26.9.17	28	Menin Gate Mem, Ypres, Belgium, P31
Cohen, S.	London, UK	DOW	22.5.17	23	St. Sever Cem Rouen, France, J A.5
Cohen, S.I.	Melbourne, Vic	KIA	1.9.18	29	Peronne Communal Cem Ext, France, V.C.18
Davis, A.	Melbourne, Vic	KIA	4.10.18	28	Prospect Hill Cem, Gouy, Aisne, France, IV.D.10
Davis, E.P.	Armadale, Vic	DOW	18.7.15	28	Lone Pine Mem, Turkey, P33
Durlacher, L.J.	Kilburn, UK	DOI	16.2.19	22	Willesden Jewish Cem, UK, KK.3
Ettingove, S.	Laidi, Russia	DOA	20.5.18	21	Brighton General Cem, Vic, J D.63 (GRM/3)
Fernandez, N.	Sydney, NSW	KIA	13.10.17	21	Menin Gate Mem, Ypres, Belgium, 45 Bn
Fink, G.	Melbourne, Vic	KIA	2.5.15	30	Lone Pine Mem, Turkey, P53
Finklestein, H.	Blackpool, UK	KIA	5.8.16	21	Villers-Bretonneux Mem, France, 20 Bn
Frankel, S.	Melbourne, Vic	KIA	15.3.18	25	Royal Berks Cem Ext, Hainaut, Belgium, II.A.7
Freadman, Z.E.	Melbourne, Vic	DOA	9.9.17	22	Willesden Jewish Cem, UK, KK.4
Freedman, A.	Johannesburg, S Af	DOW	11.6.18	27	Fouilloy Communal Cem, Picardie, France, A.I
Fromer, H.	Abbotsford, Vic	KIA	1.9.18	22	Villers-Bretonneux Mem, France, 24 Bn
Gluck, L.J.	London, UK	KIA	2.5.15	32	Lone Pine Mem, Turkey, P33
Goldring, G.	Sydney, NSW	KIA	8.8.15	30	Lone Pine Mem, Turkey, P46

Appendix 1: Memorial Roll

NAME	POB	MANNER	DOD	AGE	MEMORIAL
Goldstone, A.	Melbourne, Vic	KIA	8.6.17	24	Menin Gate Mem, Ypres, Belgium, **P**25
Goldwater, N.I.	Sydney, NSW	DOW	21.4.18	23	Outtersteene Communal Cem Ext, Bailleul, France, I.F.5
Goodman, D.W.	Lancashire, UK	DOI	27.3.19	34	Rookwood Cem, Sydney, NSW, **J** 3.3.67
Grimish, B.B.	Brisbane, Qld	KIA	11.8.18	24	Villers-Bretonneux Mem, France, 9 Bn
Grouse, R.G.	London, UK	KIA	10.6.17	27	Menin Gate Mem, Ypres, Belgium, **P**25
Gubbay, J.M.	Sydney, NSW	KIA	8.6.17	28	Menin Gate Mem, Ypres, Belgium, **Add P** 59
Hains, M.	Adelaide, SA	KIA	7–12.8.15	21	Lone Pine Mem, Turkey, **SM** C.39
Hallenstein, D.I.M.	Heidelberg, Germany	KIA	2.9.18	25	Peronne Communal Cem Ext, France, IV.E.14
Hansman, E.E.	Sydney, NSW	DOI	28.12.17	25	Hollybrook Mem, Southampton, UK, **P**86
Hansman, H.J.	Sydney, NSW	KIA	3.12.17	28	Berks Cem Ext, Hainaut, Belgium, II.B.23
Harbert, G.	Warsaw, Poland	KIA	19.7.16	28	VC Corner, Aust Cem and Mem, Fromelles, France, **P**16
Harris, C.M.	Enmore, NSW	DOW	28.8.15	24	Abbeville Communal Cem, Somme, France, II.C.10
Harris, L.H.L.	London, UK	DOI	13.9.20	48	Rookwood Cem, Sydney, NSW, **J** 4.4.73
Hart, C.H.A.	Bathurst, NSW	KIA	26.7.16	23	Villers-Bretonneux Mem, France, 18 Bn
Hart, H.	London, UK	KIA	18.5.15	19	Lone Pine Mem, Turkey, **P**28
Hart, John	London, UK	DOI	20.4.19	22	Mons (Bergen) Communal Cem, Hainaut, Belgium, X.B.20
Hart, Joseph	Melbourne, Vic	KIA	20.7.16	20	Ration Farm Military Cem, La Chapelle-D'Armentieres, France, VI.H.48
Hart, L.	Melbourne, Vic	DOW	4.5.15	20	Beach Cem, Anzac, Turkey, I.A.17
Herman, H.E.	London, UK	DOW	20.11.15	22	Lone Pine Mem, Turkey, **P**58
Herman, M.P.	Sydney, NSW	KIA	9.8.18	26	Heath Cem, Harbonnieres, France, II.J.16
Hershorn, F.	London, UK	KIA	2.3.17	22	Warlencourt British Cem, Pas de Calais, France, 4.D.18
Hojein, L.	Vadso, Norway	KIA	2.5.15	32	Quinn's Post Cem, Turkey, D.1
Hyams, W.	Melbourne, Vic	KIA	4.10.17	30	Buttes New British Cem, Polygon Wood, Belgium, XXIX.C.7
Illfeld, J.	Maitland, NSW	KIA	2.3.17	23	Warlencourt British Cem, Pas de Calais, France, VIII.C.50
Isaacs, M.M.	London, UK	KIA	2.7.18	22	Querrieu British Cem, France, C.28
Isaacs, W.W.	Fitzroy, Vic	KIA	5.8.16	21	Villers-Bretonneux Mem, France, 22 Bn
Israel, A.	Spittlefields, UK	KIA	27.7.18	24	Villers-Bretonneux Mem, France, XIII.F.1
Jacks, A.	Stockport, UK	KIA	26.9.17	22	Menin Gate Mem, Ypres, Belgium, **P**29
Jacobs, A.A.	London, UK	KIA	7.10.17	23	Tyne Cot Cem, West-Vlaanderen, Belgium, XXXVIII.B.21
Jacobs, H.	London, UK	KIA	8.8.15	34	Lone Pine Mem, Turkey, **P**46
Jacobs, L.W.	Ballarat, Vic	DOW	3.12.15	22	Ari Burnu Cem, Anzac, Turkey, I.13
Joel, S.I.	Sydney, NSW	KIA	7.6.17	19	Menin Gate Mem, Ypres, Belgium, **P**25
Jonas, B.	Timau, NZ	DOI	12.5.19	46	Willesden Jewish Cem, UK, 4.T.K
Joseph, J.D.D.	Melbourne, Vic	KIA	20.7.16	19	VC Corner, Aust Cem and Mem, France, **P**3
Joseph, S.A.	Melbourne, Vic	KIA	9.8.18	25	Rosieres Communal Cem Ext, France, II.E.12
Judell, E.	Orroroo, SA	KIA	9.8.15	24	Walkers Ridge Cem, Anzac, Turkey, II.C.6
Klein, J.	Essex, UK	KIA	20.9.17	23	Menin Gate Mem, Ypres, Belgium, **P**23
Kotton, M.	Kremenchuck, Russia	KIA	19.9.18	26	Templeux-le-Guerard British Cem, France, I.E.10
Kozminsky, M.E.	Melbourne, Vic	DOW	19.8.16	31	Worley-Baillon Communal Cem Ext, France, III.D.5
Kriesman, J.H.	Middlesex, UK	KIA	29.7.16	24	Villers-Bretonneux Mem, France, 25 Bn
Krug, D.V.	Warialda, WA	KIA	23.8.18	26	Beacon Cem, Sailly-Laurette, France, VI.J.3
Kunin, G.	Vilna, Russia	KIA	18.9.17	23	Hooge Crater Cem, Flanders, Belgium, VI.E.16
Landsler, E.L.	London, UK	KIA	19.7.16	23	VC Corner, Aust Cem and Mem, France, **P**8
Lazarus, I.	Fitzroy, Vic	KIA	8.5.15	22	Skew Bridge Cem, Turkey, II.B.9
Lazer, H.J.	Glen Innes, NSW	KIA	24.3.17	22	Cite Bonjean Military Cem, Armentieres, France, V.A.10
Lazer, L.	Sydney, NSW	KIA	11.8.18	19	Heath Cem, Harbonnieres, France, VII.J.16
Lebovich, M.	Odessa, Russia	DOW	5.5.18	23	Caestre Military Cem, France, I.B.15
Lee, D.	London, UK	KIA	27.4.15	24	Lone Pine Mem, Turkey, **P**42
Lenneberg, F.B.	Southport, Qld	DOI	20.9.18	33	Abbeville Communal Cem Ext, France, IV.F.14
Levene, A.D.	Glasgow, UK	KIA	23.7.15	20	Shrapnel Valley Cem, Turkey, I.C.12
Levi, K.M.	St Kilda, Vic	KIA	7.8.15	24	Twelve Tree Copse Cem, Turkey, I.E.20
Levy, A.	Ascot Vale, Vic	KIA	29.3.18	22	Mericourt-l'Abbe Communal Cem Ext, France, II.F.7
Levy, C.	Sydney, NSW	DOW	15.5.18	23	Daours Communal Cem Ext, France, III.B.45
Levy, E.	London, UK	DOW	15.11.16	29	Longueval Road Cem, France, I.7
Levy, F.S.	London, UK	KIA	19.4.17	30	Jerusalem Mem, Israel, **P**59
Levy, G.N.	Gwalia, WA	KIA	8.10.17	24	Menin Gate Mem, Ypres, Belgium, **P**17
Levy, H.	London, UK	KIA	21.9.17	39	Menin Gate Mem, Ypres, Belgium, **P**17
Levy, H.M.	Adelaide, SA	DOW	19.5.16	18	Estaires Communal Cem Ext, Nord, France, II.Q.4
Levy, L.	Sydney, NSW	KIA	29.9.18	25	Villers-Bretonneux Mem, France, 56 Bn
Levy, L.H.	Sydney, NSW	KIA	19.7.16	29	VC Corner, Aust Cem and Mem, Fromelles, France, **P**8
Levy, R.L.	W Maitland, NSW	DOW	8.3.18	33	Outtersteene Communal Cem Ext, Bailleul, France, II.A.34
Liggi, R.R.	London, UK	DOW	18.1.17	23	Kantara War Mem Cem, Egypt, D.53
Littmann, S.	London, UK	DOW	18.5.18	26	Crouy British Cem, Crouy-sur-Somme, France, II.B.27

Jewish Anzacs

NAME	POB	MANNER	DOD	AGE	MEMORIAL
Loewe, S.	Brisbane, Qld	DOW	9.7.18	28	Crouy British Cem, Crouy-sur-Somme, France, III.E.9
Lynes, A.	London, UK	DOW	30.8.15	24	Lone Pine Mem, Turkey, **P**62
Lyons, J.T.	Murchison, Vic	KIA	19.5.15	19	4 Bn Pde Ground, Turkey, D.11
Mandelzon, H.	Yass, NSW	KIA	29.7.16	25	Villers-Bretonneux Mem, France, 28 Bn
Marcus, R.	Cape Town, S Af	KIA	21.7.16	38	VC Corner, Aust Cem and Mem, France, **ADD P**
Marks, A.G.	Melbourne, Vic	DOW	14.8.15	30	Lone Pine Mem, Turkey, **P**24
Marks, L.	Melbourne, Vic	KIA	25–29.4.15	23	Lone Pine Mem, Turkey, **P**13
Marks, L.M.B.	Melbourne, Vic	KIA	3.5.15	33	Lone Pine Mem, Turkey, **P**36
Marks, M.	Leeds, UK	KIA	8.8.18	19	Villers-Bretonneux Mem, France, II.C.3
Marks, M.L.	Carlton, Vic	KIA	4.10.17	27	Tyne Cot Cem, West-Vlaanderen, Belgium, **SM** 78
Marquis, G.	Liverpool, UK	DOW	17.8.15	38	Lone Pine Mem, Turkey, **P**38
Marzan, W.	Havre, France	KIA	14.10.17	29	Menin Gate Mem, Ypres, Belgium, **P**23
McCarthy, F.	Parramatta, NSW	DOI	10.6.18	35	Longuenesse (St Omer) Souvenir Cem, Pas de Calais, France, V.B.60
Mendelsohn, B.L.	Esk, Qld	KIA	20.7.16	25	Fromelles (Pheasant Wood) Military Cem, France, II.F.2
Mendes, A.	Maclean, NSW	KIA	5.4.18	20	Villers-Bretonneux Mem, France, 49 Bn
Mendoza, H.K.	Melbourne, Vic	KIA	11.6.17	28	Menin Gate Mem, Ypres, Belgium, **P**29
Menser, L.M.	Sydney, NSW	DOW	10.4.17	39	Aveluy Communal Cem Ext, Picardie, France, N.37
Michaelis, F.M.	St Kilda, Vic	DOI	14.5.17	24	Willesden Jewish Cem, UK, J.F.27
Miller, J.	Leeds, UK	KIA	26.8.16	33	Villers-Bretonneux Mem, France, 21 Bn
Minor, D.	Yina, Russia	KIA	4.5.18	24	Meteren Military Cem, France, V.D.656
Mitchell, A.D.	Glebe, NSW	DOW	5.5.15	23	Old Cairo (Jewish) War Mem Cem, Cairo, Egypt, M.7
Moses, H.L.	Hamilton, NZ	KIA	31.7.17	40	Menin Gate Mem, Ypres, Belgium, **P**27
Moss, B.	Ravenswood, Qld	DOW	20.8.17	32	Trois Arbres Cem, Steenwerck, France, I.Z.33
Moss, E.E.	Bungendore, NSW	DOW	8.8.15	45	Lone Pine Mem, Turkey, **P**23
Moss, J.	Dunedin, NZ	KIA	19.7.18	41	Borre British Cem, Nord, France, II.D.23
Moss, L.	Brisbane, Qld	DOI	1.10.15	19	Brisbane General (Toowong) Cem, Qld, 3.4.14.L/596 (GRM/4*)
Myers, M.	Sydney, NSW	KIA	19.8.16	24	Villers-Bretonneux Mem, France, 4 Bn
Nathan, A.	London, UK	KIA	20.3.17	22	Lebucquiere Communal Cem Ext, Pas de Calais, France, II.G.II
Norman, A.	Melbourne, Vic	KIA	20.5.15	26	4 Bn Pde Cem, Turkey, C.14
Nyeman, C.	Fitzroy, Vic	KIA	18.8.16	27	Villers-Bretonneux Mem, France, 8 Bn
Nyman, A.	Fitzroy, Vic	KIA	11.9.18	28	Jeancourt Communal Cem Ext, Aisne, France, III.C.11
Pasvalsky, L.	Russia	KIA	3.9.16	19	Villers-Bretonneux Mem, France, 51 Bn
Phillips, S.I.	Ballarat, Vic	DOI	2.6.16	28	Old Cairo (Jewish) War Mem Cem, Cairo, Egypt, P.158
Pirani, C.S.	St Kilda, Vic	DOI	26.4.18	29	Karrakatta Cem, Perth, WA, J0.AA.227
Pirani, E.J.	Melbourne, Vic	KIA	25.7.16	19	Villers-Bretonneux Mem, France, 11 Bn
Pizer, E.	London, UK	KIA	28.9.17	22	Duhallow ADS Cem, West-Vlaanderen, Belgium, IX.C.18
Purcell-Cohen, R.R.	Sydney, NSW	DOI	8.11.17	29	Rookwood Cem (Jewish) Sydney, NSW, 3.18.281
Rabinovitch, B.	Sydney, NSW	KIA	19.7.16	18	VC Corner, Aust Cem and Mem, France, **P**17
Rabinovitch, E.H.	Sydney, NSW	DOW	31.8.18	22	Suzanne Communal Cem, France, B.15
Raphael, F.F.J.	Melbourne, Vic	KIA	15.11.16	23	Villers-Bretonneux Mem, France, 21 Bn
Ribeiro, M.	London, UK	KIA	16.4.18	27	Outtersteene Communal Cem Ext, Bailleul, France, II.H.35
Richards, C.S.	Narrandera, NSW	KIA	16.9.17	21	Perth Cem (China Wall), West-Vlaanderen, Belgium, I.E.6
Robin, D.K.	Bialystok, Russia	DOW	16.4.16	32	Erquingham-Lys Churchyard Ext, Nord, France, I.J.9
Rolbin, H.	Manchester, UK	DOI	18.1.17	28	Blackley Jewish Cem, Manchester, UK, .2856
Rosenberg, M.	Broken Hill, NSW	KIA	5.8.16	25	Kantara War Mem Cem, Egypt, B.35
Rosenfeldt, A.	Perth, WA	KIA	7.8.16	21	Villers-Bretonneux Mem, France, 48 Bn
Rosenthal, S.	Melbourne, Vic	KIA	25.9.17	35	Hooge Crater Cem, Flanders, Belgium, XI.C.9
Rosenthall, A.K.	Newtown, NSW	DOI	29.5.15	33	Alexandria (Chatby) Jewish Cem no. 3, Egypt, .3
Rosenwax, C.H.	Carlton, Vic	KIA	7.1.16	29	Villers-Bretonneux Mem, France, 19 Bn
Roth, K.C.	Deniliquin, NSW	DOI	21.7.16	46	Fawkner Cem, Melbourne and East Melbourne Hebrew, Vic, B.146
Russell, P.H.	Burwood, NSW	DOW	6.11.15	28	Lone Pine Mem, Turkey, **P**64
Sacks, S.	London, UK	KIA	8.6.17	23	Lindenhoek Chalet British Military Cem, Belgium, II.I.1
Samuel, E.	Glasgow, UK	KIA	19.7.16	28	VC Corner, Aust Cem and Mem, France, **P**17
Saunders, S.A.	Adelaide, SA	DOW	14.8.16	28	Boulogne Eastern Cem, France, VIII.B.139
Shappere, C.S.	Sydney, NSW	DOW	29.12.16	25	Bernafay Wood British Cem, Montauban, France, K.68
Sherman, G.J.T.	Sydney, NSW	KIA	25.4.15	23	Lone Pine Mem, Turkey, **P**13
Sherman, L.	Sydney, NSW	KIA	2.10.17	22	Menin Gate Mem, Ypres, Belgium, **P**23
Silberthau, R.S.	Melbourne, Vic	KIA	2–5.10.17	23	Menin Gate Mem, Ypres, Belgium, **P**7
Silverman, A.	Radum, Poland	KIA	9.10.17	24	Menin Gate Mem, Ypres, Belgium, **P**23
Silverman, J.	London, UK	DOW	23.9.17	25	Menin Road South Military Cem, West-Vlaadere, Belgium, I.S.43
Simon, O.	Melbourne, Vic	DOW	6.5.15	23	Alexandria (Chatby) Jewish Cem no. 3, Egypt, .2

NAME	POB	MANNER	DOD	AGE	MEMORIAL
Singer, S.	London, UK	KIA	25.7.16	23	Villers-Bretonneux Mem, France, 2 Bn
Solnick, E.L.	Melbourne, Vic	KIA	28.7.16	18	Villers-Bretonneux Mem, France, 23 Bn
Solomon, J.	Sydney, NSW	KIA	29.8.16	36	Courcelette British Cem, France, V.F.9
Solomon, M.	Pittsburg, USA	KIA	19.7.16	22	VC Corner, Aus Cem and Mem, France, **P**6
Springer, S.	Melbourne, Vic	DPOW	16.4.18	35	Heath Military Cem, Harbonnieres, France, II.C.14
Steinberg, I.	Perth, WA	KIA	20.4.16	20	Rue-du-Bacquerot (13 London) Graveyard, Laventie, France, F.35
Symons, E.	Richmond, Vic	KIA	4.10.17	25	Menin Gate Mem, Ypres, Belgium, **P**23
Trigger, S.W.	Macarthur, Vic	KIA	16.8.16	29	Villers-Bretonneux Mem, France, 50 Bn
Wachman, R.	Dublin, Ireland	KIA	11.4.17	23	Villers-Bretonneux Mem, France, 48 Bn
Weingott, A.	Sydney, NSW	DOW	2.5.15	26	Alexandria (Chatby) Jewish Cem no. 3, Egypt, .1
Weingott, S.	Sydney, NSW	DOW	5.6.15	21	Lone Pine Mem, Turkey, **P**16
Wertheim, J.	London, UK	DOI	13.5.19	20	Rookwood Cem, Sydney, NSW, **J** 3.27.436
White, M.	London, UK	KIA	25.4.18	28	Villers-Bretonneux Mem, France, 51 Bn
Whitfield, C.S.K.	London, UK	DOW	17.4.18	27	Ebblingham Military Cem, France, I.C.20
Wittner, H.	Deleni, Romania	KIA	21.2.17	23	Villers-Bretonneux Mem, France, 22 Bn
Woods, L.	Sydney, NSW	KIA	21.9.17	29	Menin Gate Mem, Ypres, Belgium, **P**7
Woolf, S.	Carlton, Vic	KIA	9.8.18	22	Rosieres Communal Cem Ext, France, II.A.8

EMPIRE FORCES

NAME	POB	MANNER	DOD	AGE	MEMORIAL
Abrahams, F.A.	Vic	KIA	10.9.16	24	Thiepval Mem, Somme, France, Face, 13C
Blaubaum, E.	Melbourne, Vic	KIA	3.6.16	30	NZ Army, Cite Bonjean Military Cem, Armentieres, France, II.A.18
Braun, C.L.	NSW	KIA	19.6.17	43	Nasirabad Government Cem, India, E.B.19
Cohen, C.H.	NSW	KIA	18.11.18		Willesden Jewish Cem, Brent, UK, N.I.11
Cohen, E.H.M.	Sydney, NSW	DOW	10.8.15		Embarkation Pier Cem, Gallipoli, Turkey, **SM** B.53
Cullen, R.N.		KIA	6.12.15	30	Doiran Mem, Lake Doiran, Greece, **Add P**
Davis, F.L.	Sydney, NSW	DOA	10.11.18	21	Wellington (Karori) Cem, Wellington City, NZ, **J** 132.A
Israel, R.S.	Vic	KIA	16.7.16		Delville Wood Cem, Longueval, Somme, France, **SM** B.6
Lasker, R.S.	Newcastle, NSW	KIA	20.5.18	22	Aulnoye Communal Cem, Nord, France, I.A.45
Levy, A.G.	NSW	DOA	25.4.18		Willesden Jewish Cem, Brent, UK, Cx.21.4
Levy, M.B.	NSW	KIA	12.4.18	25	Ploegsteert Mem, Hainaut, Belgium, **P**1
Lewis, B.	Melbourne, Vic	KIA	8.6.17		Wulverghem-Lindenhoek Rd Military Cem, Belgium, V.B.24
Mandelstam, J.	WA	KIA	6.3.16	37	Noex-les-Mines Communal Cem, Pas de Calais, France, I.H.2
Michaelis, G.M.	Vic	DOW	23.9.15	20	7 Fd Amb Cem, Gallipoli, Turkey, II.C.11
Myers, S.M.	NSW	KIA	29.5.16	24	Cite Bonjean Military Cem, Armentieres, Nord, France, I.B.23
Rosenfeldt, A.B.P.	W Maitland, NSW	KIA	8.5.15		Twelve Tree Copse (NZ) Mem, Gallipoli, Turkey, **P**19
Solomon, H.P.	Vic	KIA	20.10.17	34	Gainsborough General Cem, Lincolnshire, UK, B.N.C.199
Solomon, K.M.H.	NSW	DOW	18.9.15	26	Willesden Jewish Cem, Brent, UK, Cx.13.28

Post—World War I

AUSTRALIAN IMPERIAL FORCE

NAME	POB	MANNER	DOD	AGE	MEMORIAL
Packer, N.E.	Mosman, NSW	DOA	26.10.22	26	Rookwood Cem, Sydney, NSW, **J** 5.15.265

World War II

ROYAL AUSTRALIAN NAVY

NAME	POB	UNIT	MANNER	DOD	AGE	MEMORIAL
Asher, J.S.	Adelaide, SA	HMAS Kuttabul	KIA	1.6.42	20	Adelaide (West Terrace) Cem, SA, **J** 4S.26E.GRM/5
Herman, I.	Perth, WA	HMAS Perth	DPOW	24.8.43	28	Kanchanaburi War Cem, Thailand, 1.J.63
Opas, M.	London, UK	HMAS Sydney	KIA	20.11.41	38	Plymouth Naval Mem, Devon, UK, **P**62
Rothbaum, L.	Perth, WA	HMAS Sydney	KIA	20.11.41	19	Plymouth Naval Mem, Devon, UK, **P**58 **C**2

AUSTRALIAN ARMY

NAME	POB	UNIT	MANNER	DOD	AGE	MEMORIAL
Altshuler, E.	Harbin, China	8 Div Ord Corps	DPOW	14.9.44	26	Labuan War Mem Cem, Brunei Bay, Malaysia, **P**27
Barnett, K.R.	Auckland, NZ	Trg	DOI	9.5.43	31	Albury War Cem, NSW, F.B.6
Benjamin, R.	London, UK	12 Grn Bn	DOI	15.3.44	54	Springvale War Cem, Melbourne, Vic, I.N.B.4
Berliner, H.L.	Brisbane, Qld	ACS	DOI	26.2.43	49	Springvale War Cem, Melbourne, Vic, 1.T.D.6
Berliner, L.A.	Albert Park, Vic	2/21 Bn	DPOW	15.2.42	21	Ambon Mem, Indonesia, **C**3
Bernstein, H.	London, UK	2/22 Bn	KIA	1.7.42	41	Rabaul Mem, PNG, **P**19
Beth-Halevy, A.B.	Kalish, Poland	2/12 Bn	KIA	21.1.44	30	Lae War Cem, PNG, IA.D.2
Blashki, V.S.	Sydney, NSW	Aust HQ	DPOW	26.11.43	28	Kanchanaburi War Cem, Thailand, **SM** 9.M.9
Bolgraaf, S.	Bondi, NSW	2/12 Bn	KIA	1.1.43	23	Port Moresby (Bomana) Mem Cem, PNG, **P**3
Britnell, D.R.	Glenferrie, Vic	1 OBD	KIA	5.7.45	22	Labuan War Mem Cem, Brunei Bay, Malaysia, 6.C.8
Burgheim, W.S.	Fraustadt, Germany	3 Emp Coy	DOI	16.8.45	41	Forces Mem Board, Rookwood Crem, Sydney, NSW, Niche 34SB
Burman, L.	London, UK	4 Docks Op Coy	DOI	11.7.45	26	Lae War Cem, PNG, J.C.7
Ciddor, M.M.	Manchester, UK	2/7 Bn	DOW	6.2.43	23	Lae War Cem, PNG, K.B.9
Cohen, R.D.	Bowral, NSW	2/18 Bn	KIA	9.2.42	26	Singapore Mem, Singapore , **C**119
Danciger, S.	Krakow, Poland	2/15 Fd Regt	KIA	22.1.42	30	Singapore Mem, Singapore , **C**115
Davidovitz, J.	Sydney, NSW	18th A Tk Bty	KIA	30.4.42	28	Townsville War Cem, Qld, E.C.10
Deitch, M.	London, UK	109 CCS	DOI	4.6.45	34	Townsville War Cem, Qld, E.A.7
Earl, G.	Lublin, Poland	2/9 Regt Wksp	DOI	14.6.45	24	Albury War Cem, NSW, E.B.2
Fernandez, A.	Sydney, NSW	2/10 Fd Amb	KIA	1.7.42	43	Rabaul Mem, East New Britain, PNG, **P**31
Fink, T.	Melbourne,Vic	AHQ	DOA	22.11.42	45	Vic Crem Mem, Springvale War Cem, Vic, **P**2
Glass, B.B.	Sydney, NSW	2/13 Bn	KIA	5.12.41	22	El Alamein War Mem Cem, Alamein, Egypt, **C**92
Goldstone, M.	South Yarra, Vic	2/23 Bn	DOW	26.7.42	26	Hadra War Mem Cem, Alexandria, Egypt, 3.D.16
Grose, R.A.	Manchester, UK	7 Div Sig	DOI	14.3.43	32	Lutwyche Cem, Brisbane, Qld, 75.9
Harris, C.M.	Johannesburg, S Af	2/18 Bn	DOI	20.4.45	37	Labuan War Mem Cem, Brunei Bay, Malaysia, **P**10
Harris, R.	London, UK	2 AMT School	DOI	2.8.42	30	Fawkner Mem Park Cem, Melbourne, Vic, A.901.GRM/3
Harris, S.N.	St Kilda, Vic	8 Div Sig	DPOW	7.6.45	24	Labuan War Mem Cem, Brunei Bay, Malaysia, 16.D.5
Hawkins, M.J.	Dublin, UK	2/2 MCU	DOI	30.12.44	41	Rookwood Cem, Sydney, NSW, J 11.24.414
Jacobs, P.A.	Malvern, Vic	2/21 Bn	DPOW	27.7.45	29	Ambon War Cem, Maluku, Indonesia, 18.C.9
Joseph, D.E.	Caulfield, Vic	51 Comp AA Regt	DOI	9.8.44	23	Townsville War Cem, Qld, E.D.5
Klitenik, S.	Poland	2/7 Bn	KIA	6.5.45	21	Lae War Cem, PNG, LL.A.2
Kurtz, A.	Lutomirsk, Poland	4 Emp Coy	DOA	29.1.44	34	Albury War Cem, NSW, O.C.11
Lasker, J.L.	Sydney, NSW	2/2 MG Bn	DOA	17.10.41	30	Gaza War Cem, Israel, D.B.10
Laufer, U.S.	Berlin, Germany	8 Emp Coy	DOA	30.12.43	20	Tocumwall General Cem, NSW, B.A.12
Lazarus, S.A.	Elsternwick, Vic	2/21 Bn	DPOW	20.2.42	27	Ambon War Cem, Maluku, Indonesia, 23.C.15
Lesnie, N.M.G.	Sydney, NSW	2/12 Fd Amb	KIA	14.5.43	28	Sydney Mem, Rookwood, NSW, **P**2
Letwin, G.	Brunswick, Vic	13 AGH	DOI	7.10.43	23	Thanbyuzayat War Cem, Mon State, Myanmar, A2.C.3
Levey, R.E.	Hamilton, Vic	2/10 Fd Amb	DPOW	14.6.45	31	Labuan War Mem Cem, Brunei Bay, Malaysia, **P**26
Lipp, B.	Bialystock, Poland	37 Emp Coy	DOA	17.4.44	31	Lae War Cem, PNG, **P**5
Lubansky, H.	Jerusalem, Israel	2/38 Bn	MPD	12.10.42	19	Port Moresby (Bomana) Mem Cem, PNG, **P**7
Marcus, L.J.	London, UK	2/17 Bn	KIA	28.10.42	23	El Alamein War Mem Cem, Alamein, Egypt, A111.A.24
Marks, Z.J.	Melbourne, Vic	Aust HQ AIF	DOI	25.8.42	33	Gaza War Mem Cem, Israel, C.A.13
Mirmovitch, M.	Margo, Cyprus	2/11 Bn	KIA	12.5.45	30	Lae War Cem, PNG, HH.A.11
Morris, Alfred	London, UK	4 Grn Bn	DOI	13.9.40	42	Rookwood Cem, Sydney, NSW, J 10.9.153
Morris, Allen	St Kilda, Vic	2/21 Bn	DPOW	28.6.45	31	Ambon War Cem, Maluku, Indonesia, 17.C.14
Morris, M. (Levitus)	Sydney, NSW	55 Comp AA Regt	DOA	16.3.45	34	Adelaide River War Cem, NT, D.D.14
Moses, A.	Sydney, NSW	2/28 Bn	KIA	2.11.42	30	El Alamein War Mem Cem, Alamein, Egypt, A1.C.20

Appendix 1: Memorial Roll

NAME	POB	UNIT	MANNER	DOD	AGE	MEMORIAL
Nelson, M.N.	Sydney, NSW	BIPOD	KIA	12.4.43	35	Port Moresby (Bomana) Mem Cem, PNG, A1.C.19
Newman, D.C.	Junee, NSW	2/4 LAA Regt	DOW	23.9.43	20	Lae War Cem, PNG, T.D.1
Pearlman, L.	Ballarat, Vic	2/22 Bn	KIA	4.2.42	33	Rabaul (Bita Paka) War Mem Cem, PNG, P18
Platt, R.A.	Sydney, NSW	2/30 Bn	KIA	7.7.45	21	Lae War Cem, PNG, HH.C.6
Pollock, H.	Seven Hills, UK	7 PW Guard Coy	DOI	13.11.46	54	Rookwood Cem, Sydney, NSW, J 12.1.3
Raphael, G.A.	Perth, WA	2/4 MG Bn	DPOW	19.2.42	25	Singapore Mem (Kranji War Cem), Singapore, C135
Rorkin, J.	Poland	2/3 Bn	DOW	7.11.42	16	Port Moresby (Bomana) War Cem, PNG, C6.D.17
Rose, J.	London, UK	2/42 Tpt Pl	KIA	25.9.45	23	Kranji War Cem, Singapore, 3.E.19
Rosebery, S.S.	Sydney, NSW	2/1 AHS 'Manunda'	DOI	1.2.46	55	Sydney War Cem, Rookwood, Sydney, E.A.16
Rosenberg, A.	Orange, NSW	2/15 Fd Regt	DOI	26.12.43	41	Kanchanaburi War Cem, Bangkok, Thailand, 1.C.69
Rosendahl, H.	Barmen, Germany	6 Emp Coy	DOI	3.10.45	39	Springdale War Cem, Melbourne, Vic, 1.R.D.15
Roskin, N.N.	Melbourne, Vic	6 Fd Amb AAMC	DOI	7.1.45	25	Lae War Cem, PNG, K.C.10
Samuels, J.H.	Sydney, NSW	2/15 Bn	KIA	25.10.42	27	El Alamein War Mem Cem, Alamein, Egypt, AII.G.2
Sanders, H.	London, UK	2/20 Bn	DOI	30.12.42	37	Kranji War Cem, Singapore, 3.A.17
Saywell, L.P.	Neutral Bay, NSW	6th Div HQ	POW-P	8.5.45	26	Prague War Cem, CZE, IV.C.2
Schwartz, Z.	Dubrobno, Russia	4 AGH	KIA	10.4.41	43	Tobruk War Cem, Libya, 3.G.1
Schwarz, H.G.	Vienna, Austria	2/1 Bn	DOI	16.12.45	24	Goulburn General Cem, NSW, G.B.9
Schwarz, M.	Vienna, Austria	8 Emp Coy	DOA	30.12.43	26	Tocumwal General Cem, NSW, B.A.11
Sender, I.H.	Leeds, UK	2/12 Fd Amb	KIA	14.5.43	37	Sydney War Mem, Rookwood, NSW, P1
Sharp, W.	Paddington, NSW	2/18 Bn	DPOW	1.4.45	22	Labuan War Mem Cem, Brunei Bay, Malaysia, P11
Shemberg, H.	Szczugzyn, Poland	37/52 Bn	DOW	10.12.43	21	Lae War Cem, PNG, T.D.7
Shmith, R.A.	Melbourne, Vic	2/12 Fd Regt	KIA	15.6.41	21	Tobruk War Cem, Libya, 4.A.7
Silverman, H.N.	Fitzroy, Vic	Hvy Bty	KIA	30.1.42	31	Rabaul (Bita Paka) War Mem Cem, PNG, P31
Solomon, L.J.	Gundagai, NSW	28 Bde HQ	DOA	10.9.43	34	Newcastle (Sandgate) War Cem, NSW, E.C.10
Solonsch, S.	London, UK	105 GT Coy	DPOW	11.4.43	41	Jakarta (Ancol) Netherlands Field of Honour, Indonesia, II.100-101
Spero, M	London, UK	2 Grn Bn	DOI	27.8.44	54	Rookwood Cem, Sydney, NSW, J 11.21.33
Stolarski, C.D.	Warsaw, Poland	Admin HQ	DPOW	24.3.45	25	Labuan War Mem Cem, Brunei Bay, Malaysia, P8
Stone, J.E.	Arncliffe, NSW	8 Div HQ	DPOW	31.5.43	26	Thanbyuzayat War Cem, Mon State, Myanmar, A6.D.11
Victorsen, E.M.	Tarrieton, SA	21 Emp & Wks Co.	DOI	4.8.42	57	Muswellbrook General Cem, NSW, H.D.1
Weinstein, A.	Salisbury, UK	2/2 MG Bn	DOW	25.10.42	26	El Alamein War Mem Cem, Alamein, Egypt, AII.G.9
White, B.	South Yarra, Vic	4 A Tk Regt	DPOW	6.4.45	32	Labuan War Mem Cem, Brunei Bay, Malaysia, P1
Wolfson, N.	Sydney, NSW	55/53 Bn	KIA	7.12.42	21	Port Morsby (Bomana) War Cem, PNG, A5.C.25

ROYAL AUSTRALIAN AIR FORCE

NAME	POB	UNIT	MANNER	DOD	AGE	MEMORIAL
Alexander, D.S.	Waverley, NSW	466 Sqn	KIA	29.1.44	21	Berlin 1919–1945 War Cem, Germany, Coll 5.H.3-6
Alexander, J.A.	Cremorne, NSW	53 RAF	KIA	17.4.44	20	Runnymede Mem, Surrey, UK, P259
Bennett, A.	Perth, WA	148 RAF	KIA	5.8.44	29	Krakow Rakowicki Cem, Poland, Coll 1.D.6-7
Berghouse, R.	Newtown, NSW	11 Sqn	KIA	24.2.42	23	Rabaul Mem, PNG, P36
Brand, N.	Warsaw, Poland	102 RAF	KIA	24.7.44	25	Runnymede Mem, Surrey UK, P260
Chester, I.I.	Sefet, Israel	4 Tng School	DOA	21.7.43	20	Geraldton War Cem, WA, A.B.6.
Chester, L.H.	Richmond, Vic	31 Sqn	KIA	17.2.45	19	Ambon War Cem, Indonesia, 30.C.8.
Cohen, J.	Tel Aviv, Israel	160 RAF	KIA	22.9.43	21	Singapore Mem, Singapore, C429
Dent, H.I.C.	Brisbane, Qld	461 Sqn	KIA	21.1.43	21	Runnymede Mem, Surrey, UK, P187
Dyte, A.C.	Melbourne, Vic	1437 Flt RAF	KIA	31.8.42	21	El Alamein War Cem, Egypt, Coll A.IV.H.2
Fine, B.D.	Malvern, Vic	1654 RAF	DOA	27.5.44	20	Belcon Cem, Chester, UK, A.194
Flohm, L.W.	Perth, WA	460 Sqn	KIA	21.11.44	21	Durnbach War Cem, Bayern, Germany, 2.E.9
Frieze, B.S.	St Kilda, Vic	4 CF	DOA	5.3.45	23	Cairns Cem, Qld, A.C.18
Goldman, W.	Melbourne, Vic	458 Sqn	KIA	15.11.41	29	Runnymede Mem, Surrey, UK, P62
Gomes, L.C.	Paddington, NSW	172 RAF	KIA	29.9.43	20	Runnymede Mem, Surrey, UK, P192
Green, M.I.	Prahran, Vic	6 OTU	DOA	26.1.44	20	Nowra War Cem, NSW, B.B.8
Harlem, A.A.	Windsor, Vic	199 RAF	KIA	31.8.43	21	Eindhoven (Woensel) General Cem, Noord-Brabant, Netherlands, EE.104
Hoffman, A.D.L.	Melbourne, Vic	115 RAF	KIA	25.4.44	21	Heverlee War Cem, Leuven, Belgium, 5.E.9
Horne, A.E.	Sydney, NSW	408 RCAF	KIA	14.5.43	30	Flushing (Vlissingen) Northern Cem, Zeeland, Netherlands, D.32
Isaacs, G.H.	Windsor, NSW	103 RAF	KIA	7.7.43	21	Runnymede Mem, Surrey, UK, P193
Jacobs, D.	Marrickville, NSW	13 Sqn	KIA	23.4.42	24	Adelaide River War Cem, NT, P10
Jaques, F.A.	Balmain, NSW	18 RSU	DOA	18.1.45	22	Adelaide River War Cem, NT, D.D.1
Joseph, G.H.	Windsor, Vic	467 Sqn	KIA	17.6.43	25	Rheinberg War Cem, Nordrhein-Westfalen, Germany, Coll 3.B.6-14
Joseph, H.W.H.		5 FTS	DOA	17.12.40	24	Stoke-upon-Tern (St Peter Church Cem), Shropshire, UK, D.140

World War II, Royal Australian Air Force (cont.)

NAME	POB	UNIT	MANNER	DOD	AGE	MEMORIAL
Kan, A.E.	London, UK	460 Sqn	KIA	2.12.43	24	Berlin 1919–1945 War Cem, Germany, 8.K.8
Kimmel, F.G.	Vienna, Austria	RAAF HQ	DOA	2.10.45	20	Sydney War Cem, NSW, D.B.8
Klippel, J.O.	Turramurra, NSW	HQ Ferry C RAF	KIA	7.5.44	22	Runnymede Mem, Surrey, UK, P257
Levitus, S.	Sydney, NSW	460 Sqn	KIA	3.6.42	22	Runnymede Mem, Surrey, UK, P111
Malor, R.L.	Perth, WA	70 RAF	KIA	12.6.44	31	Sofia War Cem, Bulgaria, Coll 2.C.8-11
Myerson, P.	Sydney, NSW	408 RCAF	KIA	29.1.45	20	Durnbach War Cem, Bayern, Germany, 3.G.21
Opas, A.L.	Caulfield, Vic	108 RAF	KIA	12.8.42	21	El Alamein War Mem Cem, Alamein, Egypt, C266
Orbuck, L.D.	Melbourne, Vic	9 RAF	KIA	10.4.42	20	Rheinberg War Cem, Kam-Lintfort, Germany, 6.C.17
Oshlack, C.B.	Warsaw, Poland	1 ES	DOI	14.11.43	19	Springvale War Cem, Melbourne, Vic, 2.Q.A.14
Oshlack, J.	Warsaw, Poland	466 Sqn	KIA	3.6.44	27	Tourville-la-Campagne Communal Cem, France, Coll 4
Patkin, L.B.	Melbourne, Vic	467 Sqn	KIA	2.1.44	30	Hanover War Cem, Germany, 1.G.14
Pearce, W.E.	Sydney, NSW	261 RAF	KIA	9.4.42	23	Trincomalee War Cem, LKA, 2.E.13
Roden, J.H.	Clovelly, NSW	150 Sqn	KIA	20.9.42	21	Choloy War Cem, Meurthe-et-Moselle, France, Coll 2A.C.1-5
Rosalky, M.	Sydney, NSW	1 OTU	DOA	22.2.45	35	Sale War Cem, Vic, B.C.9
Rose, M.	Northcote, Vic	57 Sqn	KIA	8.7.44	21	St Maclou-de-Folleville Churchyard, Seine-Maritime, France, 9
Rosenberg, L.C.	Kalgoorlie, WA	1 EFTS	DOA	17.3.42	40	Adelaide (West Terrace) Cem, SA, Road 1s.34.37W.GRM/6
Saulwick, L.J.	New York, USA	467 Sqn	KIA	8.1.45	19	Runnymede Mem, Surrey, UK, P284
Schott, K.J.	Melbourne, Vic	467 Sqn	KIA	19.7.44	20	Brabant-le-Roi Churchyard, Meuse, France, 2
Shapir, M.W.	Melbourne, Vic	108 RAF	KIA	15.8.42	24	El Alamein War Mem Cem, Alamein, Egypt, C265
Shaw, R.	Tempe, NSW	450 Sqn	KIA	29.5.42	20	Knightsbridge War Cem, Acroma, Libya, 7.B.24
Simons, B.	Brisbane, Qld	2 STT	DOI	5.3.45	19	Woden Public Cem, Canberra, ACT, 4.0.4
Solomon, M.	Sydney, NSW	1404 Flt RAF	KIA	21.7.42	23	Plymouth Jewish Cem, Devon, UK, D.23
Wolfson, H.H.	Kensington, NSW	640 RAF	KIA	2.3.45	29	Heverlee War Cem, Vlaams-Brabant, Belgium, 10.A.8
Woolf, G.	Macksville, NSW	97 RAF	KIA	2.1.44	19	Rheinberg War Cem, Kamp Lintfort, Germany, 6.A.19
Woolf, H.	Meckering, WA	RAAF HQ	DOA	4.4.46	37	Springvale War Cem, Melbourne, Vic, 1 P.B.5

ROYAL AIR FORCE

NAME	POB	UNIT	MANNER	DOD	AGE	MEMORIAL
Cullen, R.N.	Newcastle, NSW	80 RAF	KIA	4.3.41	23	Tirana Park Mem Cem, Albania, SM E
Pincus, J.D.		602 RAF	KIA	19.7.44	22	Ranville War Cem, Ranville, Normandy, France, IX.C.10

MERCHANT NAVY

NAME	UNIT	MANNER	DOD	AGE	MEMORIAL
Rosen, H.J.	MV Macdhui	At sea	18.6.42	31	Port Moresby (Bomana) War Cem, PNG, B1.A.23
Rosen, J.L.	MV Neptuna	At sea	19.2.42	50	Northern Territory Mem, Darwin, NT, P12

Post–World War II

AUSTRALIAN ARMY

NAME	POB	UNIT	MANNER	DOD	AGE	MEMORIAL
Nathan, E.D.	Alexandria, Egypt	65 Bn	DOA	4.7.47	20	Yokohama War Cem, Hodogya Ward, Japan, Aus Sect C.A.7
Sher, G.M.	S Af	1 Cdo Regt	KIA	4.1.2009	30	Melbourne Chevra Kadisha Cem, Lyndhurst, Vic, 04.0.61

ROYAL AUSTRALIAN AIR FORCE

NAME	POB		MANNER	DOD	AGE	MEMORIAL
Adler, F.B.	UK		DOA	16.6.54	31	Lutwyche, Kedron, Qld, ANZ-8-10-34
Lester, P.J.	Melbourne, Vic		DOA	19.3.47	26	Yokohama War Cem, Hodogya Ward, Japan, C.A.5

Appendix 2:
Those who served

The following pages contain the names of 6798 Australian Jewish men and women who served in the Australian or Allied armed forces in the major conflicts from 1898 to 1945.

These lists were prepared by Russell Stern of the Australian Jewish Historical Society (AJHS) over many years of reviewing personnel records held in the National Archives of Australia and community records. Russell's review of Harold Boas' *Australian Jewry Book of Honour: The Great War 1914–1918* and Gerald Pynt's *Australian Jewry Book of Honour World War II* determined that some of those names did not qualify for inclusion here, while others needed to be added. Genealogical records also helped to determine whether some people who indicated they were not Jewish on their enlistment forms were in fact Jewish. Stern found almost 2000 more Jewish men and women than were listed in Pynt's book actually enlisted in World War Two. For background to the inclusion or omission of names, see Stern's three papers in the AJHS journal (Volume XXI, Part 4, 2014, p. 573; Volume XXII, Part 2, 2015, p. 211; third paper due June 2017). The AJHS welcomes any evidence of errors or omissions via its website: <www.ajhs.com.au>. Work on the lists is ongoing and more detailed versions are planned. It is not yet possible to scrutinise the records of all 1.5 million or so Australians who have served. In the future, such a review may add many more names to the lists.

- Some servicemen/women enlisted under an alias or married name: where known, their birth name is also given.
- A superscript 2 next to a name indicates the person enlisted twice; a 3 indicates three times.
- An asterisk next to a name means the person died on service; further details can be found in the Memorial Roll, beginning on page 360.
- Abbreviations for rank, unit and military honours can be found in the Australian War Memorial Glossary at <www.awm.gov.au/glossary/>.
- Only honours awarded during their military career are shown after names, with the exception of knighthoods which are designated as (Sir).
- For Boer War and World War One personnel, the unit with which they served is given – this is required with their service number for unique identification. For World War Two personnel, unit information has not been included; each person's number is unique, and personnel were often reassigned during their service.

Boer War

NAME	RANK	SERVICE NO.	UNIT
Aarons, Alfred			
Abraham, Cyril	Pte	921	1 Comwel Hor
Abrahams, Claude	Tpr	188	Bushveldt Carbineers
Ackerman, Laurence	Tpr	2632	3 NSW Imp Bushmen
Adler, Harry Mark	Tpr	429	Bushveldt Carbineers
Alexander, Eustace			
Alexander, J.J.	Pte/Tpr	29	1 SAMR; 2 SAMR; 6 Imp
Allen, Abraham James *	Sgt	86	SA LH
Allen, Philip	Cpl	49	1 WAMI; 5 WAMI
Allman, Daniel John	Tpr	44	5 Comwel Hor
Audat, Benjamin			Kitchener's Hor
Barnard, David L.	Tpr	199	1 Comwel Hor
Barnett, Maurice			Scottish Hor
Barnett, Samuel	Tpr	33	2 SAMR
Barnett, William	Tpr; Tpr	1123; 900	2 NSWMR; 3 NSW Imp Bushmen
Benjamin, Herbert Asher	Lt		5 Q Imp Bushmen
Bernstein, Harry (Burnstein)			Colesberg TG
Blumenthal, Herbert Edgar	Pte	327	6 WA
Braun, Benjamin Henry	Pte; Tpr	23	1 NSWMR; 3 NSW Imp Bushmen
Braun, Charles Lima	Sgt	153	1 NSWMR
Caines, Herbert	Lt		NSW ImpBushmen
Cohen, Ernest Henry	Tpr	1554	2 Imp LH
Cohen, Isidore Mark			SA LHR
Cohen, J.M.	Tpr	1752	SA LHR
Cohen, Leopold Wolfe	Dvr	1048	City Imp Volunteer Arty
Collins, Mark Frederick	L/Cpl	368	NSWMR
Davies, Frank	Lt		Rhodesian FF
Davies, Walter David (Karri) MID x 4	Col		Imp LH
Davis, Jacob John	Tpr	235	5 SA Cont
Davis, Mark	Pte	1254	5 VMR
De Pass, Ernest Simeon	Lt		11 Imp Yeo
Goldreich, Leisser			Cape Garrison Arty
Goldreich, Samuel J.	Cpl	141	Bethune's Mtd Inf
Goldring, Henry William	Sgt	316	NSW Imp Bushmen
Goldsmith, Douglas Eard	Tpr	538	6 SA Imp Cont
Goldsmith, Joseph Isaac	Pte	3055	2 Bn Rlway Pnr Regt
Goldspink, Leopold Michael	Tpr	851	2 Imp LH
Goldstein, Mark *	Tpr	728	Natal Carbineers
Harris, Samuel	Lt		2 WAMI
Hart, Alexander J.	Pte	265	NSWMR
Hart, Nathaniel	CSM	406	6 WAMI
Harte, Henry	Pte	366	6 WAMI
Herman, Lewis Cyril			
Himmelhoch, Samuel			SA LH
Hollander, Percy Eneyl	Pte	1267	NSW AMC
Ikin, James Edison	Tpr	9571	Kitchener's Hor
Joseph, Joseph Ernest			4 Qld Imp Bushmen
Joseph, Louis	Pte	1883	Mtd Sect Rlway Pnr Regt
Kensell, Isaac John	Tpr	26805	Robert's Hor
Kensell, Samuel Sampson	Tpr	1560	Bethune's Mtd Inf
Kohn, Charles Henry	Tpr	265	1 Comwel Hor (NSW)
Levi, John James *	Pte		Capetown Highlanders
Levy, Myer	Pte	1271	Imp LI
Lewis, Hyman A.	Tpr	264	5 Comwel Hor (NSW)
Lissner, I.G.			5 QMI
Loel, Bertram Benjamin	Vet Lt		2 Comwel Hor
Marks, Alfred Henry (Marsh) *	Tpr		2 Scottish Hor
Marks, Bertie			
Marks, J.C.			Imp LH
Marks, J.L.	Lt		
Menser, Leslie Maurice			Aust Bushmen
Menser, Louis	Tpr	536	3 NSW Imp Bushmen
Meyer, Ernest			3 Regt NSWMR
Moses, Herbert Charles			
Moses, Herbert Lamert	Cpl; Tpr	4494	Kitchener's Hor
Moses, Moss	Pte	7071	9 NZ
Moss, Aubrey	Tpr	3223	3 NSW Imp Bushmen
Moss, Michael George	Pte	49	NSWMR
Phillips, Fennel (Horace)	Pte	985	5 VMR
Phillips, Louis Eleazar	Pte	721	Cameron's Scouts 3 Aust Bushmen
Phillips, Woolf			Paymaster's Office Rosebank Camp Capetown
Pollock, Samuel	Pte	1460	5 VMR
Posner, Michael	Tpr	27130	J'burg MR
Raphael, Ralph	Tpr	266	1 Comwel Hor (NSW)
Saunders, Alfred Solomon			5 V Imp Bushmen
Selby, Harold Isaac MID	Pte	444	NSW Imp Bushmen; Scottish Hor
Shappere, Henry Elijah (Harry)	Sgt	99830	BB Bty Royal Horse Artillery
Shappere, Rose MID	Nurse		Princess Christian ANSR
Simmons, Albert	Pte	1401	5 VMR
Sleeman, Morris	Tpr	251	B Bs H
Solomon, Bertram Marcus	Pte	45	4 WAMI
Solomon, Herbert *	Pte	266	5 WAMI
Solomon, Judah Moss	Tpr	850	2 NSWMR
Solomon, Solomon	Cpl	77	NSW Citizen Bushmen
Solomon, Sydney Meyer	Tpr	488	2 NSWMR
Solomon, Walter Samuel	Tpr		6 Aust Contingent
Tamworth, Lewis (Louis)	Lt		ImpYeo Montgomery Coy
Visbord, Jacob John			
Woolstein, Harry More (Wollstein)	Sgt; Maj		2/6 Q Imp Bushmen

World War I

ROYAL AUSTRALIAN NAVY

NAME	RANK	SERVICE NO.	NAME	RANK	SERVICE NO.
Abrahams, Abram	C/Sto	7085	Levy, Eric Leonard		2704
Applebaum, Abraham	AB	5455	Levy, Jack MBE	CPO	3296
Barnett, [?]	OS	1430	Levy, Phillip Solomon	CPOS	2265
Berman, Charles Maxwell		6168	Levy, Sydney Joseph	OS	4210
Collins, Harold Mark DSM	AB	3157	Lewis, John		1982
Gollant, Myer	Sto	1144	Lewis, Maurice George		2485
Hammel, W.	Smn		Lewis, Mautz	Boy	6411
Harris, S.			Marks, Arthur Lewis Philip	AB	6871
Hart, Frank	Sto	760	Marks, Harold Lindsay	OS	6380
Horwitz, Henri	L/Teleg	3496	Moss, Eric Elias	AB	4727
Hough, [?]	PO		Myer, S.	AB	
Jacobs, William Walter	AB	5794	Perlstein, Leslie	WOM	411
Justice, Roy David *	Sto	3537	Rosenberg, S.	AB	
Komkomer, Emanuel	Sto	337	Rosenbloom, Victor Percy		2559
Lazarus, Myer	Smn	4263	Solomon, Louis	Boy	5411

AUSTRALIAN ARMY

NAME	RANK	SERVICE NO.	UNIT	NAME	RANK	SERVICE NO.	UNIT
Aarons, Daniel (Sir) Sidney MC & Bar	Capt		16 Bn	Allen, Bertie Horace	Pte	2619	60 Bn
Aarons, John Fullarton *	Pte	2868	16 Bn	Allen, Sydney Herbert	Capt		2 AGH
Aarons, Leslie	Pte	13251	14 Fd Amb	Alman, Israel Albert	Pte	2776	44 Bn
Aarons, Maurice Lewis *	Pte	2281	16 Bn	Altman, Samuel	Pte	6953	14 Bn
Aarons, Theodore Harold (Ashton)	Lt		3 MG Bn	Altson, David	Lt FO	10797	3 Sqn AFC
Aarons, Vincent	A/Sgt	16210	ASC	Ansell, Herbert Abraham *	2/Lt		29 Bn; 8 MG Coy
Abelson, Coleman *	Pte	2026	43 Bn	Appel, Jack	Pte	2553	13 Bn
Abraham, Walter Shachtel	Dvr	14962	ASC	Aronson, Malcolm Phillip	S/Sgt	5479; 3	Admin HQ
Abrahamovitch, Henry George	Pte	V76268	11 AGH	Aschman, Robert	Pte	4429	50 Bn
Abrahams, Benjamin	Pte	4356	2 Bn	Ash, Clive	Pte	4495	29 Bn; 5 MG Bn
Abrahams, Hyam	Tpr	1992	2 RMT Unit	Ash, Sydney	Pte	4494	29 Bn
Abrahams, John	Dvr	33941	5 DAC	Asher, Felix	Pte	1874	DAP
Abrahams, Leon Joseph	Pte	65703	3 Bn	Asher, Harold	Pte	607	9 Bn
Abrahams, Louis	Tpr	205	1 RMT Unit	Asher, John	Pte	1776	1 Bn
Abrahams, Louis Henry	Dvr	11633	28 ASC	Asher, John Henry *	Lt		4 Div Arty
Abrahams, Manuel (Emanuel)	Pte	3103A	45 Bn	Asher, Rudolph	S/Sgt	16778	AMC
Abrahams, Robert William	Pte	7073	1 Bn	Asher, Samuel *	Pte	2149	36 Bn
Abrahams, Samuel Victor	Pte	468	13 Bn	Audet, Lewis	Spr	22299	14 Fd Coy
Abramam, Leo	Pte	5646	5 Bn	Balkind, John	Pte	4943	4 Pnr
Abramovitz, Alexander	Pte	60586	27 Bn	Bannet, Nathaniel	Cpl	3362	4 Div Sig
Abromovitz, Alexander (Abrams, Henry Albert)	Pte	60586	ASC	Barcan, Hyman	Pte	113	2 Tropical
Adelson, Israel Arthur[2]	Pte; Spr	4984	32 Bn; 27 Bn	Barfield, Leopold Powell Warschauer	Pte	713A	34 Bn
Ades, Simon Albert *	Lt	3168	35 Bn	Barmes, Frank Mark	Gnr	1747A	11 FAB
Afriat, Albert Montefiore	Pte	258	2 Fd Amb; AMC	Barnard, George Jessel	Gnr	71585	APC
Alexander, Clive Reginald	Capt		AMC	Barnard, Lancelot Lee	Sgt	495	27 Bn
Alexander, Elias Bernard	Cpl	7843	AGH; AMC	Barnard, Sydney Harry *	Pte	6762	27 Bn; 48 Bn
Alexander, Isaac Solomon	S/Sgt	3020	Den Corps	Barnes, David (Barmes) *	Gnr	1748	11 FAB
Alexander, Isaac Solomon	Pte	61345	GSG	Barnett, Arthur Montague	Pte	1609	ANMEF
Alexander, Jessel Alexander MSM	ER/WO1	2872	17 Bn; Admin HQ	Barnett, Charles	Pte	5339	45 Bn
Alexander, Louis	Spr	2700	7 FCE	Barnett, David	Pte	6767	24 Bn
Alexander, Maurice Mark	Pte	3847	51 Bn	Barnett, Frank Jessell	Pte	5036	7 Bn
Alexander, Nathan Marcus Adler	Maj		AMC (Samoa)	Barnett, Frederick Cecil	MTD	30221	FAB
Alexander, Raphael David	Pte	1938	36 Bn; 34 Bn	Barnett, Jacob Leon	Pte	1042	30 Bn
				Barnett, Lewis Isaac	Pte	20	1 RMT Unit

World War I, Australian Army (cont.)

NAME	RANK	SERVICE NO.	UNIT
Barnett, Maurice	Tpr	6476; 6712	5 Bn
Barnett, Max Morris **MID MSM**	S/Sgt	4134	1 Pnr
Barnett, Phillip Aaron	SS Sgt	6536	4 FAB
Barnett, Reginald	T/Capt		5 DAC
Barrington, Lewis Harold	Pte	11	13 Bn
Barrkman, Harry	Pte	3231	14 Bn
Bass, Louis	Pte	2417A	34 Bn
Basser, Maurice	Pte	5979	19 Bn
Baumberg, Byron	Pte	2730	ICC; Pro Corps
Beaconsfield, Angel	Pte	19829	AMC
Beaver, Wilfred Norman *	Lt		60 Bn
Behrend, Oscar	Capt		Den Corps
Belfort, Alexander Eisy	Pte	58187	
Belkind, Ishai	Pte	14985	FCE
Bell, Isaak	Spr	6768	21 Bn; 5 Bn
Bell, Myer	Tpr	3386	8 LH
Bellinson, Aaron	Pte	6766	22 Bn
Benarie, Mex	Pte	4886	28 Bn; 2 Div Sig
Benjamin, Alfred Joseph	Pte	65950	4 Bn
Benjamin, Alva	Capt		RAMC
Benjamin, Aubrey	Cpl	8819a	1 Bn; 20 ASC
Benjamin, Barnett	Cpl	2379	FCE; 20 ASC
Benjamin, Cyril	Sgt	2098	9 ASC
Benjamin, David Henry	Sgt	2795	55 Bn; APC
Benjamin, Davis	Dvr	5403	ASC
Benjamin, Edward	Dvr	3002	AFC
Benjamin, Eric Louis	Gnr	8772	2 DAC; ASC
Benjamin, Ernest **MM**	L/Sgt	171	2 Pnr
Benjamin, Frank (Lenneberg)	Pte	2575	18 Bn
Benjamin, Lawrence	Lt FO	522; 9150	69 Sqn; AFC
Benjamin, Lewis	Pte	2321	5 Pnr
Benjamin, Mark	Spr	2224	Rlway Unit; Post Corps
Benjamin, Oswald Deronda	Pte	7978	6 FAB
Benjamin, Stanley Octavius *	Bdr	3959	4 FAB
Benjamin, Victor	Pte	20021	3 CCS
Benn, Jack Joshua	L/Cpl	1660	58 Bn; 57 Bn
Bennett, Gershon Berendt	Capt		Den Corps; AMC
Bennett, Miriam Adelaide	S/N		AANS
Bennett, Oscar	AM2	381	1Sqn; AFC
Bentwitch, Isidore Herbert	Pte	5972	35 Bn
Bentwitch, Solomon Barnet **MID**	ER/Sgt	1914	6 Bn; HQ AIF Deps in UK
Bercovitch, Maurice **MM & BAR**	Pte	5337	16 Bn
Berlinsky, Jack	Pte	2786	39 Bn
Bernard, Frank (Hershorn, Lesnie Bernard) *	Pte	1659A	19 Bn
Berner, Leslie	AM2	2980	AFC
Bernstein, Alexander Bernadth²	Pte	1620; 699	60 Bn; 29 Bn
Bernstein, Fairleigh	Cpl	5552	21 Bn; APC
Bernstein, Harry	Pte	501	23 Bn
Beth, Moses	Pte	3757	29 Bn
Bickart, David	Pte		AMC
Bickart, Joseph	Capt	9387	2 Fd Amb
Bier, Abraham	Pte	3356	57 Bn
Bier, Eli William	Sgt	9	67 Bn
Birnberg, Lionel	Sgt	6724	10 Bn
Bishop, Samuel *	Pte	1187	5 Bn
Black, Bernard	Tpr	N51047	7 LH
Black, Emanuel	Pte	1310	10 Bn
Black, Ernest	Pte	1516	10 Bn
Blaine, Cedric Norman	Pte	290	23 Bn
Blashki, Bertie Henry	CSM	33274	21 FAB
Blashki, Eric Phillip **MC**	Capt		RAMC
Blashki, Roy Hector * **MID**	Capt		14 FAB
Blaubaum, Athol	Capt		AMC Res
Blaubaum, F.J.	Capt		
Blaubaum, Ivan	Maj		2 AGH
Blaubaum, Otto	Lt	26212	AFA; Den Corps; AMC
Bloch, Felix Louis *	Gnr	34944	6 AFA
Bloch, Henry Scharrer	Gnr	8496	6 FAB
Bloom, Alfred	Pte	6723	11 Bn
Bloom, Arthur Arron	L/Cpl	2031	25 Bn
Bloom, Gerald Abraham	Gnr	28121	7 FAB
Bloom, Henry Montague	Spr	18861	3 LROC
Bloom, Julius Sydney *	Pte	1817	17 Bn
Bloustein, Herbert (Buxton, Herbert Morris) **MSM**	CQMS	614	5 Bn
Bloustein, Solomon	Pte	230	9 LH
Blume, Jack	Pte	3700	2 Bn
Boas, Harold	H/Lt		YMCA Rep
Bolgraaf, John Nathan		N86071	
Boock, Louis	Pte	N75002	AMC
Bortnoski, Louis Jacob	Pte	6217	AMC
Bortzell, Samuel		1140	17 Bn
Bowson, Abraham	Pte	7372	3 Bn
Bracey, David	Pte	1515	9 Bn
Braham, Algernon Charles	Cpl	5536	28 Bn
Braham, Marcus Phillip	Dvr	2460	5 Div Train
Braham, Roy Gilbert	Capt	W2690	Den Corps; AMC
Brahms, Herbert	Pte	2771	44 Bn
Brahms, Vivian	Pte	1879	42 Bn; 44 Bn
Brandt, Clement Alphonse	Pte	6924	23 Bn
Breitman, George * **MM**	Pte	4965	3 Bn
Bressler, Jack	Pte	3498	60 Bn
Britain, Samuel	Pte	314A	11 MG Coy
Brodsky, Hector Laurence	Pte	4372	24 Bn; APC
Brodsky, Louis	Pte	2957	23 Bn
Brodziak, Cecil Myer	Pte	12877	9 DUS
Brodziak, Cedric Errol Meyer * **DSO MID**	Maj		3 Bn; 3 MG Bn
Brodzky, Vivian	Pte	3109	37 Bn
Bromberg, Julius Maurice	Pte	6730	16 Bn
Broon, Hyman	Pte	9713	ADH
Brouwer, Jacob	Pte	57781	GS
Brown, Lewis	Pte	3687	13 Bn
Browne, Louis	Gnr	13034	2 DAC
Browne, Maurice Harold	Spr		Mining Corps
Browne, Roy George	Pte	370	AMTS
Browne, Sylvester Henry	SS Sgt	56	1 LH
Buchner, Hyman	Pte	5059	60 Bn
Burns, Richard Robert (Hickman)	Pte	6151	19 Bn
Buttel, Mark Albert	Pte	1030	13 Bn (POW)
Cahn, Frederick	Pte	844	18 Bn
Camp, Harry (McCarthy, Florance) *	Dvr	18848	FAB
Cantor, Adolph Conrad	Pte	5351	14 Bn
Cantor, Stanley Jacob	Capt		1 AGH
Caplan, Joe	ER/Cpl	6043	19 Bn; 3 Bn
Carey, Patrick Joseph	Sgt	1246	AVC
Caro, George Alfred	Pte	14028	3 CCS
Caro, Leslie	Pte	6727	7 Bn

NAME	RANK	SERVICE NO.	UNIT
Caro, Martin	Cpl	6058	APC
Caro, Phillip **MBE MID ×2**	Lt		1 Mining Corps
Carson, Arthur	Pte	18652	AMC
Chain, Isaac	Pte	5067	4 Bn
Cherry, Jack	Pte	3555	59 Bn
Clifford, Dudley Lionel	ER/Sgt	1290	2 ASH
Clifford, Leslie	Sgt	1211	16 Bn
Coevorden, Marcus	Pte	2452	1 Pnr
Cohen, Alexander *	Pte	6739	16 Bn
Cohen, Alfred	Pte	797A	29 Bn
Cohen, Alfred	Pte	1695	30 Bn
Cohen, Alfred	Pte	3128	48 Bn
Cohen, Alfred	Pte	6228	23 Bn
Cohen, Alfred Alexander	Pte	3280	6 Bn
Cohen, Alroy Maitland	Capt		4 Bn; 56 Bn
Cohen, Arthur	Pte	418	17 Bn
Cohen, Arthur Francis **MC MID**	Capt		2 Tun Coy
Cohen, Austin Lewis	Pte	5072	4 Bn
Cohen, Basil W.	Capt		RAMC
Cohen, Benjamin Charles	Pte	4087	19 Bn
Cohen, Bernard David	ER/SQMS	3025	Admin HQ
Cohen, Cecil	Pte	916	6 Bn
Cohen, Celian Lawrence	Cpl	20024	AMC
Cohen, Clive Phillip	Cpl	3027A	34 Bn
Cohen, Colyn Adrian Keith	Lt		33 Bn
Cohen, Cyril Wolf	S/Sgt	211	7 Bn
Cohen, David	Pte	3136	51 Bn; Aust Corps HQ
Cohen, David	Gnr	20920	8 FAB
Cohen, Eliot Tamworth	Sgt	2883	7 LH
Cohen, Ernest	Tpr	1721	7 LH; Post C
Cohen, Ernest	L/Cpl	16331	AMC
Cohen, Francis Lyon	Chap		
Cohen, Frank Joel	Pte	2637	33 Bn
Cohen, Frederick Leon	AM2	V75011	AFC
Cohen, Gabriel	Pte	62784	3 GSR
Cohen, George *	Pte	6300A	27 Bn; 28 Bn
Cohen, Gordon George	Pte	N25186; 3274	41 Bn
Cohen, Harley	Pte	37	4 Bn
Cohen, Harold	Dvr	54170	5 MT Coy
Cohen, Harold Edward **CMG DSO MID ×2**	Lt-Col		7 FAB
Cohen, Harold Francis	Capt		AE
Cohen, Henry	Pte	2359	9 Bn
Cohen, Henry	Cpl	3024	8 Bn
Cohen, Henry *	Pte	6540	19 Bn
Cohen, John	Pte	1333; 2212	6 Bn
Cohen, John	Art Cpl	1578	Div Am Park
Cohen, John *	L/Cpl	3500	23 Bn
Cohen, Joseph *	Pte	1630	59 Bn
Cohen, Joseph	Pte	5341; 5665	8 Bn; 59 Bn
Cohen, Joseph Alfred[2]	Pte; Spr	35; 5967	33 Bn; Tun Coy
Cohen, Joseph Henry	T/Sgt	397	14 Fd Amb
Cohen, Karl Morris **CdeG(B)**	Sgt	4153	6 FCE
Cohen, Leslie	Pte	2126	19 Bn; 22 Bn
Cohen, Leslie Albert[2]	Pte	3978	ANMEF; 20 Bn
Cohen, Lipman	Spr	3359	2 Div Sig
Cohen, Louis	Pte	69399	GSG
Cohen, Louis Jacob	L/Cpl	2346	20 Bn; 56 Bn
Cohen, Lyon Livingstone	Pte	216; 2546	1 Bn; 8 Bn
Cohen, Monty	Pte	1894	23 Bn
Cohen, Myer	Dvr	16795	AMC; 1 Div MT Coy
Cohen, Neville Kingsbury Purcell	Sgt	5324	19 Bn
Cohen, Norman Sidney	Cpl	1684	21 Bn; 24 Bn; 22 Bn
Cohen, Oram Edward Murray Purcell **MM**	2/Lt	29254	AMC; 117 How Bty; 12 FAB
Cohen, Percival Frederick	Pte	2500	19 Bn
Cohen, Russell Cecil	Pte	3711	8 Bn
Cohen, Samuel Mendel	AM2	S14803	AFC
Cohen, Sidney	Cpl	276	4 MG Coy
Cohen, Sidney	Pte	2895	30 Bn
Cohen, Sydney Hubert	Gnr	34720	FAB
Cohen, Sydney Israel *	Pte	3378	55 Bn
Cohen, Sydney Lionel (Sydnie)	Lt	2392	55 Bn
Cohen, Vernon Henry	Cpl	5552	20 Bn
Cohen, Victor	Pte	3026	35 Bn
Cohen, Victor	Pte	6294	21 Bn
Cohen, Victor Joseph	L/Cpl	18198	AMC
Cohen, Victor Julius	Dvr	11201	3 Div MT Coy
Cohn, Charles (Cohen, Soloman) *	Pte	6476	4 Bn
Colley, Arthur Wellesley	Pte	477	44 Bn
Colley, Leon Edward	Col Sgt	158	3 ANMEF
Colley, Reuben Harold Woolf	Pte	6014	11 Bn
Collins, Arthur	Pte; Gnr	1594A	1 AGH; 14 FAB
Collins, Harold Emanuel **MSM**	WO2	619	Fd Amb; AFC
Collins, Solomon George	Pte	3044	4 Bn
Conroy, David (Levene, Abraham David) *	Pte	708	4 Bn
Cooper, Harry	Pte	3706	3 Bn; 8 Bn
Coopersmith, Hyman	Pte	6787	23 Bn
Copeland, Charles Louis (Van-Koppelen)	Pte	4082	22 Bn
Copeland, George	Pte	6240	6 Bn
Copeland, Norman	Dvr	12419	MT Coy
Coppel, Elias Godfrey	Pte; Gnr	7854	AGH; 2 DAC
Coppleson, Victor Marcus	Maj		4 Tropical
Corrall, Joseph	Pte	1904	21 Bn
Crawcour, Isaac	Pte	16661	AMC
Crawcour, Maurice Emanuel Ralph[2]	Gnr; T/Cpl	1183; 39732	2 FAB; Ord Corps
Crawcour, Samuel Lewis	Cpl	89	MG Sect 29 Bn
Crawcour, Sydney	Capt		AMC
Cromer, Samuel	Pte	6309	27 Bn
Crook, Louis	Pte	2622A	9 Bn
Croot, Alexander	Pte	6057	22 Bn
Cyfer, Harry	Pte	951	2 Bn
Da costa, Daniel	Pte	5670	8 Bn
Da costa, Isadore	Pte	32365	14 FAB
Dalmer, Frederick	Pte	4357a	35 Bn
Danglow, Jacob	Chap Maj		
Daniels, Mark	Pte	94249	Dep
Daniels, Sophia	S/N		AMC
David, Arthur Julius	Sgt	1964	15 Bn (POW)
Davids, Louis Edward	A/Bdr	180	1 FAB
Davis, Alexander *	Pte	3823	22 Bn
Davis, Augustine George[3]	Pte; Sgt; Pte	1179; 6851; 60113	17 Bn; GSR
Davis, Cedric Fernand	Pte	3044	33 Bn
Davis, Charles	S/Sgt	799	AMC
Davis, Charles Myer	Pte	6460	16 Bn
Davis, Clyde Isaac	Capt		AMC; 5 Fd Amb
Davis, Cyril	Pte	7832	1 Bn
Davis, Cyril Brasmoff	Pte	1870	4 LH

World War I, Australian Army (cont.)

NAME	RANK	SERVICE NO.	UNIT	NAME	RANK	SERVICE NO.	UNIT
Davis, Emanuel Percival *	Pte	774	11 Bn	Fernandez, Albert	Pte	6715	8 Fd Amb; 2 AGH
Davis, Ernest Edward	Pte	813	2 Mining Corps; 2 AMT Coy	Fernandez, Nathan (John) *	Pte	4789	45 Bn
Davis, Frank John	Cpl	20	1 AGH; 1 Fd Amb	Ferstat, Aaron	QMS	1997	16 Bn
Davis, Frederick David	MTD; Pte	935	36 Bn; 1 Cyc Bn	Ferstat, Abie	Dvr	20129	8 FAB
Davis, Gerald de Vahl	Sgt	19380	Sig Serv; 6 LH	Fine, Aaron Harry	Pte	3767	2 Bn
Davis, Israel	Spr	W14279	Tun Coy	Finebert, Emile	Pte	9101	AMC
Davis, Jacob Henry	Pte	5010	29 Bn	Fineman, Louis (Simmonds)	Pte	3456	58 Bn
Davis, Mark	Lt		17 Bn	Fink, Gordon *	Pte	674	16 Bn
Davis, Maurice	Pte	1089	14 Bn	Fink, Thorold	Gnr	33148	2 FAB; 10 FAB
Davis, Oscar Harry	Pte	4099	Cyc Bn	Finklestein, Harry *	Pte	540	20 Bn
Davis, Reuben	Pte	6072	9 Bn	Finn, Paul	Pte	1644	35 Bn
Davis, Reuben	Pte	6247	6 Bn	Fischer, Percy	Pte	5819	20 Bn
Davis, Vincent Stewart	Gnr	1463	36 HAG	Fisher, Henry	Pte	5269	31 Bn
Davis, William Emile	Capt		39 Bn	Flegeltaub, Amos	Spr	1002	1 Mining Corps
De Groen, Lyonal S.	Pte	3638	18 Bn	Flegeltaub, Bertram	Pte	1539	11 Bn; ICC
Deatker, Ernest Frederick	Pte	5817	25 Bn	Flegeltaub, Travers	Pte	2881	55 Bn; 14 Fd Amb
Defries, Hamlet Leopold	Gnr	76	36 SAB	Flesfadar, Julian	Pte	62805	AMC
Defries, Samuel Henry	Pte	362	56 Bn	Frances, Sindo	Pte	4807	29 Bn; AIF HQ
Degarviller, Emil	Pte	1630a	25 Bn; MT Coy	Frank, Ernest	Pte	676	1 Div Fd Bkry
Dennerstein, Alexander	Pte	260	37 Bn	Frankel, Alan Philip	ER/Cpl	382	4 Div Cyc Coy; 49 Bn
Dennerstein, William	Pte	14861	AMC	Frankel, Simie *	Cpl	2027	24 Bn
Dennison, Harry	Pte	7079	1 Bn	Frankenburg, Edward	Pte	4786	48 Bn
Detmold, Frederick Julius	Dvr	1645	8 A Bde; AFA	Freadman, Ernest	Cpl	14017	3 CCS
Diamond, Sidney **DCM**	Lt	926	6 Bn; 60 Bn	Freadman, Zavel Ephraim *	2/Lt		4 Sqn AFC
Dimdore, Samuel	Pte	9683	8 Fd Amb	Fredman, Henry Simeon	Pte	1218	14 Bn
Doniger, Harry	Pte	2912	30 Bn	Fredman, Leonard Walter[3]	Gnr; Pte	907; 86021	36 HAG; Spec Serv (Escort)
Doniger, Samuel	Pte	2687	15 Bn	Freedman, Abe *	Pte	7244	13 Bn
Dorfman, Wolf	Pte	4477	54 Bn (POW)	Freedman, David Isaac **MID**	Chap Maj		
Drewitt, George Edward	2/Lt	29	2 LH; 10 FAB	Freeman, Arthur	Pte	53020	41 Bn
Dubrulle, Emilienne	S/N		AMC (India)	Freeman, Mark	T/Cpl	2994	5 Fd Amb
Durlacher, Leslie Joseph *	Pte	2363	47 Bn	Freiman, Nathaniel Bernard (Freeman)	Lt	880	38 Bn; AFC
D'voretsky, Frank	Gnr	2571a	4 Div Arty	Friedlander, Barnett	Sgt	3501	53 Bn
Dymond, Lewis	Dvr	1021	1 LH; FCE	Friedlander, Wilfred John	Gnr	20956	10 FAB
Eckman, Ernest Wilfred Harold Joseph	Pte	1940; 2940	4 Bn	Friedman, Leslie Harold	Cpl	108	AMC; 5 FAB; ANZAC HQ; AFA
Eckman, Frank (Bede Joseph)	Tpr	4226	12 LH	Friedman, Donald (Harris, R.L.)	Dvr	594	1 BAC
Edwards, Alan Sydney	Pte	7	4 Bn	Fromer, Harry *	Pte	1504	24 Bn
Eilenberg, Emanuel Gordon	ER/Cpl	8117	2 AGH; 4 Fd Amb	Fryberg, Horace Hyman	Pte	2304	6 Bn
Ellis, Oswald Jacob	Capt		AMC; 14 Fd Amb	Fryberg, Louis **MM**	FO Pilot; 2/Lt	4490	7 Bn; 65 Bn; 30 Sqn AFC
Ellis, Victor Barnard	H/Cpl	53717	13 Bn	Fryberg, Phillip Blashki	Pte	V80206	GSG
Ellison, Hyman Hirch Norman	Gnr	29267	117 How Bty; 3 A FAB	Galland, Bernard Rupert	Sgt	7006	18 Bn
Ellitt, Simeon	Gnr	7576	5 FAB	Garcia, George Maurice	ER/Sgt	37551	10 FAB
Elsner, Hubert Clive	Pte	8140	ASC	Garcia, Joseph	Pte	65	5 Bn
Emanuel, Herbert Louis	Pte	8360	1 Fd Amb; 5 Fd Amb	Garcia, Lou	2/Lt	323	14 Bn
Emanuel, Reginald	Pte	21008	7 Sea Tpt Sect	Gensberg, Jacob	Pte	5461	23 Bn
Epstein, Mark	Pte	V29098	Citizens A	Gershen, Morris	Pte	7742	B Reception Camp
Esserman, Ernest	Dvr	26426	DAC	Gerson, Julius	Pte	19425	AMC Dtls
Ettingove, Samuel *	Gnr	V74029	Inf B Dep	Ghananburgh, Cyril Wilson	Pte	52292	40 Bn
Eve, Phillip Leonard	Pte	2433	9 Bn; 25 Bn	Gilbert, Mark	Dvr	8865	22 How Bde
Fader, Mervyn Abraham	Gnr	34739	FAB	Gild, Samuel	Sgt	4243	32 Bn
Farchy, Lazare	Cpl	1506	1 Bn	Ginsberg, Aaron	Pte	17535	AMC
Feldman, Israel	Pte	3158	51 Bn	Glance, Albert	Pte	3465	16 Bn
Feldt, Abraham	Pte	2163	56 Bn	Glance, Alfred Maurice	L/Cpl	2470A	29 Bn; MG Coy Dtls
Feldt, Israel	Pte	4113	19 Bn	Glass, Arthur	Pte	6175	23 Bn
Feldt, Mark	Pte	2164	56 Bn	Glasser, Hyman	Pte	387	40 Bn
Feldt, Samuel	Pte	3379	51 Bn	Glick, Harry Wolfe	Pte	6425	28 Bn
Fels, Schija	Pte	1126	13 Bn	Glick, Montague Barend	Pte	3976	51 Bn
Felt, David	Pte	3299	34 Bn				

NAME	RANK	SERVICE NO.	UNIT
Glover, Reuben	Pte	2058	33 Bn; 1 AGH
Gluck, Leopold Joel *	Pte	42	11 Bn
Goffin, Ben	Pte	5014	22 Bn
Goldberg, Alfred (Lewis)	Pte	4456	26 Bn
Goldberg, Benjamin	Pte	5103	14 Bn
Goldberg, Claude	Pte	118	39 Bn
Goldberg, Harry	Pte	50182	22 Bn
Goldberg, John	Pte	3055	36 Bn
Goldberg, Joseph	Pte	5591	22 Bn
Goldberg, Joseph	Pte	62312	27 Bn
Goldberg, Sidney (Godfrey)	Pte	21033	10 Sea Tpt Sect (Mental)
Golden, Robert	ART	10931	2 Am Sub Park
Goldenberg, Abraham	Pte	8867	5 Fd Amb
Goldenberg, Leon Shalman	Pte	2291	46 Bn
Goldman, Albert	Cpl	66	30 Bn
Goldman, Louis	Pte	1704	2 Pnr; DUS
Goldman, Victor Joseph	Pte	4421	17 Bn; 63 Bn
Goldring, Eric George	Lt		3 Bn
Goldring, Gordon *	Pte	140	15 Bn
Goldring, Harold William	Lt		3 Bn
Goldring, Leslie	S/Sgt	227	Div Arty; 3 Ech
Goldring, Roy Albert	Dvr	708	2 LH; 3 DAC
Goldsmid, Joseph Albert	Capt MO		AMC (Ayrshire)
Goldsmith, Henry **MC**	Capt		13 FAB
Goldsmith, Lionel Joseph	Pte	940	6 Bn
Goldstein, Aaron	Cpl	3118	8 Bn
Goldstein, Alexander	Maj		4 San Sect
Goldstein, Daniel Hopetoun (Golding)	H/Sgt	3746	54 Bn; 5 Div AVC
Goldstein, Emanuel	Pte	5025	30 Bn
Goldstein, Frank	Pte	6153	23 Bn
Goldstein, Leon[2]	Sig; Pte	1548	16 Bn; HQ (Claremont)
Goldstein, Louis Isaac (Goldie, John)	Capt	802	16 Bn
Goldstein, Percy Hirsch	Capt		17 Bn; 55 Bn
Goldstein, Phillip	2/Cpl	16565	1 Div Sig
Goldstein, Ralph	Pte	5338	21 Bn
Goldstine, Lewis	Pte	6249	9 Bn
Goldstone, Aaron *	L/Sgt	887	37 Bn
Goldwater, Nathaniel Isaac *	Cpl	333	4 Bn
Goodman, David Walter[2] *	Pte; CSM	32; 994; 4501	ANMEF; AMC; 4 Bn
Goodman, Isaac Bernard[2]	S/Sgt; Cpl	1384	ANMEF; APC
Goodman, Mark	Pte	2045	30 Bn
Goodrich, Arthur	Dvr	525	2 FAB
Gordon, Abraham Sidney	Pte	2828	13 Bn
Gordon, Leo	Pte	6080	18 Bn
Gordon, Samuel Louis	Bdr	10766	6 FAB
Gorfine, Samuel	Pte	2671	21 Bn
Gould, Bernard[2]	Pte; Spr	20469	50 Bn; 1 Sig Corps
Gould, Nat (Gold, Nathan)	Pte	53585	53 Bn
Granger, John	Pte	3173	39 Bn
Green, Israel	Pte	4223B	1 Pnr
Green, John	Gnr	16014	24 How Bde; 10 FAB
Green, Joseph	Pte	53582	56 Bn
Green, Louis Henry Samuel	Pte	2157	7 LTMB; 5 MG Bn
Green, Louis Horace	AM2	1902	AFC
Green, Matthew Sidney	Pte	5377	13 Bn; 1 Cyc Bn
Green, Samuel	Sgt	3291	46 Bn
Green, Samuel Matthew	Pte	9609	Fd Amb
Green, Simon	Pte	3342	1 Pnr
Green, Solomon	Pte	4363	30 Bn
Greenbaum, Samuel Eric	Pte	3109	8 Bn
Greenberg, Harry	Lt	530	Sig Sqn
Greenberg, Isaac	Pte	4776	15 Bn
Greenberg, Joseph Samuel	Pte	415	19 Bn; 17 Bn
Greenberg, Leon Joseph	H/Capt		YMCA
Greenberg, Phillip	MTD	5829	22 Bn; 2 MT Coy
Greenberg, William	Pte	6057	23 Bn
Greenstein, Wolfe	Pte	60562	2 Bn
Greenwald, Samuel	Spr	6314	FCE; 4 Div Sig
Greif, Philip	Pte	7777	11 Bn
Grimish, Barney Bernard *	Cpl	1748A; 1761A	9 Bn
Grimish, Jacob Phillips	Pte	1139	9 Bn
Grimish, Joseph Jones	RQMS	3032	6 LH
Grimish, Leopold Julien	L/Cpl	9958	AMC; 3 AGH
Grinblat, Samuel	Cpl	275	HS Dtls
Groenewoud, Arthur	Pte	15806	2 Fd Amb
Gross, Alan Isidor	Pte		4 Dep Bn
Gross, Donald Alfred	Pte	21055	AMC; Sea Tpt Sect
Grouse, Reginald Charles *	T/Sgt	1827	36 Bn
Gubbay, Joseph Manasseh *	Pte	2308	36 Bn
Guinsberg, Alfred[2]	Pte; Pte	4649; 2019	23 Bn
Guss, Harry	Spr	21253	5 Sig Tp
Guss, Simon Joseph	Dvr	14173	32 ASC; Mtd Div
Haiff, Saul	Pte	3166	53 Bn
Haimson, David	Pte	563	23 Bn
Hains, Clarence Louis	Sgt	1136	9 LH
Hains, Harold Joseph	Pte	578	2 AGH
Hains, Ivan Coronel	Capt MO		AMC (Tpt)
Hains, Joel Morris	Tpr	1343	3 LH
Hains, Morris *	Pte	2150	3 Bn
Hains, Philip	ER/S/Sgt	14634	23 FAB; APC
Hallenstein, Dalbert Isaac Morris *	Lt		5 Bn; 5 MG Bn
Hamburger, Simon (Hamilton)	Cpl	62	38 Bn
Hammell, Wilton	Pte	14561	ASC; APC
Hansford, William Aaron	Pte	69386	GSG
Hansman, Edgar Emanuel *	AM2	883	4 Sqn AFC
Hansman, Hyam Joseph *	Pte	2578	37 Bn
Harbert, Gershun *	Pte	2173	4 Bn; 59 Bn
Harlap, Lion	Tpr	1098	10 LH; Pro Corps
Harlem, Bertram Julius **MM**	Pte	6825	21 Bn; 6 Bn
Harlem, David Emanuel	AM2	2707	AFC
Harlem, Ellis	Spr	2611	60 Bn; 5 Div Sig
Harlem, Julius David	Pte	19850	Sea Tpt Sect
Harris, Abraham	Pte	3406	59 Bn; 3 FAB
Harris, Benjamin	Cpl	6604	8 Fd Amb
Harris, Bernard Maurice	Pte	1592	1 AGH
Harris, Charles David	Pte	13789	AMC
Harris, Charles Montagu *	Capt		RAMC; 7 Bn RSF
Harris, Desmond David	L/Cpl	7226	2 FCE
Harris, Edgar Owen	Dvr	15	4 LH; DSC
Harris, Ernest Lionel	Pte	4140	18 Bn
Harris, Frank Alan	Gnr	39344	AFA
Harris, Herbert Jacob	Spr	2954	6 LH; 2 Sig Trp
Harris, Jack Eugene	Pte	67400	GSR
Harris, Joel Marks	2/Lt	35040	AFC
Harris, Joseph	Pte	4799	43 Bn
Harris, Laurence Levi (Herschel) *	Maj		3 AGH

Jewish Anzacs

World War I, Australian Army (cont.)

NAME	RANK	SERVICE NO.	UNIT
Harris, Louis	Pte	4454	22 Bn
Harris, Michael	Pte	18426	AMC
Harris, Phillip Lawrence	Lt	1375	ASC; 23 Bn
Harris, Reginald Lewis	Pte	3372	49 Bn
Harris, William Keith	Bdr	4811	1 FAB; 1 DAC
Hart, Cecil Hubert Aaron[2] *	Cpl; Sgt	310; 1943	ANMEF; 18 Bn
Hart, Harry	ER/Cpl	2785	58 Bn
Hart, Harry	Pte	14324	AMC Dtls; 1 AAH
Hart, Harry Julian	Pte	1227	17 Bn
Hart, Henry *	L/Cpl	1354	7 Bn
Hart, Henry Louis	Spr	2715	7 FCE
Hart, Joel Henry	A/Sgt	6582	AMC Dtls
Hart, John *	Pte	6465	7 Bn
Hart, Joseph *	Pte	190	30 Bn
Hart, Joseph	Pte	3131	28 Bn
Hart, Leslie *	L/Cpl	267	7 Bn
Hart, Lionel	Pte	3104	57 Bn
Hart, Maurice	Pte	1946	60 Bn
Hatfield, Albert Victor	2/Lt		46 Bn
Hatfield, Edward Kozminky	Lt		60 Bn
Henlein, Max Basil	Pte	6265	9 Bn
Henry, Alan	Capt		14 Bn; 39 Bn
Herman, Albert Ernest	Pte	16165	4 Fd Amb
Herman, Eric	Pte	1770	7 Bn; 4 Div HQ
Herman, Harold Ellis *	Pte	1706	17 Bn
Herman, Joseph	Pte	3800	4 Div HQ
Herman, Louis Cyril	L/Sgt	8072	18 ASC; 5 Div Train
Herman, Maurice Phillip *	Pte	4370	30 Bn
Hickman, Leonard	Pte	400	2 Pnr
Hielman, Harold	T/Cpl	2617	AFC
Hielman, Norman Nathan	L/Cpl	2635	4 Bn
Hielman, Randolph	Pte	4138	19 Bn
Higson, Ebenezer Thomas[2]	Tpr	75; 2648	7 LH
Himmelhoch, Albert	Gnr	17115	1 FAB
Hines, Mark George[2]	Pte	47	15 Bn; 31 Bn
Hoffman, Wolfe	Pte	2224	16 Bn; 9 Fd Amb
Hojein, Lauritz (Hojem) *	Pte	268	16 Bn
Honey, Samuel	Gnr	10652	AMC; FAB
Honig, Max	Pte	3551	
Horwitz, Harry	Pte	313	1 Bn
Horwitz, Myer	2/Lt	7281	11 Bn
Humberta, Abe Harris	Gnr	30925	TMB
Humberta, Jud Harris	Gnr	16053	AMC; FAB
Hussies, Walter Robert	Spr	6625	6 Fd Coy; 21 Bn
Hyams, William *	Pte	5359	24 Bn
Hyland, Alfred	Pte	4519	14 Bn
Hyman, Arthur Wellesley OBE MID ×2	Maj		7 LH; 51 Bn
Hyman, Eric Montague DSO MID	Maj		12 LH
Hyman, Herbert	Pte	2190	21 Bn
Hyman, Joseph MSM	Dvr	3925	14 FAB
Ikin, James Edison[2]	Gnr; Pte	2453; 14904	DAC; 1 FAB; ASC
Illfeld, Julius *	Pte	5666	20 Bn
Ipp, Joe	Dvr	2315	13 LH; 1 FAB
Isaacs, Aubrey	Pte	6337	19 Bn
Isaacs, David Joseph MSM	T/RQMS	505	MG Bn
Isaacs, Laurence David	ER/Sgt	2828	Admin HQ
Isaacs, Leopold Edgar	T/Cpl	3626	40 Bn

NAME	RANK	SERVICE NO.	UNIT
Isaacs, Morris Myer (Jackson, Charles Morris) *	Gnr	31011	10 FAB
Isaacs, Myer Joseph	Spr	1288	1 Mining Corps; 3 Tun Coy
Isaacs, Nellie	S/N		AMC; ANS
Isaacs, Phillip	Pte	3655	32 Bn
Isaacs, Robert Leo[2]	MTD	7264; 7514	14 Bn; 4 LTMB
Isaacs, Samuel	L/Cpl	4838	7 Bn
Isaacs, William Woolf *	Sgt	4138	22 Bn
Isaacson, Arnold	Lt	5488	4 Div Train
Isaacson, Isidor[2]	Maj		3 Div Train; Spec Serv (POW Guard)
Isen, Bennett	Dvr	14402	ASC
Israel, Alec *	Pte	3076	33 Bn
Israel, Arthur Charles	Pte	1351	2 Bn
Israel, Gershon	Gnr	867	36 HAG
Israel, Henry DCM	Lt	2543	6 Bn
Israel, Leslie Phillip	Lt	W2409	19 Bn
Israel, Louis Mark Cynal	Spr	22649	4 Div Sig Coy
Israel, Morris Samuel MM MID	2/Cpl	595	3 Sig
Israel, Norman Joseph	Sgt	2389	6 Bn; 58 Bn
Israel, Reuben	ER/Cpl	2936	50 Bn
Jacks, Abraham*	Pte	3387	49 Bn
Jacobs, Arthur Abraham (Adrien) *	Sgt	66	10 Bn
Jacobs, Charles Arthur	Cpl	6378	4 Div MT Coy
Jacobs, Charles John	Lt		21 Bn
Jacobs, Charles Norman	Gnr	26762	1 DAC; 14 FAB
Jacobs, David	L/Cpl	4359	27 Bn; 5 Fd Amb
Jacobs, Emmanuel (Martin Edward)	Pte	4807	32 Bn; 50 Bn
Jacobs, Frederick Mitchell	Pte	15343	Aust Corps HQ
Jacobs, Harold MID	Maj		1 Bn; 61 Bn
Jacobs, Harold Leslie MC	Lt		FAB
Jacobs, Henry (Kalamaski) *	L/Cpl	155	15 Bn
Jacobs, Herbert	Pte	1685	16 Bn
Jacobs, Herbert Sydney[2]	H/Capt		AMC
Jacobs, Lionel	CQMS	7853	10 ASC; 1 Cyc Bn
Jacobs, Louis William *	Pte	1772	7 Bn
Jacobs, Mark	Pte	2286	22 Bn
Jacobs, Montague Melbourne	Tpr	2363	10 LH
Jacobs, Solomon (Sullivan) William	Pte	3225A/6525	10 Bn
Jacobs, Sydney	Dvr	13438	2 DSC
Jacobson, Albert Edward	Dvr	833	44 Bn
Jacobson, Albert Henry	L/Cpl	25	1 LH; ASC Dtls
Jacobson, Louis	L/Cpl	3718	18 Bn
Jennings, William	Spr	1945	2 FCE
Joachim, Lewis Maurice	Pte	4747	53 Bn
Joel, Sidney Isaac *	Pte	1837	34 Bn
Jonas, Benjamin *	Cpl	225	Admin HQ
Jonas, Hyam Emanuel	Pte	60466	2 Bn
Jones, Albert Cosman	Pte	48	1 FAB
Jones, Benjamin George	L/Cpl	14262	DAP
Jonsen, Otto Carl MM	T/Cpl	8731	7 Fd Amb; GBD
Jonsen, William Sydney	Pte	8730	7 Fd Amb
Joseph, Albert	Dvr	2736	12 FAB
Joseph, Arthur	Pte	5	8 Bde HQ
Joseph, Benjamin Aaron	Pte	666	ASC; 65 Bn; DSC
Joseph, Coleman Henry MC MID ×2	Maj		4 Div Sig Coy
Joseph, Elias Frederick	Dvr	10629	ASC
Joseph, Francis	Dvr; Pte	1220	ASC Dtls; 17 Bn
Joseph, Frank Rintel	Pte	6399	17 Bn; 38 Bn

NAME	RANK	SERVICE NO.	UNIT
Joseph, George	Pte	2179	Dep Bn
Joseph, Herbert Lionel	Pte	3332	3 Bn
Joseph, Horace Mahratta	Pte	20051	Den Corps; AMC
Joseph, Isaac	Pte	8760	2 Fd Amb; 6 Fd Amb
Joseph, Joseph Davis DePass *	Pte	1055	31 Bn
Joseph, Lindsay Touv	T/Cpl	973	2 DAC
Joseph, Marks	Pte	6643	17 Bn
Joseph, Morris Cedric Clair	Pte	2794	58 Bn
Joseph, Sydney Alfred *	Pte	6522	7 Bn
Joseph, Walter Solomon	Gnr	24386	8 FAB
Josephson, Joseph	Pte	6758	1 Bn
Judell, Cedric	ER/S/Sgt	2392	50 Bn; 4 Fd Bkry; Admin HQ
Judell, Elias *	QMS	213	9 LH
Kalik, Louis	Pte	1783	18 LTMB
Karmel, Ellis Morris	Pte	7021	7 Bn
Katz, Samuel	Pte	48	13 Bn
Keesing, Gordon Samuel MID	Capt		FCE; 4 Div AE
Keesing, Herbert	Pte	1790	20 Bn
Keesing, Ross Alexander	Pte	2617	51 Bn
Keesing, Tobias	Tpr	2464	4 LH
Kersh, Abraham	Pte	54066	
Kessel, Izard DCM	Cpl	4450	1 Bn
Keysor, Leonard VC	Lt	958A	1 Bn; 42 Bn
King, Alfred	Lt	336	14 Bn
King, Frank	Pte	114	7 Bn
King, Thomas	L/Sgt	62	1 Fd Amb
Kino, Walter Philip	Gnr	38642	AFA
Kirk, Reuben	Pte	3529	8 Fd Amb
Kivovich, Yur (Carmichael, Victor Michael)	Pte	2690	Mtd Div
Klein, Joseph *	Pte	2133	26 Bn
Kloot, Phillip	Pte	3539	5 Bn
Kohn, Charles	Pte	3174A	67 Bn
Komesaroff, Peter	Pte	1684	56 Bn
Kopit, Abraham[2]	Cpl	3833	5 Bn; B Rec Corps
Kosky, Alfred	ER/Sgt	17349	AMC Dtls; Fd Amb
Kosky, Joseph John[2]	Pte	3937; 4465	16 Bn; 4 Pnr
Kosky, William Henry	L/Cpl	721	14 LH
Kott, Maxwell	ER/WO1	6460	APC; Admin HQ
Kotton, Moisey *	Pte	1235	LTMB; 4 Bn
Koty, George Herman	Pte	2109	40 Bn
Kozminsky, Clifford Samuel	Pte	19838	AMC
Kozminsky, Maurice Edward *	2/Lt	4649	7 Bn
Krantz, Albert	Pte	935	17 Bn
Krantz, Samuel Harold MM	L/Cpl	2281	43 Bn
Krausman, Nathan	Pte	463	3 Pnr
Kresner, Ernest (Emanuel)	Pte	19067	AMC
Kresner, Henry	Gnr	7714	5 FAB
Kriesman, John Howard *	Pte	4161	25 Bn
Krug, David Valentine *	Pte	978	44 Bn
Kunin, Gregory *	Pte	5043	22 Bn
Kurtz, David Mark	A/Sgt	11154	9 Fd Amb
Lakovsky, David (Lake)	Gnr	1304	36 HAG
Lampert, David	Pte	2176	5 Bn
Landes, Samuel	Pte	5661	AMC; 19 Bn
Landsler, Edwin Laurence *	Pte	3336	53 Bn
Langford, Louis	Pte	3836	59 Bn
Langley, Jacob Nathan	Gnr	31532	14 FAB
Langley, John Bernard Louis	Pte	718	18 Bn
Lasker, Robert Sydney *	A/Cpl	9959	2 AGH
Lawrence, Harold Sydney	Pte	56360	11 Bn
Lawrence, Keith Francis MM	Pte	6436	6 Fd Amb
Lawrence, Norman Isidore	Pte	2942	48 Bn
Lazarus, Alfred	Dvr	1892	4 LH; 4 MG Sqn
Lazarus, Arthur Moritz	Dvr	33305	1 DAC; 11 FAB
Lazarus, Edward Percy	Sgt	888	ANMEF
Lazarus, Isaac *	Pte	1578	7 Bn
Lazarus, Isaac	Pte	3904	58 Bn
Lazarus, Joseph	Pte	154	10 Bn
Lazarus, Maifred Philip	T/Sgt	1599	4 LH; APC
Lazarus, Myer	Gnr	2379	1 Pnr; FAB
Lazarus, Robert	Pte	3868	8 Bn
Lazarus, Samuel Clement	Pte	V74945	Dep
Lazarus, Samuel Emanuel	Pte	56358	11 Bn
Lazarus, Thomas Henry	Pte	2707	46 Bn
Lazarus, William	Pte	2351	38 Bn
Lazarus, Zadea	Sgt	31204	4 DAC; 11 FAB
Lazer, Henry Joseph *	Lt		33 Bn
Lazer, Lionel *	Pte	7531	25 Bn
Lazer, Simon Henry	Pte	723	6 Bn
Lebovitz, Elias	Dvr	908	28 Bn; ICC
Lebovich, Morris *	Pte	7002	2 Bn
Lee, David *	Pte	1275	14 Bn
Leedman, Charles Herbert Leopold MC & BAR	Capt		AMC
Leitner, Arthur	Pte	W16860	
Lenneberg, Frank Benjamin *	Pte	7264	16 Bn
Lenneberg, Harry Gordon	Pte	6383	22 Bn
Lentz, Leon	Pte	2828	34 Bn
Lenzer, Simeon	Pte	69290	GSG
Leven, Harry	Gnr	2706	4 DAC
Lever, Samuel	Pte	3549	4 Bn
Leveson, Robert (Levingston)	Pte	43	24 Bn
Leveson, Victor	Pte	1744	2/2 Pnr
Levy, Harold Hyman	Pte	4643	14 Bn
Levi, Herman Solomon	Cpl	22	AMC (Home Serv)
Levi, Keith Maurice * MID	Capt		1 AGH
Levi, Norman Leslie	MTD	14991	MT Coy
Levi, Rupert Nathaniel	2/Lt		23 Bn
Levin, Myer (Leleve)	Bdr	17279	TMB
Levinski, Jules	Pte	2927	14 Bn
Levinsohn, Harold Alexander	Pte	2707	17 Bn
Levinson, Benjamin	Pte	6342	25 Bn
Levoi, Joris Philip	L/Sgt	2850	59 Bn; 5 Pnr
Levy, Albert * MM	Sgt	505	39 Bn
Levy, Arthur	Pte	6349	13 Bn
Levy, Austin	MTD	1793	AFC
Levy, Cedric George	L/Cpl	1750	2 AGH
Levy, Charles Louis	Dvr	89	AMC
Levy, Clarence Henry	Pte	2904	2 Pnr
Levy, Coleman *	Pte	25562	55 Bn
Levy, David	Pte	7087	18 Bn
Levy, Douglas Alexander	Cpl	18892	1 FAB; 3 Bn
Levy, Edgar Wellington	Pte	5314	2 Sig Coy; Pnr
Levy, Elias *	Pte	4812	50 Bn
Levy, Frank	Maj		12 FAB
Levy, Frank Sidney *	L/Cpl	114	28 Bn; ICC
Levy, George	Pte	3980	28 Bn; 1 Pnr
Levy, George Newman *	Pte	7000	11 Bn
Levy, Godfrey Israel	ER/Sgt	1726	17 Bn

World War I, Australian Army (cont.)

NAME	RANK	SERVICE NO.	UNIT
Levy, Harold (Harry) *	Pte	7365	11 Bn
Levy, Harry Moss *	Pte	3531	8 Bn
Levy, Henry	Pte	6274	1 Bn
Levy, Herbert Abraham	Pte	3179	60 Bn
Levy, Jack Marks	ER/Cpl	174	Ord Corps; APC
Levy, Jacob Alfred	Pte	7995	16 Bn
Levy, Leon *	Pte	2209	56 Bn
Levy, Leonard Henry Jaques	Pte	7515	6 Bn
Levy, Lewis Lyons	Tpr	1491	4 LH; 2 Mtd REG
Levy, Lionel Harold *	Pte	2870	53 Bn
Levy, Louis	Pte	1141	3 Bn
Levy, Maurice	Pte	2349	6 LH
Levy, Michael	Pte	60243	1 Bn
Levy, Michael Samuel	L/Cpl	115	35 Bn
Levy, Reginald Michael	Spr	14344	1 Wrls Sqn
Levy, Reuben	S/Sgt	121	Den Corps; AMC
Levy, Roy Edward	Pte	752	MG Coy
Levy, Roy Leonard *	Pte	15535	3 Fd Amb
Levy, Sidney	Pte	2956	2 Pnr
Levy, Sidney Montefiore	Gnr	27041	13 FAB
Levy, Theodore Harold **MBE**	Capt	61	1 AGH Amb Dtls; Pro Corps
Lewis, Alfred (Goldberg)	Pte	4456	26 Bn
Lewis, Allan Maurice	Pte	1749	AGH; 6 Fd Amb
Lewis, Arthur	Pte	4527	49 Bn
Lewis, Arthur	Pte	18867	AMC
Lewis, Bernard	Pte	6581	17 Bn
Lewis, George	Pte	4575	25 Bn
Lewis, John	ER/2/Cpl	408	8 LH; ANZAC Police
Lewis, Julian	Pte	20043	AMC
Lewis, Louis	S/Sgt	14825	Sea Tpt Sect
Lewis, Mark **MM**	L/Cpl	77	1 Fd Amb
Lewis, Morris **MC**	Capt		44 Bn
Lewis, Norman Woodmancy	ER/S/Sgt	207	4 Bn; APC
Lewis, Reuben	Pte	6582	17 Bn
Lewis, Richard (Removitch, Morris)	Spr	424	1 Tun Coy
Lewis, Simon Henry	Pte	2627	60 Bn
Lewis, Verdi	Pte	3589	57 Bn
Liefman, Louis David	Dvr	147	14 Fd Amb
Liggi, Reginald Rachamim (Legge) *	Sig Sgt	7	10 LH
Lipert, Lewis	Pte	56103	DUS
Lipman, Alfred Emile	Pte	12632	11 Fd Amb
Lipman, Arthur Alfred	Lt		52 Bn
Lipman, Augustus	Dvr	13266	5 Div Sup Col
Lipman, Hyman	Pte	18654	AMC
Lipman, Leo Benjamin **MSM**	ER/WO1	948	3 Bn; Admin HQ
Lipman, Louis	Pte	7200	GSR
Lipman, Samuel	Pte	2608	33 Bn
Lipshut, David	Pte	2547	29 Bn
Lipshut, Louis	Lt		66 Bn
Lipstine, Eric John Simon	Tpr	3384	5 LH
Lissner, Hyman **MM**	L/Sgt	3282	1 Pnr
Littmann, Soloman * **MM**	Pte	2403	11 Bn; 51 Bn
Lobascher, Lewin David	2/Lt		32 Bn
Loewe, Luke Ormond	Pte	6340	26 Bn
Loewe, Sigismund *	Pte	4837	15 Bn
Loewenthal, Athol Vyvian	Pte	11283	ASC; 3 Div Train
Loffman, Phillip **MM**	Pte	3510	16 Bn
Luck, Sydney Ivor	L/Sgt	1148	1 ASH

NAME	RANK	SERVICE NO.	UNIT
Ludski, Ivan	Pte	6305	7 Bn
Lynes, Augustus *	Pte	259	18 Bn
Lyons, Benjamin Disraeli	Pte	17570	AMC
Lyons, John Thomas *	Pte	150	3 Bn
Lyons, Walter Maurice[2] **MSM**	L/Cpl; Pte	611; 1181	ANMEF; 33 Bn
Mackomel, Samuel (Muchomel)	Far Sgt	2052	4 DAC
Magnus, Benjamin Henry	Gnr	28418	3 DAC
Magodrick, David	Pte	4190	20 Bn; 62 Bn
Malatzky, Herbert	Pte	219	21 Bn; 7 MG Coy
Malatzky, Louis	Cpl	931	28 Bn; 7 MG Coy
Mandelson, Cyril Nathan	Gnr	3972	FAB
Mandelson, Henry	Pte	484	4 MG Coy; 8 Bn
Mandelzon, Harry *	Pte	658	28 Bn
Marcus, Reuben *	Pte	732	31 Bn
Margolin, Eliazar Lazar **DSO MID**	Maj		16 Bn
Marker, Henry Arthur	Pte	4418	1 Bn
Markowicz, Alfred Jan (Marr, De Topor)	Pte	350	3 Bn
Marks, Adelina	S/N		14 AGH
Marks, Alfred George *	L/Cpl	658	5 Bn
Marks, Asher	Pte	3756	51 Bn
Marks, Benjamin	Gnr	28	22 Bn; 5 FAB
Marks, Cecil Solomon	Pte	2681	2 Pnr
Marks, Cyril Moss	Pte	5729	58 Bn/Aust; Emp Coy
Marks, David	Gnr	V25838	FAB
Marks, Edward Percy	Pte	5633	6 Fd Amb; 16 Fd Amb
Marks, Emanuel Elias	Pte	6537	5 Bn; 1 Mob Vet Sect
Marks, George Moss	Sgt	2394	1 Bn
Marks, Herbert Edward	Cpl	8199	2 AGH
Marks, James George	Cpl	1128	28 Bn; AIF HQ
Marks, John	Pte	349	7 Bn
Marks, John Harris	Pte	3547	Pnr; Sig; 59 Bn
Marks, Lionel *	Cpl	210	1 Bn
Marks, Lionel Marcus Bernard *	L/Sgt	413	13 Bn
Marks, Marcus Leslie *	Pte	7888	1 Fd Amb
Marks, Maurice *	Pte	7099	35 Bn
Marks, Myer	Spr	1102	2 DSC
Marks, Raymond	AM2	1922	AFC
Marks, Reginald Harold	Dvr	49	LH Fd Amb; 1 Fd Amb
Marks, Reuben	Pte	3083	7 Bn
Marquis, Gordon *	Pte	1577	13 Bn
Marsden, Arthur Edward	S/Sgt	10440	AMC Dtls
Marx, Harold	Pte	2435	59 Bn
Marzan, William *	Pte	2873	33 Bn
Mayer, Robert	Pte	965	1 Bn
Mayer, Robert	Pte	6606	28 Bn
Meinrath, Julian Eric	Pte	3864	1 Pnr Bn
Mendelawitz, Abraham	Pte	4086	32 Bn
Mendelsohn, Berrol Lazar *	Lt		17 Bn; 55 Bn
Mendelsohn, Harris **MC**	Capt		AMC
Mendes, Alfred *	Pte	3972	49 Bn
Mendes, John Lewis	Pte	16336	2 HS (Kanowna)
Mendez, Isaac	Pte	3347	36 Bn
Mendoza, Clifford Lisle	Lt	2121	47 Bn
Mendoza, Howard Kingsley *	Lt		52 Bn
Menser, Leslie Maurice *	Sgt	2525	55 Bn
Mersky, Joseph	Pte	8146	Fld Bkry
Meyer, Cyril Bernard	Lt		13 Bn
Meyer, Reginald Victor	Pte	20561	AMC
Meyers, Errol Solomon	Maj		11 Fd Amb

Appendix 2: Those who served

NAME	RANK	SERVICE NO.	UNIT	NAME	RANK	SERVICE NO.	UNIT
Meyers, Leslie Hyam	Pte	2184	19 Bn	Myers, Lewis	Pte	2387	1 Bn Pnr
Michael, Cyril	Dvr	12807	ASC; 3 Div Train	Myers, Lewis	Pte	3157	25 Bn; B Reception Camp
Michael, Lewis	Pte	2924	58 Bn				
Michael, Norman B.	Dvr	12808	ASC	Myers, Mark *	Pte	3848	4 Bn
Michael, Reginald Samuel	Pte	69118	16 (V) Rfts	Myers, Ralph	Cpl	96	10 MG Coy
Michaelis, Frank Moritz *	Gnr	31586	FAB	Myslis, Henry Samuel	Pte	902	ASC; Pro Corps
Michaelson, Jack Frank	Pte	55507	6 Bn	Myslis, Moss	ER/2/Cpl	1044	Rlway Corps; APC
Michelly, Percy	Pte	836	7 Bn				
Michelson, Morris	Pte	4646	Corps Schools	Nable, Harry	Pte	7768	1 Bn
Middlemass, Andrew Rupert	ER/Sgt	3830	4 Bn; APC	Napthali, Walter	L/Sgt	12213	5 FAB
Milewski, Harold	Gnr	35645	1 FAB	Narr, Richard	Pte	13851	11 Fd Amb
Miller, Joseph *	Sgt	3984	21 Bn	Nathan, Alfred *	Pte	4909	8 Bn; 60 Bn
Millingen, Arthur Claude	Pte	1874	42 Inf Bn	Nathan, Arthur Joseph	A/Bdr	33159	2 FAB; 1 DAC
Millingen, Cedric MID	L/Sgt	1599	55 Bn AMC; 14 Fd Amb	Nathan, Bertram	S/Sgt	6553	4 FAB; AIF HQ
				Nathan, Edward	Pte	2829	34 Bn; 2 Bn
Millingen, Hubert Stanley	Pte	1688	14 Fd Amb; Admin HQ	Nathan, George Aaron	Pte	3410	4 Bn
Mills, John	Dvr	3184	60 Bn; 59 Bn	Nathan, Harold	Pte	3325	18 Bn
Minor, David *	Pte	6051	1 Bn	Nathan, Lewis	Pte	18323	AMC
Mirls, Arthur	Cpl	371	31 Bn	Nathan, Louis Percy	H/Capt		22 Bn
Mirls, Roy Lewis	Lt	3532	7 Fd Amb; 11 FAB	Nathan, Percival Montague	Pte	1809	2 Bn
				Nathan, Richard	Pte	2368	33 Bn
Mirls, Theodore	Pte	2179	2 Bn	Neal, Joseph	Pte	1505	2 Bn
Misch, Eric John	Pte	1690	ICC	Nelken, Ferdinand Adrian[2]	Pte; Cpl	6322; 261	7 Bn; B Rec Corps
Mitchell, Alan David *	Pte	1323	1 Bn				
Mitchell, Albert	Pte	671	24 Bn	Nelson, Arthur Percy	Vet Sgt	112	1 Vet Sect
Mitchell, Clive Harry	Spr	18588	3 LH; Sig Tp	Nelson, Clarence Leslie	QM; H/Capt	250	30 Bn; 5 Div Base Dep
Mitchell, Ernest Meyer	Lt	2042	1 MG Bn				
Mitchell, Karl Arthur	Tpr	64081	7 LH	Nemirovsky, Michael (Arnold)	MTD	4865	51 Bn; DSC; 3 MT Coy
Monash, Sir John GCMG KCB VD	Gen		4 Bde; 3 Div				
Morris, Alfred Levy	Pte	7118	14 Bn	Netter, Henry	Pte	725	43 Bn
Morris, Frank David	Sgt	2436	AMC	Neustadt, Julius Leonard	Sgt	1142	23 Bn; AIF HQ (Cairo)
Morris, Harry	Pte	4557	6 Bn				
Morris, Jack	Pte	3000	1 Pnr Bn	Nimenski, Coleman Frederick	Pte	9406	21 ASC
Morris, Lewis George	Pte	5307	AMC	Nimenski, Martin	Pte	11266	ASC Train; 13 DUS
Morris, Michael	L/Cpl	3547	8 Bn	Nimon, Joseph	L/Cpl	55	8 Bn
Morris, Roy Albert	Cpl	4352	27 Bn	Norman, Alfred (Marks) *	Sgt	1303A	4 Bn
Moses, Hamilton Leslie *	Cpl	497	44 Bn	Nyeman, Charles *	Pte	3882	8 Bn
Moses, Harry Ernest	Dvr	7438	15 ASC	Nyeman, George	Pte	3104	4 Pnr
Moss, Alexander	L/Cpl	1573	ASC	Nyman, Abraham[2] *	Pte	297; 7021	2 Bn
Moss, Alfred Michael	Pte	21025	1 HS	Nyman, Soloman	Pte	5400	24 Bn
Moss, Aubrey Moton	Capt	167	3 FAB; 2 Pnr; 41 Bn	Oberman, Edward	Pte	6090	11 Bn
				Opitz, Horace	Gnr	11881	FAB
Moss, Benjamin *	Pte	2471	47 Bn	Orbuck, Louis	Lt	1650	37 Bn
Moss, Edward Elias *	Pte	1585	4 Bn	Ormiston, Clifton	Cpl	782	39 Bn
Moss, Ephraim Henry	Pte	3107	39 Bn	Ormiston, Gerald	Bdr	7106	6 (A) Bde; FAB Am Col
Moss, Henry	Pte	7768	35 Bn				
Moss, John *	2/Lt		11 Bn	Ornstein, Phineas Samuel	H/Capt		39 Bn
Moss, Lewis	AM1	2397	AFC	Packer, Norman E. *	Capt		RAMC
Moss, Louis *	Pte	301	13 Bn	Pasvalsky, Louis (Walters) *	Pte	4872	51 Bn
Moss, Nathaniel	Spr	13667	Tun Coy	Payton, Frank	Pte	4200	28 Bn
Myer, Nahum	Lt	28342	2 FAB	Perlstein, Angelo	Bdr	6803	4 FAB
Myers, Abraham	Tpr	727	1 LH	Perlstein, Edward Phillip	Pte	69091	Spec Serv
Myers, Carlisle David	Tpr	302	6 LH; Pro Corps	Pertzel, Charles Alfred	Pte	65813	3 Bn
Myers, Edward Leonard (Lipman)	Pte	3881	1 Bn; 1 MT Coy	Pesmany, Thomas	Pte	12041	9 Fd Amb
Myers, Harry Malden	Gnr	54549	12 A Bde; AFA	Phillips, Arthur Herbert	Pte	6858	17 Bn
Myers, Henry Mark	Gnr	58605	AFA; 55 Bn	Phillips, Clive	Pte	3227	AMC Dtls
Myers, Isaac	Spr	21828	FCE	Phillips, David	Pte	245	MG Bn
Myers, Isaac Jack	Dvr	13176; V54178	1 Aux MT Coy	Phillips, David Abraham	Cpl	4758	20 Bn
Myers, Isaiah Myer	Pte	1148	5 Mob Vet Sect	Phillips, Elias Adrian	Lt		AFC; 34 Bn
Myers, Isaiah Myer	Pte	V20990	Permanent Guard	Phillips, Ernest Maurice	ART	15429	AMTS
				Phillips, Fennel	Sgt	2099	18 DUS
Myers, Joseph Lazarus	ER/2/Cpl	6519	4 Bn	Phillips, Jacob Nathan	Pte	91907	GSR
				Phillips, John Alfred MID	Lt	927	23 Bn; 7 Fd Amb

World War I, Australian Army (cont.)

NAME	RANK	SERVICE NO.	UNIT	NAME	RANK	SERVICE NO.	UNIT
Phillips, Max	Pte	1518	ANMEF	Rosengarten, Leopold Jubille Gersham	Lt	9495	6 FAB
Phillips, Morris **DCM**	Sgt	3103	56 Bn	Rosenthal(l), Jack Lewis	Tpr	2047	12 LH
Phillips, Moss	L/Cpl	623	18 Bn	Rosenthal, Jacob	Capt		RAMC
Phillips, Philip David **MM**	2/Cpl	22561	25 How Bde; 3 Sig Coy	Rosenthal, Joseph	Pte	10385	2 Fld Amb
Phillips, Samuel Isaac *	Pte	2016; 4959	7 Bn	Rosenthal, Morris	Pte	7780	51 Bn
Phillips, Sidney	Lt		6 LH	Rosenthal, Norman	Pte	12056	9 Fd Amb
Phillips, Walter	Pte	2898	1 Bn	Rosenthal, Samuel *	Lt		58 Bn
Pimentel, Morton Parker	Pte	15938	AMC	Rosenthal, Samuel	S/Sgt	116	11 Bn; APC
Pincus, Cecil	Dentist		AMC	Rosenthall, Arthur Kingston *	Pte	50	1 LH Fd Amb
Pincus, Frank Fabian	Pte	5427	ASC	Rosenwax, Charles Henry *	Pte	2236	19 Bn
Pincus, Paul	Dentist		AMC	Roth, Karl Chaskel*	Sgt (Dispenser)	537A	22 Bn; 4 Fd Amb
Pinto, Reuben	Pte	4443	48 Bn	Roth, Sydney	Dvr	530	59 Bn
Pirani, Carl Simeon *	Pte	218	16 Bn	Rothbaum, Harry Isaac	Pte	2442	4 MG Bn
Pirani, Ernest John *	Pte	3924	11 Bn	Rothbery, Harry	L/Cpl	7370	2 CCS
Pirani, Max Gabriel	Gnr	52466	6 FAB	Rothberg, Max	Spr	21859	FCE
Pizer, Edward *	Pte	5433	14 Bn	Rothstein, Jacob Solomon	Pte	W10313	Depot Coy
Platkin, Haim Samoilovich (Platt, Edward)	Gnr	37448	FAB	Rothstein, Morris	Gnr	3425	2 Pnr; 10 FAB
Pollock, Emanuel	Pte	2747	23 Bn	Rubinowich, Hyman Samuel	Pte	2128	8 Bn
Pollock, Lewis	Pte	4775	21 Bn	Rubinowich, Lewis Judah	Pte	18729	AMC
Preshner, Morris	Pte	2893	39 Bn	Ruschin, Leopold²	Pte	1132; 1389	14 Bn; ANMEF
Price, Harold Clyde	Lt	1151	6 LH	Russell, Phillip Henry *	Bugler	661	20 Bn
Proosov, Isaac (Pruss)	Pte	705	68 AFC	Saber, Alan Maurice	Pte	5414	21 Bn
Purcell-Cohen, Rupert Raphael *	Capt		ANMEF; 3 Bn	Saber, Kenneth Woolf²	ER/2/Cpl	6479; 1406	23 Bn; 14 Bn
Pyke, Clarence Abraham **MC MID**	Maj; DAAG			Sacklove, Barney	Pte	712	24 Bn
Pyke, Goodman Joel	Lt	336A	3 Div Train	Sacks, Bennett Solomon	Pte	3376	46 Bn
Rabinovitch, Bezelle *	Pte	1798	8 Bn; 59 Bn	Sacks, Simon (Charles) *	Spr	4341	13 Fd Coy
Rabinovitch, Eliezer Hurst *	Pte	17708	AMC; 9 Fd Amb	Saffar, Morris	Pte	132	51 Bn
Raphael, Fredrick Felix John *	Pte	1590	21 Bn	Salek, Louis	Pte	3154	4 FCE; 8 San Sect
Raphael, Harold Julian Wilberforce	Tpr	57014	GS	Salom, Bertram Philip	ER/Sgt	2736	Admin HQ
Raphael, Henry	Lt		Cyc Bn	Samins, Abe	Gnr	35587	6 FAB
Raphael, Keith Simeon	Dvr	13448	2 MT Coy	Samuel, Aubrey George	Pte	1132	1 FA Bde; ICC; ASC
Raphael, Phillip Morris²	Pte; L/Sgt	1644; 243	7 Bn; B Rec Corps	Samuel, Edward * **MID**	Pte	3911	59 Bn
Rapke, David	ART	7571	AMTS	Samuel, Rudolph Meyer	Pte	19078	AMC
Rappeport, Samuel	Pte	2659	43 Bn	Samuels, Harry	Pte	12728	ASC
Ribeiro, Michael *	L/Cpl	1617	4 Bn	Samuels, Louis **MC**	Gnr; Lt	11408	1 FAB
Rich, Vivian M. **CdeG**	Maj		RAMC	Sander, Cyril **MM**	Cpl	2640	33 Bn; 30 Bn
Richards, Clifford Sydney *	Cpl	18530	5 FAB	Sanders, Algernon Benjamin **MM**	Pte	7902	6 Fd Amb
Rischin, Harry	Bugler	6816	5 Bn; 67 Bn	Sanders, Frederic Roy	Pte	7901	6 Fd Amb
Rischin, Phillip	Pte	3001	Pnr Bde	Saphir, Abraham	Pte	2450	11 Bn
Robin, David Kalman *	Pte	2002	18 Bn	Sarfaty, Alfred	Spr	5022	1 Fd Coy
Rolbin, Harris *	Pte	1613	3 Bn	Satinover, Jacob	Cpl	2531	16 Bn; 48 Bn
Romain, Hyam Anidjar	T/CSM	6893	24 Bn	Saunders, Abe	Pte	6627	17 Bn
Rosebery, Sidney Solomon **MID**	Capt		RAMC	Saunders, Albert Barnett	Pte	147	7 Bn
Roseberg, Maurice	Spr	7541	AE & MM & B Coy	Saunders, Alfred Solomon	Cpl	35	3 LH
Roseman, Abraham	Pte	1328	37 Bn	Saunders, Harry	Cpl	1005	17 Bn
Roseman, Sydney	Spr	21128	Div Sig Coy	Saunders, Montifiore David	Pte	2630	44 Bn
Rosen, Joseph	Pte	6582	14 Bn	Saunders, Samuel Archie *	Sgt	6831	ASC; 14 MG Coy
Rosen, Morris Louis	Gnr	20104	8 FAB	Schneider, Abraham	Pte	1185	4 Bn
Rosenbaum, Dudley	ER/Cpl	3446	58 Bn	Schoenheimer, Rudolph Sydney	Sgt	1662	2 ASH; Con Dep; AMC
Rosenberg, Adolph	Dvr	2431	10 ASC; ASC Dtls; 5 Div Train	Schwartz, Harry	Pte	55220	GSG; 8 Bn
Rosenberg, Julius Myer **MM**	Pte	4737	2 Pnr	Scott, Henry Louis	Gnr	33065	10 FAB
Rosenberg, Mark *	Tpr	1678	7 LH	Seager, Frederick	Pte	1798	15 Bn
Rosenberg, Solomon	Pte	2868	6 Bn	Seeligson, Camillo Cyrus	Pte	2865	48 Bn
Rosenfeldt, Aaron (Rose, John) *	Pte	4449	48 Bn	Seeligson, Joseph Henry	Pte	4130	32 Bn
Rosenfield, Reuben Laman²	Maj		AMC	Seigel, William Wallace	Pte	3459	45 Bn
Rosengarten, Arnold Leslie	Pte	10244	AMC (Shoobra)	Selig, Maurice	Pte	5665	19 Bn; 3 BN
Rosengarten, Leopold	Pte	10241	AMC (Shoobra)	Selig, Oscar Moritz **MM**	Pte	3917	13 Bn
				Selig, Reginald Reuben	Gnr	21295	1 FAB

NAME	RANK	SERVICE NO.	UNIT
Shapir, Reuben	Pte	1053	8 Bn
Shapir, Reuben	Pte	3925	21 Bn; 24 Bn
Shappere, Cyril Solomon *	Lt		3 Bn
Sharp, Lewis	Pte	5763	13 Bn; GBD
Sharp, Samuel Sydney	Spr	19102	AE Dtls; 46 Bn
Sharp, William	Spr	1914	1st FCE
Sherick, Joseph	Pte	6880	28 Bn
Sherman, Godfrey John Thaman *	Pte	206	9 Bn
Sherman, Leslie *	Pte	5108	33 Bn
Shilony, Jack	Pte	19629	10 Fd Amb
Shinberg, Izzie	Pte	2139	29 Bn; 58 Bn
Shineberg, Hyman	Pte	4611	39 Bn
Shineberg, Samuel Albert	Pte	72008	Clerical Corps (Egypt)
Shmith, Arthur Herman	Dvr	16203	5 MT Coy
Shonthall, Isedore	Pte	7774	2 Bn
Shuter, Samuel Charles[2]	L/Cpl	377; 3646	14 Bn; 22 Bn; 58 Bn
Silberberg, Montefiore David	Capt		14 AGH
Silberthau, Henry	Pte	6311	1 Bn
Silberthau, Rudolph Samuel *	Pte	6312	1 Bn
Silver, Harold Ivan	Pte	2881	35 Bn
Silverman, Abraham *	Pte	2815	20 Bn
Silverman, Joseph *	Pte	1994	AMC
Silverman, Myer	Pte	1259	14 Bn
Silverston, Lewis Israel	2/Lt		28 Bn
Silverstone, Francis	Pte	6248	AMC Dtls
Silverstone, Neville Rothschild	Spr	63914	Wrls Tng School
Simberg, Abraham	Pte	645a	44 Bn
Simmons, Aubrey Mitchell	Cpl	14015	CCS
Simmons, Daniel Mendoza Brixton[3]	Pte	3979; N36470; 6152	3 Bn; 8 Bn; 26 Bn
Simmons, Elias Benjamin	Pte	3921	8 Bn
Simmons, Ernest **MM**	Pte	960	29 Bn
Simmons, Israel	Pte	4905	6 Bn; 57 Bn
Simmons, Leon	Pte	50157	22 Bn
Simmons, Norman Henry	Pte	1086	7 Bn
Simmons, Victor Ephraim	L/Cpl	12402	10 Fd Amb
Simon, Oscar *	Pte	105	9 Bn
Simons, Samuel[2]	Pte	566; 86102	13 Bn; Spec Serv (Escort)
Simons, Samuel	L/Cpl	2678	1 Pnr
Simonsen, Martin	Pte	1419	7 Bn; 14 Bn
Simonson, Eric Landon	Capt FO		14 Bn; AFC
Simonson, Paul William **OBE MID**	Capt	2247	22 Bn
Simpson, Benjamin	Pte	53555	54 Bn
Singer, Lewis	Pte	3432	3 Bn; 2 Bn
Singer, Samuel *	Pte	1621	2 Bn
Sloman, Louis	L/Cpl	558	18 Bn; 45 Bn
Smoishen, Abraham	Pte	14827	2 LH Fd Amb
Soeff, Samuel	Pte	3450	54 Bn
Solnick, Alexander Isidor	AM	50	AFC
Solnick, Ernest Lawrence *	Pte	1999	23 Bn
Solomon, Albert	Pte; Dvr	5641	20 Bn; 4 Div Sig
Solomon, Albert Yuba	Cpl	1096; 2902	16 Bn; 6/43 Bn
Solomon, Alfred Henry	Cpl	34830	FAB
Solomon, Edward Jack	Sgt	1203	10 Bn
Solomon, Emanuel	Gnr	11406	1 FAB
Solomon, Harold Isaac	Lt		25 Bn
Solomon, Harry Octavius	Pte	321	13 Bn
Solomon, Henry Abraham	Pte	16228	ASC
Solomon, Herbert John	Pte	94595	Depot

NAME	RANK	SERVICE NO.	UNIT
Solomon, John *	L/Cpl	1411	13 Bn
Solomon, Joseph Henry	Pte	1825	6 Bn
Solomon, Joseph Lionel	A/Sgt	6978	Tun Coy
Solomon, Lewis Victor (Louis)	L/Cpl	214	2 Fd Amb; AMC
Solomon, Melbourne	Gnr	31183	DAC
Solomon, Morris[2]	L/Cpl; Dvr	415; 1071	ANMEF; 4 Div Sig
Solomon, Morton *	Pte	1367	32 Bn
Solomon, Percy Montefiore[2]	Pte	1004; 86206	17 Bn; Spec Serv
Solomon, Sidney Gordon	L/Cpl	6101	27 Bn
Solomon, Sidney Norman	Sgt	1267	18 Bn
Solomon, Sydney	Pte	775	ANMEF
Solomon, Sydney John	Cpl	7101	10 Bn
Solomon, Victor	Dvr	15765	FCE
Solomons, Judah Henry	Sgt	304	4 Bn
Solomons, Leslie Emanuel	Spr	20831	ACS
Solomons, Maurice **MM**	Pte	3415	19 Bn
Solomons, Solomon	CQMS	976	21 Bn
Soltan, Harry	Pte	3947	2 Pnr Bn
Soltan, William	Pte	1810a	17 Bn; 2 Pnr Bn
Spanjer, Henry	WO1	418	1 Bn; A Ord Corps
Spear, Ernest Emanuel	Pte	239	1 Sqn; AFC
Spiegel, Jack	Pte	6566	15 Bn
Springer, Simon *	Pte	6884	19 Bn; 35 Bn
Stanton, Albert Henry	Spr	21370	5 LH Sig Tp
Steenbhom, Harold Moses	Pte	53556	AIF Dep
Steigrad, Max **MID**	T/CSM	7561	ASC; CTC
Stein, Peter	Pte	5107	29 Bn
Steinberg, Isadore *	Pte	2218	9 Bn
Steinberg, Laurence Solomon **MM**	Pte	2887	44 Bn
Stern, Bernard	2/Cpl	1848	8 ASC; 12 FAB
Stern, Jacob	Pte	2255	6 Bn
Stern, Norman Nathan	Pte	W16882	Depot
Sternberg, Alexander Barnet	Lt		Mail Censor's Office
Sternberg, Oscar Joel	Lt		3 Tun Coy
Sternberg, Simeon Herman	Cpl; WO2	7903; 2040	6 FAB; 6 Fd Amb; ANMEF
Sternheim, Alfred	Pte	2904	57 Bn
Susman, Harold Stainfeld	Lt		33 Bn
Sussman, Maurice	T/WO2	1240	6 LH; 3 FAB
Symonds, Hyman	Capt		AMC
Symons, Emanuel *	Pte	2371	22 Bn
Taylor, David	Pte	59601	GSR; 3 Bn
Thomas, Henry Lamert **MM**	A/Sgt	2466	30 Bn; 2 FAB
Thomas, Hubert Carl	ER/Sgt	6930	24 Bn
Thompson, Jack	Pte	21771	AMC
Thorley, Charles David	Pte	487	42 Bn
Tofler, Louis Judah **MC**	Lt		56 Bn; 53 Bn
Topal, Henry James Isaac	Pte; Cpl	404; 87892; 591	3rd Fd Amb; AMC; ANMEF
Tortsan, Max	Pte	3957; 6127	2 Bn; 1 Bn
Trager, Samuel	Pte	74967	ICC
Traub, Aron	Pte	54999	59 Bn
Trenn, Lionel Harold	Tpr	3317	1 LH
Treweeke, Lewis Cohen Hosking	Gnr	853	36 HAG
Trigger, Samuel	Dvr	909	4 ASC
Trigger, Samuel Winifred *	Pte	1750	50 Bn
Turner, Joseph Alexander	Pte	3894A	11 Bn
Van der Velde, Benjamin	Pte	3244	11 Bn; Post Corps
Van-Emden, Jacob	Pte	6897	19 Bn

Jewish Anzacs

World War I, Australian Army (cont.)

NAME	RANK	SERVICE NO.	UNIT	NAME	RANK	SERVICE NO.	UNIT
Van-Gelder, Sidney Joseph	Pte	3961	2 Bn	Weiss, Israel	Pte	3730	51 Bn
Vandenberg, Alfred Ernest	Dvr	5511	1 FAB	Weiss, Joseph	Pte	7091	16 Bn
Vandenberg, Joachim	Pte	5467	4 Bn	Wertheim, Jacob *	Pte	3491	56 Bn
Vernon, Michael Hyams	Pte; MTD	53826	13 Bn; MT Coy	White, Joseph (Solomon, Simon)	Pte	1106	2 LH Fd Amb; 10 Bn; 50 Bn
Victorsen, Albert Joseph	Spr; Dvr	85	3 Fd Coy	White, Morris *	Pte; Dvr; Pte	545	28 Bn; 51 Bn
Victorsen, Ernest Max[2]	Pte; Dvr	552; 5457	ANMEF; 1 LH Fd Amb; 5 Fd Amb	White, Roy	Pte	1136	21 Bn
Victorsen, Louis Charles	Pte	3641	6 Pnr	Whitfield, Charles Stanley Kalman * MSM	Sgt	1792	4 Bn
Victorsen, Talbot George	MTD	41	1 MT Coy	Wineberg, Harry	Pte	5470	16 Bn
Visbord, Jacob	Pte	2109	24 Bn	Wishman, David	Pte	58912	18 Bn; 24 Bn
Vurhaft, Joseph	Pte	6327	9 Bn	Wittner, Hyman *	A/Cpl	3963	22 Bn
Wachman, Abram	Sgt; Pte	66553; 86781	21 GSR	Wittner, Maurice Bertram	Pte	55012	59 Bn
Wachman, Robert *	Cpl	4451	16 Bn; 48 Bn	Wolff, Harry	Sgt	2898	Pro Corps
Wachman, Simon Daniel	Pte	826	44 Bn	Wolff, Percy Peter Allen	Pte	14853	AMC Dtls
Walters, Isidore (Roswalski)	Pte	6835	11 Bn	Wolfson, Heyman	Pte	221	32 Bn
Walters, Jack	Sgt	1066	32 Bn	Wolfson, Jacob	Pte; Gnr	53832	4 DAC
Walters, Philip MM	Sgt	6763	28 Bn	Wood, Gus Raymond	ER/Cpl; Pte	64901	Aust HQ (Egypt); 2 LH Bde HQ
Warner, Jack	MTD	13341	6 MT Coy	Woods, John Philip (Wadley)	Pte	3009	57 Bn
Wass, Henry John	Pte	7380	14 Bn	Woods, Louis *	Pte	4585	3 Bn
Watchman, Nathan	Pte	1881	6 Bn	Woolf, Samuel *	Pte	2226	9 Bn
Waxman, Clive Raymond MM	Sgt	3969	22 Bn	Woolf, Sidney	Pte	7337	14 Bn
Waxman, Ernest Cecil	L/Cpl	4250	21 Bn	Woolfe, Hyman Ellman MM	Pte; Dvr	300	59 Bn; 5 FAB
Waxman, Samuel	Pte	5905	24 Bn	Woolman, Simon	Pte	138	9 MG Coy
Weinberg, David Julyan (Orlov, Julian)	Sgt	581	34 Bn	Yako, Benjamin	Pte	6303	20 Bn
Weinberg, Ralph	Gnr	11129	3 (A) Bde; AFA	Young, Louis	Pte	3345	59 Bn
Weiner, Samuel	Pte	4517	23 Bn	Zander, Lindo Herman	AM	1589	12 LH; 67 Sqn; AFC
Weingott, Abraham	Bdr; Sgt	389	3 Bty; AFA; Emp Coy	Zander, Waldo Hyman MID	Capt	805	30 Bn
Weingott, Alexander *	Pte	695	13 Bn	Zeeng, Wolfe	Dvr	12442	10 Fd Amb
Weingott, Barron	Dvr	7741	1st FCE	Zeffert, Maurice Emanuel	A/Sgt	2612a	51 Bn
Weingott, Samuel *	Pte	127	1 Bn	Zeffertt, Samuel Walter	Pte	3546	9 Bn; 49 Bn
Weinrabe, Lewis Byron	Pte	2494	3 Bn; 55Bn	Zeltner, Isard	Pte; Dvr	16202	ASC
Weisberg, Thane (Whitehill)	QMS	2134	3 Bde Am Col	Zines, Joseph Maurice	Pte	1435	12 Bn; 52 Bn
				Zmood, William (Wolfe)	Pte	5793	2 Bn

EMPIRE FORCES

NAME	RANK	SERVICE NO.	UNIT	NAME	RANK	SERVICE NO.	UNIT
Abrahams, Frederick Alfred *	Rfn	4684	Queen's Westminster R	Brodziak, N.L.	Lt		RGA
Afriat, Albert Montefiore			15 Hamps	Cohen, Sefton L. (Drummond)	Capt		YLI
Alexander, Harold	Lt-Col		Imp	Cohen, B.H.	Lt		RAF
Asher, Felix	2/Lt		5 Seaforth	Cohen, Cecil Hope *	Capt		Yorks Regt
Bauer, Oscar	Pte	133015	RF; NRRF	Cohen, Cedric K.	Capt		RAMC
Benjamin, Arthur C.	Lt		RF; RFC	Cohen, Ernest G.	Lt		Imp
Benjamin, Athol	Lt		India	Cohen, Ernest Henry Melmotte *	Sgt	12/1048	NZ A
Benjamin, Laurie	Maj		RGA	Cohen, Eveline	Dvr		RAMC att
Benjamin, Lionel William				Cohen, Hamilton Richard			
Benjamin, Rudolf			Imp	Cohen, Harold F.	Capt		Imp
Bennett, Rosey	Nurse		RX; VAD	Cohen, Leon			
Bercove, S.	SM			Cohen, Lewis G.	Lt		Imp
Bercovitch, Solomon	Cpl	1104	King Edward Hor	Cohen, R.R.			RF
Bergman, Harry			USA	Cohen, R.S.			RASC
Berkovitz, C.	L/Cpl		King Edward Hor	Cohen, Sidney	Pte	276	Imp
Bernstein, Henry Lawrence				Cowen, J. DCM	Pte		Border
Blaubaum, Eric (Bowden) *	Pte	8/3495	Otago Inf Regt; 2 Bn	Cullen, Ralph Neville *	2/Lt		R Ir R
Blaubaum, Ivan	Capt		NZEF	Davies, Mervyn	Capt		
Bloom, [?]	Pte	1641	RAMC	Davis, Frank Lewis *			NZ Tng Unit
Brash, Alfred Falk	Lt		62 Inf	Davis, Maurice Levene	Lt		IA
Braun, Charles Lima *	Capt		Essex	De Jong, Edward Meyer			
Brodziak, Henry Jacob	Pte		NZEF	Edwards, Alan Sydney			RFC

NAME	RANK	SERVICE NO.	UNIT
Friedman, Maurice			Belgian Fd Arty
Goldstein, Herbert Myer			
Harris, Austen	Pte		Pro 38 Bn
Harris, Phillip L.	Lt		
Hart, E.	Pte		Imp
Herrman, B.	Pte	8154	Jewish Bn
Isaacs, Hubert D.			E Lan Regt; 10 Bn
Isaacs, Kenneth	Lt		
Israel, Reuben S. *	L/Cpl	4999	SA Inf
Jacobs, Charles Henry	Pte	69243	WIR
Jacobs, H.S.			Imp Reservists
Joseph, Cyprian Charles			SA Medica
Joske, Clive	Lt		
Kaye, Arthur E.			Imp
Kaye, Gerald S. MC CdeG	Capt		RFA
Krantz, Cyril			SA
Krantz, Leon			SA
Lasker, Robert Sydney *	2/Lt		25 Sqn; RAF; [ex AIF]
Lenneberg, F.B.	SM		SA Motor DR
Lenzer, Reuben	Capt		Imp (USA)
Lesnie, S.	CQMS	4325	RAMC
Levinson, B.A.	Capt		Imp
Levinson, E.R.	Capt		Cdn Inf
Levy, A.L. MC	Capt		Cdn Inf
Levy, Alwyn Gordon *	FL		42 Sqn; RFC
Levy, Bernard	Rfn	24/2025	NZ Rifles Bde
Levy, Douglas Alexander			Imp
Levy, Isaac DCM			Mx
Levy, Maitland Ben *	Capt		IG
Levy, Reginald			Indian
Lewis, Banett *	Pte	11688	Canterbury Inf Regt; 2 Bn
Luck, Sidney Ivor OBE	Capt		RE
Mandelstamn, Joseph *	Sgt		Imp
Margolin, Eliazar Lazar	Lt-Col		38 Bn; RF
Marienthal, W.L.	Dvr		ASC
Marx, S.			Lab Corps
Michaelis, Archie			Arty
Michaelis, Grant Moritz *	Lt		R East Anglia Regt
Michaelis, L.M.	Gnr		Imp
Michaelis, Roy	Lt		RGA
Morris, Lazar	Lt		Imp
Myer, E.B.			Imp
Myers, Sidney Myers *	Tpr	11/1729	Wellington MR Regt
Myslis, Henry Samuel (Samson)			RAPC
Pezaro, Marcus George	Sig	46242	NZEF
Pezaro, Samuel Alfred	Rfn	77445	RB
Phillips, Isaac	Pte	3/3517	FA
Phillips, L.D.	Cpl		SA
Phillips, Louis			1 Wellington MR Regt
Platkin, Haim Samoilovich			42 Jewish Bn
Plottel, F.			Imp
Rich, Carrick	Pte		
Rich, Ruby			
Rosenfeldt, Augustus Bernard Paul *	L/Sgt	10/92	Wellington Bn
Rosenfeldt, Henry Ernest	Cpl	45740	RB
Rosenthal, Leah ARRC	Nurse	WO372/23	QAIMNS
Sampson, Isadore	Pte	74350	4 Bn
Shmith, Frank	Dvr		Imp
Shmith, Harry	Dvr		Imp
Sinauer, Esmond MC	Capt		RE
Solomon, Hubert Philip *	Lt	11564	RFC
Solomon, Kenneth Maurice Halgren*	Lt		11 Glosters
Solomon, Nathan	Pte	23/1818	2 Canterbury Inf Regt
Solomon, Phillip Born	Rfn	26/970	4 RB
Sorokiewich, Harold			RAMC
Spiro, Joseph	Pte	31373	1 Wellington MR Regt
Steigrad, Max	2/Lt		CTC (post-AIF)
Trenn, A.			SA A
Trenn, Norman Theodore	S/Sgt		7 SA Inf
Weinberg, David Julyan (Orlon)			Zion Mule Corps
Whelan, Cyril (Waxman)	FL		RFC

World War II

ROYAL AUSTRALIAN NAVY

NAME	RANK	SERVICE NO.
Aarons, Raymond Albert	T/LDGSTO	R22549
Abraham-Wilms, Sydney Joseph Leon	Sg Lt Cdr	
Adelstein, Elvira Ruth (Sloman)	3rd O	
Adler, Henry	AB	PM8353
Altson, Bruce Harold	PO RADMECH	26919
Amsberg, George Frederick	Lt	
Asher, John Samuel *	STO2	PA1913
Balaam, Frederick John	Sig	S7373
Balon, Victor Bernard	Coder	26267
Baume, Alan Charles MID	A/PMR Lt Cdr	
Benjamin, Edward	PO	F1512/98
Blaubaum, Peter Eric	Sg Lt	65011
Blievers, Zeeva (Halperin)	Wtr	WR/1812
Brendon, Jill Kate	A/Wtr	WR/2623
Burman, Lloyd John	Wtr	PM7510
Cowen, (Sir) Zelman	Lt	
Crawcour, Jack Athol	Lt	
Crawcour, Neil Alfred	Ord Smn CB V/S	F5693
Davis, Colin Louis	T/LS	B/2442
Diamond, Richard Leigh	Store A	PM8536
Dorin, David Albert	Smn	PM5060
Ensly, Joshua	AB	F4995
Epstein, David	AB	F3823
Epstein, Harry		R27476
Epstein, Jacob Lewis	AB	PM2051
Falk, Balfour Amiel	Ord Tel	S4785
Feldman, Renee	Wtr	WR/831
Fienberg, Bennett Jacob	Sup A	S8852
Glass, Harold Hyman	Lt	
Goldberg, Sid	CANMGR	
Goldenberg, Freda Gertrude Sara	WRANS Tel	WR/1075
Goulston, Edna Maude	3rd O	WR/627

World War II, Royal Australian Navy (cont.)

NAME	RANK	SERVICE NO.	NAME	RANK	SERVICE NO.
Greenberg, Jack	AB	F2680	Opas, Maurice *	CANMGR	
Halsted, Victor Michaelis	Lt	PM2133	Orken, Aaron	PO Ck	17028
Harris, Maurice	Ldg Ck	S3875	Paltie, Joseph	Constable (GS)	795
Hart, Eric Joseph	Lt		Patkin, Norma	Wtr	WR/2369
Herman, Hyman (Hymen)	Smn	F/V291	Rapke, Trevor George	PMR Lt	
Herman, Isaac *	AB	F2692	Rischin, Lewis	AB	S8099
Hickman, Ann Elizabeth	Ldg WRANS Store A	WR/948	Robin, Dudley Joseph	Lt	PM2870
Hoffman, Harry Aaron	SBA2	F2672/12	Rosanove, Ivan	PO RADMECH	26957
Holzman, Samuel Abraham	Ord Smn	F2689/20	Rose, Sydney Brozel	Constable	1130
Hyams, Louis Joseph	Coder	27051	Rosebery, Marion Olive	Store A	WR/2465
Isaacs, Basil Maurice	AB	PM7349	Rosenbloom, Victor Percy	AB	2559
Joel, (Sir) Asher Alexander **BSM** (USA)	Lt		Rothbaum, Lionel *	STWD	24576
Joel, Joseph	Lt		Roubin, Phillip	Tel	B/2650
Katz, David Morris	L/S	S/V03	Samuel, Victor	Sto	W2012
Kaye, William	Lt		Saunders, Alan Neil	Ldg Smn	PA1573
Kensell, Jacob Rolfe	Sto	20709	Schenberg, Morris	ERA3	F3623
Klein, Eric John	AB	PM8443	Schott, Frank Joseph	AB	PM8308
Klippel, Robert Edward	AB	S3211	Segal, Juliet	Coder	WR/1195
Kohane, Hans Jack	Lt	PM4931	Sharp, Philip	Lt	F3649
Kops, Mark Abraham	SBA2	S/3977	Shaw, Kenneth David	AB	PM8308
Kronenberg, Reuben	Ldg RADMECH (S)	26924	Shilkin, Berny Nathan	SBA	F2679
Lands, Stanley George	Sub	S/4402	Shineberg, Emanuel	AB	PM5051
Lane, Edward	PO Ck	11310	Shmith, Nona Hannah	Ldg Wtr	WR/1440
Lazarus, Lewis	LDGSTO	PM1174	Silberberg, Frank Gerald	Ldg RADMECH	26827
Lazarus, Maurice Henry	Sto	PM2019	Simons, Philip Neville	Sg Lt	
Lenny, Harold Joseph	Sto PO	S/10305	Sleeman, Douglas	Ord Sig V/S	S/3527
Levin, Carmel	Joiner 3	F2682	Slutzkin, Frank Albert	Lt	PM5471
Levin, Harry	AB	F2777	Solomon, Benjamin Morris	Sto	PM1773
Levy, Jack **MBE** (WWI)	Wdr; Lt Cdr	3296	Solomon, Loris	Ldg Smn	PM2186
Levy, Joe	Sub	02835	Solomon, Myer Jacob	Lt	
Levy, Keith Michael	Lt Cdr	PM5758	Solomons, Jacques Delmonde	Sgt2	648
Lewis, Hyman	CERA	R30861	Solomons, Samuel Lewis	PO STWD	10336
Lipman, Gwendoline Lois	Ldg TPHONEOP	WR/1533	Steinberg, Matthew	Joiner 4	F2705/19
Lipman, Kenneth **MID**	Ldg SBA	S3695	Stennett, Albert Edward	Sub	
London, Jack Huskell	Ord Smn	F3648	Sternberg, Alexander	Mot Mech 4	26036
Markovitch, Reuben Israel	Ldg Tel	R28306	Symonds, Leonard Douglas	AB	S/10015
Marks, Martin Charles	Ord Smn	PM8082	Symons, Yetta Rae	PO Wtr	WR/125
Marks, Sabbathe Zalman	Lt	PA/VI8	Thau, David Leon	Ord Smn	F2725/20
Masel, Leigh	Ldg Sup A	PM5458	Trobe, Rosmond	Ord Smn	F4413
Meyers, John Robert	Lt	B2332	White, Myer	AB	PM5661
Meyers, Rodney Ian	Lt	42958	Wolfe, Frederick Levi	EA3	S3370
Michael, Kenneth Samuel	Sub (E)	PM	Wolfson, Abraham	Constable (GS)	1091
Michael, Ronald Joseph	Ldg Store A	PM6110	Woolf, Moss	Ldg Tel	S1225
Millman, Woolf	Ord Smn	F/2681/19	Zeffert, Paul	AB	F5205
Munz, Hirsch	Lt (Sp)		Zusman, Solomon	Ldg STWD	F3438
Newstead, Nanette	Wtr	WR/2092			

AUSTRALIAN ARMY

NAME	RANK	SERVICE NO.	NAME	RANK	SERVICE NO.
Aaron, Albert	L/Cpl	N452492	Abadee, Jack Stanley	Pte	N225589
Aaron, Edward	Cpl	N120525; NX126548	Abel, Edward Maurice	Pte	VX74849
Aarons, Gershon	Pte	V310723	Abeshouse, Jack	Sgt	N46372; NX150890
Aarons, Harry Montague	Dvr	V310840	Abeshouse, Lionel Isaac	Pte	N263782; NX150891
Aarons, Henry	Pte	VX27149	Abraham, Amandus Leopold	Pte	N237380
Aarons, Lionel Isaac	Sgt	V206171; VX130823	Abraham, Joachim	Pte	V378192
Aarons, Louis	Pte	V517699	Abraham, Leo	Pte	V377402
Aarons, Morris Joseph	Gnr	V306265; VX124091	Abrahams, Abraham	Dvr	VX10039
Aarons, Phillip	S/Sgt	V83355	Abrahams, Braham Ernest	L/Sgt	N11446; NX100295
Aarons, Sydney	Sgt	V281489; VX130588	Abrahams, Burt Leopold	Pte	Q265189

Appendix 2: Those who served

NAME	RANK	SERVICE NO.
Abrahams, Eric Weston	L/Cpl	N218995
Abrahams, Frances	Pte	VF510172
Abrahams, Joseph Saltiel Gilbert	Pte	N439636
Abrahams, Leon Joseph	Capt	N74728
Abrahams, Reuben	S/Sgt	V12545; VX36440
Abramczyk, Siegbert	L/Cpl	V377401
Abramovich, Leslie	Capt	N105109; NX70660
Abramowicz, Maskymilian	Pte	VX95470
Abramson, Myer Isaac	Pte	V275306
Absolom, James Emanuel	S/Sgt	V76714; VX122582
Ackerman, David	Pte	N465980; NX177471
Ackman, Denis Samuel	Cpl	N14673; NX180724
Acton, Egon Herbert	Pte	N321013
Adair, Ronald Isadore Shafto	Cpl	NX40093
Adams, Joseph	Pte	NX206246
Adelstein, Charles Harold	Gnr	NX105310
Adelstein, Ephraim	Capt	NX109060
Adelstein, Neville	Lt	N55077; NX103938
Adler, George	Cpl	NX90500
Adler, Gustav Joseph	Pte	V377087
Adler, Henry	Pte	V367034
Adler, Henry Max	Cpl	N231025
Adler, Herbert	Pte	V377628
Adler, Herman	Pte	W48517
Adler, John	S/Sgt	V502057
Adler, Louis Philip	Pte	N226405
Adler, Louise	Pte	WF93739
Adler, Ludwig	Cpl	N321001
Adler, Morris	Pte	NX190823
Adler, Siegbert	Cpl	N261076
Adler, William	Pte	V53764
Adonis, Nathan	Gnr	WX25359
Adunaj, Israel Josek	L/Cpl	V378062
Ajzensztejn, Jakub	Sgt	V377159
Akerman, John (Akkerman)	Capt	V57036; VX91344
Akkerman, Maurice	Bdr	VX33578
Alexander, Aaron Victor	Sgt	N271520; NX177209
Alexander, Egon	Pte	V377730
Alexander, Henry	Pte	VX47624
Alexander, Henry Samuel	S/Sgt	NX20582
Alexander, Jessel Alexander	Capt	N78134
Alexander, John Sheridan	Cpl	VX63931
Alexander, Lionel Jacob	Pte	NX82096
Alexander, Millicent Julia	Pte	VF508491
Alexander, Norman (Absolom)	Gnr	VX30535
Alexander, Rex	Cpl	NX9421
Alexander, Roy	Tpr	NX84262
Alexander, Symon Julius	Sig	NX43886
Alford, Eric Thomas	L/Cpl	V377049
Allen, Edward	Sgt	N7019
Allen, Maurice	Pte	N323675
Allen, Phillip	Sgt	N456894
Allert, Paul	L/Sgt	V377473
Alman, Donald Leslie	Pte	WX40465
Alman, Robert Arthur	Pte	W10242; WX27344
Alman, Sydney Arthur	Pte	W49787; WX39247
Alman, Thomas David	Pte	WX14635
Alpert, Herbert	Pte	V377584
Alpins, Oscar	Maj	V146428; VX114239
Alsberg, Peter Kurt	Pte	V377949
Altman, Lionel Louis	S/Sgt	VX2516
Altman, Maurice Leopold	Sgt	VX2515

NAME	RANK	SERVICE NO.
Altman, Myer	Gnr	NX134596
Altmann, Andrew Houston	Pte	N173181
Altmann, Herbert	Cpl	N321142
Altmann, Siegfried	Pte	N321140
Altschul, Heinz	Pte	V378396
Altshul, Moses Aron	Pte	V156820
Altshuler, Evsik *	L/Sgt	NX38959
Altshuler, William	S/Sgt	QX15245
Amstead, James	L/Cpl	V206795
Anderson, Leslie Lewis	Gnr	NX85405
Ansbacher, Joseph	Pte	V377472
Anschel, Klaus	Pte	V37772
Anson, Manfred	Cpl	VX129127
Antman, Benjamin	Pte	V377585
Anton, Charles William	Pte	N221503; NX131034
Appelboom, Myer	Pte	N469457
Applebaum, Trevor Zola	Gnr	NX10908
Arane, John (Jehosua)	Tpr	N321288; NX172972
Arber, Norman	Pte	V377972
Arber, William	Pte	VX22469
Arkin, Aharon	Pte	W55897
Arndt, Kurt	Pte	V377924
Aronoff, Benzion Bernard	Pte	V377400
Aronovski, Judelis Jehuda	Pte	NX88660
Aronson, David	Lt	VX89668
Aronson, Malcolm Phillip	Lt	N323615
Aronstein, Fritz	Pte	V378386
Ash, Clive	WO2	NX13943
Ash, Harry	Cpl	S1508
Ashkanasy, Maurice **MID**	Maj	VX43608
Ashkinazy, Harry	Pte	N219016
Asman, Icchok Benjamin	Pte	N237388
Aubor, Samuel	Pte	V377091
Audet, Lewis	Lt	N393033
Auer, Emil	Pte	V377645
Auer, Georg	Pte	V377646
Austerlitz, Hans Joachim	Pte	V377644
Ausubel, Abraham Bensch	Pte	V377130
Ausubel, Josef	Pte	V377292
Axelgrad, Josef	Pte	V378333
Axelrad, Hans	Pte	V378375
Bach, Moses Abraham	WO1	N390494
Bacharach, Lotar	Pte	V378301
Baer, Herbert Herman	Pte	V377511
Baer, Werner	Sgt	V377627
Bailin, Morris	Sgt	N255883; NX150915
Bailin, Wallace	Cpl	NX127792
Baitz, Edward Isaiah	Cpl	V43437
Baitz, Paul	Pte	V56526
Baker, Erich	Pte	N394627; NX180751
Baker, John Mendel	Cpl	2191600; NX19296
Baker, Louis	Dvr	N225628
Baker, Maurice Hyman	Sgt	N271294; NX140655
Balbierer, Emanuel	Pte	V377507
Ball, Gerald	Pte	N463361
Ball, Raphael	Pte	V502446
Ball, Stanley	Pte	V14449; VX143784
Bancroft, Henry Cyril	Lt	VX76979
Banczewski, Eljasz	Pte	V515160
Baramovitch, Samuel	Pte	248352; N248352
Barasch, Lewis	Pte	V35737
Barasch, Myer Hyman	Pte	V206186

385

Jewish Anzacs

World War II, Australian Army (cont.)

NAME	RANK	SERVICE NO.
Barasch, Solly	Dvr	V60982; VX138461
Bardas, Brae	Pte	V66523
Barfield, Lao	Pte	S34703
Barfield, Leo	Pte	S212389
Barme, Rolf	L/Cpl	N221535
Barnbaum, Abraham	Pte	Q203365
Barnbaum, Harry	Cpl	Q144871; QX58971
Barnbaum, Samuel	Pte	Q16122
Barnett, Adolphe Henry	Pte	V509033
Barnett, Alan David	Tpr	N180639; NX101251
Barnett, Charles Maurice	Gnr	V6327; VX26970
Barnett, Edward Elias	Sgt	VX23859
Barnett, Joseph Joshua	Lt	V2034; VX83607
Barnett, Keith Joel	Pte	V69501
Barnett, Keith Joel	Sig	V143779; VX121789
Barnett, Keith Reginald *	L/Cpl	NX69234
Barnett, Lewis	Gnr	VX10706
Barnett, Maurice	Pte	V11614
Barnett, Montague	Pte	N271151
Barnett, Samuel Joseph	Sig	V255453; VX140105
Barnett, Sydney Joseph	Dvr	V125039
Baron, Jack	Pte	NX51279
Barr, Alfred	Pte	V378290
Barrington, Bernard	L/Cpl	N101011
Barripp, Samuel	Pte	NX87351
Barrow, Samuel	Pte	V74646
Bartak, Percy	Capt	V147225
Bartak, Samuel	Dvr	VX63064
Barton, Norman Benjamin	Pte	VX100766
Basger, Boris Burnett	Pte	NX5103
Basger, Robert	Pte	NX73587
Basil, Michael	Pte	V206845
Bass, Jack	Pte	SX8536
Bass, Leonard	Cpl	N13097; NX135808
Bass, Nathan	Pte	N227574
Basser, Adrian Gustave Nelson	Lt	NX110242
Basser, Leo Wolf	Lt	NX151705
Bauer, Franz	Capt	SX33401
Baum, Heinz	Pte	NX59986; N221646
Baum, Samuel	L/Sgt	NX59986
Baumwald, Rodolf	Pte	N321143
Baxter, Paul	Cpl	VX129143; V502345
Bayer, Alfred Israel	Pte	N463565
Bayer, Arnold	Pte	V377638
Bazar, Egon	Pte	V500736
Beaconsfield, Howard Isadore	Pte	VX95349
Bear, Alfred	Sig	V185713
Bear, Colin Leslie	Capt	N278486
Bear, Myer	Pte	V370686
Beare, Irwin	Pte	V156266
Becher, Michael	Sig	V510289; VX127352
Becher, Michuel	Pte	V378345
Becher, Moris	Pte	V378128
Beck, Emil	L/Cpl	V378108
Beck, Karl	Pte	N221735
Beck, Kurt	Pte	N321026
Becker, Hans	Pte	V377720
Becker, Raymond	Pte	NX3813
Becker, Theodore	Gnr	N218699; NX132650
Beckman, Theodore	Pte	N106929
Beer, Fred	Pte	V377410
Beer, Halsahluv	Pte	V378249

NAME	RANK	SERVICE NO.
Beer, Jack	Pte	V39580
Beer, Karl	Pte	V377583
Beerman, Stephen	Pte	N261073
Begach, Klaus	Pte	V377642
Behrendt, Werner	Cpl	V377474
Behrendtsohn, Jakob	Pte	V507450
Beirman, Judah	Sgt	N273033
Belfer, Jacob	Cpl	S26510
Belinfante, Leslie	Pte	N239581
Bellamy, Benjamin	Pte	V377188
Bellinson, Aaron		V157405
Benary, Leslie (Bewary)	Sig	VX93507
Bender, Mark	Pte	V377038
Bender, Max	Pte	V378036
Bender, Mosek Dawid	Pte	V377033
Bendit, Walter	Pte	N224772
Bendit, Werner Kurt	Pte	N224965
Benedikt, Walter	Pte	V377508
Benet, Samuel Izak	Pte	V377106
Benjamin, Alan Lionel **MID**	Capt	V55296; VX117096
Benjamin, Arthur Lewis	Sig	WX1282
Benjamin, Bruce Stanley	Gnr	VX146010
Benjamin, Cyril	Pte	NX86066
Benjamin, David Errol	Pte	NX7729
Benjamin, David James	Lt-Col	NX12267
Benjamin, Edward	S/Sgt	V10634
Benjamin, Ernest David	Pte	V76725
Benjamin, Felix	Sgt	QX22690
Benjamin, Harold	Dvr	NX23321
Benjamin, Harry	Sgt	V85513
Benjamin, Heinz	Pte	V378387
Benjamin, Leslie Hyam	WO2	Q123625; Q230648
Benjamin, Rudolph *	Pte	V82706
Benjamin, Sidney	L/Cpl	NX137214
Benjamin, Sydney Albert Bernard	Sgt	V206632
Benjamin, Sydney Colin	Sgt	NX15642
Benjamin, Victor Myer Julius	Pte	NX79941
Bennett, Alexander	Pte	V206011
Bennett, Alexander	Pte	V378102
Bennett, David Monash	Pte	VX124761
Bennett, Gershon Berendt **OBE**	Lt-Col	V5927; VX89047
Bennett, Herman Adler	Cpl	V206441
Bensky, Benjamin	Pte	W19511
Bensky, Hyman	Bdr	WX10105
Bensky, Jack	Bdr	WX10106
Bentley, Harry Isadore	Sgt	NX93755
Benton, Alan David	L/Sgt	VX15740
Berah, Maurice	Capt	V146913; VX108216
Bercove, Solomon David	WO2	WX1679
Berenholtz, Elka	Pte	VF508214
Berenholtz, Isaac	Pte	V55660; VX119741
Berenholtz, Morris	Cpl	V158384; VX125040
Bereson, Harry (Beresinsky)	Capt	VX88178
Berg, Benjamin	Capt	VX16234
Berg, David	Pte	N270973
Berg, Maurice Alexander	Capt	2905033; NX65384
Berg, Myer Joseph	Lt	V13549; VX18550
Berger, George Martin James	Pte	N237381
Berger, Hermann	Pte	N321054
Berger, Peter	Capt	NX77177
Berger, Theo	Pte	V377639
Berger, Walter	Pte	V377431

NAME	RANK	SERVICE NO.	NAME	RANK	SERVICE NO.
Berghouse, John Alexander	L/Cpl	N226071	Blitz, Erich	Sgt	V377350
Bergl, Francis	Pte	V504844	Blitz, Paul	Pte	V515976
Bergman, Arthur Ansel	Gnr	N387984	Blitz, Walter	Sgt	V377349
Bergman, Hugo	Pte	N221695	Bloch, Adolf	Pte	V377509
Bergman, Leopold	Pte	Q272802	Bloch, Bernard	Spr	N216866
Bergman, Norman	Gnr	NX16401	Bloch, Max	Pte	V158291
Bergmann, George	L/Cpl	N191519	Bloch, William	Gnr	N283573
Bergmann, Gerhard Salomon	Pte	V378353	Block, Samuel	Sig	NX164444
Bergner, Vladomir Josif	Pte	V377459	Blondin, Archie	Pte	NX27251
Berinshan, Hyman Solomon	Capt	W96738; WX36171	Bloom, Dan	Gnr	NX92181
Berinson, Hyman	Pte	V377043	Bloom, David	S/Sgt	N323506
Berinson, Sam	Pte	W90547	Bloom, Gerald Abraham	Lt	NX151322
Berkman, Gerszon Gary	Pte	V377025	Bloom, Harold Maurice	L/Sgt	N225447
Berl, Sanel	Spr	TX5626	Bloom, Harry	Pte	V158656
Berlin, Jack	Gnr	V33492; VX115115	Bloom, Jack	Pte	V357536
Berliner, Harris Lionel *	Sgt	V6364	Bloom, Meryl Louise	Sig	NF409448
Berliner, Kenneth Lewis	Lt	NX76303	Bloom, Morris	L/Cpl	N225570
Berliner, Leon Alfred *	Pte	VX65015	Bloom, Roy Towers	WO1	QX49928
Berlinsky, Harry Lewis	Gnr	N461128	Bloomfield, David Maurice	Gnr	N109549
Berlinsky, Jack	Pte	W16258	Bloomfield, Solomon	Pte	W7761
Berman, Harold	Sgt	NX37063	Bloomfield, Stanley Bernard	Pte	N321002
Berman, Isadore	L/Cpl	NX58213	Bloustien, Albert	Pte	SX26694
Berner, Phillip	Maj	N60358; NX12421	Blum, Hellmut	Pte	N221505
Bernhardt, Abraham John	Pte	V19303	Blum, Herbert Adolf	Pte	N463180
Berns, Harold	Pte	NX42671	Blumann, Ernest	Pte	W60818
Berns, Robert	Pte	V377978; VX129163	Blumenfeld, Gerd Adolf	Cpl	V377426
Berns, Sol	Cpl	N225891; NX164213	Blumenfeld, Kurt	Pte	V377850
Berns, William	Cpl	N224336	Blumenfeld, Leopold	Pte	N224806
Bernstein, Gerd	Pte	V377513	Blumental, Zavel	Pte	V378189
Bernstein, Harry *	Pte	VX28109	Blumental, Zvi	Pte	V351149
Bernstein, Helmut Michael	Pte	V377637	Blumenthal, Henry Joachim	Pte	V377640
Bernstein, Horst	Pte	V377200	Blumenthal, Joseph	Pte	N251693
Bernstein, Phillip	Pte	VX39509	Blumenthal, Ludwig	Pte	N443480
Berrick, Alan Ellis	Gnr	NX56394	Blumenthal, Theodor	Pte	N303741
Bershatzky, Israel	Pte	Q151074	Bluthal, Israel Leib	Pte	V378228
Berstein, David Henry	Cfn	N236374; NX149054	Boan, Clive Harry **BEM**	Sgt	VX18698
Besser, Fritz	Pte	N221536	Boan, Norman Maurice	L/Bdr	VX25177
Beth-Halevy, Abraham Bezalel *	L/Sgt	VX77341	Boas, Bernard Abraham	Pte	V367007
Bettelheim, Martin	Pte	V502447	Boas, Harold John Pulver	Lt	VX39194
Biegler, Robert	Pte	N221621	Boas, Norman Samuel	Sgt	VX21717
Bier, Herbert	Pte	N244838	Boas, Philip Victor	Pte	S85182; S29048
Biner, Israel	Pte	VX65356	Boehm, Franz Wilheim	Pte	N268500
Bing, Martin Leo	Pte	N321003	Boehm, Gerhard Mauritz	Pte	V378153
Birnberg, Lionel	Pte	V4875	Boehm, Heinrich Samuel (Symon)	Pte	V377635
Birsztejn, Yosel	Pte	V378037	Boehm, Kurt	Pte	N261075
Bischofswerder, Felix	Pte	V509763	Boehm, Ralph Albert	Pte	V377636
Blach, Kurt	L/Cpl	V377362	Bogan, Phillip	Cpl	QX688; Q19091; Q70606; QX48394
Black, Emanuel	Pte	S212153	Bogan, William	Pte	Q28502
Black, Norman	Cpl	NX169543	Bogan, Wolf	L/Sgt	QX41475; Q90980
Blackman, Edward Isaac	Pte	N390225	Bogatin, Abram	Pte	V377036
Blaine, Cedric Norman	Capt	V80577	Boggatt, Isaac Ian	Pte	V377028
Blake, Jack	Pte	V156129	Bohm, Frederick	Pte	V378070
Blaschke, Walter Siegfried Sigermund	Pte	N444901	Bolgraaf, Charles	Sig	NX153613
Blashki, Arnold Roy	Cpl	V56535	Bolgraaf, Eva	Sig	NF409447
Blashki, Kenneth Edward	Sig	VX134361	Bolgraaf, Simon *	Pte	NX105247
Blashki, Phillip	Lt	V106058; VX114202	Bolloten, Michael	Pte	V500965
Blashki, Ronald Reginald	Gnr	V185012; VX114865	Bolot, Aaron	WO2	NX141786
Blashki, Victor Samuel *	WO2	NX50505	Bolot, Boris (Robert)	Pte	N47047
Blau, Franz Eduard	Cpl	N321016	Bolot, Leon	Sgt	NX41580
Blau, Hans	L/Cpl	V501725	Bondy, Ernst	Pte	N237041
Blau, Otto	Pte	V502458	Boock, Louis Michael	L/Sgt	Q194909
Bleier, Peter	Pte	V512815			

World War II, Australian Army (cont.)

NAME	RANK	SERVICE NO.	NAME	RANK	SERVICE NO.
Borchardt, Markus	Pte	V502448	Brooks, Leon	Cpl	V500323; VX147555
Borensztejn, Syalon Leib	Pte	VX92872	Brooks, Max	Pte	V354636
Boritz, Ozjasz	Pte	V377181	Broslovsky, Abraham	Pte	N273081
Born, Heinz Julius	Pte	V377715	Brovman, David Leon	Capt	N74462; NX115988
Bornstein, Joseph	Capt	VX138726	Brown, Alan	Pte	V377783
Bornstein, Maurice John	Pte	V66484; VX147994	Brown, Cyril	Pte	WX41859
Bornstein, Siegfried	Pte	V377363	Brown, George William	WO2	VX84949
Borowich, Raymond	Pte	V357328	Brown, Isaac	Pte	W60670
Borys, Majer	Pte	V377460	Brown, Jack	Sig	VX58576
Botfai, John (Balfour)	Pte	V378191	Brown, Joseph	Spr	VX102524
Boulton, Charles Ewart	S/Sgt	VX1992	Brown, Norman	Spr	vx4306
Boulton, David Derick	Capt	VX16908	Brown, Robert	Pte	NX92694
Boulton, John Trevor Cornwall	Pte	VX15022	Browne, Adrien Alexander Adolph	Gnr	NX168965; N7001
Bower, Fred	Pte	V377811	Browne, Barbara Esther	Lt	NFX207388
Boymal, Sam	Cpl	VX84357	Browne, Roy George	Lt	N278433
Braham, Jack Mortimer	Pte	VX2167	Bruch, Herbert	Pte	V377395
Braham, Martin Arnold	Pte	VX9856	Bruck, Hugo	L/Cpl	W60809
Braham, Norman	Gnr	V51240	Bruckner, Myer	Cfn	QX47834
Bramd, Isaac	L/Cpl	V18787	Brudo, Pierre Robert	Sig	N319371
Brand, Norman	Pte	V61354	Bruell, Kurt	Pte	V377510
Brand, Sol	Pte	V158547	Bruhand, Daniel	Pte	V377307
Brand, Victor **MC**	Capt	VX39085	Brukarz, Baron	Pte	N323561
Brandman, Frederick	Pte	N221538	Brukarz, Raphael Nathan	Sgt	N442495
Brandmann, Hans	Pte	N221539	Brull, Alfred	Pte	V378006
Brandon, Berrima	Gnr	NX112937	Brull, Jack	Pte	N452442
Brandon, Joseph Myer	Pte	NX161745	Brummer, Leo Manfred	Pte	V378389
Brandon, Myer	Sgt	NX105657	Brunswick, Kurt	Pte	V377828
Brandstatter, Jakob	Pte	V378203	Brunton, Mark George	Lt	V19714
Brandt, Gerhard	Pte	V377641	Brustman, Solomon	Pte	V377257
Brash, Robert Alfred	Cpl	NX15794	Brygel, Joseph	Cpl	VX88340
Bratspies, Gustav	Pte	V378297	Brygel, Morris	Pte	VX107004
Bratspies, Herbert Harry Israel	Pte	V377369	Brzezinski, Abram	Pte	V504654
Braude, Bernhard Walter	Pte	V377798	Brzezinski, Moroka	Pte	N321112; NX164320
Braun, Benjamin Joseph	L/Sgt	N76417	Buch, Gunther	Pte	V377366
Braun, Josef	Pte	N224859	Buchanek, Manuel	Pte	Q153417
Braun, Paul	Pte	V377512	Buchanek, Ted	Pte	Q153416
Brecher, Erich	Pte	N221647	Buchanek, Victor	Pte	Q153415
Breckler, Alec	Lt	W400165	Buchatsky, Emanuel	Pte	VX144512
Breckler, Alexander	Capt	WX31093	Buchler, Joseph	Pte	N230315
Breit, Johannes	Pte	V377834	Buchner, Hyman	Pte	N99186
Brem, Louis	Sgt	NX173774; NX16596	Buchner, Jack	Pte	VX108753
Brenner, Adolf	Pte	V501546	Buchner, Leslie	Pte	VX100531
Bressler, Jack	Pte	V354868	Buchner, Morris	WO2	VX126477
Bretler, Moshe	Pte	V377961	Buckland, Henry John	Sgt	V377739
Bridgland, Walter Lewis	Capt	437277; SX20841	Buechenbacher, Otto	Pte	V503908
Brill, Rudolf Emanuel	Pte	V378186	Bueno De Mesquita, Edgar David	Cpl	VX35005
Brill, Walter	Pte	N224618	Bullen, Benjamin Enoch	Tpr	NX114648
Briner, Jack **MID**	Sig	QX59068	Bund, Herbert Jacob	Pte	N218990
Briner, Nash	Pte	QX40627	Buniak, Izrael	Cfn	NX93065
Britnell, David Robert *	Tpr	VX61625	Bunzl, Erich	Pte	V377418
Broben, Athol John	Sgt	V4004	Bunzl, John Stephen	Pte	N237042
Broch, Alfred	Pte	V378261	Burger, Franz	Pte	V378190
Brodie, Albert Peter	Cpl	VX119471	Burgheim, Walter Siegmund *	Pte	N456838
Brodie, Harry	Pte	N321289	Burke, Bernie	Spr	VX77291
Brodkin, David	Pte	V378144	Burke, Sophy	Cpl	VF345705
Brodsky, Alexander Gregory	Lt	N463156	Burlakov, Albert	Sgt	N464004
Brodsky, George	Gnr	N221607	Burlakov, Alex	Cpl	V315989
Brodsky, Isadore Irvine	Lt	N463157	Burman, Benjamin Joseph	Pte	V354845
Brodziak, Henry Jacob	Pte	N279055	Burman, Donald Daniel	Cpl	VX39538
Brodziak, Innes Albert	Lt-Col	NX34848	Burman, Leonard *	Cpl	V44373; VX102564
Bronstein, Norman	Pte	V13525	Burman, Paul	Pte	V377992
Brook, Henry	Sgt	1997; QX32102	Burman, Stuart John	Pte	N71302

NAME	RANK	SERVICE NO.
Burnham, Emanuel Maurice	Pte	NX150282
Burns, Gabriel Athol	Pte	N468350
Bursztyn, Hono Wolf	Pte	W56127
Butow, Hans Joseph	Pte	N463651
Buxton, Sidney	Gnr	NX31053
Byk, Chaim Mordko	Cpl	V377309
Cahn, Albert Hyman	Pte	W17112
Cahn, Walter	Pte	V377796
Cahn, Willy	S/Sgt	V146930
Caminer, Edward	WO2	V15218
Cann, Arthur	Pte	V378363
Cantor, William	Pte	V4807; V82378
Caplan, Harry	Cpl	VX113137
Caplan, Jack	Pte	V504946
Caplan, Philip	Dvr	NX191612
Caplan, Raymond	Pte	VX151885
Caplan, Simon	Cpl	VX133513
Carew, John Clive	Pte	V378181
Caro, Albert Edward	Lt-Col	WX3373
Caro, George Alfred	Pte	4028
Carstens, Guenter (Carson, Frederick Edgar)	Pte	V377505
Carvin, George	Pte	N463655
Casan, Michel	Lt	VX100072
Casparius, Heinz	Pte	V377748
Casper, Alfred	Pte	V377020
Casper, Athol Louis	Lt	WX11019
Casper, George Mendel **MID**	WO2	VX106504
Cass, Alick	Pte	W55774
Cass, Frederick	L/Cpl	V377005
Cass, Jacob	Pte	W49185
Cass, Namon Lewis	Capt	W52
Cass, Solomon	Sgt	WX32505
Cassell, Abraham Herman	Sgt	Q45063
Castle, Harry Philip	Lt	NX99739
Catts, Alfred	Pte	V377279
Catts, Fred	Pte	V377734
Catts, Herbert	Pte	N76771
Catts, Leonard Irwin	Lt	NX91605
Catts, Louis William	A/Bdr	N225593
Ceber, Szmul Zalman	Pte	V377138
Cebon, Leon	Pte	V158682
Ceen, Albert Marius	Sgt	V378098
Chain, Isaac	Pte	N105842
Charles, Gunter Harald	Pte	V377735
Charmatz, Erwin	Pte	N231022
Charmatz, Harold	Pte	N231026
Chaskel, Max	Pte	V378110
Chass, Julian	Pte	V377048
Chebel, Solomon	Pte	V378139
Chernow, Nathan	Cpl	NX145574
Cherny, Leon	Pte	N321155
Cherny, Myer	Pte	V158003
Chester, Ivan	Pte	W16080
Chester, Morrie Bernard	Spr	VX144294
Chester, Walter	Spr	W34224; WX28839
Chikin, Max	Sgt	NX27099
Chinn, Ben **MM**	Cpl	NX38196
Chodziesner, Georg Frederick Wilhelm	Pte	V501963
Chojnachi, Abram	Tpr	NX73526
Chosid, Dov	Pte	W61031
Ciddor, Harold	Pte	N180066

NAME	RANK	SERVICE NO.
Ciddor, Merton Mark *	Lt	VX15617
Ciddor, Norman	Cpl	N13113
Clements, Charles	Pte	N221677
Cohen, Alan Jack	Pte	NX103297
Cohen, Albert	Pte	V36815
Cohen, Albert Mendel	Pte	NX49782
Cohen, Alexander	L/Cpl	N248881
Cohen, Alfred	Pte	N70369
Cohen, Alroy Maitland	Lt-Col	N30142
Cohen, Anthony Neil	Sig	NX144505
Cohen, Arthur	Bdr	QX16512
Cohen, Arthur	Pte	V156812
Cohen, Arthur Joseph Phillip	Sgt	VX42078
Cohen, Arthur Peel	Sgt	NX19069
Cohen, Arthur Stanley	Pte	VX8983
Cohen, Aubrey Lewis	Gnr	NX28504
Cohen, Avon	Spr	WX25764
Cohen, Baron	Spr	V63256
Cohen, Bernard David	WO1	N65905
Cohen, Bertram Clarence	H/Maj	W56795
Cohen, Betsy Hilda	L/Cpl	NF409542
Cohen, Charles Joseph	Pte	NX202902
Cohen, Clive Phillip	S/Sgt	N77274
Cohen, Colyn Adrian Keith	Lt-Col	N60114
Cohen, Cyril	Pte	NX193870; N219371
Cohen, Cyril	Sgt	VX62360
Cohen, Cyril Wolf	WO2	V80616
Cohen, David	Pte	N225710
Cohen, David	Pte	V36603
Cohen, David Ian	Pte	VX127645
Cohen, Dorothy Rose	Pte	VF395600
Cohen, Douglas Harry	Capt	N429535; NX200300
Cohen, Edward	Pte	V144751
Cohen, Edward	Capt	VX43099
Cohen, Emanuel	Cpl	N240800
Cohen, Emanuel Edward	Pte	V15938
Cohen, Francis Lionel	L/Cpl	N29162
Cohen, Fritz (Fred)	Pte	N248253
Cohen, Gabriel	Capt	VX111296
Cohen, Geoffrey	Maj	VX291
Cohen, George	L/Cpl	W51126
Cohen, George David	Gnr	N223255
Cohen, Harold	Sgt	W29875
Cohen, Harold	Capt	WX32639
Cohen, Harold Edward	Bdr	VX80699
Cohen, Harold Francis	Maj	NX114733
Cohen, Harry	Sgt	N213796; NX167886
Cohen, Harry	L/Cpl	N226294
Cohen, Harry	Sig	NX164819
Cohen, Harry	Pte	VX69513
Cohen, Henry	Pte	V206826
Cohen, Henry	Cpl	V365413
Cohen, Hyman Louis	Cpl	NX160533; N255294
Cohen, Ian Athol Lawrence	Sgt	NX144845
Cohen, Isaac	Cpl	NX52198
Cohen, Jack	S/Sgt	S1172
Cohen, Jack	Lt	VX126042
Cohen, Jack Beresford	Pte	N323742; NX200619
Cohen, James Frederick	Sgt	NX15793
Cohen, Joel Joshua	Pte	W67235; W78741
Cohen, John	Sgt	WX39842
Cohen, Joseph	Cpl	N218705

Jewish Anzacs

NAME	RANK	SERVICE NO.	NAME	RANK	SERVICE NO.
Cohen, Joseph	Pte	V65481	Cohn, Herbert Paul Israel	Pte	N221648
Cohen, Joseph	Lt	V350291	Cohn, James	Pte	N440022
Cohen, Keith Frederick	Sgt	QX27288	Cohn, Kurt	Pte	V377768
Cohen, Leon	Sgt	V509654	Cohn, Louis Ludwig	Pte	N321359
Cohen, Leon	S/Sgt	W31876	Cohn, Max	Pte	N196496
Cohen, Leonard	Pte	NX202209	Cohn, Seigfried Salomon	Pte	V378390
Cohen, Leonard Leslie	Pte	VX46192	Cohn, Siegbert Simon	Pte	N199747
Cohen, Leslie	S/Sgt	VX124482	Cohn, Werner	Cpl	V377880
Cohen, Leslie Lyon Livingstone	L/Sgt	N447352	Cohn, Werner Julius	Pte	N286843
Cohen, Lionel	Lt	VX124044	Colley, Leon Edward	WO2	N65587
Cohen, Lionel Frederick	Gnr	N223410; NX178360	Colman, Gerald John	Cpl	N221501; NX179410
Cohen, Lou	Pte	VX27679	Colman, Jack	Capt	NX203771
Cohen, Louis	L/Cpl	N382506	Colman, Walter Ulrich	Pte	N221507
Cohen, Louis David	Pte	VX48371	Conway, Harold Jack	S/Sgt	N222402; NX126018
Cohen, Lysbeth Rose	Lt	NF464059	Copeland, Norman Charles	Pte	V38152; VX135429
Cohen, Mark	Gnr	NX55613	Coper, Fritz	Pte	N221540
Cohen, Mathew	Cfn	W96922	Coper, Willy	Pte	N321329
Cohen, Maurice	Sgt	V5216	Copolov, Alan	Pte	V370797
Cohen, Maurice	Lt	V513452	Copolov, Myer	Gnr	V310215
Cohen, Maurice	Bdr	W19606	Coppel, Keith Raymond	Pte	V501623
Cohen, Maurice Kerry	Cpl	NX79797	Coppel, Wilfred Allan	Cpl	VX146502
Cohen, Maurice Leonard	Pte	VX126602	Coppleson, (Sir) Victor Marcus	H/Lt-Col	NX35069
Cohen, Max	Pte	V377506	Corden, Ralph Simon	Cpl	V378193
Cohen, Max	Dvr	WX38266	Corrick, Ralph Joseph	Cpl	N83353
Cohen, Max Charles	Lt	NX203599	Cossmann, Richard	Pte	N221541
Cohen, Maxwell Michael	Pte	N256765	Court-Rice, Lewis Sinclair	Tpr	NX40005
Cohen, Mendal Bershoft **MID**	WO2	WX2641	Couzins, Henoch (Keziwoda)	Pte	V512581
Cohen, Mendel	Pte	VX113768	Couzins, Samuel	Pte	V280383
Cohen, Meryl Derham	Capt	V345046	Cowen, Harold Phillip	Lt	VX114289
Cohen, Meryl Louisa	Sgt	VF389714	Cowen, Harris	Cfn	NX142797
Cohen, Michael Ernest	Sgt	VX117521	Cowen, Lionel Hyman	Pte	VX502044
Cohen, Mourice	Pte	Q124282	Cowen, Mark	Cpl	VX23898
Cohen, Norman	L/Sgt	NX66055	Coyne, Franklin John	Gnr	VX21486
Cohen, Norman Benjamin (Cullen)		V511980	Coyne, Graham Maxwell	Cfn	VX51587
Cohen, Norman Marcus	Sgt	VX39155; V81842	Coyne, Ralph Joseph	Sgt	VX64527
Cohen, Norman Stuart	Cpl	VX50254	Crafti, Edward	Pte	Q203103
Cohen, Oram Edward Murray	Lt	N278749	Crafti, Jacob	WO2	Q191467; QX37462
Cohen, Pamela Ramsay	Sig	VF512514	Crafti, Mathew	Sgt	QX43658
Cohen, Percy Harris	Pte	V158492	Crafti, Pearl	Pte	QFX64362
Cohen, Phillip	Sgt	VX96515	Craig, David Ralph	Capt	VX104376
Cohen, Phillip Moses	Pte	V62127	Crawcour, Edwin Sydney	Sgt	VX148289
Cohen, Reginald George	Pte	N225506	Crawcour, Jack Athol	Pte	V56807
Cohen, Ronald Lewis	Sig	NX2163	Crawcour, Jean Audrey	Cpl	N391146
Cohen, Roy David *	Lt	NX34909	Crawcour, Joseph Aubrey	L/Sgt	N324015
Cohen, Roy Samuel	Capt	QX59539; Q119895	Crawcour, Sydney	Capt	VX226
Cohen, Russell Alexander	L/Cpl	N202229	Cremer, Samuel	Sgt	NX67585
Cohen, Samuel	Gnr	NX145634	Croot, Alexander	Pte	NX24711
Cohen, Samuel	Spr	W55580	Crowne, Joseph Miar	Bdr	NX131896
Cohen, Samuel	Pte	W60895	Crownson, Sidney Kadish	Capt	V147212
Cohen, Samuel Bernard	Pte	N439649	Crystal, David	Cpl	VX119413
Cohen, Samuel Herbert	Pte	V66126	Csalan, Ernest	Pte	N221508
Cohen, Samuel Victor	Pte	V506089	Csalan, Ladislas	Pte	N463177
Cohen, Sydney Michael	Pte	V27228	Cukierkan, Jankiel	Pte	V377093
Cohen, Thomas Burnett	S/Sgt	NX59282	Cullen, George Jocelyn **MBE**	Maj	NX12334
Cohen, William David Kerry	Cpl	NX104445	Cullen, Paul Alfred **DSO & Bar**	Maj Gen	NX163
Cohen, William Jacob	L/Cpl	V18192	Curzon, Maurice	Lt	V147223
Cohen, Wolf	Sgt	V13745	Czesny, Pinkus	Pte	V378057
Cohn, Alfred Theodor	Pte	N221624	Da Costa, Alfred Lucien	Spr	VX83455
Cohn, Arnold	Pte	V377731	Da Costa, Louis	Sgt	N282461
Cohn (Rothstadt), Betty Augusta	Capt	SX10647	Dabscheck, Jacob	L/Cpl	VX121995
Cohn, Hans	Pte	N286897	Dabscheck, Morris Barnett	Pte	V281373
Cohn, Heinz Hermann	Cpl	N221502	Dahan, Bernard	Pte	V363833

Appendix 2: Those who served

NAME	RANK	SERVICE NO.
Dahl, Hans	Pte	V377581
Daltrop, Rolf Bernd	L/Cpl	V377503
Dalvean, Louis	Pte	V156984
Dalvean, William	Pte	VX120508
Danby, Fred	Pte	S83020
Danby, Peter	Pte	V377504
Danciger, Sigmund *	Gnr	NX38170
Dane, Mario	Pte	V378010
Danglow, Frank Dalbert	Lt	VX117041
Danglow, Jacob	Chap Col	V507442
Dankowitz, Robert (Norbert Naftali)	Pte	V377351
Danzig, Felix	Sgt	V377964
Danziger, Gerhard (Dunn, Gerald)	Pte	V377502
Danziger, Herbert	Pte	N437738
Danziger, Max	Pte	V377733
Dare, Jacqueline	Sig	NF409554
David, Max	Pte	N436692
Davidovitz, Joseph (Davis) *	Gnr	NX17457
Davidson, Hans	L/Cpl	V378271
Davies, Judah John (Shwabsky, Judah David)	Pte	NX21545
Davis, Albert Louis	Pte	VX123839
Davis, Alexander Simeon	Pte	NX97697
Davis, Alfred Sydney	Sgt	VX916
Davis, Archie Wolfe	Cpl	VX66478
Davis, Arthur Davis	Sgt	N50843
Davis, Cecil	Pte	VX126200
Davis, Cecil Abraham	Pte	N462485
Davis, Charles Alexander	Pte	NX179729
Davis, David Isadore	Pte	Q28518
Davis, David Samuel	Pte	V363516
Davis, Eric Lewis	Maj	NX243
Davis, Geoffrey Edward	Gnr	NX15043
Davis, Harold Lewis	Capt	NX203551
Davis, Harry John	Sgt	N388747
Davis, Herschel	Pte	VX101396
Davis, Hyman Aaron	Lt	NX138558; N105256; NX59250
Davis, Hyram	Pte	VX144428
Davis, Ian Mark Percival	Pte	NX24229
Davis, Jack	Cpl	NX82657
Davis, John Lewis	Gnr	NX110088
Davis, Joseph Henry	S/Sgt	50646; NX16394
Davis, Joy Gertrude	Pte	WFX17052
Davis, Louis (Marcus)	Pte; Gnr	NX54394; N454810
Davis, Myer	Spr	P127
Davis, Phillip	Cpl	N391533
Davis, Rufus Solomon	Sgt	W7227; WX35887
Davis, Samuel	Pte	N442496
Davis, Samuel	Pte	V195460
Davis, Winston Joseph	S/Sgt	NX9320
Davis, Wolfe	Maj	V147216
Deane, Nathan	Pte	NX18737
De Groen, Geoffrey	Sgt	NX67344
Dehn, Heinz	Pte	V503914
Deitch, Abraham	Sig	NX112011
Deitch, Bernard	Dvr	N464117
Deitch, Lewis	L/Bdr	N257001
Deitch, Myer *	Pte	N461375
Dengler, Erwin	Pte	N461375
Dessauer, Gerhard	Pte	N226706
Deutsch, Alfred	L/Cpl	V500734
Deutsch, Felix	L/Cpl	N303744
Deutsch, Frederick Michael	Pte	V502449
Deutsch, Joseph	Pte	V377409
Deutsch, Norbert	Pte	N303742
Deutsch, Walter	Pte	N221543
Devries, Max Adolf	Pte	V377738
Diamond, Bertram Hershell	Capt	NX130565
Diamond, Frank Jacob	Pte	NX190221
Diamond, Henry	Pte	N224853
Diamond, Herbert Maurice	Pte	N457459
Diamond, Richard	S/Sgt	N281476; NX131825
Diamond, Ronald Braham	Pte	NX190222
Diksztejn, Abraham	Cpl	NX164799
Dinte, Alexander Julius	Pte	Q267242
Director, Max	Pte	V378111
Doctor, Walter	Pte	N321145
Dodge, Frederick	Pte	V378100
Dodge, Kelvin Howard	Pte	N221544
Don, Louis	Cpl	N219122
Doobov, Jacob Jankel	Cpl	Q266394
Dorevitch, Alexander	Pte	V46464
Dornberg, Kurt	Cpl	V377582
Dorsen, Frederick	Pte	N221625
Drach, Otto	Pte	V377413
Dresdner, Heinz	Pte	N237039
Dresler, Max	Pte	V378257
Dreyfus, Alfred	Pte	V377455
Drezner, David	Pte	V377149
Driels, Hans Juergen	Pte	V377500
Drucker, Heinz	Pte	VX151786
Dryen, Edward	Pte	N278844
Dryen, Leonard	Pte	NX80933
Dryen, Ronald Gordon	Maj	N23825; NX104704
Duband, Samuel	Sig	VX110972
Dubiner, Edgar	Pte	V377877
Dubsky, Hugo	Pte	V377911
Duldig, Karl	Pte	V377986
Durlacher, Gordon Louis	WO2	V81069
Durlacher, Hans Merman Moritz	Pte	V377701
Dushak, John Morris	Pte	N447325
Dvoretsky, David	Capt	W13217
Dvoretsky, Harold	L/Cpl	W15421; WX37475
Dzienciol, Israel Szymsol	Pte	W60820
Dziwak, Ber	Pte	V377855
Earl, Eddie	Pte	V377105
Earl, George *	Cfn	VX58940
Eaton, David Norman	Sgt	NX100487
Ebel, Bernhard	Pte	V377905
Ebstein, Walter George	Pte	V378175
Eckstein, Erich	Pte	V377904
Edel, Erwin	Cpl	NX116367
Edel, Waldemar	Cpl	N226519
Edelhofer, Friedrich	Pte	V377495
Edelman, Alwyn David	Sgt	SX15052
Edelman, Harry Jacob	Cpl	WX39445
Edelman, Howard John	Maj	SX13896
Edelman, Joseph Robert	Pte	WX34797
Edelman, Simon	Pte	N456528
Edelstein, Leib	Pte	V378302
Edelstein, Ludwig	Cpl	V377399
Edelsten, Hymie	Gnr	V196672
Edwards, Harry Bernard (Eibuschitz)	Pte	N445182
Edwards, Henry	WO2	NX171909

World War II, Australian Army [cont.]

NAME	RANK	SERVICE NO.	NAME	RANK	SERVICE NO.
Edwards, Samuel	Cpl	NX108941	Epstein, Ludwig	Cpl	V377718
Efron, Keith Ephram	Pte	V517535	Epstein, Phillip Jacob	Sgt	VX17609
Efron, Solly Henry	Pte	V206713	Epstein, Raymond	Pte	V504822
Eglitzky, Benzion Charles	Capt	NX203798	Epstein, Samuel	Cpl	NX100273
Ehrlich, Karl Wolfgang	L/Cpl	V377415	Epstein, Stanley Leonard	Cpl	NX190808
Ehrlich, Walter	Pte	V377408	Epstein, Walter	Pte	V377580
Ehrmann, Kurt	Pte	V377498	Esser, Alfred Adolph	Capt	V147741
Eichler, Paul	Pte	V377336	Ettinger, Siegimond Wolf	Pte	V377771; VX129021
Eigenberg, Szmul Leib	Pte	V377966	Eule, Heinrich	Pte	V377416
Eilenberg, Alen Henry	S/Sgt	V35109	Exiner, Robert	Cpl	VX129206
Eilenberg, Emanuel Gordon	Sgt	V366723	Eynstone, Herbert Horace	Sgt	VX79365
Eilenberg, Jim Albert	Sig	VX94047	Fabian, Erwin	S/Sgt	V377518
Eilenberg, Ronald Lewis Mid	Lt	VX19620	Fabian, Leo	Pte	V377790
Einbinder, Max	Pte	V378272	Factor, Abraham Joseph (Andy)	Pte	V377173
Einfeld, John Isidore **MID**	Capt	NX102512	Faerber, Hans Artur Benno	Pte	V377046
Einfeld, Joseph	Sgt	NX25531	Fagen, Leon	Sgt	NX170462
Einfeld, Lawrence	Pte	N217842	Fagen, Walter	Pte	N27254
Einhorn, Joseph	Pte	W5890	Faifer, David	Cpl	V206716
Eisen, John Harold	Cpl	NX141271	Faigen, Harry	Spr	WX40978
Eisen, Otto	Pte	VX129141	Faigen, Maxwell	Pte	N226754
Eisenberg, Adolf	Cpl	V378112	Faigenbaum, Aron-Zelik	Pte	W60946
Eisenberg, Charles	Pte	N220082	Faigenbaum, Harry	Pte	W60812
Eisenstein, Otto	L/Cpl	W78014	Fajnsztejn, Naftoli Bert	Pte	V377329
Eisinger, Erich	Pte	V377826	Fajwlowicz, Mark (Lovett)	Pte	V377744
Eisler, Hans	L/Cpl	N321028	Faktor, Szulem	L/Cpl	V378229
Eisler, Robert	Pte	N455701	Falk, David	Sgt	NX120815
Eismann, Jakob	Pte	V377342	Falk, Frederick Albert	Pte	N452612
Eisner, Arnold	Pte	V377808	Falk, Gerald Y.	Capt	N60400; NX70784
Eisner, Hans	Pte	N224619	Falk, Leib Aisack	Chap	N393221
Eizenberg, Leonard Isadore	Sgt	NX118194	Falk, Norman	Sgt	N75265; NX67761
Eizenberg, Leslie	Pte	VX142522	Falkenstein, Hans	Pte	V377549
Eizenberg, Morris Victor	S/Sgt	QX12146	Farkas, George	Gnr	N467146
Elbaum, Leon	Sgt	V60988	Faust, Barry	Sig	NX190117
Elbaum, Phillip	Pte	V206714	Faust, Gerald	Sig	N219976
Elboz, Jack (John)	S/Sgt	N36250	Feder, Ela	Pte	V377070
Elfman, Frederick	Cpl	VX130874	Federbusch, Markus Abraham	Pte	V378304
Elias, Stanley	Pte	V175182	Feher, Emeric	Pte	V377875
Ellis, Archie Samuel	Maj	VX117132	Feibes, Fritz Henry	Pte	V378334
Ellis, Joshua Harry	Cpl	NX148580	Feigen, Dennis	Sgt	NX157508; N17869
Ellis, Robert	Pte	N244846	Feinberg, Hyam	Gnr	VX121666
Elsner, Hubert Clive	Pte	W31779	Feistman, Heinz Peter	Pte	V513560
Eltham, Walter	Pte	V377826	Feld, Cyril	Pte	V113380; VX135834
Elton, Henry Joseph	Pte	V377794; VX129248	Felder, Adolph	Cpl	V377492
Elton, William	Pte	V378319	Felder, Henry	L/Cpl	V377340
Emanuel, Joseph Solomon	Capt	V147622	Feldheim, Sydney Solomon	Pte	N71535
Emanuel, Leslie	Sgt	NX91479	Feldman, Simon Ferdinand	Capt	WX30806
Emden, Walter Heyman	Sgt	V377979	Feldman, Solomon A.	Pte	V212163
Encel, Ezyrel	Pte	V377018	Feldmann, Julius	WO2	VX110712
Engel, Rudolf	Pte	N221627	Feldmann, Robert	Pte	V55001
Engelander, Aaron	Pte	N323689	Feldt, Cecil (Felot)	Pte	NX23743
Engelmann, Hans Robert	Pte	V509762	Feldt, Ernest Louis	Sig	NX3705
Engelmann, Max	Pte	V377497	Feldt, Henry Harris	Pte	SX18972
Englander, Eric Simon	WO2	VX143926	Feldworm, Rubin	Pte	V378061
Ensly, Joshua	Pte	WX11911	Feller, Alfred	Spr	N217938
Epshtein, Alack	Pte	V156999	Feller, Raymond Woolf	Lt	NX117564
Epstein, David	Pte	W6556	Fellner, Emeric	Pte	V515159
Epstein, Garth Leon	Sgt	VX62705	Fernandez, Albert *	Pte	NX19620
Epstein, George Isadore	Pte	W69513	Ferstat, William	Maj	WX30988
Epstein, Harry	Pte	NX168180	Festberg, Alfred	Pte	V378269
Epstein, Herbert Samuel	Pte	W48553	Feuerstein, Franz Wolfgang	Pte	V377519
Epstein, Joshua	Sgt	VX88087	Feuerstein, Hans Gerhard	Pte	V377589
Epstein, Keith Wolfe Newington	Maj	VX81051	Fichmann, Hans	Pte	V377480

NAME	RANK	SERVICE NO.	NAME	RANK	SERVICE NO.
Fichtmann, Walter	Cpl	N316916	Fowler-Smith, Hyman	Sgt	NX112118
Fidler, Elja Noeh	Cpl	V377784	Fowler-Smith, Norcom	Lt	NX108129
Fidler, Jack David	L/Cpl	V378348	Fox, Solomon	Gnr	N237372
Fidler, Wolf	Pte	VX123834	Foxman, Abraham	Cpl	VX121667
Fiegel, Bernhard	Pte	N465070	Foxman, Samuel	Gnr	VX144893
Field, Eric Leslie	Pte	V377810	Fraenkel, Kurt	Pte	W60838
Field, Gerald	Capt	NX110240	Frajman, David Chaim	Pte	V377295
Fienberg, Isaac Woolf	Pte	N323548	Frajman, Rafel	Pte	V350976
Fienberg, Stanley Selwyn	Cpl	N99067	Frampton, Phineas Edward	Pte	N275762
Fienberg, Sydney Hyman Victor	WO2	N65897	Frank, Louis	Pte	N303608
Figdor, Alfred	Pte	V378298	Frank, Peter Robert	Pte	N237040
Fine, Bernard David	Pte	V280610	Frank, Rudolph Carl Otto	Pte	V378371
Fineberg, Harold	Cpl	VX125147	Frank, Werner	Pte	V377481
Fink, Brahm	L/Cpl	NX103207	Frankel, Eskel	Lt	VX3567
Fink, Jack	Pte	V366072	Frankel, Joseph	Pte	W61802
Fink, Morris	S/Sgt	VX23398	Frankel, Keith Louis	Cpl	Q125525
Fink, Rudi	Pte	N463341	Frankel, Leo	Sgt	VX44366
Fink, Samuel	Sig	VX145938	Frankel, Leslie	Pte	V350900
Fink, Sydney	Pte	V357142	Frankel, Lou	Pte	VX145342
Fink, Thorold *	Capt	VX111255	Frankel, Morris	Pte	VX82099
Fink, Wolf	Pte	V366073	Frankel, Norman	WO2	V123024
Finkel, Salomon	Pte	V378114	Franken, Ernest	Cpl	N321138
Finkelstein, Abe	Cfn	WX10924	Frankenberg, Aaron	Pte	N22129
Finkelstein, Beatrice	Pte	WF96162	Frankl, Fritz	Pte	N221628
Finkelstein, Ernest Hyman	Pte	VX82959	Franks, Phineas	Sgt	VX118434
Finkelstein, Francis Sydney	Lt	NX100206	Freadman, Ernest	S/Sgt	V350778
Finkelstein, Frank Albert	Pte	W86783	Freadman, Ralph	Capt	VX14188
Finkelstein, Harry	Pte	V156541	Freadman, Roy Joseph	Pte	V280836
Finkelstein, Harry	Pte	WX4637	Fredericks, Irvin Joseph	L/Cpl	N221511
Finkelstein, Maurice	Cpl	NX191659	Freedman, Abraham	L/Sgt	V82509
Finkelstein, Nathan	Cfn	VX138018	Freedman, Barnett Emanuel	Sig	VX147145
Finkelstein, Ralph	Tpr	WX32713	Freedman, Claude Nathaniel	S/Sgt	WX1469
Finkelstein, Saul	Gnr	W32859	Freedman, George	Pte	W13702
Finkelstein, William	Pte	W75832	Freedman, Harry	Chap	V
Finkelstein, William	Pte	W236671	Freedman, Harry	Pte	V156054
Finkelstein, William George	Pte	WX4008	Freedman, Hedley John **MID**	Maj	WX3393
Finsterbusch, Arnold	Pte	N221510	Freedman, John	Dvr	W32829
Firer, Max	Cfn	V157568	Freedman, John Nathaniel	Lt-Col	VX62097; VX80969
Firstenberg, Michael David	Pte	V501194	Freedman, Joseph Abraham	Cpl	VX102274
Fischbach, Max	Pte	V378113	Freedman, Lionel Henry	Pte	V35118
Fischer, Hans	Sgt	V377361	Freedman, Michael	Cpl	VX9819
Fischer, Hans	Cpl	V515089	Freedman, Morris	Pte	W77642
Fischer, Karl	Pte	V377869	Freedman, Nancy Amelia	Sgt	VF345369
Fischer, Karl Heinz	Pte	N221589	Freedman, Samuel Joseph	Sgt	V65881
Fischl, Eugen	Pte	V502450	Freedman, Yankiel (Jacob Abraham)	Sgt	VX83943
Fish, Joseph Louis	Spr	N247992	Freeman, Armand Jules	Sig	N220381
Fishelson, Joshua	L/Sgt	VX25228	Freeman, Nathan	Cpl	NX132086
Fisher, Bernard	Capt	V500114	Freiberg, Samuel	L/Cpl	N321331
Fisher, Solomon	Pte	V205554	Freiberger, Walter	Pte	V506034
Fitzer, Nathan		N324068	Freilich, Oscar	Tpr	NX34102
Flatau, Gert	Cpl	V377591	Frenkel, Erwin	Pte	V378230
Fleischer, George	Pte	N445181	Freudenthal, Bernhard	Pte	V377987
Fleischer, Oskar	L/Cpl	V377364	Freund, Carl	Pte	V502451
Fliece, Howard	Sgt	N221547	Frey, Fred	Cfn	W55790; WX39760
Flohm, Harry Abraham Lewis	Pte	NX151763	Frey, Horst	Cpl	QX29117
Flohm, Lionel Wilfred	Pte	W21528	Frey, Walter	L/Cpl	W96503
Flugelman, Herbert	Pte	N460171	Friedberg, Otto	Pte	N221697
Flussmann, Kurt	Pte	V514787	Friede, Hans Hugo	Pte	NX179892
Foldes, Lajos	Sgt	S82972	Friedeberger, Klaus	Pte	V377653
Foot, Reginald Reuben	Pte	N95442	Friedhofer, Arnold	Pte	V503911
Foreman, Hyman	Pte	W12395	Friedhofer, Karl	Pte	V503910
Forman, Solomon	Pte	W12452	Friedlaender, Bruno Ernest	Cpl	V377372

World War II, Australian Army (cont.)

NAME	RANK	SERVICE NO.	NAME	RANK	SERVICE NO.
Friedlaender, Paul	Pte	V378338	Gilbert, Molly Estelle	Pte	SFX25471
Friedlander, Gunter	Pte	N221514	Gilbert, Raymond	Pte	V354884
Friedlander, Ignaz	Cpl	V377419	Gill, Leslie Pejsach	Capt	VX150049
Friedlander, Martin	Pte	N221629	Gilovitz, Emanuel	Sig	N435835
Friedlander, Neville	Gnr	NX80364	Gilovitz, Samuel	Lt	N245625
Friedlander, Philip Myer	Pte	N457211	Gilray, Louis	Cpl	N9803
Friedlander, Sidney Jack	Pte	N342012	Ginges, Lionel Solomon	Cpl	N217589
Friedlander, Walter Herman	Pte	N231001	Ginges, William	Cpl	N413139
Friedlich, Ernst	Pte	V377625	Ginges, William	Spr	NX152621
Friedman, Arnold	Pte	V377352	Gingold, Henoch	Cpl	NX92721
Friedman, Henry Marcus	Cpl	VX145246	Gingold, Lejb	Pte	N321161
Friedman, Hyam	L/Sgt	V37631; VX146849	Ginsberg, Maurice William	Capt	NX108197
Friedman, Jonas	Pte	V501588	Ginsberg, Werner Ewart Israel	Pte	V377755
Friedman, Max David	Pte	V354651	Ginsburg, Walter	WO2	NX94834
Friedman, Percy	Pte	W78986	Ginter, Richard Abraham	Lt	VX94183
Friedmann, Kurt	Pte	V377569	Ginter, Samuel	Pte	V78293
Friedmann, Manfred	Pte	V377935	Gishen, Marie	Pte	VF519009
Friedmann, Walter	Pte	V377398	Glance, Alfred Maurice	Pte	V91919
Frieze, David Archibald	Pte	VX139629	Glance, Harold Harris	Spr	N73753
Frischer, Adolf	Pte	N464017	Glance, James Henry	Pte	W69502
Frischer, Emanuel	Pte	N464028	Glance, Samuel	Pte	W68850
Fritz, Geza	Pte	N464323	Glaser, Marks	Pte	N437797
Frohlich, Fritz	Pte	V378173	Glaser, Siegfried Peter	Pte	N221551
Frohlich, Heinz Alfred	Pte	NX179217	Glass, Alfred	Pte	V377230
Frosz, Josef	Pte	V378032	Glass, Bruce Barnet *	Pte	NX23202
Fryberg, Abraham **MBE MID**	Lt-Col	QX6379	Glass, Edward Gabriel	L/Sgt	N443760
Fryberg, Joseph	Sgt	VX25229	Glass, Harold Hyam	Pte	N42118
Fuerst, Walter	Pte	V377347	Glass, Kenneth Maurice	Gnr	N42203
Fuks, Jakob	Pte	V378115	Glass, Richard Lewis Barnet **MC**	Lt	VX45395
Fulop, Herman	L/Cpl	N346412	Glass, Robert Barnet	Cpl	NX23203
Furedi, Leopold	Pte	N464545	Glass, Rudolph	Spr	NX108682
Furhmann, Arthur	L/Cpl	V377626	Glassel, Joseph Myer	Lt	VX56930
Gabler, Arnold David	Pte	V377907	Glassel, Norman	Gnr	VX79745
Gabor, Martin	Pte	N221512	Glasser, Daniel	Sig	N53406
Gabriel, Werner Baer	Pte	V377567	Glasser, Maurice	Cpl	V145057
Galewski, George Manfred	Pte	N231008	Glasser, Samuel	Pte	T14923
Gans, Siegfried Samuel	Pte	Q230619	Glat, Marian	Pte	V377840
Gantman, Joseph	Pte	N280026; NX73742	Glattauer, Erwin	Pte	N221552
Garber, Meilach	Pte	V377192	Gleedman, Abraham Louis	S/Sgt	VX101626
Garcia, Bernard	Pte	W6790	Glick, Leopold Albert	L/Sgt	VX84733
Garcia, Dudley Abraham	Pte	S110147	Glick, Lionel	Pte	Q270240
Garcia, Joseph Nathanael	Maj	V16497	Glogau, Alex	Pte	V377545
Garcia, Maurice	Pte	WX37824	Glogowski, Nochum	Pte	V377017
Garcia, Raphael	Sgt	VX10354	Glover, Alfred	Pte	VX8308
Garden, Leslie James	Pte	NX30762	Gluck, Albert	Pte	VX111519
Gardener, Arthur	Pte	N303400	Gluck, Max	Cpl	N221513
Gardener, John	Pte	NX179927	Gluckman, Albert	Capt	NX76244
Garrick, Samuel	Gnr	Q125055	Gluckman, Carl Benjamin	Pte	V366995
Gayst, Henry	Capt	NX207586; 240131	Gluckman, Lasky	Pte	V363675
Gecht, Mendel	Pte	V378349	Glueck, Hermann	Pte	V377370
Geist, Hans	Cpl	V378160	Glueck, Salomon	Cpl	V377538
Gelbart, Benjamin	Pte	V155124	Goffin, Maurice	Pte	VX93654
Gelfand, Samuel	Pte	W60835	Goffin, Solomon	Pte	VX93653
Gerber, Walter	Pte	N221550	Gold, Abraham	Pte	VX55760
Gero, Joseph	Sgt	NX90199	Gold, Andor	Pte	N221553
Gershon, Jack	Sig	WX18486	Gold, Ernst	Pte	V377536
Gershon, Jack Lester	Lt	NX86790	Gold, Hyme	Cpl	VX77294
Gerstl, Fritz	Pte	N321147	Gold, John	Spr	VX71443
Gerstman, Samuel Rudolph	Maj	VX135228	Gold, Josef	Pte	V378116
Gertler, Albert	Pte	N452873	Gold, Maurice	Pte	VX56050
Geschmay, John George	Cpl	SX16469	Gold, Max	Pte	V36883
Gilbert, Cecil Henry	Maj	N280262	Gold, Rufus Manuel	A/Bdr	NX141609

Appendix 2: Those who served

NAME	RANK	SERVICE NO.
Goldberg, Abraham	Pte	VX78583
Goldberg, Alroy Harold Cedric	Pte	N380133
Goldberg, David	Dvr	N215577
Goldberg, Ellis Myer	Sgt	TX15836
Goldberg, Emanuel	Cpl	V206099
Goldberg, Ernest	Pte	SX28358
Goldberg, Geoffrey Mark	S/Sgt	V146684
Goldberg, Hyam Hirsch	Cpl	N154435
Goldberg, Inez	Pte	NF455799
Goldberg, Jack	Pte	VX128002
Goldberg, Joseph	Cpl	V379050
Goldberg, Leon Braham	Dvr	VX111712
Goldberg, Leonard Keesing	Pte	S66049
Goldberg, Leslie Claude	Pte	VX18523
Goldberg, Maxine Leah	Pte	NF453037
Goldberg, Morry	Cpl	NX178973
Goldberg, Myer		V52067
Goldberg, Nathan	Pte	SX5800
Goldberg, Percy	Pte	W95171
Goldberg, Reuben	Dvr	NX146076
Goldberg, Ronald Solomon	Pte	TX14354
Goldberg, Simon	Pte	VX74628
Goldberg, Solomon	Pte	VX145332
Goldbloom, Samuel Mark	Pte	V39658
Goldburg, Maxwell Alan	Sgt	Q194546
Goldenberg, Abe	Pte	WX42094
Goldenberg, Abraham	Pte	V505409
Goldenberg, Alfred	Pte	V357199
Goldenberg, Dan	Cpl	VX109529
Goldenberg, Norman	Sig	V53876
Goldflam, Mordka	Pte	W55863
Goldhar, Mordcha David	Pte	V350897
Goldhill, Vera Pearl	Lt	VF398041
Golding, Morris	Pte	V205171
Goldman, Alfred	Pte	V507195
Goldman, Herbert Joseph	Sgt	S75565
Goldman, Joseph	Capt	N393186; NX77297
Goldman, Kenneth	Cpl	SX20608
Goldman, Lazarus Morris	Maj/Chap	VX354
Goldman, Mary Patricia	Pte	NF454465
Goldman, Maurice	Capt	WX11063
Goldman, Max	Pte	V502075
Goldman, Norman Naphtaili	Pte	Q201994
Goldman, Percy Jehonation	Pte	Q137247
Goldman, Philip	Gnr	NX53961
Goldman, Reginald	Cpl	NX192256
Goldman, Richard		V500471
Goldman, Rudolf	Sgt	W60813
Goldman, Samuel	Sgt	N391705; NX193484
Goldman, Samuel	Pte	NX43942
Goldman, Samuel	Capt	WX32690
Goldman, Shalom	Pte	W60972
Goldman, Szyja	Sgt	Q149302
Goldman, Walter	Pte	N321139
Goldmann, Arnold	Pte	N221724
Goldmann, Bernhard	Pte	N463176
Goldmann, Bernhard	Pte	V377484
Goldmann, Joachim Friedrich	Pte	V377699
Goldmann, Leo Werner	Pte	V377534
Goldner, Fritz	Pte	Q272891
Goldring, Max	Cpl	NX18708
Goldring, Woolf Jack	Pte	N225601

NAME	RANK	SERVICE NO.
Goldschmid, Ervin	Pte	N463219
Goldschmidt, Hans	Pte	N221592
Goldschmidt, Henry	Pte	N186822
Goldschmidt, Eric	Pte	V377550
Goldschmidt, Richard	Pte	N231015
Goldsmith, Arthur Joseph	Pte	V62143
Goldsmith, Herbert Henry	Sgt	VX70154
Goldsmith, Leslie Joseph	Pte	VX3518
Goldstein, Aaron	WO2	V167200
Goldstein, Alexander	Maj	N78775
Goldstein, Alexander	Pte	V83884; VX22081
Goldstein, Alfred David	Cpl	NX25703
Goldstein, Benjamin	Pte	VX59993
Goldstein, Bernard	Pte	N324095
Goldstein, Cecil Mitchell	S/Sgt	N469715
Goldstein, Cyril	Sig	V72788
Goldstein, Ernst	Pte	N463182
Goldstein, Fritz	Pte	V378268
Goldstein, George Henry	Pte	N218783
Goldstein, Hans Alfred	Pte	V377977
Goldstein, Hans Felix	Pte	V377587
Goldstein, Harry Morris	Cpl	V156685
Goldstein, Harry Sidney	Capt	NX120166
Goldstein, Jack	Cpl	NX44038
Goldstein, Julius	Pte	Q153421
Goldstein, Louis Barnett	Sgt	VX73670
Goldstein, Mark	Pte	N291418
Goldstein, Mark	Cpl	NX200305
Goldstein, Neville Joseph	Sgt	NX98294
Goldstein, Otto	Pte	V378267
Goldstein, Phillip	Cpl	NX203849
Goldstein, Ralph Saul	Cpl	NX123063
Goldstein, Solomon	Pte	N176930
Goldstein, Werner Julius Max	Pte	N224767
Goldstone, Morris *	Lt	VX25259
Goldsvaig, Israel	Pte	W64403
Goldsztat, Szjya	Pte	V378051
Goldwasser, Szlama	Pte	V377153
Gollant, Myer	S/Sgt	VX19796
Golomb, Gilbert	Lt	NX3359
Golomb, Lewis Goodman	Lt	N455531; NX173017
Gonsiorowski, Manfred	Pte	V378335
Goode, Eli	Cpl	W81329
Goode, Herman	Cpl	WX14880
Goodman, Bernard	Spr	NX73881
Goodman, Bernard Frederick	S/Sgt	NX120127
Goodman, Clive Ernest	Bdr	VX114795
Goodman, David Arnold	Pte	N213573
Goodman, Henry (Gutfeund, Heinz)	Pte	NX179875
Goodman, Hyam Eric	Gnr	N442466
Goodman, Isador	Lt	V146311; VX117152
Goodman, John David	Gnr Sp Gp 2	N213417; NX153748
Goodman, Solomon	Pte	V78621
Goran, Barnett Maurice	S/Sgt	N261727
Goran, Leon	Pte	N69489; NX12728
Goran, Phillip Robin	Pte	NX33535
Gordon, Alec	L/Sgt	VX113393
Gordon, Bernard Isaac	Pte	S62649
Gordon, Cecil	Pte	N457460
Gordon, Egon Lyon	Pte	N221725
Gordon, Henry	WO2	NX139424

World War II, Australian Army (cont.)

NAME	RANK	SERVICE NO.	NAME	RANK	SERVICE NO.
Gordon, James Martin	Pte	VX1147	Greenberg, Mack	Gnr	WX41865
Gordon, Reuben Henry	Sgt	3135022; NX42754	Greenberg, Tony Samual	Pte	NX175326
Gordon, Samuel Lewis	Lt	N76923	Greenberg, William	Pte	WX39143
Gore, Herbert	Pte	N224804	Greenberg, William David	Sgt	NX166685
Gorney, Samuel	Pte	N215527	Greenfield, Joshua	Cpl	WX3546
Gorodkin, Abraham	Pte	V15451	Greenstein, Cyril	Dvr	N256415
Gorodnaski, Frederick	WO2	WX26400	Greenstein, Esther	Sgt	NF460437
Gorr, George	Capt	VX90835	Greenstein, Jean	Pte	NF460814
Gorr, Gershon	Pte	V395203	Greenstein, Leonard	Dvr	N255997; NX130992
Gotowizna, Israel Ber	Pte	V378035	Greenstein, Sidney	Pte	N461858
Gotowizna, Pajwel	Pte	V501800	Greenstein, Wolfe	L/Cpl	NX19573
Gottinger, Peter Martin	Pte	V510305	Greenwald, Arthur Douglas	Cpl	NX25387; NX155088
Gottleib, Otto	Sgt	V377367	Greif, Philip	WO2	W243223
Gottlieb, Hugo	Cpl	V502452	Gries, Heinz	Pte	V377763
Gottlieb, Leon	L/Cpl	V377588	Griff, Ben	Pte	S33478
Gottlieb, Walter	L/Cpl	N224966	Griff, Bernard Gordon	Sgt	SX5690
Gottschalk, Kurt	L/Sgt	W55796	Griffin, Alphonse	Pte	N333901
Goulston, Eric H.	Lt-Col	NX70332	Grinblat, Lazar	Pte	V205763
Goulston, Gordon Cedric	Cpl	NX53894	Grinblat, Malcolm	Pte	VX96959
Goulston, Roy Frank (Goulstow)	L/Bdr	NX78937	Grinblat, Raymond	Pte	V29282; VX130494
Goulston, Stanley Jack Marcus **MC MID**	Maj	NX12269	Grinstein, Adolph William	Pte	V503403
Gouttman, Alec	Spr	N467356	Grinston, Michael	Sgt	NX119192
Gow, Jack	Gnr	V151385; VX126993	Grischa, Sergius	Pte	VX77776
Grace, Eric Louis	Cpl	N224746	Grochowski, Calel	Pte	V378223
Grace, Leslie Percival	Pte	NX172838	Groenewoud, Arthur	L/Cpl	V354717
Gradsztejn, Baines	Pte	V378056	Groenewoud, Joan Margaret	Sig	VF389625
Graetzer, Fred	Pte	V377371	Gronner, Fred Georg	Pte	N410863
Graf, Eugen Peter	Pte	N221696	Grose, Harry	Sig	QX26263
Graf, Helmut Alex	Pte	V506887	Grose, Ralph Alexander *	Sgt	QX4724
Granek, Moszek	Pte	V378320	Grose, Samuel Henry	WO2	QX12850
Grange, Paul	Sgt	V143811	Grose, William	Sig	QX4614
Granger, Isadore Elias	Spr	VX91176	Gross, Dudley Alfred Edmund	L/Sgt	VX92245
Grasyan, Salomon	Lt	VX121036	Grossbard, Jacob	Pte	V377486
Gray, Hyman	Pte	V501810	Grossman, Joseph	Sgt	VX52073
Gray, Max	Pte	N93955	Grosvero, Edward John	Pte	VX25570
Gray, Wulf Hans	L/Cpl	V377857	Grouse, Madge	Cpl	NX145140
Green, Alfred	Sgt	N450795	Gruen, Fritz Henry Georg	Sgt	V377485
Green, Anne	Pte	WF56829	Gruenbaum, Kurt	Cpl	V513682
Green, Benjamin Morris Julius	Lt	V261051	Gruenbaum, Ludwig	Cpl	V377358
Green, Bernard Reuben		VX132681	Gruenebaum, Kurt Max	Pte	V377537
Green, Ernest Leslie (Eichengrun, Ernst)	L/Cpl	V377499	Gruenebaum, Manfred	Pte	N221554
Green, George Alfred	WO2	VX3355	Gruenfeld, Robert	Pte	V377388
Green, Harold Godfrey	Cpl	V187089	Grunberg, Mieczylaw	Pte	V377152
Green, Israel	WO2	N225603	Grunfeld, Alfred	Pte	N221556
Green, Jacob Neville	Cpl	NX174728	Grunseit, Fery	Capt	VX504193
Green, Leslie	Spr	N89258	Grunseit, Friedrich	Cpl	N191518
Green, Maurice	Pte	WX21073	Grunthal, Wolfgang	Cpl	QX29118
Green, Max Simeon	Sig	VX63352	Gruszka, Izaac	Pte	V378137
Green, Myer Barnett	Sig	V101790; VX126732	Gruszka, Perec	Pte	V377457
Green, Nathan	Pte	V156745	Gruzman, Laurence Charles	WO2	NX41591
Greenbaum, Louis	Pte	V44829	Grynberg, Max	Pte	V377882
Greenbaum, Raymond Simeon	Pte	V357411	Gubbay, Norman Albert	Gnr	NX100258
Greenbaum, Samuel Eric		V400546	Gubbay, Solomon	Cfn	NX99131
Greenberg, Alan Abraham	Pte	VX127668	Gumbert, Heinz	Pte	N410903
Greenberg, Alec	Bdr	WX38930	Gunsberger, Hans	Pte	N212135
Greenberg, David	Cpl	WX42479	Gunzberg, Michael	Pte	W66856
Greenberg, David Reuben	Pte	NX205642	Gunzburg, Benjamin	Pte	W66781
Greenberg, George	Pte	WX11928	Gunzburg, Samuel	Pte	W79340
Greenberg, Harry	Sgt	V186745	Gurewicz, Lew	Pte	V1205
Greenberg, Joseph	Pte	VX122387	Gurvich, Abrams	Pte	V377463
Greenberg, Leon	Pte	VX148571	Guss, Harry	Sgt	N274583
Greenberg, Leslie	Sgt	W12380; WX35298	Gust, Isaac	Cpl	V354522; V501869

Appendix 2: Those who served

NAME	RANK	SERVICE NO.
Guter, Leo	Pte	V378336
Gutman, Gerhardt	Pte	V377533
Gutmann, Felix	Pte	V509557
Gutnick, Hyman	Pte	NX79021
Guttenberg, Fritz	Pte	V377535
Guttmacher, Max	Pte	V377355
Guttmann, Karl	Pte	V377487
Haarburger, Manfred	Pte	V377547
Haarburger, Walter Paul	Pte	V377531
Haarburger, Werner	Cpl	V377532
Haas, Erich	Pte	N221558
Haas, Siegfried	Pte	N221630
Haase, Bruno	Pte	V377548
Hacker, Arnold	Pte	V378082
Hagenow, Kurt	Pte	V377546
Haim, Marcel (Haisea)	Pte	N346753
Hain, Mossy	Capt	VX145106
Hains, Robert Myer	Capt	SX15734
Hajos, Charles	L/Cpl	N221649
Halasi, Thomas	Pte	N452195
Halber, Jacob	Pte	NX172788
Halbert, Robert	Pte	VX129208
Hallenstein, Albert Richard	Pte	VX40599
Hallenstein, Ernest Michaelis	Pte	N460904
Hallenstein, Rolf William	Cpl	V377765
Halperin, Amran	Lt	WX36709
Halperin, Simon	Pte	NX153232
Halpern, Benjamin	Pte	V502453
Halpern, Berthold	L/Cpl	V377530
Halpern, Edward	Pte	W61920
Halphen, Peter	Pte	V377806
Halprin, Absalom	Sgt	N282658
Halprin, David	L/Sgt	VX2450
Hamery, Samuel	L/Cpl	V377012
Hamilton, Bertram Alfred	L/Cpl	VX18137
Hammer, Heinz	Cpl	QX41755
Hammerschmidt, Arthur	Pte	V377624
Hammerschmidt, Harry Heinz	Sig	VX503121
Hammond, Frank	Gnr	NX150104
Hammond, Walter	Sgt	NX88170
Hanemann, Sundel	Pte	N321020
Hanf, Israel Klaus Peter	Pte	N286896
Hannes, Eva Elizabeth	Pte	NFX207147
Harber, Joseph Lewis	Pte	V35490
Harlem, Bertram Julius	Pte	S70108
Harlem, Donald Alfred Lawrence **MID**	Lt	69252; SX1719
Harp, Samuel	Cpl	NX152476
Harris, Bernard Maurice	YMCA WLFO	
Harris, Cecil	Spr	VX113459
Harris, Clyde Jack		V340354
Harris, Cyril Montefiore *	Pte	NX56235
Harris, David	Pte	N221683
Harris, Edward Walter	Pte	NX161606
Harris, Jack Crownson	Pte	V504531; VX125612
Harris, Joel Mark	Maj	S15973
Harris, Joseph	Sig	VX6425
Harris, Leslie Samuel	Pte	VX79851
Harris, Louis Leslie	Capt	NX101918
Harris, Mark	Sgt	NX102733
Harris, Michael Henry	Pte	NX154836
Harris, Paul Leopold	S/Sgt	NX150001

NAME	RANK	SERVICE NO.
Harris, Reuben *	Pte	V157009
Harris, Ronald Ernest	Pte	V352604
Harris, Samuel	Gnr	VX1040
Harris, Syme Newell *	Cpl	VX63884
Harrison, Noel Edward	Pte	NX43679
Hart, Dorothy Caroline	Cpl	VF345058
Hart, Ivor	Cpl	VX61558
Hart, Jack	Sig	N219983
Hart, Norman Godfrey	Gnr	N248435
Hart, Solomon	Pte	VX36443
Hartman, Bernard Joseph	Pte	V311618
Hartman, Leo Alfred	Pte	V44495
Hartman, Neville	Pte	V507714
Hartstein, Hans	L/Cpl	N171950
Hartstein, John	Gnr	NX16480
Hartstein, Zedekiah	Pte	W20155
Hartwich, Guenter Julius	Pte	V377379
Hartz, David Solomon	Pte	W11862
Hartz, Ron Henry		WX2962; WX12567
Hartz, Sydney Abraham	L/Cpl	WX5106
Harvey, Edward Louis	Lt	NX31284
Hasenberg, Gerd Jacob		WX42042
Haskin, Norman	Pte	V36491
Haskin, Samuel Lionel	Pte	V185180
Hasson, Moses	Pte	N215294
Hatfield, Albert Victor	Capt	N60191
Hatfield, Edward Kozminsky	Maj	N60148
Hatfield, Roy Hyndes	Sgt	NX121951
Hatfield, Royston Hyndes	Capt	2101703; NX177995
Hatfield, Samuel Bolam	Capt	NX115376
Hausman, Berisch	Gnr	N323640
Hausman, Solomon	Pte	N230361
Haven, Samuel Michael	Pte	V55693
Havin, Daniel	Cpl	V76974
Havin, Samuel	Sig	V205308
Hawkins, Michael Joseph *	Cpl	NX98910
Hayat, Joseph	Pte	V395188
Hayman, Gilbert Samuel	L/Cpl	NX115391
Hayman, Marcus	Sgt	VX57101
Hearsch, Bernard	Pte; Sig	NX87494; VX64571; V38154
Hearsch, David	Pte	V55602
Hearst, John	Pte	V515572
Hecht, Robert	Sgt	QX42955; Q146806
Heckler, Max	Pte	V378158
Heidemann, Egon (Hayden)	Pte	N191520
Heimann, Warren Henri (Hyman, Werner)	Pte	V377357
Heine, Walter Paul Rudolf	Pte	V377541
Heinemann, Karl Heinz	Pte	V377695
Heiser, Solomon Barnett	Pte	Q200814
Helfand, Monty	Pte	VX500223
Helfgott, Elias Peter	Pte	V206139
Heller, Ernst	Pte	N437739
Helman, Charles John	Capt	SX34515
Helmer, Hyman	Cpl	N219498
Helmer, Izrael	Pte	V378069
Helmer, Jack	Cfn	V157014
Henry, Felix	Pte	N323733
Henry, Maurice Salmonow	Capt	NX203587
Herbst, Guenter Philipp	Pte	V500732
Herman, Andrew	Pte	N224969
Herman, David Kurt	Pte	V501375
Herman, Eric	Lt	N334078

World War II, Australian Army (cont.)

NAME	RANK	SERVICE NO.	NAME	RANK	SERVICE NO.
Herman, Esther Erna	Pte	NF462723	Hofbauer, Fritz	Pte	V378266
Herman, Harold Ellis	Pte	NX142729	Hoffman, Aaron Lipman	Capt	VX112065
Herman, Hymen	Pte	W68842	Hoffman, Benjamin	Cpl	W96087; WX39464
Herman, Louis Cyril	L/Cpl	V1544	Hoffman, Bruce	Pte	W96686
Herman, Maurice Kurtz	Pte	V146927	Hoffman, Bruce	Pte	WX26207
Herman, Sali	Sgt; Lt	NX102781; VX138789	Hoffman, Hyman Judah	Capt	WX39609; W93056
Herpe, Arno	Pte	V377323	Hoffman, Leo	Pte	N231019
Herr, Williams David	Pte	V377488	Hoffman, Myer Solomon	Cpl	VX118689
Herrmannsohn, Heinz	L/Cpl	V377544	Hoffman, Nathan	Pte	W82305
Herrnstadt, Arthur	Pte	V501545	Hoffman, Valda Victoria	Pte	NF461938
Hersh, Gus	Pte	V201494	Hoffman, William	Pte	V357562
Hertz, Cyril Sidney	Pte	N73019	Hoffman, Wolfe	WO1	5264; W244379; W2535; WX30572
Hertz, Rich	Capt	WX29078; W29856	Hoffman, Wolfe	Pte	V148000
Hertzberg, Albert Abraham	WO2	2522; NX8711	Hofman, Paul	Pte	V378306
Hertzberg, Gordon Lionel		N323560	Hofstaedter, Walter	Pte	V378274
Hertzberg, Harold Raymond	Sgt	N95756	Hohenstein, Siegfried	Pte	N221732
Hertzberg, Reuben	Capt	QX22735	Hollander, John Barnett	L/Cpl	NX137078
Hertzka, Hermann	Pte	N450611	Holloway, Billie Collins	Cpl	NX60016
Herz, Edgar	Capt	W61404	Holman, Simon	Capt	WX35266
Herz, Sophoni	Pte	V377981	Holzbauer, Hans	Sgt	V377339
Herzog, Herbert	Pte	V378305	Holzman, Isaac Wolfe	Pte	W23061
Heselev, Marcus	Pte	V158073	Holzman, Samuel Abraham	Pte	W22679
Heydemann, Walter	Pte	V377736	Homburg, Julius	Pte	V378117
Heymann, Fritz	Pte	V378382	Honig, Mattus	Pte	V155586
Heymann, Herbert	Pte	N321141	Honigsberg, Kurt	Pte	V377762
Heymanson, Arthur Henry Benjamin	Capt	VX104034	Hopkins, Fred	L/Cpl	V377021
Heynemann, James Guy	Sgt	V377529	Horin, Jack	Pte	VX113987
Hielman, Randolph	Pte	N236543	Horin, Maurice	Pte	VX124924
Hielman, Randolph	Pte	N236543	Horinack, Henry	Pte	V310897
Higson, Geoffrey William	Tpr	NX118235	Horowitz, Fred	Pte	V377346
Higson, Henry Russell	Sig	NX123943	Horowitz, Samuel	Pte	WX34640
Hildebrand, John	Pte	V310932	Horrvitz, Louis Myer	Pte	W78637
Hillel, Abraham Leslie	Pte	WX41487	Horry, Harry Rockman	Sgt	W8071; W19077; WX36504
Hillman, Gerszon	Pte	NX203163	Horwitz, Leon	Cpl	NX179539
Hillman, William Arnold	Capt	W28584	Horwitz, Myer	Lt	Q119190
Hilton, Artur (Heitler)	Pte	V377516	Huber, Leopold	Pte	N463199
Himmelhoch, Enid Sylvia	Capt	NX34833	Humberta, Judah Harris	WO2	N75213
Himmler, Ernst	Pte	N224778	Hunt, Eric Alfred	Pte	NX156556
Hirsch, Amnon	Pte	WX19516	Huppert, Eugene	Pte	V378366
Hirsch, Ernst Hermann	Pte	V506032	Hurst, Eric	L/Cpl	NX92432
Hirsch, Heinz	Pte	V377991	Hurtwitz, Huffshi	Pte	VX94167
Hirsch, Kurt	Pte	N221560	Hurwitz, Robert	Pte	VX53273
Hirsch, Walter Manfred	Pte	V377950	Hyams, Frederick	Pte	V1050
Hirsch, Walter Max	Pte	V377696	Hyams, Harry	Pte	V146727
Hirsch, Walter Simon	Pte	N460601	Hyams, Harry	Pte	W75620
Hirschberg, Gerdt	Pte	V377698	Hyams, Henry Barnett	Tpr	NX162681
Hirschberg, Gunter	Pte	V377539	Hyams, Leslie Albert	Gnr	VX139339
Hirschberg, Hans Ulrich	Pte	V377976	Hyams, Samuel Lawrence	Pte	V187202
Hirschel, Kurt Josef	Pte	V377016	Hyman, Arnold	Sgt	NX153569
Hirschfeld, Ludwig	Pte	V510829	Hyman, David	Pte	V366201
Hirschfeld, Werner	Pte	V377543	Hyman, Eric Montague **DSO MID** (WWI)	Maj	N75495; NX71049
Hirschfeld, Werner	Pte	V377959	Hyman, Harry	Gnr	NX100220
Hirsh, Brian Jack (Guenter, Jack Brien)	Sgt	VX129174	Hyman, Hyman	Pte	V337007
Hirsh, John	Pte	V206220	Hyman, Jack	L/Sgt	N219405
Hirsh, Phillip Sol	Sgt	VX130078	Hyman, John Philip	Lt	VX96099
Hirsh, Sam	Pte	V378134	Hyman, Simon (Simie)	Cpl	VX140029
Hirsh, Steven David	Pte	NX139053	Hymans, Sydney	Cpl	V503683
Hirst, Walter Menny	Cpl	N338805	Inberg, Mordka Aron	Pte	N321290
Hochberger, Simon	Pte	V377697	Indyk, Maurice	Pte	NX149277
Hochstadt, Abraham Hersch	Pte	N264572	Inlander, Rudolf	S/Sgt	VX146786
Hocmuth, Harry	L/Cpl	NX179646	Innes, Claude (Israelik, Klaus Abraham Samuel)	Pte	NX180923
Hoenig, Rudolf R.	Pte	N221561			

Appendix 2: Those who served

NAME	RANK	SERVICE NO.	NAME	RANK	SERVICE NO.
Irom, Josef	Pte	N231014	Jacobs, Ethel	Sgt	NF409156
Isaac, Saul	Pte	WX41058	Jacobs, Frank	Tpr	NX178983
Isaacman, Myer	S/Sgt	NX506139	Jacobs, Frederick Mitchell	Lt	N393230
Isaacs, Aby	Sig	VX119883	Jacobs, Herbert Sydney	Maj	VX133032
Isaacs, Emanuel	L/Cpl	NX191511	Jacobs, Jack-Zaky	Pte	V378129
Isaacs, Ernest Abraham	Sig	V53894	Jacobs, Joseph	Pte	NX7563
Isaacs, Eskill Nathan	Cpl	368030; VX16158	Jacobs, Leonard Myer	Sgt	V54969; VX66636
Isaacs, Geoffrey (Isles, Geoffrey Kenneth)	Pte	N218907; NX27075	Jacobs, Mark	S/Sgt	N71727
Isaacs, George Alfred	Sgt	SX39323	Jacobs, Mervyn	Pte	NX144231
Isaacs, Harold Ernest	S/Sgt	V205810	Jacobs, Morris	Lt-Col	VX138508
Isaacs, Harry	Cpl	VX20991	Jacobs, Otto	L/Sgt	V377420
Isaacs, Hila Evi	Sgt	VF396860	Jacobs, Peter Acland *	Sgt	VX37066
Isaacs, Jack Alexander **MBE**	Maj	V85274; VX39391	Jacobs, Raechel Miriam	Lt	NX122660
Isaacs, Jacob	Cpl	N82158	Jacobs, Robert George (George)	Lt	VX3362
Isaacs, John Henry	Cpl	V144259; VX85610	Jacobs, Samuel Joshua	Capt	SX10999
Isaacs, John Solomon	Pte	VX117944	Jacobs, Sydney	Lt	NX100527
Isaacs, Joseph	Gnr	N230183	Jacobs, Victor	Sgt	NX162137
Isaacs, Joseph	Pte	N252531	Jacobsohn, Heimann	Pte	WX42381
Isaacs, Joseph Myer	Sig	V205509	Jacobsohn, Walter	Pte	N463198
Isaacs, Marcus Woolf	Pte	VX78218	Jacobson, Isadore	Gnr	N50110
Isaacs, Maurice	WO1	N319555	Jacobson, Maurice	Pte	V508584; V53092
Isaacs, Michael Barnett	Sgt	N219509	Jacobson, Samuel	Gnr	V307443
Isaacs, Phillip Alfred	Cpl	V146568	Jacoby, Jacob	Pte	V377988
Isaacs, Robert Grouse	Gnr	N222593	Jaeger, Robert	Pte	N224858
Isaacs, Wallace Frederick	Spr	WX16820	Jaffe, Lewis Hyman	Pte	V36897
Isaacs, William	Sgt	V186436	Jagoda, Szyja Mordka	Pte	V377128
Isaacson, Arnold	Pte	V350861	Jakubowicz, Hellmuth	Pte	V377338
Isaacson, Arthur	L/Sgt	VX86626	Janover, Alec Wolfe	Sgt	VX127911
Isaacson, Barbara Joan	Cpl	VF391191	Janover, Perry	Pte	V60881
Isaacson, Edward	Cpl	VX116707	Jaques, Frank Arnold	Pte	N468469
Isaacson, Lynka Caroline	Capt	V388729	Jaretzky, Walter	Pte	N463169
Isaacson, Mathew	Pte	VX1123	Jarvis, Joseph William	Pte	N444385
Isaacson, Philip	Cpl	V83984; VX78526	Jarvis, Lewis	Pte	N463434
Isaacson, Samuel	Pte	VX1152	Jassniger, Walter	Pte	V377007
Isaak, Harry Joseph	Pte	N321149	Jayton, Harry (Jacobson, Hans)	L/Cpl	N221729
Isen, Bennett	WO2	Q164810	Jedwab, Israel	Pte	VX120299
Isenberg, Ben	Gnr	NX15881	Jedwab, Max	Pte	V378054
Isenstein, Robert Abraham	Maj	SX11585	Jedwabinski, Mashik	Pte	VX74979
Isles, John Neville	Sgt	NX190926	Jeffery, Joseph Simeon	Pte	NX119965
Israel, Abraham	Spr	Q124709; QX58960	Jeidels, Harry	Pte	V377345
Israel, Henry Ernest **DCM**	Maj	V144513	Jenkins, Phillip	L/Sgt	N236515
Israel, Joseph	Pte	N270945	Joachim, Alexander	Gnr	VX113743
Israel, Leslie Phillip	Pte	N61083	Joachim, Raynor Ralph	Capt	V132437; VX108491
Israel, Lionel Benjamin	Pte	N289084	Joachim, Ronald	Pte	NX165720
Israel, Michael Judah	Pte	V504073	Joel, Asher Alexander [Refer RAN list]	L/Cpl	NX113532
Israel, Miriam	Pte	VFX121993	Joel, Bernard Newton	Lt	W12182; WX29258
Israel, Morris Samuel	L/Col	VX108402	Joel, David	Lt	NX165688
Israel, Nathaniel Bert	Pte	Q200071	Joel, Isaac	Gnr	VX83199
Israel, Norman Joseph	Capt	V357212	Joel, Morris Samuel	Pte	V5078
Jablonsky, Alfred	Pte	V377572	Jona, Anna	Sig	VF397043
Jachounsky, Moris	Pte	V378210	Jona, Judah Leon	Capt	VX50843
Jack, Seeyon Michael	Tpr	NX114567	Jonas, Lewis	Cpl	NX24292
Jackman, Harry Hans **MBE**	WO2	859596; VX147583	Jonas, Seigbert	Cpl	N244840
Jacks, Sydney Orvell	Cfn	QX47650	Jones, John	Lt-Col	VX108487
Jackson, Louis Alfred	Lt	3107674; VX45541	Jones, Norma Dorothea	Lt	VX29699
Jackson, Martin Harold	Pte	V511642	Jontofsohn, Harry	Pte	V378307
Jackson, Victor	Spr	NX56357	Joseph, Abraham Isaac	Gnr	NX8534
Jacob, Ferdinand	Pte	V506030	Joseph, Albert	Pte	S212514; S31311; S110854
Jacob, Heinz Herbert	Pte	N321005	Joseph, Benjamin	S/Sgt	NX12855
Jacobinski, Horst (Jacobs, R.H.)	L/Cpl	V377952	Joseph, David Emanuel *	Gnr	VX85886
Jacobius, Heinz	Pte	V377540	Joseph, Ernest Arnold	WO2	VX19771
Jacobs, Charles Philip **MBE**	Capt	VX17859	Joseph, Harry	Dvr	N233175

Jewish Anzacs

NAME	RANK	SERVICE NO.
Joseph, Hilton Lindsay Laing	Pte	N206915
Joseph, Joel	L/Sgt	NX94642
Joseph, Kenneth	Pte	N187218; NX100685
Joseph, Leonard	Pte	NX33599
Joseph, Leslie	Dvr	NX87904
Joseph, Lewis	Sig	VX141756
Joseph, Louis	Pte	NX23871
Joseph, Lynn Harvey	Capt	NX77338
Joseph, Maxwell Deane	Sgt	NX101190
Joseph, Maxwell Harry	S/Sgt	V502418; VX124624
Joseph, Neil	Capt	N271536; NX70954
Joseph, Norman Joseph	Lt	NX13802
Joseph, Phillip Herman	Pte	N324195
Joseph, Raymond	Pte	NX104420
Josephson, Warwick Selig	Cpl	NX166644
Judell, Kurt	Pte	V378273
Judenberg, Heinz Werner	Pte	V377526
Juhn, Hans	Pte	N460906
Julius, Jack	Pte	N72644
Julius, Max Nordau	Pte	Q16732
Juni, Max	Pte	V16943; VX128643
Jurberg, Gabriel	Pte	V378084
Jurberg, Maurice	Pte	V205655; VX131036
Just, Frederick	Pte	V377694
Justitz, Alfred	Pte	V377515
Kacen, David	Pte	N228060; NX154329
Kaczynski, Gerhard	L/Cpl	V378378
Kadden, Gerd	L/Cpl	V377521
Kadisch, Julian	Cpl	V377422
Kadner, Ernst	L/Cpl	V377870
Kaffebaum, Hersch Elimelech	Pte	V377773
Kagan, Aron	Pte	V69289
Kahan, Maurice	Cpl	V9128
Kagan, Maurice	Pte	V65581
Kahn, Fritz	Pte	N261074
Kahn, Julius	Pte	V378314
Kahn, Robert Leo	Pte	V377348
Kahn, Rudolph Anselm	Pte	V378308
Kahner, Martin Max	Sgt	W94442
Kaiser, Frank Phillip	Sgt	NX114158
Kalcher, Fredrick	Pte	N450769
Kalik, Maxwell	Pte	VX3715
Kalisch, Paul	Pte	N463192
Kallenstein, B. (Stewart, R.B.)	Sgt	NX172294
Kamer, Edgar	Pte	V377325; VX129224
Kamien, Abe Joe	Pte	W2836; WX25362
Kaminski, Kurt	L/Cpl	V514769
Kaminsky, Menachin	Pte	V502327
Kaminsky, Soli	Pte	V12326; VX145633
Kamsler, George Hugo	Pte	NX180424
Kan, Alexander Elias	Pte	V46185
Kanatopsky, Abner	Pte	V55533
Kann, Herbert Carl	Pte	V377377
Kanter, Emil	Pte	V377558
Kantor, Theodore	Pte	N221563
Kantorowicz, Walter	Pte	V377982
Kaplin, Henry Arthur (Kapelnikoff)		N154102
Karpin, Colin	Cpl	VX104636
Kary, Hans Siegfried	Pte	N450796
Kasriel, Helmut	Spr	NX180187
Katschke, Heinrich	Pte	N450799
Katz, Aaron	Pte	V501193

NAME	RANK	SERVICE NO.
Katz, Albert	Pte	V377686
Katz, Alfred Felix	L/Sgt	V377577
Katz, Artur	Pte	V377421
Katz, Eli Aleck	Cfn	V516869
Katz, Ernest	Cpl	V377523
Katz, Frederik Manfred	Pte	V377827
Katz, George	Pte	W65177
Katz, Manfred	L/Sgt	V377921
Katzmann, Joseph	Pte	N435640
Kaufman, Abraham Sam	Pte	VX120288
Kaufman, Ernst Leo	Capt	V505945
Kaufman, Hans Guenther	Pte	N321334
Kaufman, John Alfred Morton	Pte	V507582
Kaufman, Norman	Pte	N391466; N389970
Kaufman, Sam	Pte	V378178
Kaufmann, Ernest	Pte	N321150
Kaufmann, Georg Edward Justus Hugo	L/Cpl	V515980
Kaufmann, Hans	Pte	V377693
Kaufmann, Walter	Pte	V377561
Kaufmann, Willy	Pte	V377573
Kay, Ralph Stanley	Cpl	NX161171
Kaye, Geoffrey Alfred	Maj	VX357
Kaye, Leonard Joseph	Sig	NX140499
Kaye, Maurice	Sig	NX178718
Kaye, Peter	Capt	350211; V16613; VX59291
Kaye, William	Pte	V66167
Kayne, Victor Abraham (Abrahams)	Sgt	VP7235; VX85136
Kayser, Norman	Lt	VX80949
Kedzier, Boruch Barry	Cfn	NX175508
Keen, Charles	Cpl	NX205122
Keen, Jack	Pte	NX141056
Keen, John Alexander	Capt	NX203493
Keesing, Albert	S/Sgt	NX165468
Keesing, Arthur Lewis **ED**	Capt	NX128654
Keesing, Roy Selwyn	WO1	NX25888
Keidan, Alec	Sig	VX81564
Keil, Hans Jurgen	Pte	V377688
Keisner, Aaron Harry	Pte	VX27729
Kellerman, Maurice Herman		N225609
Kellerman, Solman	Sgt	NX116157
Kelman, Sol	Pte	W79247
Kelson, Edgar Joe	Capt	NX65311
Kempe, Hermann	Pte	V378397
Kempler, Edward	L/Cpl	VX20217
Kempler, Heinz	Pte	N465160
Kenigsberg, Hersz Majer		N323656
Kennett, John (Katzner, Jakob)	Pte	V147354
Keonigsberger, Heinz Martin	Pte; L/Cpl	V501248
Kerpen, Leopold	Pte	V070007
Kersh, Cecil Isadore	Sgt	N281650
Kersh, Jack	Pte	NX29001
Kersh, Sydney	Pte	QX20396
Kessler, Albert	Cpl	N456949
Kessler, Heinz Peter	Pte	V378277; VX127547
Kezelman, Bernard Samuel	Bdr	NX106263
Khuner, Alfred	Pte	V377912
Kiefel, Rudolph	Pte	N481601; N384901
Kiffer, Jacob	Cpl	V504106
Kikis, Fred	Pte	N321017
Kinderlehrer, Les	Pte	V378101
Kindler, Rael Hyman		V55152
King, Marcus Lionel	Sig	NX102632

Appendix 2: Those who served

NAME	RANK	SERVICE NO.
Kingsley, Robert Walter (Kraus)	Cpl	N224786
Kingston, John Braham	Pte	NX178406
Kino, Walter Philip	Cpl	W48136
Kinstler, Izrael Hersz	Pte	W61059
Kirchhausen, Julius	Pte	V377597
Kirschner, Guenter (Kirsner, Gordon)	Pte	V377524
Kirschner, Stephen	Pte	N467841
Kirsner, Marcus **ED**	Lt-Col	VX81020
Kiss, Lazar Isaac	Pte	NX149154
Klajnsztajn, Szaja	Pte	V377848
Klarsfeld, Fritz (Field, Peter)	Pte	V377944
Klausner, Hans Stephen	Pte	V378278
Kleeberg, Albert	Pte	V378289
Kleiman, Charles	Pte	V155993
Kleiman, Josef	Pte	V377282
Klein, Eric	Cpl	N319435
Klein, Joseph	Gnr	VX52985
Klein, Manfred	Pte	V377690
Klein, William	Sgt	WX36692
Kleinermann, Albert	Pte	V377801
Kleinman, Simon Yudel	Gnr	VX88845
Klement, Frederick	L/Cpl	N346522
Klepfisz, Idel Leon	Capt	V513946
Klepner, Frank Herbert	Pte	V377296
Kliger, Sam	WO2	VX54962
Klimont, Georg Carl	Sgt	S82967
Klineberg, David	Capt	NX137121
Klitenik, Szymon *	Pte	VX92357
Klooger, Barnett	Pte	VX96955
Klooger, John	Pte	V311658
Klooger, Joseph	Pte	V156181
Klooger, Keith	Pte	VX149518
Klooger, Myer	Pte	V55707
Kluger, Bruno	Cpl	V377514
Klyne, Jeffrey Gehajak	Pte	V377010
Knopman, Szlama	Pte	NX103201
Knopp, Cecil	Pte	V502404
Knopp, Myer George	Pte	V198700; V505208
Knothe, Hans Walter	Pte	V377520
Koch, Hans Reinhard	Pte	N221723
Koenig, Hermann	Pte	N321046
Kohn, Frederick	WO2	V1457
Kohn, Hans	Pte	V377575
Kohn, Robert	Pte	V377359
Kolben, Felix	Pte	V378309
Koll, John	Pte	V378012
Komesaroff, Judah Leib	Pte	V364912
Komesaroff, Morris	Pte	V158273
Komesarook, Peter	Pte	V512320
Kommel, Barry Bennett	Pte	N223718
Komorner, Leo	Pte	V378399
Konewka, Pejsach	Pte	V378063
Konigsberg, Harry	Dvr	WX38254
Konigsberg, Nahman	Pte	W13972
Kooperman, John	Spr	WX41251
Kooperman, Max Joseph	L/Cpl	W50728
Koppel, Heinz	Pte	V377687
Koppstein, Heinz Adolf Henry	Cpl	N237045
Korman, Harry	Spr	NX174176
Korman, Jack	Pte	V39694
Korn, Fritz	Pte	V377684
Korngold, Benjamin	Pte	V377689

NAME	RANK	SERVICE NO.
Kornhauser, Jacob	Pte	V378066
Kosky, Albert Judah	Dvr	WX18037
Kossmann, Heinz	Pte	V377394
Kosterlitz, Rudolf	Pte	W57112
Kovacs, Gabon	Pte	N460911
Kowadlo, Leslie	Pte	V158646
Kozminsky, Geoffrey Carlisle	L/Cpl	VX14418
Kramer, Harry	Pte	N385837
Krantz, Henry	Pte	V377311
Krantz, Kenneth David	Capt	SX26147
Krantz, Sydney	Maj	SX13978
Krasenstein, Maurice Abraham	Pte	WX32654
Krasey, Sid	Gnr	V31494
Krasnostein, Amechi	Lt	WX33460
Krasnostein, Jacob Jack	Sgt	W59945
Krasnostein, Leslie	Pte	WX7446
Krasnostein, Solomon	Sgt	WX25433
Krass, Norman	Cpl	N482022
Kraus, Henry Paul	L/Cpl	N224961
Kraus, Walter	Pte	W64765
Krause, Aaron Samuel	Cpl	VX121462
Krause, Lothar	Pte	V377750
Krebs, Gunter	Pte	W94607
Krebs, Werner	Pte	N463121
Kreitzer, Harry	Pte	V206277
Krell, Isydor	Pte	V378206
Kremer, Joseph	Capt	VX138511
Krew, Maurice	Pte	V310609
Krieger, Sigmund William	L/Cpl	N321237
Kristianpoler, Max	Pte	N221726
Kristianpoler, Siegfried	Pte	N221730
Kriszhaber, Kurt	Pte	V377522
Kronach, Fritz Israel	Pte	N321325
Kronenberg, Reuben	Pte	V56668
Krug, George	Pte	N226654
Krug, Max Bruno	L/Cpl	N215591
Kruglak, Solomon	Pte	V377842
Krul, Mailach	Pte	V377852
Krupa, Leon (Leibert)	Gnr	N220356
Kuchmar, Norman	Pte	V158967
Kugel, Otto	Pte	N221719
Kuhn, Werner Julius	Pte	N221529
Kuner, Julius John	Pte	S86297
Kuner, Maurice	Pte	N393805
Kuperstein, David	Pte	V500956
Kupper, Paul	Pte	V378262
Kurlender, Berek	Pte	V378227
Kurtz, Abraham *	L/Sgt	V377849
Kurzki, Harry	Pte	N435764
Kurzmann, Fred Siegfried	Pte	V377737
Kux, Victor	Pte	V504474
Labisch, Kurt Simon	Pte	N221525
Lachman, Itamar	Sgt	VX121259
Lachman, Sumer	Pte	V378238
Lachter, Harold	Gnr	NX174203
Lake, Alan Victor (Lukner, Elie Wigda)	Pte	N224781
Lamm, Erwin	Pte	V501961
Lampert, Bernard	Pte	NX56574
Lampl, Willi (Wilhelm Wolfgang)	Cpl	V377680
Landau, Ivan Samuel	Pte	VX54868
Landau, Izrael Jakob	Pte	V377031
Landauer, Albrecht August	Pte	N221593

Jewish Anzacs

World War II, Australian Army (cont.)

NAME	RANK	SERVICE NO.
Landauer, Alfred	Pte	V502454
Landauer, John Louis	Pte	WX14928
Lander, Alexander	Pte	NX119945
Lander, Arnold William	Lt	NX107462
Lander, Jonathan	Lt	NX106354
Lander, Lewis	Spr	N73761
Landis, Jack	Cpl	N222607
Landman Lionel	Sgt	V61236
Landman, Jules	Sig	VX53057
Lane, Morrie (Koblentz, Moshe)	Pte	NX93064
Lang, Jack	Cpl	N218787; NX128297
Langfelder, Richard	Pte	V514939
Langford, Alfred Ernest	Pte	VX63270
Langley, Keith (Isaacs)	Cfn	VX123727
Langstein, Peter	Pte	V378263
Lapin, Allenby Abraham Michel	Lt	VX13848
Lapin, Charles	Pte	N410893
Lapin, James Michael	Pte	N47096
Lapin, Muir Jack Meyer	Capt	VX62200
Lapin, Norman	Gnr	NX50870
Laqueur, Rudi	Pte	V377682
Lash, Simon	Pte	N221656
Lasica, Wolfe	Pte	V158650
Lasker, Jack Lewis *	L/Sgt	NX50826
Lasker, Noel Emmanuel	Bdr	NX100350
Lasker, Sam	Pte	N221657
Lasky, Ella	Pte	VF395685
Lasky, Harold	WO1	VX112381
Lasky, Jack Lyons	Gnr	N348586
Lasky, Peter George (Laske)	Pte	V377651
Laufer, Ernst	Pte	V377674
Laufer, Kurt	Pte	V377675
Laufer, Moritz	Pte	V507319
Laufer, Richard	Pte	N221666
Laufer, Ulrich Siegmund *	Pte	V510654
Lawrence, Boris	Sgt	VX74348
Lawrence, Daniel Agranovich		A11794
Lawrence, Donald Samuel	L/Sgt	VX111485
Lawrence, Harold Sydney	Sgt	V91005
Lawrence, Herbert Abraham		VX23927
Lazarus, Desmond **MID**	Lt	NX83909
Lazarus, Ellen	Capt	VX272
Lazarus, Joseph	Pte	N324148
Lazarus, Keith Joseph	Capt	NX203809
Lazarus, Leo	Pte	VX112873
Lazarus, Leo Sydney	Sig	VX109466
Lazarus, Maifred Philip (Maifried / Marfried)	WO2; Lt	N70075; N76071
Lazarus, Ronald	Spr	V21064
Lazarus, Samuel Alexander *	Lt	VX19346
Lazer, Cyril Basil	Sgt	VX119074
Lazer, Marcus Lyon	S/Sgt	NX45865
Le Bransky, Baron	Cpl	VX142315
Lea, Harris	L/Cpl	V186977
Leber, Aaron	Pte	V186694; V39696
Lebrecht, Franz	L/Cpl	V377633
Lederer, Ernest	Pte	W78238
Lederer, Walter	Pte	N173077
Lederman, Peter	Pte	N224770
Lederman, Peter	Pte	VX150155
Lee-Bernstein, Marcus Henry	Lt	VX2585
Leedman, Charles Herbert	Lt-Col	WX29062

NAME	RANK	SERVICE NO.
Leedman, Harry	Lt	WX32375
Leedman, Robert Louis	Capt	WX38710
Lefcovitz, Henry	Pte	NX3103
Leffmann, Erich	Pte	V377663
Lehmann, Helmut	Pte	N221633
Lehmann, Kurt	Pte	N221522
Lehmann, Siegfried	Pte	V377435
Lehrer, Harry	Pte	VX96375
Lehrer, Isaac Henry	Pte	NX140009
Lehrer, Leo	Pte	V377742
Leicht, Ernoe Martin (Ernest)	Pte	V377743
Leidert, Wolfgang Josef (Leighton, Peter Warren Joseph)	Pte	V377659
Leighton, Harry	WO2	WX37136
Leiser, Kurt	L/Cpl	V377667
Lejderman, Montague Mordcha	Pte	V377300
Lemberg, Walter (Frederick)	Pte	N171953
Lemish, Aaron	Pte	V146257
Lemish, Lazarus	Cpl	VX116219
Lemish, Myer	Pte	VX140916
Lenn, Ernest	Cpl	NX158012
Lenny, Ivan	S/Sgt	WX34658
Lenny, Leonard Isaac	L/Cpl	W9853
Lenthen, Lewis Harris	Pte	N324041
Lenthen, Simon Solomon	Pte	NX83900
Lenzer, Mischa	Sgt	NX65167
Lenzer, Simeon Jacob	Pte	N223077
Leon, Gordon Mark	WO1	VX35882
Leonard, Julius	Sgt	N380159
Leopold, Heinz	Pte	V377740
Leschnitzer, Guenther	L/Cpl	V377761
Leser, Ernest	L/Cpl	V377437
Lesnie, Allan	Cpl	NX86020
Lesnie, Norman Moss George *	WO2	NX65478
Lester, Frederick	Pte	VX129226
Lester, Montague Cecil	Cpl	V501397
Letwin, Gerald *	Pte	V12886; VX56712
Letwin, Leonard Victor	L/Cpl	V300955; VX128103
Levant, George	Pte	S70279
Levenson, Harry	Pte	N465250
Lever, Jack	Gnr	N255367
Levey, Alfred	Pte	V4616
Levey, Athalstane George	Maj	NX107681
Levey, David Victor	Cpl	QX64173
Levey, Harris Charles	Pte	V158138
Levey, Joseph	WO2	Q426
Levey, Marcus	Pte	VX100961
Levey, Robert Edwin *	Pte	NX47023
Levi, Alfred Morris Ronald	Sgt	VX128769
Levi, Claude	Cpl	N224025; NX164461
Levi, Leslie Maurice	Sgt	NX181050
Levi, Lionel Phillip	Cpl	N224299; NX111521
Levi, Marcus	L/Sgt	VX52862
Levi, Max	Pte	V377676
Levi, Myer	Pte	VX139212
Levi, Zalman	Pte	W79293
Levien, Neville Keith	Sig	N218112
Levin, Daisy Francis	Cpl	VF396927
Levin, Harold	Bdr	WX25363
Levin, Jacob Solomon	Pte	W68718
Levin, Joseph	Gnr	N217757
Levine, Aaron	Sgt	NX144902

Appendix 2: Those who served

NAME	RANK	SERVICE NO.	NAME	RANK	SERVICE NO.
Levine, Boris Bernard	Cpl	VX118332	Lew, Pincus	Pte	V142457
Levine, David	Sgt	VX75155	Lew, Robert	Cpl	VX128564
Levine, John Louis	Cpl	Q136389; QX20974	Lewenberg, Henry	L/Cpl	V377027
Levine, Leiba	Pte	V378138	Lewin, Chaim	Pte	V377174
Levine, Sydney	Maj	NX111950	Lewin, Hans	Pte	N221566
Levitus, Albert	Pte	NX56682	Lewin, Rudolf Martin	Pte	V377920
Levitus, Reuben	Pte	N324058	Lewin, Walter	Pte	N221674
Levy, Alec	Sgt	V144303	Lewinski, Kurt	Pte	V377664
Levy, Alexander	Spr	SX8855	Lewinsky, Alfred	Cpl	V377662
Levy, Alexander	Spr	SX19646	Lewinsohn, Siegmund	Pte	V503913
Levy, Alexander	Cpl	V4414	Lewis, Allan Stanley	Sgt	N410874
Levy, Alfred Myer	Lt	VX86393	Lewis, Braham Ralph	Capt	VX91932
Levy, Derek Jack Marco (Levi)	Pte	VX56827	Lewis, Charles	Pte	NX93522
Levy, Donald Wilton	Tpr	NX168990	Lewis, Charles Bernhardt	Sgt	N27100
Levy, Edward Henry (Ted)	WO2	NX175338	Lewis, David	S/Sgt	VX135741
Levy, Elja Haims	Capt	SX22156	Lewis, Ernest Frederick **MID**	WO2	VX74469
Levy, Ernst	Pte	V377677	Lewis, Geoffrey John	S/Sgt	NX35220
Levy, Faith	Lt	VFX138621	Lewis, Harry	Pte	2121806; NX55095
Levy, Fritz	Pte	V377650	Lewis, Israel Jack	Pte	2122024; NX140616
Levy, Gary	L/Sgt	SX30294	Lewis, John	Pte	VX83242
Levy, George	Cpl	V4921	Lewis, John Moseley	Sgt	N25657
Levy, Gerhard	Pte	N467927	Lewis, Joseph	Cpl	V501341; VX64005
Levy, Hans Jakob	Pte	V377994	Lewis, Julian	Pte	NX54202
Levy, Henry	Spr	N73130	Lewis, Louis	Cpl	N225471
Levy, Henry Edward (Harry)	L/Cpl	VX64492	Lewis, Loulie Maxine	Pte	SF84159
Levy, Hyman	Pte	V206228	Lewis, Montague Bernard	L/Cpl	N7040
Levy, Israel	L/Sgt	N391573	Lewis, Morris	Pte	N219083
Levy, Jack	Pte	NX91790	Lewis, Morris	Pte	NX123772
Levy, Jack Leopold	Pte	NX24416	Lewis, Morris	Pte	V75104; VX116869
Levy, Jacob Alfred	Pte	W232670	Lewis, Phillip	Lt	NX89636
Levy, Jacob Lewis	Sgt	NX86286	Lewis, Ralph Abraham	S/Sgt	NX131237
Levy, Jerome	Pte	N25446; NX111126	Lewis, Robert Maurice	L/Cpl	VX44872
Levy, Joseph Neville	Sgt	TX14791	Lewis, Samuel	Cpl	NX69503
Levy, Keith Joseph	L/Sgt	VX125137	Lewis, Samuel	Bdr	WX32228
Levy, Kenneth Sydney	Sgt	V146902	Lewis, Solomon Andrew Phineas	Capt	N463704
Levy, Kurt Paul	Pte	V377963	Lewis, Woolfe	Gnr	WX25296
Levy, Lance Henry	Sig	SX3017	Lewisohn, Gerhard	Pte	V377889
Levy, Lazarus	Pte	VX151681	Lewkowicz, Jankel	Pte	V378059
Levy, Leonard	Cpl	VX56295	Libhaber, Pincus (Pinkus / Peter)	Spr	NX79029
Levy, Leonard Henry Jaques	Cpl	N65973	Libow, Leonard	Pte	NX109603
Levy, Leopold Michael	WO2	N223473	Lichtenstein, Fritz Peter	Pte	WX40340
Levy, Lewis	Pte	N275819	Lichtenstein, Kurt Caspar	Pte	V377344
Levy, Lewis		V205819	Lichtheim, Ludwig (Layton, Louis Simon)	Pte	V377436
Levy, Lewis Joseph	Capt	NX147865	Lieberman, Abraham Samuel	Gnr	Q149008
Levy, Lionel Hilton	Pte	N100576	Lieberman, Sydney Israel	Lt	V6080
Levy, Louis	WO2	N107664	Liebmann, Fritz Heinz	Pte	V377231
Levy, Louis	Pte	N229893	Liebrecht, Guenther	Pte	V501724
Levy, Maximillian	Gnr	N452946	Liebrecht, Heinz	Pte	V515367
Levy, Mayer Henry	Cpl	VX76874	Liefman, A.H.	Pte	V357540
Levy, Philip Michael	Lt	NX79949	Liefman, David	Spr	VX66100
Levy, Raphael Ernest	Pte	N468176	Liefman, Lionel	Spr	VX103940
Levy, Reuben	Sgt	V16010	Liffmann, Erich	Pte	V377494
Levy, Robert	Spr	WX4587	Lightstone, Gerhard (Lichtenstein, Gerhard Moritz)	Pte	N221594
Levy, Samuel	Pte	NX88665	Lilienfeld, Kurt	Pte	N221634
Levy, Shraga Phillip	Pte	W47991	Lilienthal, Herbert	Gnr	NX100253
Levy, Sydney Joseph	WO2	V83010	Lilienthal, Noel	Capt	NX205159
Levy, Victor Michael	Pte	N223190	Lilienthal, Victor	Pte	NX105241
Levy, Walter	Pte	W79267	Lindemann, Alfred	Pte	V378395
Levy, Walter Herman Theodor	Pte	N221595	Lindenberg, Alfred	Pte	N221698
Lew, Harold Ellis	Pte	NX8215	Lindner, Leopold	Pte	N191921
Lew, Harry	Pte	V55712	Lindner, Manfred	L/Cpl	V377673
Lew, Hyman	Pte	V60885			

Jewish Anzacs

NAME	RANK	SERVICE NO.	NAME	RANK	SERVICE NO.
Linz, Walter	Pte	V501249	Lubransky, Myer	Sgt	V206567
Lipman, Leo Benjamin	Pte	N105808	Ludski, Joel Lewis	Gnr	NX176268
Lipman, Peter Robert	Pte	Nx201197	Lurje, Ber	Pte	V377872
Lipman, Rex John (Eric) **MID**	Capt	VX69785	Luster, Louis Colman	Pte	N213885; NX73682
Lipman, Robert Allen	Sig	NX153615	Lustgarten, Simon	Pte	V377841
Lipman, Robert Loewe	L/Cpl	NX15832	Lustig, Fred	Pte	V515519
Lipman, Rodney Arthur	Sgt	NX167328	Lustig, Henry Hugh	Pte	V377892
Lipman, Vivian David	Capt	WX32443	Lustig, Kurt	Pte	V377891
Lipovitz, Solomon	Pte	W79340	Lustig, Paul	Pte	N244847
Lipp, Bancion (Ben) *	Pte	VX47535	Lux, Charles Israel	Pte	V61243
Lipp, Leo	Pte	V129130	Lyons, Frederick Graham Leonard	Cpl	VX58836
Lippmann, Heinz	Pte	V377661	Lyons, Jack Solomon	Lt	VX38456
Lippmann, Herbert	Cpl	V377819	Lyons, Stanley Louis	S/Sgt	VX120092
Lippmann, Kurt Eduard Bernhard	Sgt	V377890	Lyons, Zelda	L/Bdr	VF391304
Lippmann, Robert Leopold	L/Cpl	NX179637	Maas, Ludwig	Sgt	V378310
Lipsfield, Leslie	Cpl	VX126383	Maas, Robert	Pte	N321049
Lipshut, Albert Louis	Lt	V28009; VX83837	Maas, Willi	Cpl	NX194855
Lipshut, Jack Keith	WO2	VX126816	Magnus, Basil	Sgt	V144701
Lipshut, Keith Jacob	Capt	V56955; VX94716	Magnus, David Emanuel	A/Sgt	N219085
Lipshut, Louis	Lt	V83670	Mainzer, Herbert	Pte	V378264
Lipson, Menzie	Spr	N441825	Majer, Hans	Pte	N221569
Lipton, Joseph	Pte	V65555; VX133939	Malinowicz, Abram Alosek	Pte	V378132
Lisman, Desmond Bertram	Tpr	WX16832	Malins, Harry Leon	Spr	N232545
Lisman, Michael	Cpl	NX58385	Mandel, Michael	Pte	V374513
Lisman, Nanette Lillian	Cpl	WF90112	Mandel, Thomas (Tully)	Cpl	VX115908
Lissek, Harry	Pte	V157043	Mandelberg, Albert Alfred	Sgt	NX135063
Littauer, Herbert Israel	Pte	V377683	Mandell, Francis Gordon	Pte	N195268; NX119660
Littauer, Martin David	Dvr	NX66363	Mandell, Jack	Pte	N440207
Litthauer, Ernst (Linton, Ernest)	Pte	N321057	Mandell, Leon	S/Sgt	NX49158
Litthauer, Fritz	Pte	N221650	Mandelson, Lewis Folk	Capt	QX29429
Lobascher, Joseph Francis	S/Sgt	V145898	Mandelson, Roy Boaz	Pte	N460944
Lobl, Johann	Pte	N454365	Mandie, Emmanuel	Pte	V206410
Loewald, Klaus Gunter	Pte	V501250	Mandl, Edmund	Pte	V377939
Loewe, Hans	Pte	V377660	Mane, Samuel	Pte	NX179567
Loewenstein, Alfred	Pte	N224744	Mangold, Kurt Joseph	Cpl	V377803
Loewenstein, Hans	Pte	V377666	Mann, Joseph	Gnr	N275848
Loewenstein, Hans Joachim	Cpl	N463948	Mann, Oswald	Gnr	NX100254
Loewenstein, Kurt	Pte	V501544	Mann, Samuel (Mandelbaum)	Dvr	WX35444
Loewenstein, Robert Leopold	Pte	V377665	Mannheim, Hans	Pte	V377957
Loewenstein, Werner Julius	Pte	V377954	Mansfield, Alan Lewis	Sgt	V53912; VX63249
Loewenthal, John	Maj	NX70261	Mansfield, George Joseph	Lt	VX63707
Loewenthal, Louis Samuel	Lt-Col	NX70154	Marantz, Sulim	Pte	V377822
Loewenthal, Siegbert	Pte	V377672	Marcus, Leon Jack *	Pte	NX22101
Loewy, Alfred	Pte	V377423	Marcuse, Ernst Henry	Pte	V377746
Loffelholz, Markus	Pte	V377777	Marcuse, Heinz Herman	Pte	V513192
Lohde, Sigismund Sigurd	Sgt	V377393	Margolis, George	Pte	V517351
Lomnitz, Menko	Pte	V377592	Margolis, Maurice	Pte	NX111205
Lopata, Jack Charles	Pte	NX23966	Margulius, Hermann (Martin, Harry Herman)	Pte	V377894
Lopata, Louis	Sgt	NX162876	Marienberg, Leonhard (Martin, Leonard)	Pte	V378380
Lorant, Anthony	Spr	WX16004	Marin, Stanley	Pte	VX75111
Lorge, Frederick	Pte	V377681	Markov, Bray	Pte	V158143
Louwisch, Joseph Abovy	Capt	NX194833	Marks, Abraham	Pte	V14626
Love, Benjamin	Tpr	NX55604	Marks, Alan	Pte	VX133572
Lowe, Alan	Pte	N385844	Marks, Albert Charles	Pte	V187394
Lowe, Egon (Loewenstein)	Cfn	N224780; NX180752	Marks, Alexander	Pte	NX152580
Lowe, Helmut (Loewenstein)	Pte	N456871	Marks, Benjamin	Pte	V350025
Lowenstein, Erich	Pte	V515279	Marks, Benjamin	Pte	VX119383
Lowenstein, Fritz	Pte	V378259	Marks, Benjamin Berendt	Sgt	V350810
Lubansky, Harry *	Pte	V155173	Marks, Bernard John	Gnr	VX31329
Luber, Ronald David	Pte	NX155778	Marks, Charles Edward	Pte	VX140196; V56682
Lubo, Peter	Pte	N226655	Marks, Cyril Moss	Pte	V357348
Lubransky, Jonas	Pte	V156609			

Appendix 2: Those who served

NAME	RANK	SERVICE NO.
Marks, David	Pte	NX6195
Marks, David	Gnr	VX121519
Marks, Emanuel Elias	Pte	V81208
Marks, Geoffrey Lionel	Cpl	VX24786
Marks, George	Pte	NX104454
Marks, George David	Maj	VX104011
Marks, Harry Joseph	Sgt	VX86882
Marks, Henry	Pte	VX138359
Marks, Howard Alfred	Cpl	VX104853
Marks, Jack	Pte	N219086
Marks, Jack Barnett	Lt	V66189
Marks, John	S/Sgt	NX120844
Marks, Keith David	Pte	VX124042
Marks, Lionel	Pte	V39708
Marks, Lylie	Gnr	NX54901
Marks, Myer Reuben	Cfn	VX141815
Marks, Ralph	Cpl	V325918
Marks, Sadie	Pte	NF437627
Marks, Solomon	Gnr	V51820
Marks, Sydney	Pte	V354509
Marks, Victor	Lt	V31279
Marks, Zalick Joshua *	S/Sgt	VX8366
Markson, Nathan Bernard	Pte	N83532
Markus, Walter	Pte	N251552
Marshall, Clarence Maurice	Capt	VX92157
Marshall, Samuel Simon	Capt	VX133113
Marx, Benjamin Rudolph	Gnr	NX141246
Marx, Gunther	Pte	N321051
Marx, Hermann	Pte	V377745
Marx, Leopold	Pte	N221667
Marx, Otto	Pte	V378120
Marx, Walter	Pte	V377376
Maschler, Fred Robert	Pte	V377382
Masel, Philip MID	Maj	WX3392; 515952
Masel, Samuel	Capt	W29809; WX34352
Masel, Walter Jona	Maj	WX31733
Mases, Hans	Pte	V377385
Mass, Ernest	Pte	V377383
Mass, Robert	Pte	V377631
Massarik, Frank (Franz)	Cpl	VX147488
Masur, Julius	Pte	V377186
Matlin, Saney Izaak	Pte	QX23257
Matsdorf, Wolf Simon	Pte	NX179475; N173079
Mattersdorf, Michael	Pte	N318920
Max, Leo	Cpl	V377914
May, Albert		N324263
May, Charles Karl	Pte	N446664
May, Gerd (Gerald)	L/Cpl	V377374
May, Klaus	Pte	N321035
May, Paul	Pte	N321036
Mayer, Edgar Jacob	Pte	V377893
Mayer, Henry	Pte	V377470
Mayer, Jacob	Pte	N321341
Mayer, Kurt Alexander	Pte	V378398
McClean, Leslie	L/Sgt	NX119464
Mears, Clifford William	Pte	N219095
Meerkin, Boris	Pte	V377293
Meerkin, Jack Henry Gregory	Pte	QX17143
Meerkin, Maurice Moses	Pte	Q203380
Meerkin, Myer	Pte	V517567
Meier, Bertold	L/Cpl	V378338
Meininger, Fritz Josef	Cpl	N221526
Meinrath, Clive David	Pte	N248733
Meinrath, Julian Eric	Capt	N483110
Meisner, David	Pte	N321022
Meister, Karl	Pte	W60825
Melov, John	Sgt	NX175722
Melov, Mendel	Cpl	NX105307
Melovitch, Maurice Bernard	Gnr	V52349
Meltzer, Jules	L/Cpl	V54995
Mendel, Fritz	Pte	V377758
Mendel, Karl	Pte	N435091
Mendel, Leslie	Pte	QX33129
Mendel, Paul	Pte	NX128244
Mendelawitz, Abraham	S/Sgt	W243041
Mendelawitz, David	Pte	W74932
Mendelawitz, Mervyn Maurice	Lt	WX10565
Mendels, Allan	Pte	N465491
Mendels, Julius	Pte	N224803
Mendelsohn, Albert Clive	Lt-Col	VX48626
Mendelsohn, Arthur Mark	Sgt	N79561
Mendelsohn, Braham Coleman	Capt	NX208067
Mendelsohn, David Berrol	Sgt	N36389
Mendelsohn, Gwen Esther	Cpl	VF395846
Mendelsohn, Paul Gerald	Bdr	N73504
Mendelsohn, Ronald Sali	Sgt	NX90939
Mendelson, Norman	Capt	V158668; VX95080
Mense, Johann	Pte	V377942
Merksamer, Markus	Pte	N249514
Messer, Colin Coleman	Lt	N78593
Messer, Harry	Cpl	VX102301
Meth, Max Ludwig	L/Sgt	V377386
Meth, Rudolf	Pte	V377943
Metsch, Ignatz	Pte	N346408
Meyer, Albert	Pte	V377469
Meyer, Asher	Gnr	N440452
Meyer, Bernhard	Pte	V377685
Meyer, Erich Emanuel	Pte	N321342
Meyer, Gerhard	Pte	V377830
Meyer, Hans	Pte	V377632
Meyer, Herry	Pte	V377818
Meyer, Karl Heinz	Pte	N464396
Meyer, Leo	Sgt	V500321
Meyer, Max	Pte	V377726
Meyer, Otto Martin	L/Cpl	V377387
Meyer, Paul Heinz	Cpl	N321023
Meyer, Rudolf	Pte	N221722
Meyer, Siegfried	Pte	V377724
Meyer, Waldemar	Pte	N321343
Meyer, Walther Kurt Herbert	Pte	N221644
Meyerowitz, Werner	Pte	N321025
Meyersberg, George	Cpl	V378071
Meyerstein, Werner	Pte	V377003
Meyrowitz, Kurt Gunther	Pte	N221668
Michael, Arthur (Ernest)	Lt	NX113175
Michael, Cyril	Cpl	V18516
Michael, Henry Ray	Pte	VX42628
Michaelis, Alan	Capt	V145772; VX47597
Michaelis, Alfred	Pte	V378369
Michaelis, Archie	Pte	V357416
Michaelis, Joan Elizabeth	Lt	VFX95841
Michaelis, Roy Louis	Lt	VX114284
Michaelis, Rupert	WO1	NX55395
Michaels, Joseph	Cpl	V335530

Jewish Anzacs

NAME	RANK	SERVICE NO.	NAME	RANK	SERVICE NO.
Michels, Werner	Pte	V377563	Morris, Harry Abe	Pte	WX16169
Michelson, David Enoch	Capt	NX320	Morris, Henry	Sgt	NX149896
Michelson, Harry	Cpl	V378364	Morris, Isaac	Gnr	N240410
Michelson, Ronald	Sig	V35362	Morris, Jack	Cpl	V206362
Midalia, Max	Sgt	WX41386	Morris, John Israel	Sig	T26828
Midalia, Roy	Pte	WX25706	Morris, Louis	Pte	VX113608
Middlemass, Andrew Rupert	Cpl	N273153	Morris, Louis Solomon	Sgt	N225190
Midler, Issy	Pte	V377024	Morris, Manny (Emanuel Percival)	Pte	NX173821
Miedzwinski, Gerhard (Mitchell)	Pte	V509236	Morris, Maurice (Levitus) *	Sgt	NX81840
Milecki, Wolf	Pte	V377125; VX125044	Morris, Myer	Gnr	NX46055
Milecki, Wolf	Pte	VX113984; V377767	Morris, Percy	Pte	W11046
Miller, Hyman	Pte	V506415	Morris, Percy Hyman	L/Cpl	N323661
Miller, Joshua	Pte	VX137143	Morris, Sidney	Cpl	NX90778
Miller, Louis Elijah	Pte	V350929	Morris, Solomon	Pte	V370789
Miller, Maurice	Pte	V506926	Morris, Stanley Alfred	Pte	NX91996
Miller, Noel	Pte	NX52976	Morris, Stanley Hyman	L/Cpl	NX101089
Miller, Phillip	Pte	V366211	Morris, Victor Joseph	Pte	N284016
Miller, Simon John	L/Sgt	VX105528	Moser, Rudolf	Cpl	V377751
Millet, Josef	L/Cpl	V377365	Moses, Arthur *	L/Cpl	QX1463
Millingen, Colin Charles	Lt	NX24604	Moses, Braham Lewis	Gnr	NX87014
Millingen, Hubert Stanley	WO1	N66007	Moses, Harry	Pte	V504105
Millman, Bert (Zeitlin)	Cfn	WX1276	Moses, Hubert Phillip	Lt	SX372
Millman, Leon	Spr	W6294	Moses, Motel Max	Pte	V377161
Millman, Woolf	Sig	W6483	Moses, Victor	Cpl	V377373
Milman, John	Pte	NX67940	Mosler, Rolf	Pte	V377023
Milov, Ben	Pte	W80218	Moss, Morris	Cpl	NX93204
Milston, Neville Hyman	Sig	NX10477	Moss, Theodore Hertzl	Sgt	V19193
Minden, Alfred	Gnr	NX56007	Mossenson, Nissan	Gnr	W2792
Mintz, Marcel	Pte	V377332	Moszkowicz, Benjamin	Pte	VX59081
Mirjam, Martan	Pte	V377291	Mottek, Heinz Ludwig Israel	Pte	N221699
Mirmovitch, Menahem *	Pte	WX19590	Mottek, Ronald Wolfgang	Pte	VX129118
Mirsky, Myer Harry	Sgt	V156690	Munz, Cheska	Sgt	V378176
Mischkowski, Leopold	Pte	V506033	Munz, Isak	Pte	N191638
Mish, John Norman	Gnr	VX42515	Murkies, Nathan Naftoli	Spr	VX55310
Mitchell, Clive Harry	L/Sgt	N79352	Mutz, Barnett	Pte	VX86158
Mitchell, Keith Myer	Pte	N463392	Mutz, Havis Harry	Cpl	VX139681
Mitchell, Mathew	Sgt	V9138	Myer, Leslie Baevski	Lt	VX22128
Mitchell, Norman	Gnr	N233386	Myers, Arthur George Stanley	WO1	Q124244
Mitelman, Henry	Cpl	VX23881	Myers, Benson Joseph	S/Sgt	NX14794
Mittler, Kurt	Pte	V377381	Myers, Cedric Alexander	Sig	N216401
Moalem, Nissim Joseph	Cpl	NX156107	Myers, Esther Gertrude	Pte	NF456006
Moddel, Bruno	Pte	N447391	Myers, Harry Maldon	WO2	N390156
Moddel, Harry	Pte	N447427	Myers, Joseph Lazarus	Cpl	N334086
Model, Hans Werner (John Warner)	Pte	VX146256	Myers, Joseph Myer	S/Sgt	QX45214
Modern, Paul	Pte	V378339	Myers, Leon	L/Sgt	N324169
Mohliwer, William	Pte	N221602	Myers, Mark	Cpl	N81551
Mohrenwitz, Martin Bernardt	Pte	V377936	Myers, Mark	Lt	N220419
Mondschein, Ernst	Pte	V377378	Myers, Morris	Gnr	NX100262
Morgenstern, Isak	Pte	V505139	Myers, Philip	Pte	N223106
Morley, Richard	Pte	N464019	Myers, Ronald Joseph	Cpl	NX65161
Morley, Solomon	Pte	V508282	Myslis, Harold Joseph	Maj	NX70800
Morris, Abraham Stanley	Bdr	NX37798	Nable, Abraham Philip	Sgt	N46875
Morris, Albert	Capt	NX168619	Nable, Jack	Sgt	QX47632
Morris, Alfred *	Pte	N71621	Nable, Louis	S/Sgt	QX48387
Morris, Allan *	Cpl	VX38634	Nable, Marcus	Pte	Q90165
Morris, Basil Edward	Pte	N217805	Nadel, Ludwik	Spr	Q124270
Morris, Betty Louise	Pte	NF481257	Nagelberg, Max	Sig	VX52820
Morris, David	S/Sgt	VX17753	Nagler, Isidor	Pte	V377384
Morris, David Walter	Spr	NX137978	Naidel, Samuel	Pte	N247875
Morris, Emanuel	Cpl	N25606	Nassau, Leopold	Pte	V377390
Morris, Geoffrey	Spr	WX36765	Nassau, Otto Erich Gerhard	Pte	V377709
Morris, Geoffrey Gerson	Lt	VX42579	Nathan, Alan Gordon	Sgt	VX61496

Appendix 2: Those who served

NAME	RANK	SERVICE NO.
Nathan, Albert Nathaniel	Cpl	S212113
Nathan, Arthur Joseph	Maj	VX135246
Nathan, Bryan Solomon	Pte	NX203512
Nathan, Edward David *	Pte	VX96635
Nathan, George Saltiel	Lt	WX29788
Nathan, Hans	Pte	N221520
Nathan, Harold Henry	Spr	V36912; VX60780
Nathan, Leonard Edward	S/Sgt	WX35810
Nathan, Lewis	L/Sgt	W18911; WX28293
Nathan, Myer	Maj	VX112062
Neilson, Leonard (Goldstein, Leopold)	L/Sgt	Q186913
Nelken, Edward	Sgt	VX129155
Nelken, Ferdinand Adrian	Lt	V60836
Nelson, Abraham	Pte	V156623
Nelson, Earle	Sig	NX140653
Nelson, Morris Norman *	Pte	NX96008
Nemenoff, Matthias	Sgt	VX128259
Nerichow, Karl Heinz	L/Sgt	V377467
Nettheim, Arthur Noel Felix	S/Sgt	NX51408
Nettheim, Keith Salomon	Cpl	NX28286
Nettheim, Leslie Roy	Sgt	N281613
Neufeld, Michael	Pte	V378001
Neufeld, Wilhelm	Pte	V377610
Neuhaus, Jacob	Pte	V503909
Neumann, Erich	Pte	V377525
Neumann, Franz	Pte	V514451
Neumann, Hans Friedrich	L/Cpl	V377749
Neumann, Heinz Peter	Pte	V377571
Neustaedter, Helmut	Pte	V377945
Neuwahl, Hans	Pte	V377375
Newman, David Charles *	Gnr	NX34412
Newman, Eric	Pte	V377900
Newman, Hans	L/Cpl	N318921
Newman, Henry Paul	Pte	Q153515
Newman, Horace Bohmer	Lt	N225584
Newman, Jessel Albert	Tpr	NX56902
Newman, Joseph	Cpl	W51145
Newman, Joseph Konrad	Cpl	NX179804
Newman, Maurice Leslie	L/Cpl	NX78546
Newman, Ronald	Pte	N217715
Newmark, Ariel	Sgt	VX106269
Newmark, David	WO1	VX79690
Newmark, Sydney	L/Cpl	N53485
Newton, Richard	Pte	N221733
Niechcicki, David I.	Pte	V378355
Ninedek, Samuel	Tpr	VX74727
Nirens, Maurice	Pte	V377302
Noble, Charles Maurice	Cpl	NX59149
Norman, George Solomon	Sgt	N273472; NX82335
North, Paul	Sgt	V378146
Nothmann, Kurt	Pte	N224783
Notkin, Dov	L/Sgt	3133715; VX25944
Oberlander, Alfred		V377427
Odelski, Motel	Pte	V378022
Oderberg, Albert	Pte	V39747
Oderberg, Harold	Sgt	VX544
Ohlberg, Kurt	Pte	N321238
Oliver, Sol	Pte	V505447
Opas, Roberta Judith	Pte	VF345938
Opit, Leon Benjamin	Pte	N218036
Opit, Manis	Sgt	N103301
Opitz, Laurence Louis	L/Cpl	NX95089
Opitz, Marcus	Pte	N220030
Opoczynski, Benjamin	Pte	V377996
Opoczynski, Max	Cpl	N248185
Oppenheim, Rolf	Pte	V378400
Oppenheim, Semmi	Pte	N221570
Oppenheimer, Alfred	Pte	N221571
Oppenheimer, Hans Max	Cpl	V377916
Oppenheimer, Lincoln Menny	Pte	V377466
Oppenheimer, Paul Erwin Ludwig	Pte	V378152
Orbach, Alfred	Pte	N231020
Orbuck, Lawrence David	Pte	VX4540
Orken, Marcus Benjamin Bartholomew	Lt	VX44039
Orloff, Elieser (Alec)	Pte	V378127
Orloff, Shimshon (Samson)	Pte	V377967
Osborne, Bernard Cecil	Gnr	W33668
Osborne, Harold (Olsberg)	Cfn	V34878
Oschinsky, Heinz Frederick	L/Cpl	V377465
Oshlack, Abraham	Pte	V205791
Oshlack, Joseph	Pte	V39749
Oviss, Harry	Pte	V205817
Ovitch, Julius	Sgt	NX163196
Owen, Alexander	Maj	N393239; NX115475
Owen, Hyam Maurice	Lt-Col	NX130975
Owen, Morris David	Capt	NX200878
Packer, Leopold Henry	WO1	VX146599
Page, Henry	Pte	V367028
Page, Honnon	L/Cpl	VX134443
Page, Joseph	Pte	VX28816
Page, Lewis	Pte	V357982
Pahoff, Leslie	Pte	VX64508
Pahoff, Phillip	Pte	V155306; VX139707
Pallis, Julius	Pte	VX148007
Palmbaum, Fred	Pte	N224851
Paltie, Himey Harry	Dvr	NX81722
Parasol, Kalman	Pte	V507939
Parish, Nelson	Pte	V378030
Parker, Benjamin Abraham	S/Sgt	N283408
Parker, Lindsay	Lt	NX108623
Parkin, Cyril Morwick	Maj	340043; VX23471
Pasmanik, Samuel	Pte	V357474
Patkin, Michael MID	Sgt	VX9508
Patkin, Robert	L/Sgt	VX7615
Pauson, Adolf	Cpl	V377915
Pazaky, Maurice	Pte	NX205192
Pearce, William Ernest	Gnr	N73431
Pearlman, Celia	Capt	VX45572
Pearlman, Cyril Solomon MM	Capt	VX6746
Pearlman, Henry	Pte	N294492
Pearlman, Hyman	Tpr	NX22740
Pearlman, Leslie *	L/Cpl	VX30758
Pearlman, Lloyd Samuel	Pte	V132542
Pearlman, Mark	Pte	N164759
Peck, Alexander	Capt	V85248; VX56587
Pecker, Samuel	Pte	NX155560
Peisah, Nathan	Spr	NX2138
Pell, Szulim	Pte	V518260
Pellach, Froim	Pte	N437288
Penn, Lewis	Pte	N12382
Perec, Charles	Capt	WX17035
Perger, Gustav Rudolph Imre		V377902
Perkins, Joseph	Sgt	VX143645
Perl, Erich	Pte	N321319

World War II, Australian Army (cont.)

NAME	RANK	SERVICE NO.
Perl, Michael Mathias	Maj	VX39227
Perlberger, Ferdynand	Pte	N321247
Perlman, Edward	Capt	V158620; VX95022
Perlman, Joseph	Gnr	W22949
Perlman, Max	Pte	W81713
Perlow, Maurice Hyam	Dvr	WX40728
Perlstein, Alan Roy	Pte	V205952
Perlstein, Louis Henry	Lt	VX24370
Pertzel, Charles Alfred	Pte	VX42272
Peter, Aby	Pte	V378292
Peter, Morris	Pte	V378029
Peters, Harry	Spr	NX180318
Peters, Kurt Sydney	Pte	Q153428
Peysack, Leo	Pte	V509764
Peyser, Thomas	Pte	N221523
Pfeiffer, Rudolf Alfons	Pte	N221727
Philipp, Franz Adolf	Pte	V377579
Philipp, Werner	Pte	V377424
Philippsohn, Otto	Pte	N464809
Phillips, Abraham Eleazer	Pte	NX40070
Phillips, Aubrey Norman	Pte	NX109972
Phillips, Cecil	Cpl	NX2296
Phillips, David Abraham	Pte	N78751
Phillips, Edward	Pte	NX6386
Phillips, Geoffrey Lewis	WO2	NX26136
Phillips, Gerald Solomon	Capt	V55270; VX117239
Phillips, Harry Cecil	Pte	N166632
Phillips, Henry Hope	S/Sgt	V281246
Phillips, Hirsch	Sgt	QX35265
Phillips, Jack Delmont	Pte	N36370
Phillips, Jacob Nathan	L/Sgt	N77089
Phillips, John Louis	Dvr	NX143117
Phillips, Leslie Montague	WO2	VX18575
Phillips, Lewis	Tpr	NX45035; NX47675
Phillips, Mark	Sgt	NX15141
Phillips, Morris	Sig	N322788; NX57592
Phillips, Neville	Sgt	NX2297
Phillips, Norman	Cfn	N153580
Phillips, Orwell Edward	Capt	NX139102
Phillips, Ronald Asher	S/Sgt	NX140561
Phillips, Samuel Judah	WO1	NX128505
Phillips, Solomon	Cpl	N274895
Phillips, Walter	Pte	V515349
Pianka, Osher Mendel	Pte	V378142
Pieck, Hans	Pte	N231021
Pietruschka, Najei (Maier)	Pte	V378151
Pilpel, John	Pte	WX4212
Pilpel, Percy	Pte	WX33310
Pincus, Hans Ivo	Maj	VX80886
Pinkus, Numan	Pte; Capt	V158417; VX97981
Pinto, Reuben	Pte	N77415; V15037; V84511
Pisarevsky, Noah	Sgt	VX964
Pisarevsky, Ralph	Gnr	VX115257
Pisarevsky, Solomon	Sgt	VX26620
Pisk, Karl	Cpl	N385839; NX179122
Piski, Paul	Pte	V377630
Pizer, Henry Ian	Lt	VX96340
Plager, Ernest	Pte	N171944
Platt, Robert Arthur *	Pte	N219648
Platt, Selig	Pte	N77716
Platus, Leon	Pte	NX124231
Platz, Ernst	L/Cpl	V377825

NAME	RANK	SERVICE NO.
Plaut, Fritz	Pte	V510652
Plaut, Hans	Pte	N221527
Plessner, Karl	Pte	N321348
Plotke, Walter	Pte	N463190
Plotkin, Irving	Pte	VX121932
Plotnek, Joseph	Pte	SX2247
Plottel, Eric	Gnr	NX103263
Plunkett, Edward Henry Coules	Pte	WX298
Pogany, Theodore	Pte	V377999
Pokorny, Frederic Edward	Cpl	W60831
Polack, John Robert	S/Sgt	VX100357
Polack, Peter Joseph	Lt	VX22286
Polak, Aaron	Sig	NX161964
Pollack, Julius	Pte	V354794
Pollak, Felix	Pte	N221530
Pollak, George	L/Sgt	V378214
Pollak, John Kurt	Pte	N375296
Pollak, Rafael Felix	Pte	V506031
Pollak, Walter Paul	L/Cpl	V377464
Pollak, William	Pte	N375295
Pollard, Dennis	Gnr	N76789
Pollock, Harry *	Cpl	N77644
Pollock, Israel	Pte	VX15000
Polonsky, Ephraim Roy	Pte	V155960
Pordes, Josef	Cpl	N221573
Portnoj, Heinrich	L/Cpl	V378240
Posaner, Michel	Pte	NX118478
Posluszny, Kazinierz	Pte	N480735
Posner, Lewis Davis	Pte	V187487
Posner, Michael	Pte	V4068
Postle, Maurice (Harold)	Pte	NX206730
Preis, Leo	Pte	V378265
Preshner, Oscar Sydney	Pte	QX7649
Press, Lily	Pte	N390389
Press, Reubin	Pte	N218043
Priester, Kurt	Pte	V377878
Prince, Jack	Pte	VX122382
Proosov, Phyllis	Pte	NF461885
Proosov, Victor	Gnr	NX165759
Prosser, Thomas	Sgt	NX98922
Pszenny, Benjamin Dawid	Pte	N221659
Pura, Colin Geoffrey **MID**	Lt	NX65551
Pyke, Robert Elias	Lt	VX29873
Pynt, Gerald	Lt	NX111333
Pynt, Hyman	L/Cpl	N226236
Rabinov, Alan Simeon	Sig	VX46027
Rabinov, Cyril	S/Sgt	VX83275
Rabinov, Joseph	L/Cpl	NX81986
Raboy, Alexander	Pte	V28172
Radinger, Joseph	Pte	N221637
Radinowski, Erwin Israel	Pte	N286901
Rael, Benjamin	Sgt	V144994
Raffkiss, Louis	Pte	V508995
Raiter, Samuel	Spr	WX41321
Raleigh, Herbert William	Pte	V377206
Raphael, Geoffrey Alfred*	Lt	WX3447
Raphael, Louis	Pte	VX62209
Raphael, Richard Hyam	Pte	TX500028
Rapke, Ralph	Pte	V335693
Rapken, Simon Abraham	Pte	N225198
Rappaport, Emanuel	Pte	N215695
Rappaport, Emil	Capt	NX173655

NAME	RANK	SERVICE NO.	NAME	RANK	SERVICE NO.
Rappeport, Samuel	Pte	W69489	Robinson, Daniel	Sgt	VX10171
Rappeport, Samuel	Pte	W242711	Robinson, Louis	Sgt	VX16693
Raszba, Jewsiej	S/Sgt	NX41797	Roby, Alexander **ED**	Lt; Brig	139906; QX60076
Ravdell, Maurice	Pte	VX64145	Rochlin, Charles Shalmon	L/Sgt	NX121461
Ravech, Martin Charles	S/Sgt	VX136864	Rochlin, Oscar	Capt	VX133274
Raven, Maurice	Pte	W90805	Rockawin, Hyme	Pte	V503452
Rawicki, Abram	Pte	V378027	Rockman, Abraham Louis	Pte	V60948
Rawson, Roma Isabel	Bdr	WF90869	Rockman, Barnet	Pte	VX116704
Raymond-Reschovsky, Frank Samuel	Pte	N221720	Rockman, Danil	Pte	V377319
Raynor, Harry	Pte	V377757	Rockman, Elia Ber	Pte	V378344
Redapple, Joseph	Pte	V357451	Rocks, Harry	Pte	N248252
Redapple, Leon	Capt	TX6488	Roden, Hyam	Lt	NX41830
Redelman, Shya	L/Cpl	NX176007	Roden, Wallace Woolfe	Gnr	NX3402
Redlich, Julius	Pte	V377874	Roehricht, Horst David (Reed, Harry Bernard)	Pte	N261077
Rees, Frederik Manfred	Pte	V377760	Rogalsky, Sydney Solomon	Pte	VX126958
Regent, Walter	Pte	V377853	Rogers, Alfred Lipman	Maj	WX1578
Reich, Friedhelm	Pte	V377552	Rogers, Kalman	Pte	V357182
Reich, Leopold	Cpl	N321180	Rogers, William	Sgt	V156819
Reichenberger, Hans	L/Cpl	V377617	Romain, Leonard	Pte	VX59625
Reichman, Joseph	Cpl	VX64086	Ronai, Fritz Eugene	Sgt	N231007
Reichwald, Alfred	Pte	V378381	Ronai, Otto	Pte	V378079
Reichwald, Martin	Pte	V501247	Rood, Alfred	Pte	VX120703
Rein, Ernst	L/Sgt	V378229	Rood, Benjamin	Pte	V350985
Reismann, Rudolf	Pte	V377428	Rood, Lewis	Pte	VX131040
Reiss, Hans	Pte	V377453	Rorkin, Joseph (Rovkin) *	Pte	NX73811
Reisz, Andre	Pte	N321152	Rose, Irene	Sig	VF398010
Reitzes, Ludwig	Pte	N321350	Rose, Jack *	Dvr	VX78145
Renensson, Timothy George	Pte	V146741	Rose, Leo	Sgt	VX61586
Reston, Samuel	Pte	N215749	Rose, Norman	Capt	WX11118
Retter, Arthur	Pte	N321153	Rose, Solomon **MID**	Capt	VX39118
Reuben, Eli William	Pte	QX151	Rosebery, Arthur Lionel	Cfn	NX21861
Reuben, Elias	L/Cpl	WX42024	Rosebery, Sidney Solomon *	Maj	NX70851
Reuben, Ronald Harold	Gnr	NX110185	Rosefield, Clifford Leslie	Maj	VX111103
Revelman, Alec	Gnr	N216635	Rosefield, Marcus Melbourne **MID**	Lt-Col	VX108488
Revelman, Morris	Pte	VX77888	Roseman, Edward Myer William	Capt	VX16045
Rheuben, Eric Lionel	Pte	N225616	Roseman, Ernest	L/Cpl	N233509
Rheuben, Norman Mark	Pte	NX91573	Roseman, Harold Harris	Dvr	VX17017
Rheuben, Percy Edward	Pte	N219267	Roseman, Myer Abraham	Pte	NX82257
Rhodes, Roy Alexander	Sgt	N18376; NX123697	Roseman, Solomon	Pte	W74466
Ribush, David	Pte	V207129	Roseman, Sydney	Pte	VX18427
Rich, Joshua Saul	L/Cpl	W67702	Rosen, Albert	Lt	NX15968
Rich, Louis	Pte	N216327	Rosen, Alexander Eli	Pte	VX4837
Rich, Malcolm (Myer)	Pte	NX151953	Rosen, Bernard	Gnr	N248532
Rich, Martin Sally	Pte	N463193	Rosen, Bernard Wolfe	Pte	N455286
Rich, Norman	Lt	VX94168	Rosen, Clarence Alexander	Gnr	V31455
Richards, Harold Joseph	Capt	NX77286	Rosen, David	Pte	N453812
Richardson, Arnold	Maj	V10676	Rosen, David Elia	Spr	N173073
Richmond, Neville Leslie	Sig	VX52898	Rosen, Emanuel	Dvr	NX87296
Richter, Ernst	L/Cpl	V377040	Rosen, Leslie	Cpl	W55391
Ridge, Jacob Asias (Reich)	Sgt	V377306	Rosen, Louis	L/Bdr	NX165052
Rieder, Werner	Pte	V377752	Rosen, Marcus Joseph	Capt	WX35046
Riesenfeld, Eric (Carey)	Pte	N321262	Rosen, Maurice	Pte	W51134
Riner, Rachmiel	Pte	N464810	Rosen, Murray	Spr	WX36833
Rischin, Henry Isaac	Pte	N239238	Rosen, Nathan	Lt	2152111; WX36716
Rischin, Isadore	S/Sgt	VX122905	Rosen, Victor	Pte	V377429
Rischin, Philip (Emanuel P.)	Spr	NX53718	Rosen, Woolfe	Pte	NX89244
Rizeman, David	Pte	N92301	Rosenbaum, Cyril	Pte	N323552
Rizeman, Solly	Pte	N260003	Rosenberg, Abraham	Pte	V366932
Robe, Stanley	Pte	VX61400	Rosenberg, Alan *	Gnr	NX23803
Robey, Frederick	Cpl	N463186	Rosenberg, Albert	WO2	NX42990
Robin, Stanley Gordon	Pte	V158187	Rosenberg, Alexander Moses	Pte	V159406
Robins, Harold Boris	Gnr	VX148234			

Jewish Anzacs

NAME	RANK	SERVICE NO.
Rosenberg, Clive Simpson	Lt	VX15357
Rosenberg, David	Pte	N226599
Rosenberg, Emanuel	Pte	VX131895
Rosenberg, Eric	Pte	N224968
Rosenberg, Gerald	Pte	VX50896
Rosenberg, Hans Cecil	Cpl	V377304
Rosenberg, Heinz	Pte	V377629
Rosenberg, Ian Albert	Pte	W61905
Rosenberg, Isaac	WO2	Q106850
Rosenberg, Joshua	L/Cpl	WX4482
Rosenberg, Julius Myer	Bdr	W48385
Rosenberg, Kurt	Pte	V378276
Rosenberg, Leon	Cpl	VX143011
Rosenberg, Marcus	Pte	V502972
Rosenberg, Marcus Harry	Capt	TX15201
Rosenberg, Neville	Cpl	V55492; VX119235
Rosenberg, Paul Theodore	Pte	QX63381; Q202020
Rosenberg, Philip	Cfn	WX31432
Rosenberg, Phyllis (Rose)	L/Cpl	VX116457
Rosenberg, Preston	Sgt	V5653
Rosenberg, Samuel	Gnr	NX200271
Rosenberg, Sydney	Pte	V354585
Rosenberg, Walter	Pte	N463713
Rosenbergs, Hirss Bers	Pte	W55872
Rosenblum, Alec	Pte	NX31291
Rosenblum, Arnold (Abraham)	Bdr	NX149848
Rosenblum, Felix	Sgt	NX105990
Rosenblum, Gerhard	Pte	V377614
Rosenblum, Lawrence	Sgt	N436683; NX169198
Rosenbluth, David	Pte	QX27840
Rosenbund, Walter Louis Israel	L/Cpl	N321360
Rosenbusch, Berthold	Pte	V378123
Rosencweig, Morrie Leon	Pte	N216860
Rosendahl, Hans *	Pte	V378083
Rosendorff, Hans Gunther	Pte	W93180; WX39841
Rosenewajg, Majlech	Pte	N221660
Rosenfeld, Clifford Marcus	Pte	N220286
Rosenfeld, Leon	Pte	VX113986
Rosenfeld, Vernon Keith	Spr	NX42983
Rosenfield, Frederick	Capt	NX204415
Rosenfield, Lionel Nathan	Sig	VX142663
Rosenfield, Max	Sig	VX502055
Rosenfield, Maxwell Samuel	Gnr	Q146329
Rosengarten, Alfred Bernard	L/Sgt	V206818
Rosengarten, Lionel	Sgt	VX104851
Rosenstein, Heinz	Pte	N321040
Rosenthal, Alfred	Pte	V377616
Rosenthal, Cecil Zalman	Pte	N445568
Rosenthal, Fritz	Pte	V377611
Rosenthal, George	Pte	V378340
Rosenthal, Hans	L/Cpl	V377618
Rosenthal, Hans Walter	Pte	N303403
Rosenthal, Haym	Pte	V377804
Rosenthal, Helmuth	Pte	V378280
Rosenthal, Isaac	Sgt	N234344
Rosenthal, Jack Emanuel	Pte	V78762
Rosenthal, Leo Lipman (Lipucaccu)	Pte	N221638
Rosenthal, Leon	Cpl	NX148306
Rosenthal, Leon Israel	Cpl	NX111409
Rosenthal, Lindsay Kenneth	S/Sgt	SX10241
Rosenthal, Ronald Joseph	Lt	SX5611
Rosenthal, Sam	Pte	WX38543

NAME	RANK	SERVICE NO.
Rosenthall, Lyle	S/Sgt	N347742
Rosenwald, Leo Marcus	Pte	N264438
Rosenwax, Alec Samuel	WO2	WX31891
Rosenwax, Mark Hertz	Dvr	VX84335
Rosenwax, Max Hedley	Cfn	NX195231
Rosenwax, Samuel	Pte	V36447
Rosenwax, Victor Samuel	Cpl	VX116065
Rosham, Abraham	Spr	WX26900
Roshkoff, Alexander	Pte	QX352
Roskin, Nathaniel Neville *	Capt	NX201219
Rosner, Heinrich	Pte	V354809
Ross, Jack Samuel	Pte	W51115
Ross, Norman Clive	Pte	VX18092
Ross, Robert Bruno (Rosenberg)	Pte	N321214
Ross, Samuel	Pte	N51772
Ross, Samuel Noah	Pte	V69211
Rossen, Bennie	WO1	N27811
Rosset, Fritz	L/Cpl	N410843
Rostkier, Icko	Spr	VX129094
Rostkier, Szmul	Pte	VX52759
Rotenstein, Abraham Jacob	Pte	V377185
Roth, Hermann	Pte	V377829
Roth, Otto	Pte	S83023
Roth, Sydney	Pte	V16403
Rothbaum, Harry Isaac	L/Cpl	W243592
Rothberg, David Leonard	Sgt	VX87329
Rothberg, Harry	Pte	V350826
Rothberg, John Julius	Pte	VX94944
Rothenberg, Konrad	Pte	V377612
Rother, Salo	Pte	N221524
Rothfield, Jessel Meyer	Cfn	VX71619
Rothfield, Norman	Pte	V365585
Rothfield, Raymond David	Capt	2100752; NX206859
Rothfield, Thomas Lewis	Lt	V127190; VX84686
Rothman, Aaron	Pte	N21858
Rothman, Maurice	Pte	VX139448
Rothman, Philip	Cfn	NX193889
Rothman, Philip	Pte	V55557
Rothman, Samuel	Pte	Q42076; QX50068
Rothman, Samuel	Pte	V378172
Rothmuller, Erich	Pte	N464580
Rothschild, Julius	Pte	V378311
Rothschild, William	Pte	V378258
Rothstadt, Leon Eric	Lt-Col	VX222
Rotman, Icek Uszer	Cfn	WX41367
Rotstein, Yegal	Pte	WX40870
Rottell, Bernard	Pte	V62171
Rottell, Isaac	Sgt	V155537
Roubin, Rebecca	Pte	QX57749
Roudner, Maurice	Pte	VX132197
Roussin, Israel	Pte	N100512
Rovkin, Gregory	Pte	N323515
Roxon, Emanuel	Pte	Q273870
Rozenbaum, Mosze Szymen	Pte	V378358
Ruben, Felix	Pte	V378086
Ruben, Rudolf	Pte	V377615
Rubenstein, Frank MID	WO1	VX2602
Rubenstein, Norman	Cpl	VX129079
Rubenstein, Sampson	Pte	V60300
Rubin-Zacks, Louis	Capt/Chap	WX1544
Rubinsohn, Max	Pte	V377619
Rubinstein, Harry	Pte	V378359

Appendix 2: Those who served

NAME	RANK	SERVICE NO.
Rubinstein, Kusiel	Capt	NX200954
Rubner, Phillip	Sig	NX150785
Rubner, Ron	Dvr	NX168596
Rudin, Leopold Montague	Pte	VX140884
Runds, Stanley	Pte	W96838
Ruskin, Alfred	Sgt	VX129205
Rybak, Edward Leslie	Sgt	NX116850
Rybak, John Sydney	Gnr	N275923
Rybicki, Mordchaj	Pte	V378141
Ryner, Fritz Erwin (Schwerin)	Pte	N237386
Ryner, Gerhard Gunther Israel (Schweriner)	Pte	N321188
Ryter, Phillip		V158449
Ryvitch, Emanuel	S/Sgt	V206827
Ryvitch, Michael (Rich)	Gnr	V33598
Ryzman, Dov	Gnr	VX123381
Rzezak, Israel Isak	Pte	VX76376
Sabatzky, Horst	L/Cpl	N221640
Sabor, Hans Egon	Pte	V502455
Sachs, Edward Lewis	Pte	N463127
Sachs, Rudolf	Pte	V377555
Sack, Harry	Pte	N213546
Sack, Leo	Pte	V501251
Sackville, Reuben	Cpl	VX124638
Sadka, Frederick Samuel	Lt	NX170900
Saffer, David	Pte	V400129
Saffron, Abraham Gilbert	Cpl	N217771
Safra, Samuel	Pte	S70181
Sainken, Benjamin	Lt	WX34751
Sainken, Solomon	Pte	W58035
Saks, Harry	Pte	V351075
Salek, Alan Crownson	Gnr	VX33756
Sallmayer, Ernst	Pte	V377656
Salman, Gersz	Pte	V378318
Salmon, Colin	Lt	2139094; VX51592
Salomon, Ernest Gunther	Pte	S85550; SX38257
Salomon, Ernst	Pte	V377778
Salomon, Gerd Hugo	Pte	S85556
Salomonis, Hans (Selwyn)	Pte	V511048
Salon, Alfred	Pte	V378074
Salonsky, Norman	Pte	NX92724
Salter, Robert	Pte	V378187
Same, Emille Aminadum	L/Sgt	W19658
Same, Leo	Cpl	W23116
Same, Phillip	Dvr	W51610
Same, William	Cpl	W56091
Samelowitz, Isaac	Pte	W73638
Samelowitz, Leon	Dvr	W95784
Samuel, Alwyn Ruta	Gnr	NX24230
Samuel, Erich	Pte	N221641
Samuel, Harry Myer	Pte	VE446474
Samuel, Phyllis Catherine	Pte	NF453191
Samuel, Ralph Aaron	Pte	VE446490
Samuel, Wilhelm	Pte	V377475
Samuels, Harry Alexander (Henry)	Sig	NX17966
Samuels, John Harris *	Capt	QX6407
Samuels, Meyer Jacob	Pte	N339514
Sander, Hans Adolf	Pte	NX179657
Sanders, Harry *	Pte	NX952
Sandlers, Abraham Barnett	Pte	VX142580
Sandor, Ernst	Pte	V377832
Sandor, George	Cpl	V146359

NAME	RANK	SERVICE NO.
Saper, Morris	Pte	N389515
Sapier, Leslie	Pte	NX175419; N442353
Sapier, Reuben	Pte	NX180353
Sapirsztejn, Chaim Lejb (Sapir)	Pte	V378177
Sarfaty, Gordon Alfred	Pte	NX203408
Sarfaty, Peter Mark	L/Bdr	NX135413
Saslawski, Josef	Pte	V377482
Sassoon, Joseph	Pte	N213475
Satinover, John	Cpl	WX28042
Sauer, Leo	Pte	V506029
Sauerstrom, Leib	L/Cpl	V378124
Saunders, Alfred Lewis	WO2	SX2432
Saunders, John Paul Maxwell	Cfn	WX39145
Saunders, Maurice	Sgt	VX118796
Saunders, Maurice Elias	S/Sgt	NX79326
Saunders, Nathaniel Solomon	Cfn	SX26874
Saywell, George Montague	Cpl	NX98282
Saywell, Lawrence Philip *	Pte	NX6461
Saywell, Preston Greenwald		NX103654
Sazonov, Aaron	Pte	WX23044
Schab, Felix	Pte	N460985
Schack, Erich	Pte	V377554
Schaechter, Otto	Pte	V378286
Schaffer, Johann	Pte	V377607
Schafranek, Karl Peter	Pte	V377894
Scharf, Martin	Pte	N237385
Scharf, Martin	Pte	N321187
Schatzki, Paul	Pte	V377985
Schaye, Hans	Pte	V377658
Scheiner, Frank	Pte	V377770
Schenberg, Arthur	Cpl	WX38865
Schenberg, Isaac	Pte	W69142
Schenk, Hans	Pte	V377854
Schenkel, Majer	Pte	V378224
Schermann, Richard	Pte	V377897
Schetzer, Harry	Pte	V42925
Schetzer, Leslie Maurice		V66357
Schiff, Hans	Pte	V377341
Schiff, Max	Pte	V377596
Schimetschek, Leo	Pte	N463138
Schischa, Eugen	Pte	N231016
Schlachcic, Martin	Pte	V378341
Schlaff, Jacob Osias	Bdr	NX101501
Schlafrig, Robert	Spr	W55804
Schlam, Moritz	Pte	V378394
Schlam, Saul	Pte	V378383
Schlesinger, Erich	Pte	V377451
Schlesinger, Franz Ludwig	Pte	V377901
Schlesinger, Kurt	Pte	V377595
Schlesinger, Michel	Pte	N463369
Schlesinger, Paul	Pte	V378296
Schlosser, Heinrich	Pte	N455210
Schmahl, Kurt	Pte	V378384
Schneeweiss, Hans George	Pte	N221577
Schneeweiss, Walter (Snow)	Pte	N161885
Schnock, Walter	Cpl	V378072
Schoenfeld, Ernst	L/Cpl	V377600
Schoenheimer, Rudolph Sydney	WO1	Q67063
Scholem, Erich	Pte	N321324
Scholem, Guenter David	Cpl	NX179912
Schonbach, Fritz	Pte	V377433
Schonfeld, Montague	Pte	VX9495

Jewish Anzacs

NAME	RANK	SERVICE NO.
Schott, Keith Jacob	Gnr	V206195
Schreiber, Marcel Sofer	Maj	NX157618
Schreiber, Mendel Sofer	Capt	N303472
Schreiber, Robert	Pte	V378105
Schrugin, Hyman	Cpl	WX40098
Schubert, Rudolf	Pte	V377998
Schuftan, Henry (Heinz)	Pte	N191521
Schultz, Lipman	Pte	V504339
Schultz, Mark	Lt	NG2500
Schulvater, Harry Moritz	Pte	N385841
Schureck, John (Jacob)	Pte	N233657
Schwab, Heinz	Pte	V377443
Schwarcz, Josef	Pte	V377843; VX151753
Schwarcz, Julius	Pte	V378288
Schwartz, Albert	Pte	V350927
Schwartz, Alexander	Pte	Q203294
Schwartz, Isaac	Pte	V144125
Schwartz, Maurice	L/Cpl	V16359
Schwartz, Monty	Pte	V4064
Schwartz, Zelman *	Maj	VX14799
Schwartzberg, Mordka	Pte	V378026
Schwarz, Alan Mark	Gnr	V110315
Schwarz, Harry George *	Pte	NX146473
Schwarz, Herbert	S/Sgt	V506875
Schwarz, Julius	Pte	V377929
Schwarz, Max *	Pte	V510653
Schwarz, Werner	Pte	V377553
Schwarzfeld, Siegfried	Pte	N321358
Schweiger, Gerhard	Pte	N231029
Schwerin, Paul	Pte	N463684
Scott, Maurice Herbert	Maj	N10002; NX71032
Seckel, Heinz	Pte	V378125
Seelig, Julius	Pte	V377879
Seeligson, Lionel Alexander	Pte	V510357; WX13806
Seeligson, Nathaniel Edward	Pte	V389481
Segal, Abraham	Pte	S82938
Segal, Arthur	Pte	N349223
Segal, Asher	Gnr	N468599
Segal, Chaim	Pte	V378085
Segal, Gordon	Pte	W80991
Segal, Harold	Pte	N217762
Segal, Harry	Capt	NX157654
Segal, Harry	Pte	VX136626
Segal, Harry Aaron	Pte	V18182
Segal, Isaac	Sgt	NX69673
Segal, Lewis	WO2	N30107
Segal, Maurice	Spr	NX164798
Segal, Michael	Dvr	V205449; VX89694
Segal, Moshe	Pte	W60815
Segal, Nathan	Pte	N462623
Segal, Norman	Pte	N217763
Segal, Reuben	Pte	WX41344
Segal, Rose (Shilkin)	Sig	WF90730
Segal, Solomon David	Sgt	WX40508
Segall, Alfred	Pte	N256793
Segall, Julius	Pte	N444386
Seifmann, Efrojem	Pte	N251551
Seigell, Aby	Pte	VX30442
Seknow, Bert	Pte	V378046
Selby, Benn Atherton **MID**	Capt	NX116815
Selby, Clive Herbert **MID** x 3	Lt-Col	NX22
Selby, David Mayer	Maj	NX142851

NAME	RANK	SERVICE NO.
Selby, Doris Adeline	Capt	N108185
Selby, Esmond John	Maj	NX119319
Selby, Victor	Pte	N224774
Selig, Albert Edmund Alexander	Bdr	NX102606
Selig, Herman	Pte	N230218
Selig, Martin	Pte	V377934
Selton, Peter Leo	Cpl	V377708
Sender, Isidor Harry *	Maj	NX12304
Sender, Leslie	Cpl	NX137479
Sernack, Maxwell	Lt	NX156368
Sernack, Sidney	Capt	NX76382
Sessler, Egon	Pte	V377785
Sessler, Kurt	Pte	V377793
Shadur, Jack Israel	Pte	V512350
Shapero, Arnold	Bdr	N219826
Shapir, Ivan	Pte	VX23925
Shapira, Louis	Pte	V350881
Shapiro, Sol	Sgt	W60839
Shappere, Arthur Joseph	Capt	N278473
Shappere, Phillip Harold	WO2	VX61057
Sharhon, Nissim	Sgt	N321190
Sharp, Abraham Harry	Sig	WX34856
Sharp, Alexander	Cfn	W81059
Sharp, Edward	Pte	NX116165
Sharp, Israel	Pte	NX21280
Sharp, Phillip	Pte	V378053
Sharp, Ronald	Cpl	WX39545
Sharp, Sydney William	Dvr	NX503549
Sharp, William *	Pte	NX33739
Sharpe, Samuel	Pte	W67070
Shatten, Reginald Jack	Pte	NX34118; NX6879
Shaw, Allan (Szuster, Alter)	Pte	W55805
Shaw, Simon Alexander	Pte	V377836
Sheezel, Marcus Stanley	Cpl	V187306
Sheldon, Ernest	Pte	N321041
Sheller, Abraham	Pte	V78760
Sheller, Peretz	Pte	VX116034
Shemberg, Henry *	Pte	VX74833
Sher, Boris	Pte	V56743
Sher, David Elroy	Pte	V186721
Sher, Sollomon	Pte	V507678
Sherman, Augustus	Pte	Q143801
Sherman, Leon	Sgt	NX115099
Sherr, Mendel Benjamin	WO2	V185281; VX142376
Sherwin, Otto	Pte	VX120504
Sherwood, Maurice	Sgt	NX34202
Shiffron, Samuel	Pte	V158620
Shifreen, Louis	S/Sgt	N65596; NX10628
Shilkin, Joshua	Capt	WX31304
Shilkin, Philip	Sgt	WX38748
Shilkin, Saul	Sgt	W95369
Shilkin, Solomon	Pte	W46113
Shilkin, Wolf	Cpl	W48170
Shimshoni, Max	Pte	V377812
Shinberg, Simon	Pte	V213322
Shineberg, Samuel Albert	S/Sgt	N273832
Shipper, Ralph	L/Cpl	N191523
Shirley, Sybil Rosalind (Eule)	Sgt	VF395883
Shmith, Clive Samuel	Capt	VX59685
Shmith, Ernest Clive	Cfn	VX15749
Shmith, Robert Alick * **MID**	Bdr	VX18085
Shmith, William Gerson	Pte	VX107800

Appendix 2: Those who served

NAME	RANK	SERVICE NO.
Shnanider, Abram	Pte	V378041
Shneider, Abe	Pte	V511671
Shnookal, Lawrence	Pte	V56856
Shnukal, Michael	Pte	VX124490
Shnukal, Philip	S/Sgt	NX44239
Shonthall, Isidor	Pte	N105875
Shoolman, Alec Mark	Pte	NX123720
Shoolman, David	Pte	NX169980
Shore, Martin Leon	Pte	VX1022
Shostak, Roy Solomon	Cpl	NX204593
Shott, Wolf	Pte	N226690
Showman, Cecil	Sig	NX51569
Showman, Morry	Pte	NX109095
Showman, Myer	Pte	NX104472
Shulman, Jack	Pte	NX90430
Shulman, Solomon	Pte	W68625
Shuster, David	Pte	V378171
Siegal, Sam	Pte	V377458
Siegelberg, Mark	Pte	V378205
Sife, Herbert Samuel	L/Cpl	N321039
Siglin, Alec	Maj	WX29300
Silber, Kurt	Pte	V377622
Silberberg, Alfred	Pte	N221604
Silberberg, Frank Gerald	Pte	V159233
Silberberg, Fritz Victor	Pte	N248190
Silberman, Aaron	Gnr	WX40998
Silberman, Hans Bernd	Pte	N221642
Silbermann, Herbert	Pte	V378392
Silberstein, Ernest Peter Jacob	S/Sgt	VX100129
Silberstein, Otmar	Pte	V377623
Silbert, Alexander	Cpl	WX38375
Silbert, Keith Alexander	Lt	W233894; WX26958
Silberthau, Max	Pte	V378088
Silkin, Norman (Shilkin)	Pte	N463718
Silman, Leon **MID**	Pte	VX55757
Silman, Norman Israel	Pte	V377164
Silver, Edward	Pte	VX121043
Silver, Henry	Pte	V156643
Silver, Irving Joseph	Cpl	V4615
Silver, Jack Isidore	Pte	N96076
Silver, Josek Szyja (George)	Pte	V503860
Silverman, Herbert Nathan * **MID**	Capt	VX129333 (POW)
Silverman, Jacob	Pte	V357186
Silverman, Jacob Samuel	Lt-Col	VX8325
Silverman, Leon Woolf	S/Sgt	V13717
Silverman, Morris	Pte	V377971
Silverman, Myer	Pte	V357286
Silverman, Simon Lewis	Gnr	SX24787
Silvers, Henry	L/Cpl	V377298
Silverstone, Jessel	Maj	NX12297
Simenauer, Kurt	Cpl	V377610
Simenauer, Alfred	Cpl	V377657
Simenauer, Hans Ludwig	Pte	V377599
Simmelmann, Arthur	Pte	V377791
Simmenauer, Bernhard	Pte	V378002
Simmonds, Sydney	Pte	NX86449
Simmons, Charles	Sgt	N220407
Simmons, David	Lt	VX21049
Simmons, David Henry	Sig	VX96309
Simmons, Donald Samuel	Pte	VX29018
Simmons, Lewis	Cpl	V5837
Simmons, William	Cpl	28189; NX31209

NAME	RANK	SERVICE NO.
Simon, Amelia	L/Cpl	VF388485
Simon, Brund (Bruno)	Pte	V377556
Simon, Ernest	Pte	V377821
Simon, Ernest Ludwig	Sgt	V377652
Simon, Ernst	Pte	N231002
Simon, Felix	Pte	N221711
Simon, Karl Heinz	Pte	V377655
Simon, Maurice	Lt	W236655
Simon, Mouritiu	Cpl	W81745
Simon, Paul	Cpl	V500753
Simon, Peter	Pte	N321011
Simon, Philipp	Pte	V378126
Simon, Raymond Gustave	Spr	VX121273
Simons, Alexander Arthur	Pte	V84056; VX2595
Simons, Bernard Ronald	Pte	V61167
Simons, Harold	Lt	VX46039; VX104061
Simons, Harry	Spr	N119804
Simons, Raymond Emerson	Sig	NX129135
Simons, Sol	Cpl	VX2475
Simonsohn, Erich	Pte	W55791
Singer, Fritz	Pte	V377820
Singer, Jack	Pte	NX100838
Singer, Leonard	Sig	VX133503
Singer, Marks	Pte	V350908
Singer, Martin Simeon	Pte	N225521
Singer, Maurice Samuel	Cpl	NX30161
Sklarsh, Harry	Pte	V378143
Skurnik, Alter	Pte	V378048
Skurnik, Emanuel	Cpl	N246999
Skurnik, John	L/Sgt	NX194850
Skurnik, Josek	Pte	V378346
Slade, David	Gnr	N324257
Slade, Hyman	Pte	V206499
Sleefrig, Anold Isadore	S/Sgt	N5507
Sleefrig, Henry George (Selby)	S/Sgt	NX151710
Slonim, Alexander Mark	S/Sgt	VX101163
Slonim, Maurice	Sgt	VX128762
Sluice, Henry Van Der	Lt	VX124663
Slutzkin, Alan	Sgt	VX108837
Slutzkin, Frank Albert	Pte	V158986
Slutzkin, George Quentin	WO2	V151312; VX21029
Slutzkin, Ivon Myer (Sage)	Capt	V60433
Slutzkin, Leo Phillip **MID**	Capt	V36203; VX117018
Slutzkin, Robert Eliot	Pte	V82841
Smiley, Walter	Pte	V377844
Smith, Betty	L/Cpl	VF346733
Smith, Eric Arthur Joseph	Cpl	V501133
Smorgon, George	Pte	V112216
Smorgon, Samuel	Pte	V159053
Snader, Hyman	Pte	WX38859
Snider, Aaron Samuel	Pte	V357578
Snider, Joseph	Pte	V330214
Snider, Mack	Pte	V159240
Snyder, Samuel	Sig	N80499
Soffer, Joshua Leib	Pte	V296405
Soffer, Samuel	Cfn	V13804; VX64246
Sohn, Hans	Pte	V377654
Solmitz, Felix Carl	Pte	V501245
Solomon, Albert	Pte	N218216
Solomon, Albert Alfred	Pte	V4425; VX55896
Solomon, Benjamin	L/Sgt	NX141784
Solomon, Carl Abraham	Capt	2164321; NX70959

World War II, Australian Army (cont.)

NAME	RANK	SERVICE NO.	NAME	RANK	SERVICE NO.
Solomon, David	Pte	NX43546	Spicer, Nathan	Pte	V350888
Solomon, David	Tpr; Spr	NX84440	Spiegel, Alwin	Pte	VX55718
Solomon, Eric Robert	Capt	NX32986	Spiegel, Edgar	Pte	N464957
Solomon, Eric (Sydney)	Dvr	NX48805	Spiegel, Ernst	Pte	V378370
Solomon, George Herbert	Maj	SX26444	Spielman, Saul	Capt	VX108275
Solomon, George Samuel	Cpl	QX8346	Spigelman, Harry	Pte	V357585
Solomon, Herbert John	Maj	NX122807	Spigelman, Samuel	Pte	V201607
Solomon, Howard Austin	Maj	WX1565	Spielvogel, Lasselle Harris	Pte	VX3269
Solomon, Jack	Sgt	NX84303	Spilkowicz, Jacub	Pte	V377334
Solomon, Joseph	WO1	NX15001	Spindler, Alfred	Pte	N464985
Solomon, Joseph	S/Sgt	NX15928	Spira, Heinz	Pte	N346428
Solomon, Joseph	Pte	NX116961	Spira, Jacques	Capt	NX100971
Solomon, Lewis Joseph *	WO2	NX101544	Spitz, Hans	Sgt	V377719
Solomon, Lloyd Victor	Capt	237536; NX67008	Spitzer, Victor David	Gnr	VX127428
Solomon, Louis	Pte	N339146	Spizer, Mannie	Pte	V205312
Solomon, Louis	Cfn	NX148336	Spizer, Sydney Solomon	Dvr	VX90952
Solomon, Mark	Pte	NX120428	Spruch, Leopold	Pte	V377604
Solomon, Mervyn Harris	L/Cpl	N180001	Stafford, William	Capt	PX124
Solomon, Morris	Pte	N103665	Stander, Josef	L/Cpl	V377805
Solomon, Nathan Reuben	Pte	NX17014	Stanton, Albert Henry	Maj	VX23299
Solomon, Raymond Joseph	Sgt	SX31244	Stanton, Alma Gwynneth	Lt	VF346904
Solomon, Rupert Clifford	Capt	W6503	Stanton, Sydney Ralph	Pte	VX69784
Solomon, Samuel Bert	WO1	NX136018	Star, Enoch	Tpr; Spr	NX19714; N101001
Solomon, Sara	Pte	SF64816	Stark, Hermann	L/Cpl	N221643
Solomon, Stanley Alexander	Spr	NX39587	Stark, Martin	Pte	N456072
Solomon, Victor Abraham	S/Sgt	NX19649	Stark, Nathan	Pte	V518004
Solomons, Jack	Pte	N323651	Starke, Joseph Gabriel	Gnr	N450283
Solomons, Lewis Joel	Gnr	NX81050	Starke, Samuel	Capt	WX41839
Solomons, Maxwell	Pte	NX56825	Starke, Trevor	Pte	W7258
Solomons, Michael	Pte	V354544	Steen, Keith Maurice (Steenbhom)	Lt	NX143971
Solomons, Phillip	Pte	WX4851	Steigrad, Joseph **CBE MID**	Brig	NX212
Solomons, Phillip Roland Nathan	Pte	SX3646	Stein, Albert (Stone)	Pte	V515678
Solonsch, Samuel (Douglas John) *	Pte	VX15035	Stein, Harry	Pte	V38622
Soltan, Milton	Pte	NX169393	Stein, Kurt	Pte	N221721
Somen, Harry	Sig	N206941; NX155492	Stein, Max	Pte	N435802
Somen, Joseph	Sig	N205920; NX155493	Stein, Stefan	Pte	V377621
Somers, Harry Walter	Pte	V377871	Steinberg, Leon	Pte	V377034
Sommer, Erich	Pte	N224749	Steinberg, Reuben	Pte	W68848
Sommer, Frederick	Pte	N249550	Steinberg, Walter (Stanley)	Pte	V377445
Sommer, Fritz	Pte	N221670	Steiner, Leo	L/Cpl	N248186
Sondheim, Guenter	Pte	V377389	Steiner, Leopold	Pte	N286844
Soneberg, Israel	Pte	V377974	Steiner, Ludwig	Pte	V378287
Sonenberg, August Jacob	Pte	VX77475	Steiner, Walter	Pte	N221731
Sonenberg, Leopold Pincus	WO2	VX86625	Steinhardt, Ernest	Sgt	WX35443
Sonenfild, Abraham	Pte; Sig	N444404; N464703	Steinhardt, Kurt	Cfn	VX129192
Sonenfild, Keith Malcolm	Pte	N218319; N469984	Steinitz, David	L/Sgt	VX15101
Sonnenberg, Arthur	Pte	V514504	Steinmetz, Heinz Wolfgang	Pte	V377446
Sonnewald, Gerhard	Pte	V377444	Stekel, Wolfgang	Pte	V377560
Sor, William Paul	Pte	W94425	Stencel, Alec	Pte	V378047
Sorsky, Jack	Sig	VX64715	Sterberg, Harry	Pte	VX116980
Sostheim, Gerd	Pte	V377605	Sterling, Juliet (Coupland)	Cpl	VX112511
Southwick, David Michael	Cpl	V205451; VX143644	Stern, Erwin	Pte	N231000
Spagat, Erich	Pte	V502456	Stern, Frederick Hugo	L/Cpl	N226668
Spak, Salli	Pte	V378384	Stern, Hellmut	Pte	V377452
Spaniel, Henry August Abraham	L/Sgt	V378208	Stern, Iser David	Pte	V62186
Specteman, Solomon	Pte	NX90454	Stern, Joachim	Pte	W59176
Spencer, Bernard Sidney	WO1	V15309	Stern, Juda Leib	Pte	W64295
Spencer, Jack Myer	Capt	VX23886	Stern, Manfried	Pte	V377606
Sperling, Juraj	L/Cpl	NX92179	Stern, Nathan	Pte	N266067
Spero, Marcus	Gnr	NX165285	Stern, Otto	Pte	N256794
Spero, Maurice *	S/Sgt	N69522	Stern, Rolf Alfred	Pte	V377391
Spicer, Leo Gary	Pte	V205617; VX131323	Stern, Rudolf	Pte	NX152844

NAME	RANK	SERVICE NO.	NAME	RANK	SERVICE NO.
Sternberg, Kurt	Sgt	V377396	Symonds, Bruce Braham	Capt	NX201971
Sternberg, Siegfried	Pte	N321352	Symonds, Dudley Cecil	Gnr	NX48913
Sterne, Kurt Albert	Pte	V377717	Symonds, Hyman Reuben	Pte	NX100178
Sterne, Lionel John	Pte	V377716	Symonds, Kenneth	Pte	NX80707
Stevens, Edward John	Sgt	NX140974	Symonds, Leslie Julius	S/Sgt	NX141694
Stewart, Ronald Barnett	Sgt	NX172294	Symonds, Lewis	Sig	NX193298
Stillman, Harry	Pte	VX109685	Symonds, Maurice Isidore	Pte	V56968
Stiwelband, Micsha	Pte	V378300	Symonds, Naomi	S/Sgt	NX145216
Stiwelband, Oswald	L/Cpl	V377551	Symonds, Neville David	Gnr	NX78006
Stock, John	Spr	VX116617	Symons, John Emanuel	L/Bdr	VX13992
Stolarski, Chaim David *	Pte	VX52764	Szafran, Maurice	Pte	V377305
Stone, Alfred	Pte	NX52829	Szapiro, Izaak-Lejb Lou	Pte	N321105
Stone, Joseph Ernest *	Pte	NX26513	Szekely, Simon	Cfn	NX6575
Stone, Julius	Maj	N393191	Szklarz, Aron	Pte	V377456
Stone, Leon	Sgt	VX3509	Szmulewicz, Szaja	Pte	V502983
Stone, Marcus Nahum	Capt	VX114231	Sztajnic, Herzlik (Stafford, Harry)	Pte	V377275
Stone, Michael	Spr	NX66102	Sztarkstein, Mark (Stark)	Pte	V508849
Stone, Noah	Gnr	Q143387	Szwarc, Abram	Pte	V378225
Stone, Ronald Nathan	Gnr	NX27765	Szwarc, Gitman	Pte	V378322
Storozum, Hans	Cpl	N221591	Szwircpelc, Gerszon (Shor)	Pte	VX75052
Strasser, Frank	S/Sgt	NX65440	Tabak, David	Pte	V377937
Straton, Manfred	Pte	N298308	Taft, Hyman Pincus	Capt	VX93919
Strauss, Carl Hans	Pte	V377479	Tait, Hyman	Sgt	VX145326
Strauss, Erich	Pte	N453241	Tarry, Sidney	Cpl	V378076
Strauss, Erich	L/Cpl	V377602	Tartakover, Alexander Ralph	L/Bdr	VX21757
Strauss, George	Pte	N321156	Tate, Leon	Gnr	W233941
Strauss, Jack	Pte	V377754	Taubman, Abram Josef	Pte	V378044
Strauss, Richard	Sgt	V377574	Tauman, Jacob	Pte	N215652
Strauss, Siegfried (Steven)	Pte	V377940	Tauman, Maurice		V147637
Strauss, Walter Salomon	Pte	V377910	Tauss, Paul	Pte	W55802
Straussler, Egon	Pte	V377930	Taussig, Emil	Pte	V377725
Strelec, Harry	Pte	V36262	Taussig, Wilhelm	Pte	N463165
Strum, Heinz Ernest	Pte	N171962	Taylor, Bernard	Pte	NX168828
Strunin, Maurice	Pte	VX149012; V55503	Teitel, Werner Wolf	Pte	V377845
Strunin, Sam	Cpl	VX90403	Temple, Harry	Gnr	NX17202
Stuckgold, Blessing	Cpl	N388981	Temple, Louis	Pte	N224429
Stuckgold, Frederick	Pte	NX4110	Tenenbaum, Icko Szloma	Pte	V158910
Sturm, Maximilian	Pte	V377368	Tenenbaum, Leo David	Pte	V377786
Sturtz, Frederick	L/Cpl	V377759	Terry, Daniel	Cpl	N65798
Suchowolski, Lazar	Pte	V506680	Tetel, Sabina Helen	Cpl	NF456348
Suesskind, Kurt	Pte	V509760	Thalhiemer, Ruben	Pte	V378393
Suessmann, Gerson	Pte	V500735	Thomas, Arthur Lionel	WO2	VX34623
Sullivan, Arthur Irving MID	WO2	QX9896	Thomas, Colin David	Sgt	VX15875
Sulman, David Eber	Spr	NX161789	Thompson, Jack	Pte	N387505
Sulman, Leslie	Lt	N323568	Tichauer, Erich	Pte	V503912
Sultan, Werner	Pte	V377948	Tichauer, Ernest Joseph (Thompson)	Pte	V377896
Summerfield, Warner	Cpl	VX77283	Tichauer, Heinz	Pte	V377568
Super, Alfred Newton	WO1	V502629	Tichauer, Herbert	L/Cpl	V377833
Super, David Cecil	Cpl	NX21772	Tichauer, Salo Max	Pte	V377990
Super, Montague Albert Benzion	Pte	VX13039	Tikotin, Peter	Pte	V377565
Surgel, Myer	Pte	V503462	Tisch, Leo	Pte	V378285
Susman, Harold Stainfield	Lt-Col	S33136	Tishler, Harold	Sgt	N102981
Suss, Hans Hubert	Pte	V377774	Tishler, Leonard Lawrence	Pte	VX13650
Sussman, Gerald George	Pte	N221581	Tittman, Arthur	Pte	NX144805
Sussman, Heinz Julius Isidor	Cpl	NX110994	Tofler, Louis Judah	Capt	N76060
Sussman, Leslie Mendelssohn	L/Sgt	NX154196	Tofler, Victor	S/Sgt	NX103836
Sward, Clive Max	L/Cpl	V281485	Toister, Samuel	Pte	W50559
Sward, Geoffrey Joseph	Cpl	VX138983	Toister, Samuel	Pte	W55800
Swartz, Joseph	Pte	WX4924	Toltz, Abraham Jock	Lt	NX132532
Swift, David	Pte	V37848	Tonn, Gerhard Adolf	Pte	N231010
Swinburne, Max	Pte	VX72451	Tooler, Cyril	Pte	NX100179
Symon, Joe	Pte	483154; N26437	Tooler, Harry	Cfn	NX138374

NAME	RANK	SERVICE NO.	NAME	RANK	SERVICE NO.
Tooler, Isador	L/Cpl	NX26825	Vogel, Hans Paul	Pte	V377766
Topal, Henry James Isaac	Sgt	N101602	Vogel, Henry	Cpl	N221585
Topelberg, Ephraim	Sgt	W60995	Volk, Alexander	Pte	V501958
Topor, Tsaji-Sam	Pte	V378131	Vollweiler, Heinz (Tait I.)	Pte	V378385
Torda, Charles	Pte	N221582	Voss, Herbert	Pte	V377594
Torda, Severin	Pte	N321042	Wachman, Ernest	Cpl	V500094
Tortsan, Max	Pte	N72608	Wachman, Ronald	Pte	NX111127
Toster, Harry	L/Cpl	W33031	Wachsmann, Gerhard Julius	Pte	N453564
Toster, Joseph George	Lt	WX33587	Wachsmann, Walter	Pte	V377923
Trainor, Carl	Pte	V378049	Wachtel, Otto	Pte	V377593
Traub, Alfred	Pte	WX858	Wainrib, Colin	Pte	V378291
Traub, Michael	Pte	W15638	Wainrib, Henry	Cpl	VX93320
Traugott, Max	Pte	V378342	Wajnrajch, Abraham	Pte	V378091
Trebitsch, Walter	Pte	V377380	Wajntraub, Mojzesz	Pte	N321163
Treidel, Herbert	Pte	V504065	Wajsbord, Elazar Isaac	Pte	V377099
Treitel, Kurt	Sgt	V377441	Waligora, Jankiel	Pte	V378003
Trenn, Berrot David (Berel)	S/Sgt	NX27716	Walker, Charles	Capt	V147368
Trethewie, Rachel Crownson	Lt	VF388024	Walker, Simpson	Pte	NX16715
Trevaks, Hyman	Gnr	VX74129	Wallis, George	Pte	V377576
Trigger, Charles Gabriel	Tpr	QX31406	Walter, Joseph	Sgt	WX27779
Trigger, Maurice	Pte	NX23245	Walters, Isidore	Sgt	W48223
Trobe, Donald	Pte	WX22661	Walters, Philip	Pte	W43417; W55957
Trobe, Rosmond	Gnr	W39790	Walvisch, Leonard Morris	Gnr	VX134451
Tropp, Theodore	Pte	VX121827	Wand, Maurice	Pte	QX40287
Troy, Jack	L/Cpl	N103351	Wantoch, Albert Edward	Cpl	N273598
Trunkowski, Max	Pte	V378009	Warburton, Thomas Robert Claude	Pte	VX2461
Tryster, George	Pte	V378064	Ward, Russell Henry	Sgt	NX145502
Trytell, Joseph	Pte	VX116874	Warner, James	Pte	V377310
Tweg, Hyim Shaoul	Gnr	VX52768	Wartecki, Hertz	Pte	V507324
Ulman, Percy	Cpl	V155485	Wassermann, Albert	L/Cpl	V377477
Ulman, Phillip Roy	Pte	VX100332	Wassner, Mescalem Max	Pte	N230360
Ulman, Simon	L/Sgt	V500819	Wawrinetz, Adolf	Pte	N264387
Ulmer, Alfred Felix Reginald	Spr	N450800	Waxman, Rafael	Cpl	VX77290
Ulmer, Herbert	Pte	NX179821	Webberley, Leslie	Lt	VX94524
Underwood, William Dixon	Gnr	NX162632	Weidenbaum, Fritz Werner (Carter)	Pte	V377941
Unger, Abraham	Pte	Q151144	Weil, Kurt	Pte	N231028
Upfal, Max	Pte	V404796	Weil, Rudolf Ludwig	Pte	V377722
Upfal, Mojsze Max	Pte	VX56494	Weill, Hans Leopold	Pte	V377229
Urbach, Franz Joseph	S/Sgt	V377354	Weinberg, Coleman	Sig	NX51457
Urban, Tibor Urban	Pte	N346784	Weinberg, Franz Stefan Max	Pte	V377700
Vago, Valentine Balint	Pte	N463124	Weinberg, Hans Hermann	Pte	V377440
Van Cleef, Friedrich	Pte	N455215	Weinberg, Louis Henry **MM**	WO2	VX4492
Van Coevorden, Simeon William	Sgt	NX119193	Weiner, Otto	Pte	V377432
Van Gelder, Mordecai	Pte	V144379	Weingeist, Julius	Pte	V377490
Vander-Sluys, Aaron	Pte	SX5734	Weingott, David	Cpl	NX193108
Vanpraag, Joel Barney **MID**	Lt	WX6886	Weingott, Gilbert	Gnr	NX119508
Vanpraag, Margaret Dora	Cpl	VF398108	Weingott, Issy	Sig	VX19707
Varro, Egon	Pte	V377015	Weingott, Jack	Pte	NX16701
Vause, Michael Harry	Cpl	QX2125	Weingott, Rieka	L/Cpl	NFX200355
Velik, Jacob David	Gnr	V270293	Weinsheink, David Lezar	Pte	V512617
Velik, Leon	Bdr	VX135573	Weinstein, Alexander *	WO2	NX15397
Velik, Mayer Morris	Capt	V144548	Weinstein, Percival	Cpl	N108025
Victorsen, Ernest Max *	Pte	N26359	Weinstein, Samuel	Sgt	N464152
Vince, Robert Edward	S/Sgt	VX60447	Weinstock, David	Pte	V377567
Vinson, M.B.	S/Sgt	VX948	Weinstock, Myer	Pte	V310654
Vinternicz, Karl	Pte	V378077	Weinwurm, Paul	Pte	W90233
Visbord, Abraham Wolf	Gnr	V51044	Weis, Isador Ludvig	Pte	V377960
Visbord, Jacob	Pte	S2575	Weiss, Albert Harold	Sgt	W48730
Visbord, Monte	Pte	QX9256	Weiss, Erich	Pte	V503915
Voet, Hartog	Pte	N323753	Weiss, Fritz	Pte	N463189
Voet, Phillip	Pte	N323754	Weiss, Kurt Manfred	Pte	QX27700
Voet, Simon Phillip **MID**	S/Sgt	NX150039	Weiss, Max	Pte	N221579

Appendix 2: Those who served

NAME	RANK	SERVICE NO.
Weissberg, Leon	Pte	V378005
Weisser, Mendel	Pte	V510254
Weisz, Hans August	Pte	V377906
Wellner, Arthur	Pte	V377927
Wende, Zelig Icek	Pte	W95104
Wenger, Franz Stanley	Pte	N321355
Werner, Eliasz	Pte	V378812
Werner, Jakob Kurt	Pte	N321164
Werner, Moses Josef	Pte	N455700
Werthauer, Dietrich (Werth)	Pte	V377204
Wertheim, Julius	Cpl	V377908
Wertheim, Lutz Hans	Pte	N461441
Wertheimer, Felix	Pte	V377926
Wertheimer, Herbert	L/Cpl	N221671
Westheimer, Fritz	Pte	N248187
Westheimer, Joachim Joseph	L/Cpl	N221703
Westheimer, Josef David	Pte	NX179723
Wetzler, Edgar	Pte	V378283
Weyl, Walter	Pte	V377570
White, Bernard *	Gnr	VX32051
White, Egal	Capt	VX117057
White, Gershon	Pte	VX84700
White, Harold	Spr	V71009
White, Myer	Pte	V36258
Whiteman, Stanley Joseph	Cpl	NX25574
Whitman, Howard	Pte	N221704
Whitman, Samuel	Pte	N108080
Whitmont, Cecil George	Lt	NX146801
Wickens, Abraham Bert	Pte	V207132
Wicks, Jokel	Pte	V362641
Wiener, Lewis	Pte	VX55613
Wiener, Lorenz Max	Pte	V147322
Wieselberg, Saul	Pte	V502457
Wieselmann, Ladislaus	Cpl	V377406
Wieselmann, Victor	Pte	V377417
Wilczynski, Klaus	Pte	V378282
Wild, Efraim Bernard	Pte	N321300
Wildberg, Max	Pte	V378140
Wilks, Lewis	Sgt	V503895
Will, Hans Joachim	Pte	V377578
Will, Harry	Cpl	372857; VX95159
Willer, Harry Wolfe	Pte	N107564
Willner, Aron Wolf	Pte	W61902
Willow, James	Pte	N251616
Willow, Max	Pte	N251893
Wilner, Harry	Pte	WX33153
Wilson, Robert Henry	Gnr	VX20963
Wineberg, David	Pte	WX38170
Wineberg, Leslie Bertram	Sgt	NX130645
Wingens, Bruno	L/Cpl	W55798
Winn, Samuel	Gnr	VX50900
Winter, Richard	Pte	V377404
Winthrope, Leopold	Capt	V147367
Wise, Colin Marc	Capt	NX101912
Wiseman, Joel	Spr	VX77286
Wisniewski, Jankew	Pte	V378295
Witman, Edgar	Pte	V514515
Wittels, Simon	Pte	V377403
Wittenberg, Emil	Pte	V377405
Wittenberg, Harry	Sgt	NX131443
Wittenberg, Maurice	S/Sgt	N256943; NX174943
Wittner, Braham	Sig	VX121241

NAME	RANK	SERVICE NO.
Wittner, Charles Jacob	Pte	V379816
Wittner, Hyman	L/Cpl	VX25881
Witton, Emil Hans	Pte	NX180376
Witton, Paul	Pte	NX178632
Woelz, Sidney Isadore	Pte	N213737
Wohlgemuth, Leon Edward	Pte	V377947
Wohlmuth, Herbert Joseph	Pte	N321215
Wolf, David	Pte	V378356
Wolf, Ernst	Pte	V377353
Wolf, Helmut Kuno	L/Cpl	N224964
Wolf, Henry Morris	Spr	NX163479
Wolf, John Rupert	Pte	N221599
Wolf, Kurt	Pte	N211801
Wolf, Max	Pte	N321356
Wolf, Reginald Sydney	Gnr	NX15807
Wolf, Sam	Pte	V377114
Wolfe, Hugo Alexander	Capt	VX149204
Wolfe, Kaufman Samuel	Cpl	NX29203
Wolfe, Paul	Pte	V377993
Wolff, Alfred	Pte	V377489
Wolff, Gottfried Frederick	Pte	N224748
Wolff, Guenter Rudolf Ludwig (Geoffrey Ronald)	Pte	V377832
Wolff, Hugo	Pte	V378221
Wolff, Theodor	Pte	V512570
Wolffs, Walter	Cpl	V377491
Wolffsberg, Heinz	Pte	V378159
Wolfsohn, Hugo	Pte	V378157
Wolfson, Norman *	Pte	NX79953
Wolheim, Charles Mortimer	Lt	SX2535
Wolifson, William	Spr	NX57177
Wolinski, Kenneth Eric	Sgt	NX23546
Wolinski, Philip	Pte	W39579
Wolinski, Werner Siegfried	Pte	N244850
Wollan, Maurice	Pte	V377860; VX90919
Wollff, Eric Marks	T/Maj	VX134865
Wollff, Valerie Rachel	Cpl	VF345273
Wolman, Bernard	Cpl	V206542
Wolman, Joseph	Chap 4	Q69032
Wolman, Ruth	Pte	QF271349
Wolper, Harry	Pte	V517639
Wood, J. (Holzbauer, Hans)		
Woolf, Ellis Barnetti	Dvr	VX23128
Woolf, Geoffrey	Pte	V206991
Woolf, Harry	Pte	N454378
Woolf, Henry Alexander	Spr	NX21177
Woolf, Herman (Harry)	Sgt	V31067
Woolf, Israel	Pte	N186880
Woolf, Jack	Sgt	VX43570
Woolf, Jacob Stanley	Pte	V380657
Woolf, John Cyril	Pte	N176745
Woolf, Maurice Emanuel	Pte	V315747
Woolf, Montague Julius	Pte	VX21365
Woolf, Phineas Joel	Pte	VX136334
Woolf, Solomon	Pte	N468179
Woolf, Vincent William	Pte	V83027
Worms, Adolf	Cpl	N321202
Woss, Rudolf	Pte	W60833
Wright, David	Pte	WX33325; WX20022
Wurzburger, Walter	L/Cpl	V377946
Wylozny, David Mejer	Spr	W60830
Wyner, George	Pte	QX2845

World War II, Australian Army (cont.)

NAME	RANK	SERVICE NO.	NAME	RANK	SERVICE NO.
Wyner, Jack	Pte	NX26318	Zemelman, Hamey Leon	Pte	N266470
Wynn, Joe (Waintrob, Josek)	Pte	V377097	Zent, Oscar	Pte	V158461
Wynn, Victor	Capt	VX96328	Zentner, Heinrich	Pte	V377356
Wynne, Nathan	Pte	VX2986	Zentner, Hermann	Pte	V377411
Wynstanly, Roy	Pte	VX10659	Zentner, Kurt	Pte	V377343
Wysokier, John	Capt	VX151528	Zerman, Percy	Capt	TX6484
Wysokier, Raphael	Pte	VX119416	Zimmerman, Henry	Sgt	V508951
Yaffe, William	Pte	V206610	Zimmermann, Leo	Pte	V378185
Yaffie, George	Pte	N214409	Zimmermann, William	Pte	V506647
Yaffie, Morris	Pte	N215971	Zinader, David	Cpl	N93244
Yaffie, Nathan	Pte	N215970	Zinader, Maurice	Cpl	NX160946
Yass, Emmery John	Cpl	N221672	Zines, Jack	Cpl	NX148459
Yescovitch, Abraham	Pte	V157321	Zines, Maurice	Pte	W16021
Yoffa, David Leslie	Maj	VX112191	Zinner, Heinz	L/Cpl	N221673
Yoffa, Henry Herbert	Maj	VX108370	Zinner, William Otto	Pte	W55795
Yoffa, Isaac Valvyl	Capt	V147982	Zions, Albert	Gnr	N218103
Younger, Mark	S/Sgt	NX86920	Zions, Jack	Pte	NX94111
Yugoviitch, Isaac	Pte	N101705	Ziporkin, Maurice	Gnr	VX25879
Zablud, Ruwin	Pte	V377205	Zipper, Bernhard	Pte	V501722
Zachariah, Henry Alfred	Cpl	VX16289	Zipper, Hans	Cpl	V515398
Zachariah, Jack Vernon	Cpl	NX22367	Zipper, Wilhelm	L/Cpl	V377721
Zadek, Moritz Israel	Pte	V378313	Zmood, Felix	Pte	V46729
Zaks, George Joseph	Spr	VX77024	Zmood, Maurice	Sgt	V34654; VX93208
Zamek, Nuchin Leib (Nathaniel)	Gnr	N219261	Zoladz, Gutman George	Pte	V378058
Zamek, Syndria	Pte	V377162	Zollshan, Arthur	Pte	V378073
Zamel, Morris	Sgt	N74384	Zucker, Alan Asher	Cpl	V186850
Zander, Alec	Pte	NX106428	Zuckermann, Chiel	Pte	V378281
Zavelsky, Moses Isaac	Pte	QX42963	Zuckermann, Fritz	Pte	N231009
Zavod, Edward	Sgt	NX129667	Zukerman, Ezekiel	Cpl	NX177790
Zeeng, Samuel	Pte	VX472	Zukerman, Harry	Cpl	NX173973
Zeffert, Jacob Meyer	Lt	WX31496	Zukerman, Maurice	Lt	VX42917
Zeffert, Jules Emanuel	Lt	WX30836	Zusman, Abraham	Pte	S2861
Zeffert, Julius Harold	Pte	W31716	Zusman, Jack	Sgt	WX27815
Zeffert, William	Cpl	W236653	Zusman, Leslie	Sgt	W51335
Zeffertt, Edward Aaron	Gnr	WX40959	Zusman, Nathan	Sgt	WX34503
Zeffertt, Francis Jack	Cpl	WX25771	Zutrauen, Ernst Rudolf	L/Sgt	V377397
Zeidenberg, Charles	Pte	WX31571; WX18485	Zutrauen, Hermann	Pte	V516366
Zeif, Solomon	Pte	V503463	Zwier, Cyril	Pte	V517408
Zeissl, George	Pte	N173069	Zwierzynski, David	Pte	V500322
Zeligman, Harry Reuben	Cpl	VX65269	Zwinger, Hans	Cpl	V377214
Zeller, Joseph	Pte	Q143864	Zygier, Fiszel Laib	Pte	V378008
Zeltner, Henry	Pte	V377789	Zylberblat, Abram	L/Cpl	V377301
Zemel, Boruch	Cpl	V378133	Zysman, Myer	Pte	V378052
Zemel, Theodore	Pte	V378251			

BRITISH ARMY

NAME	RANK	SERVICE NO.
Cohen, P.E.	Capt	256964
Joseph, Zeryl	Sister	QAIMNS

Appendix 2: Those who served

ROYAL AUSTRALIAN AIR FORCE

NAME	RANK	SERVICE NO.	NAME	RANK	SERVICE NO.
Aarons, Cyril Samuel	LAC	49168	Bernstein, Alexander	LAC	145785
Aarons, Phineas John	LAC	126603	Bernstein, Montague Rufus	WO	430006
Abadee, Solomon **MID**	F Sgt	4193	Berrick, Harold Nathan	Cpl	33982
Abrahams, Frank Victor	WO	20081	Bershatzky, Israel	LAC	435661
Abrahams, Joseph Lyon	LAC	131161	Best, Jack	Sgt	125241
Abrahams, Norman Joseph	FO	265949	Biner, Henry Harris	LAC	162635
Abramson, Myer Isaac	LAC	118513	Birnbaum, Abram	LAC	53571
Abromwich, Albert	Cpl	55774	Black, Paul	LAC	56791
Adelstein, Alexander	LAC	62226	Blashki, Loris Phillip	FO	267136
Alexander, David Sydney *	F Sgt	420109	Blashki, Phillip		1434
Alexander, Florence Essie	ACW	177533	Bloch, Max	AC1	145021
Alexander, Jack Arnold *	F Sgt	421874	Bloom, Benjamin	LAC	56483
Allen, Ian Percy Albert **AFC**	Wg Cdr	0374; 315	Bloom, Doreen Louise	ACW	101157
Allen, Louis Sydney	Cpl	71559	Bloom, Jack	F Sgt	431121
Allen, Nita Gertrude Anne	Sgt	92381	Bloom, Keith	LAC	137794
Altshuler, Alfred Abraham Lionel	LAC	67810	Bloom, Leon	Cpl	127435
Altson, David	FO	255341	Bloom, Philip Arthur George	FO	0210837; 444061
Amber, Naim Shoul	LAC	83442	Blumenthal, Cecil Bernard David	FO	0210119; 60880
Applebaum, Alexander Joseph	Cpl	73384	Boas, Naomi	Str	501221
Applebaum, Ralph Joseph	LAC	440169	Boas, Patricia May	Sgt	93360
Apte, Harold Mayer	LAC	165917	Boock, Bertram Maurice	AC1	171655
Ash, Leonard Philip	LAC	445953	Borsht, Cyril	FO	426416
Asher, Raymond Clifford	FO	412094	Bourne, John	AC2	450691
Asman, Icchok Benjamin	FO	265956	Boymal, Bernard	LAC	127648
Baffsky, Harry	LAC	161044	Braham, Marc	LAC	122946
Baitz, Sampson	AC1	428591	Braham, Norman	LAC	156976
Baker, William	Cpl	55301	Brand, Norman *	F Sgt	410443
Balkind, Abraham Elimelech	F Sgt	421877	Braun, Maurice Jacob	LAC	53275
Bardas, Charles Henry	Cpl	13198	Breckler, Leona	ACW	113251
Barnard, Harry Louis Joseph	LAC	72097	Bresinski, Myer	LAC	64213
Barnbaum, Samuel	F Sgt	434572	Bressler, Ronald Phillip	LAC	409788
Barnett, Diana Rebecca	ACW	105591	Briggs, Arthur Robert Newton	Cpl	16752
Barnett, Harold	AC1	38011	Bristow, Harry Woolf	LAC	120992
Barnett, Jack	AC1	40319	Britton, Neville Samuel Woolf	Cpl	60208
Barnett, Joel	LAC	12062	Brodsky, Alexander Gregory	FL	3896
Barnett, Peter Samuel	Sgt	41779	Brodsky, Isadore Irvine	FL	3895
Baron, Nathan	AC1	157422	Brodziak, Kenneth Leo	FL	403632
Barr, Lawrence Mark	LAC	A210889; 66846	Brook, Barry Arnold	LAC	42170
Barrington, Joseph Arthur James	FO	420520	Brooke, Victor	LAC	143655
Barrow, Samuel	LAC	143024	Bross, Leon	LAC	69751
Basser, Leonard	FO	425480	Brott, Myer	LAC	119724
Batagol, Samuel	LAC	125181	Brown, Maurice	FL	413511
Bear, Alexander	Cpl	51685	Browne, Stuart Francis	FO	429297
Becher, Abram	F Sgt	42473	Browne, Wesley Edward	LAC	71703
Belkin, Joel	LAC	127974	Brukowicz, Marisha	ACW	95358
Belkin, Sam	LAC	157064	Brustman, Allan Bruce	Cpl	56516
Bellock, John **DFC**	FO	410140	Bund, Lieselotte Shirley	ACW	105454
Benjamin, George	LAC	66372	Burd, Joe	LAC	59547
Benjamin, Lloyd George	FL	408953	Cain, Ray	LAC	450463
Bennett, Alexander *	F Sgt	418698	Camberg, Maurice	LAC	67480
Bensky, Benjamin	AC1	442213	Caminer, Edward	AC1	33515
Bentley, George Cecil	F Sgt	34525	Carroll, Jack Leslie	LAC	171593
Bentwitch, Bruce Henry	Cpl	69986	Cebon, Leon	FL	257654
Berghouse, Raymond (Maxwell Dawson) *	LAC	14840	Chani, Samuel	LAC	53574
Berinson, Shim	LAC	441338	Chester, Ivan *	LAC	429693
Berkon, Benjamin	AC1	69158	Chester, Leonard Harry *	PO	438593
Berliner, Leon Joshua Samuel	LAC	21557	Chirlian, Barnett	FL	264425
Bernhardt, Abraham John	AC1	41260	Chirlian, Brian Nathan	F Sgt	133621
Bernhardt, Marcus	LAC	62093	Chuisano, Dodo	Cpl	101652

Jewish Anzacs

NAME	RANK	SERVICE NO.	NAME	RANK	SERVICE NO.
Church, Eva Leila	ACW	95841	Davis, Dudley Augustus	Sgt	50760
Ciddor, Ella	ACW	98524	Davis, Jacob	LAC	159110
Ciddor, Eric	Cpl	51646	Davis, John Lewis	F Sgt	440150
Ciddor, Harold	LAC	436880	Davis, Kenneth Joseph	F Sgt	444005
Ciddor, Henry Hyam	FO	410951	Davis, Phillip Henry	Cpl	36542
Cohen, Abraham	STWD	160558	Davis, Reginald Henry Saville **OBE**	Gp Capt	O329; 67
Cohen, Albert	WO	427871	Davis, Roy Brasmere	Gp Capt	O33026; 251167
Cohen, Alfred Adolph Livingston	F Sgt	439337	Davis, Shirley Katherine	ACW	176659
Cohen, Aubrey Lewis	SL	262374	Davis, Zena Phoebe	ACW	109137
Cohen, Barney	AC1	86025	De Groen, Evan Benjamin	FL	263464
Cohen, Basil Hast	LAC	1264	De Groen, Leonard Lewis		207242
Cohen, Beryl	F Sgt	92648	De Groen, Lyonel Sampson	PO	6927
Cohen, Cecil Susman	LAC	72072	De Vere, Hyman	FL	416914
Cohen, David	FO	427772	De Vere, Solomon	LAC	133893
Cohen, David	FO	429091	De Young, Louis Cecil	LAC	47465
Cohen, Derrick Simeon	FL	405573	Dent, Hal Ian Comer *	FO	411428
Cohen, Francis Lionel	FO	423643	Diamond, Oscar Nathan **DFC**	FL	270544
Cohen, Geoffrey Michael	FL	424725	Dizick, John	Cpl	73939
Cohen, George Victor	Sgt [T]	A210202; 60161	Dizick, Maurice Nathan	LAC	138656
Cohen, Henry Joseph	FL	255405	Don, Basil	LAC	161092
Cohen, Joseph *	FO	401104	Don, Bernard	AC1	423080
Cohen, Judah	WO	413074	Don, Bessie	ACW	108102
Cohen, Julius Allan **DFC**	FL	117	Don, Michael	LAC	63979
Cohen, June	ACW	97558	Drechsler, Moritz	LAC	77570
Cohen, Leah	ACW	106021	Dryen, Mervyn	LAC	64731
Cohen, Leon Ralph	Cpl	35742	Dunn, Harry Joshua	LAC	56872
Cohen, Marcia	Sgt	93063	Dvoretsky, Harold	LAC	436717
Cohen, Marie	Cpl	105644	Dyte, Alan Charles *	Sgt	400920
Cohen, Mark	Cpl	52417	Edelman, Alwyn David	LAC	407703
Cohen, Maurice	AC1	436870	Edelman, Howard John	FL	
Cohen, Morris	FL	297484	Edelman, Jack	LAC	71171
Cohen, Neil Alan	Sgt	71433	Edelman, Lionel Samuel	FO	411884
Cohen, Samuel Henry	Cpl	69159	Edwards, Ronald Simon	LAC	118318
Cohen, Solomon Morris	Cpl	15503	Efron, David Herman	LAC	126612
Cohen, Sydney	F Sgt	1204	Eisen, Abraham	Sgt	10014
Cohen, Sydney	LAC	161501	Eizenberg, Louis	LAC	135990
Cohen, Trevor Montague	Cpl	33710	Elfman, Wolf	LAC	121385
Cohen, William Myer	LAC	82845	Elias, Desmond Ellmore	LAC	147828
Cohney, Ben	LAC	82050	Elias, Lionel Frankelyn	LAC	118394
Colley, Hannah Lilian	ACW	113209	Elias, Vernon Montrose	LAC	118383
Collins, Frank Zavel	LAC	444438	Elkman, David Bruce	LAC	445769
Collins, Robert	LAC	23227	Ellinson, Jacob Barnet	LAC	419841
Cooper, John Gordon	LAC	148788	Ellis, Neville Leonard	WO	421656
Cooritz, Morris	LAC	150054	Ellison, Rodney Hyman	F Sgt	422916
Corrick, Sylvia Estelle	Cpl	105962	Emanuel, Alexander	LAC	148271
Court-Rice, Ruby Miriam	ACW	98274	Emanuel, Cedric Raymond	FL	266681
Cowan, Neville	LAC	73546	Emanuel, Lawrence	LAC	76119
Cowen, Percy Harris	SL	O33058; 257700	Encel, Solomon	LAC	147791
Cowper, Leon Wallace	WO	433638	Engel, Albert Emanuel	Sgt	65585
Crafti, Rachel	ACW	102839	Epstein, Benjanim	SL	261714
Crafti, Reuben Robert	AC1	76082	Epstein, Betty Ruth	ACW	106401
Crawcour, Murray Mayer	FL	401270	Epstein, Julius **DFC & B**ar	FL	423687
Crewe, Morris	Cpl	210040; 300510	Epstein, Les	LAC	81130
Croker, Golda Amelia	Cpl	108236	Fabian, Samuel	LAC	70664
Da Costa, Isadore	FL	254151	Faigen, Maxwell	LAC	433762
Dabscheck, Conrad	LAC	125715	Falstein, Sydney Max	FO	423690
Dabscheck, Ronald Samuel	Cpl	430690	Feldman, Harry Charles	WO	41919
Davis, Alexander Simeon	LAC	420338	Feldman, Maurice Joseph	Cpl	16494
Davis, Alfred Israel	FL	36067	Feldman, Robert	F Sgt	41819
Davis, Alfred Sydney	FO	129822	Feldmann, Julius	Sgt	10581
Davis, Coleman Joseph	LAC	131401	Feyn, Benjamin	LAC	65763
Davis, David Ernest	LAC	132049	Fienberg, Alan Lewis	LAC	165333

Appendix 2: Those who served

NAME	RANK	SERVICE NO.	NAME	RANK	SERVICE NO.
Fine, Bernard David *	F Sgt	419304	Golding, Norman	FO	265084
Fink, Julian David	LAC	149329	Goldman, Douglas John	LAC	21981
Finkelstein, Ernest Isaac	LAC	46963	Goldman, William *	PO	400403
Finkelstein, Harry	Cpl	436867	Goldsmith, Hubert Daniel	Cpl	54221
Finkelstein, Joseph	WO	16099	Goldsmith, Joseph Arthur	Sgt	40323
Finkelstein, Leslie	Sgt	17392	Goldstein, Alexander	LAC	434152
Finkelstein, Lionel	LAC	82080	Goldstein, Elizabeth	ACW	98255
Finks, Maxwell James	LAC	116782	Goldstein, George Leon	WO	433588
Finley, Robert Reuben	Cpl	51896	Goldstein, Marks	LAC	41077
Flegeltaub, Hector Charles Wolf	Cpl	5927	Golomb, Sarah M.	Cpl	97562
Flegeltaub, Sydney Myer	Cpl	56875	Gomes, Lewis Charles *	F Sgt	420659
Flohm, Lewis Herman	Sgt	38185	Goode, Aaron	LAC	57432
Flohm, Lionel Wilfred *	F Sgt	427760	Goode, Don	FL	427642
Foley, Judah Jacob	LAC	157241	Goodman, Albert Abraham	Cpl	66904
Fonda, Victor	LAC	118145	Goodman, Maxwell	F Sgt	430089
Forbes, Jack (Farbsztein)	LAC	53582	Gordon, Benjamin Louis	F Sgt	A24427; 11109
Frack, Zellmar Joseph	Sgt	130137	Gordon, Clifford	LAC	64738
Frank, James	PO	432147	Gorodnaski, Roy	LAC	81913
Frazer, Ronald	LAC	74977	Gotlib, Majer	LAC	53589
Freadman, Paul	FL	418824	Gouttman, Reuben	WO	420934
Freadman, Roy Joseph	Cpl	428399	Granger, Elias	LAC	129514
Frederick, Hugh	LAC	130760	Grant, Samuel	LAC	411019
Freedman, Harold Emanuel	FO	41616	Green, Alfred	LAC	11149
Freedman, Lionel Henry	Cpl	42419	Green, Gordon Henry	LAC	132751
Freedman, Sydney	LAC	161116	Green, Maurice Isaac *	F Sgt	423717
Friedlander, Neville	WO	439717	Green, Naomi	Sgt	99457
Friedman, Ellis Solomon	LAC	77975	Green, Rachel Rae	Sgt	99650
Friedman, Harold Godfrey	FO	33507	Greenberg, Ben	LAC	76498
Frieze, Berrol Samuel *	WO	409400	Greenberg, Harris Neville		267907
Frosh, Henry	LAC	51773	Greenberg, Harris Phillip	T/SL	0211481; 267761
Frumar, Neville Raphael	FL	024662; 420814	Greenberg, Leslie Leonard	FL	267569
Gadsby, Adeline (Solomon)	Sgt	93406	Greenstein, Cyril	LAC	130263
Garber, Mendel	LAC	145224	Greenstein, Ralph	LAC	166267
Garcia, Sydney Isaac	LAC	83189	Greenwald, Lionel	LAC	164742
Gertler, Martin	Cpl	18856	Griff, Harold Hirsh	AC1	115824
Getzler, Leon	LAC	54868	Griff, Sydney Leslie	Cpl	115866
Gild, Alfred Louis	LAC	141138	Grinblat, Aaron Morris	WO	401434
Giligicz, Mejer	LAC	53586	Grinblat, Hannah Dora	ACW	174189
Gingold, Berech	AC1	53587	Grinblat, Leslie	WO	428545
Ginsburg, Reba Felice	Cpl	106958	Grinblat, Sidney	LAC	142050
Glance, Henry Francis	LAC	420183	Gubbay, Joseph	LAC	71503
Glance, James Henry	LAC	441686	Gubbay, Joseph Albert	LAC	36270
Glass, Adrian Hertzl	Cpl	34330	Gurewitz, Max	F Sgt	28126
Glass, Kenneth Maurice	FO	69542	Haimson, Lazar	Sgt	51908
Glass, Maurice Jacob	Sgt	14280	Hallenstein, Albert Richard	SL	251735
Glasser, Daniel	Sgt	20332	Halliday, Clifford	LAC	71802
Glick, Phineas	WO	434631	Halpin, Samuel Thomas	Sgt	25942
Gluck, Nathan Woodrow	FL	401033	Harlem, Athol Asher *	F Sgt	408833
Gluck, Stanley Samuel	LAC	147905	Harris, Arnold	LAC	148268
Godfrey, Harry	Sgt	80891	Harris, Clyde Jack	FL	419420
Gold, Rufus Manuel	WO	436292	Harris, Joseph	Sgt	62914
Gold, Samuel	AC1	159070	Harris, Liela Crownsen	Cpl	104689
Goldberg, Austin Simon Lewis	LAC	72149	Harris, Maurice Samuel	LAC	444284
Goldberg, Bernard	LAC	53784	Harris, Stanley	AC1	52369
Goldberg, Betty Shina Isabel	Cpl	104486	Harrison, Lawrence Neville	LAC	148470
Goldberg, David Joseph	WO	420184	Harrison, Matthew	LAC	127040
Goldberg, Jacob	Cpl	57856	Harrould, Edwin James Maurice	LAC	124539
Goldberg, Max	LAC	127062	Hart, Harry Manuel	Sgt	37533
Goldberg, Philip	Cpl	61799	Hart, Norman Godfrey	LAC	445115
Goldberg, Raymond Gershon DFC	FL	407422	Hartman, Leo Alfred	FO	428459
Goldbloom, Max	F Sgt	11946	Hartstein, Zedekiah	WO	436222
Goldbloom, Samuel Mark	LAC	49615	Hartz, Alexander	Cpl	45211

Jewish Anzacs

NAME	RANK	SERVICE NO.
Hartz, Freda	ACW	103287
Hartz, Samuel Zangwill	Cpl	80707
Harvest, Benjamin Myer	PO	408992
Haskin, Norman	AC2	450808
Haskin, Norman Ralph	LAC	41789
Haskin, Samuel Lionel	Cpl	53664
Hatfield, Arthur Albert	Sgt	17697
Hatfield, David Henry	LAC	A210063; 166746
Hayes, Joseph Bruce	AC1	158625
Hearsch, Dany	LAC	120954
Hearsch, David	LAC	50698
Hearsch, Harry	LAC	144854
Hearsch, Harry Edward	LAC	123346
Henry, Leon Simon David	Sgt	20633
Henry, Maurice Philip	FO	444459
Herman, Keith		415655
Hertz, Cyril	LAC	20758
Hertzberg, Lionel Gordon	LAC	131980
Hertzberg, Raphael Lewin	FO	124904
Heselev, Tamara	Sgt	90526
Hickman, Peter Leonard	FO	72803
Hillel, Katie Ethel	ACW	99516
Hillman, William Arnold	FL	263735
Hirst, Edmond	LAC	421730
Hoffman, Adolf David Leon *	FO	426598
Hoffman, Bertha Evelyne	ACW	103933
Hoffman, Ernest	Cpl	17350
Hoffman, Hayim Judah	WO	9230
Hollaway, Vena Dorothy	Sgt	106728
Horinack, Barnett	LAC	410666
Horne, Albert Elliott * **DFM**	PO	402461
Horry, Solomon Levy	LAC	82534
Housey, Aaron Michael	LAC	159429
Hunt, Harry Richard	WO	68089
H'Watkin, Eric Leonid	LAC	63660
Hyams, Bruce Godfrey	FL	255921
Hyman, Eskell Herbert	LAC	119219
Irving, Phillip Sydney	Cpl	70158
Isaacs, Alexander Reginald	Sgt	13902
Isaacs, Beryl Lilian	ACW	110947
Isaacs, David Ralph	AC1	50315
Isaacs, David Sassoon	LAC	84544
Isaacs, Ernest Abraham	Cpl	410339
Isaacs, Frederick Raymond	Cpl	12936
Isaacs, Gerald Henry *	F Sgt	409550
Isaacs, John Lyle	LAC	127173
Isaacs, Marcus Woolf	LAC	400003
Isaacs, Samuel	AC1	4396
Isaacs, Samuel Joseph	LAC	74978
Isaacson, Dorothy	ACW	105293
Isaacson, Peter Stuart **DFC AFC DFM**	FL	035959; 401068
Isenberg, Maurice	LAC	162667
Israel, Bertram Francis Norman **Medal of Freedom MID** [USA]	SL	262817
Israel, Ronald Albert	LAC	142959
Jackman, Harry Hans	PO	277700
Jacobs, Clifford Samuel	FO	41164
Jacobs, David *	Sgt	411328
Jacobs, Doreen Miriam (Bridges)	Sect Off	114320
Jacobs, Henry	LAC	119729
Jacobs, Joseph	FL	263519
Jacobs, Morris Bernard	AC1	160161

NAME	RANK	SERVICE NO.
Jacobs, Philip Abraham	AC1	167039
Jacobs, Rodney Samuel	LAC	132153
Jacobson, Isadore Marquis	WO	403344
Jacobson, Lionel	FO	70536
Jacobson, Samuel	LAC	449992
Jaques, Frank Arnold *	LAC	162397
Jona, Walter	LAC	158876
Jones, Ian Cosman **MID**	WO	401696
Joseph, Clive Emanuel	LAC	53596
Joseph, Graham Harris *	FO	400415
Joseph, Harold Walter Harris *	LAC	956834
Joseph, Ralph Thomas **MID**	FL	403516
Josephs, Alexander	Cpl	54117
Kagan, Freda	Cpl	95155
Kahana, Herbert Lionel	AC1	168117
Kahn, Alexander	SL	262787
Kaiser, Paul Frederick	FO	411581
Kan, Alexander Elias * **MID**	F Sgt	409716
Karmel, Richard Ellis	F Sgt	438446
Katz, Bernhard	FL	265051
Kay, Sam	Cpl	64221
Keesing, Betty	ACW	176431
Kessler, David Norman	Cpl	17474
Kimmel, Frederick George *	LAC	134295
Kindler, Israel Hyman	F Sgt	418851
Kindler, Jacob	FO	430809
King, Abraham	LAC	156644
King, Henry Myer	LAC	69075
King, Lionel Louvian	Cpl	59221
Kingston, Leigh Maurice	LAC	74932
Kino, Phyllis Esther	ACW	97049
Kleiman, Abraham	LAC	55937
Kliman, Hyman Isaac	LAC	53737
Klippel, John Owen *	FO	412149
Kommel, Barry Bennett	LAC	68061
Kooperman, Max Joseph	F Sgt	441377
Korn, Kenneth	LAC	156341
Korn, Leslie	LAC	160112
Kosterlitz, Harry	LAC	85105
Koszminsky, Ronald Marks	LAC	150814
Kowadlo, Leslie	SL; Dvr	257662
Krasenstein, Harry	WO	433600
Krause, Johann	LAC	145742
Krew, Wolfe	LAC	156409
Kruger, Michael Gordon	Sgt	300159
Krycer, Sam	LAC	54849
Kuchmar, Norman	LAC	127929
Kurzer, Henry	Sgt	64742
Labowitch, Bernard	AC2	446141
Laiser, Israel	LAC	64907
Langley, Jacob	F Sgt	14025
Lapin, Herman	LAC	52124
Lawson, Frederick Henry	FL	416585
Lazarus, Abraham Desmond	LAC	403057
Lazarus, Cecil	LAC	132792
Lazarus, Frederick George	FO	5186
Lazarus, Henry Sherratt	FL	418962
Lazarus, Keith Rothwell	LAC	41549
Lazer, Alfred Lionel	LAC	148480
Lee, Jacob Joseph	LAC	137665
Lee, John Joseph (Lachter)	LAC	125446
Lee, Valmai	Cpl	94276

NAME	RANK	SERVICE NO.	NAME	RANK	SERVICE NO.
Lehrer, Ruben	LAC	159557	Mandel, Drazel Grace	ACW	98568
Leicester, John Dudley	Cpl	11696	Mandel, Enid Bertha	Sgt	95175
Lester, Michael Joseph	Cpl	135888	Mandel, Sylvia Noelene	Sect Off	90084
Lester, Phillip Joseph *	PO	10373	Mandelberg, Jack Pond	AC1	167044
Levenson, Lewis	LAC	139185	Markov, Bray	Cpl	52738
Lever, Jack	AC1	85792	Markovitch, Maurice John	LAC	58132
Leveson, Leo Morris	PO	257608	Marks, Bertram Maurice	LAC	42252
Levey, Phillip	WO	A3776	Marks, Colin Barrington	LAC	445029
Levey, Rahel Elizabeth	ACW	97934	Marks, David	F Sgt	14180
Levi, Zauls Alexander	LAC	417586	Marks, Eric Frank	SL	251925
Levien, Harold Bruce	LAC	165647	Marks, Frederick Cecil	LAC	432625
Levien, Neville Keith	WO	424834	Marks, Hyman	LAC	130318
Levin, Benjamin	LAC	81951	Marks, Joseph Frederick **DFC**	FO	419079
Levitus, Solomon *	F Sgt	402910	Marks, Kenneth Henry	FO	430180
Levy, Anita Beryl	Sect Off	92421	Marks, Leslie Magnus	FO	400372
Levy, Aubrey Michael	Cpl	61566	Marks, Maurice Edward Jack	WO	430118
Levy, Colman Joseph	LAC	164571	Marks, Maxina Isobel	ACW	92364
Levy, Donald John	AC2	445884	Marks, Reginald	LAC	136054
Levy, Douglas Alexander	SL	262015	Marks, Rodney	Sgt	49241
Levy, Enid Yvonne (Yetta)	Sgt	105675	Marks, Rodney Stuart	WO	422280
Levy, Harry	WO	422960	Marsden, Douglas Herbert	SL	261636
Levy, Leon	LAC	121230	Marshall, Rothchild	LAC	83291
Levy, Lewis Keith	WO	207834	Masel, Colin Copel	WO	052821; 441361
Levy, Lindsay Nathan	Cpl	130334	Matison, Victor Charles	PO	416774
Levy, Lionel Hilton	FL	433005; 0211747	Maver, Arthur George	LAC	143359
Levy, Lloyd EBE	Sgt	6081	Mclean, Neil James	LAC	135288
Levy, Moya Miriam	ACW	178111	Mecoles, Samuel David	SL	253432
Levy, Susan Laura	Cpl	105747	Meerman, Leon	LAC	120863
Levy, Victor Michael	LAC	65773	Meldelson, Isaac	LAC	120233
Lew, Max Myer	LAC	146145	Melovitch, Maurice	LAC	157013
Lewis, Benjamin Sydney	F Sgt	A2423	Mendelsohn, Oscar Adolf	FL	254898
Lewis, Elizabeth	ACW	106675	Mendelsohn, Paul Gerald	WO	413316
Lewis, Maurice Saul	Sgt	10317	Mendelson, Harold	LAC	143908
Lewis, Morris	LAC	66298	Mendelson, Solomon	LAC	49946
Lewis, Philip	FO	72679	Menzies, George Benjamin	LAC	53840
Lewis, Ralph	LAC	129674	Messiah, Mordecai Ezra	AC1	71806
Lewis, Sara Maisie	Cpl	97562	Metz, Miriam	ACW	91083
Lieberman, Robert Abraham	FO	405749	Meyer, Kenneth Edward	LAC	116008
Liefman, Charles Edward	FL	400634	Michelin, Michael Charles	LAC	67059
Lilienthal, Victor	FL	424620	Michelson, David Solomon	LAC	120302
Lipman, John Edward	FO	21893	Milecki, Alexander	LAC	142742
Lipman, Trevor Abraham	FO	20050	Miller, Maurice	Sgt	41799
Lipp, Leo	AC1	127596	Miller, Simon John	WO	439254
Lipshut, Maurice	LAC	54439	Miller, Zalman	LAC	53204
Lipson, Jacob	Cpl	56905	Milston, Alan Kaufman	FO	139867
Lloyd, Vivian Leon Colley	Sgt	A51609; 38369	Mish, Eric John	FO	252166
Lubansky, Maurice	LAC	58069	Mitchell, Alexander	LAC	144657
Lubransky, Albert	LAC	58169	Mitchell, George	Cpl	64018
Lubransky, Solomon James	LAC	145002	Mitchell, Joseph Ellis	LAC	160192
Lukav, Ronald	LAC	117468	Mordecai, Lionel Joseph	FL	254964
Lurie, Matthias	FO	403478	Moritz, Abraham	WO	401012
Luster, George	LAC	164121	Morley, Bennie	Cpl	41289
Lux, Charles	FO	40326	Morris, Benjamin	Cpl	35731
Lyons, Ian Alfred **OBE, BSM** (USA) (Korea)	FL	033072; 400095	Morris, Bessie Esther	ACW	98512
Lyons, Kenneth	LAC	120269	Morris, Harold	Cpl	68014
Magnus, Errol Henry **DFC**	FL	413216	Morris, Harris Samuel	FL	264225
Maizels, Sidney	LAC	157119	Morris, John Harry	LAC	147441
Maller, Joseph	LAC	125857	Morris, Mark Solomon	FL	294936
Malor, Herbert Julius	Cpl	35476	Morris, Maurice	SL	251267
Malor, Ronald Lewis *	F Sgt	423246	Morris, Maurice	FO	406304
Manasseh, Moses	AC1	86060	Morris, Morris Louis	LAC	158562
Mandel, Ada	ACW	105204	Morris, Samuel Boaz	LAC	139469

Jewish Anzacs

World War II, Royal Australian Air Force (cont.)

NAME	RANK	SERVICE NO.	NAME	RANK	SERVICE NO.
Morrison, Stanley	Cpl	33902	Piraner, Samuel	Sgt	20850
Moses, Harry Ernest	Cpl	32216	Pizer, Denis Solomon	Cpl	125948
Moss, Abraham Nathaniel	Cpl	41682	Pizer, Ian Philip	F Sgt	431368
Moss, Isidore Ernest	F Sgt	76767	Pizer, Norman Eric	FL	408514
Moss, Lewis	FL	1072	Platus, Max	LAC	69902
Moss, Solomon	Sgt	401626	Plotkin, Murray	LAC	158868
Moss, Solomon Joel	Cpl	63427	Podem, Harold	LAC	146025
Moss, William Benjamin	LAC	125605	Polack, Margaret Ruth	Sect Off	90862
Mossenson, Nisson	WO	427532	Pollard, Dennis	LAC	133968
Murphy, Patricia (Goldman)		104615	Power, Clavering Joseph Samuel	LAC	52650
Myers, Alfred Hubert	Sgt	115798	Press, Jack Juvall	Cpl	67063
Myers, Mark Joseph	LAC	137167	Presser, Ruby Rika	Cpl	101099
Myers, Maurice	FO	2053	Prince, Dennis Aubrey	LAC	159019
Myerson, Leon Benjamin	F Sgt	445319	Prokhovnik, Nathan	LAC	56680
Myerson, Philip *	PO	432398	Pura, Anne	Sect Off	90086
Myres, Nathaniel Albert	Sgt	34910	Pura, Samuel	LAC	132244
Naphtali, Harold Isaac	Cpl	19825	Rabin, Solomon	LAC	71124
Napolsky, Paul Arthur	Cpl	A23648; 66956	Rapke, Betty Pearl	FO	350249
Nathan, Alfred	LAC	69743	Rapken, Simon Abraham	WO	433858
Nathan, Clifford Barnett	SL	264257	Rappeport, Philip	LAC	82291
Nathan, Raymond Samuel	LAC	84192	Ratner, Samuel David	FO	133805
Nathan, Reginald Vivian Edward	FL	418458	Ravdell, Mischa	Cpl	120237
Neistat, David	LAC	121171	Raynor, Robert Albert Solomon	FL	254469
Newburg, Richard	AC1	167860	Revelman, George	LAC	50152
Newburg, Yzia	ACW	176594	Rich, Joseph Geoffrey	Sgt	406044
Newman, Edgar Yitzhak Seitel	Cpl	36850	Rich, Michael (Ryvitch)	Sgt	50983
Newstead, Maurice Nathan	Cpl	69042	Richards, Clifford Solomon	FL	402397
Nissen, Alfred	Cpl	49350	Rischin, Henry Isaac	LAC	434537
Nissen, Harry	LAC	55460	Rischin, Marcia	ACW	104412
Novic, Harry	LAC	142427	Ritchie, William	AC1	439378
O'Brien, Jack Barnett	F Sgt	22047	Roberts, Harry	WO	433055
Oderberg, Albert	LAC	118408	Robin, Stanley Gordon	WO	430289
Oderberg, Harold	FO	128347	Robinson, Betty (Lewis)	ACW	108827
Oderberg, Israel Manuel	Sgt	119349	Rochawin, Anna	ACW	110312
Opas, Athol Louis *	Sgt	400354	Rochlin, Roy	FL	420060
Opas, Philip Henry Napoleon	FL	255040; 10732	Rockman, Barnet	FO	430768
Orbuck, Laurance David *	Sgt	400029	Roden, Berenice Fay	ACW	93542
Orbuck, Rita Miriam	Cpl	104926	Roden, Jacob Henry *	Sgt	411053
Orken, Marcus Benjamin		300181	Rogalasky, Samuel Coleman	Sgt	14007
Orloff, Bertie	FO	16294	Rojzenfeld, Solomon (Rosenfield)	LAC	52935
Osborne, Bernard Cecil	Cpl	80277	Romain, Joseph Wallace	LAC	135642
Oshlack, Charles Bernard *	LAC	56853	Rosalky, Lionel	LAC	66962
Oshlack, Joe *	F Sgt	410560	Rosalky, Marcus *	F Sgt	72799
Oviss, Frank	LAC	158819	Rose, Harold	LAC	50340
Owen, Francis Septimus	FO	403280	Rose, John	AC1	10670
Patkin, Leo Braham *	F Sgt	401146	Rose, Lou	A Cam O	
Patrunin, Harris Joseph	LAC	157467	Rose, Max*	FO	418179
Pearce, William Ernest *	Sgt	402825	Rose, Norman Kendal	LAC	148411
Pearl, Jack	LAC	125729	Rose, Phyllis Marcia	Cpl	97777
Pearlman, Lloyd Samuel	LAC	145306	Rose, Victor Allenby	Sgt	419483
Peckarsky, Boris David	LAC	56682	Rosebery, Beryl Maureen	F Sgt	92610
Penn, Hyman	LAC	137426	Rosen, Emanuel	F Sgt	21332
Perl, George	LAC	52520	Rosen, Louis	FO	443472
Philips, Jack Delmont	WO	422692	Rosenberg, Ian Albert	Sgt	16885
Phillips, Athol Sidney	LAC	136519	Rosenberg, June	ACW	101734
Phillips, Harry	Cpl	13589	Rosenberg, Lewis Conway *	LAC	29877
Phillips, Julius Walter	FL	68926	Rosenberg, Louis Jack	LAC	418682
Phillips, Leo	AC1	21734	Rosenberg, Marcus	FL	401804
Phillips, Lewis	AC1	411601	Rosenbluth, Alexander Samuel	F Sgt	6942
Phillips, Lewis (Aaron)	AC1	167258	Rosenbluth, David	LAC	440759
Phillips, Lionel Solomon	LAC	162390	Rosenfeld, Allan Lloyd	LAC	422712
Pinch, Wolfe	F Sgt	54070	Rosenfeld, Arnold	FL	264501

Appendix 2: Those who served

NAME	RANK	SERVICE NO.	NAME	RANK	SERVICE NO.
Rosenfeld, Eric	FL	421629	Sherbanee, Stanley Abraham	LAC	70940
Rosenfeld, Froin	Cpl	18701	Sherman, John	LAC	72271
Rosenfeld, Max	SL	262265	Shertock, Arthur Abraham	LAC	152485
Rosenfield, Geoffrey Gregory	LAC	78940	Shertock, Maxwell John	LAC	141686
Rosenfield, Joyce Eileen	ACW	101049	Shimenson, Joshua	FL	296223
Rosenfield, Maxwell Samuel	F Sgt	440242	Showman, Cecil	Cpl	36551
Rosengarten, Bernard	LAC	50854	Showman, Douglas Arthur	LAC	144768
Rosenthal, Bruce Victor	ACM rec	155162	Showman, Norma Olivette	Cpl	93204
Rosenthal, Newman Hirsh (Henry)	SL	253779	Shulman, Joseph	Cpl	17551
Rosner, Morris	Cpl	50580	Silberberg, Berthold Julius	LAC	65678
Ross, Samuel	AC1	85819	Silberberg, John David	FO	419975
Ross, Samuel	FL	424346	Silbert, David	LAC	81456
Roth, Benno	Sgt	449399	Silbert, Eric Abraham DFC	FO	427030
Roth, William	LAC	118640	Silman, Izrael	LAC	55387
Rothberg, Mossie	LAC	42985	Silver, Albert	FO	139936
Rothfield, Jessel Myer	FO	129814	Silver, Henry	LAC	53858
Rothman, Rose Ray	Sgt	97364	Silver, Howard Basil	LAC	128868
Rothstadt, Maurice	F Sgt	41802	Silver, John Lang	F Sgt	32576
Rottell, John	LAC	52449	Silver, Leslie	FO	442285
Roubin, Cyril	Sgt	79124	Silverstone, Reginald Myer		149328
Roubin, Ruth Rachael (Rosebery)	ACW	98250	Simons, Bertram *	AC1	440963
Roussin, Israel	LAC	67065	Simons, Frank David	FO	119568
Rozen, Edward	LAC	146082	Simons, Harry	Cpl	82931
Rubner, Sidney	AC1	167737	Simons, Isador	LAC	139348
Saffer, Michael Myer	Sgt	54365	Simons, Joan		94059
Saffir, Samuel	T/Sgt	58480	Simons, Myra	ACW	177141
Saks, Israel	LAC	129682	Simons, Paul Joseph	LAC	59793
Salinger, Ronald	LAC	83103	Simpson, James	LAC	423513
Salmon, Horace Abraham	Sgt	32707	Singer, George Edward	LAC	132025
Salzfass, Joseph	LAC	449771	Singer, Sarah	Sgt	90430
Same, Saul	Cpl	17313	Slade, Lewis	Cpl	10788
Samuel, Alwyn Ruta	FO	405113	Sleeman, John David DFC	FL	423912
Samuel, Benjamin Kenneth	Sgt	449601	Sleeman, Reginald Leman	FO	413907
Samuel, Henry Myer	Sgt	12529	Sloman, John Harold	Cpl	51446
Samuel, Ralph Aaron	F Sgt	18216	Sloman, Zara	Str	501248
Samuels, Jack DFC	FL	412845	Smith, Charles	Sgt	22072
Samuels, Lewis Jacob	LAC	55953	Smith, David Myer	LAC	150689
Samuels, Maurice Gilbert	FL	267371	Smith, Maurice	WO	430064
Sapier, John	LAC	62806	Smith, Mendel George	Cpl	19804
Sasson, Rachael	ACW	111818	Smith, Neville Francis	LAC	64592
Saulwick, Laurance Julius *	F Sgt	431186	Smorgon, Samuel	LAC	127607
Saunders, Hartley Moses	LAC	450040	Snyder, Samuel	LAC	423914
Saunders, Naomi (Keesing)	Cpl	106285	Solomon, Albert	AC1	440243
Saunders, Victor	Cpl	6303	Solomon, David Henry	Cpl	A22137
Schenberg, Robert Isaac	LAC	16480	Solomon, David Joseph	FL	75752
Schoeneimer, Ruby R.	Cpl	101099	Solomon, Dorothy	Sgt	108060
Schott, Keith Jacob *	F Sgt	419594	Solomon, Henry Ackman	Sgt	4775
Schureck, Carol Mathew	Cpl	21500	Solomon, Jessie	Cpl	95270
Seamonds, Henry	FL	267692	Solomon, Leslie	FO	33298
Segal, Isaac	AC2	445894	Solomon, Louis Henry	Cpl	8374
Segal, Israel Lionel	LAC	145848	Solomon, Morris *	Sgt	402679
Segal, Joseph	FL	267406	Solomon, Myer Louis	LAC	169327
Segal, Louis	LAC	53529	Solomon, Neville David	LAC	35647
Segal, Solomon	LAC	125928	Solomons, Douglas Arthur	LAC	418688
Segal, Victor Myers	Cpl	72835	Solomons, Lewis Joel	LAC	68254
Seigel, Abraham	LAC	149265	Solomons, Simon Stanley	F Sgt	432281
Selig, Victor Clyde	LAC	135454	Spero, Frank Arnold	LAC	131020
Shapir, Morris William *	F Sgt	400357	Spero, Harold Bernard	LAC	157892
Shapiro, Alec	Cpl	13906	Spielvogel, Frederick Phillip	Cpl	18504
Sharp, Aaron Ronald	LAC	82084	Spielvogel, Newman Laurence	FO	40386
Shaw, Lorraine Paula	ACW	109108	Spitz, Rudolf	LAC	150508
Shaw, Raymond *	PO	402139	Stabey, Nubert Solomon	AC1	146545

World War II, Royal Australian Air Force (cont.)

NAME	RANK	SERVICE NO.
Stamper, Louis Albert Emanuel	FO	424935
Stanfield, Edward Max (Szajnfeld)	LAC	59665
Stanton, Clive James	WO	A3684
Stanton, Gilbert Victor	FL	295166
Stanton, Norman George	FO	74852
Stanton, Roy Alan Julian	FL	253731
Starke, Joseph Gabriel	H/FL	2467
Steigrad, Allenby	Cpl	67439
Steigrad, Seeyon	LAC	73257
Stein, Wolfred	AC1	148087
Stern, Jack	AC1	130243
Stern, Samuel Bennie	LAC	125535
Stone, Maurice Lionel	WO	431793
Stone, Norman	LAC	56779
Stone, Norman	AC1	445842
Stone, Victor	SL	257596
Stuart, Judith Elliott (Meyer)	Cpl	93312
Susman, Lyle John Graham	LAC	128310
Swift, David	LAC	55261
Symonds, Lewis	LAC	138550
Symonds, Maurice Isadore	FL	257508
Symonds, Maurice Kenneth	AC1	432906
Symonds, Myer Leslie	FO	403882
Symonds, Neville	LAC	136906
Symons, Israel Arthur	LAC	145458
Symons, Nathan	LAC	138864
Szekely, Simon	LAC	444895
Tait, Alexander	AC1	125624
Tannenbaum, Hinda	ACW	95308
Tanner, Frederick Edward	LAC	136157
Tanner, Harold	LAC	164011
Tate, Leon **DFC**	FO	051830; 415594
Taylor, Samuel Bruce	LAC	149216
Thau, Judah Leon	LAC	84655
Thomas, Samuel	LAC	119223
Tishler, Keith	LAC	120166
Tofler, David Henry	LAC	151980
Tofler, Lionel Davis	FO	422319
Tooler, Norman	Cpl	20583
Toster, Harry	Sgt	80275

NAME	RANK	SERVICE NO.
Trobe, Arthur John	FO	406632
Upfal, Maxwell	AC1	149340
Van Gelder, John Lewis	WO	432698
Van Praag, Lionel Maurice **GM**	FL	60431
Vander-Velde, Jack	PO; ATC	6731
Walters, Ronald Boston	LAC	427964
Warman, Szlama Nuta	Cpl	53684
Waxman, David Leonard	LAC	115837
Waxman, Edward Moss	LAC	167924
Wayne-Traub, Leslie	Cpl	8185
Waysman, Boris	LAC	157864
Weingott, Owen Ash	Cpl	422333
Wexlear, Hyman	LAC	82415
White, Harold	FL	118464
White, Sidney	Sgt	41361
Willer, Harry Wolfe	Sgt	36902
Wills, Mervyn Abraham	FO	428811
Wolfson, Harold Harry *	FO	424253
Wolifson, Hyman	LAC	33856
Wolinski, Eric	LAC	67514
Wolinski, Kenneth Eric	FL	267900
Wolper, Morris	AC1	157865
Woolf, Charles Solomon	LAC	137829
Woolf, Godfrey *	F Sgt	421345
Woolf, Hyman *	Sgt	4063
Wynn, David	LAC	54864
Wynn, Reuben	Cpl	142572
Yaffe, Charles	Sgt	40614
Yaffe, Reuben	Cpl	63628
Yescovitch, Samuel	FL	257517
Young, Martin	LAC	154022
Young, Monica Phoebe	ACW1	93552
Younger, Maurice	LAC	53303
Zachariah, Olga (Landau)	Sect Off	91073
Zaltzman, Joseph	Cpl	51892
Zamel, Morris	Sgt	70251
Zent, Oscar	WO	419245
Zimbler, Peter Joseph	F Sgt	400049
Zions, Albert	LAC	402901
Zions, Jack	LAC	444479

ROYAL AIR FORCE

NAME	RANK	SERVICE NO.
Cullen, Richard Nigel * **DFC**	FL	39967
Pincus, J.D. *	WO	1332709

Index

Note: Footnotes are shown as, for example, 90n. Picture sections are indexed by caption number as, for example, *image 1*.

Index

Index